# THE LEGENDARY

# PORSCHE 911

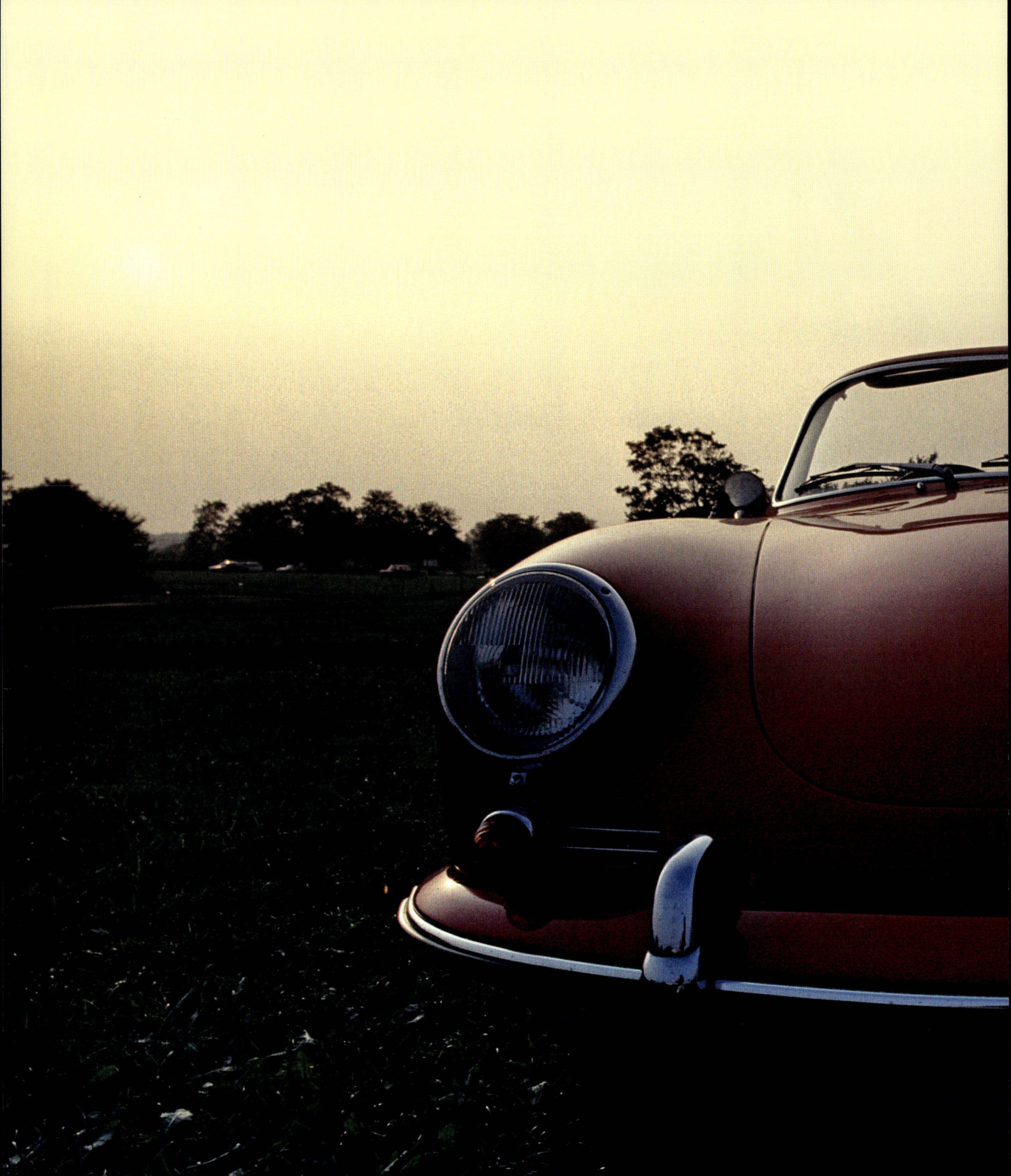

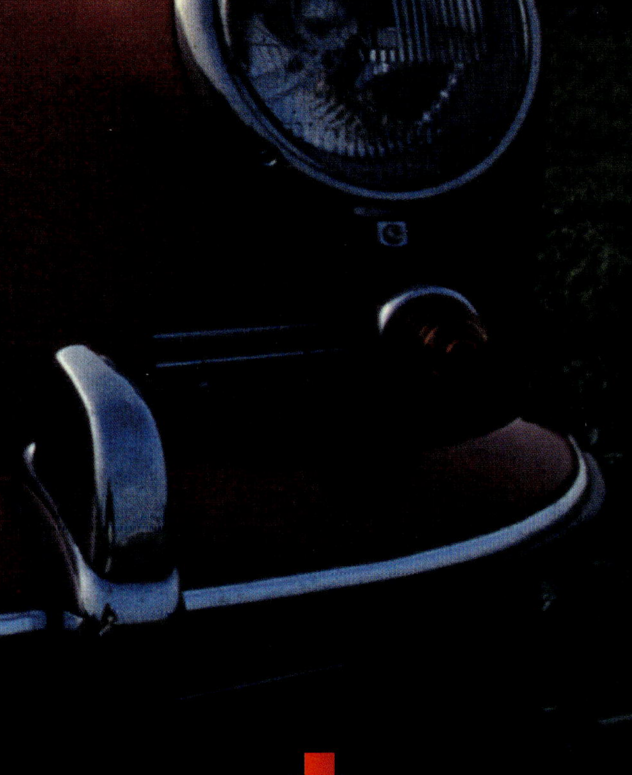

# THE LEGENDARY
# PORSCHE 911

sona
BOOKS

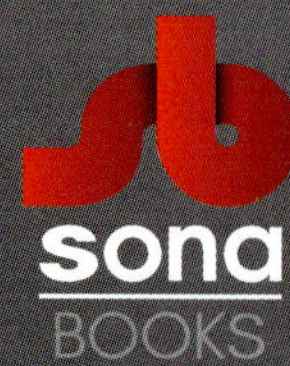

# CONTENTS

# A STYLE ICON

of days, while its rear-mounted engine has been a perennial mechanical talking point, but the 911 has always been greater than the sum of even these pleasingly idiosyncratic parts. From the start, the 911 has unapologetically followed its own path.

Launched on an unsuspecting public in 1964, the car took its first tentative steps into the realms of racing at the famed Monte Carlo Rally the following year. Ever since, the 911 has led an audacious double life clocking up the miles on the road in its own inimitable style, while simultaneously accumulating a glittering array of motorsport trophies.

The 911's global profile has only grown over the years courtesy of its legion of celebrity devotees. Hollywood legend Steve McQueen was one of the first to fall in love with Porsche's tour de force, immortalising the car in *Le Mans* in the early 1970s, while fellow silver screen big-hitters Tom Cruise and Keanu Reeves have subsequently been seduced by its unique design and drive.

There is no argument that the 911 has been a divisive car over the years, rarely failing to split motorists into opposing camps. For those seduced by its looks and performance, the 911 is an undisputed classic, while there remain those who are vocally unconvinced by its considerable charms. But as Oscar Wilde famously said, "there is only one thing in life worse than being talked about, and that is not being talked about."

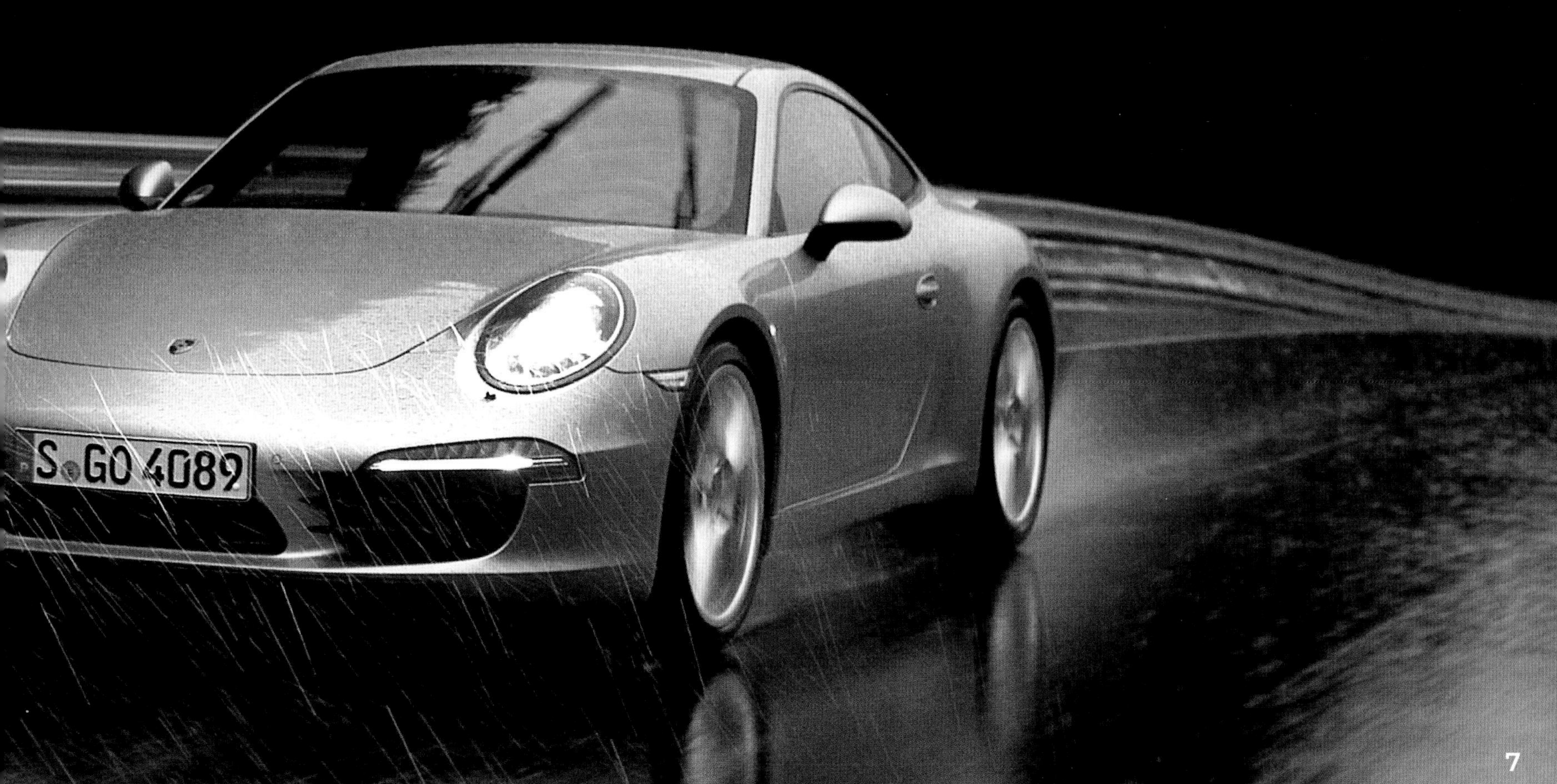

# THE HISTORY OF THE
# PORSCHE 911

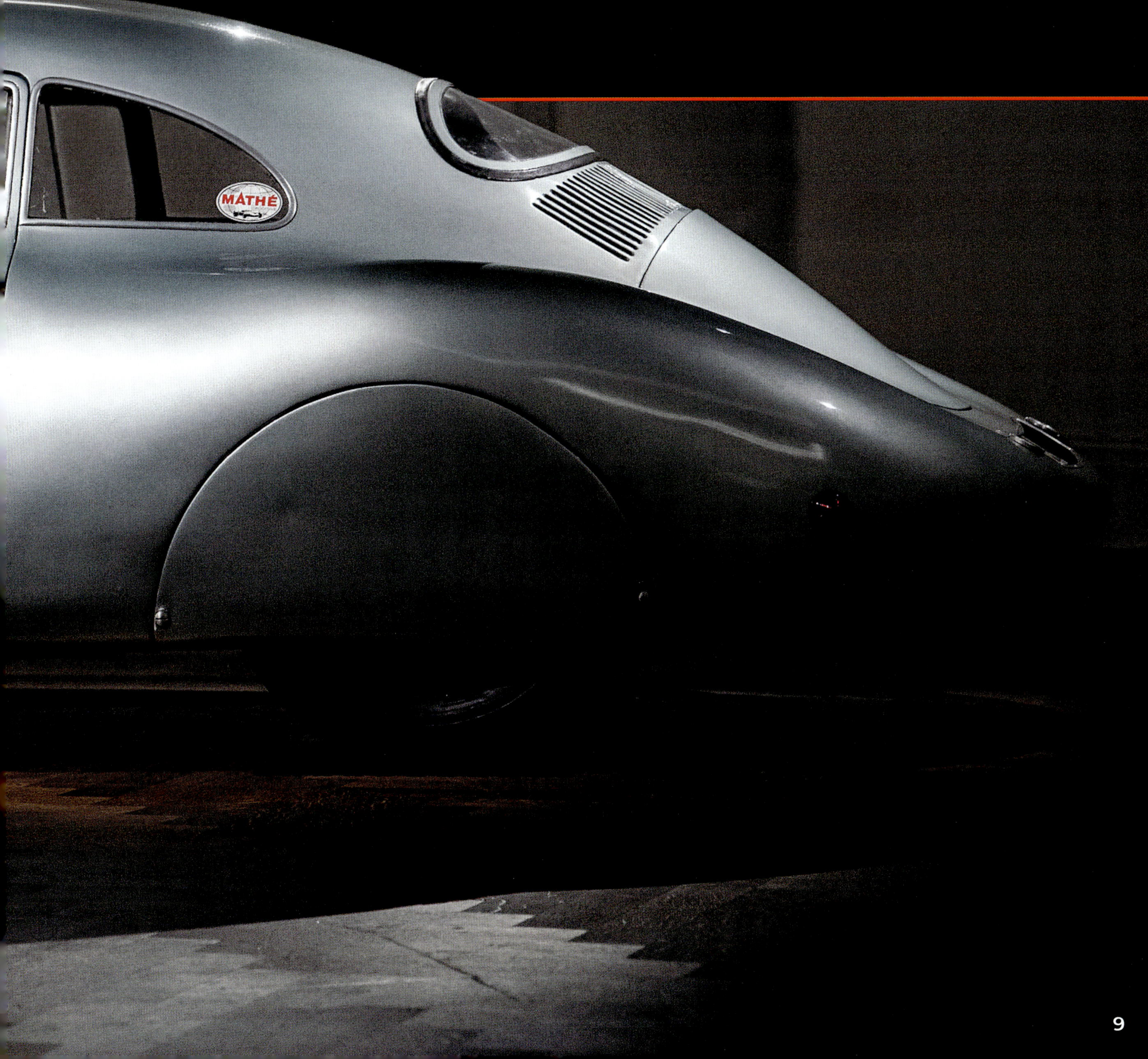

Born in Stuttgart in the 1960s, Porsche's long-lived signature series of two-door, rear-wheel drive masterpieces rewrote the motoring rulebook with its mesmeric combination of unique styling and mechanical innovation.

"**D**esigners need to be part engineer," Ferdinand Alexander 'Butzi' Porsche once said, outlining his philosophy on the creation of a truly great sports car. "Good design only exists in concert with engineering. That is because form has to follow function, so you focus on function and then give the object a shape to make it appealing." The 911 was Butzi's baby and more than six decades after he gave it life, the iconic car continues to embody his vision of stunning looks and performance in perfect harmony.

The genesis of the 911 began in the late 1950s as Porsche turned its collective thoughts to a replacement for the 356 roadster, the company's first production model which was launched by Butzi's father Ferry in 1948. Butzi headed up the design team for a project which would have a profound impact on the nascent company's fortunes and, by the early 1960s, the plans for a more spacious, powerful and comfortable update on the 356 were well advanced.

A boot with sufficient room for a set of golf clubs was far from Ferry's only contribution to the development process, but his son was the mastermind behind the eye-catching, sweeping curves that were to define the appearance of every subsequent 911. Porsche's decision to mount the 356 engine in the rear had been contentious, but the company did not waver the second time around and the 911 was duly equipped with the beating heart of the car once again at the back.

## METHOD IN THEIR MADNESS

The debate about the wisdom or otherwise of such an approach was well worn even before the 911 rolled off the production line. "What are some of the arguments against the rear-engine design?" Bernard W. Crandell had written in *Mechanix Illustrated* magazine as early as 1949. "One of the principal ones is weight distribution. With the heavy motor over the rear axle, the centre of gravity of the car is shifted to the rear. This means that when not under complete control, the car will have a tendency to turn around and travel backwards, like an arrow shot tail-first. When skidding on ice, for example. Then, too, in case of an accident, the heavy rear moves forward, telescoping the car and its occupants.

Even the rear-engine boys recognised this. In almost all models, the front hood has been retained. The driver is minus the protection of the heavy engine and its frame, it is claimed. Steering will not be as positive since not enough weight will bear down on the front wheels. Engine cooling, too, is another problem."

Unperturbed by the naysayers, Porsche pressed ahead and handed the blueprints for the 911's bodywork to Reuters, the Stuttgart coachwork company founded at the turn of the century which had manufactured the skeleton of the 356. By 1963 the car was ready for its official unveiling at that year's Frankfurt Motor Show and the public had its first glimpse of the 2.0-litre, air-cooled, flat-six newcomer, which boasted 130bhp, and a top speed of just north of 130mph.

Porsche initially christened their creation the 901 but Peugeot were not happy with the moniker. The French giant already owned the trademark on three-digit names with a zero in the middle of the combination and in order to avoid unnecessary litigation, Porsche backed down. The 911 badge may have been second choice, but the unplanned rebrand did nothing to lessen its immediate success after the first models left the factory at the end of 1964.

The public quickly fell in love with the 911 and its reception in the media was equally enthusiastic. "The subdued and pleasing noise from the back tells you where the engine is and so does the freedom from wheel spin and the ability to use a lot of the power on corners," reported *Motor* magazine. "Rear-engined handling characteristics have virtually disappeared – there are many front-engined cars which are more sensitive to crosswinds and very fast roll-free cornering can be enjoyed with no worries about losing the tail. It really comes into its own on long high-speed journeys when the very smooth six-cylinder power unit can be kept continuously in its best torque range. Above all, it has that effortless feeling which suggests that hard driving is what it is designed for."

**Early years (clockwise from top left): Ferdinand 'Ferry' Porsche; a 1967 Porsche 911R; original 901 Porsche owner's manual; 901 prototype manufactured in 1963.**

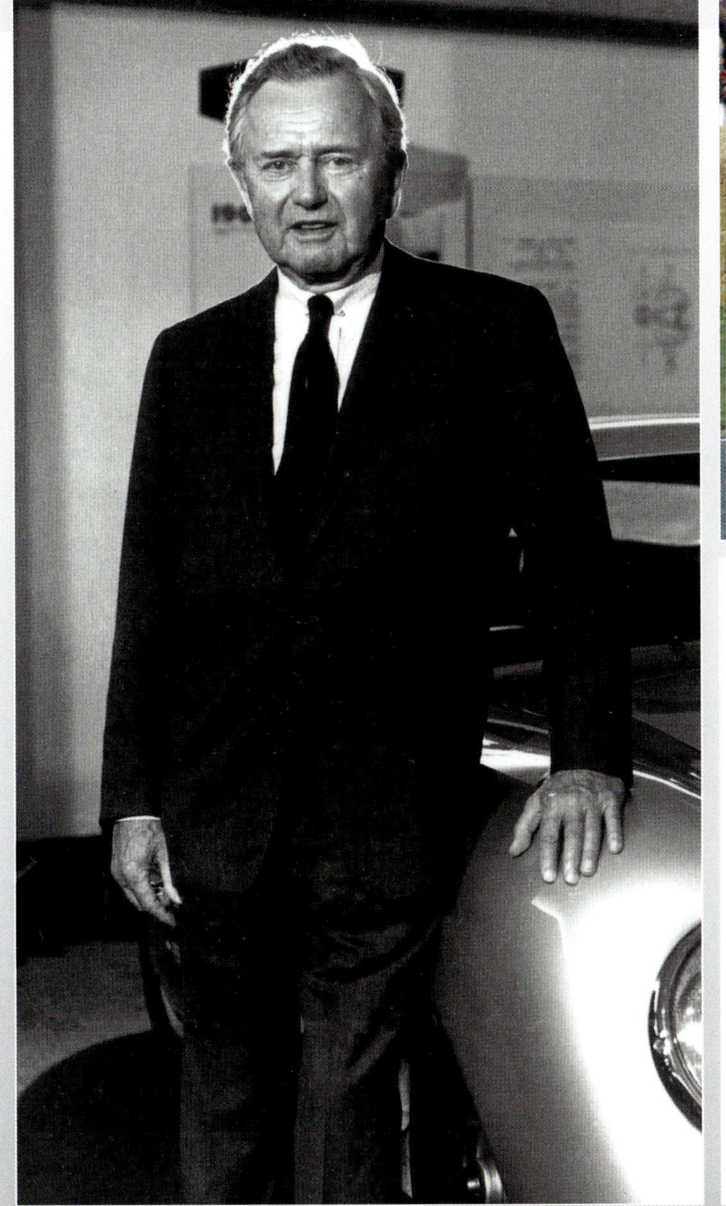

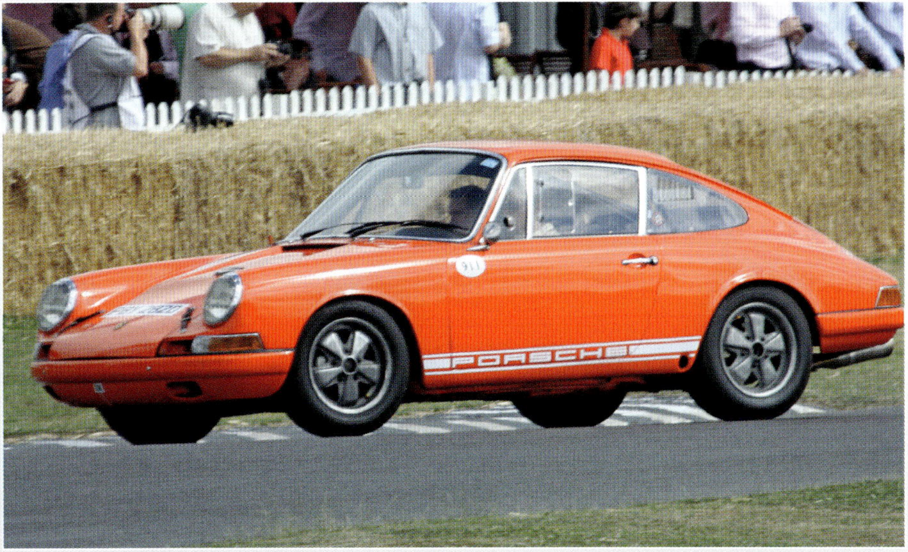

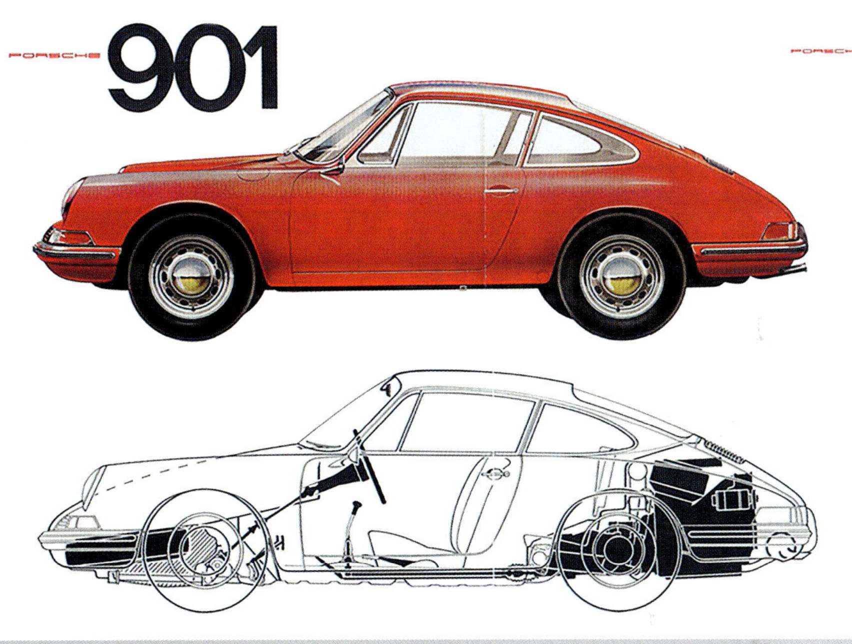

901

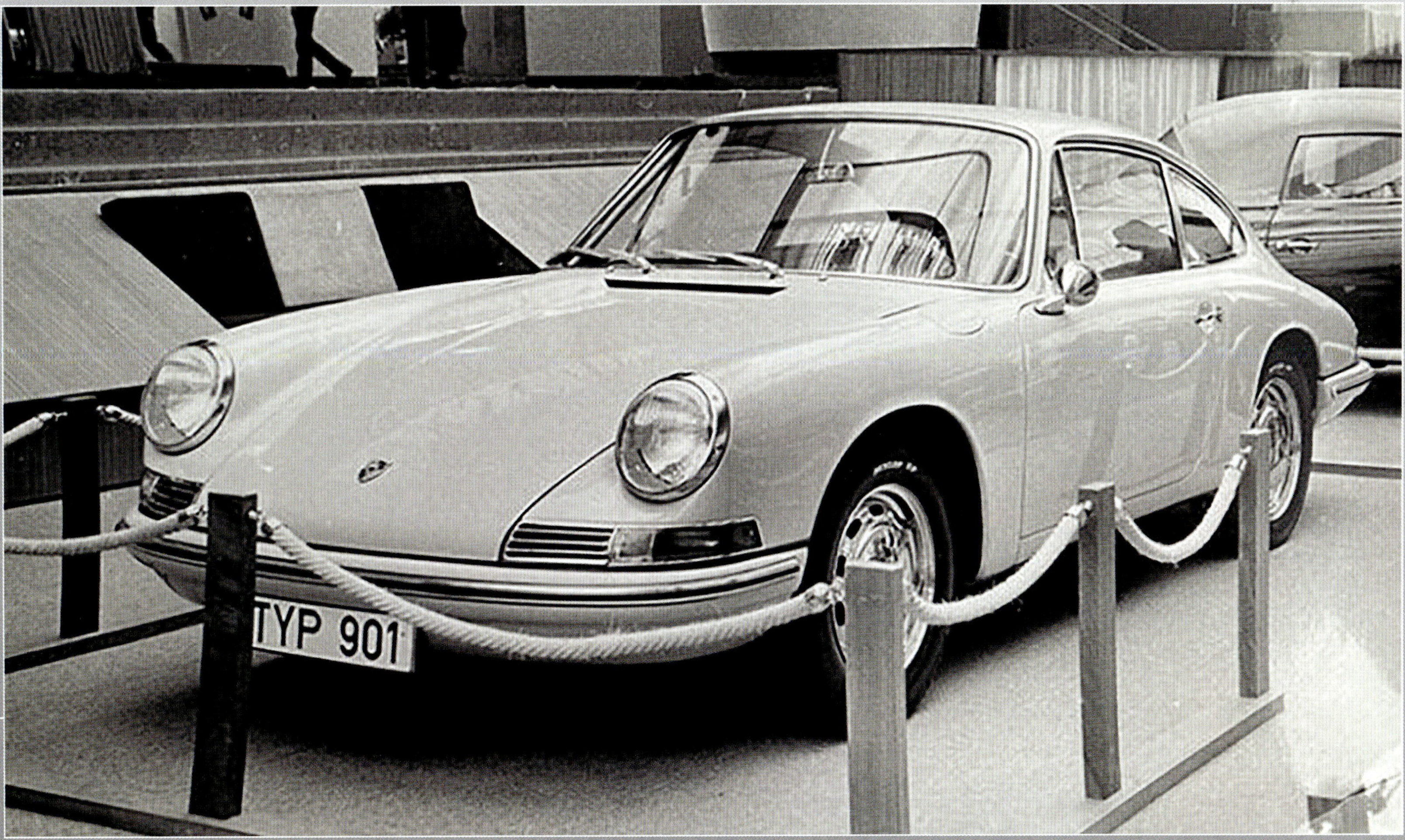

Although Porsche already had a commercial hit on their hands, Butzi was reluctant to rest on his laurels and in 1966 the 911S was launched with a more powerful 160bhp engine which elevated the top speed to 140mph, making it the fastest production car on sale in Germany. The upgrade also featured improved suspension while Porsche's legendary Fuchs alloy wheels became an option for the first time.

Further modifications followed but the 911's next major milestone came in 1972 when Porsche lodged an application at the German Patent Office in Munich. Porsche engineer Hermann Burst had been tasked with reducing the car's lift at high speeds and had concluded the back of the 911 needed more downward force. "The invention relates to a passenger car with a rear spoiler," the resulting patent application read, "one preferably mounted between side panels."

Dubbed the Entenbürzel – the 'Ducktail' – the iconic spoiler proudly debuted on the new 911 Carrera RS 2.7 at the 1972 Paris Motor Show. Porsche had taken naming inspiration for the latest edition of the 911 from the Carrera Panamericana, a road race staged in Mexico in the 1950s where one of their 550 Spyders had recorded a class victory, but it was the stunning architecture at the back of the new model that really captured the imagination. For many devotees the first Carrera is the definitive 911, even though Burst was initially blissfully unaware of the significance of his work. "At the time, I thought the spoiler was just a solution to a technical problem," he later said. "It took me a long time to realise that we had created an icon."

**(Below)** A 1973 Carrera RS2.7, the first 911 to feature the iconic 'ducktail' rear spoiler; (right) Louise Piëch, daughter of Ferdinand Porsche, with her historic 911 Turbo in 1974.

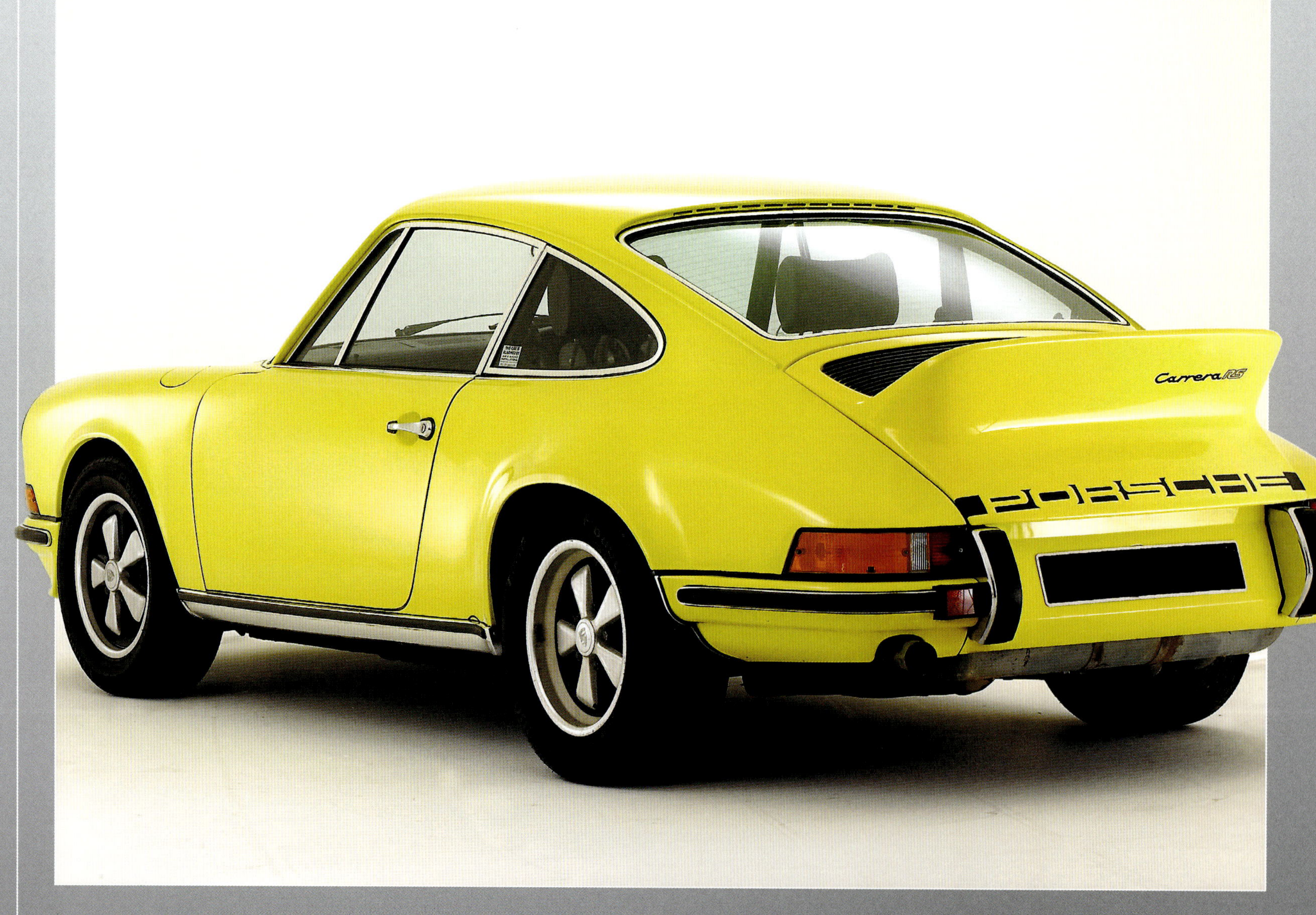

## GETTING TURBO-CHARGED

By the time the 911 celebrated its 10th anniversary in 1974, it had already firmly established itself on the motoring landscape, firstly in Europe and then inexorably further afield, but Porsche were mindful their creation's first decade could all too quickly be consigned to the automotive history books if they did not continue to innovate and evolve. The 911 needed to move with the times to preserve its embryonic status as one of the most coveted sports cars on the planet.

The second generation of 911s, known within Porsche HQ as the G-Series, began in 1974 with a relatively modest development and the introduction of impact-absorbing bumpers in response to stricter safety regulations. Twelve months later, however, the company played its ace in the shape of its new 911, the 930 Turbo. The first in the series to feature a turbo-charged, three-litre engine which generated 260bhp and such was the blistering acceleration on offer from the configuration, it was not long before the new model had been dubbed 'The Widowmaker'. Perhaps not the nickname the Porsche marketing department would have opted for – it derived from the moniker German pilots had bestowed on the accident-prone American F-104 Starfighters they flew during the Cold War – but the 911's popularity was undimmed by the association.

"While Porsche had successfully used turbocharging in racing since 1972, it was not until 1975 that the company implemented the technology for road-going models," wrote the Porsche Club of America. "Characterized by its flared fenders and whale-tail rear spoiler, the 911 Turbo became the performance benchmark for the sports car industry upon its introduction. Since that time, every successive generation of 911 has had a turbocharged derivative."

The first ever recipient of a 911 Turbo was Louise Piëch, Ferry Porsche's sister and Butzi's aunt. She was gifted a prototype as a 70th birthday present in August 1974 and although her thoughts on the car have been lost in the mists of time, the public loved it and, allied with the introduction of a Bosch fuel injection system and an improved five-speed gearbox through the 1970s and into the 1980s, Porsche irresistibly went from strength to strength.

The next chapter in the story began with the launch of the Porsche 964 in 1989. The third iteration of the 911 was a technical rather than styling milestone in the unfolding history of the model and saw the company embrace power steering, ABS brakes and airbags. The 911 Carrera 4 was a watershed with its all-wheel drive system.

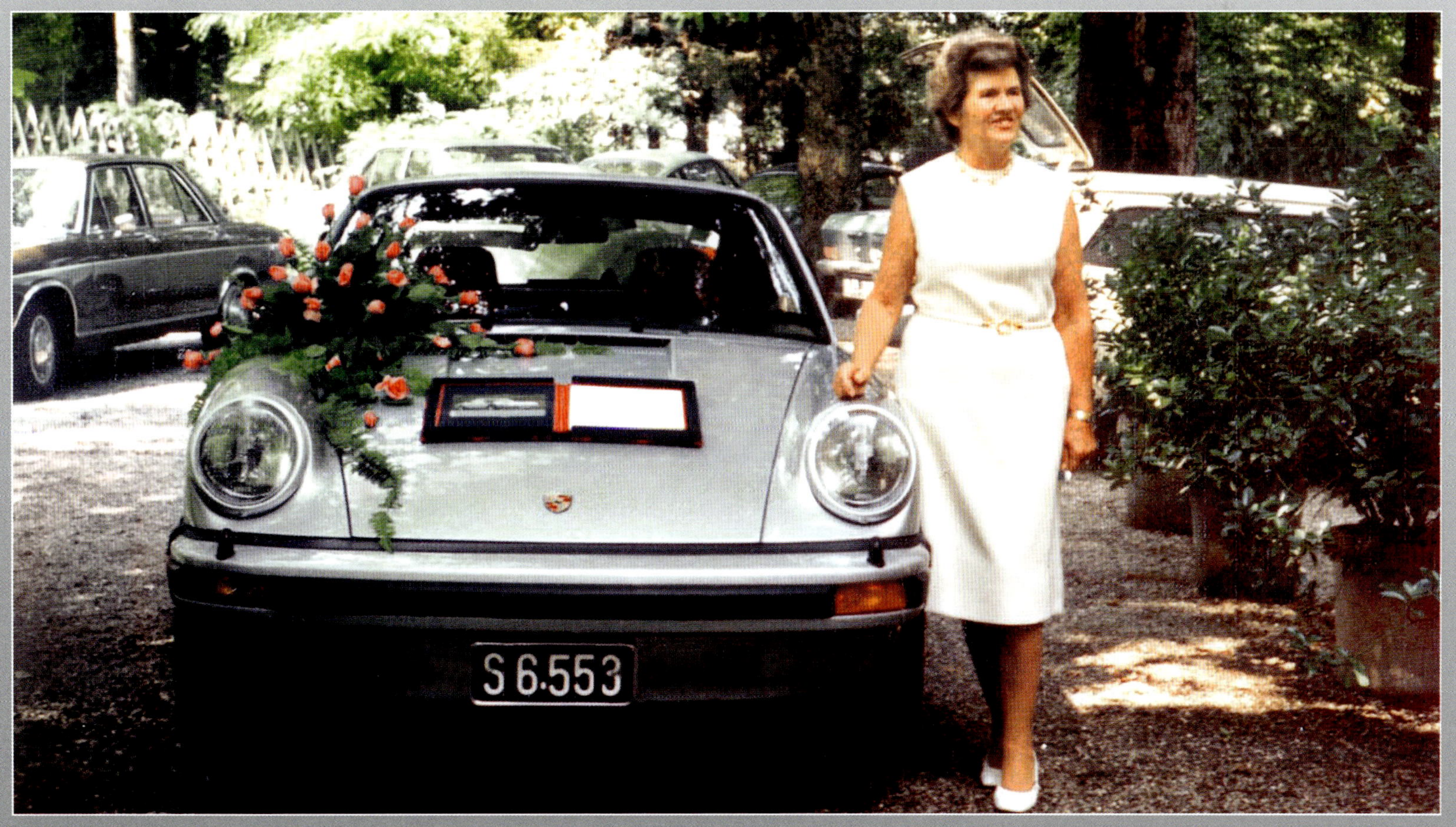

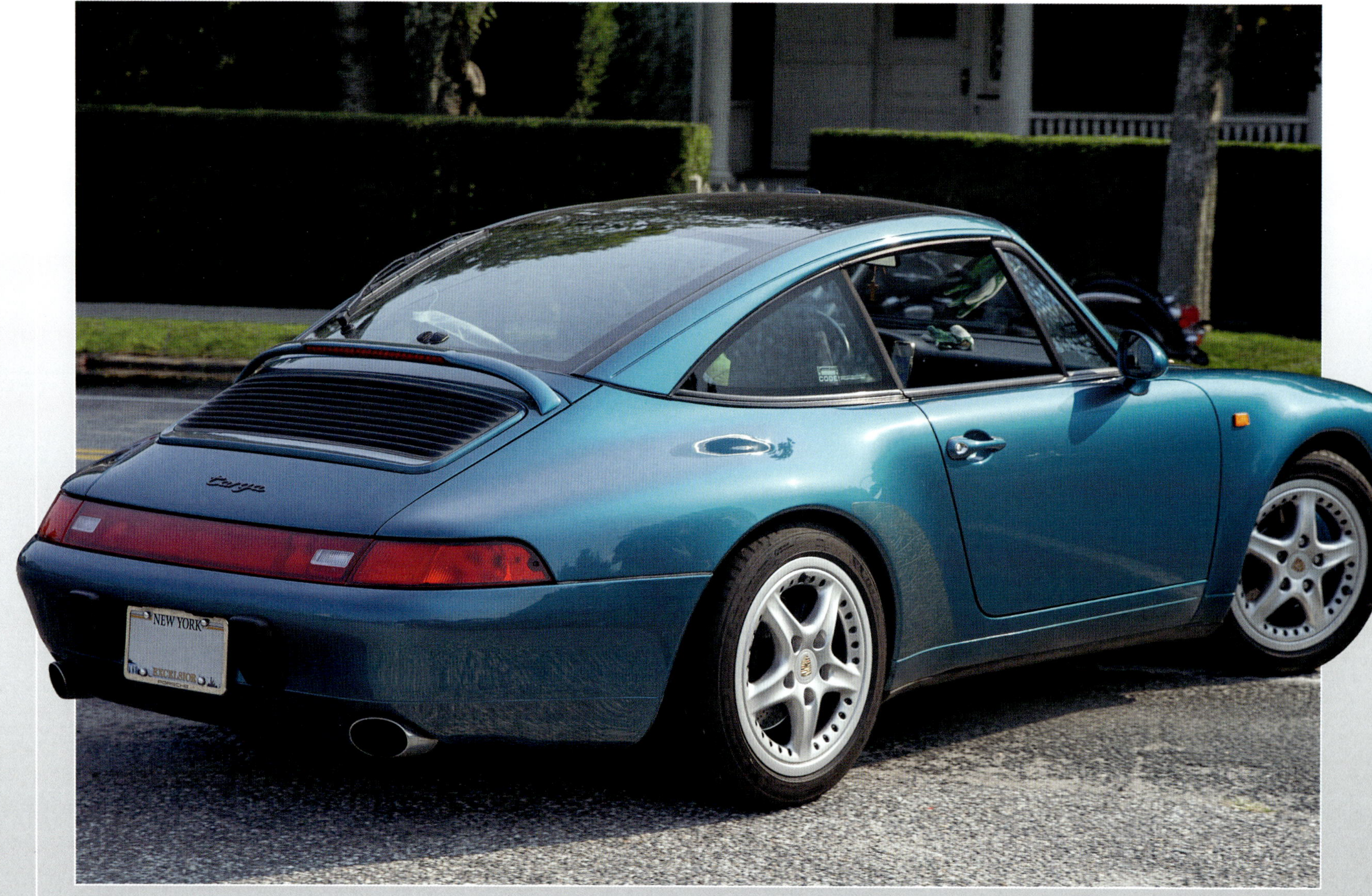



As the end of the 20th century loomed, Porsche embarked on the fourth phase of the 911 with the development of the short-lived 993 generation of cars. Unveiled in 1994, the 993 was subjected to a significant design overhaul and boasted smoother lines which many aficionados immovably maintain make it the most aesthetically pleasing in the lineage, while there was also a major step forward in the car's aerodynamic performance. Handling and ride comfort were enhanced with a multi-link rear suspension, while the 993 Turbo boasted twin turbochargers, resulting in 408bhp. Although no one who drove a 993 knew it at the time, it was also to be the last of the family to propel itself courtesy of an air-cooled engine.

## WATER-COOLER MOMENT

There is, in any walk of life, a natural and perfectly logical temptation not to abandon a winning formula. The 911's air-cooled engines had served Porsche well in terms of performance, while the signature noise the original system created had become a reassuringly familiar soundtrack

**The 993 Tiptronic-equipped, Targa version of the Porsche 911 debuted in 1994 and remained in production until 1998.**

beloved by 911 owners. However, increasingly strict emission standards exposed the inefficiency of the existing set-up of heat exchangers, fans and metal cooling fins to lower temperatures. A radical solution was required and when Porsche were ready to reveal the new 996 in 1998, they presented the motoring world with their first ever 911 with a water-cooled engine.

Perhaps predictably given such a seismic, albeit enforced shift in its engineering ethos, the switch received a mixed reception. Many mourned the passing of the air-cooled era but it was not long before the latest generation of Porsche's marquee model began to win over even the most sceptical.

"With the launch of the 996 series, the 911 had 'malevolent' and 'air-cooled' struck from its vocabulary," read a retrospective RAC review. "These water-cooled Porsches were a huge step forward, their dynamic excellence silencing most of the critics who felt it heretic to liquid cool a 911. The handling was transformed as well, giving the 911 a more mature, benign personality. Aural accompaniment, however, is a different matter altogether. The 911's noise has always been an integral part of its appeal. That flat six has always produced the most marvellous mechanical music. At full throttle, there was never a finer automotive ensemble. Nor is there still. Though the orchestra has been tempered somewhat at lower revs, press the new pendant-mounted throttle a little further and the engine is restored to full voice. It will transform you into a motoring malcontent, cursing your previous car's flabby steering and gutless throttle response."

The metamorphosis of Porsche's favourite child, however, was not finished. The water-cooled engine may have been out of sight, if certainly not out of mind, but the decision to alter the shape of the car's famed headlights was one that could not be conveniently concealed beneath the bonnet. It was Dutch engineer Harm Lagaay who jettisoned almost 25 years of 911 tradition, replacing the previously elliptical headlights in favour of what critics unflatteringly dubbed 'fried eggs' to provide the illumination, but the outcry from certain quarters did not diminish the 996's commercial success – with over 175,000 cars bought worldwide it became the best-selling 911 since the G-Series.

Despite these impressive numbers the company performed a volte-face when the 997 hit the market in 2004. The fried eggs headlights had been dispatched and their elliptical predecessors made a triumphant comeback. Every variant packed more than 300bhp – the GT2 broke new ground with 530 before the GT2 RS upped the ante even further with an eye-watering 611bhp on offer.

**The 997-era Porsche 911 Speedster was the fourth generation Speedster. It was a limited edition model of 356 units, available only in two colours Pure Blue and Carrera White.**

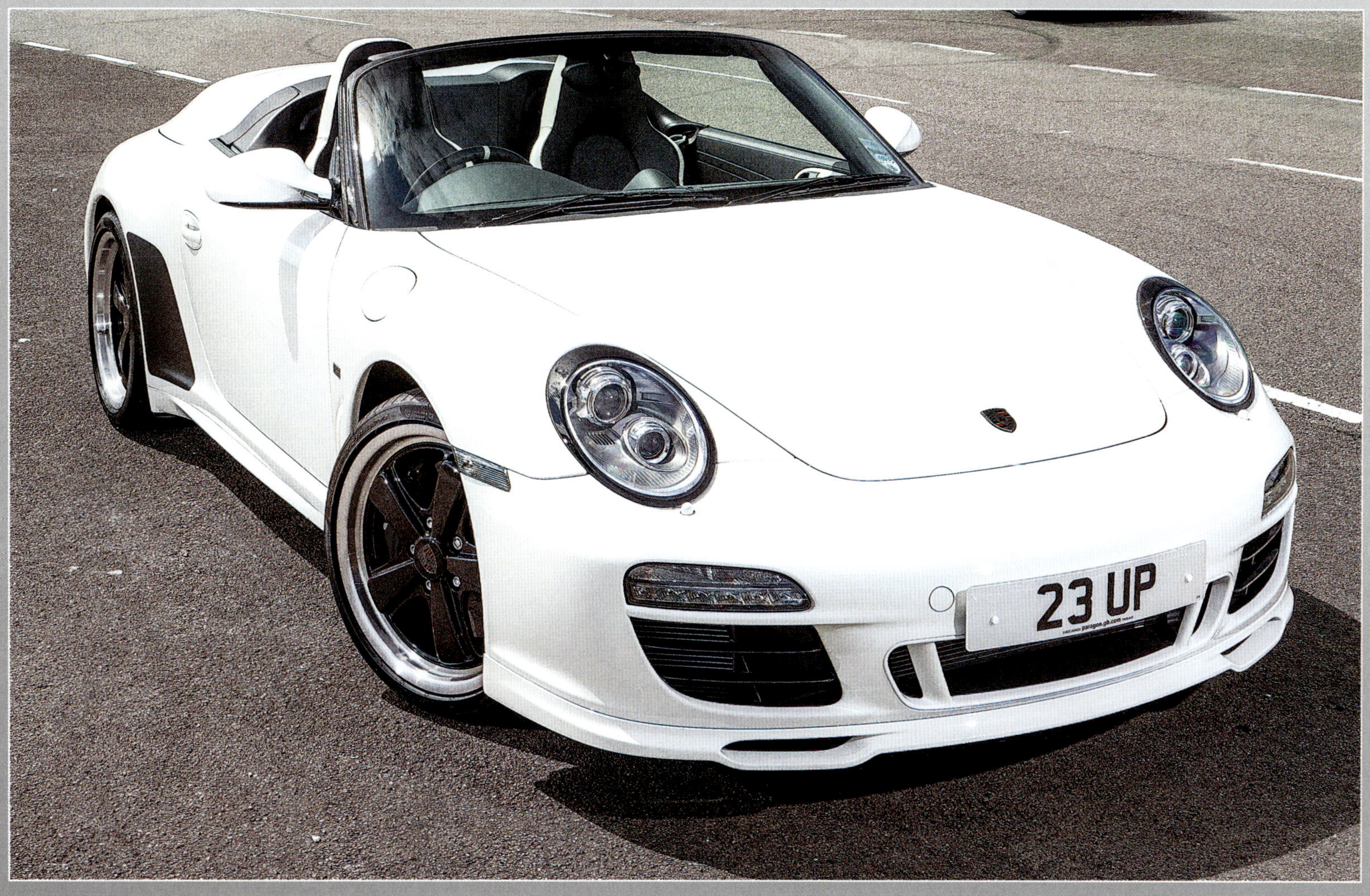

## THE MILLIONTH 911

The sixth generation of the 911 gave way to the seventh in 2011 with the advent of the 991. More muscular than its forebears but deceptively fleet-footed courtesy of its weight-shedding aluminium-steel composite exoskeleton, the 911's party trick was its marked improved acceleration thanks to its dual-clutch transmission. The 991 era also marked a monumental milestone in the company's history when, in May 2017, the millionth 911 emerged from the factory floor in Stuttgart. Resplendent in what Porsche called 'Irish Green', the special Carrera S embarked on a celebratory global tour, taking in the sights of the Scottish Highlands, the United States, China and, of course, the twists and turns of the Nürburgring, before taking up permanent residence in the Porsche Museum in the city of its birth.

By 2018 the time had come to welcome the eighth – and current – edition of the 911. The 992 is unashamedly a child of the digital age with all that was analogue banished from the cockpit, but while the internal makeover speaks to the modern era, the wide wheel base and turbochargers on every model ensure the latest incarnation of the all-conquering sports car is still suffused with the unmistakable 911 DNA.

**Built in 2017 and now housed in the Porsche Museum in Stuttgart, the Carrera S was the millionth 911 to roll off the production line.**

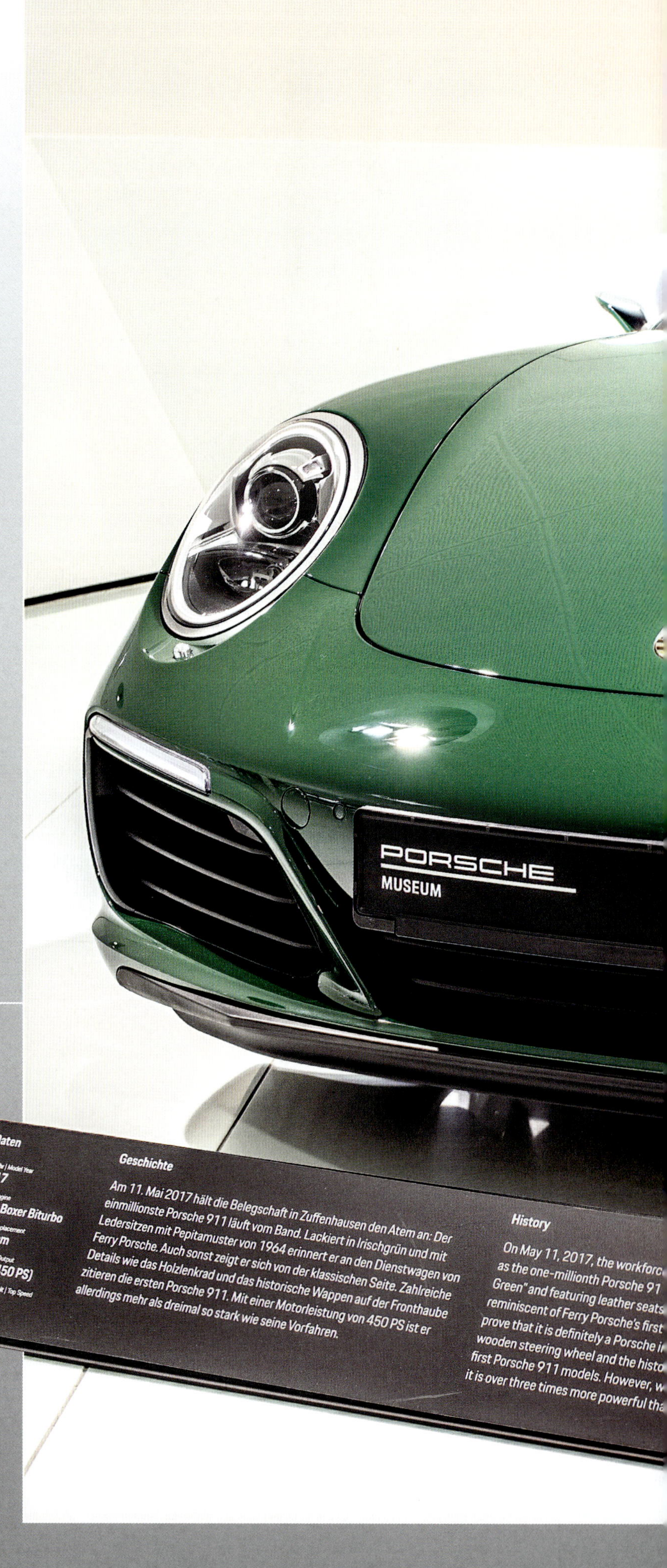

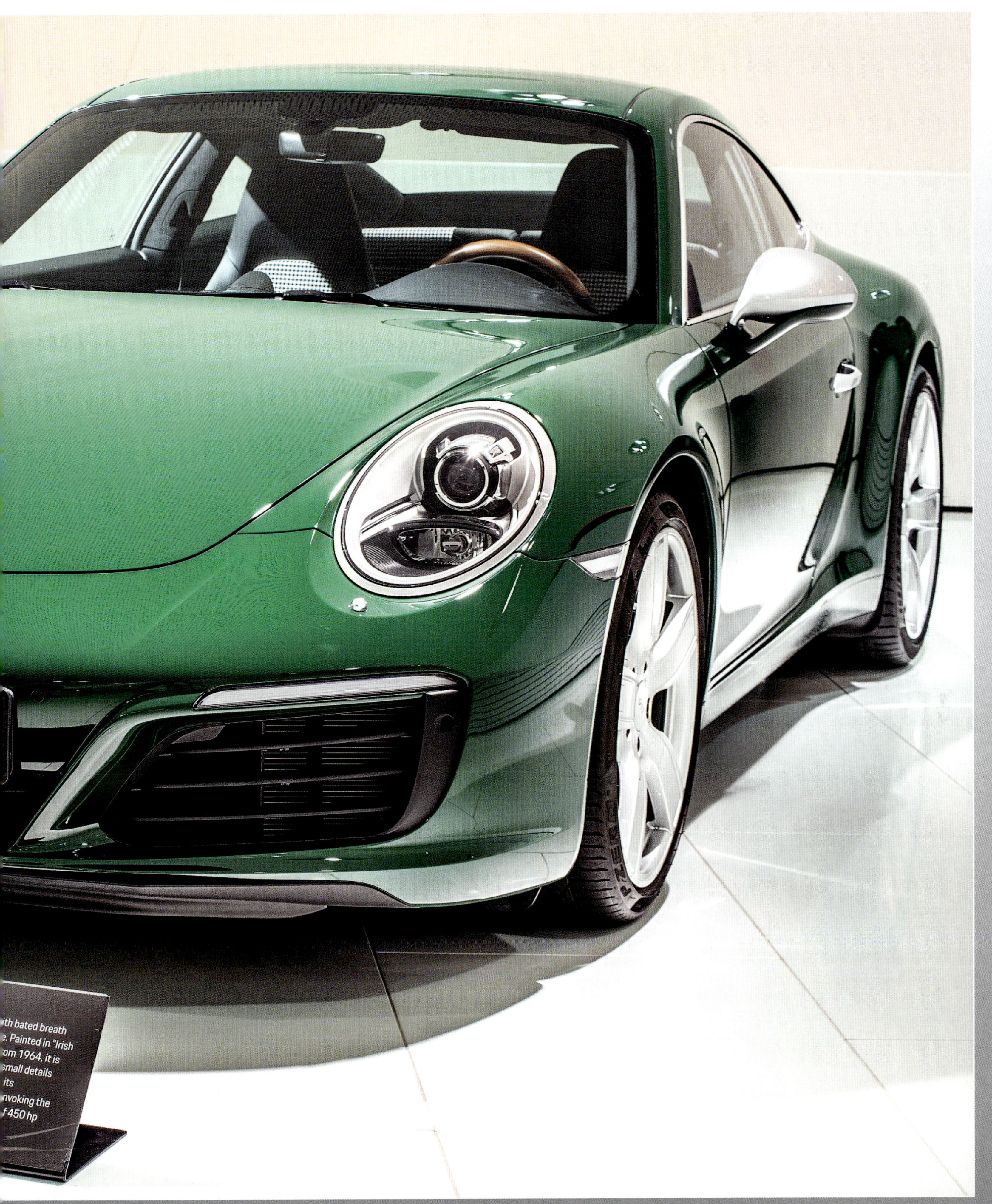



ith bated breath
e. Painted in "Irish
om 1964, it is
small details
its
nvoking the
f 450 hp

# FERDINAND 'BUTZI'
# PORSCHE



Nature versus nurture is a debate that dates back as far as Greek philosophy. English polymath Francis Galton first coined the enduring phrase in the mid-19th century and whichever side of the argument you favour, it is one that is frequently attached to 'Butzi' Porsche and the story of his 911. Whether he was born or subsequently bred to imagine the timeless curves of one of his legendary sports cars, however, is largely incidental and over 60 years since the first 911 went on sale, his creation's longevity and legacy is the final word in any discussion.

His early design flair was evidenced by a young Butzi's love of making toys. As a child he spent many hours in his grandfather Ferdinand's workshops and after completing his compulsory education in Germany during the 1940s, he enrolled at the prestigious Ulm School of Design. He failed to graduate but after a two-year internship with Bosch, one of the country's leading industrial design companies, he finally joined the family business in 1958 at the age of 22.

"I was already sure what I was going to do one day," Butzi later reflected. "It was definitely to work with the car body in relation to the engine, and in connection with that, the design." His initial role in the Porsche engine development department was short-lived before he assumed a more design-focused brief in an automotive era in which the engineers were king and styling the poor relation. Butzi, however, was now in his element.

His early projects included Porsche's 1962 Type 804 Formula One car, as well as the 2000GS Carrera 2 and the 904 Carrera GTS, but the company's most pressing issue remained a long-term replacement for his father Ferry's 356.

First on paper and then in modelling clay, Butzi's vision for the 911 gradually began to take shape. His promotion to head of the Porsche design studio in 1962 accelerated the process, and the following year, at the Frankfurt Motor Show, the company unveiled the car that would secure its fortunes for decades and indelibly etch Butzi's name into design folklore.

Known at work by his initials F.A. rather than Butzi, his family nickname, he became deputy managing director in 1968, but four years later Ferry Porsche floated the company and members of the family were excluded from executive positions. Butzi's response was the foundation of the 'Porsche Design Studio' in Stuttgart and for the remainder of his career he turned his artistic talents to creating industrial products, household appliances and high-end gentlemen's accessories, such as watches and spectacles proudly featuring the legend 'Design by F.A. Porsche'.

He spent his final years in Austria, where he had relocated his company's HQ in 1974. In 1999 the President of Austria awarded him the honorary title of Professor and in 2005 – increasingly suffering from the ravages of Alzheimer's – he retired. Butzi passed away aged 76 in Salzburg seven years later, but his most famous creation, his much-loved 911, survived him.

**Family business (clockwise from top left): Ferry Porsche and his son Butzi; Butzi famously worked with clay to make his 911 dream a reality; circa 1969, the 911 E was in the vanguard of Porsche's exponential growth.**

The third generation of his famous family to make an indelible mark on the automotive industry, Ferdinand Alexander 'Butzi' Porsche had significant shoes to fill following his grandfather's work on the iconic VW Beetle and his father's creation of the era-defining 356 Roadster.

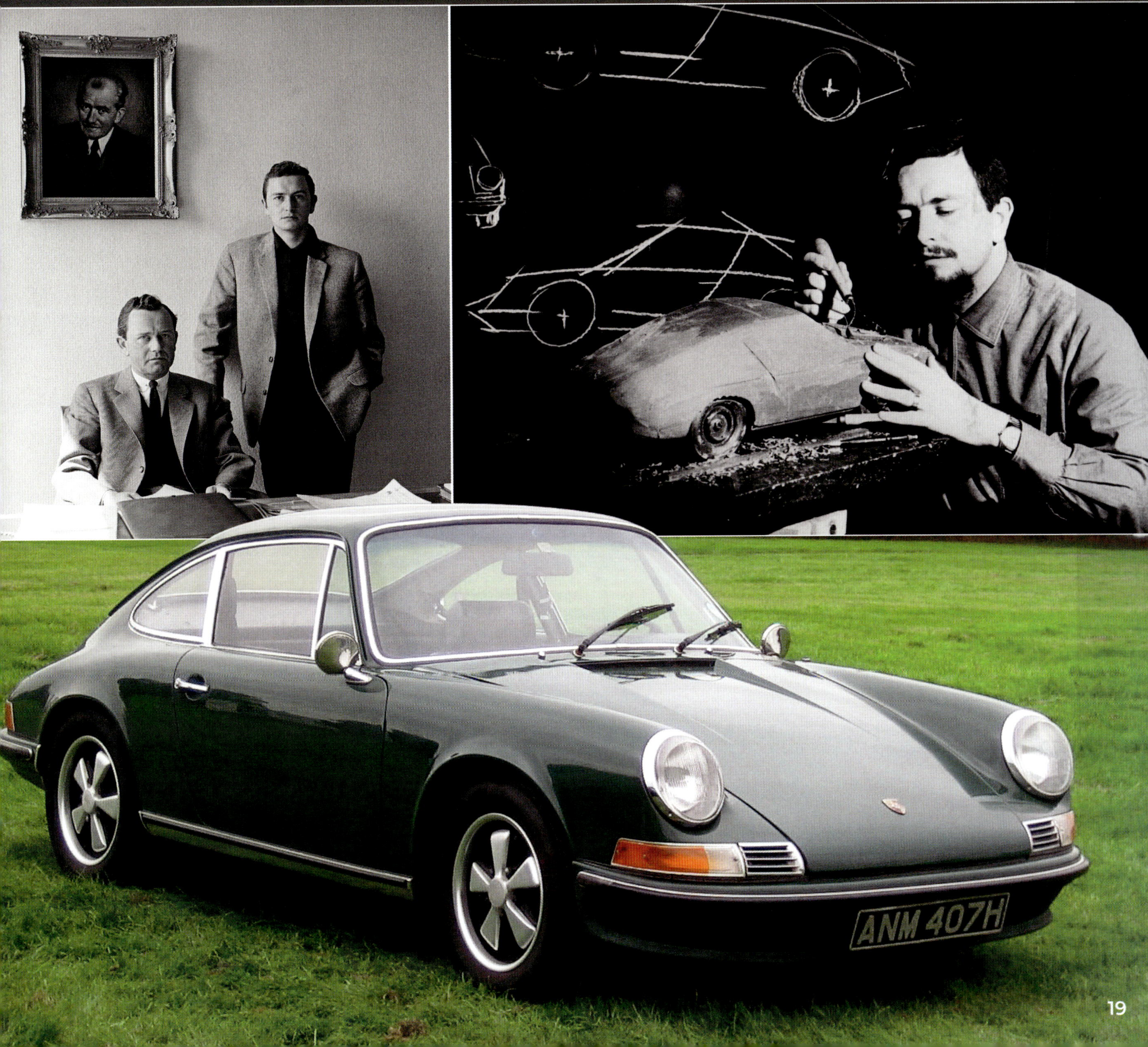

# PORSCHE 911
# MILESTONES

## 1963

Timelessly styled by Ferdinand 'Butzi' Porsche, the third generation of the family to work for the company, the first prototype two-litre, flat-six 911 is unveiled on 12 September at the Frankfurt Motor Show. The new car goes on sale the following year.

## 1966

Porsche expands its new offering with the launch of the Targa, complete with a removable roof panel.

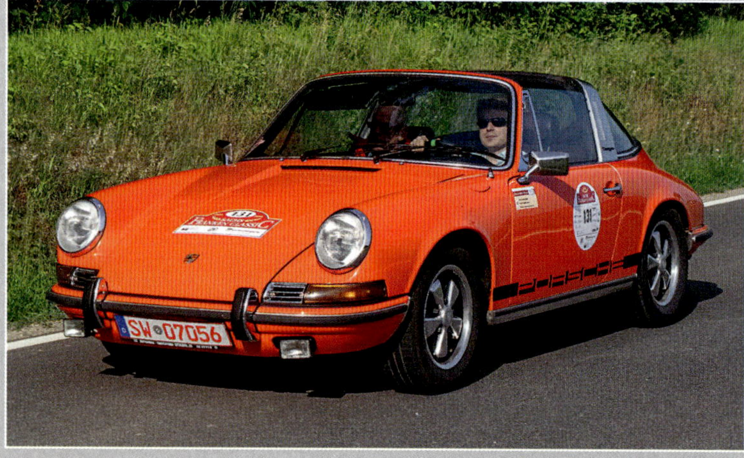

## 1967

Launch of the slimline 911R, a six-cylinder, naturally aspirated 210bhp sports car, which makes its racing debut in July at the Mugello Circuit in Tuscany.

## 1974

After a decade on sale the 911 undergoes its first regeneration as Butzi's original makes way for the G-Series, making its debut at the Paris Motor Show.

## 1975

The 911 Turbo goes on sale, the world's first ever production sports car to feature an exhaust turbocharger and pressure regulator.

## 1983

The successful series welcomes its first model to feature a folding roof, the 911 Cabriolet.

## 1984

With Frenchman René Metge behind the wheel, the 911 Carrera 4x4 triumphs at the Paris–Dakar Rally for the first time.

## 1986

The Porsche Carrera Cup, the first race event especially for 911s, is launched. German Joachim Winkelhock is the inaugural champion.

## 1987

The 250,000th 911 emerges from the Porsche factory in Stuttgart.

## 1989

To mark its 25th birthday, Porsche unleashes the 911 Carrera 4, featuring all-wheel drive.

## 1990

Technical innovation continues with the introduction of Tiptronic transmission for the 964 series, making both fully automatic and clutchless manual gear changing possible.

## 1995

The Porsche era of twin turbos is ushered in with the launch of the new 911 Turbo.

## 1996

The millionth Porsche – a 911 Carrera – rolls off the production line in Zuffenhausen. The historic car is gifted to the Stuttgart police department.

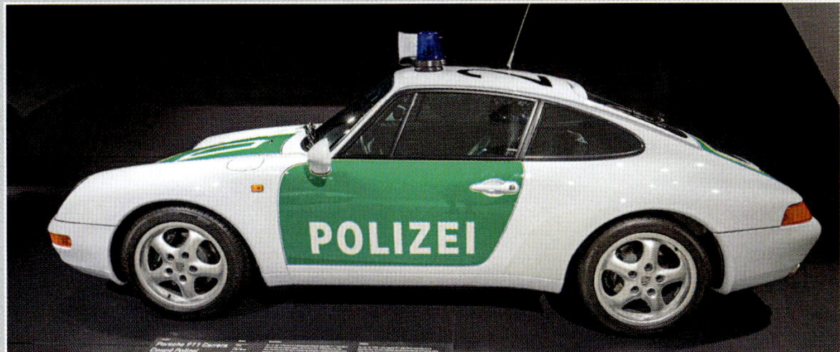

## 1998

Porsche embraces seismic change with its new 996 edition of the 911 – the first in the series to boast a water rather than air-cooled engine.

## 2009

Prominently featuring a number of iconic 911s, the Porsche Museum in Stuttgart opens its doors to the public for the first time in January.

## 2010

Updating a conventional GT3 R, adding an electrically powered front axle, Porsche unveils the company's first hybrid 911 for the track.

## 2017

The millionth Porsche 911, a Carrera S with bespoke 'Irish Green' paintwork, is unveiled.

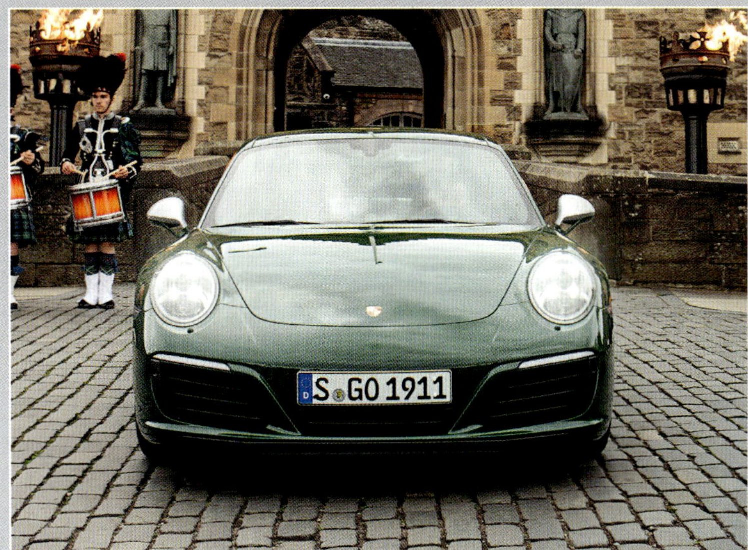

## 2018

The latest, and to date current, generation of the 911 is launched. The eighth edition in the series, the 992, replaces the 991 after eight years of service.

## 2022

A one-off '911 Sally Special', based on a Carrera GTS, sells at a charity auction in California for £2.9m – a world record for a new Porsche.

## 2024

To celebrate the 50th anniversary of its first turbocharged 911, Porsche unveils the 992 Turbo S with a top speed of 205mph. The company also reveals the new 911 Carrera GTS, the first ever road-legal 911 to feature a hybrid powertrain.

# AWARD WINNER
# EXTRAORDINAIRE

**W**hen the Porsche 911 celebrated its birthday in 2023, 60 years after the car had first emerged from the factory and onto the floor of the Frankfurt Motor Show, it was a significant milestone. The occasion was, of course, marked in its hometown of Stuttgart but not for the first time in the car's storied history, there was wider recognition of the 911s ongoing journey.

*The Sunday Times* celebrated the anniversary by naming the 911 Sport Classic, a nod to the vintage Carrera RS 2.7 of 1972, as its Car of the Year. "Porsche has built a retro version and it's so good it has roared away with our overall prize," the paper's motoring editor wrote. "The Sport Classic manages to be the quickest manual in the Porsche stable yet easy-going enough to take to the shops. Buy it in the understated grey that was the favourite of Steve McQueen, Hollywood actor and 911 enthusiast."

It was only the latest in a long line of accolades. Voted for by more than 100 leading motoring journalists from 30 countries, the prestigious World Car of the Year Awards first paid tribute to the icon when it was named the Performance Car of the Year for 2012 at a glittering ceremony at the New York International Auto Show, relegating the Lamborghini Aventador LP 700-4 and McLaren MP4-12C into second and third places respectively. The 911 GT3 won the award again in 2014, while the 911 Turbo made it a triple triumph in the same category seven years later.

The influential Evo Car of the Year awards have handed their trophy to various editions of the 911 no less than 12 times since they were inaugurated in 1998. The 911 Carrera (996.1) was the winner of the first award, with Evo noting "this rear-engined institution of complex contradictions may not be for everyone, but there aren't many who can avoid falling under its spell at some point."

The GT3 version of the 996.1 was crowned Evo's favourite again the following year, while its most recent win came in 2024 when the 911 S/T came out on top in the magazine's annual rankings, leaving among others the Aston Martin Vantage, Audi RS 6 GT, BMW M4 CS, Ford, McLaren Artura Spider and Morgan Plus Four in its wake. "What a flat-six it is," Evo wrote, "somehow more vibrant and visceral being hooked up to a six-speed manual. It is set up to be fun and engaging and it is a riot on the road."

The list of the 911's other domestic and international awards is as long as it is illustrious. They are too extensive to detail individually, but the highlights include the 911 coming fifth in the Car of the Century poll, announced in 1999 and organised by the Global Automotive Elections Foundation, and in 2012 the Carrera was named the best sports car in a vote by over 100,000 readers of German magazine *Auto Zeitung*. Back in 1995 the Porsche 911 Carrera 4 featured in *Guinness World Records* for the 'Toughest 100,000 kilometre test run of a sports car', while *The New York Daily News* crowned the 911 its Best Luxury Performance Car in 2018.

**One of the most decorated models in history, the 911 was named World Performance Car of the Year in 2014.**

The epitome of timeless styling and engineering excellence,
the Porsche 911 has been honoured multiple times by its automotive
peers with a host of prestigious awards.

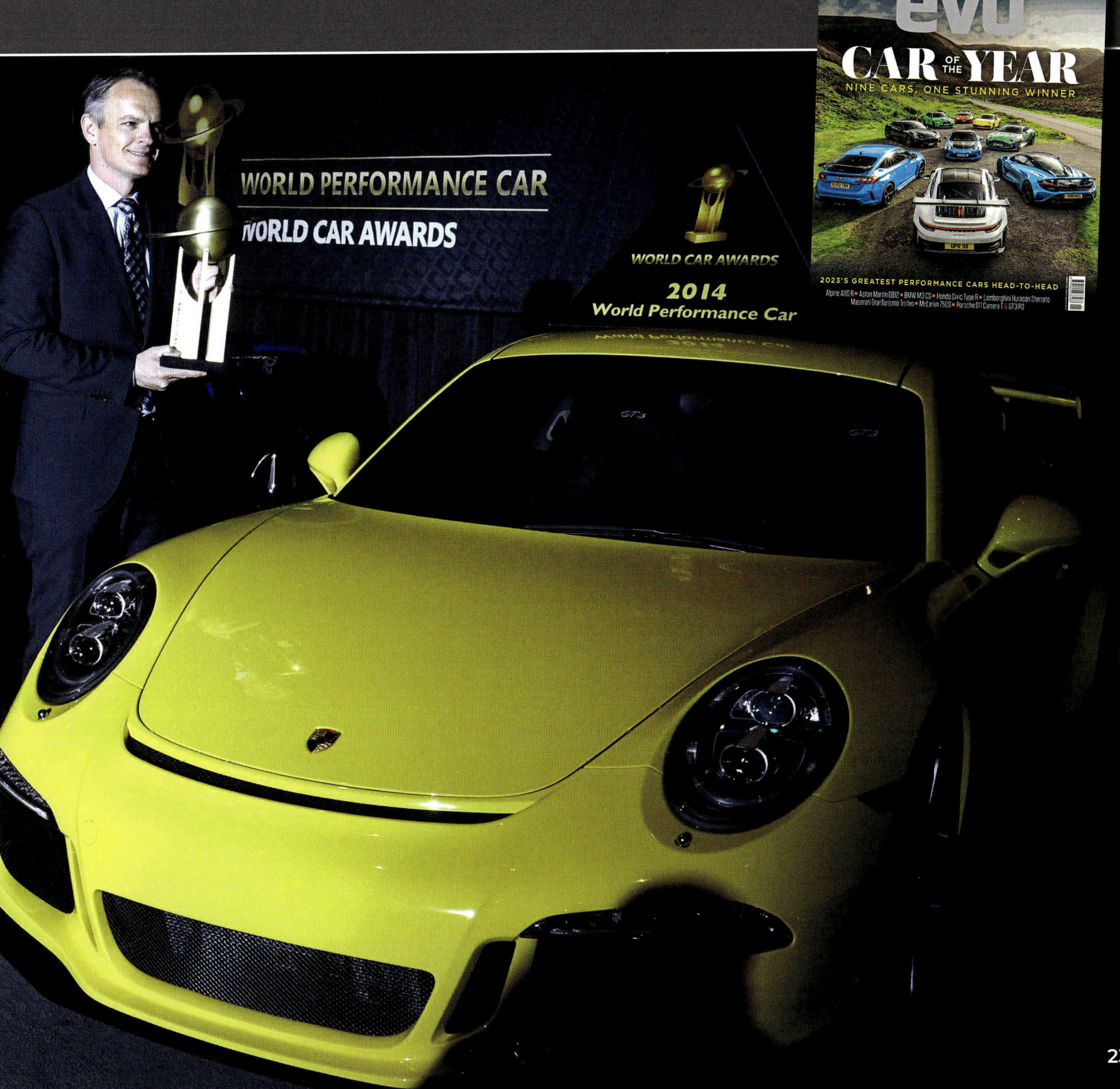

# RENNSPORT
## ICONS

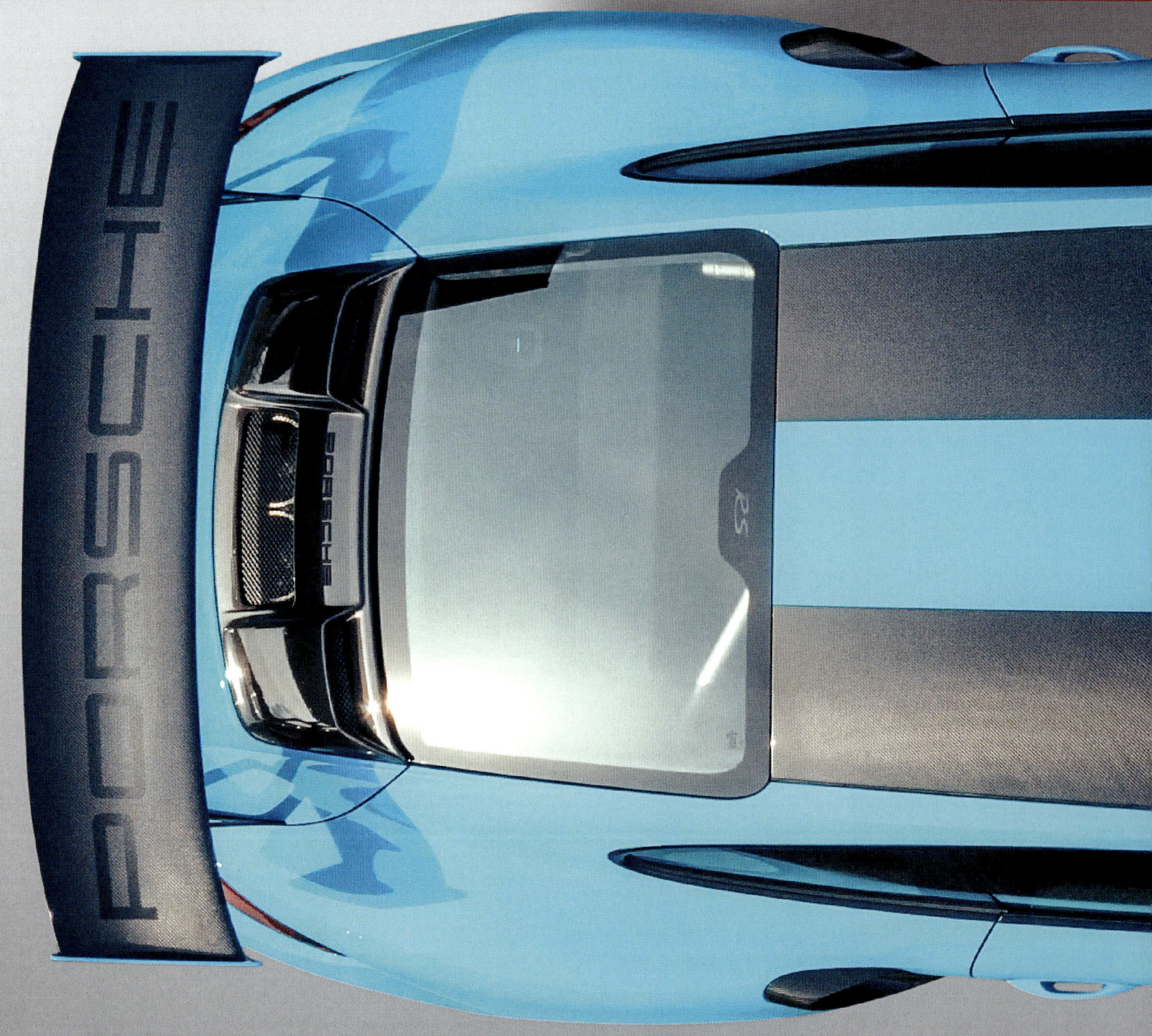

**There are few motoring legacies as rich as the Porsche 911 Rennsport.**

For most people, think 'race car for the road' and a Porsche 911 will be one of the first super sports cars that comes to mind. Various iterations of Porsche 911 race cars throughout the model's existence are responsible for an unprecedented 30,000 race victories on circuits all around the world, providing the perfect platform for the company to market its coveted road cars. When it comes to the 911 Rennsport, the cars are as close to their motor-racing counterparts as is feasibly possible. They are extremely lightweight, with reduced equipment, boasting the very best performance engines, gearboxes and chassis technology to make them as competitive as possible, be it on a circuit or even for fast road driving on the public road.

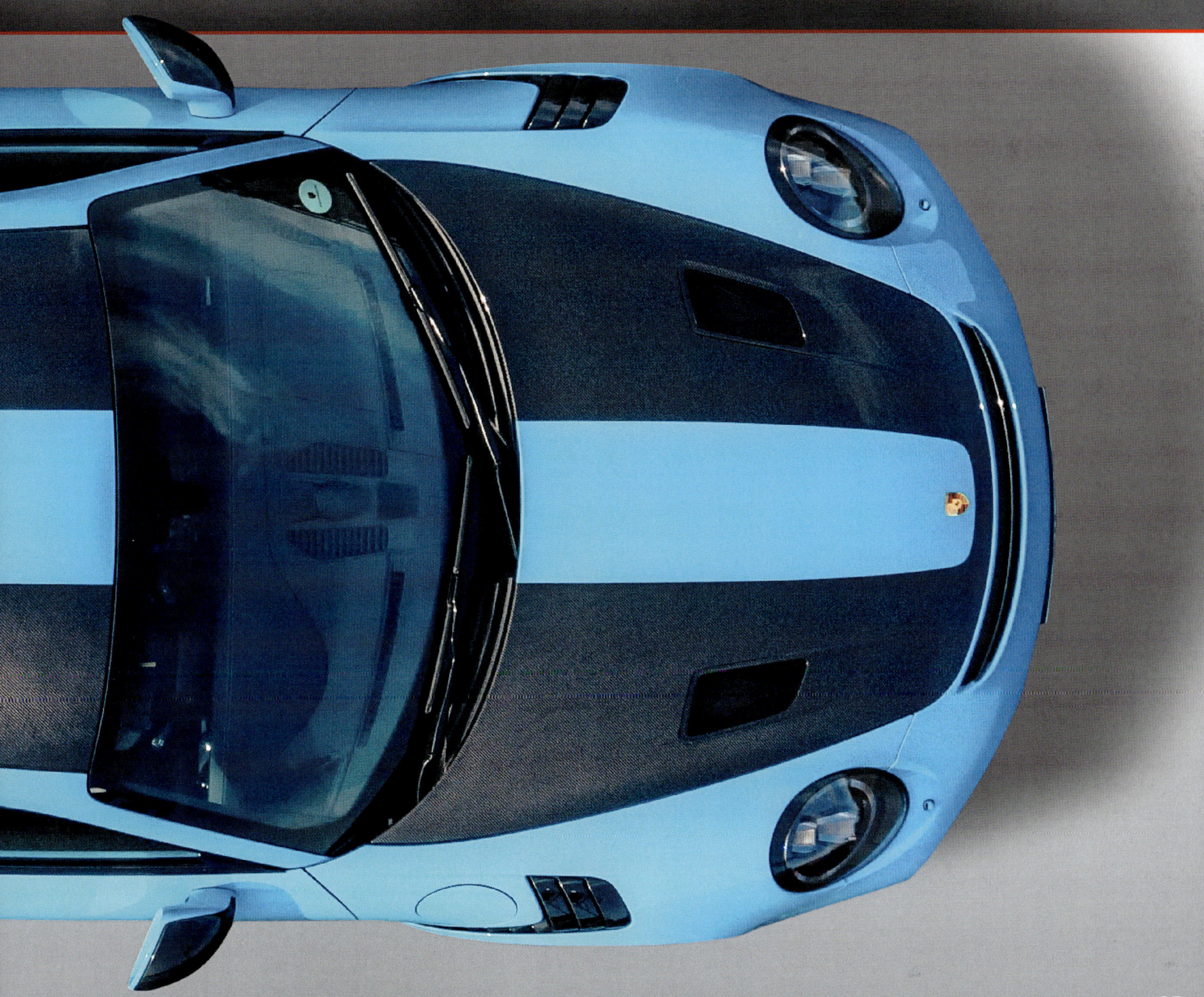

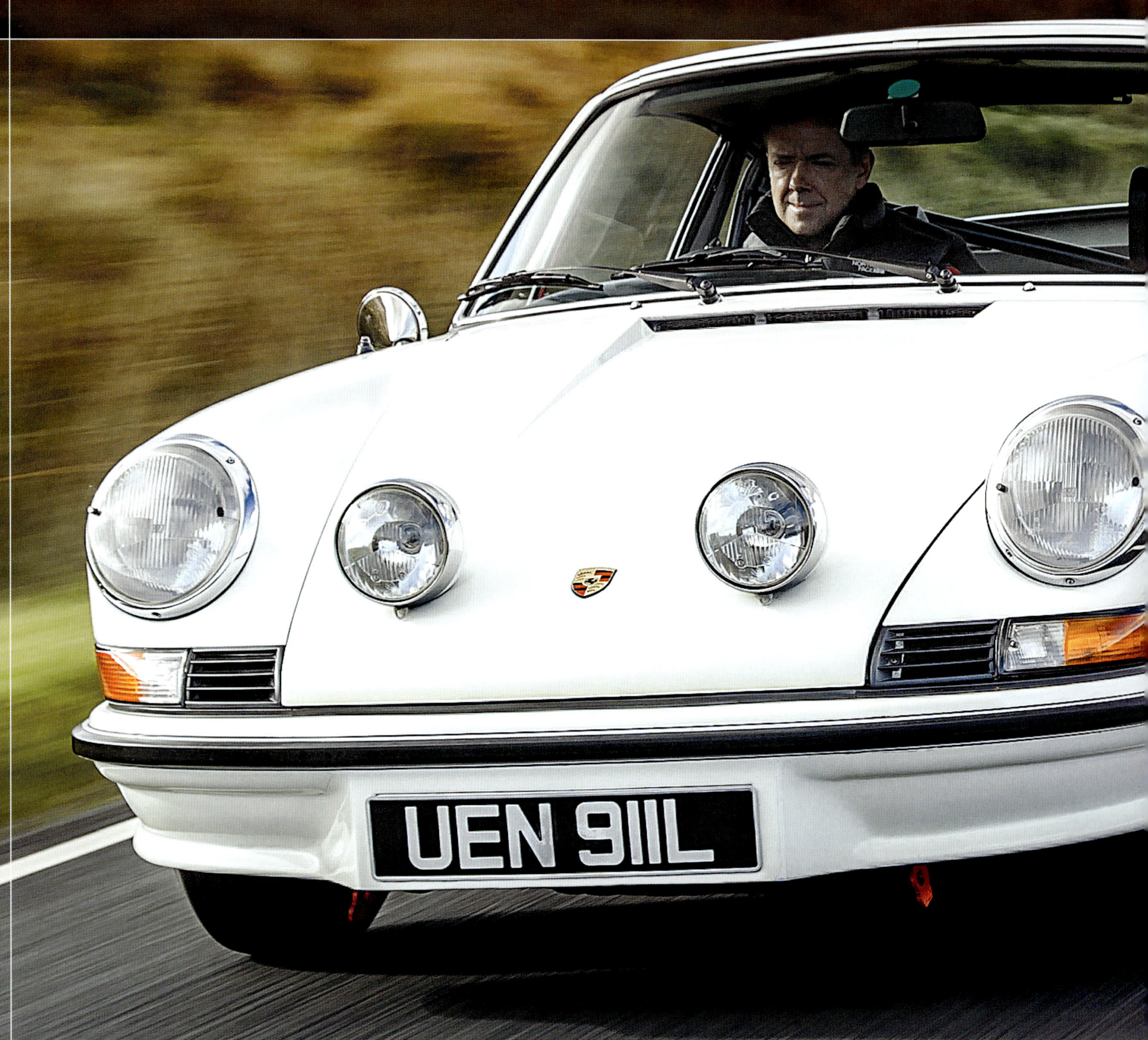
RENNSPORT
CARRERA 2.7 RS
FOR THE ROAD
UEN 911L

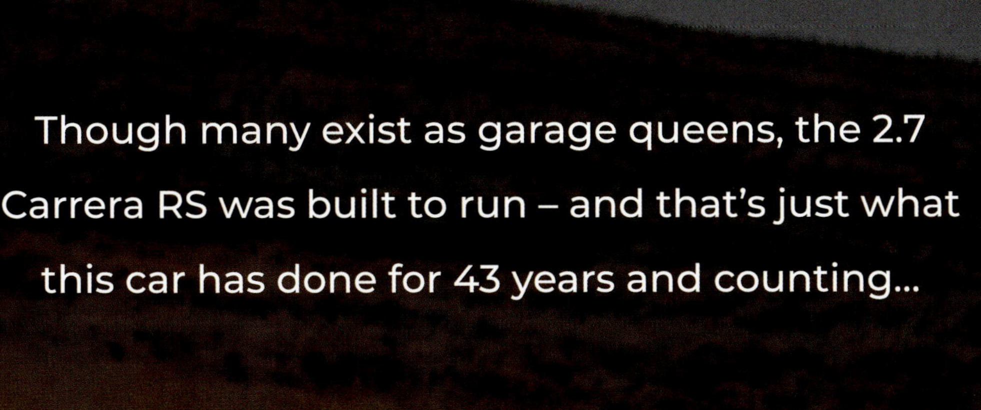


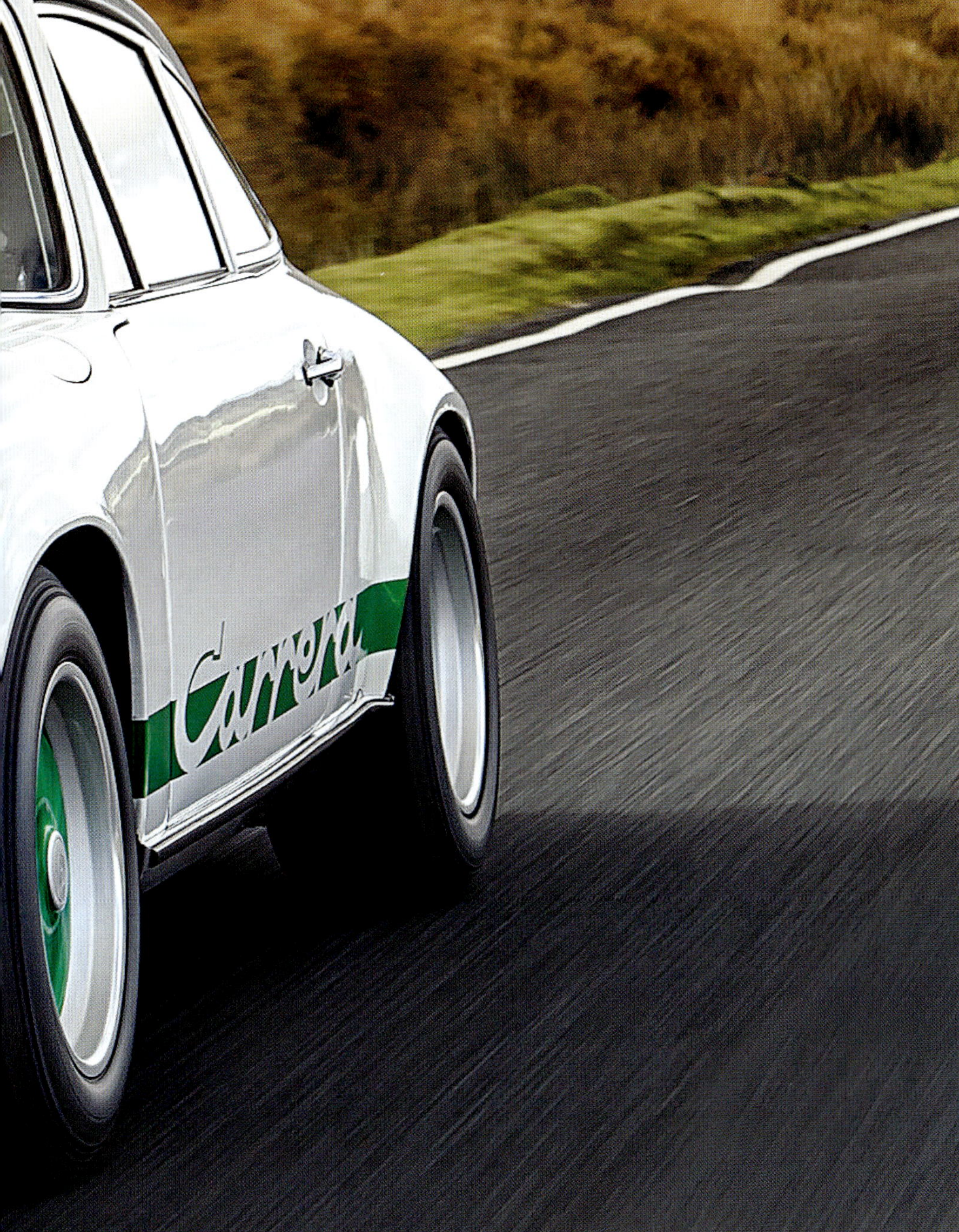



# CARRERA 2.7 RS

(1973)

### ENGINE

**Capacity:** 2,687cc

**Compression ratio:** 8.5:1

**Maximum power:** 210bhp @ 6,300rpm

**Maximum torque:** 255Nm @ 5,100rpm

**Transmission:** Five-speed manual

**Engine modifications:** Fuel metering modification, which has lifted maximum power to 229bhp

### SUSPENSION

**Front:** Independent suspension with wishbones and MacPherson struts; one round, longitudinal torsion bar per wheel; hydraulic double-action shock absorbers; anti-roll bar

**Rear:** Independent suspension with semi-trailing arms; one round, transverse torsion bar per wheel; hydraulic double-action shock absorbers; anti-roll bar

### WHEELS & TYRES

**Front:** 7x15-inch Fuchs, Avon Radical CR6ZZ 185/70/R15 tyres

**Rear:** 8x15-inch Fuchs, Avon Radical CR6ZZ 215/60/R15 tyres

### DIMENSIONS

**Length:** 4,147mm

**Width:** 1,652mm

**Weight:** 1,075kg

### PERFORMANCE

**0-60mph:** 6.3 secs

**Top speed:** 149mph

The history of the iconic Porsche 911 Carrera RS of 1973 is as lengthy as it is fascinating. Introduced to the public at the Paris Motor Show in October 1972, it was a typical example of early 1970s motor trends, ushering in a brave new outlook on life, characterised by loud and colourful products. The RS was a motoring pioneer from launch, its illustrious reputation carried forward with distinction right to the present day, where it is regarded as one of Porsche's most iconic 911s.

It is remarkable, then, to think that initially Porsche was worried about selling even the first batch of 500 cars: in their calculation of expected market demand, the rather conservative marketing department estimated that they should make only the required 500 homologation units of the new Carrera RS. Concerned that they would otherwise sit with large quantities of unsold vehicles, the RS was priced at just DM 34,000 (about £5,230) compared to the DM 31,180 (about £4,800) for the 2.4-litre 911 S. Although the Carrera RS was aimed at the sporting fraternity, the marketing department hoped that many of them would find homes as road-going cars, thus boosting sales. When most of the first batch of 500 cars sold out soon after the Paris launch, a second batch of 500 was authorised by Ferry Porsche. When they too cleared the order books, a third batch was commissioned, resulting in 1,590 units being produced in just ten months.

With the benefit of hindsight, we might wonder why Porsche didn't commit to a much bigger production run but, at the time, this model represented a big step for the company.

The Carrera RS was the first 911 to wear the 'Carrera' badge, a name which drew on the brand's early days competing in the Carrera Panamericana race in the 1950s. This model was also the first road-going car to feature the 'RS' moniker (this stood for Rennsport or Racing Sport), a powerful indicator of the car's sporting potential and ability to go racing. Although the Carrera 2.7 RS was only around 12mph faster than the 2.4-litre 911S, the bigger-engined car was 42mm wider in an effort to cope with much higher cornering speeds. The Carrera RS was also the first production car to feature a fixed rear wing, which was nicknamed 'ducktail' by the press. This rear wing, together with a front air dam, helped the RS to attain higher top speeds as well as, significantly, improved stability at those higher speeds.

The value of the Carrera RS rose modestly through the 1980s as many were still used for endurance and, later, club racing competitions, and by the 1990s it was shadowing the Ferrari Dino at around the £30,000 mark. In the early 2000s, this figure had trebled, but in recent years £600,000 to £700,000 (and more) seems to be the average value of a 2.7 RS Touring. This figure has slipped back last year, more reflecting a market correction rather than a fall in value, but the first Carrera RS is nevertheless one of the most sought-after Porsche 911s to ever leave the factory. This means that many examples of this icon are consigned to the garages of exotic car collections, with few being driven in anger today.

**A rare sight on the road today, what's more remarkable is this 2.7 RS is a first-500 homologation model**

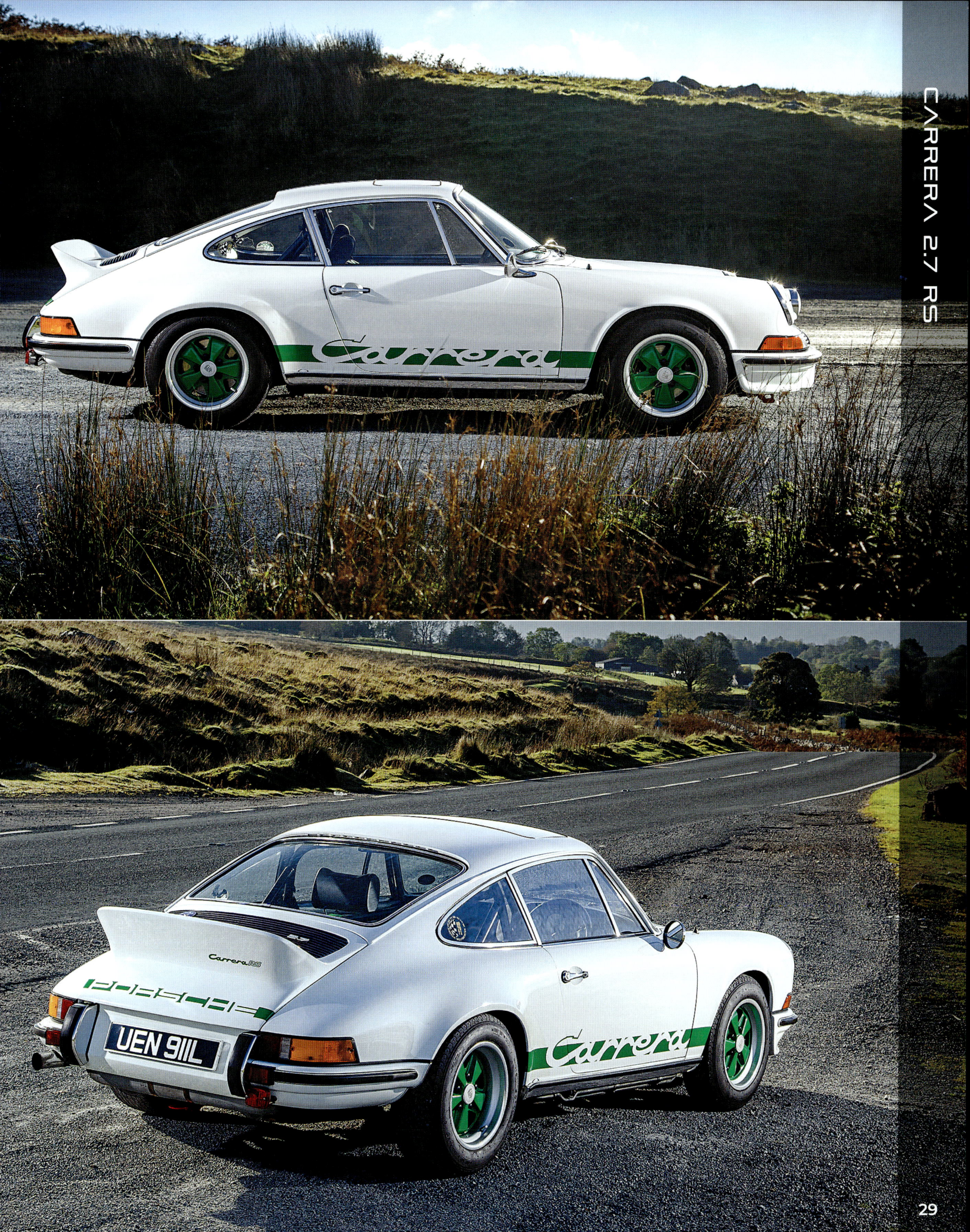

The 2.7-litre flat-six engine of the RS produced 20hp more than the 2.4-litre 911 S and featured a top speed of 152mph

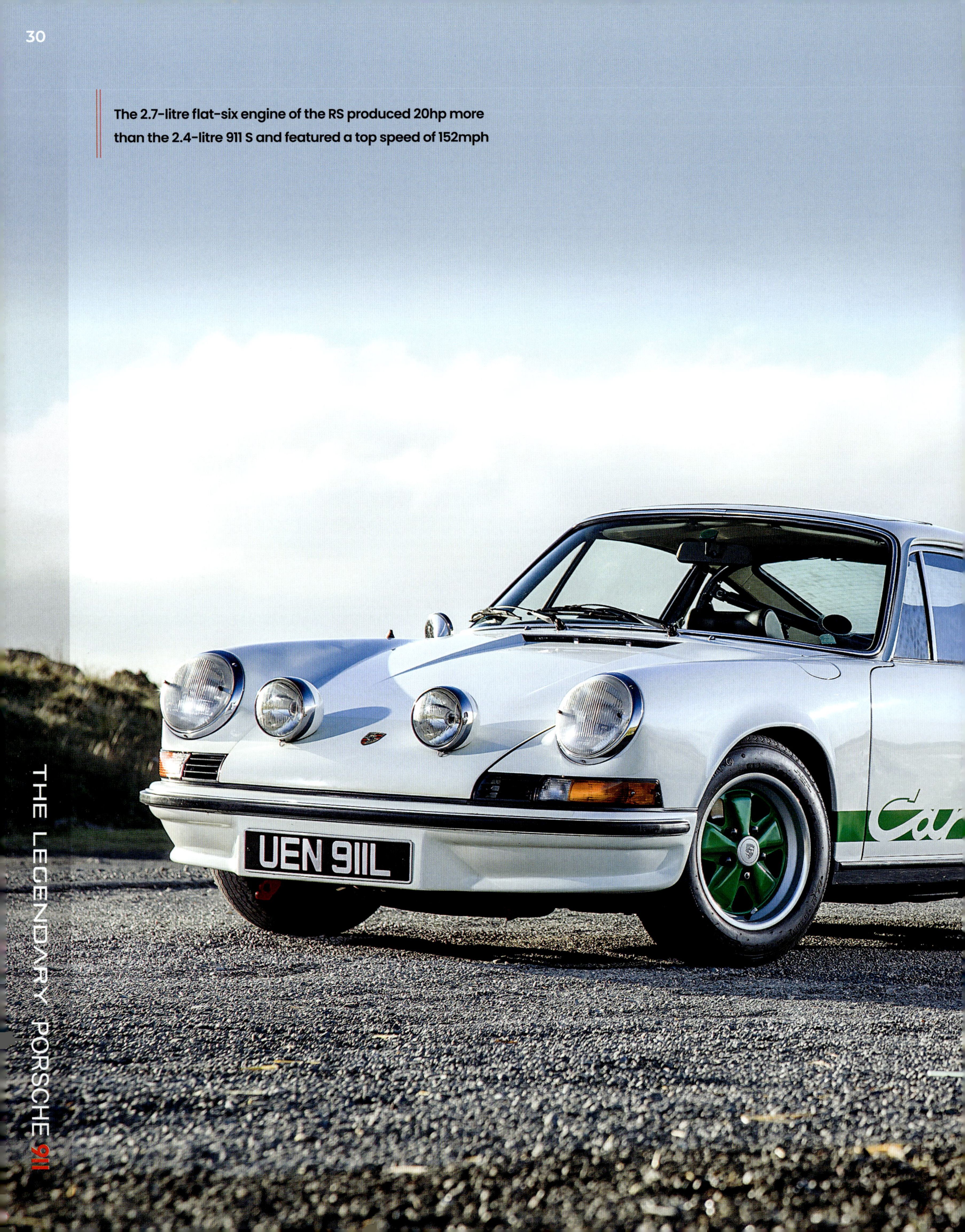

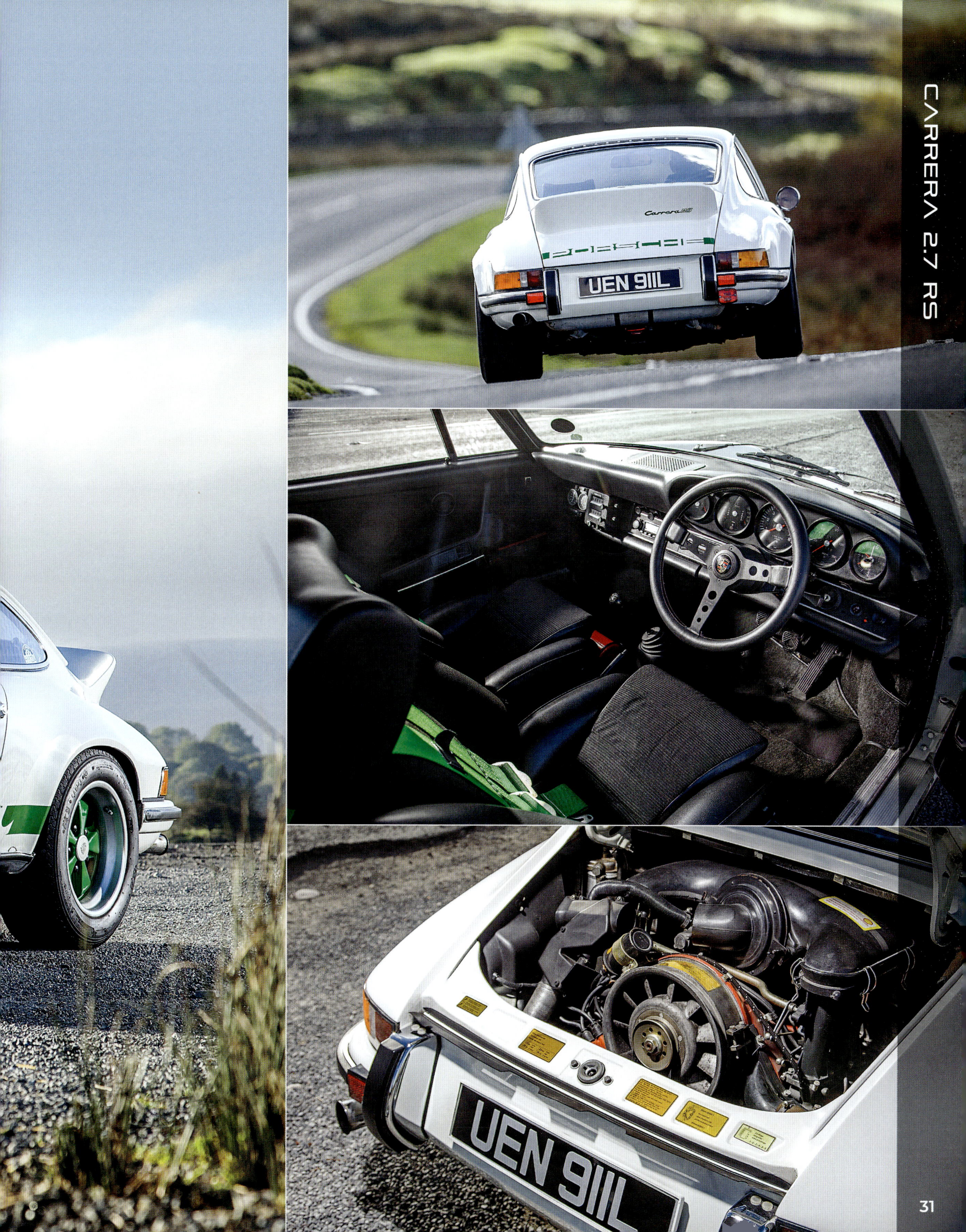

One of 20 RS N/GT 'Racing Package'

# PEAK 964 RS N/GT PERFORMANCE

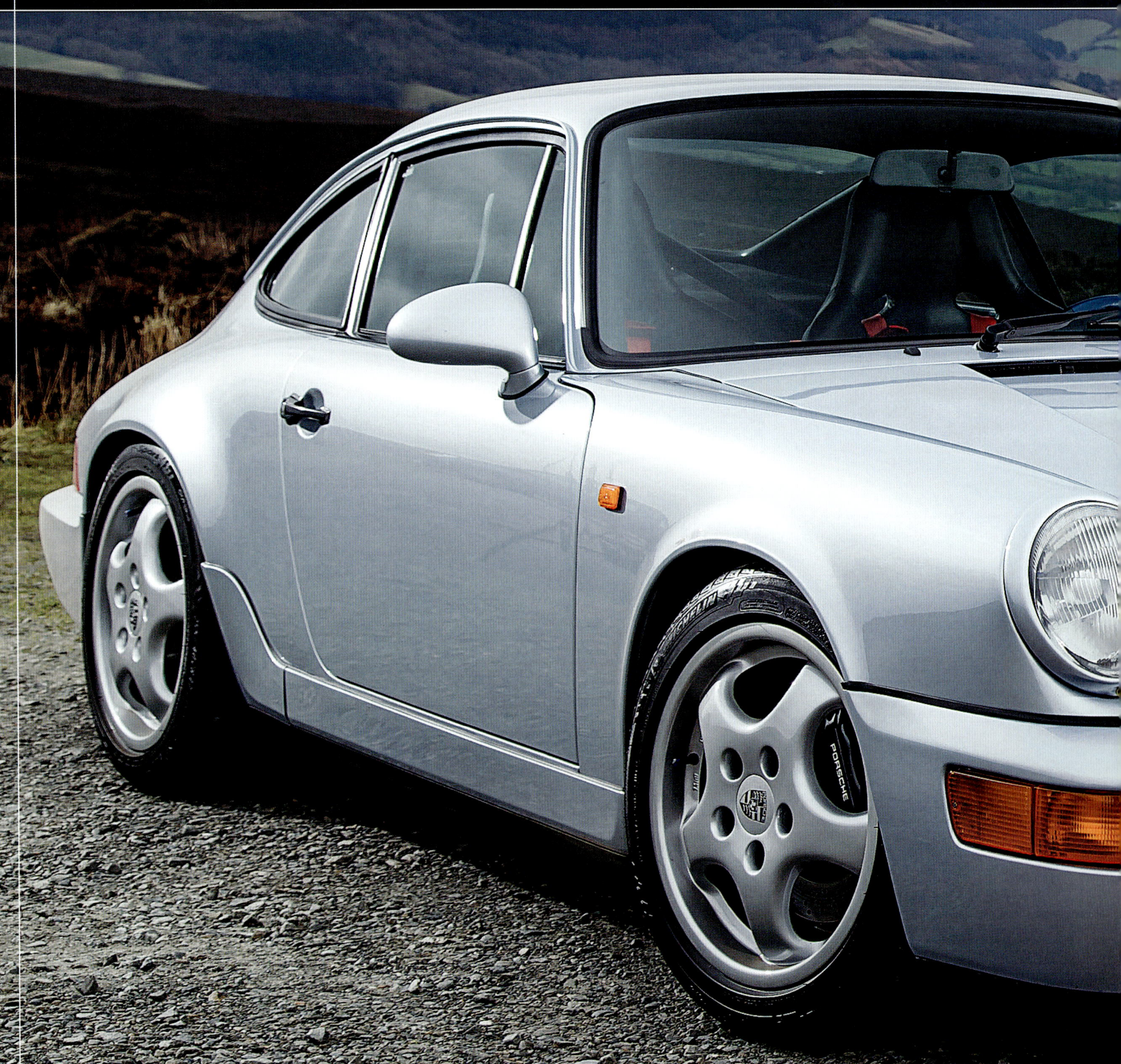

A firecracker road car with race-ready pedigree, an N/GT is a scintillating 964 Rennsport. Uncover the story of a unique example with a mysterious yet fascinating history.

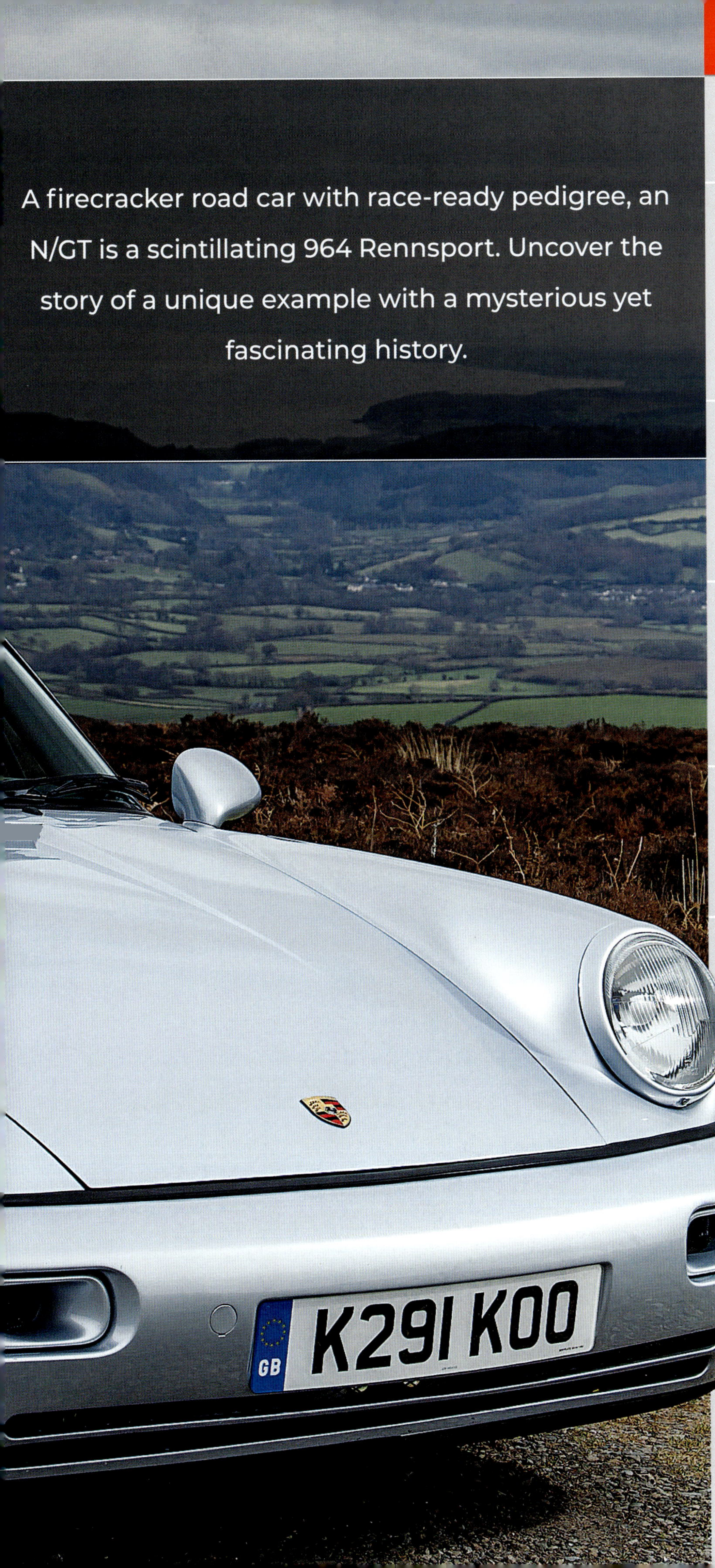

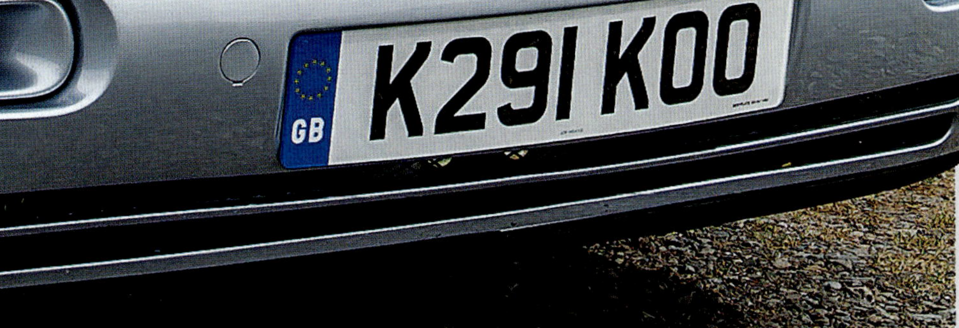

With only 290 units ever produced, the 964 RS N/GT is fairly rare by Porsche standards, accounting for around 12 per cent of total 964 Rennsport production. However, the example featured isn't merely a standard N/GT, but an extra special and substantially rare sub-production model straight from Weissach.

Just 20 examples of this particular model were made, each finished in a different colour. They went on sale for 8.8 million Yen, which was substantially cheaper than the 13.5 million Yen a 964 RS Lightweight cost at the time. All were sold in Japan and most are believed to still be in the Land of the Rising Sun. An example was recently sold at Pannhorst Classics in Germany, and the Polar silver car pictured here is the sole known example residing in the UK.

Originally a lightweight homologation special of the 964 Cup cars, the N/GT was a competition-ready fire breather permitted on the public road. A true performance thoroughbred, the suffix attached to that famous 'Rennsport' moniker simply denoted the competitions it was applicable for, this being FIA group 'N' (ostensibly production vehicles in competition), and GT racing.

Denoted from the factory as a 964 RS with option code M003 (M001 being a Cup car and M002 being the Touring model), the specification of an N/GT was Rennsport in its purest form. On top of the usual RS liturgy of a strengthened, seam-welded shell, an alloy front boot lid, no rear seats, front bucket seats with no electrical adjustment, thinner glass for side and rear windows, magnesium wheels and a lightweight rear bumper, M003 stipulated a complete removal of sound deadening (which, as well as the engine compartment cladding, meant the removal of all interior carpets and headlining, as well as carpeting in the front boot).

A sun visor was only present on the driver's side, and a welded Matter roll cage was installed as standard equipment. Carpets in the front of the N/GT's cabin were replaced with plywood footboards, and the bucket seats, colour-coded and covered in leather in the RS Touring, were covered by flame-retardant Nomex material. Schroth harnesses held the driver in place and a bigger-capacity fuel tank was installed, along with an onboard fire extinguisher and cut-off switch.

Like the 964 RS Touring and Lightweight, power was boosted for the N/GT by 10bhp, the result of modified pistons and cylinders as well as the deletion of catalytic converters, though the DME was relocated on N/GTs. The result is an aggressive Rennsport that's an uncompromising if not brilliantly exhilarating race car that, somehow, was deemed fit for the public road.

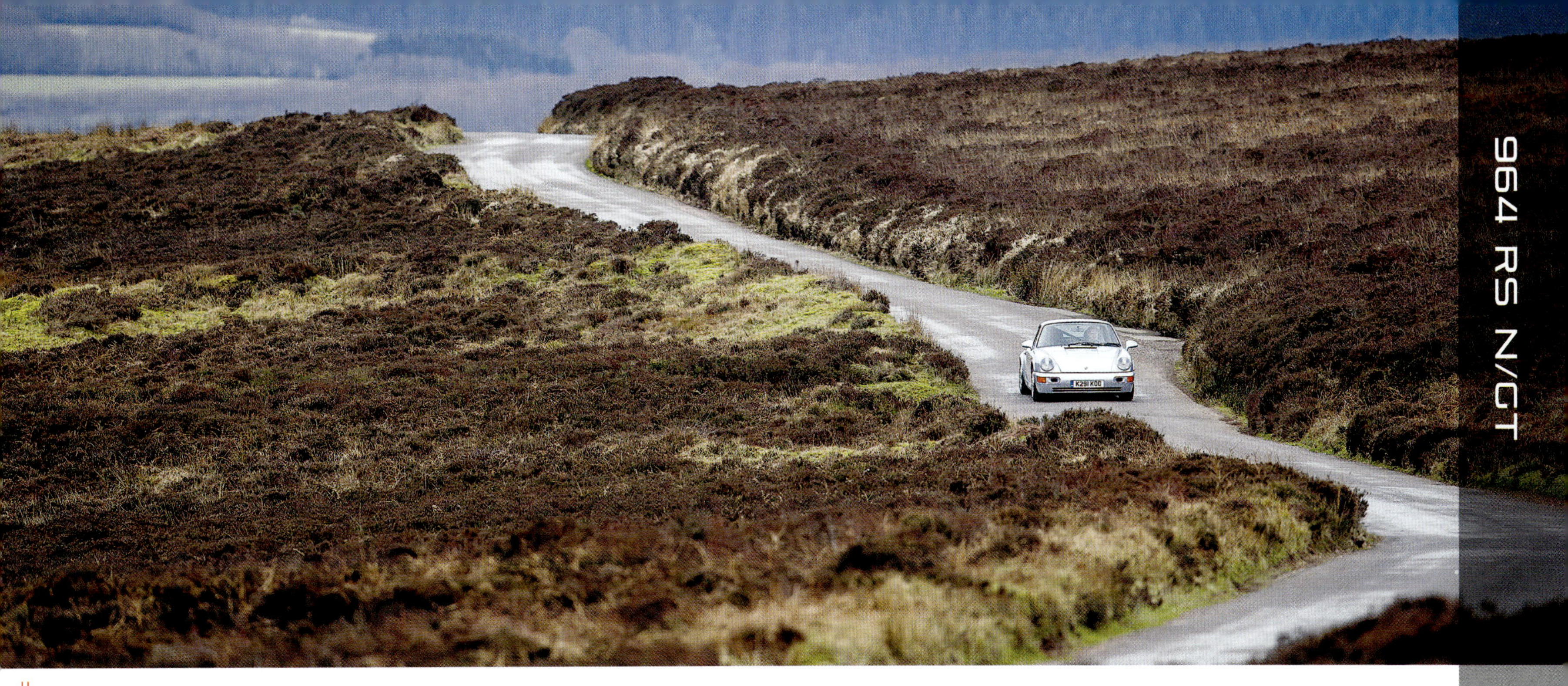

Rotated tacho clock, 75-litre fuel tank and lightweight magnesium wheels are all part of this special N/GT

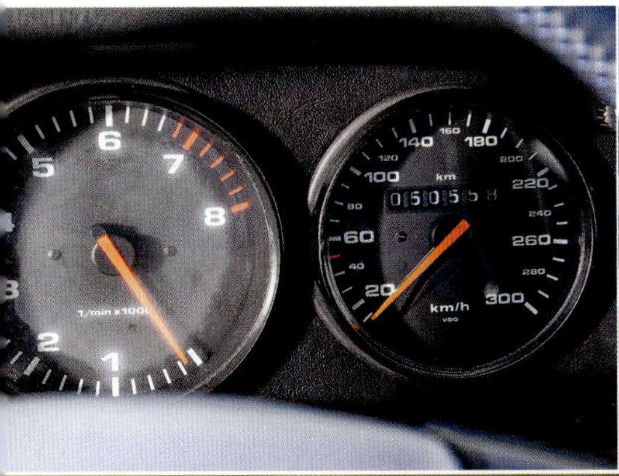

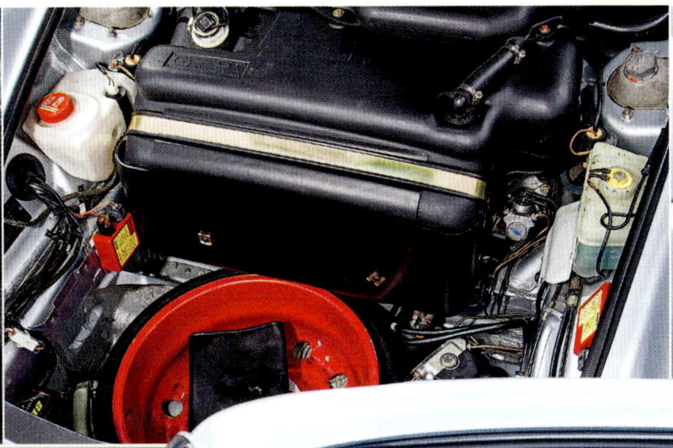

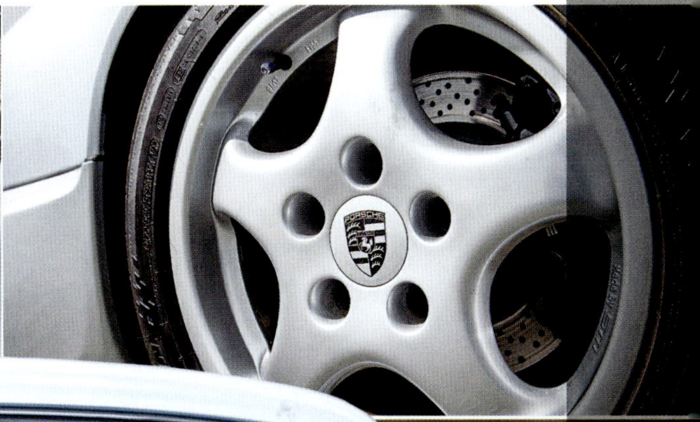

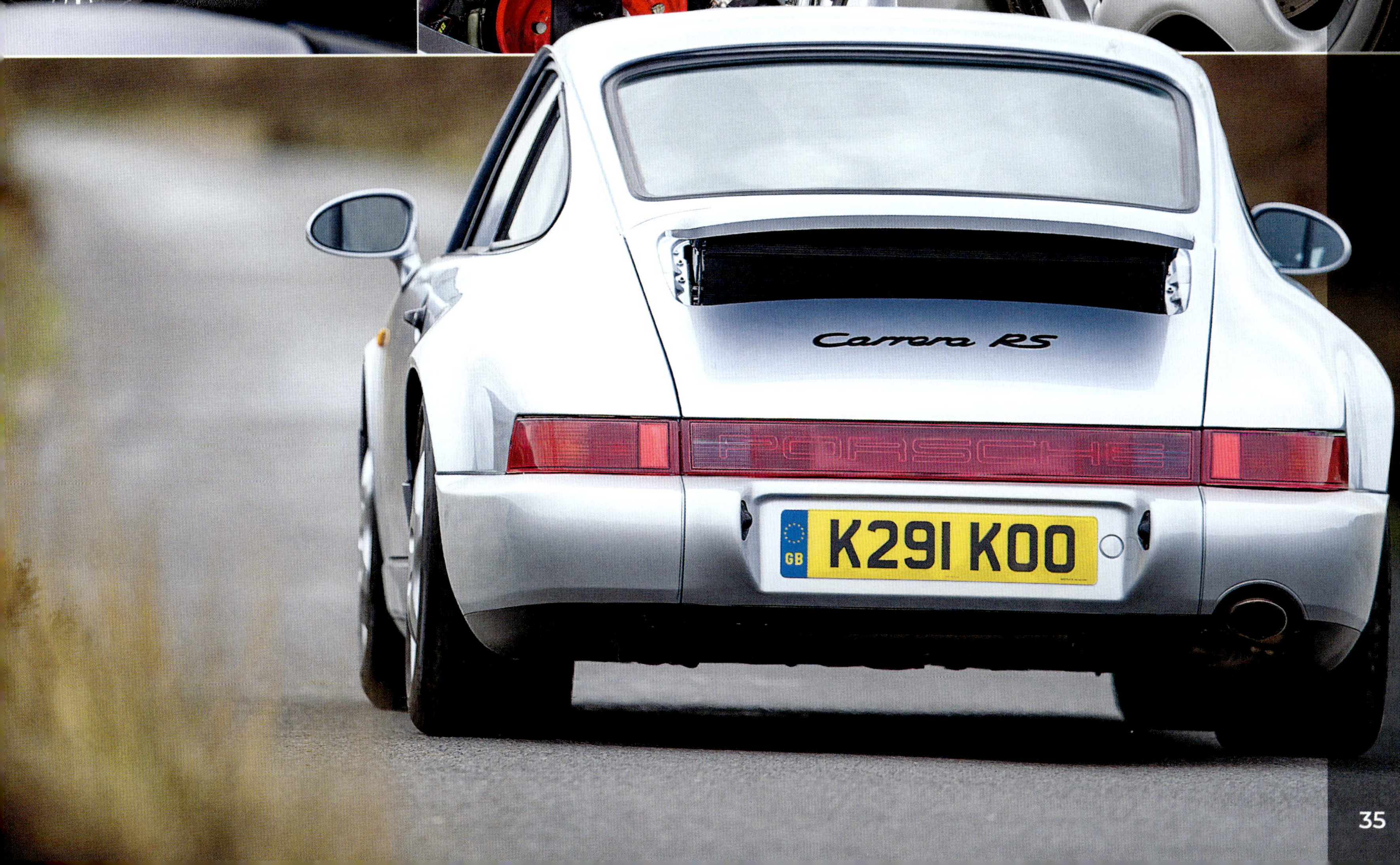

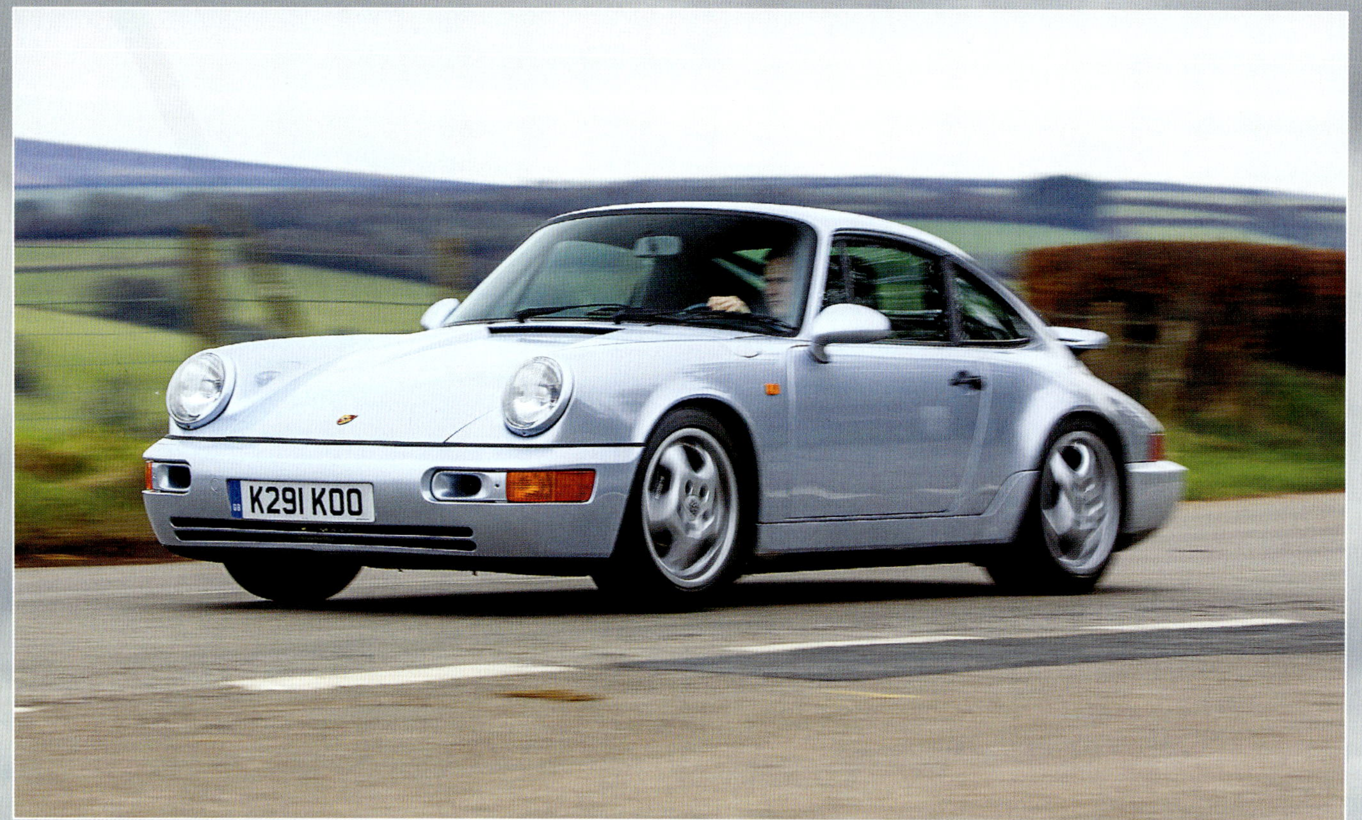

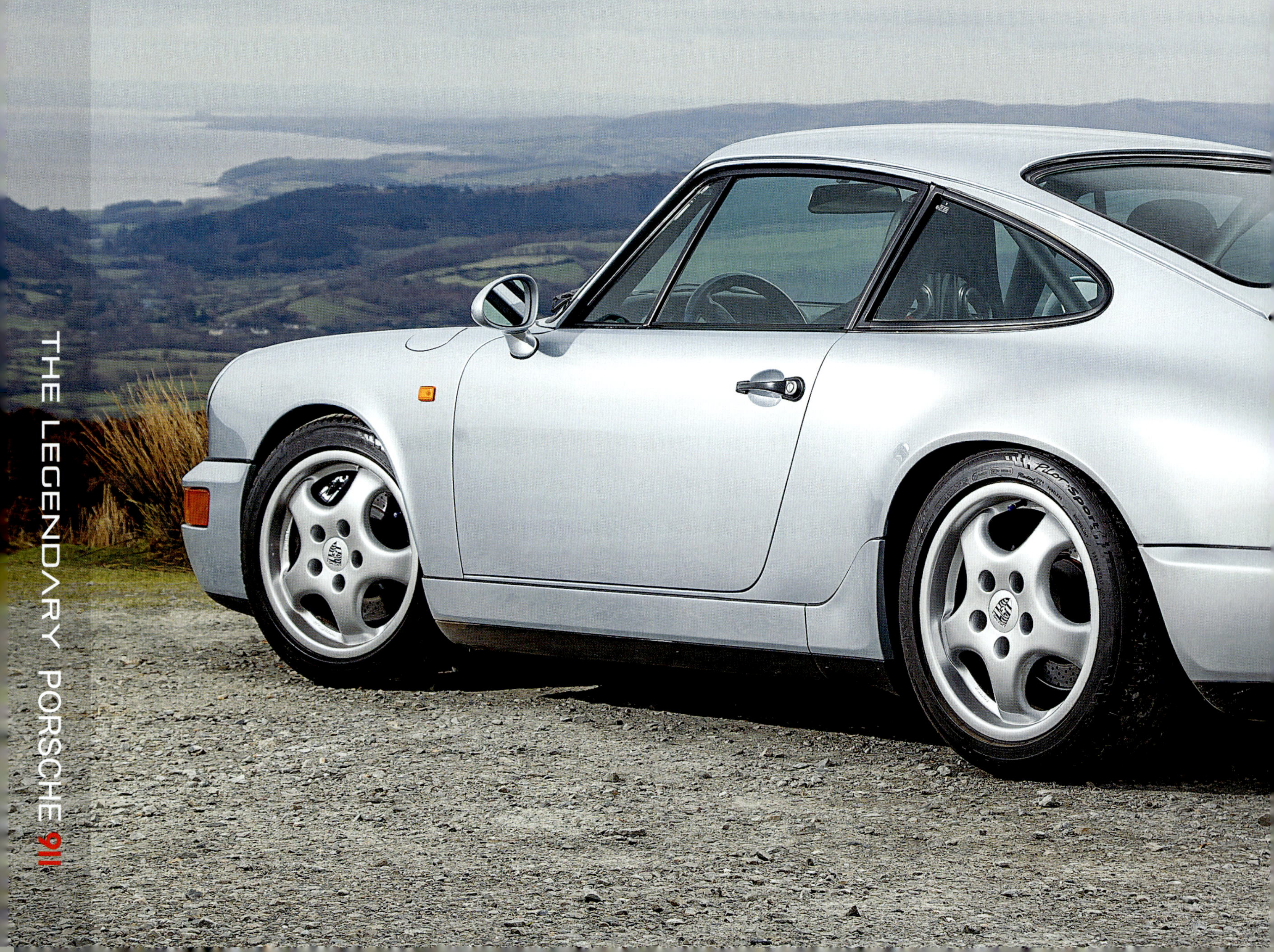

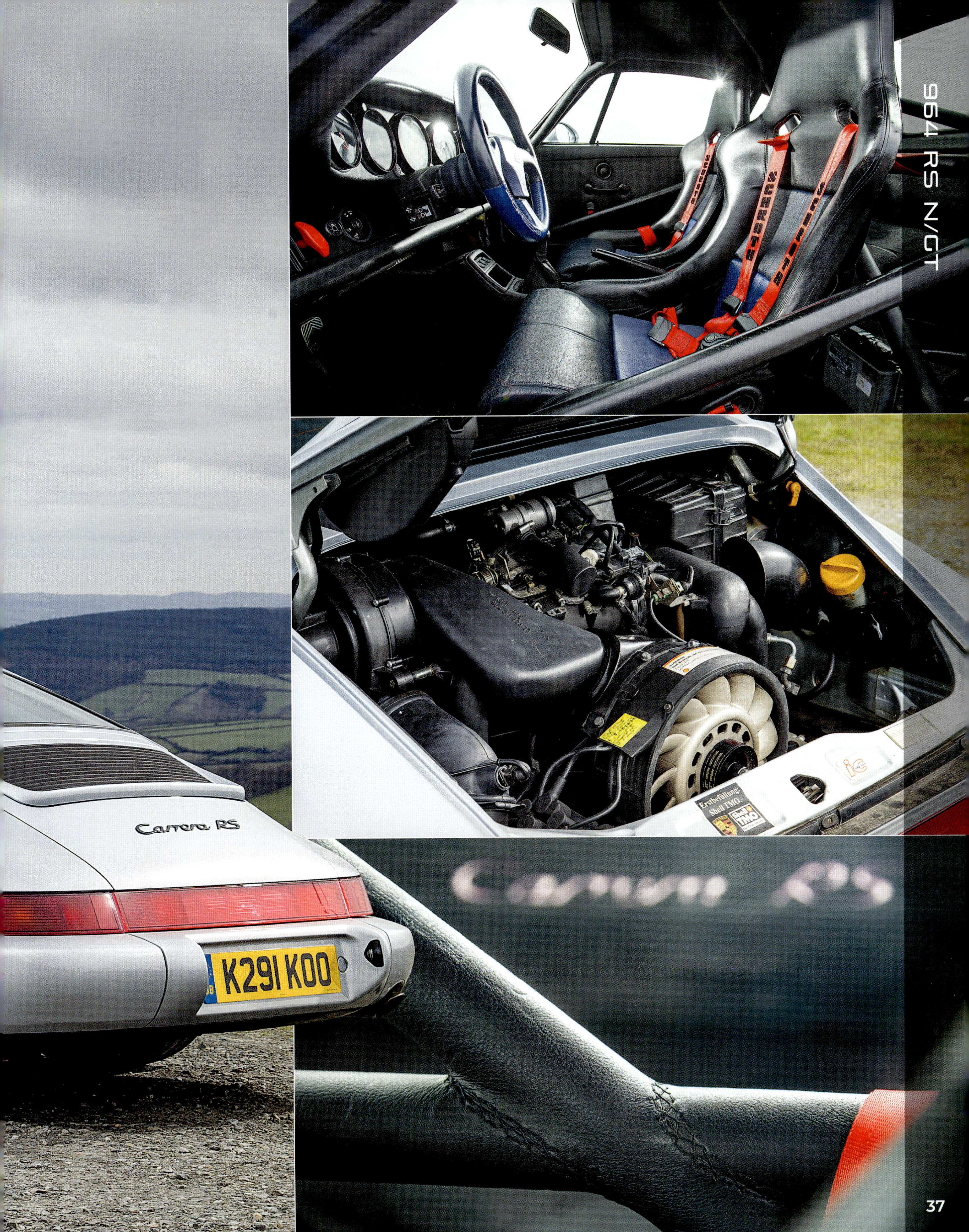

# 993 RS

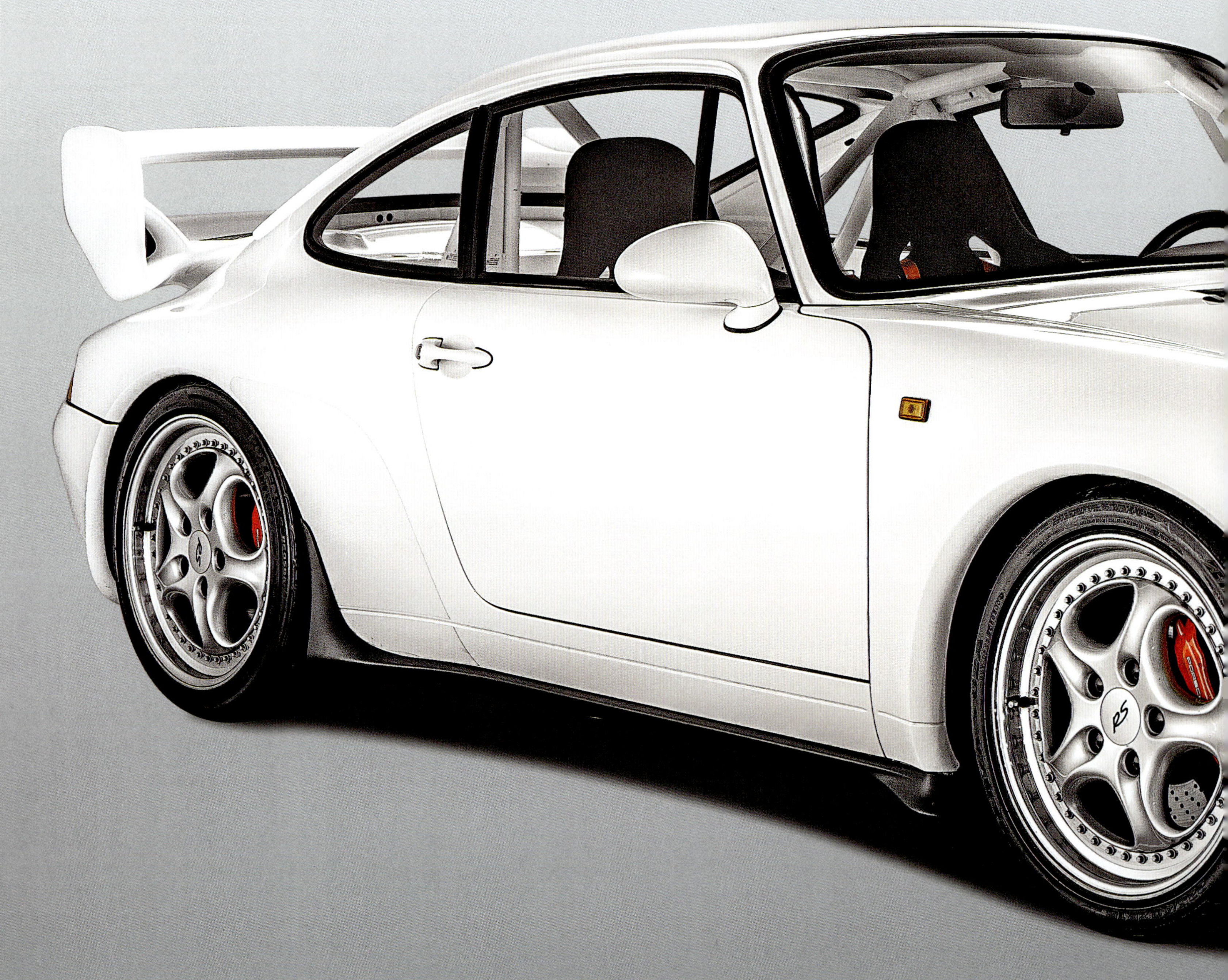

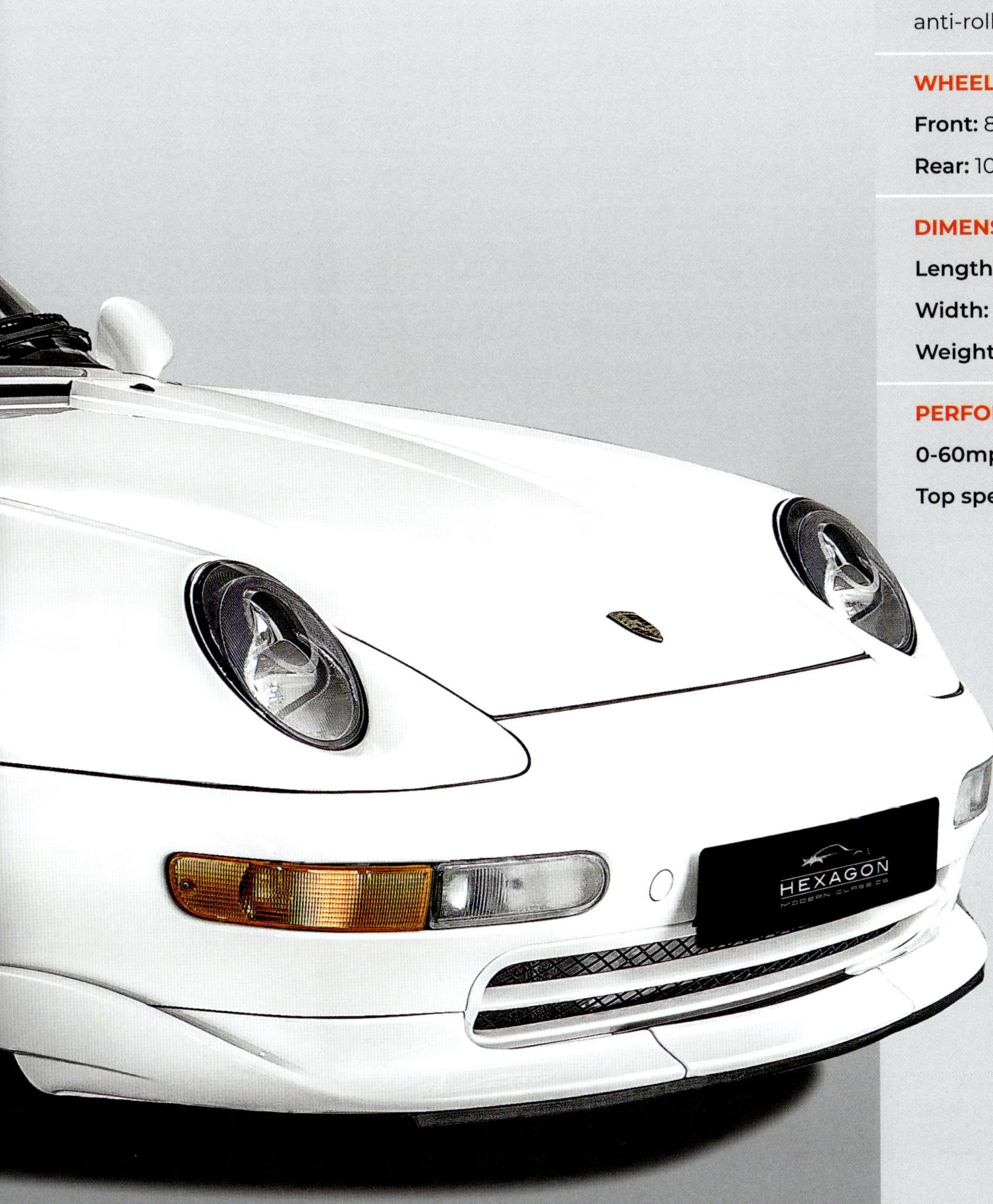




## 993 RS

(1995-1996)

### ENGINE

**Capacity:** 3,746cc

**Compression ratio:** 11.5:1

**Maximum power:** 300bhp @ 6,000rpm

**Maximum torque:** 355Nm @ 5,400rpm

**Transmission:** Six-speed manual, rear-wheel drive

### SUSPENSION

**Front:** MacPherson struts with coil springs; anti-roll bar

**Rear:** Multi-link with telescopic dampers; coil springs; anti-roll bar

### WHEELS & TYRES

**Front:** 8x18-inch; 225/40/ZR18

**Rear:** 10x18-inch; 265/35/ZR18

### DIMENSIONS

**Length:** 4,245mm

**Width:** 1,735mm

**Weight:** 1,279kg

### PERFORMANCE

**0-60mph:** 5.0 secs

**Top speed:** 172 mph

**G**et behind the wheel of the 993 RS and you'll be mightily impressed by the combination of rawness and purity on offer. That shouldn't really come as any surprise as this last of the air-cooled Rennsport cars is a special model indeed, and that makes it incredibly sought after today.

Launched in 1995, just 1,104 were built – with 227 of those produced in more hardcore Clubsport trim – and only 38 examples arrived in the UK in right-hand drive form. The Clubsport version of the 993 RS was admittedly more full on, but for those buyers that ticked the option box marked M003, this was the ultimate incarnation of this special 993. Representing around 20 per cent of total production, the variant, also referred to as the RSR in some markets, wasn't really intended for road driving, although some of the more committed owners did use them in that way. Instead, it was aimed at those that intended to wring the maximum enjoyment out of the RS on the race circuit, and here it excelled.

Costing in excess of £70,000 when new, just about all unnecessary kit was cut to maximise the weight saving, so you'd struggle in vain to find the likes of air-conditioning, electric windows, or carpets. Full harnesses were fitted as standard along with a Matter roll cage that was welded into place, and the seats gained fire-resistant Nomex coverings. Meanwhile, on the outside was an improved aero package that featured a deeper front splitter and bi-plane rear wing with substantial end plates. Highly sought after today, it's the ultimate embodiment of the RS philosophy.

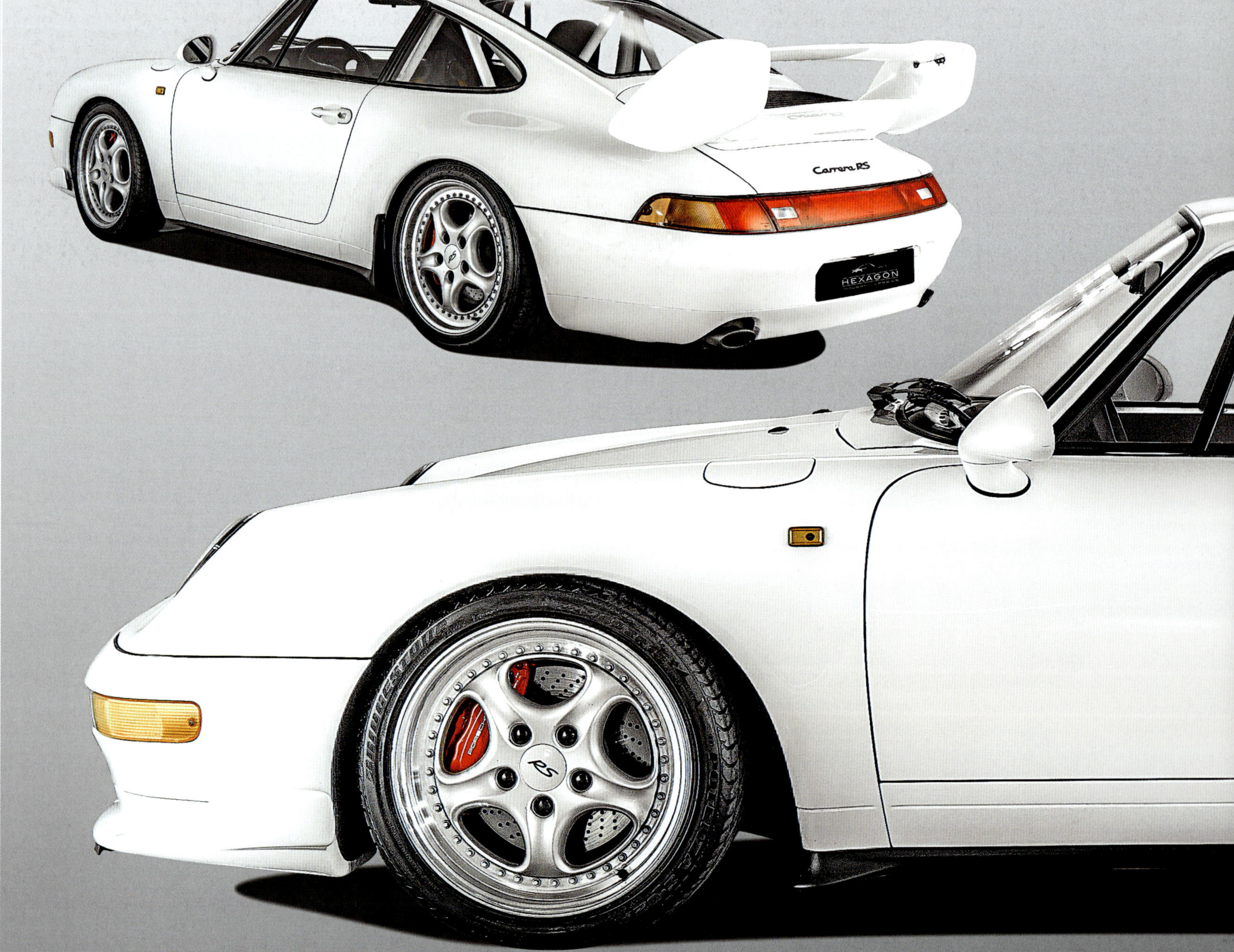

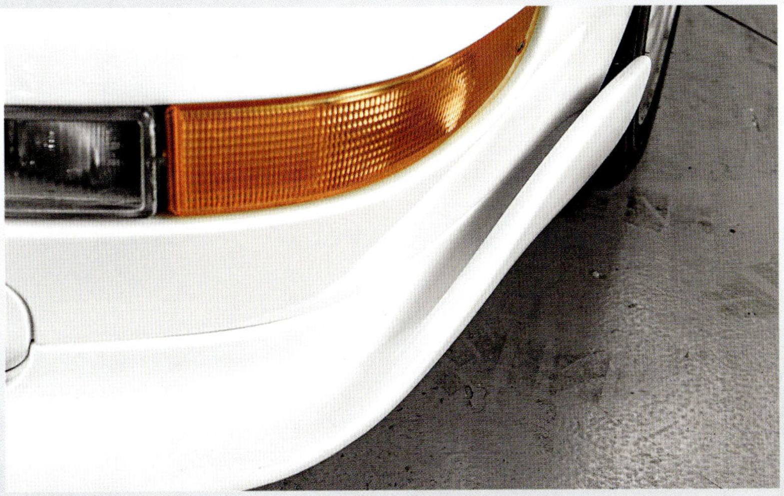

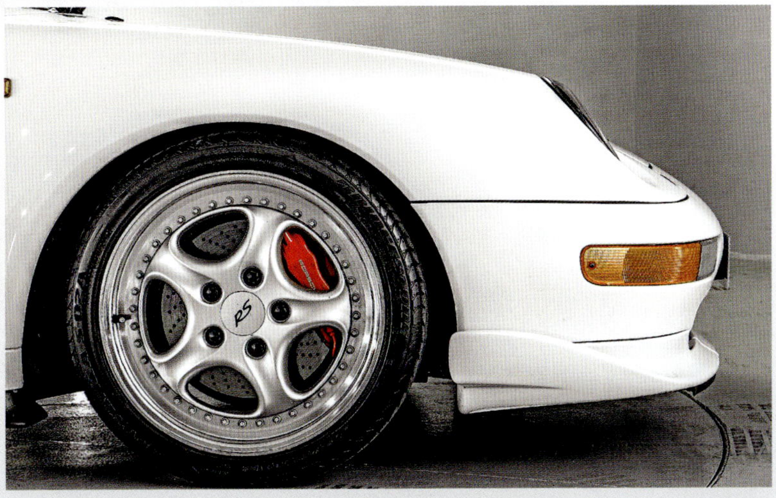

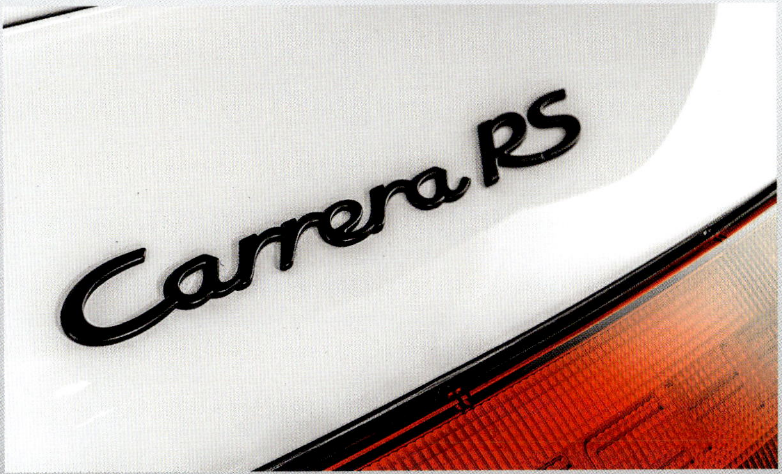

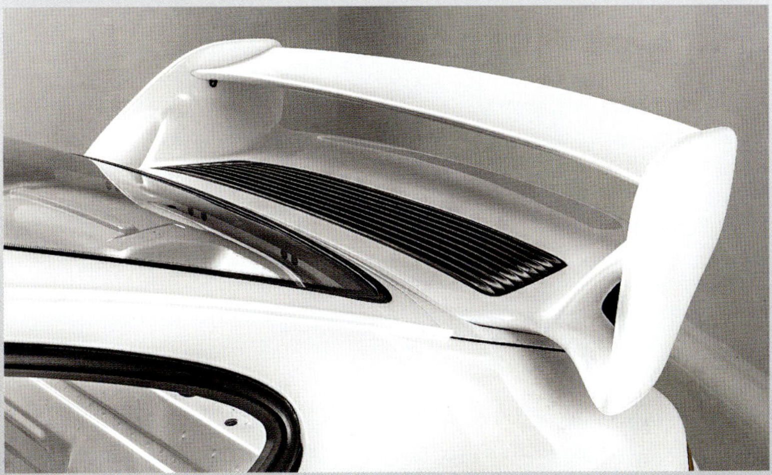

Externally, the hardcore Clubsport differed visually from the Comfort spec thanks to a larger bi-planed rear wing with air intakes, plus a front spoiler with a more extreme curvature at its sides

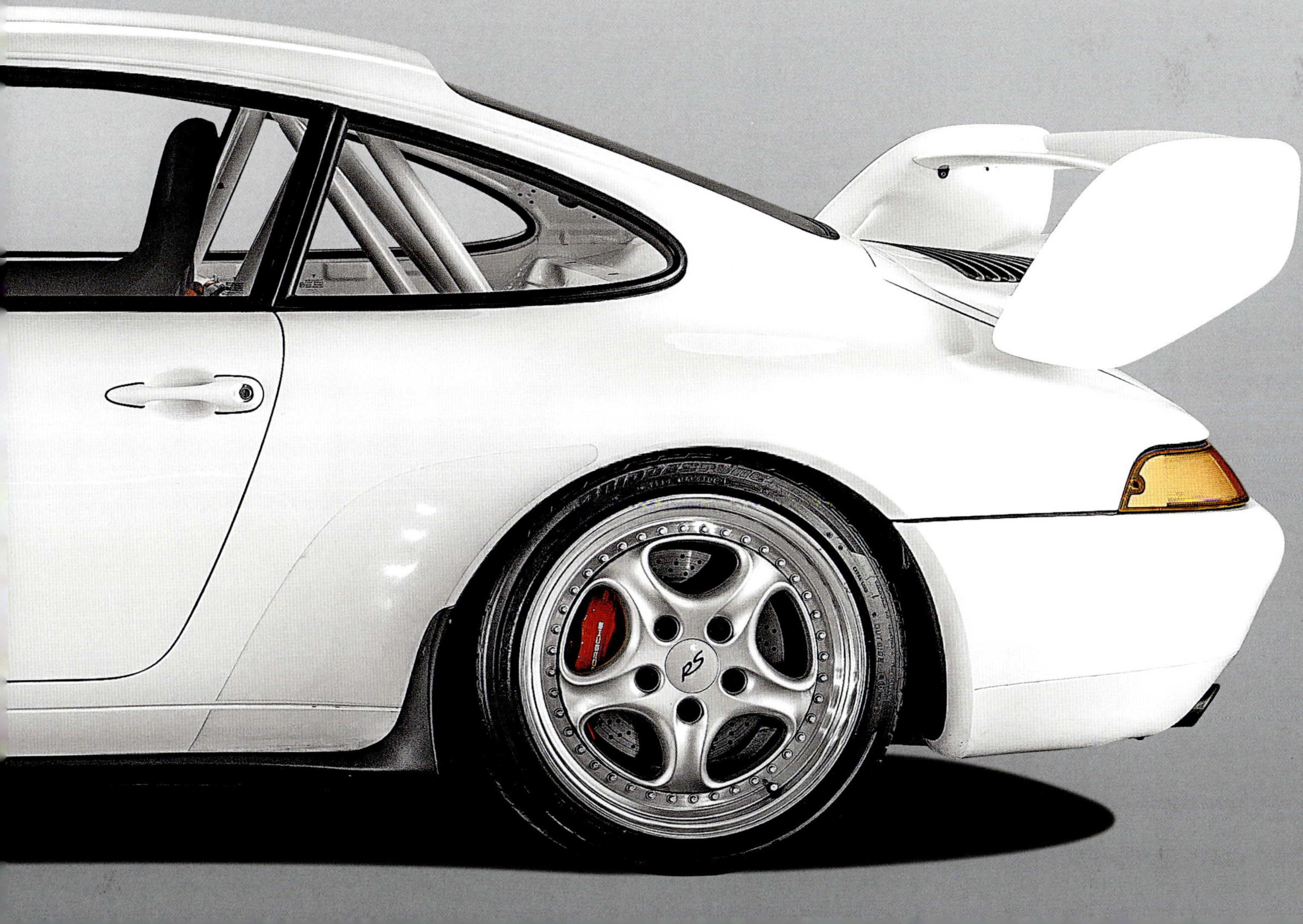

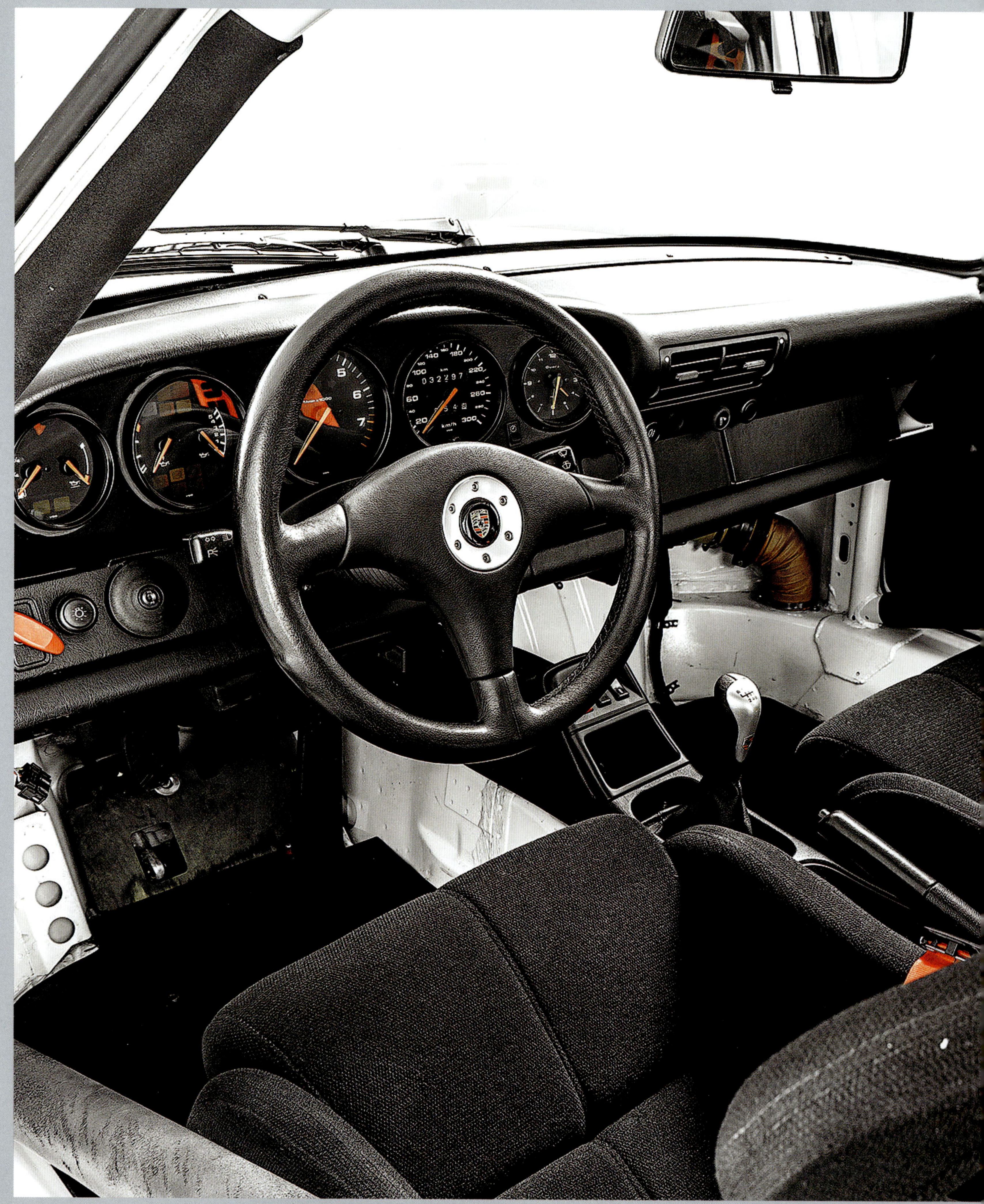

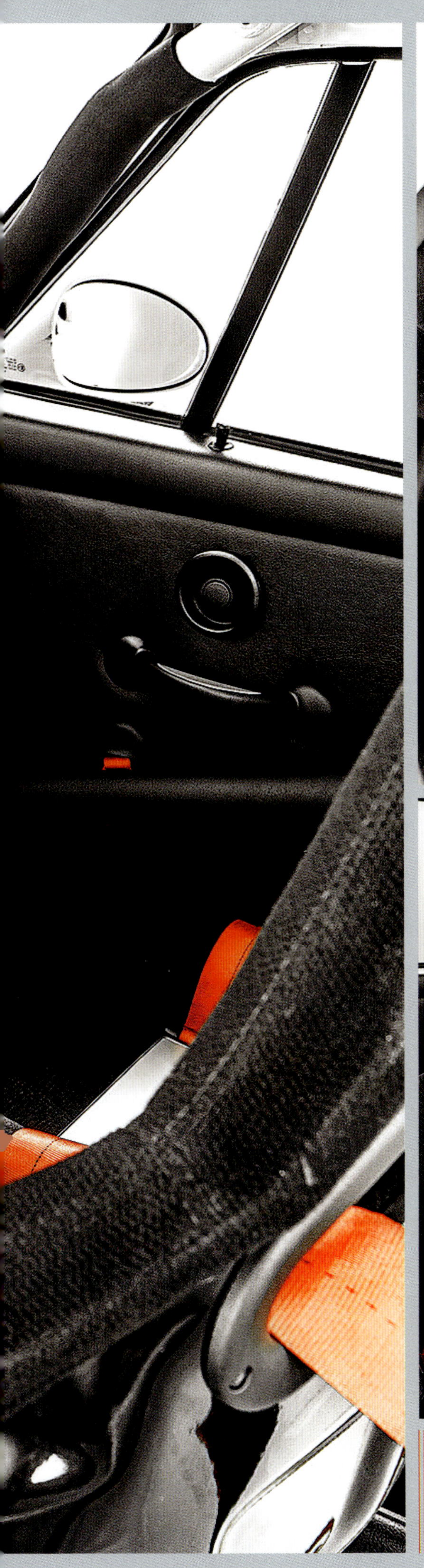

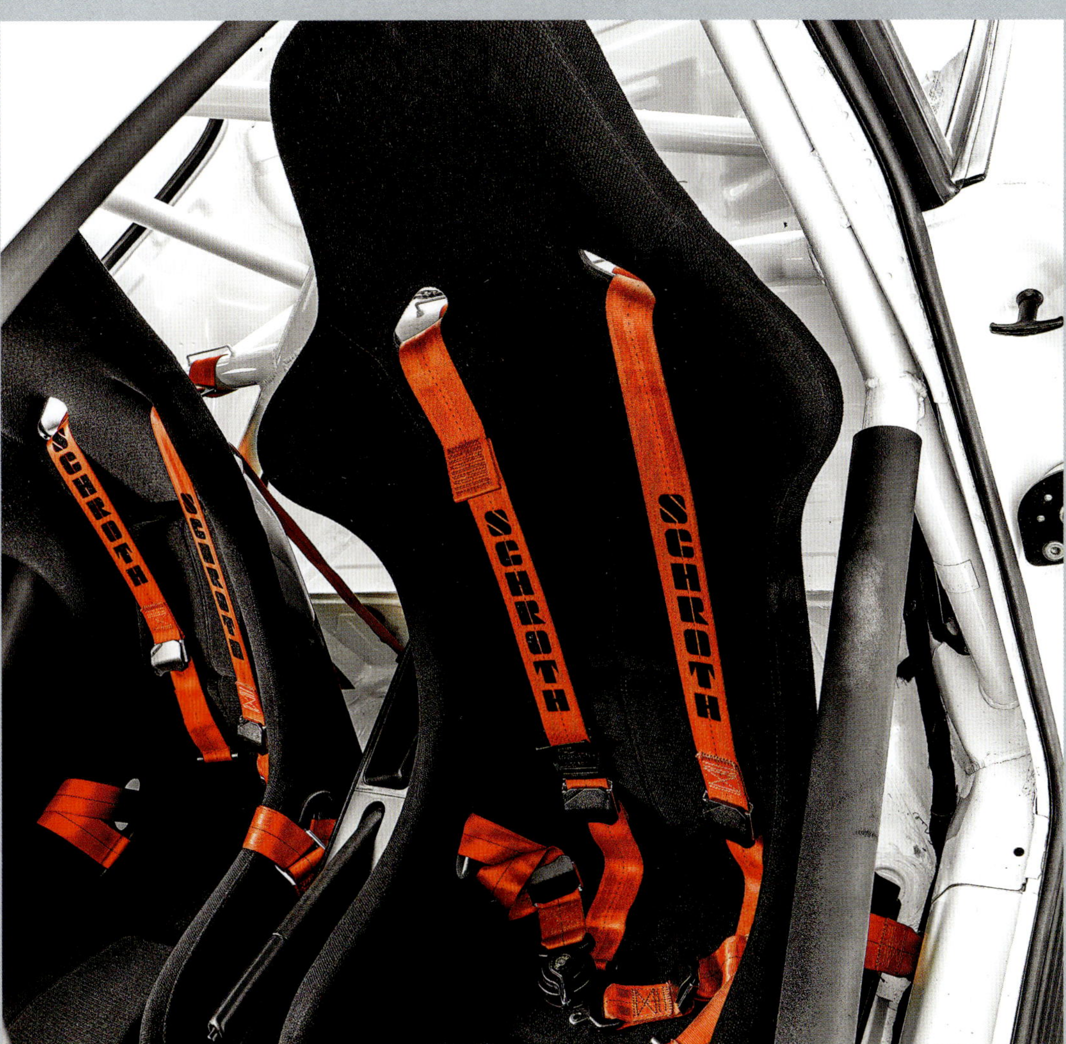

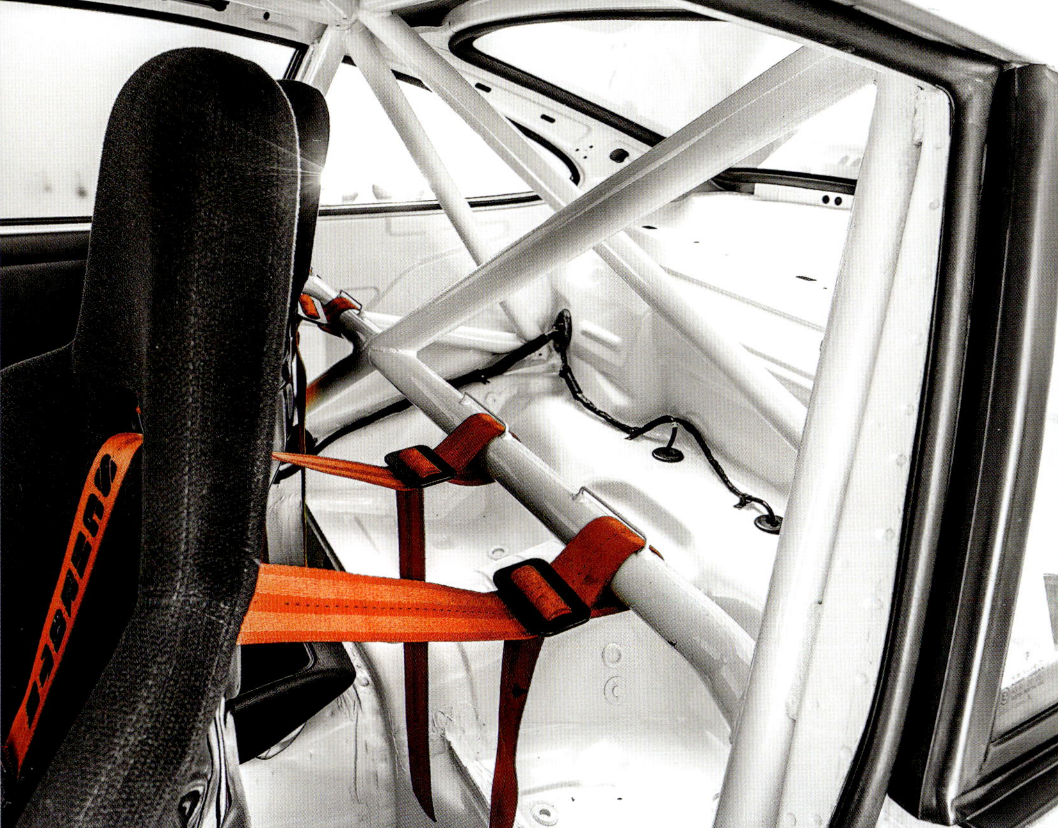

Inside, the Clubsport is sparce, with only extremely necessary equipment remaining. Nomex bucket seats offer a tight hold and a comprehensive cage including door bars offers protection and rigidity

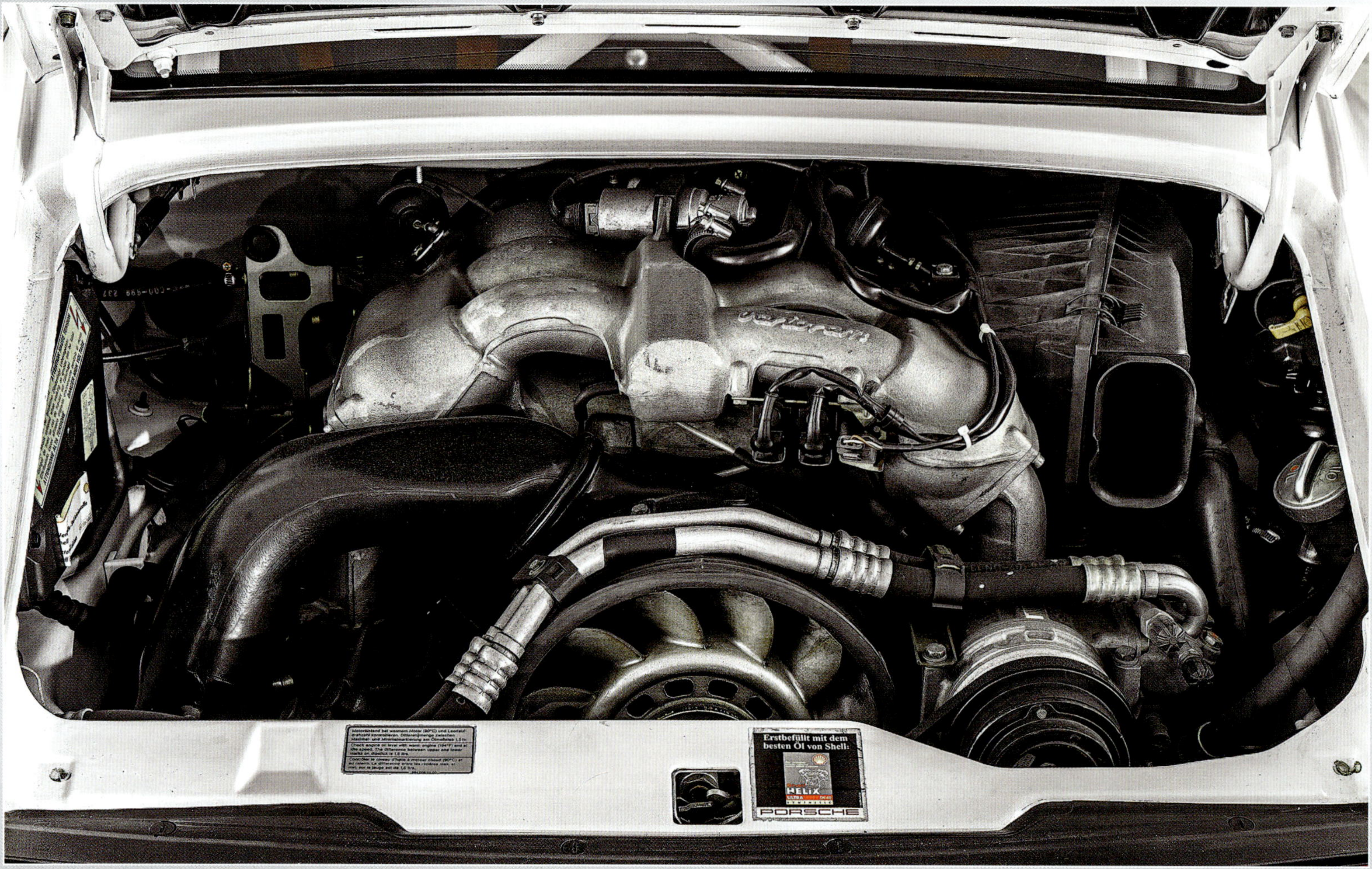

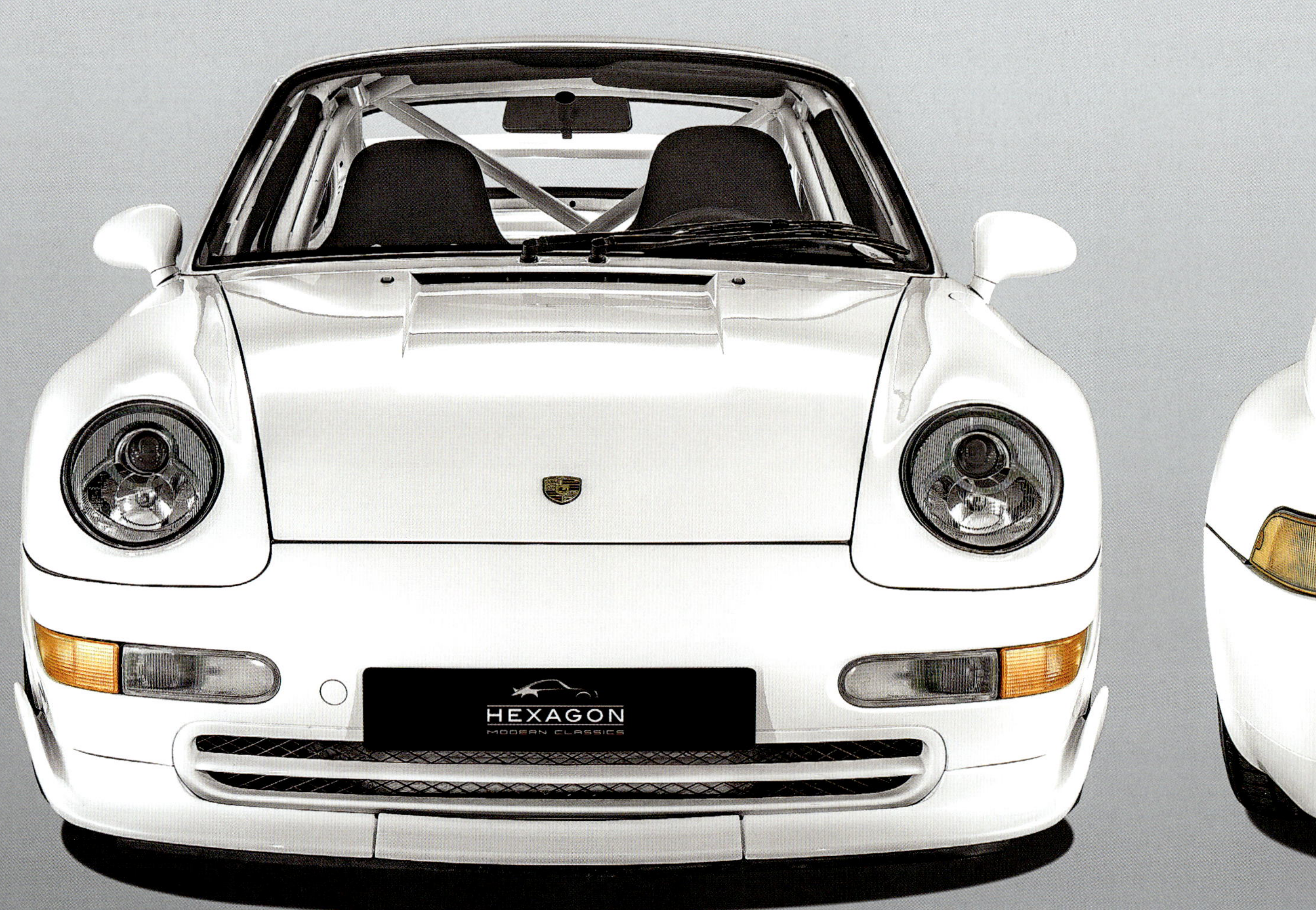

# BUYING TIPS

Make no mistake, the 993 RS is a specialist proposition and one that commands increasingly high prices. It's a car that demands respect, and that goes for buying one, where researching the history and condition would be crucial. It would be very unwise to take the plunge without seeking the advice of an Official Porsche Centre or respected specialist.

**HISTORY:** The most important aspect of buying an RS. It's vital to ensure that numbers and mileage all tally up, and extra care is needed with imported cars. Any doubts or gaps in the history, and you should tread extremely carefully.

**CRASH DAMAGE:** Hard to believe now, but when these cars were cheaper many were subjected to circuit use with all the risks that implies. Crash repairs aren't a deal-breaker as long as you know exactly what's been done and how well.

**BODYWORK:** RS parts are eye-wateringly expensive so examine them closely and carefully for any damage. Corrosion isn't a major concern, thought it can take hold around the windscreen.

**ENGINE:** Strong and with few inherent problems, the 3.8-litre unit should have been fastidiously maintained. Check for flat spots in the rev range. Oil leaks are common, though rocker cover leaks are an easy fix.

**TRANSMISSION:** Very strong if used sensibly, but hard use will take its toll. Odd noises from the gearbox will end in a big bill, so be careful – especially check for crunching synchromesh.

**BRAKES/SUSPENSION:** Refurbishing a tired set-up will cost plenty, so if an owner has skimped here what else hasn't been done? And original Speedline wheels in perfect condition are a real plus given the huge cost of their replacement.

**INTERIOR:** Condition here is a good indicator of previous ownership, so be wary of a scrubby cabin for Comforts. There's less equipment than other 911s, but make sure what's there works properly.

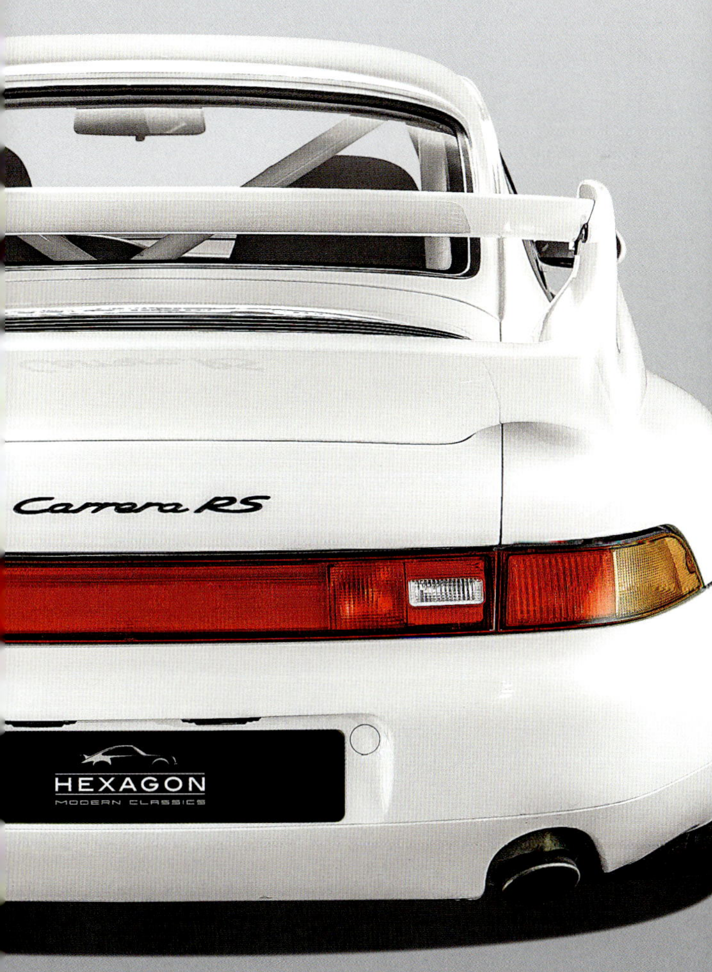

# 997.1
# GT3 RS

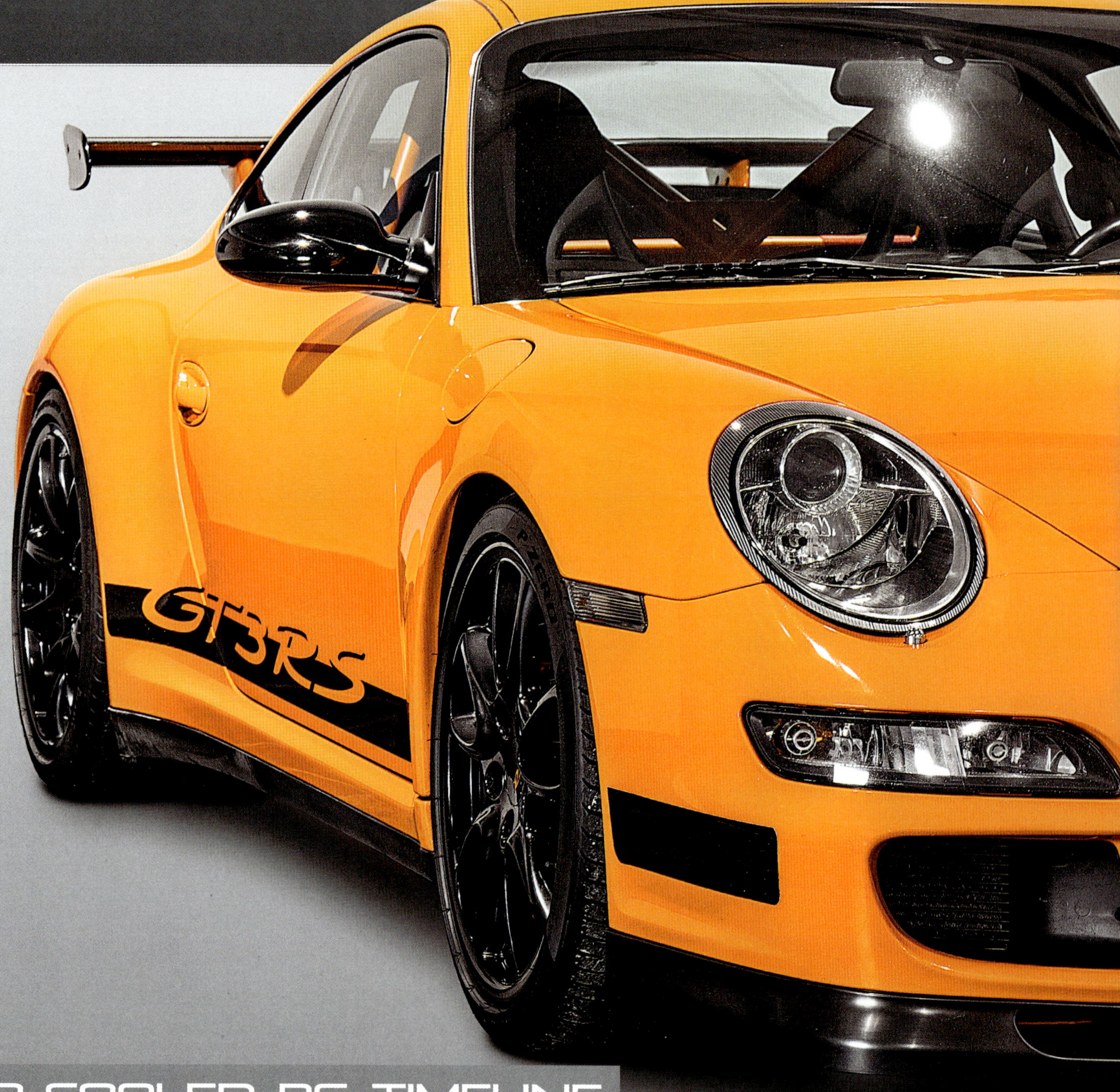

## WATER-COOLED RS TIMELINE

### 2004
The 996 GT3 is the first water-cooled Neunelfer to get the RS treatment. The 3.6-litre engine produces 381bhp, enough to despatch the 0-62mph sprint in just 4.4 seconds. 682 produced

### 2006
Porsche follow up with the 997 GT3 RS, with essentially the same engine as the 996. Power is raised to 415bhp though, and a weight-saving regime saves 20kg. 1,106 produced

### 2009
It's the turn of the Gen 2 997, this time the RS getting a larger 3.8-litre engine with 450bhp that cuts the 0-62mph time to just 4.0 seconds. Aero tweaks and dynamic engine mounts feature. 1,500 produced

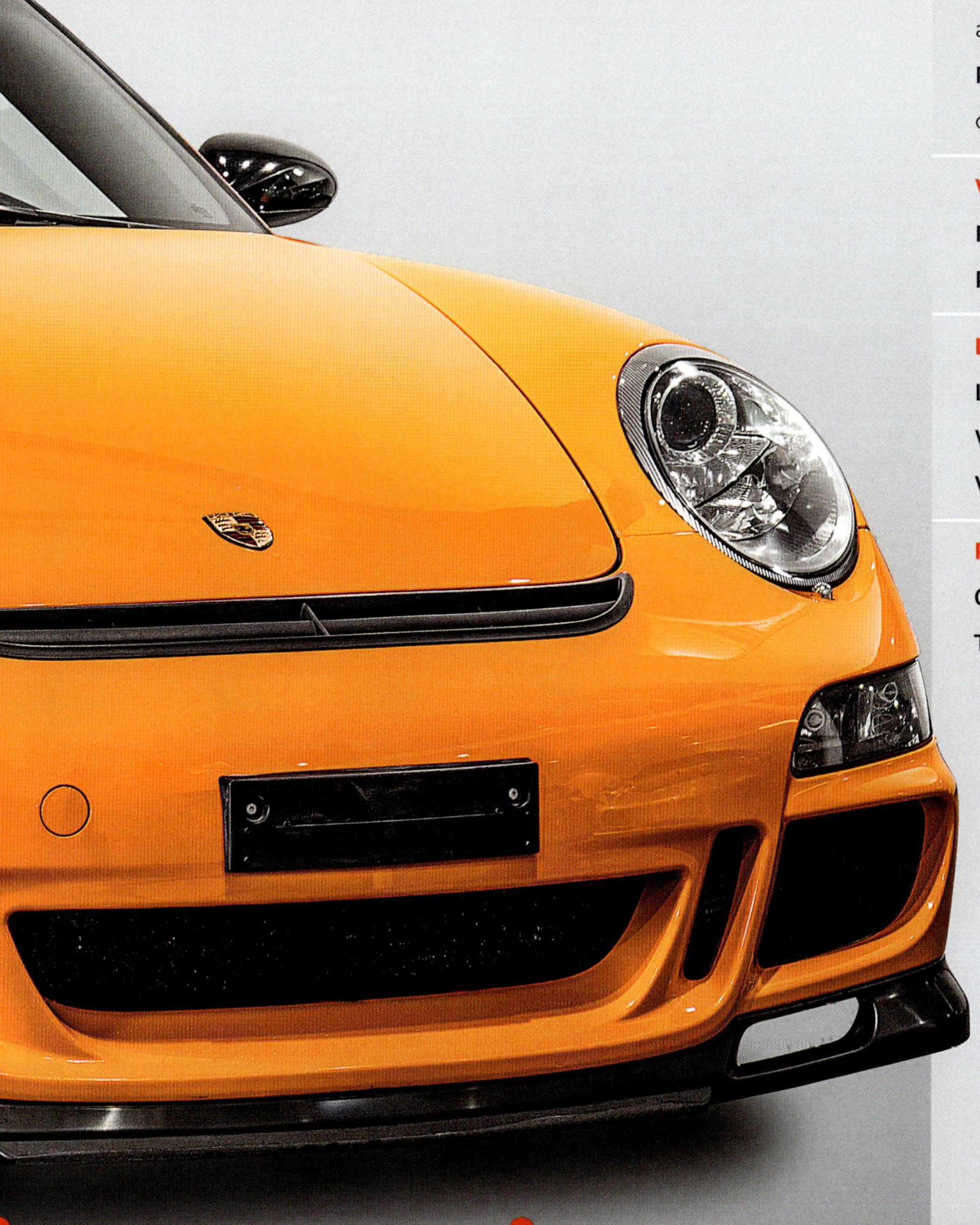





# 997.1 GT3 RS

2006-2007

### ENGINE

**Capacity:** 3,600cc

**Compression ratio:** 12.0:1

**Maximum power:** 415bhp @ 7,600rpm

**Maximum torque:** 405Nm @ 5,500rpm

**Transmission:** Six-speed manual, rear-wheel drive

### SUSPENSION

**Front:** MacPherson struts with coil springs and anti-roll bar

**Rear:** Multi-link with telescopic dampers; coil springs; anti-roll bar

### WHEELS & TYRES

**Front:** 8.5x19-inch; 235/35/R19

**Rear:** 12x19-inch; 305/30/R19

### DIMENSIONS

**Length:** 4,460mm

**Width:** 1,808mm

**Weight:** 1,375kg

### PERFORMANCE

**0-60mph:** 4.2 secs

**Top speed:** 194mph

## 2010

A sure-fire future classic arrives in the shape of the 997 GT3 RS 4.0. Boasting a stunning 500bhp, it's the quickest RS yet. 600 produced

## 2010

It's the 997 GT2 that gets the RS treatment. There's 620bhp from the 3.6-litre engine, a 205mph top speed, and plenty of tasty carbon fibre bits. 500 produced

## 2015

Huge road presence marks out the RS in 991 GT3 form. Substantially lighter than Turbo variants, the 4.0-litre engine makes 500bhp. 42 sold in the UK last year

**G**iven the desirability of the car you see here, it's no real surprise that the second-generation 997 range would include a GT3 RS. It was no mild refresh though, as the new model would receive some substantial changes, not least of which was a 3.8-litre motor that sat on active engine mounts.

With power and torque both increased – to 450hp and 430Nm respectively – the 0–60mph time was cut by 0.2 seconds to 4.0 seconds dead, and both response and mid-range shove were boosted. VarioCam Plus and a higher 8,500rpm redline also featured. Further revisions included gorgeous new centre-lock wheels and suspension that featured stiffer spring rates and tweaks to the anti-roll bars. Externally, the new model boasted various subtle changes, including redesigned air intakes, and there was a new aero package to improve downforce. 1,500 examples were produced before the 997 disappeared in 2012.

You have to head back a little over a decade, to 2004 in fact, to find the first GT3 to benefit from the legendary RS suffix. Then, it was attached to the rump of the 996 with around 680 lucky buyers getting to experience the delights of a 381bhp flat six allied to a useful weight reduction.

It would hardly come as a surprise, then, when Porsche announced that the 997 GT3 would also get the Rennsport treatment, although this time both models would arrive together in August 2006. 996 buyers had to wait five years or so for the same development. Even with an eye-watering £94,280 price tag, this new generation would prove immediately popular, so much so that 1,106 examples would leave the production line before the Gen2 version arrived three years later. Like the 996 incarnation, the first 997 GT3 RS was all about weight saving. The first-generation GT3 RS featured the wider rear bodyshell of the Carrera 4 and Porsche shaved a healthy 20kg off the weight of the Gen1 GT3.

Ultimately, the 997 generation is renowned for its usable, reliable nature and the GT3 RS does nothing to dispel that view. Yes, it was designed for the ultimate in thrills on road or track but the quality of its construction means there's little to worry about if you're considering buying one today. Find one that has been maintained regardless of cost and it'll prove an immensely rewarding experience. That said, it's worth mentioning that the RS was available in some pretty extrovert colours, so you might want to consider whether you'd be happier with black or silver rather than the Orange or Viper green!

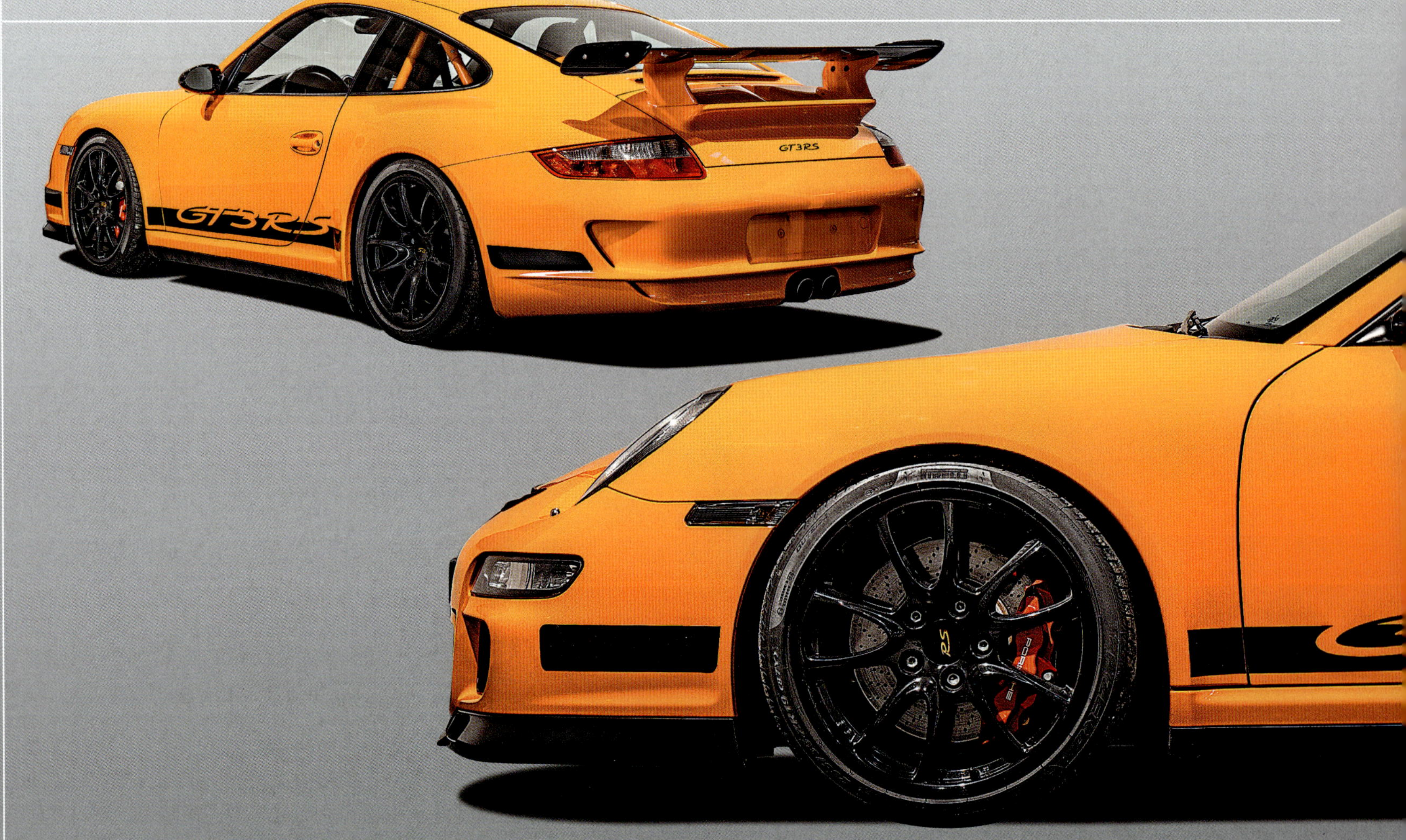

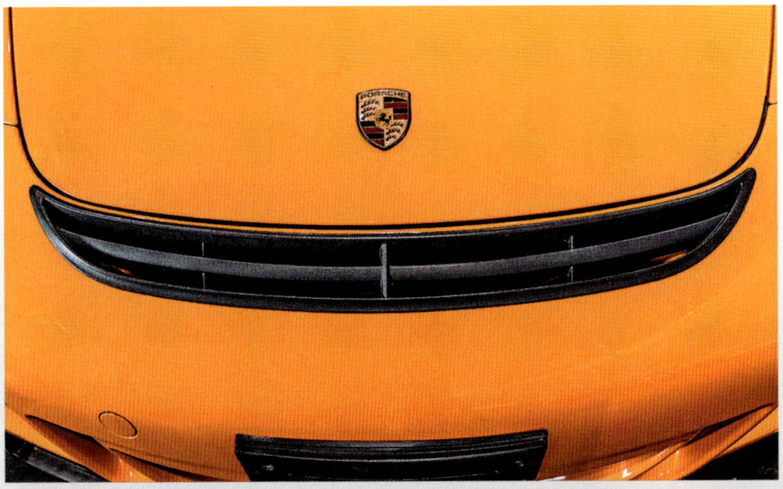

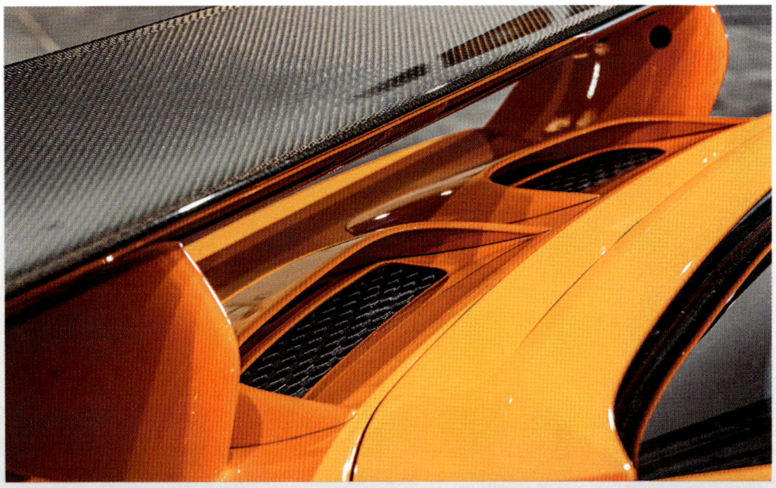

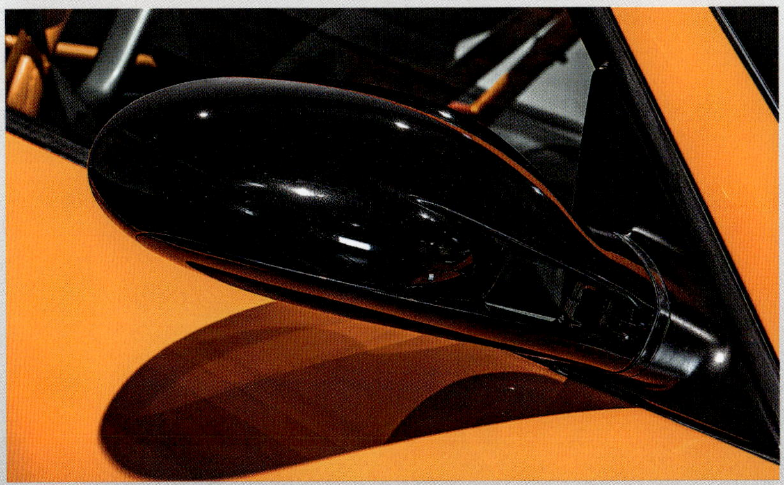

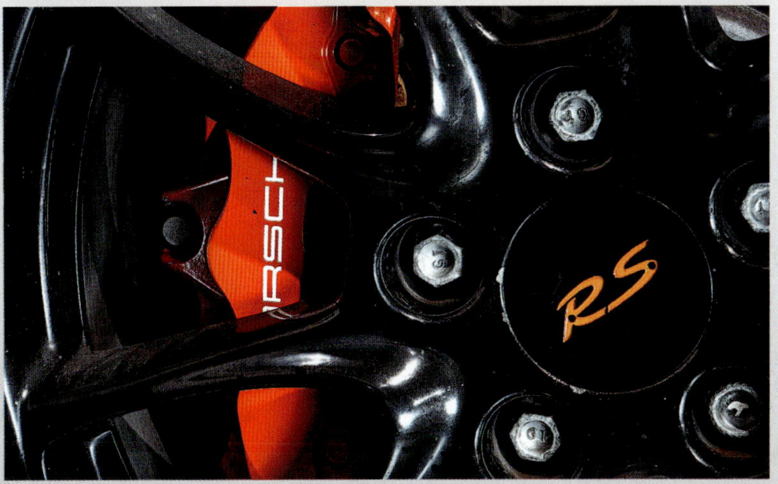

The 997.1 GT3 RS standard specification included 350mm steel discs clamped by six piston monoblock aluminium calipers at the front, and four piston items at the rear. Customary front bonnet vents and carbon rear wing aids downforce

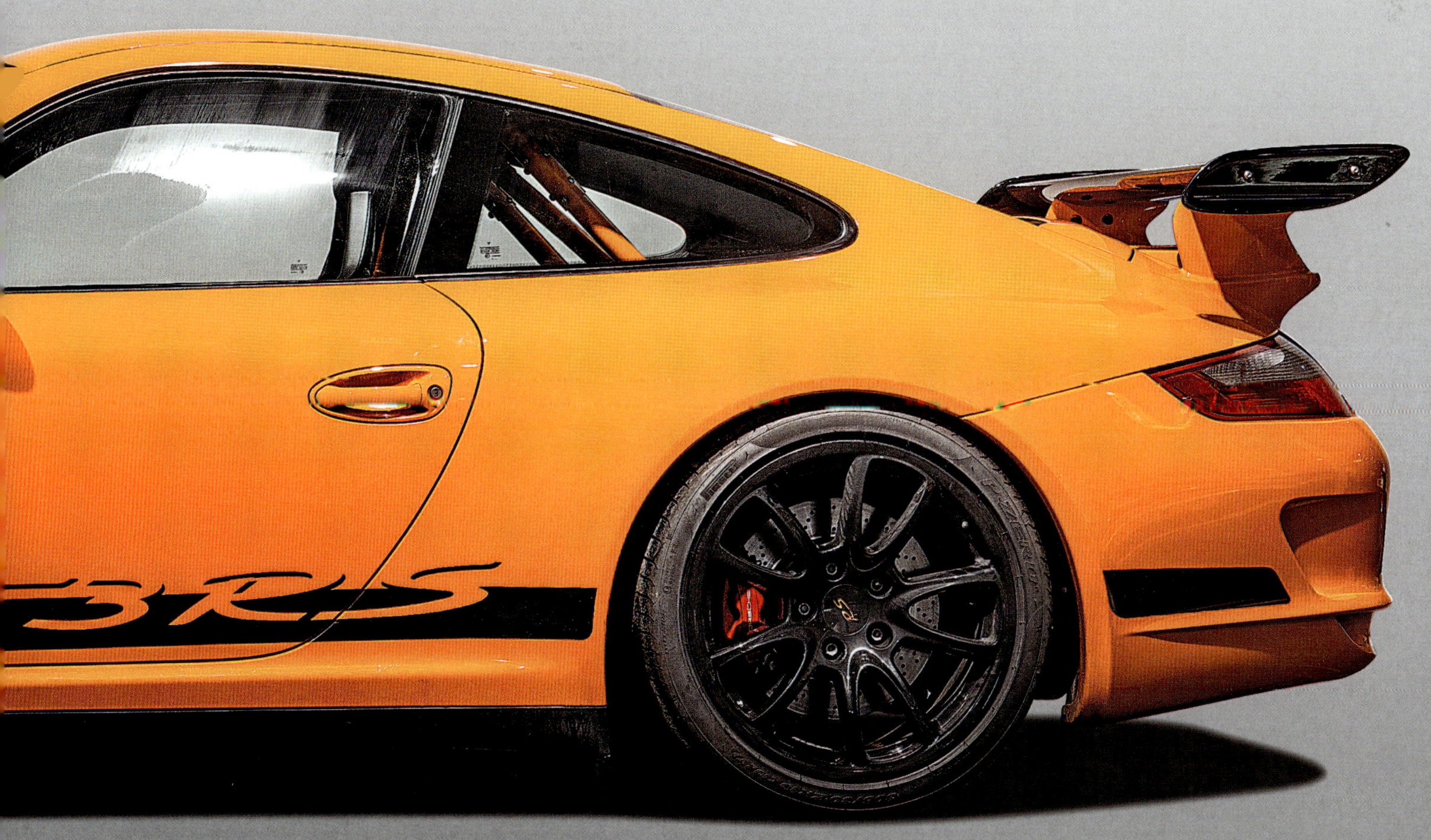

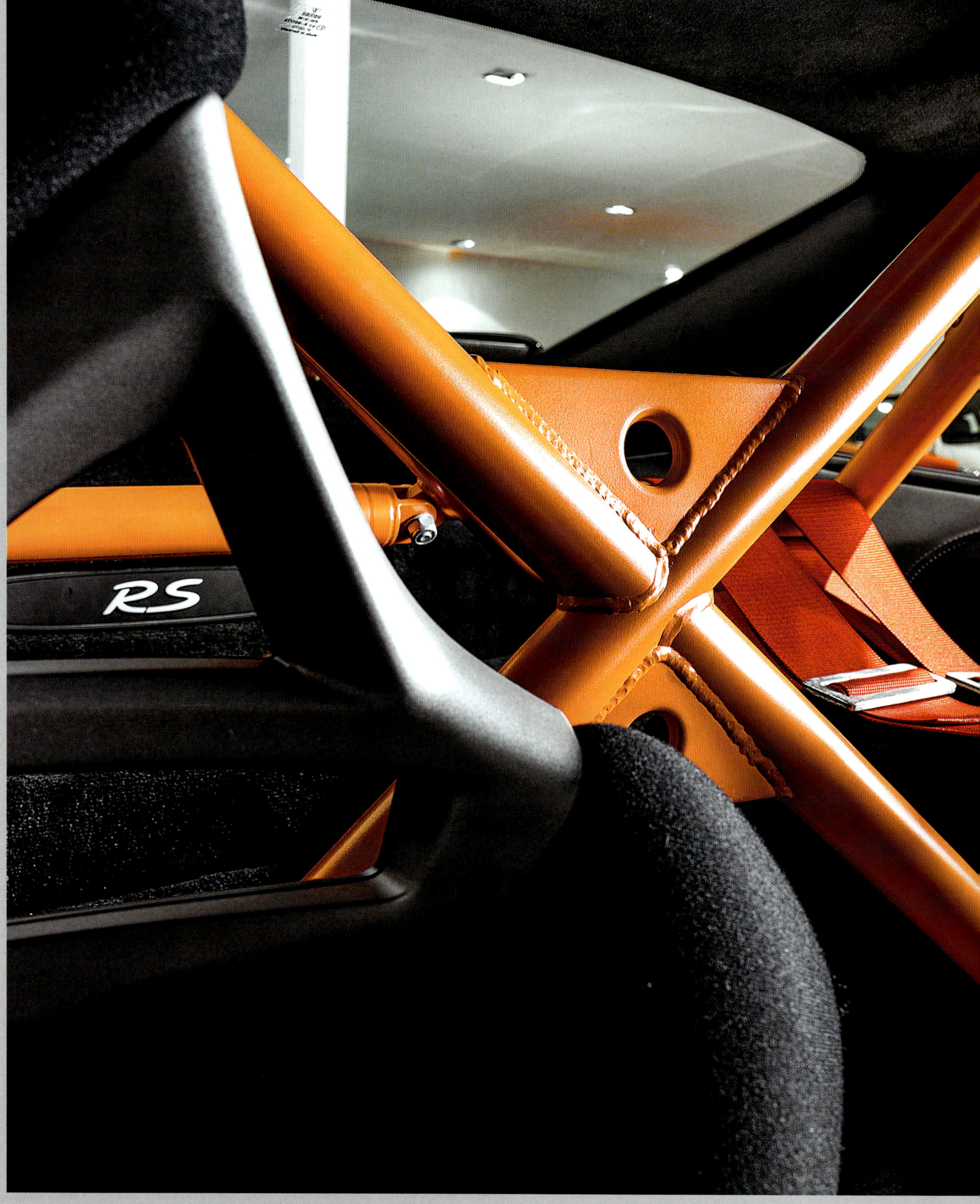

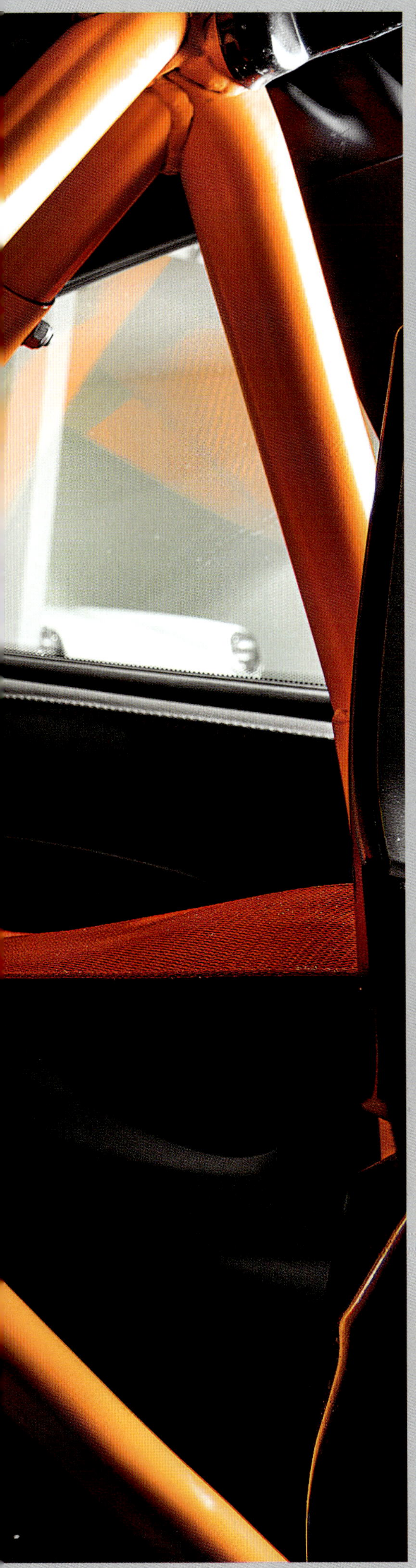

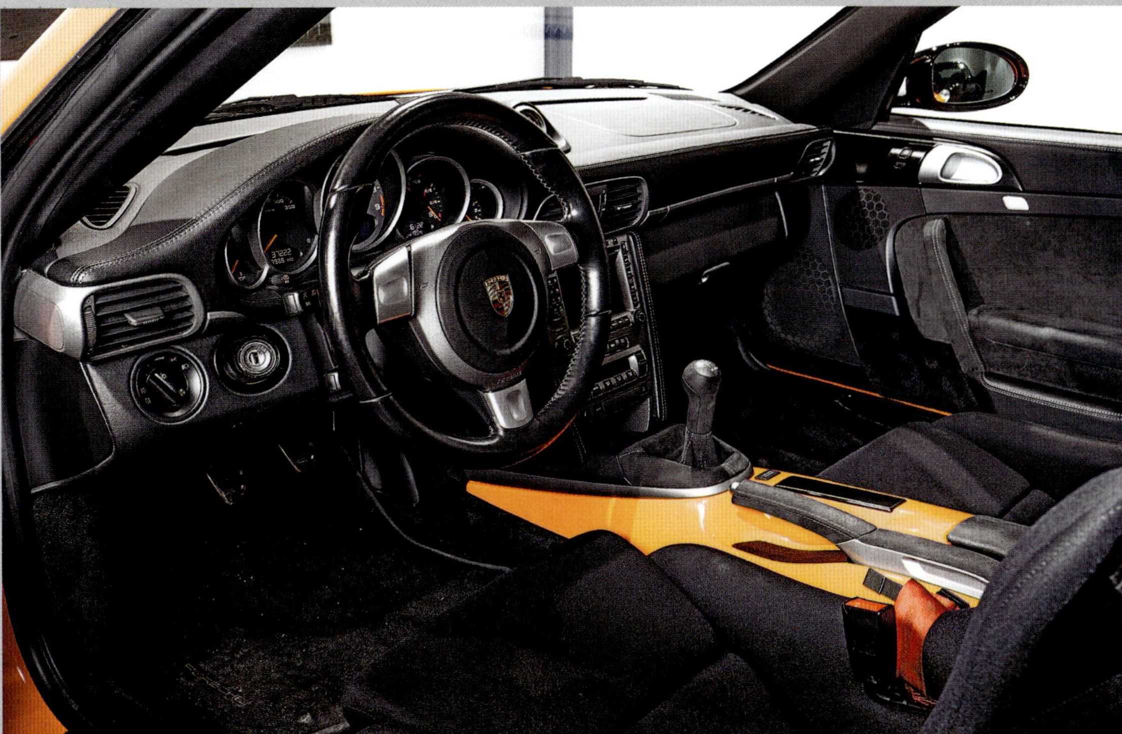

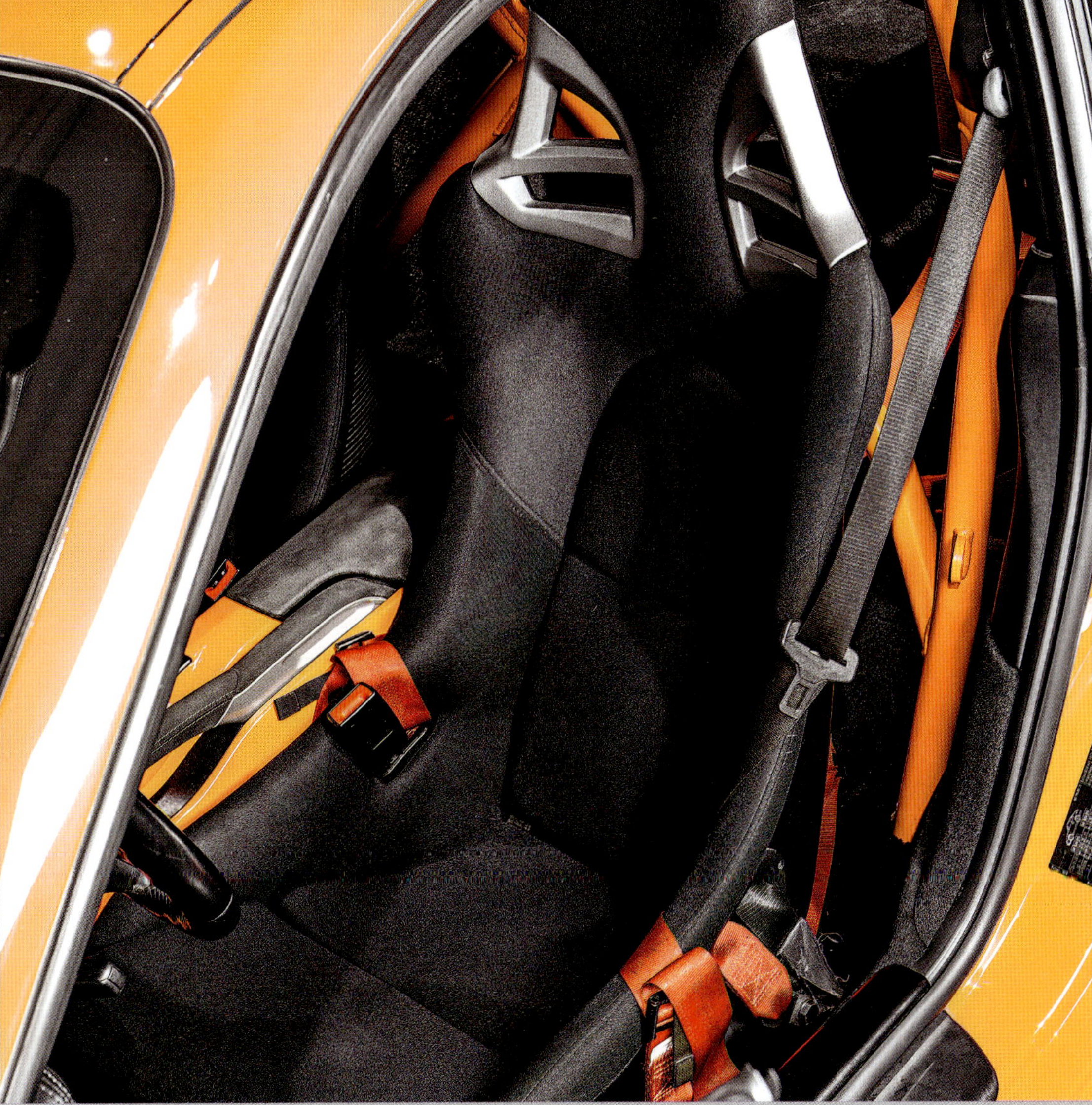

Lightweight carbon-shelled seats in flame retardant fabric came as standard and saved around 10kg compared to the GT3 items. Despite having a track-focused interior, luxury Alcantara covered the surfaces and steering wheel

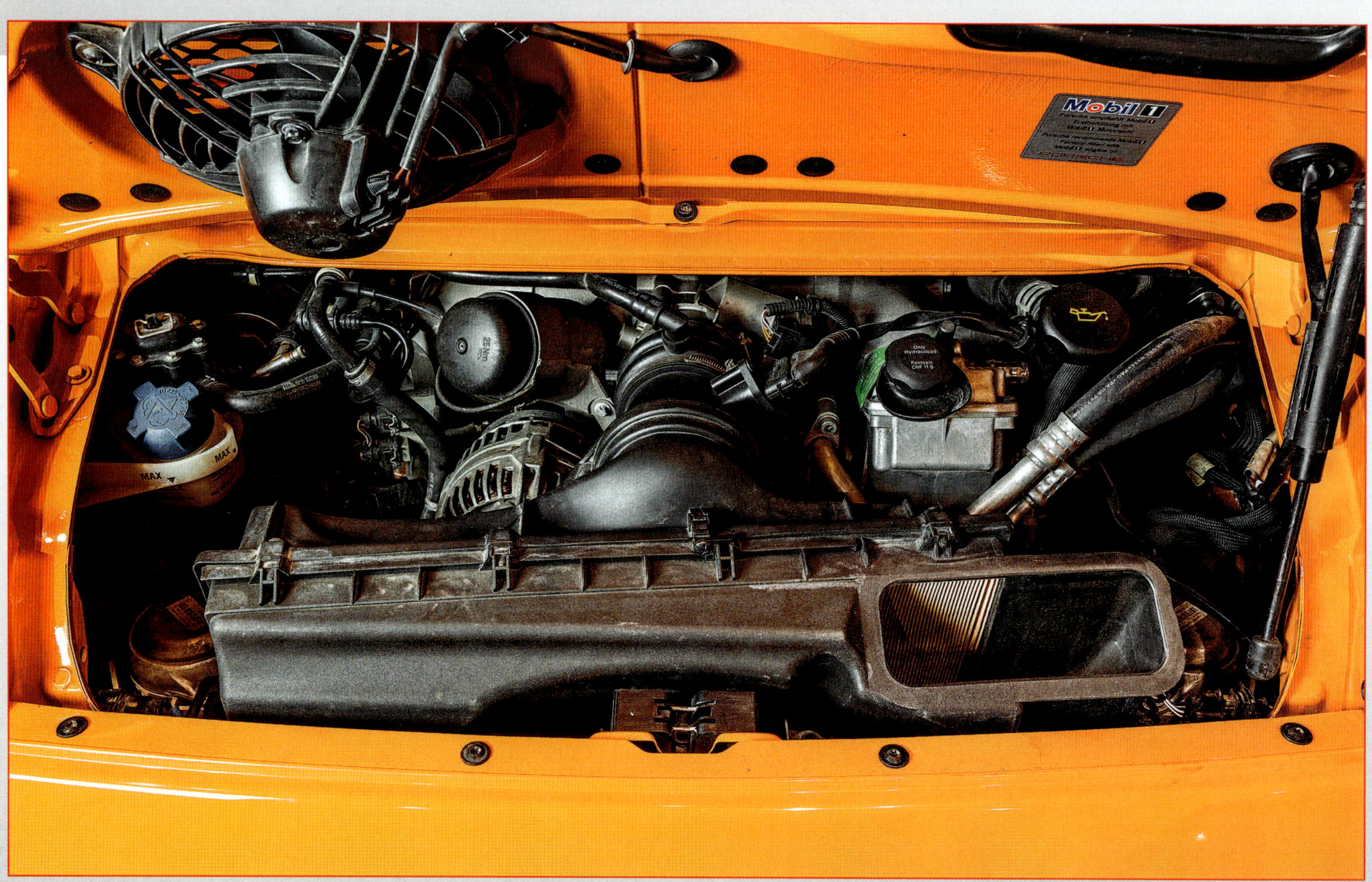

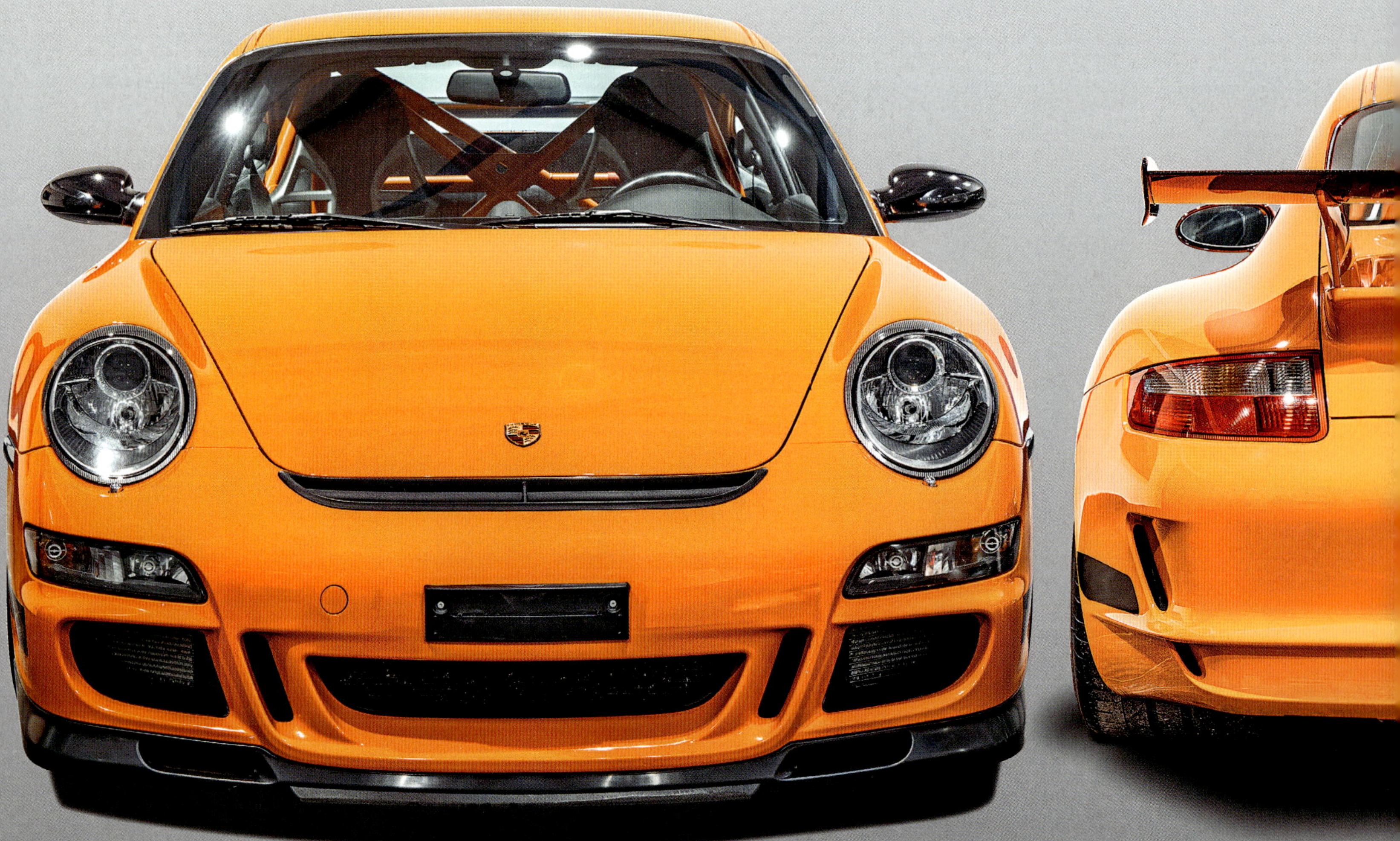

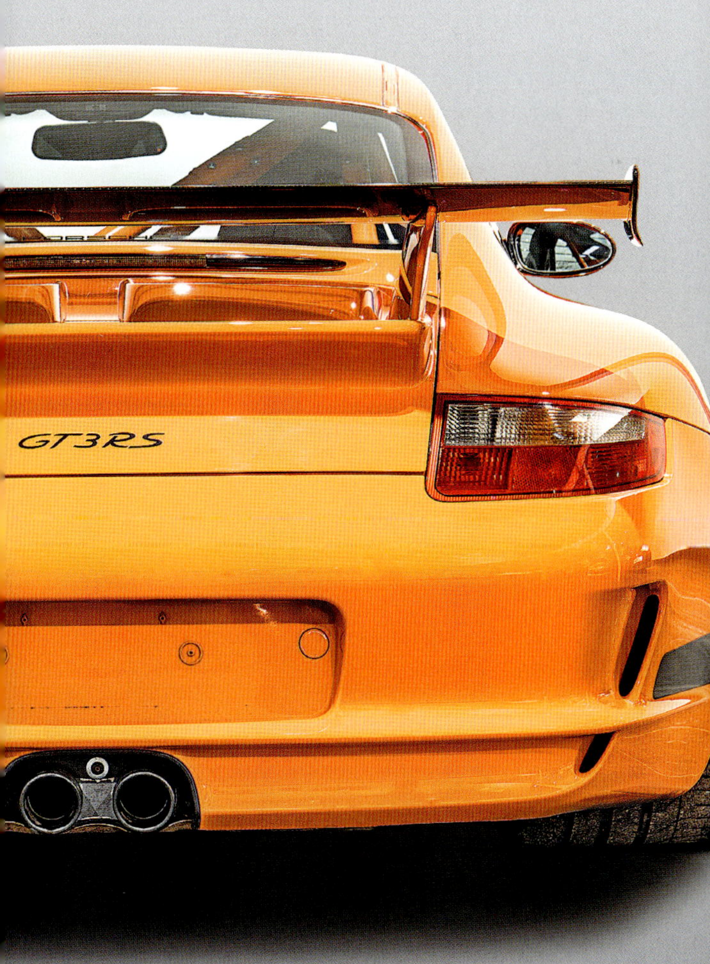


# BUYING TIPS

Ultimately, the 997 generation is renowned for its usable, reliable nature and the GT3 RS does nothing to dispel that view. Yes, it was designed for the ultimate in thrills on road or track but the quality of its construction means there's little to worry about if you're considering buying one today. Find one that has been maintained regardless of cost and it'll prove an immensely rewarding experience.

**HISTORY:** A track-focused nature means that extra care in needed. Diligence is crucial to ensure you're not looking at a tired or crashed trackday warrior.

**BODYWORK:** Corrosion isn't a concern, so spend time examining the panels for any sign of previous repair or replacement. Ensure there's no damage to the RS-specific carbon fibre parts, and look for evidence of damage to the undertrays, which points to circuit-offs.

**ENGINE:** If it's been religiously maintained, there's little to worry about. Check for oil leaks and make sure you see the results of a recent over-rev check.

**TRANSMISSION:** The gearbox is tough and shouldn't be suffering from weak synchromesh unless abused. More likely is clutch wear, so check the history to see if it's already been done as it's not a cheap job.

**BRAKES/SUSPENSION:** Hard use will take its toll on the brakes, so be sure to check their condition carefully; extensive cracking around the cross-drillings indicate a hard life and imminent replacement. Adjustable suspension may have been fiddled with, so an alignment check is advisable.

**INTERIOR:** Aside from being sure you can live with the Clubsport arrangement, the interior wears well. Just look for scuffed trim and overly smooth Alcantara upholstery.

# THE GREATEST
## 997 GT3 RS 4.0
## RENNSPORT



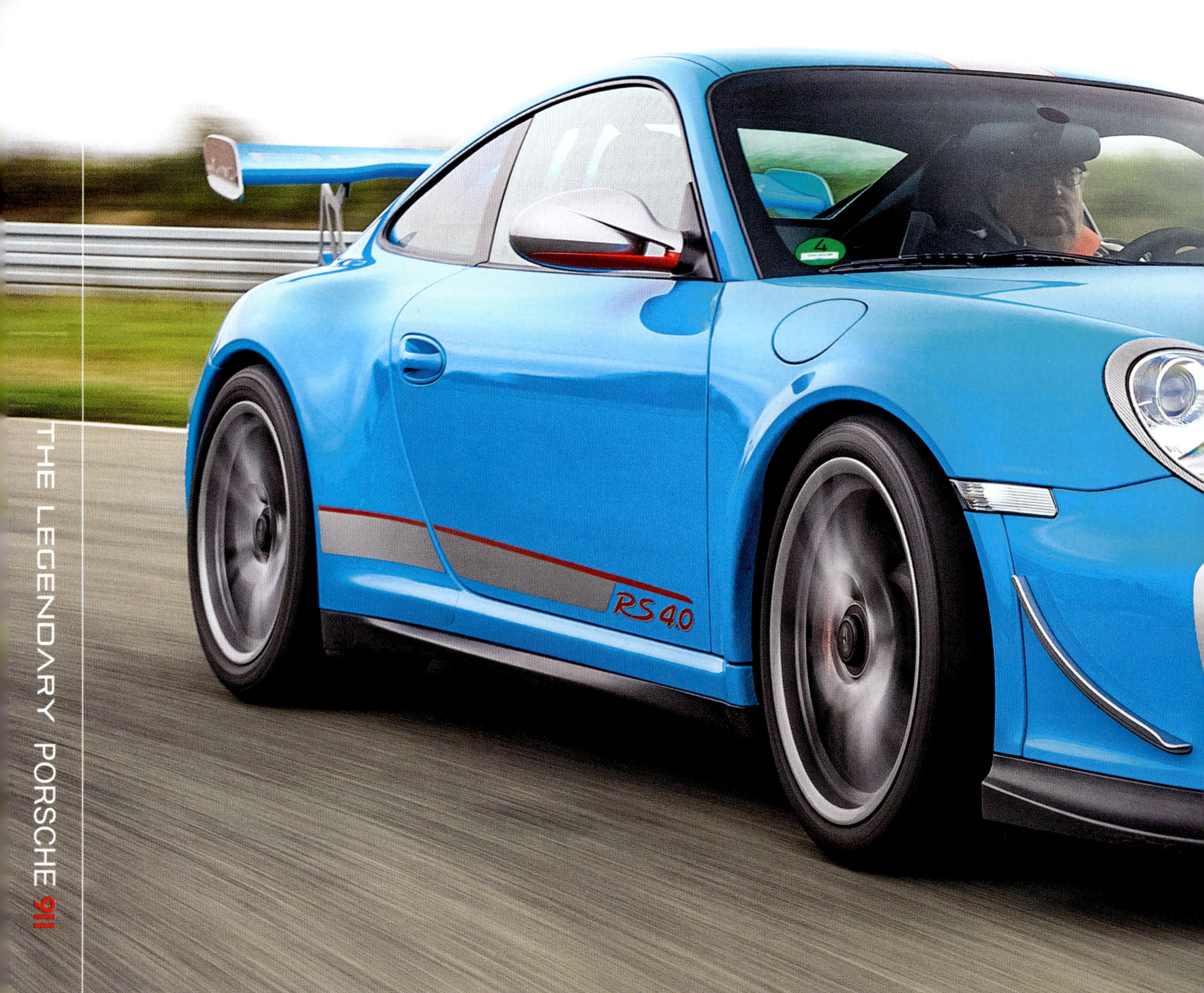

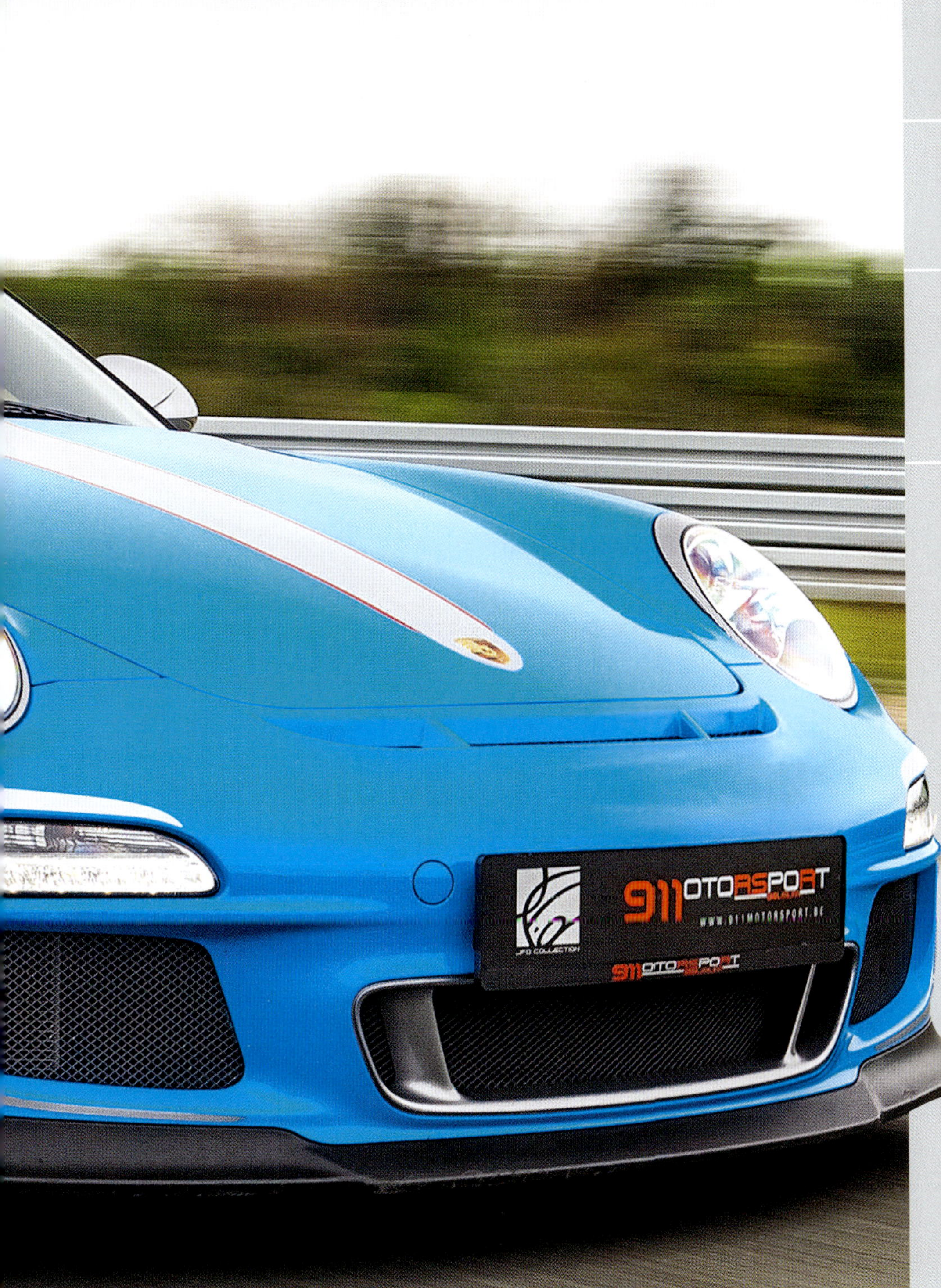

Here's why the 997 GT3 RS 4.0 remains one of the finest 911s of all time, right where it matters: on the track.





# 997 GT3 RS 4.0

(1995-1996)

## ENGINE

**Capacity:** 3,996cc

**Compression ratio:** 12.6:1

**Maximum power:** 500hp @ 8,250rpm

**Maximum torque:** 460Nm @ 5,750rpm

**Transmission:** Six-speed manual

## SUSPENSION

**Front:** Independent; MacPherson strut; PASM; anti-roll bar

**Rear:** Independent; multi-link; rose-jointed; PASM; anti-roll bar

## WHEELS & TYRES

**Front:** 9x19-inch centre-locks; 245/35/ZR19

**Rear:** 12x19-inch centre-locks; 325/30/ZR19

## DIMENSIONS

**Length:** 4,460mm

**Width:** 1,852mm

**Weight:** 1,360kg

## PERFORMANCE

**0-60mph:** 3.9 seconds

**Top speed:** 193mph

If you asked a speed freak to name their top three Porsche 911 Rennsports of all time, there'd be a very good chance the 997 GT3 RS 4.0 would be in the mix. Its presence in our top three is guaranteed and, as you're about to find out, would likely take the crown as the best of all time.

Building on the prowess of the 997.2 GT3 RS 3.8, another car which history will be very kind to, the RS 4.0 was reserved only for those with a rich and unblemished record of buying – and keeping – Porsche GT3 and GT3 RSs because, unbelievably, the company made no money from the €178,000 it decided to sell each RS 4.0 for.

The RS 4.0 was unlike anything Porsche had made before. As the company itself declared on launch: "The 911 GT3 RS 4.0 brings together in a road car all the attributes that have made the Porsche 911 GT3 a serial winner on the race track." This was a proper parts-bin special, and sheds light on the reason a numbered production run of just 600 units was decided upon: it's simply all the components Porsche still had laying around.

The numbers game was always going to dictate this to be an exceedingly special car that would attract the attentions of collectors. But, regardless, it's still gone down in Porsche folklore as one of the most desirable 911s ever made, despite the fact that Andreas Preuninger and the GT Department he leads has already moved the Rennsport denomination on rather significantly.

After all, by today's standards the specs and stats of the special-edition 997 GT3 RS 4.0 aren't actually that special anymore. Sure, it's the last Mezger engine in a GT car, and the inclusion of a crankshaft taken directly from the RSR race car is a cool move, but the flat six's circa 500hp output – the first for an RS – is now par for the course for a 911 GT3, while its 4.0-litre engine capacity is now seen on a host of GT-derived *Neunelfers* from the R, to the GT3 RS, even down to the GT3 itself.

The RS 4.0's maximum downforce was doubled by the very next Rennsport to roll out of Weissach in the 991.1 GT3 RS, and its rose-jointed rear suspension seems a little meek compared to the fully Heim-jointed, Cup-spec chassis on the 991.2 GT3 RS. Even the 997 GT3 RS 4.0's Nürburgring lap time, ever the yardstick as to a sports car's real-world performance capabilities, has been usurped by most things since. Whisper it, but even the 991.2 Carrera GTS is faster around the "Green Hell" with a time of 7:23.77 compared to the RS 4.0's 7:27.

The point should by now be clear: the 997 GT3 RS 4.0 is no longer anywhere near the summit of Porsche Motorsport-derived engineering. And that's exactly why it's so revered.

This is because what the GT3 RS 4.0 lacks in outright performance, it more than makes up for in the way this performance is delivered, and the emotion it conjures in doing so. Equipped with a manual gearbox, a passive rear axle and mechanically assisted steering, it's the pinnacle from a golden era of the 911, the last of the 997s offering a positively analogue experience in arguably the very last iteration of a classic *Neunelfer* set-up.

The stats, therefore, only tell one side of the story and, let's face it, as sports cars – Porsche sports cars included – migrate ever further towards digitisation, e-mobility and even autonomous driving outright, the reputation of the 997 GT3 RS 4.0 will only become more evergreen.

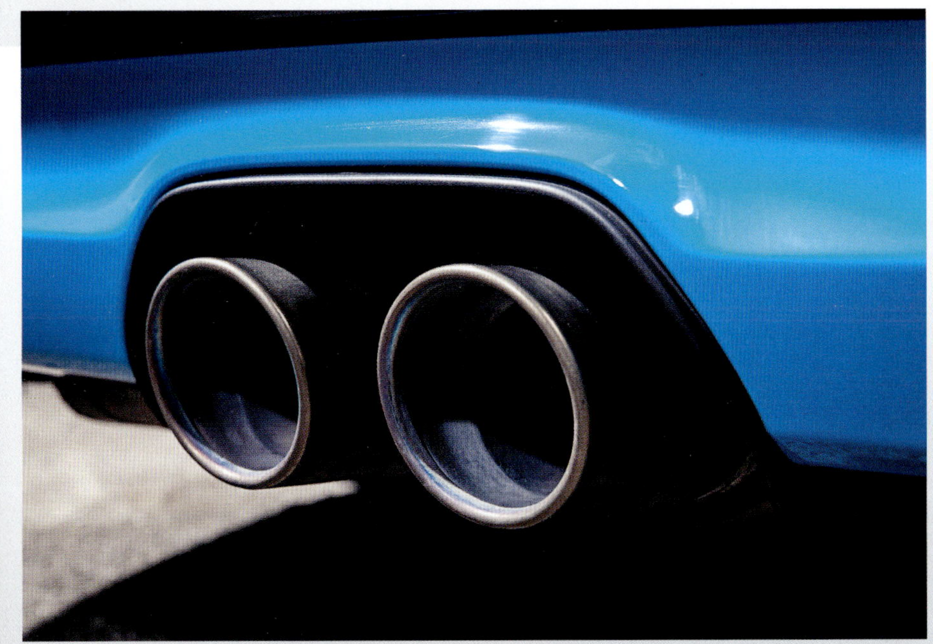

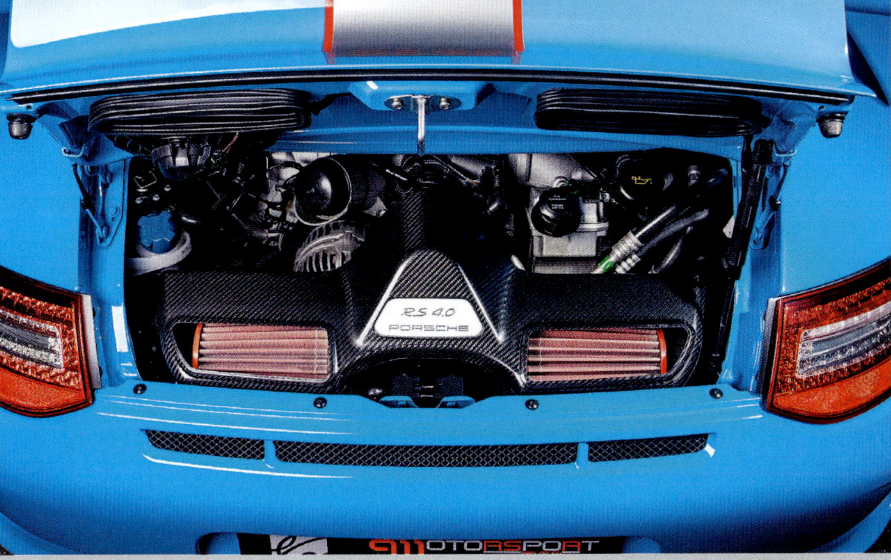

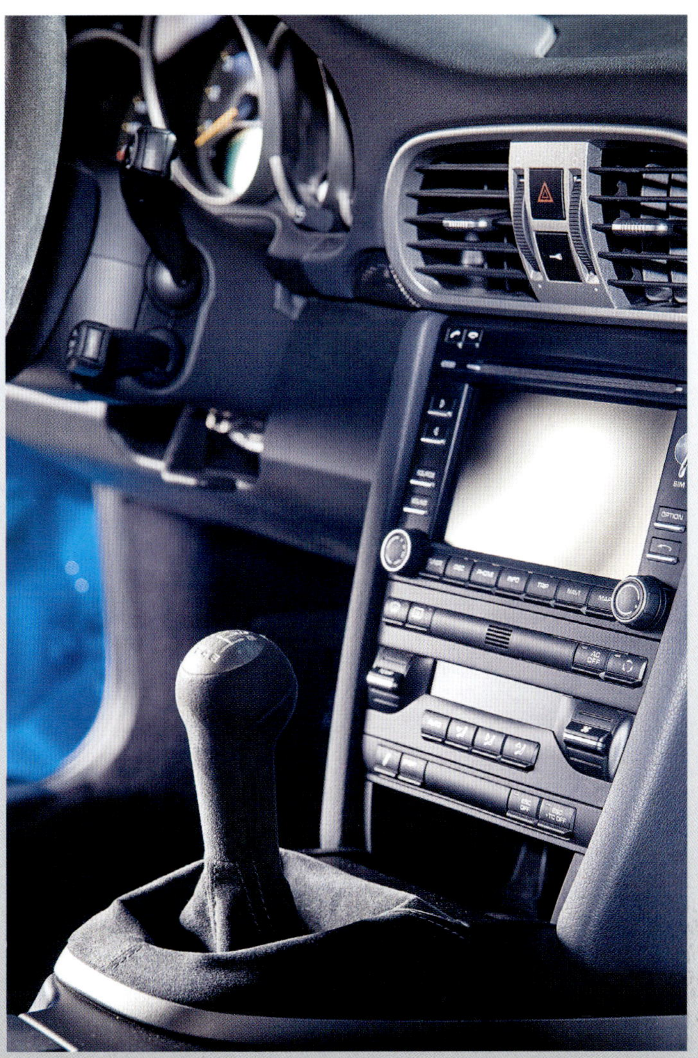

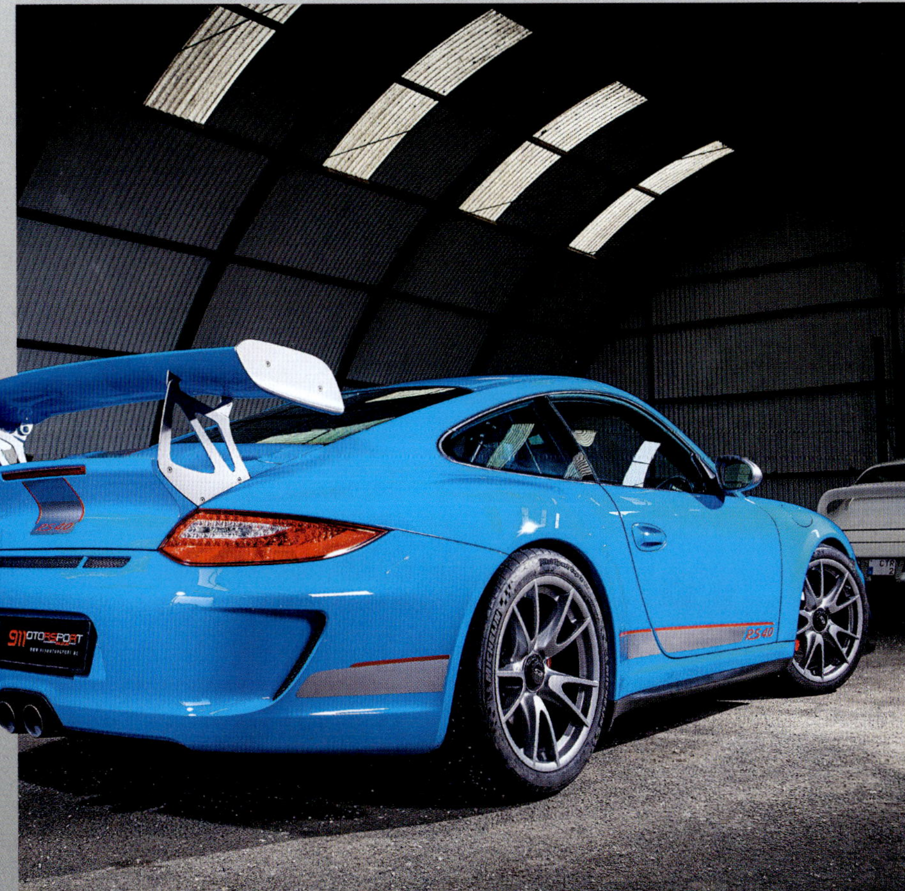

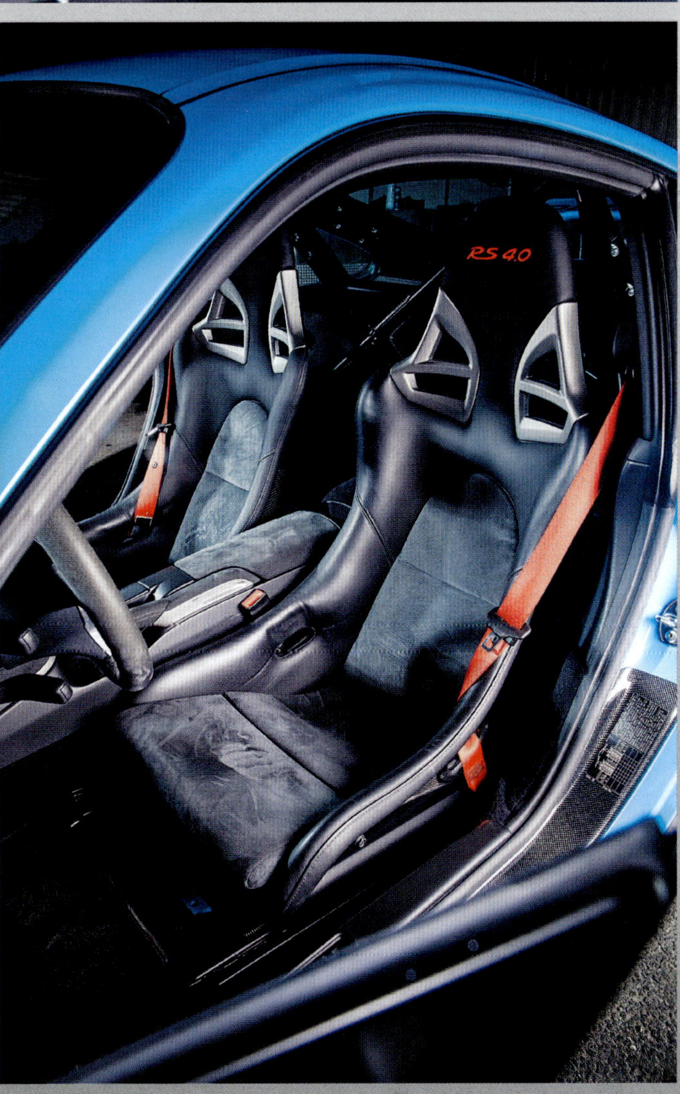

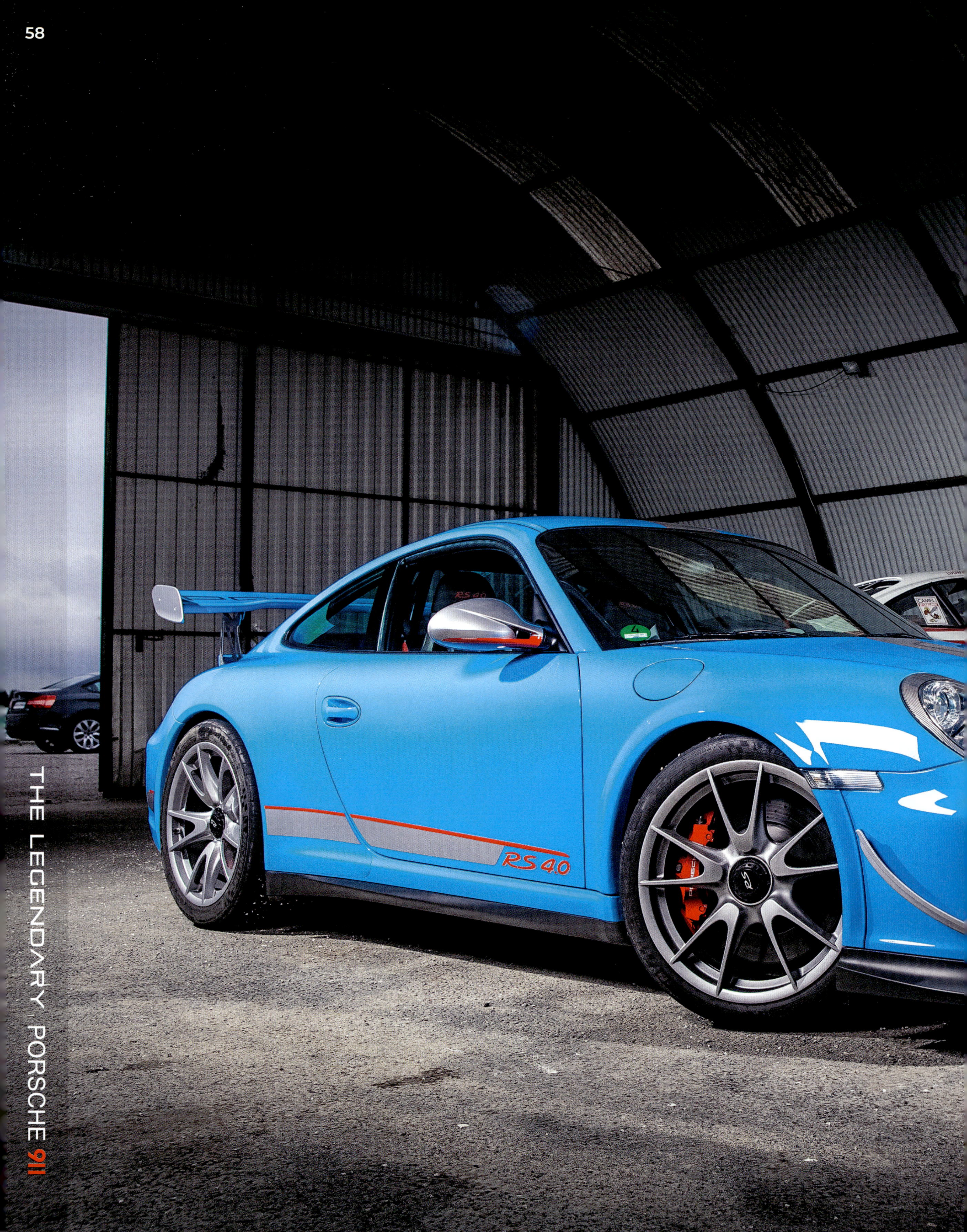
RS 4.0

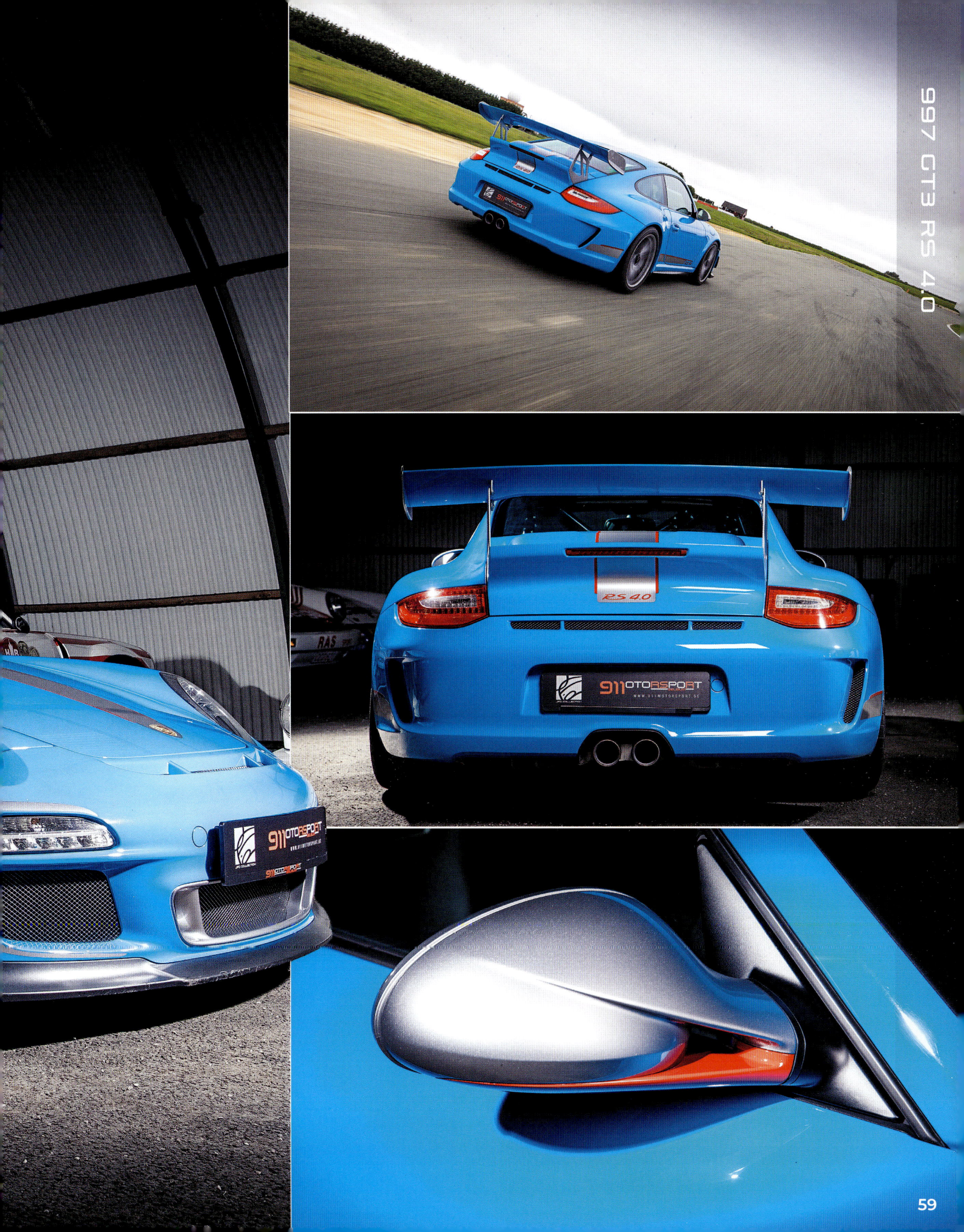

# MAN'S BEST FRIEND
# 991 GT3 RS

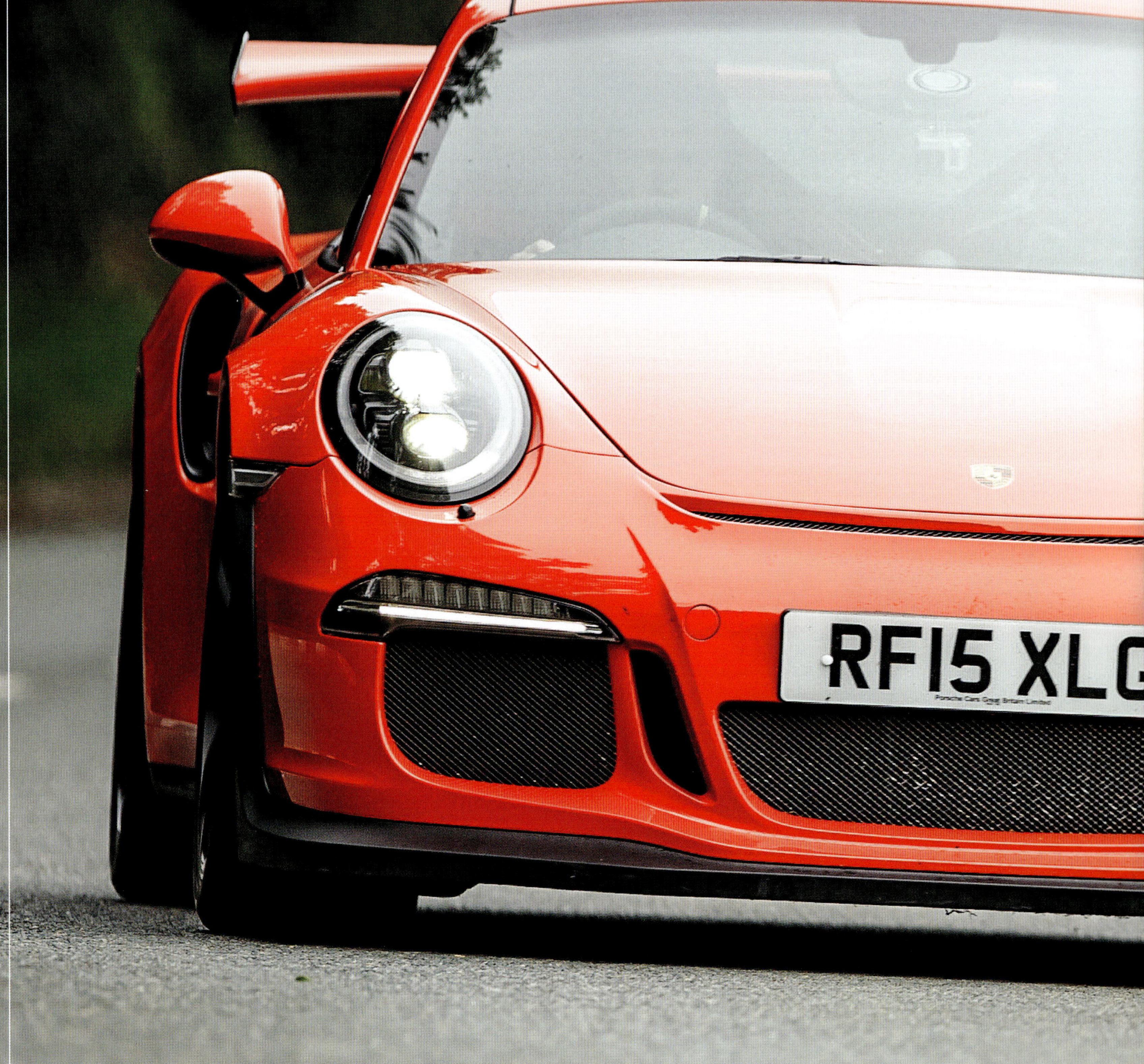

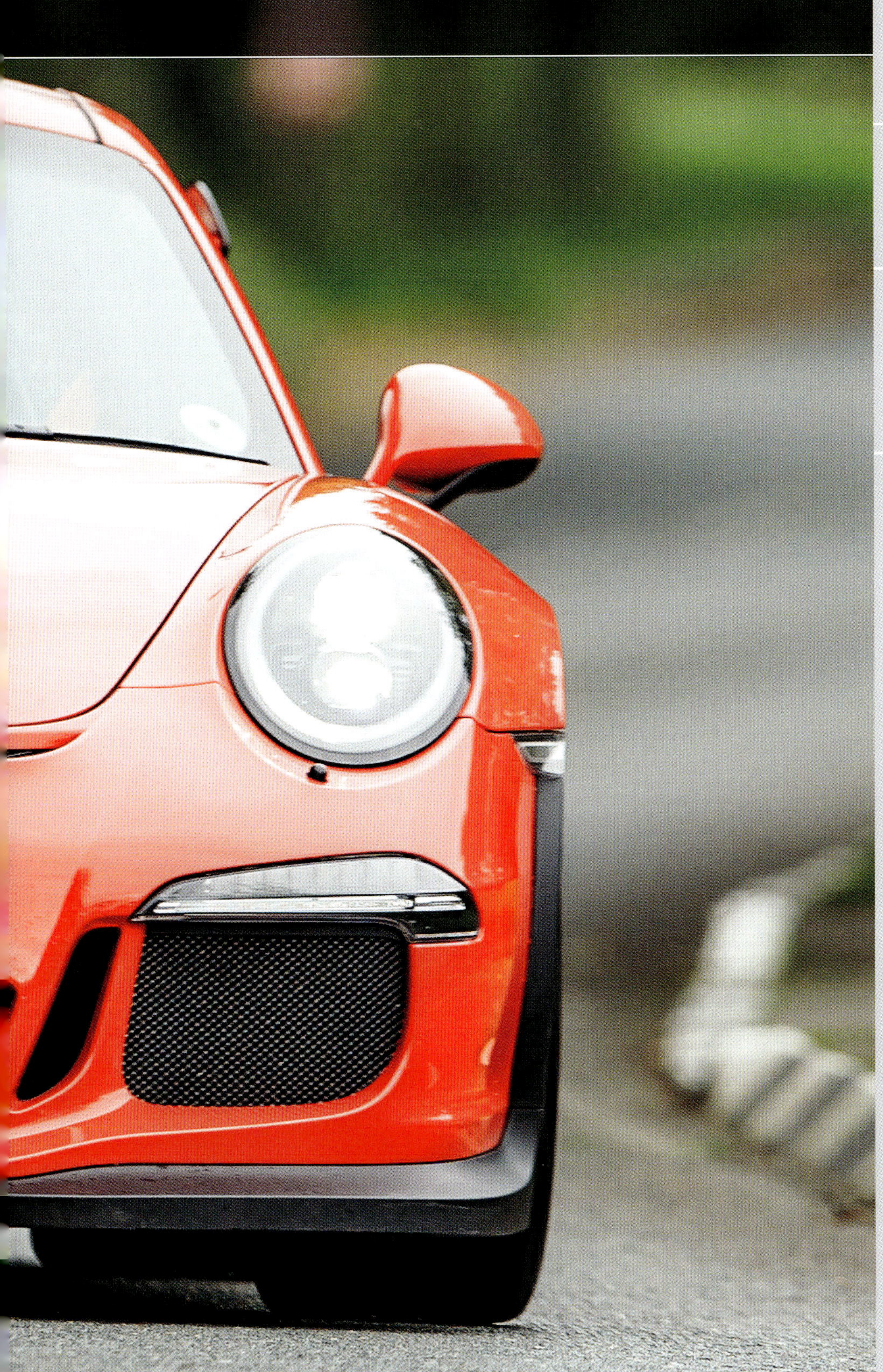

The Isle of Man's TT course offers one of the world's best driving roads, so what better way to tackle it than in Porsche's superlative naturally aspirated Rennsport?



## 991 GT3 RS

(2015)

### ENGINE

**Capacity:** 3,996cc
**Compression ratio:** 12.9:1
**Maximum power:** 500hp @ 8,250rpm
**Maximum torque:** 460Nm @ 6,250rpm
**Transmission:** Seven-speed PDK

### SUSPENSION

**Front:** Independent; McPerson strut; PASM
**Rear:** Independent; Multi-link; Rear-axle steering; PASM

### WHEELS & TYRES

**Front:** 9.5x20-inch centrelocks; 265/35/ZR20
**Rear:** 12.5x21-inch centrelocks; 325/30/ZR21

### DIMENSIONS

**Length:** 4,545mm
**Width:** 1,880mm
**Weight:** 1,420kg

### PERFORMANCE

**0-60mph:** 3.3 seconds
**Top speed:** 193mph

When it was launched in 2015, Porsche's 991 GT3 RS moved the Rennsport game on substantially from its predecessors. Equipped with a 4.0-litre flat six engine producing 500hp in a body that generated more than double the downforce of the 997 GT3 RS 4.0, the 991 also boasted rear-axle steering, a seven-speed PDK gearbox and huge 21-inch rear wheels borrowed from the 918 Spyder.

The caveat, of course, was the biggest, widest and heaviest RS ever, but that didn't matter. The car was quicker, faster and more efficient than ever before, with a 'Ring lap time of seven minutes 20 seconds to endorse it as the most accomplished Porsche Rennsport of the time. Those in the know say it's the nearest thing to a Cup car you're ever likely to get. The 991 GT3 RS is a monster – and therein lies its problem. Topping out in second gear sees 73mph register on the RS's speedometer, which is enough to break the UK speed limit. Redline in third takes you past 100mph, which will guarantee the loss of your driving licence if caught – yet the RS still has another four forward ratios to go.

It may well come with licence plates affixed to its front and rear bumpers, but the reality is you won't even begin to tap into the 991 GT3 RS's capabilities on a public road. This is a race car, born and bred, and a race car needs a race track to call home. Or does it?

If we were to proffer the idea that a suitable playground for one of Porsche's most iconic RS awaits just the other side of a ferry ride from the UK, to a challenging public road that can have disastrous – perilous, even – consequences for those who get it wrong, then you may well assume we're talking about the Nürburging Nordschleife. And, while it's true the 'Ring is a happy hunting ground for many a GT3 RS, on this occasion the chosen destination lies on a ferry east of the UK mainland, not west. We're, of course, talking about the Isle of Man.

Home to the famous TT motorcycle race held annually since 1907, its 37-mile course is made up entirely of public roads around the island, which is a self-governing territory with British Crown dependency. For two weeks per year in either May or June, these roads are closed to the public, metamorphing into a world stage for two-wheeled speed freaks to test their talent and nerve on a timed run of the circuit. For the other 50 weeks, however, the roads are just that, helping to transport some 83,000 inhabitants around the island. Much of the motor-racing paraphernalia remains though, and as for the speed limits, well, out of town there aren't any.

What's more, the course offers plenty for the driving enthusiast by way of challenges. Longer than the Nürburgring by some 24.1 miles, Isle of Man's TT has plenty in common with it: there are a number of surface changes throughout, its weather is as famously interchangeable, the track varying in altitude by some 1,400 feet, while a vast array of corner types and cambers are thrown in along the way. In short, it's a proper driver's playground, surely the best place on earth to take a 991 GT3 RS outside of a track.

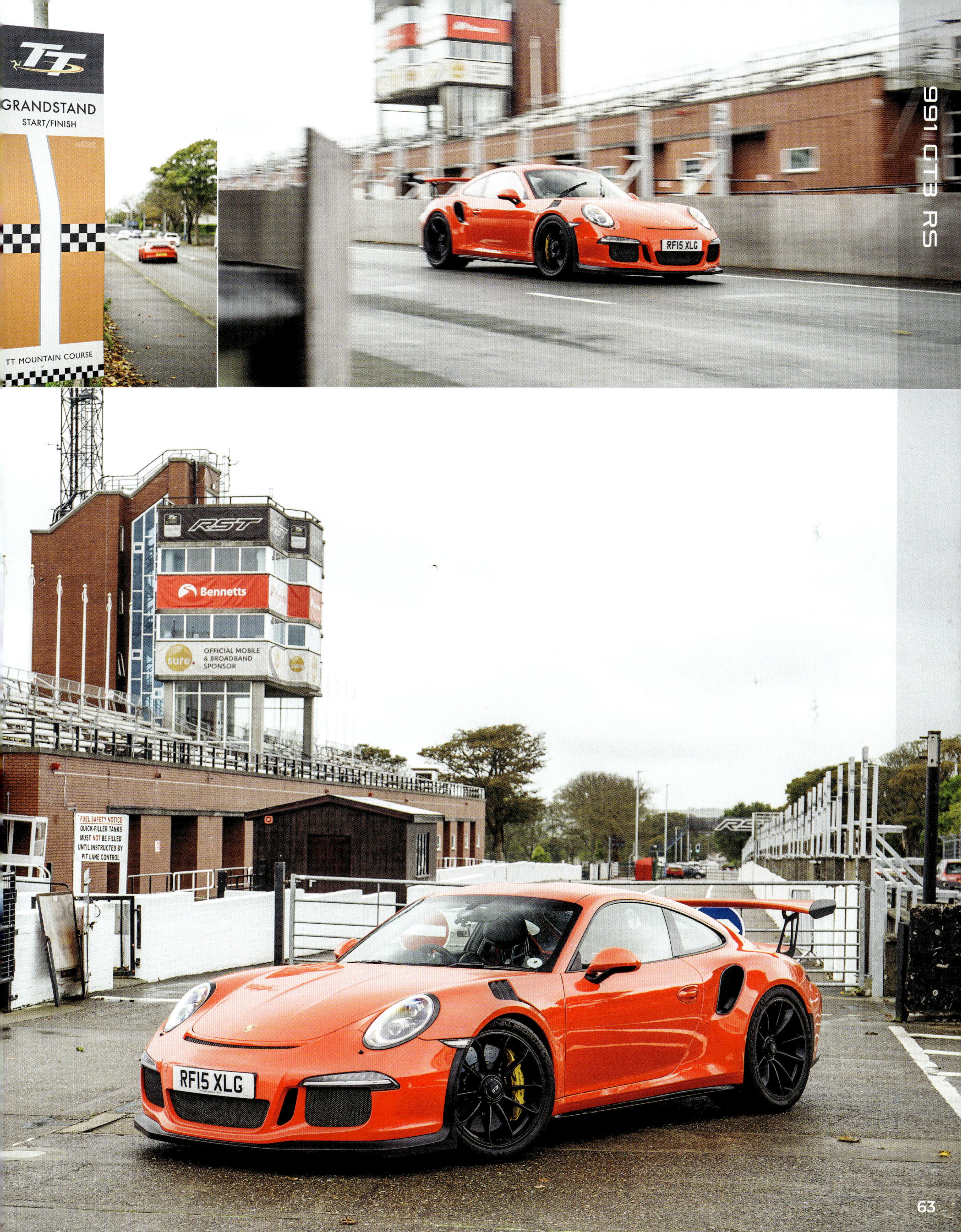
TT
GRANDSTAND
START/FINISH
TT MOUNTAIN COURSE
RF15 XLG
RST
Bennetts
SURE OFFICIAL MOBILE & BROADBAND SPONSOR
FUEL SAFETY NOTICE
QUICK-FILLER TANKS
MUST NOT BE FILLED
UNTIL INSTRUCTED BY
PIT LANE CONTROL
RF15 XLG

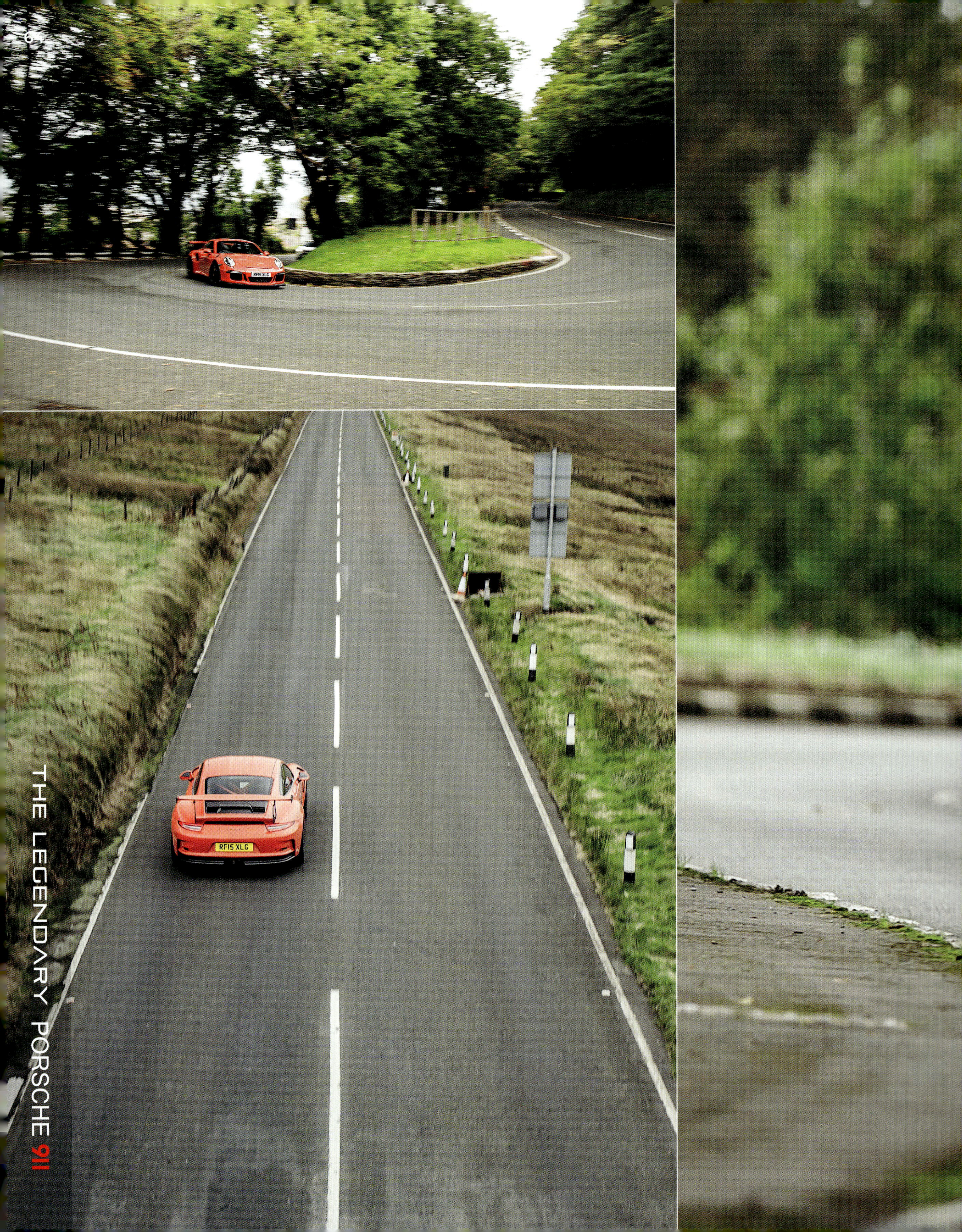
THE LEGENDARY PORSCHE 911

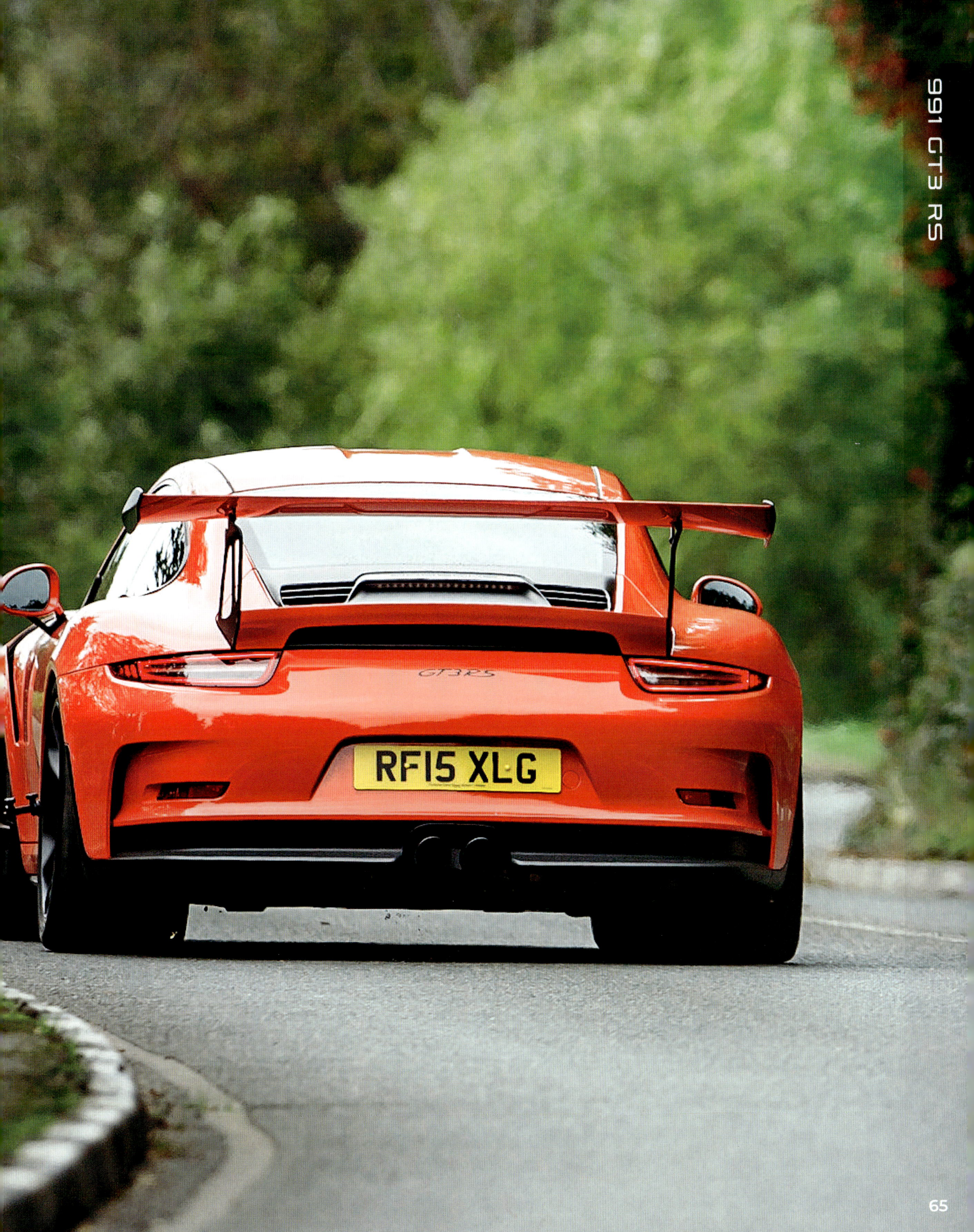

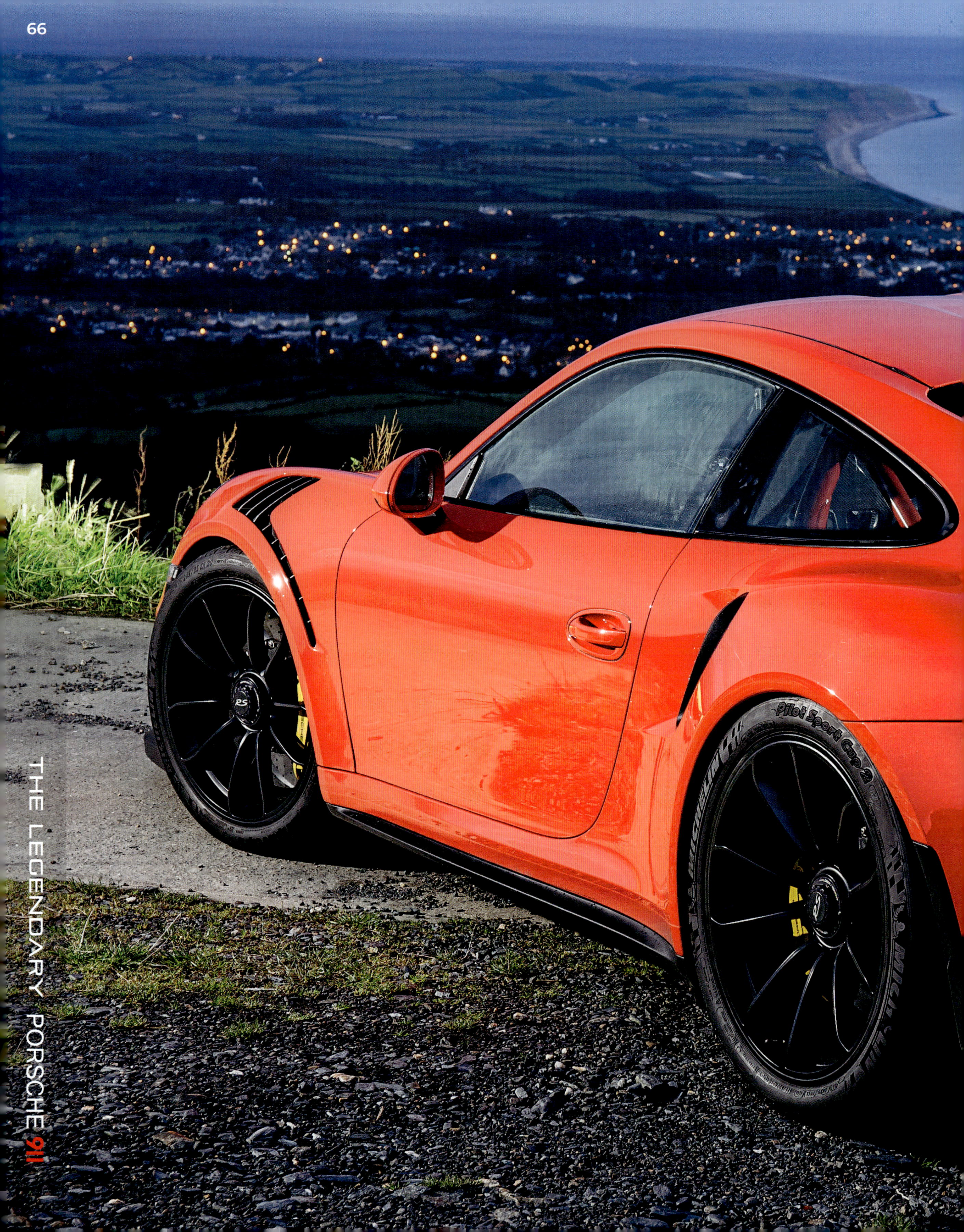
THE LEGENDARY PORSCHE 911

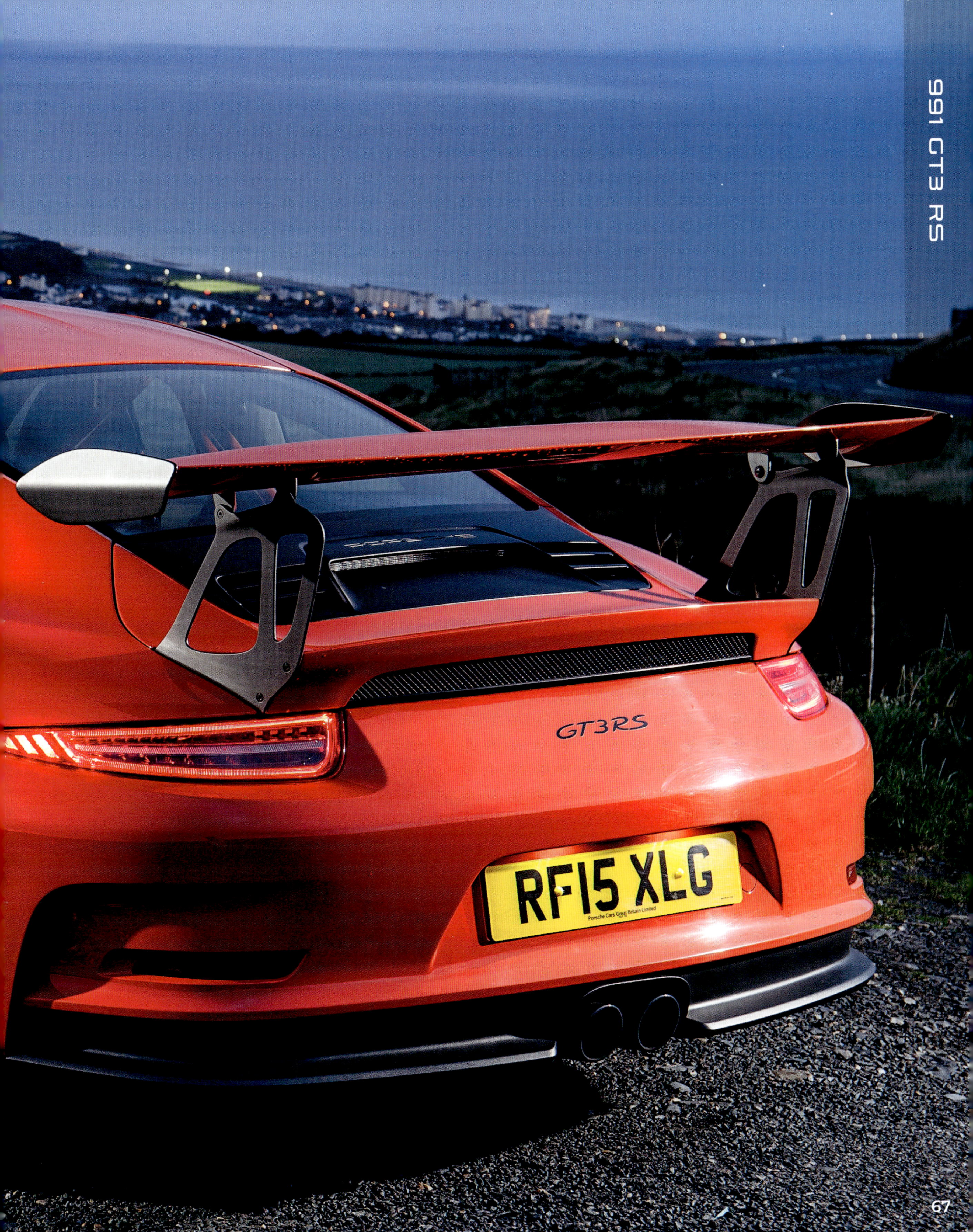
GT3RS
RF15 XLG
Porsche Cars Great Britain Limited

# SACRÉ BLEU!
# 991 GT2 RS

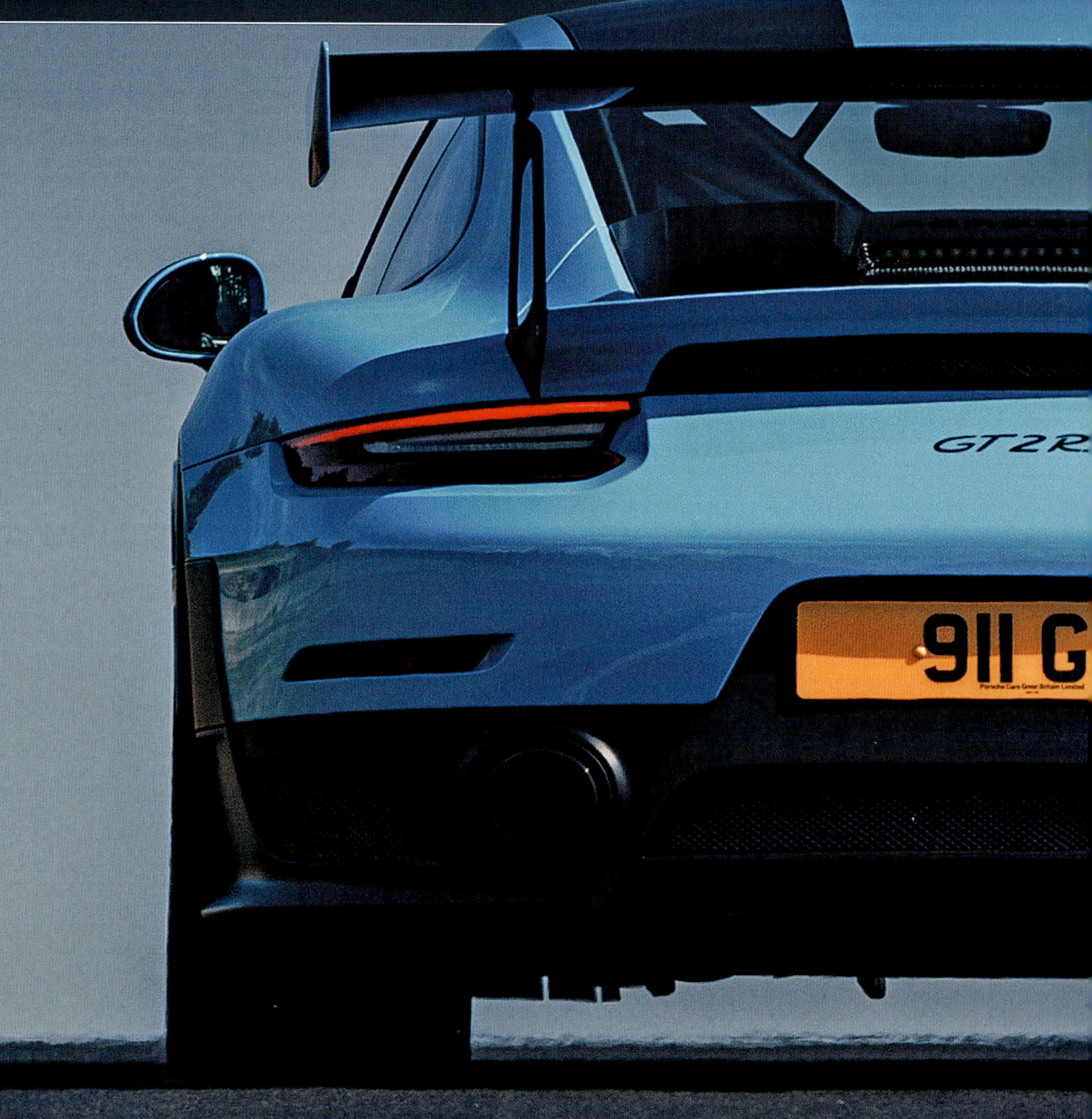

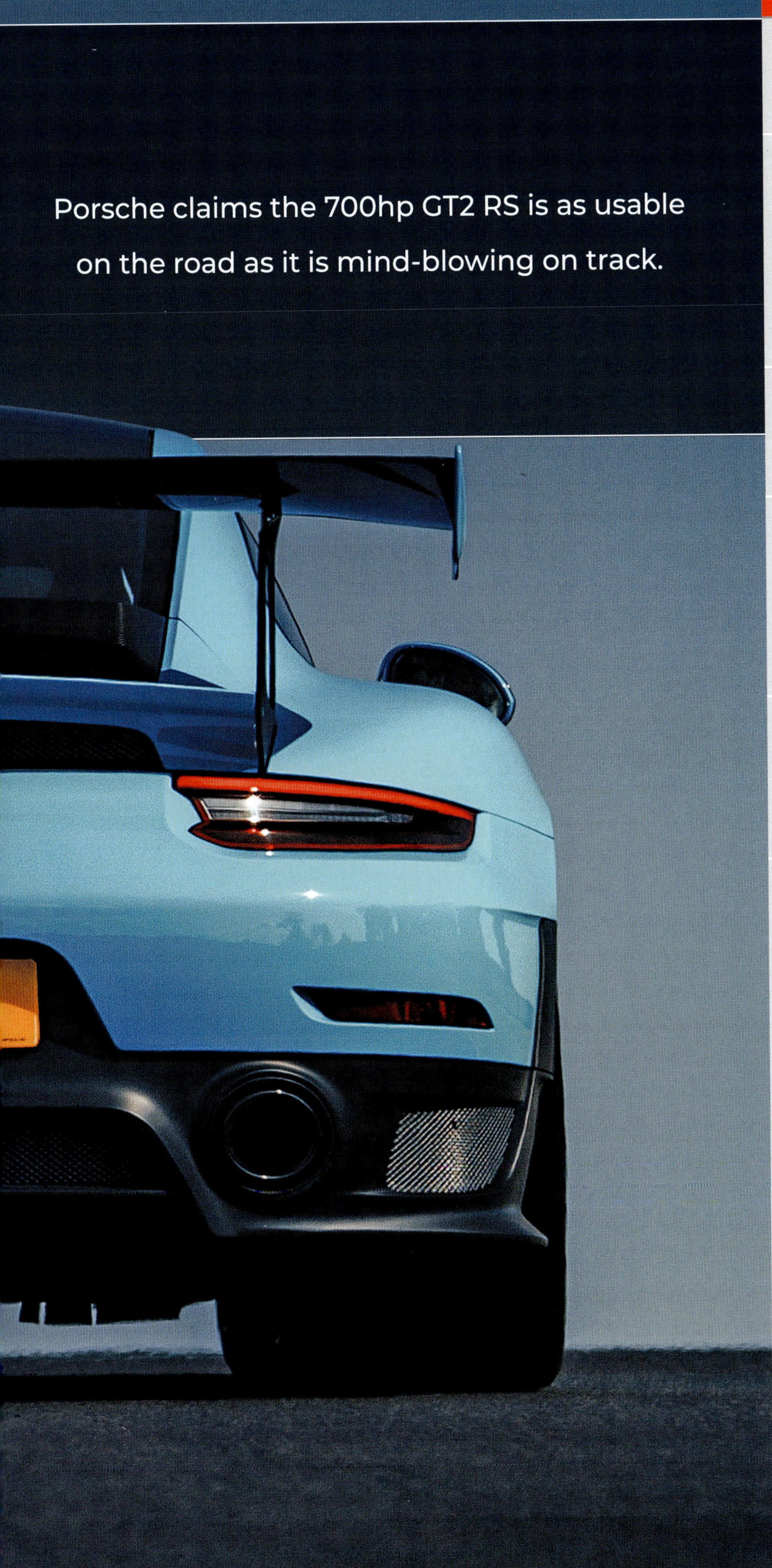




# 991 GT2 RS

WEISSACH PACKAGE

2018

## ENGINE

**Capacity:** 3,800cc

**Compression ratio:** 9.0:1

**Maximum power:** 700hp @ 7,000rpm

**Maximum torque:** 750Nm @ 2,500-4,500rpm

**Transmission:** Seven-speed PDK

## SUSPENSION

**Front:** MacPherson struts

**Rear:** Multi-link

## WHEELS & TYRES

**Front:** 9.5x20-inch magnesium alloys; 265/35 ZR20 Michelin Pilot Sport Cup 2 tyres

**Rear:** 12.5x21-inch magnesium alloys; 325/30 ZR21 Michelin Pilot Sport Cup 2 tyres

## DIMENSIONS

**Length:** 4,549mm

**Width:** 1,880mm

**Weight:** 1,430kg

## PERFORMANCE

**0-60mph:** 2.8 seconds

**Top speed:** 211mph

There's never been a more powerful, more expensive road-going 911 than the 991 GT2 RS. It essentially takes the GT3 RS's super-wide body, two-seat interior, rear-drive/PDK drivetrain and rose-joined suspension, and throws in a hand grenade in the form of the 3.8-litre Turbo S engine.

It then tunes it for an extra 108bhp to give 690bhp and 750Nm total. That represents huge gains of 177bhp and 279Nm over a GT3 RS, and with significantly different turbo characteristics too. It's enough to rocket the 1,430kg 911 from 0 to 62mph in 2.8 seconds, to 124mph in 8.3 and then on to 211mph. More relevantly, it also enabled the GT2 RS to break the then-production car record of the Nürburgring with a 6:47.03 lap back in September 2017.

The model featured has the optional and 30kg lighter Weissach Package that also featured on the factory record-breaker, including a titanium roll cage that saves 9kg. The cage tops off a seemingly contradictory if successful combination of luxury materials and perfect fit and finish layered over a hardcore race car feel – the seats, the Alcantara rim, the cage – and yet it all gels in practice. A good proportion of GT2 RS buyers would probably accept a significant degradation in comfort for a car that not only looks like it just drove off the Le Mans grid, but could put in a decent account of itself to boot, yet there's no scrimping

here. Then again, you'd probably expect that given the £207,506 price of entry – or £228,548 with the Weissach Package.

The GT2 RS strikes a similarly sweet balance at a steady-state cruise as it does with its interior. Of course, this pseudo-racer isn't as civilised as a Carrera – it's firmer, there's more road and exhaust noise too – but you can still listen to the excellent Bose stereo and chat without shouting, and the dual-clutch transmission glides through its higher ratios where a real racer would thunk. With the adaptive dampers set in Comfort there's also compliance to the suspension, an ease to the way it deals with cambers and ruts where the spec suggests it might tug about like a divining rod locked on an oasis. It continues the trend begun with its 997 GT2 RS predecessor, which actually felt cushier than the rather jagged 997 GT2 despite ostensibly being more hardcore.

The GT2 RS quickly instils confidence, the approachability that defines a Carrera still present despite such an excess of power and torque – it's a combination of the low-set driving position, excellent visibility and the controls' easy, feelsome weighting. Sat in the driver's seat, you're a key component locked into the heart of this machine like a plug in a socket.

**The GT2 RS's interior somehow manages to successfully blend luxury with a Motorsport finesse**



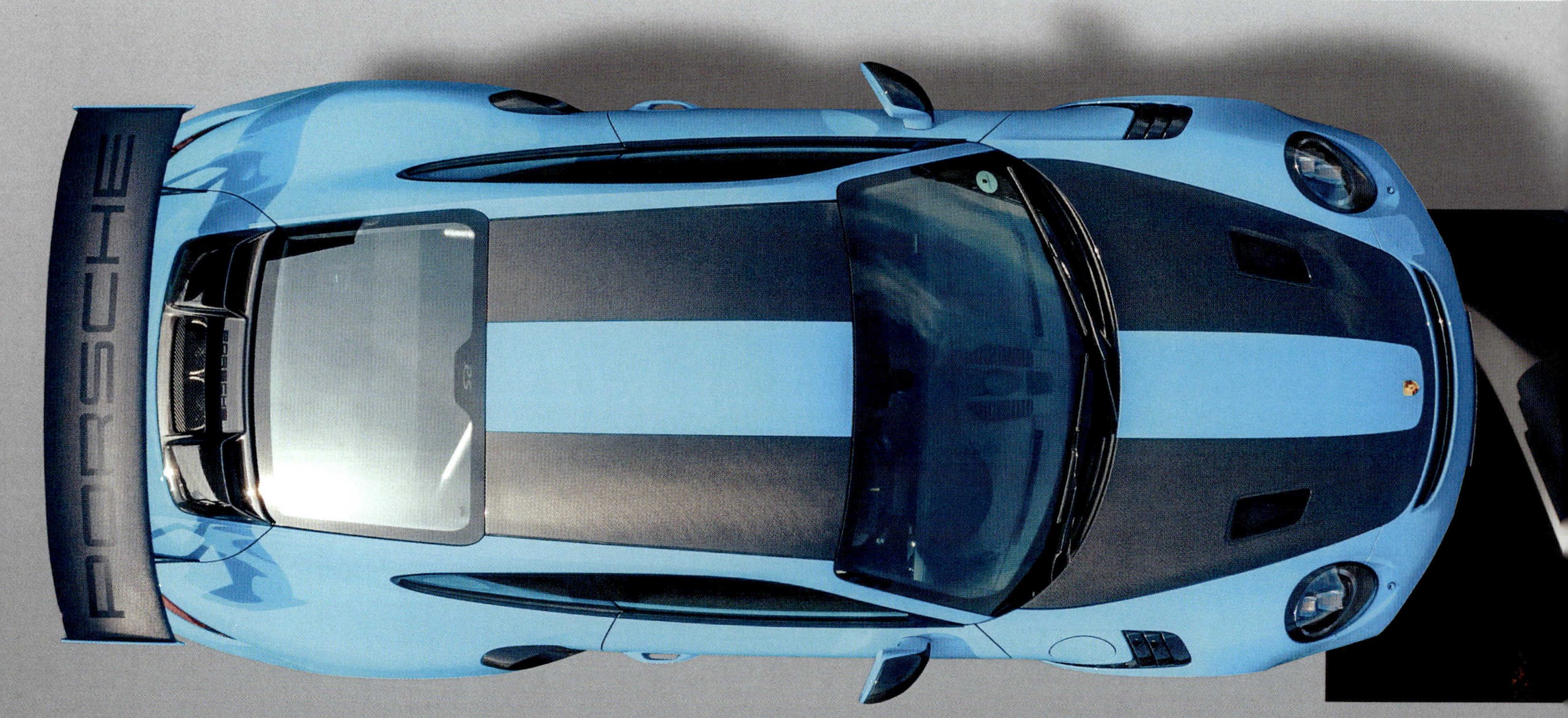

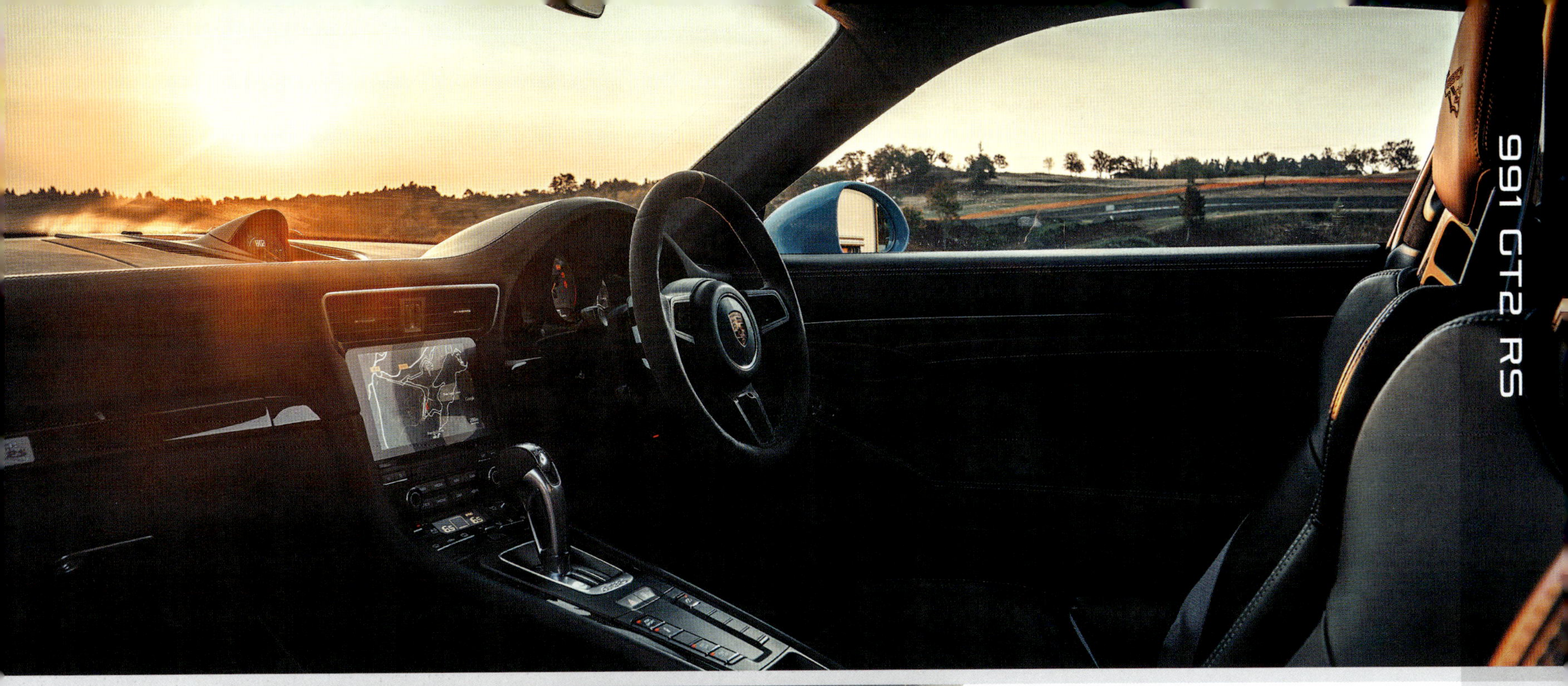

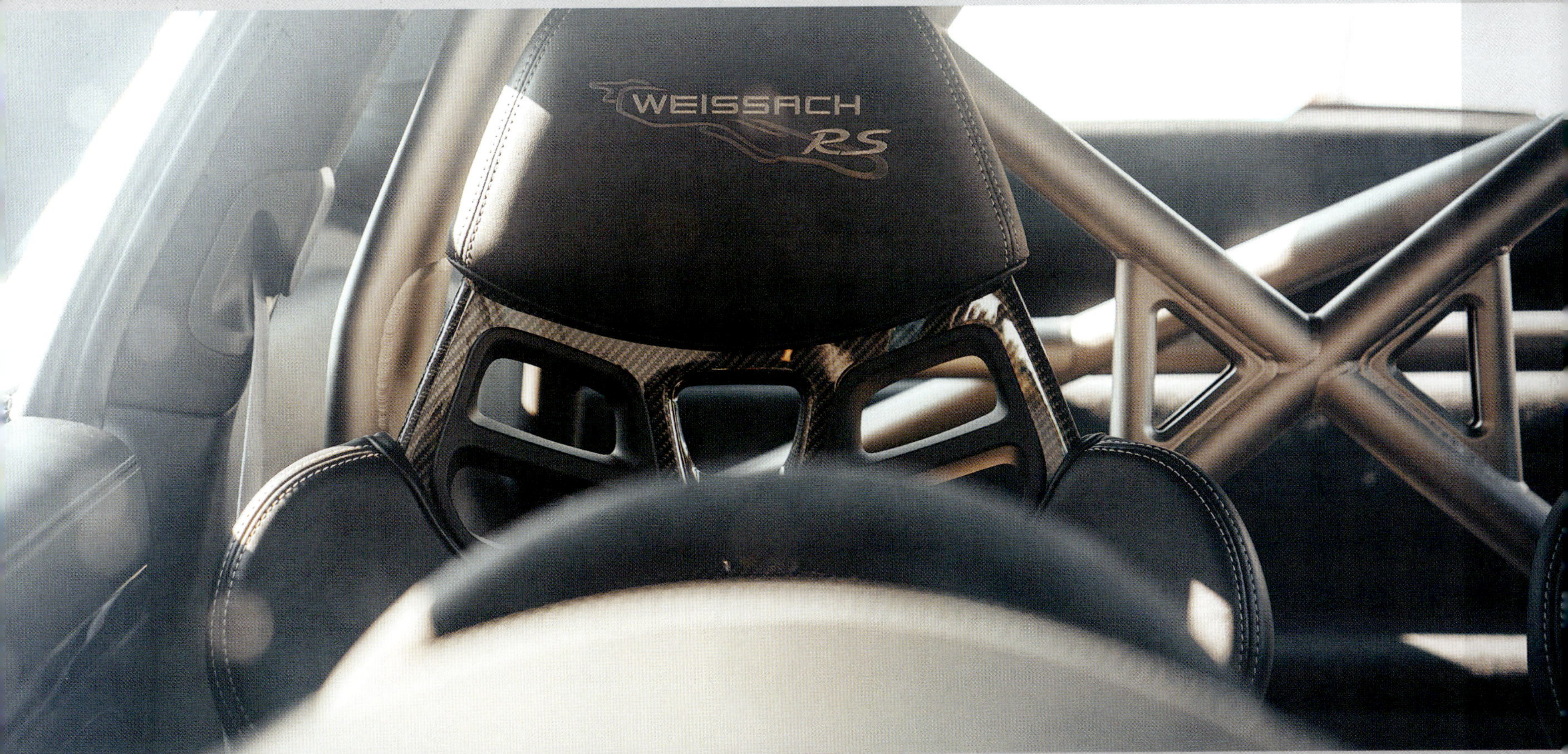

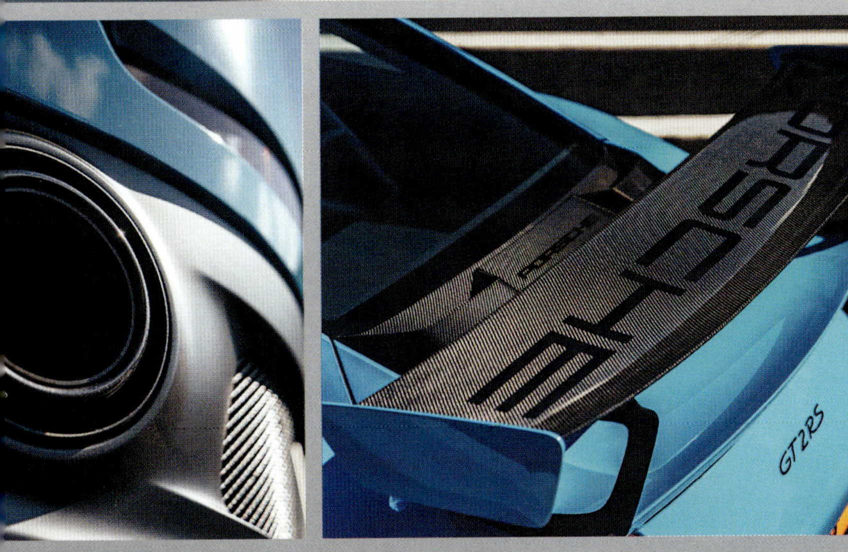

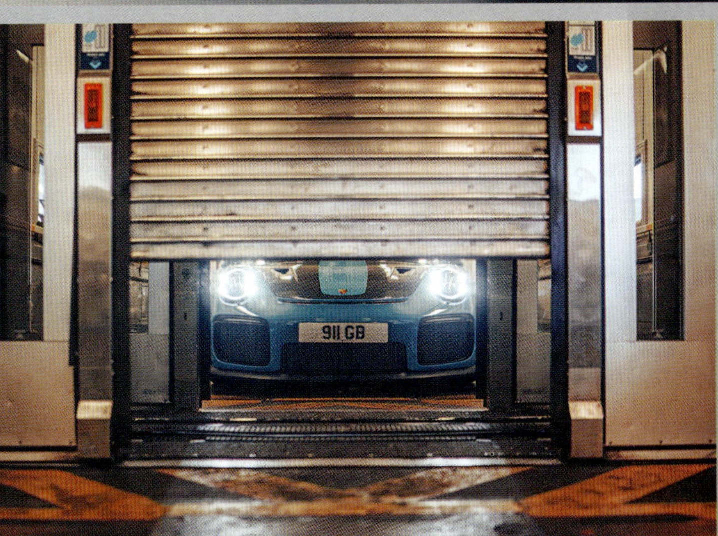

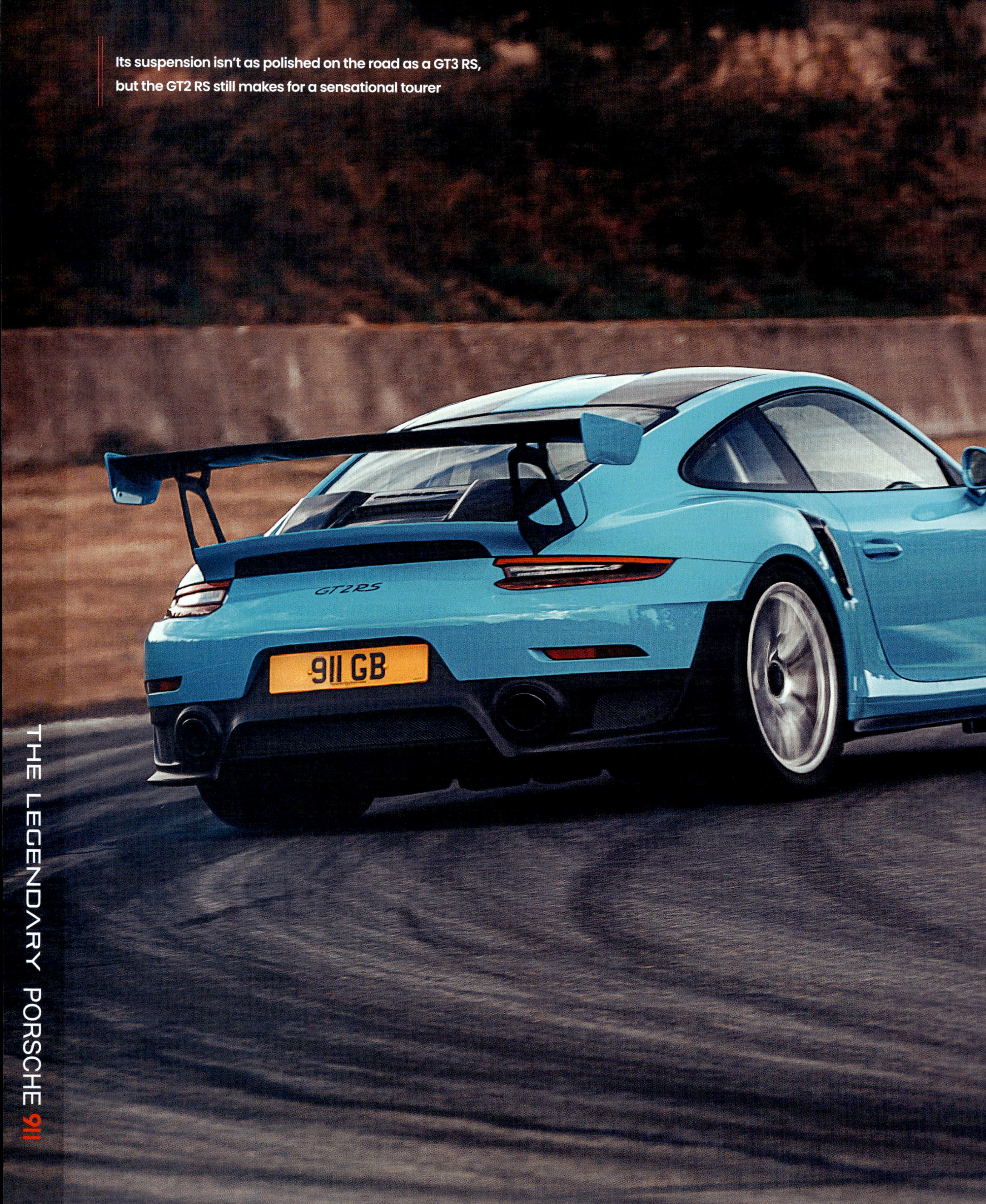

Its suspension isn't as polished on the road as a GT3 RS,
but the GT2 RS still makes for a sensational tourer

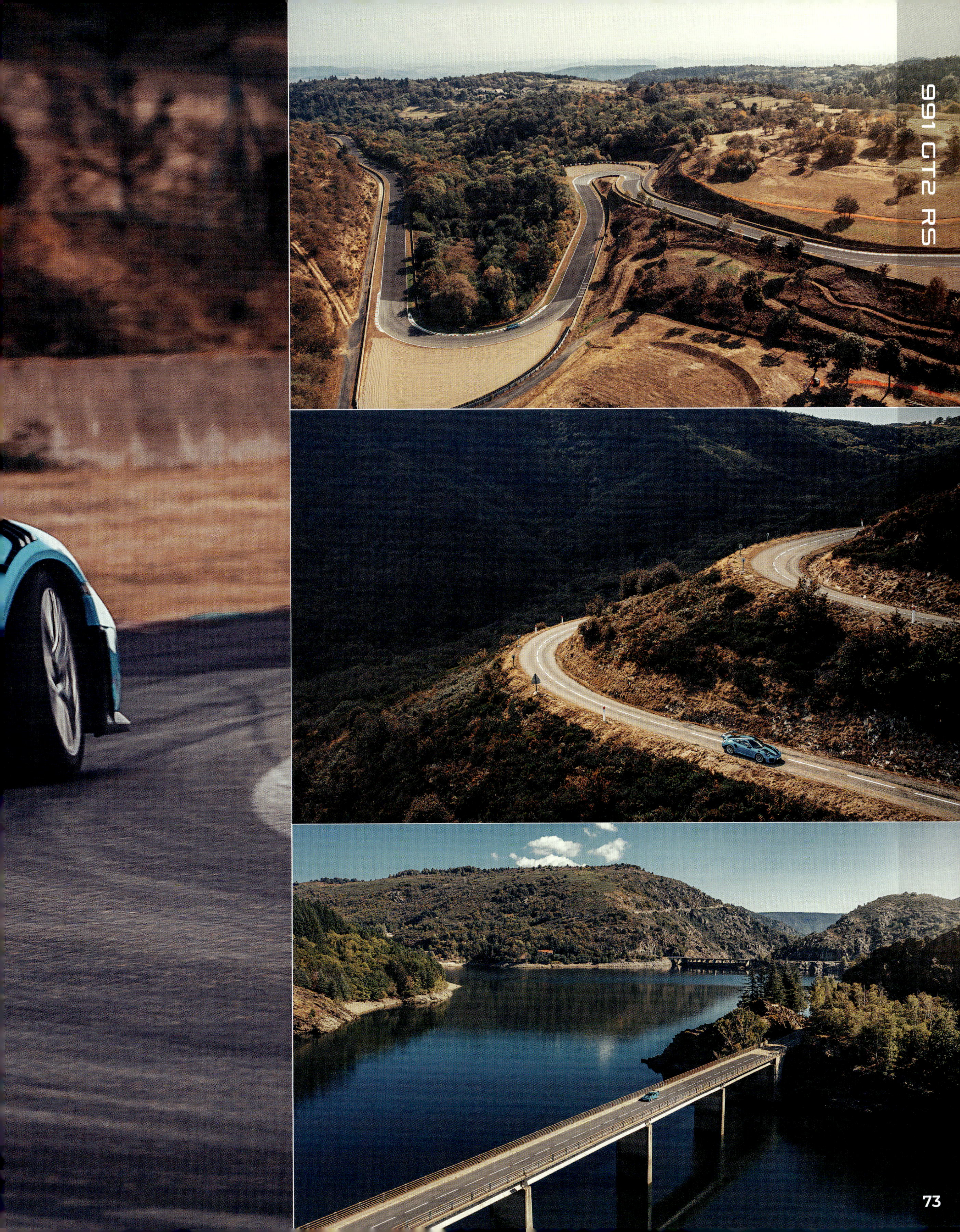
991 GT2 RS

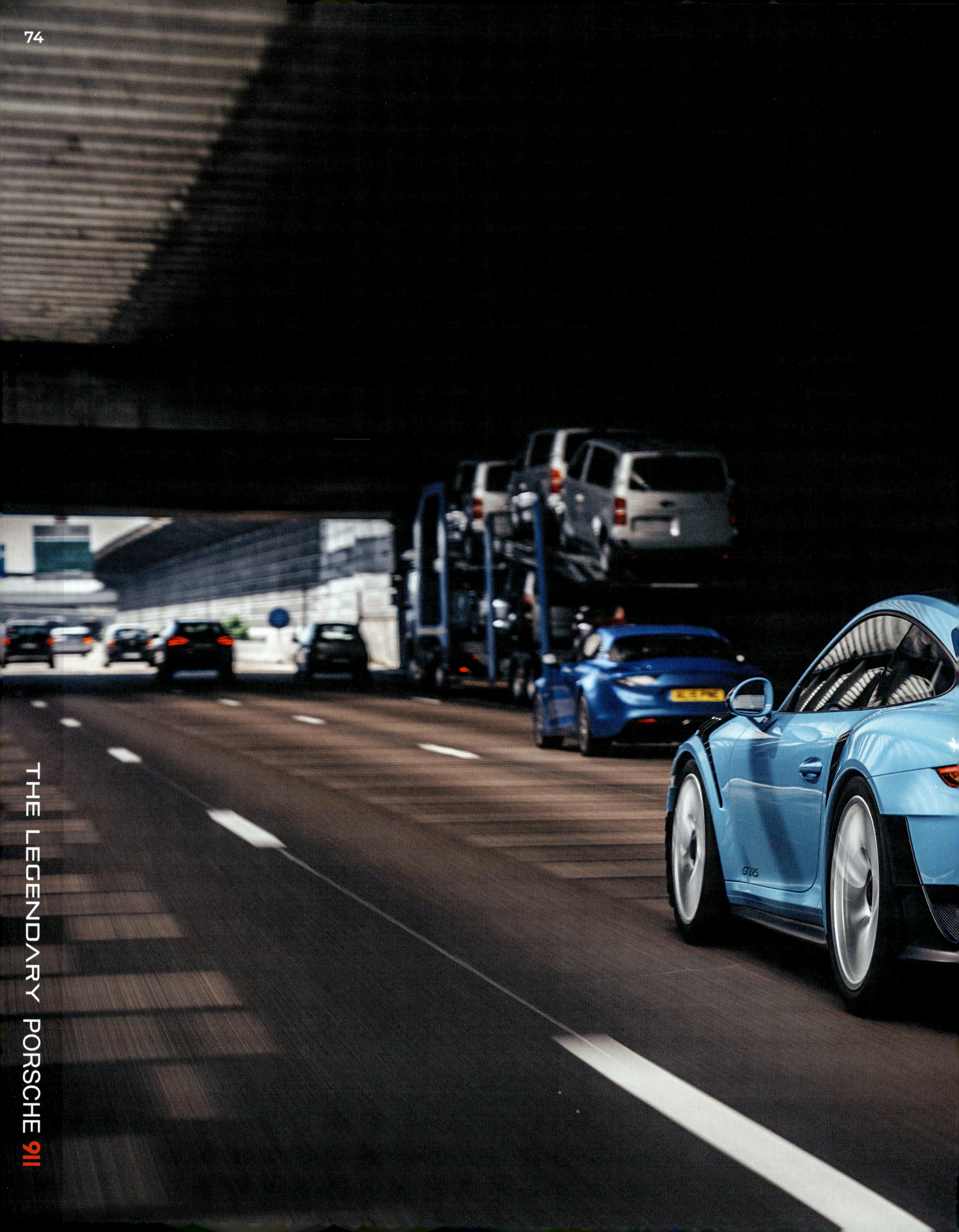

THE LEGENDARY PORSCHE 911

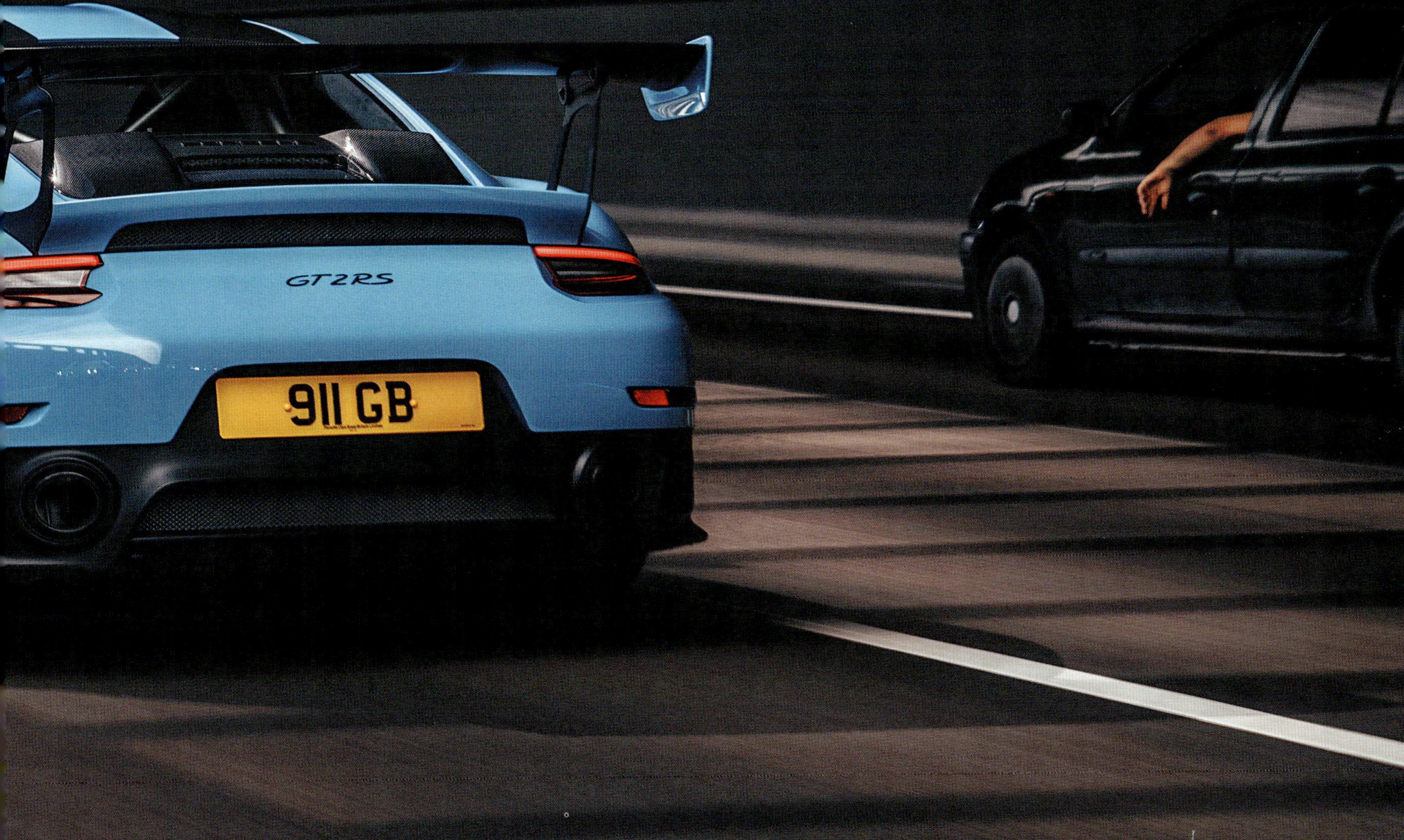

# IN A CLASS OF ITS OWN
# 992 GT3 RS

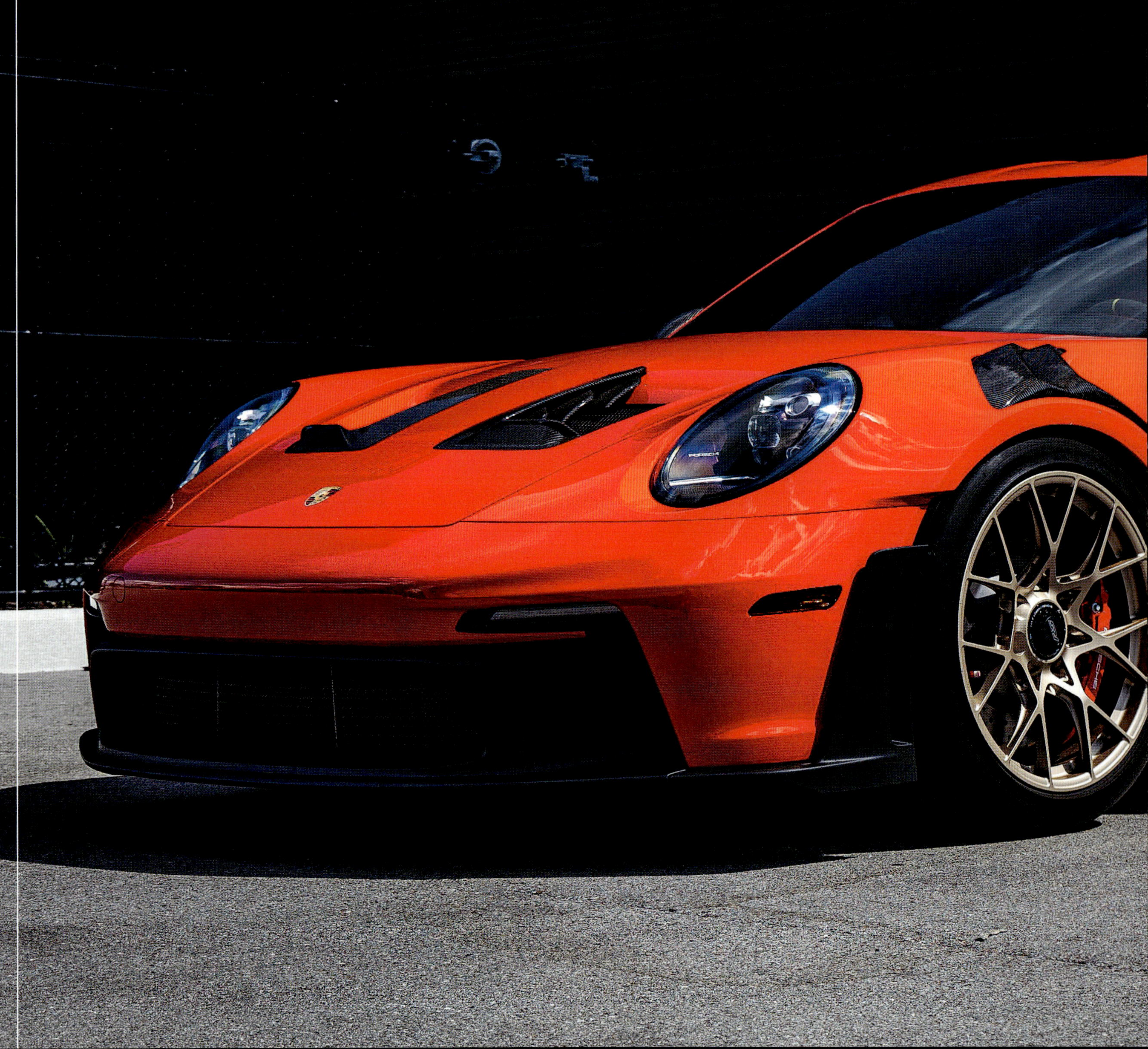

Unapologetically created for speed and adrenaline-inducing performance, the poster boy of the eighth generation of the 911 was unleashed at the end of 2022 and wasted little time in establishing its credentials.

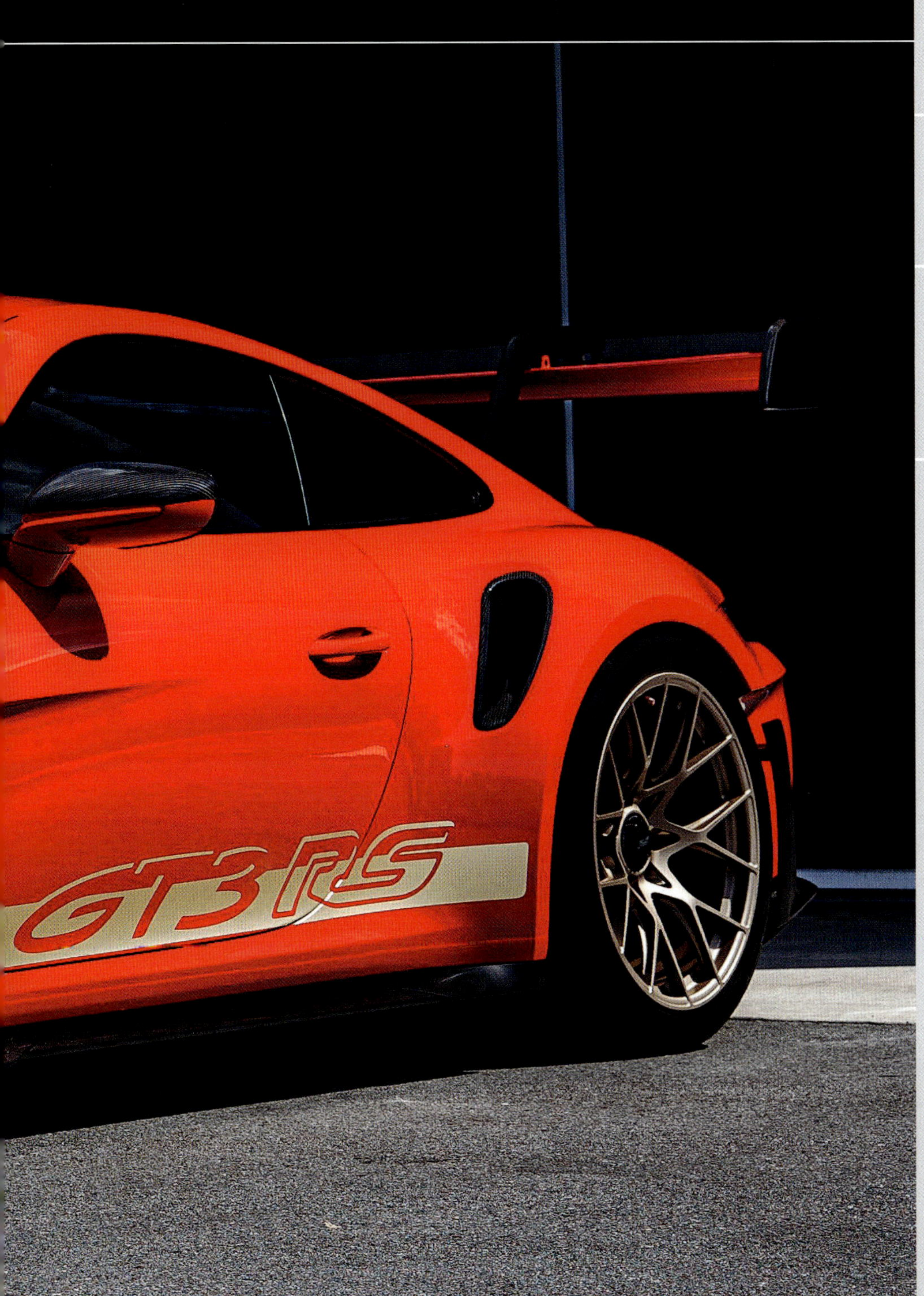




# 992 GT3 RS

2022

### ENGINE

**Capacity:** 3,996cc
**Compression ratio:** 13.3:1
**Maximum power:** 518hp @ 8,500rpm
**Maximum torque:** 465Nm @ 6,300rpm
**Transmission:** Seven-speed PDK

### SUSPENSION

**Front:** Double wishbone
**Rear:** Multi-link

### WHEELS & TYRES

**Front:** 9.5x20-inch magnesium alloys; 255/35 ZR20
**Rear:** 12x21-inch magnesium alloys; 315/30 ZR21

### DIMENSIONS

**Length:** 4,572mm
**Width:** 1,900mm
**Weight:** 1,450kg

### PERFORMANCE

**0-60mph:** 3 seconds
**Top speed:** 184mph

When Porsche were finally ready to unveil the GTS RS, the company proudly proclaimed their new offering was "clear in its intentions". Those intentions were "maximum performance", while the company waxed lyrical about "its high-revving, naturally aspirated engine with racing DNA and intelligent lightweight construction." For once the fanfare that inevitably accompanies the launch of any eagerly anticipated, high-end sports car was not hyperbole.

It took the company four years, following the introduction of the 992-series of 911s, to uncage the GT3 RS. The GT3 moniker had been first used back in 1999 on early editions of the 996 range, but almost two decades after its maiden appearance, it now badged an altogether different and markedly more ferocious animal. Its immediate predecessors – the Carrera GTS, Carrera 4 GTS, and Targa 4 GTS – had made their bow in 2021 but the trio of earlier Porsches were all eclipsed by their younger relative.

Before anyone could begin to delve in any depth into the car's impressive numbers, all eyes were drawn to the GT3 RS's imposing rear wing. Extreme was the first word that sprang to mind, but the design was far from an aesthetic affectation and in combination with a relocated radiator and clever engineering concealed within that prominent wing – the first to sit higher than the roof of a Porsche production model – it afforded the car with such dramatic aerodynamic grip that it almost welded itself to either road or track.

"It's time to restore the 911 to the top of the pecking order because, as sure as night follows day, a 911 GT3 is followed by a 911 GT3 RS," the PistonHeads website said. "Rennsport is back. With a vengeance. Let's begin with downforce. There is a lot of it. Its production begins at the front, with that centrally mounted radiator. This is the first time that the radiator has sat in the front where the boot would normally be.

"These work in tandem with the twin-element rear wing to deliver 490kg of downforce at 124mph. For the record, that's twice what the 991.2 GT3 RS made, and three times as much as the 992 GT3. The rear wing itself is a swan-neck design, just like the GT3's. Here, for the RS, there's a fixed main wing and a hydraulically adjustable upper element that extends higher than the roofline. That's never been the case before on a 911."

The control of the moveable section of the rear spoiler was also new and could be opened or closed automatically. For the manual purists, however, there was succour, as the GT3's wing could also be operated by the driver via a button on the steering wheel, a set-up inspired by Formula One's Drag Reduction System (DRS).

This all meant Porsche were not boxed into a corner when it came to the GT3 RS's engine. A naturally-aspirated, 4.0-litre, flat-six, it produced 518bhp. This was 180 less than the GT2 RS but with the new car in seventh, it could nonetheless hit 184mph, while three seconds were all that were required to hit 60 mph.

"Most Porsches, especially quicker 911s , tend to be defined by their engines," said *Auto Express*. "Not so the new GT3 RS. For despite being propelled by one of the all-time great flat-six motors – the latest RS is defined not by its incredible 4.0-litre unit but by its aerodynamics."

Glowing reviews are, of course, gratefully received, but the GT3 RS had to test its mettle on the track and this inevitably meant taking it to the Nürburgring in late 2022. The latest RS did not disappoint on the Nordschleife, setting a time of 6:49.328 minutes, 10.6 seconds quicker than the most recent 911 GT3. The lap meant the RS proudly claimed the record as the fastest ever naturally aspirated production car around the famous circuit. There will inevitably be new GT3 versions as Porsche looks forward with future generations of the 911, but without a crystal ball, it is difficult to envisage a more dynamic or intelligent sports car.

**The 911 GT3 was put through its paces at the renowned Mugello Circuit in Tuscany in late 2022.**

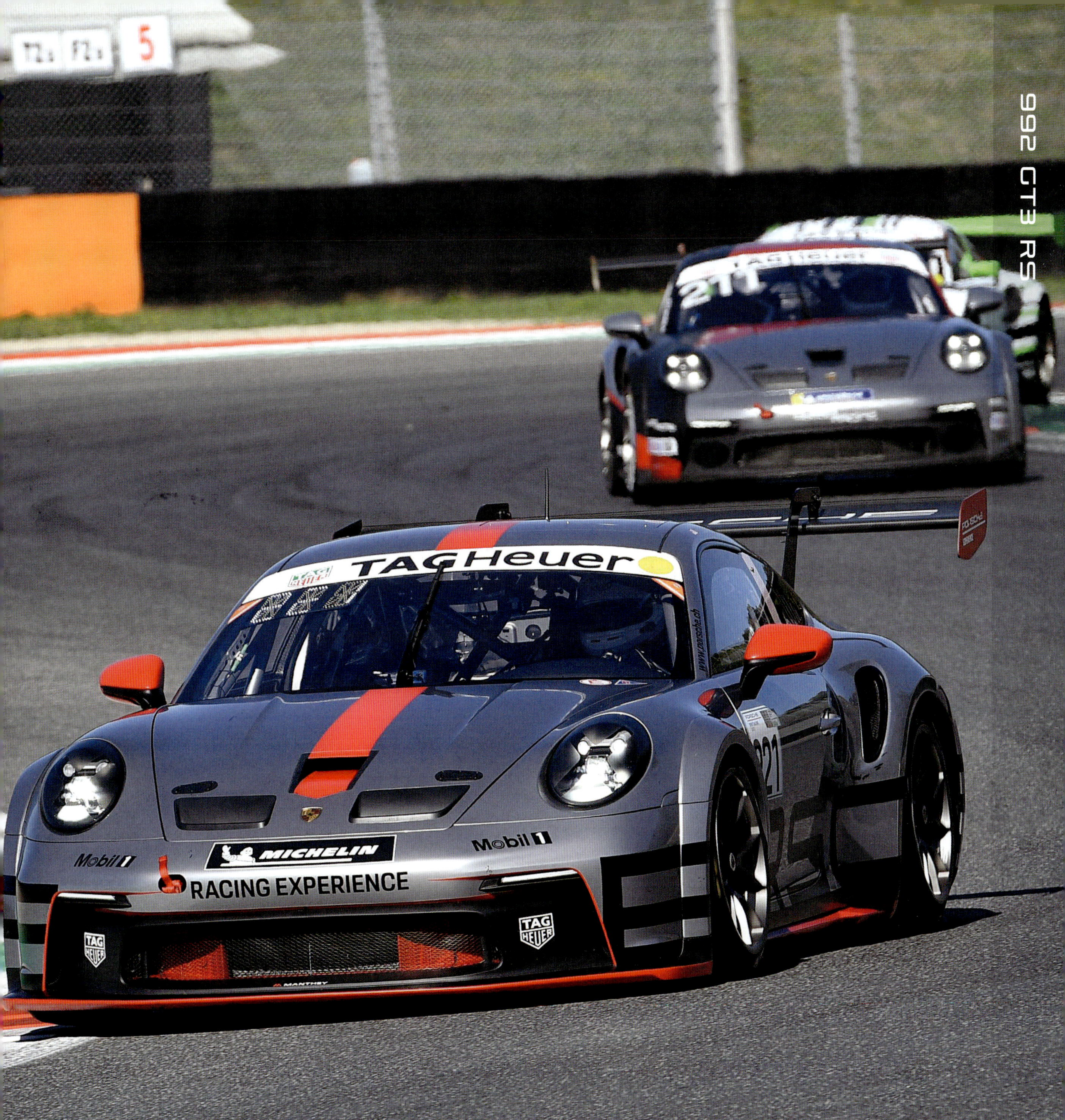

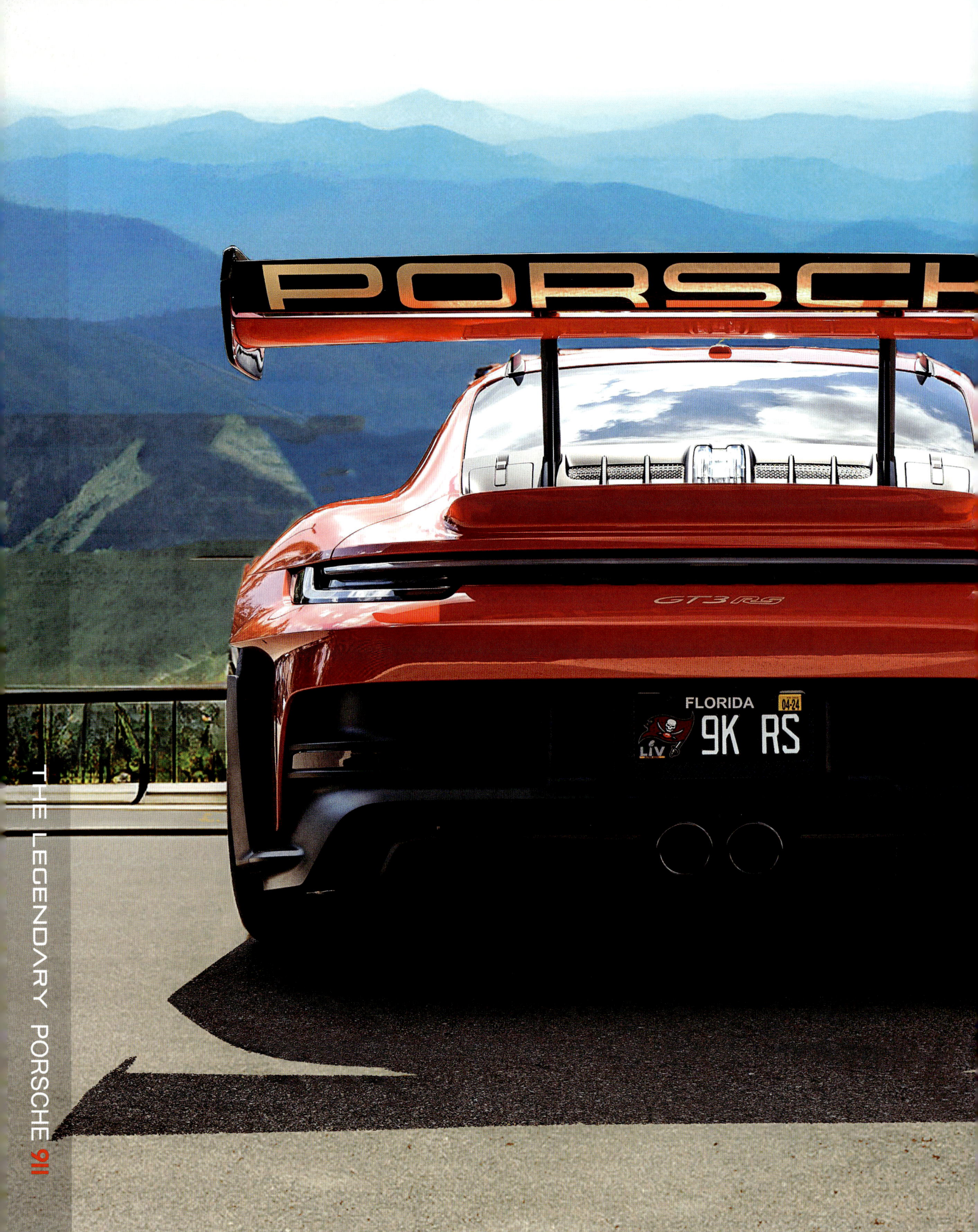

PORSCH
FLORIDA
04-24
9K RS
GT3RS

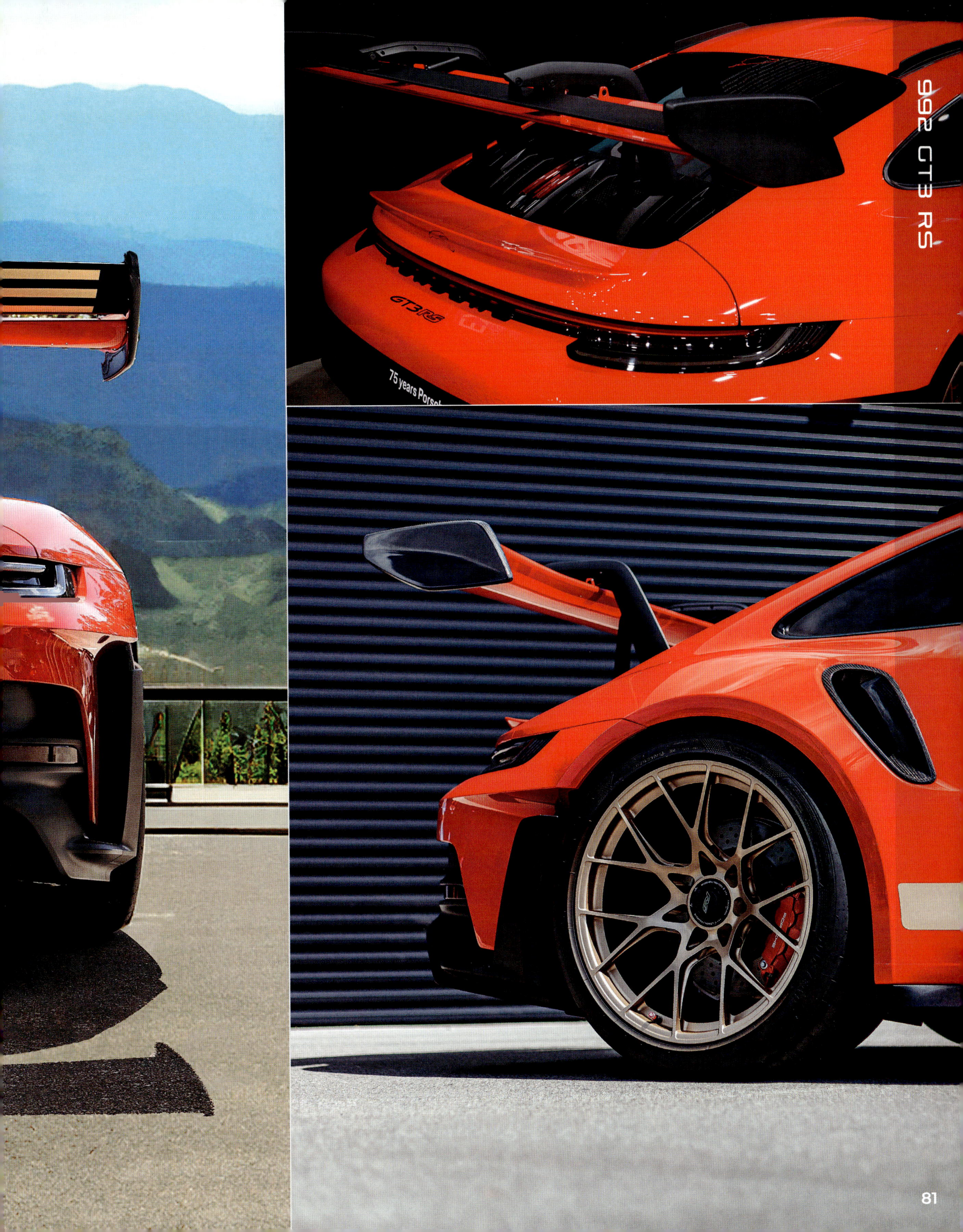
992 GT3 RS
GT3 RS
75 years Porsche

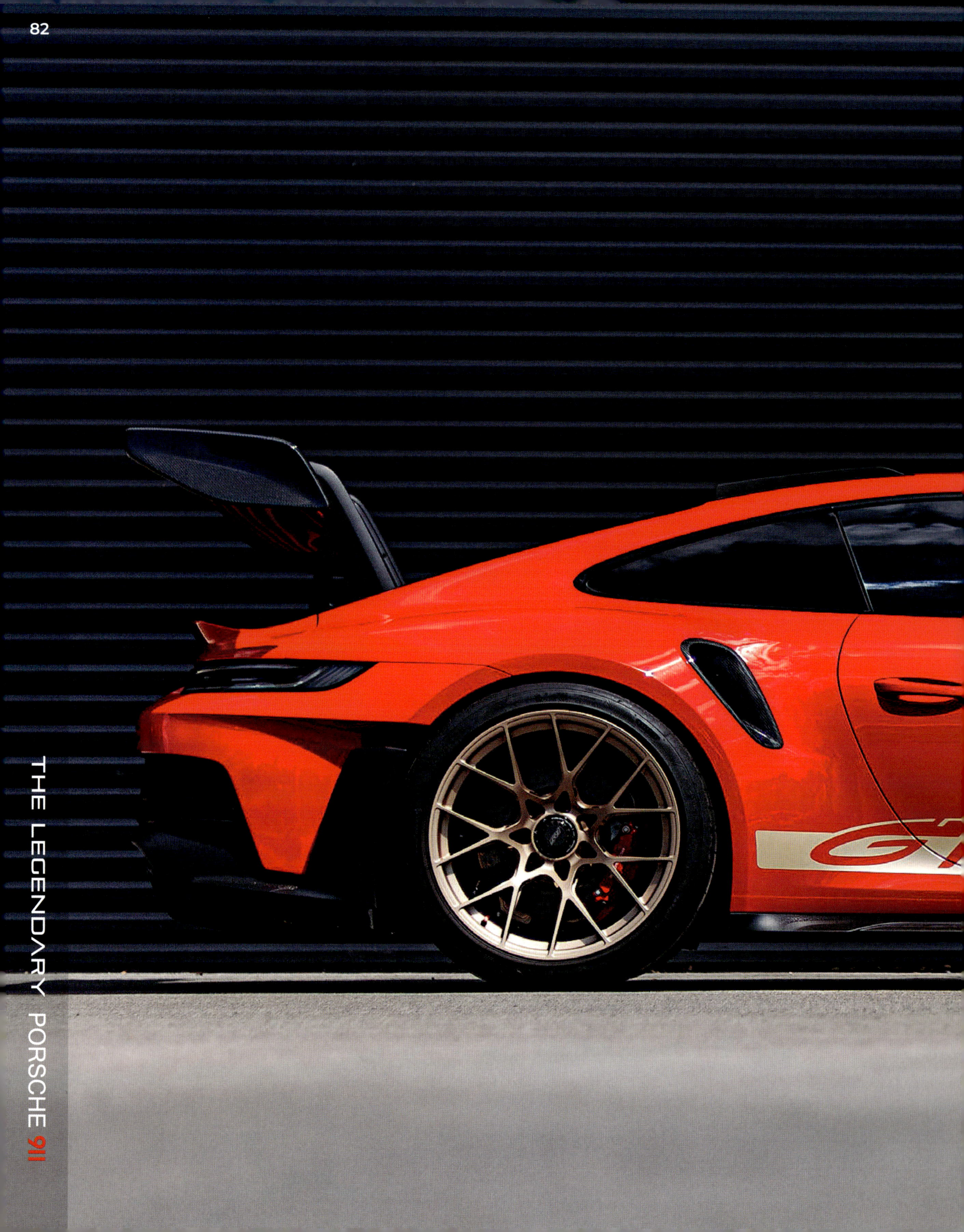

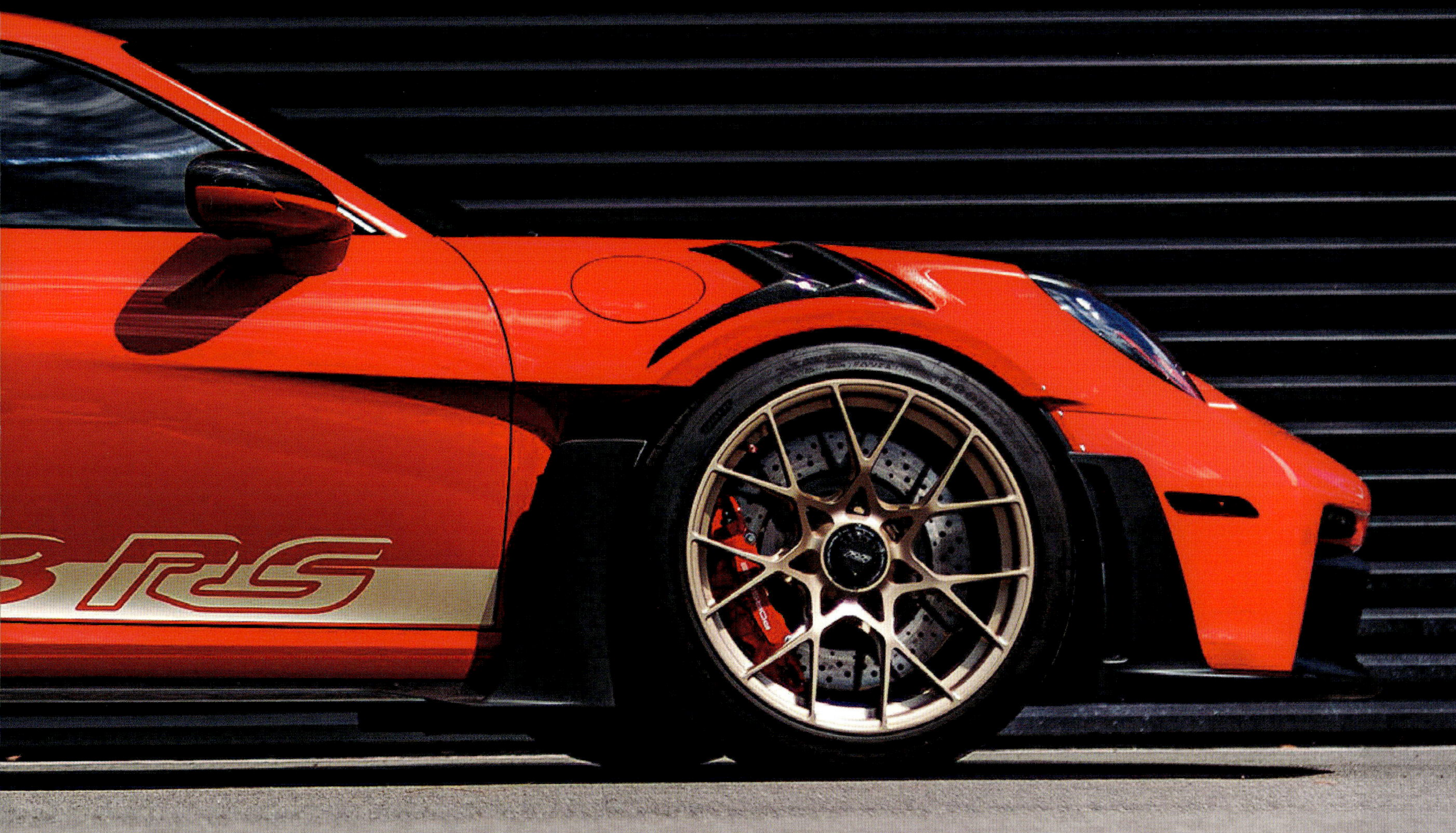

# PORSCHE
# FAMILY CARS

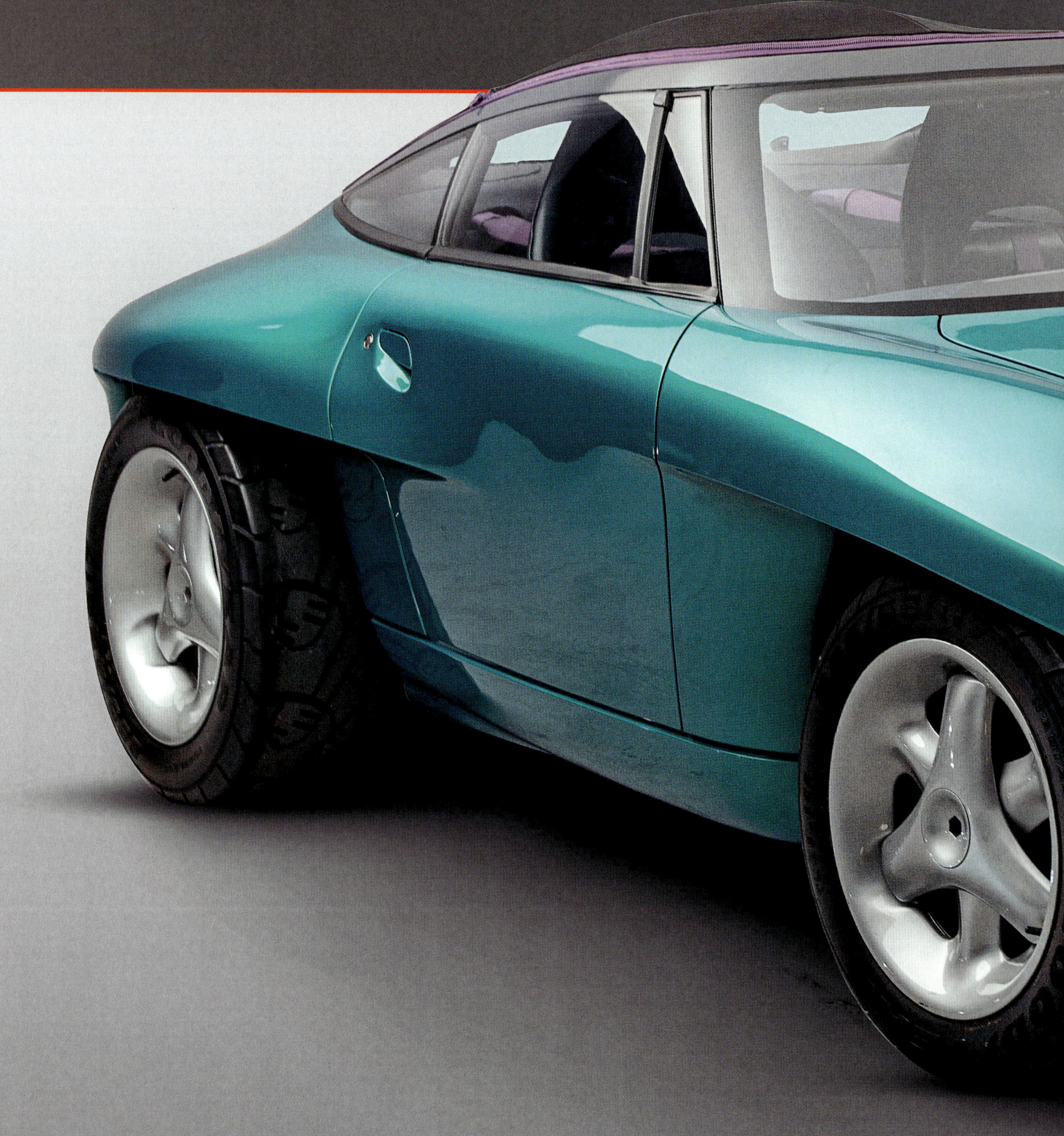

It's a family affair: showcasing the 933 Speedster presented to Ferdinand "Butzi" Porsche on his 60th birthday, the Panamericana concept car given to Ferry Porsche on his 80th birthday and the first 911 Turbo gifted to Louise Piëch, Ferry's sister, on the occasion of her 70th birthday.

Here we also pay tribute to the millionth Porsche 911 to roll off the Zuffenhausen production line; name-check a host of celebrity Porsche 911 owners; celebrate the starring role of the Porsche 911 in the movies; and recall the slick advertising campaigns that enhanced the 911 as the ultimate automotive object of desire. All in all, just like the car itself, quite a spectacular package.

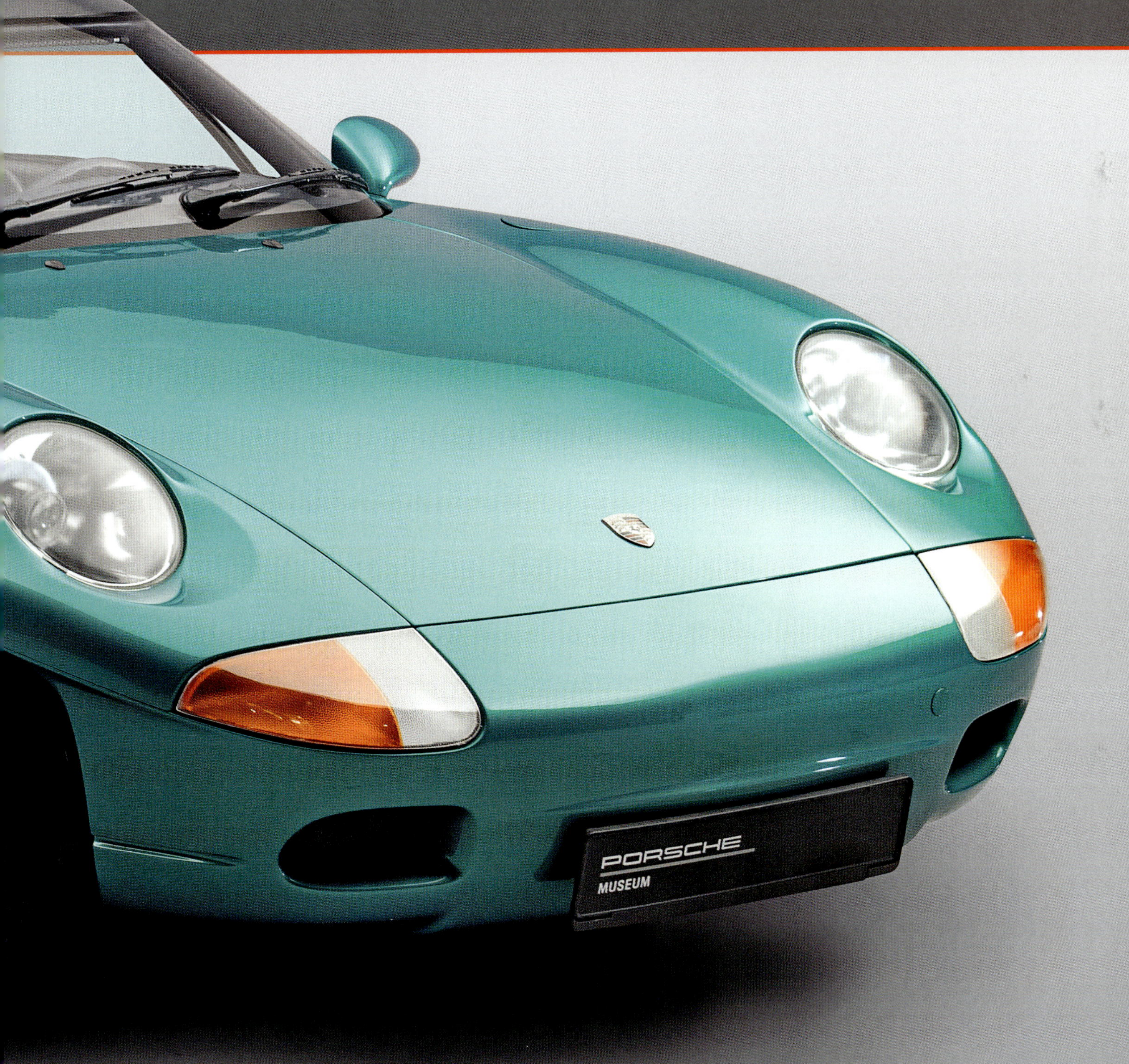

# THE FIRST TURBO
# 911 TURBO

Achieving exclusivity is rarely a simple matter, but few Turbos can carry the same clout as being one of the first examples built, with Louise Piëch a former owner.

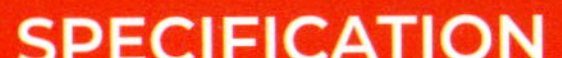

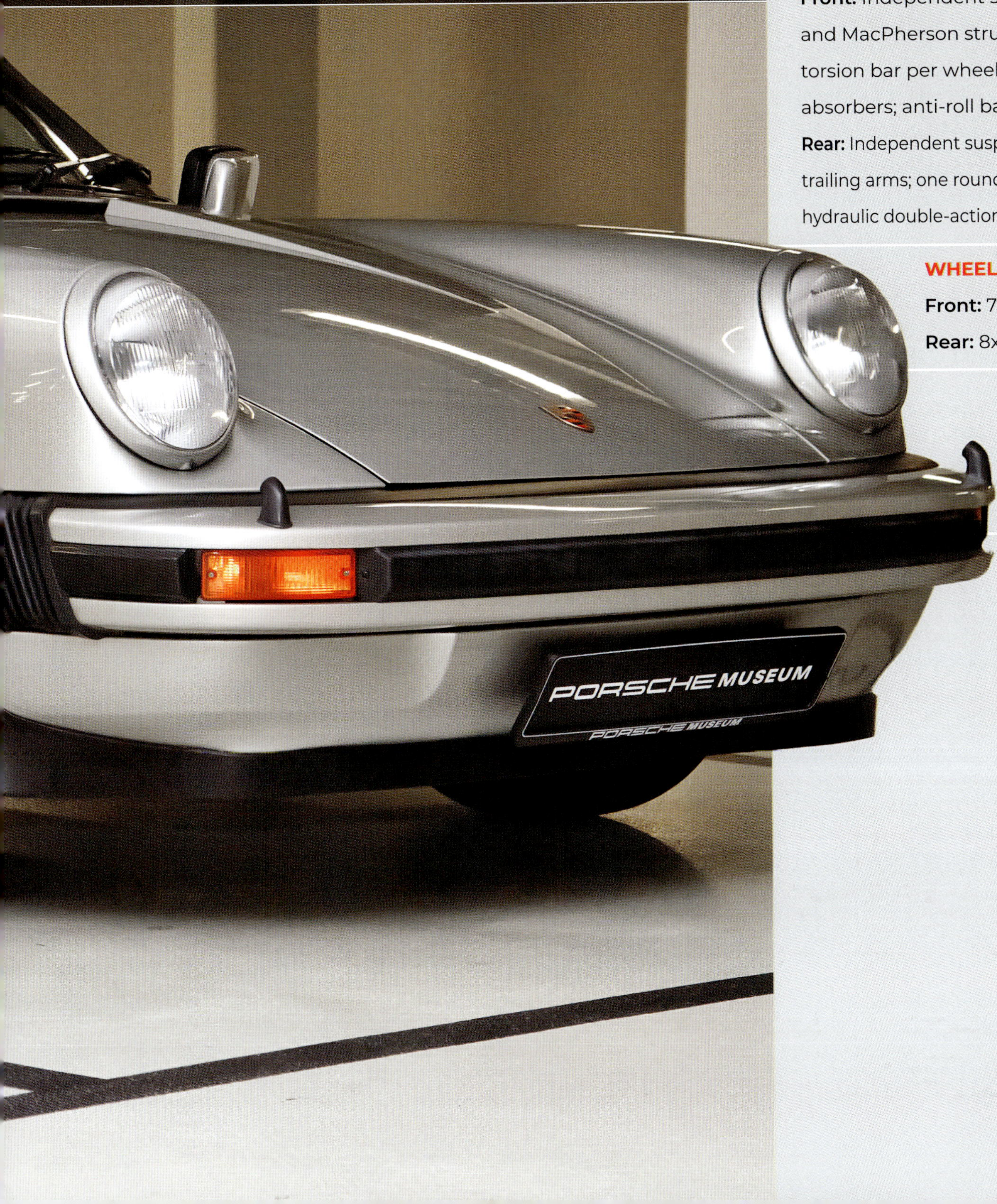

## 911 TURBO

(1974)

### ENGINE

**Capacity:** 2,687cc
**Compression ratio:** 8.7:1
**Maximum power:** 240bhp (176kW)
**Maximum torque:** 345Nm @ 4,000rpm
**Transmission:** Four-speed manual

### SUSPENSION

**Front:** Independent suspension with wishbones and MacPherson struts; one round, longitudinal torsion bar per wheel; hydraulic double-action shock absorbers; anti-roll bar

**Rear:** Independent suspension with light-alloy semi-trailing arms; one round traverse torsion bar per wheel; hydraulic double-action shock absorbers; anti-roll bar

### WHEELS & TYRES

**Front:** 7x15-inch Fuchs; 205/50/15 tyres
**Rear:** 8x15-inch Fuchs; 225/50/15 tyres

### DIMENSIONS

**Length:** 4,291mm
**Width:** 1,775mm
**Weight:** 1,195kg

### PERFORMANCE

**0-60mph:** 5.5 seconds
**Top speed:** 155mph

**B**ack in 1973, the world was changing. Russia sent its Luna 21 module to the Moon, the USA launched Pioneer 11 to study Jupiter and Saturn, and the first mobile phone call was made in New York. While these big events made headlines around the world, a relatively small Stuttgart-based motor manufacturer called Porsche was about to launch its own big-news model: the 911 Turbo.

The principle of forcing air into combustion chambers to boost power may seem like an obvious solution to us today, but getting this system working in an efficient and cost-effective manner on a production car in the Seventies was not without its difficulties. This not-insignificant obstacle might account for the reason why, up to this point, no other manufacturer had really put this technology into practice on a production car – until, that is, Porsche proved it could be done.

The story of turbo power at Porsche started with the 917/10 Can-Am Spyder race car in 1972, which proceeded to pulverise the American series in that year and the next, when the 1,100hp Sunoco 917/30 of Mark Donohue dominated so completely. Of course, development and testing on these race cars would have taken place during 1971 in order for the turbo system to be ready for the 1972 season, so the engineers without question had one eye on a production car application.

Following the success of turbo power in competition, it wasn't long before the technology found its way into the realms of the production department, and in 1973 the 911 Turbo prototype was shown at the Frankfurt Motor Show. This was a decade after the introduction of the 911 model at the same show, and a year later the polished Turbo was unveiled in Paris.

Delivery of the first Turbos to customers started in March 1975 – but initially the factory only planned a production run of 500 units. This decision must be seen in context with the times, as at around 65,000 Deutschmarks each, the Turbo cost almost the equivalent of two 911 Carreras, and the automotive world had just been turned on its head by the infamous oil crisis of the previous year. The response of the public to the 911 Turbo was nevertheless overwhelming, and the first batch of 500 cars was sold quickly. A second run of 500 units was commissioned, and before long so was a third. However, long before the early 3.0-litre 930s captured the imaginations and bank accounts of affluent petrolheads, Porsche had built an early Turbo derivative as a birthday present for none other than the late Louise Piëch.

Louise Piëch (née Porsche) was Ferry's sister and married to Anton Piëch, the one-time head of the Volkswagen factory at Wolfsburg. For Louise's 70th birthday on 29 August 1974, the Porsche factory gave her the very first 911 Turbo to be produced in Stuttgart-Zuffenhausen.

Turbocharging was responsible for much of Porsche's success throughout the Seventies as the company sold 2,850 units of the 3.0-litre model (1975–77) and 14,500 of the 3.3-litre model (1978–88). From this first model, the Turbo has expanded over the years to include Targa, Cabriolet and Turbo-look derivatives, as well as powerful versions like the 'Slantnose' cars. On the race track in the Seventies and Eighties, the 934 and 935 models rose to such prominence that they were almost unbeatable, as the victory of the Kremer 935 K3 in the 1979 24 Hours of Le Mans stands testament to.

The Porsche 3.0-litre engine had reached its development ceiling, but turbocharging would open a world of new opportunities for the 911, and from humble beginnings the 911 Turbo has grown into one of the most evocative sports cars in the world. Long may its success continue.

**Unlike later 930 Turbo models, the first Turbo was a narrow body 'Carrera' shell**

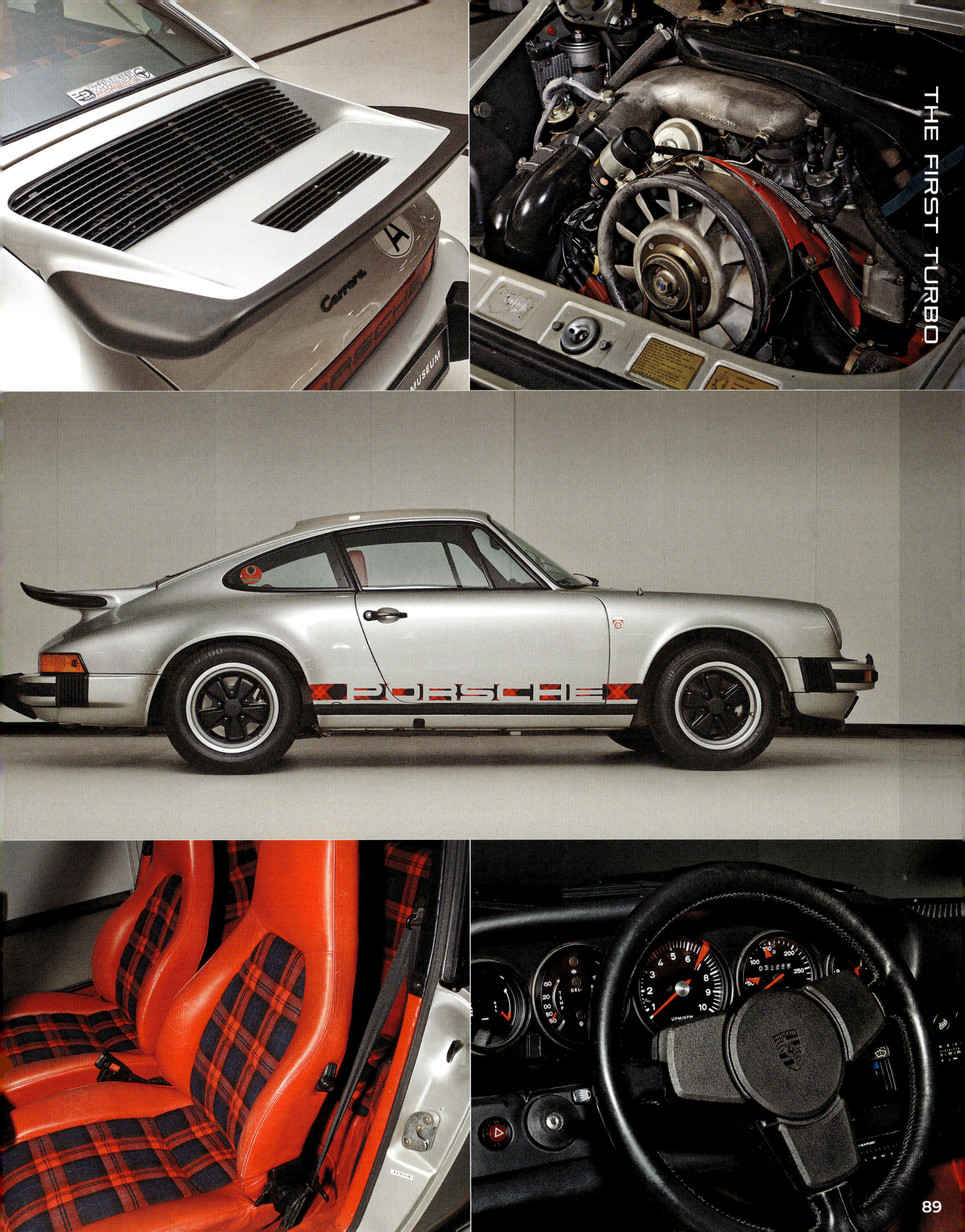

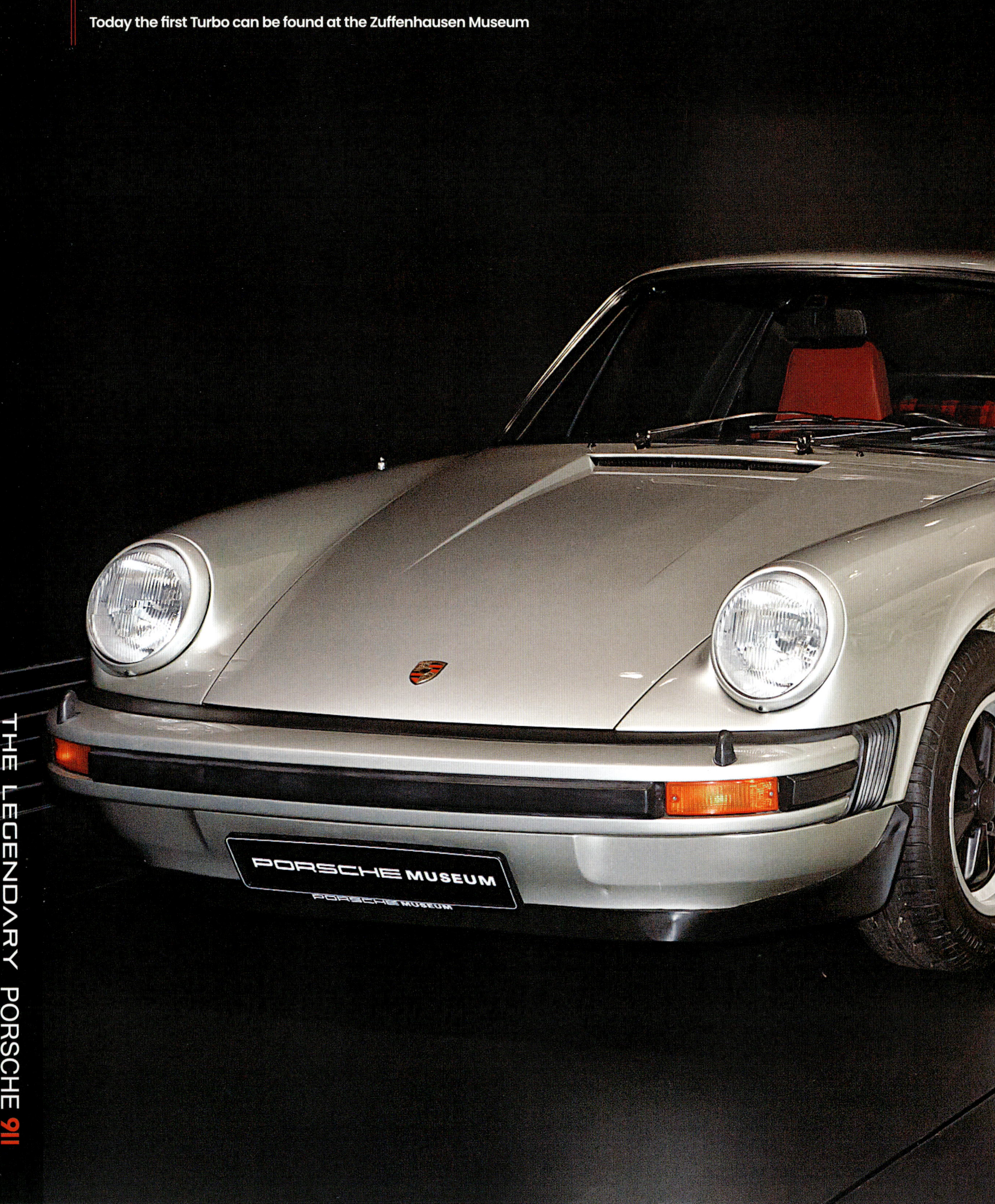


THE LEGENDARY PORSCHE 911

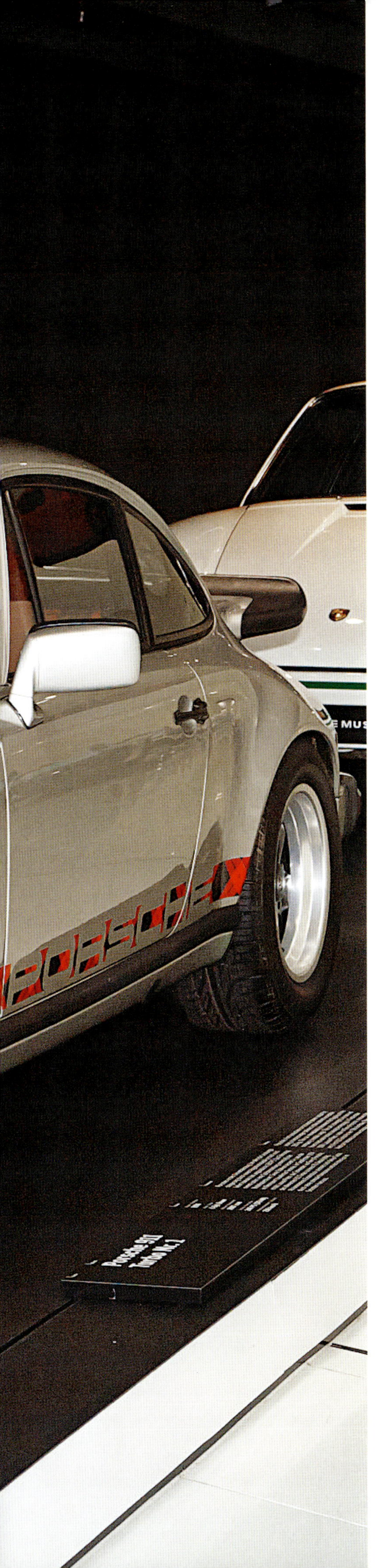



## THE ESSENTIAL FACTS

- Chassis 9115600042 is the first turbocharged 911 production car made by the factory
- The first prototype Turbo used a standard 911 Carrera narrow body and chassis
- Initially fitted with 2.7-litre turbo engine, it was later replaced with a 3.0-litre powerplant
- The car was presented to Louise Piëch by the factory on the occasion of her 70th birthday, on 29 August 1974
- The first Turbo features the familiar five-dial dashboard but, uniquely, sports a 10,000rpm race car rev counter

## OTHER PORSCHE RARITIES

### 'Carrera RS 2.7' in the making (1972)

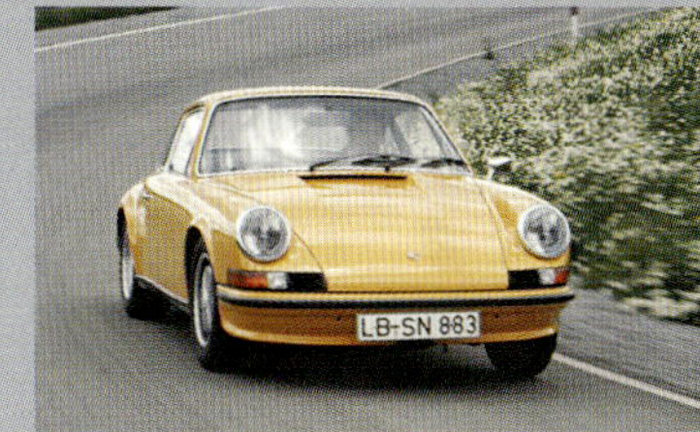

With the 911 model established in the market, it was time to produce what Porsche called a 'hammer' model. The Seventies were all about colour and radical ideas, but it had been almost a decade since the last road-going Carrera model was in the product line-up. To throw snoopers off the trail, Porsche prepared a squadron of nine standard 911S 2.4-litre cars and fitted them with 2.7-litre engines for testing and development in spring and summer of 1972. Looking like any other 911S without any engine badging, the cars were aimed at a group of enthusiasts who wanted to compete on the track at amateur level. In typical fashion, the Porsche sales department completely underestimated the market response when they decided to sell 500 of these cars, and eventually around 1,580 units were produced.

### 911 Carrera Speedster Study, IAA (1987)

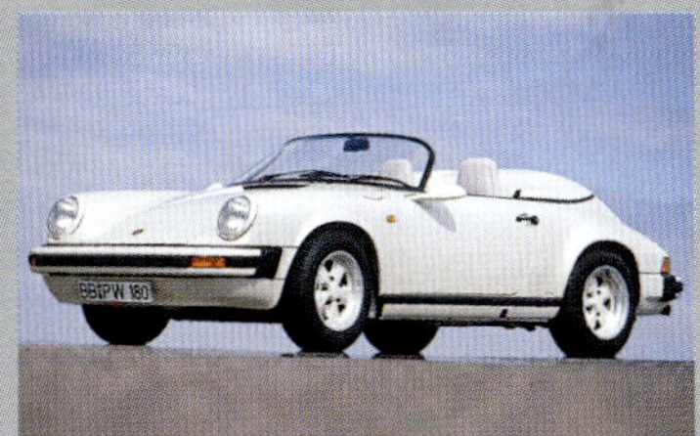

West Coast agent Johnny von Neumann persuaded Porsche's American importer Max Hoffman to get Stuttgart to make a stripped-out, low-cost 356, and the Speedster was born in 1956: a lightened, no-frills version of the 356 aimed at the performance-orientated young buyer. 30 years later, Porsche revealed its 3.2-litre 911 Carrera Speedster Clubsport, a one-off concept car built for the 1987 Frankfurt Motor Show. Based on the 911, the engine produced 231bhp, but the Speedster was 70 kilograms lighter than the Cabriolet and laid out as a two-seater. Intended to be more sport-orientated, the Clubsport featured a top that was hinged behind the occupants, and swung upwards in one piece. While it couldn't be road-registered, the Speedster could. Over 2,000 of these were made in 1989.

### Panamericana Concept (1989)

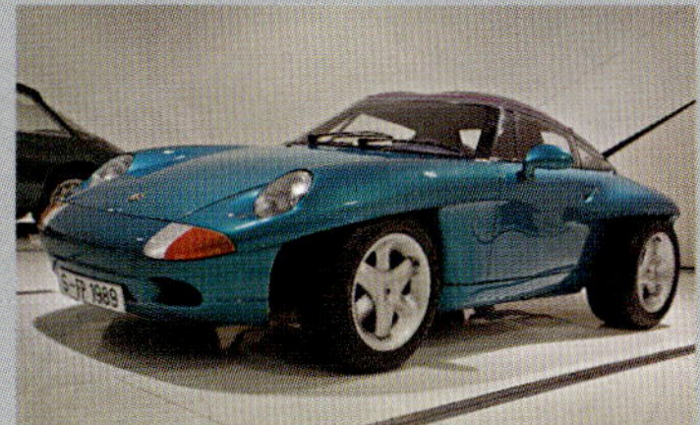

Based on the 964 Carrera 4 platform, the Panamericana concept represented fresh thinking by Dr Ulrich Bez and Harm Lagaaij. Created by Style Porsche, the Panamericana concept was intended to represent a study in future-orientated thinking, creativity and competence in technology, but such abstract marketing terminology only created confusion. The concept car was presented to Ferry Porsche at the 1989 Geneva Motor Show on his 80th birthday. It was reported that he wasn't impressed with it, but it's fair to say that the Bez/Lagaaij team probably developed it more as a test of the public's reaction than anything else. Looking more like a beach buggy on steroids, the word 'pretty' doesn't instantly spring to mind, but it is an interesting representation of some broad Eighties thinking.

# THE CONTROVERSIAL CONCEPT

# PANAMERICANA CONCEPT

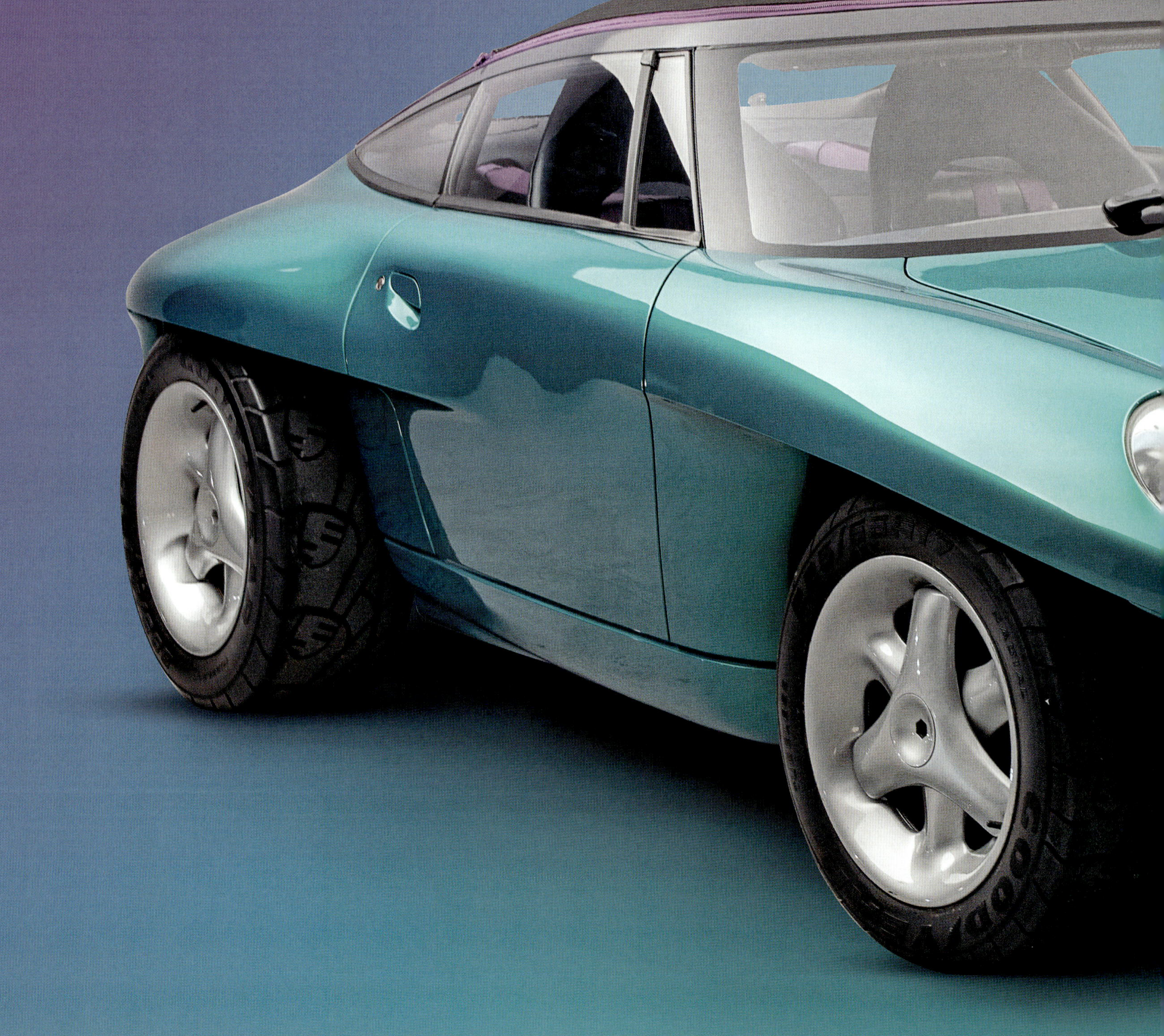

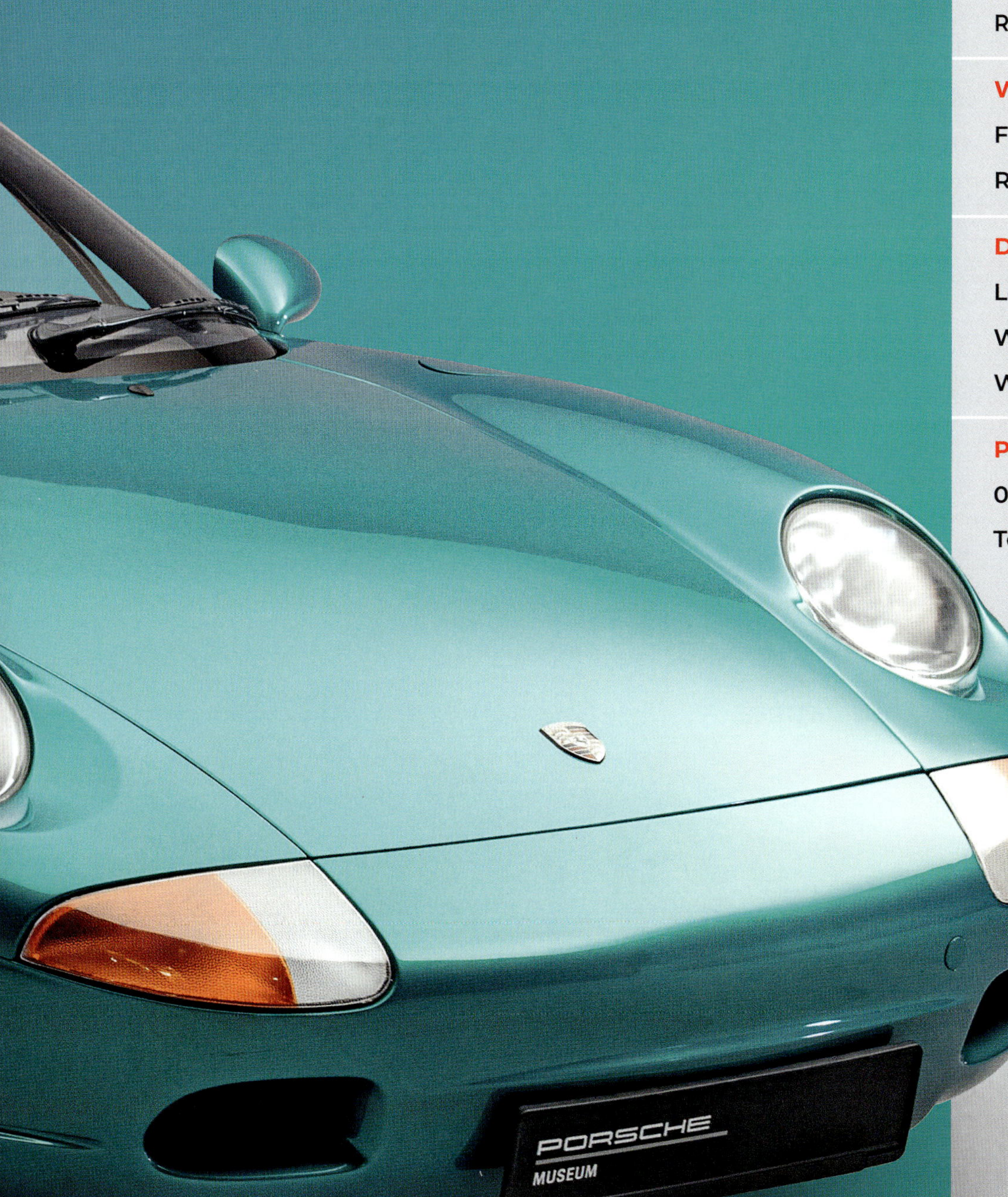

Ferry Porsche's 80th birthday present, the Panamericana, was a concept car that would signpost his company's design and engineering strategy from 1989 into the New Millennium – and beyond…





## PANAMERICANA CONCEPT
(1989)

### ENGINE
**Capacity:** 3,600cc
**Compression ratio:** 11:3.1
**Maximum power:** 250bhp @ 6,100rpm
**Maximum torque:** 310Nm @ 4,800rpm
**Transmission:** Five-speed G64 manual

### SUSPENSION
**Front:** Independent; MacPherson strut; anti-roll bar
**Rear:** Independent; trailing arm; anti-roll bar

### WHEELS & TYRES
**Front:** 8x17-inch custom six-spoke; 225/55/VR17
**Rear:** 10x17-inch custom six-spoke; 255/40/VR17

### DIMENSIONS
**Length:** 4,200mm
**Width:** 1,850mm
**Weight:** 1,474kg

### PERFORMANCE
**0-60mph:** 5.8 seconds
**Top speed:** 130mph

The notion of the concept car really does represent a fascinating yet often downright crazy corner of car culture. Wheeled out for motor shows (if indeed wheels are present), any new styles or technologies are usually expressed through utterly radical designs where manufacturers can gauge public opinion under the premise of it being a one-off. It's not uncommon, however, for a popular concept to make production, albeit with often significant changes in order for it to comply with legislation. Porsche has a rich track record in this regard, with recent, notable examples including the 918, Taycan and 986 Boxster.

However, there is another concept, which can lay a claim to being as successful as the aforementioned trio to realise production, for its impact on the company at large is, without doubt, just as profound.

Based on a Porsche 911, its aesthetics offered a wild departure from the Neunelfer's altogether more reserved profile and styling: the Porsche Panamericana drew on past success in competition on rough terrain. And, though it never made production (nor was it ever intended to do so), elements of its design and engineering would continue to permeate throughout Porsche in the 911 lineup – and beyond – in the years prior to and after the new Millennium.

Unveiled in 1989 at the Frankfurt Motor Show, the idea was to design a Carrera Panamericana-compatible vehicle, commissioned 35 years after the famous Mexican race was cancelled for good. With most of this notorious race taking place on rough terrain, the function of this one-of-one vehicle necessitated all-wheel-drive, a technology which Porsche had adopted just one year earlier with its first 911 Carrera 4. It will therefore come as no surprise that it is the 964 Carrera 4's all-wheel-drive system installed on the Panamericana, but what many will not know is the 964's influence on the Panamericana goes further still. The base car itself is a 964 Carrera 4 Cabriolet, powered by the requisite factory M64 flat six engine, producing the usual 250hp, with power fed to all four wheels via a G64 five-speed manual gearbox.

As it is known, there were never any serious plans to put the car into production but regardless, the Panamericana is a concept of huge historical significance. It offered a snapshot of company trajectory in terms of future 911 styling, but also revealed intrigue from those at the top at Porsche to diversify into other markets with its model lineup – exemplified by designer Murkett's eventual promotion to head both the Cayenne and Panamera projects. A project which, really, shaped the future of sports car engineering at Porscheplatz, the Panamericana is as important to company history as those aforementioned 918, Taycan and Boxster studies – a remarkable feat given it never actually turned a wheel on the public road.

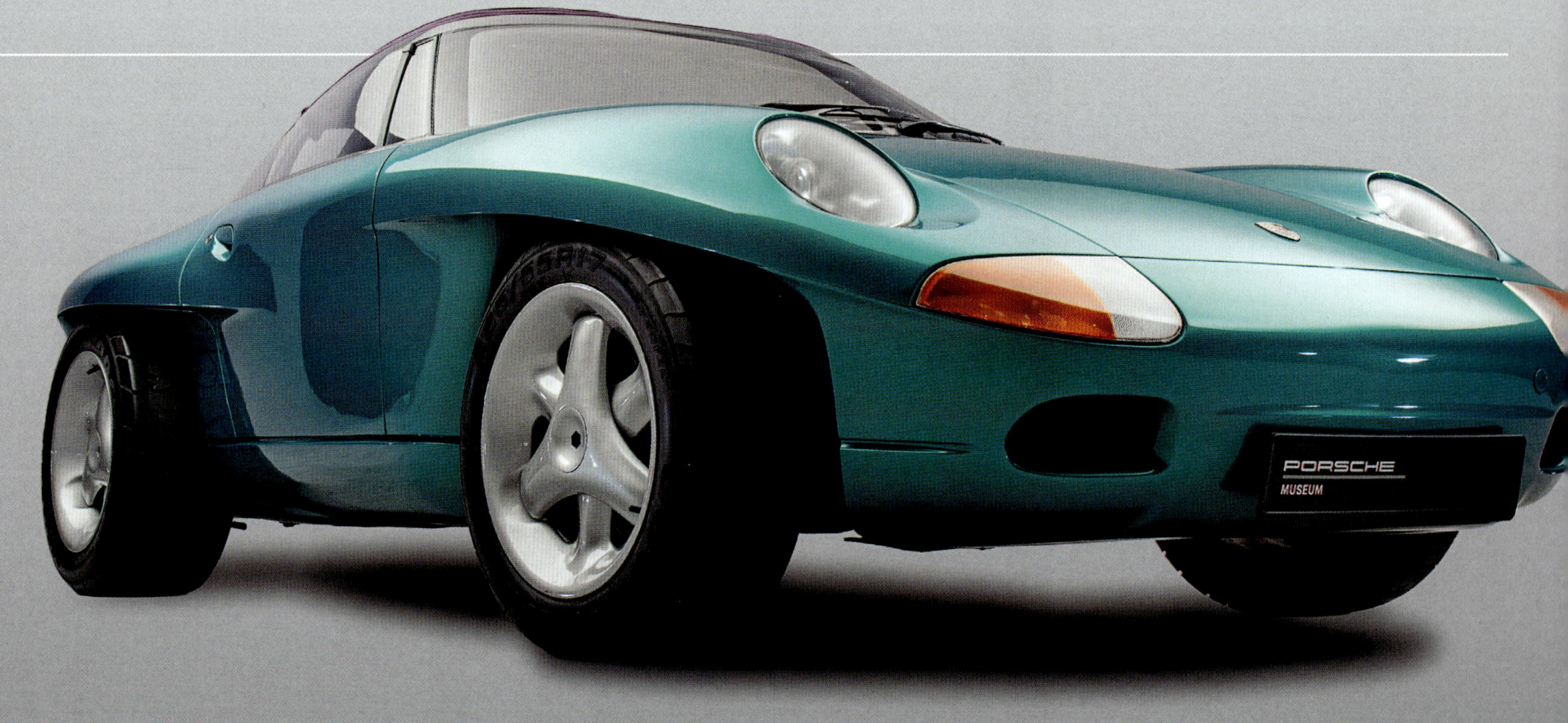

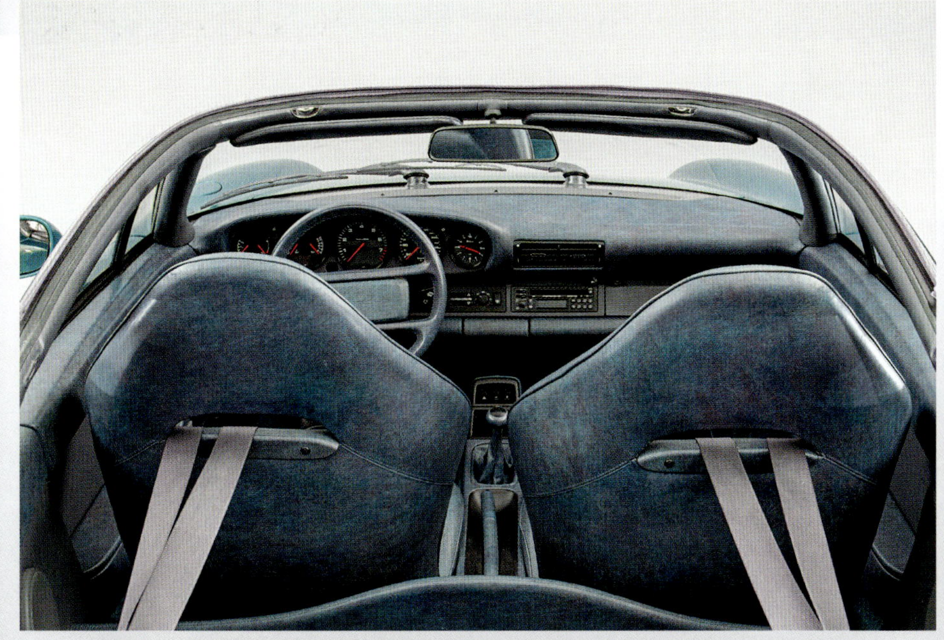

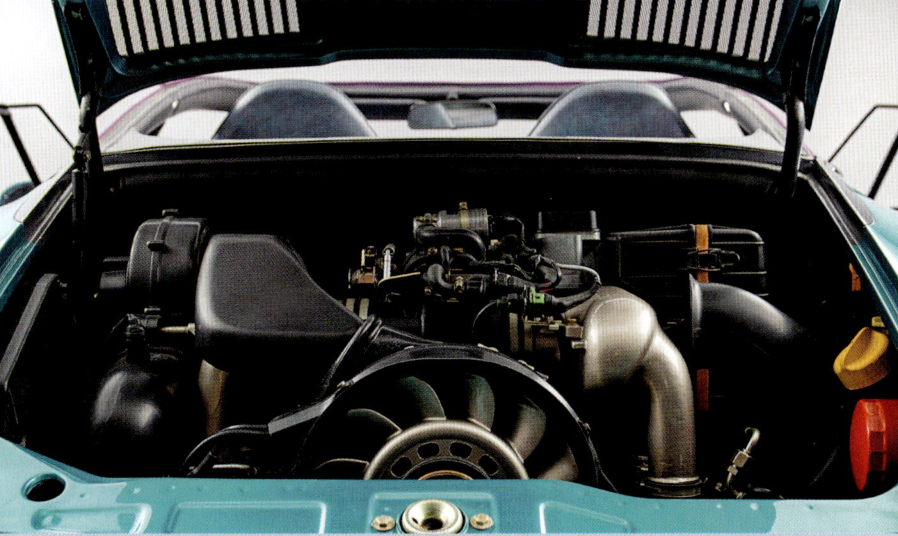

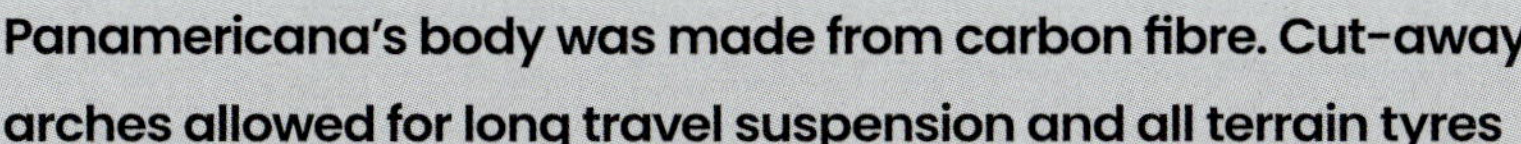

Panamericana's body was made from carbon fibre. Cut-away arches allowed for long travel suspension and all terrain tyres

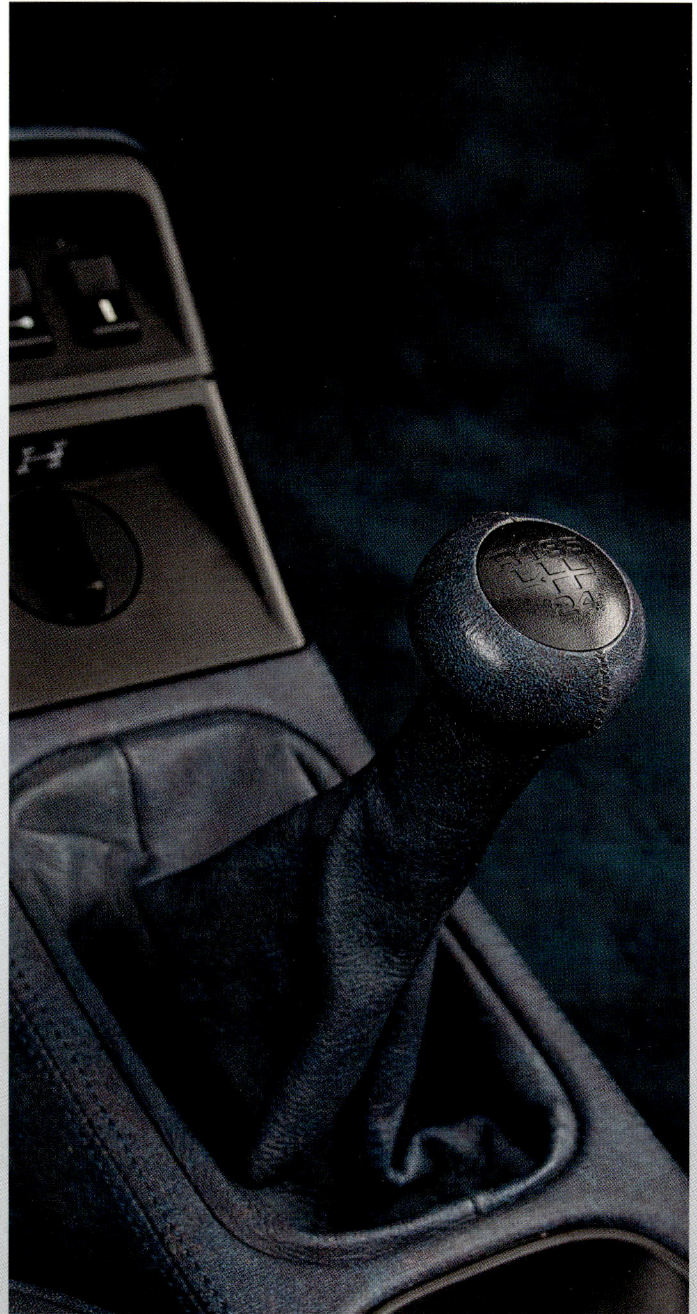

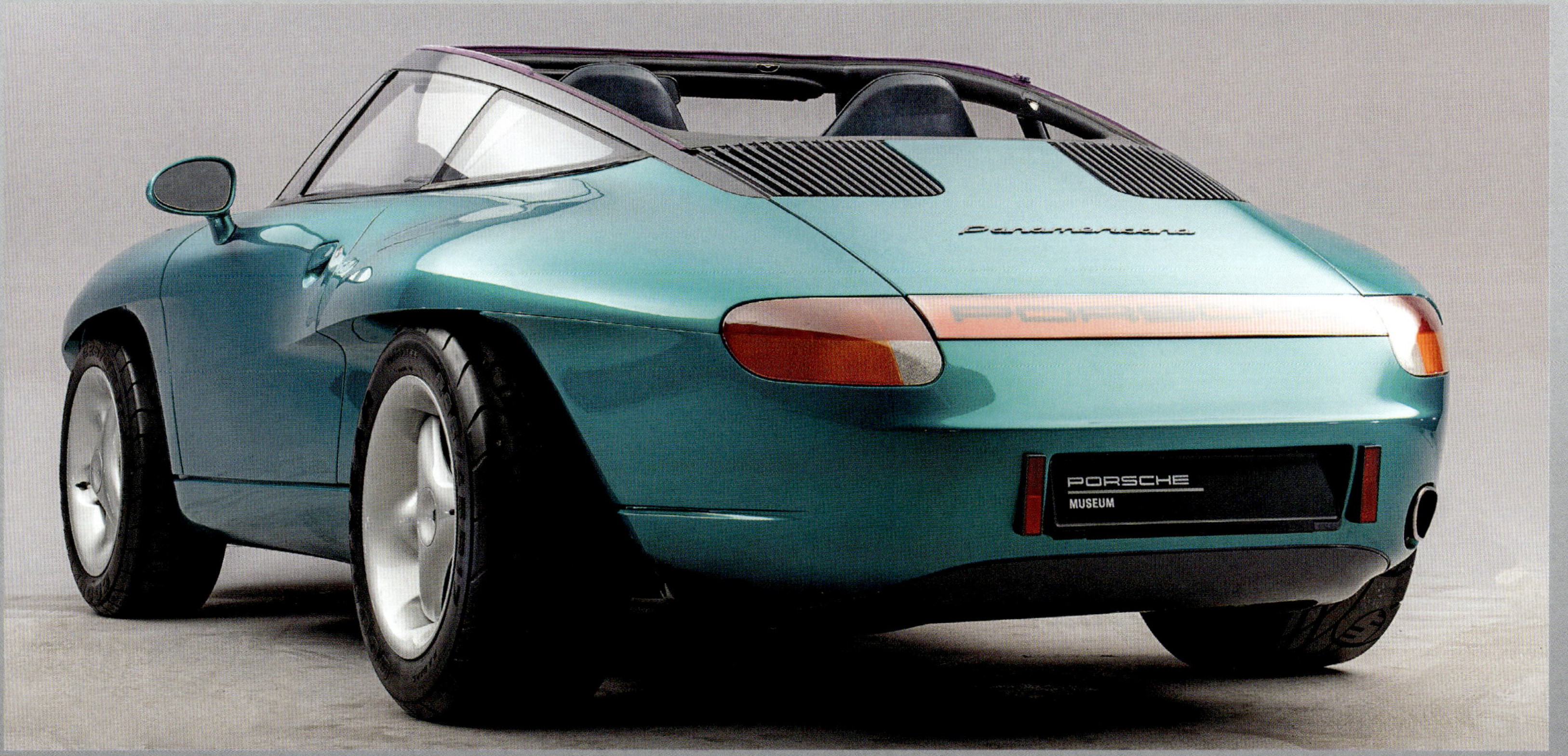

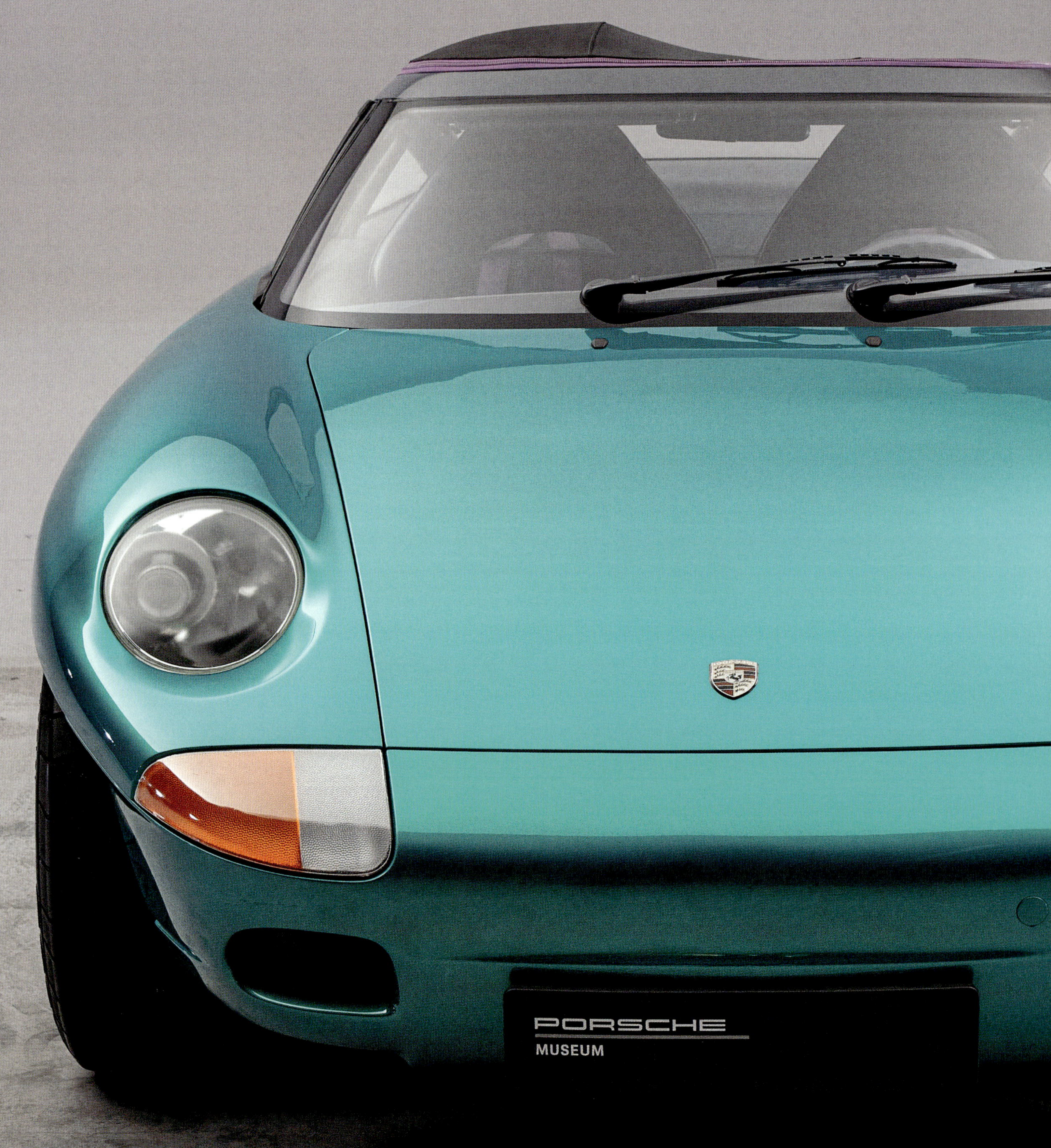
PORSCHE
MUSEUM

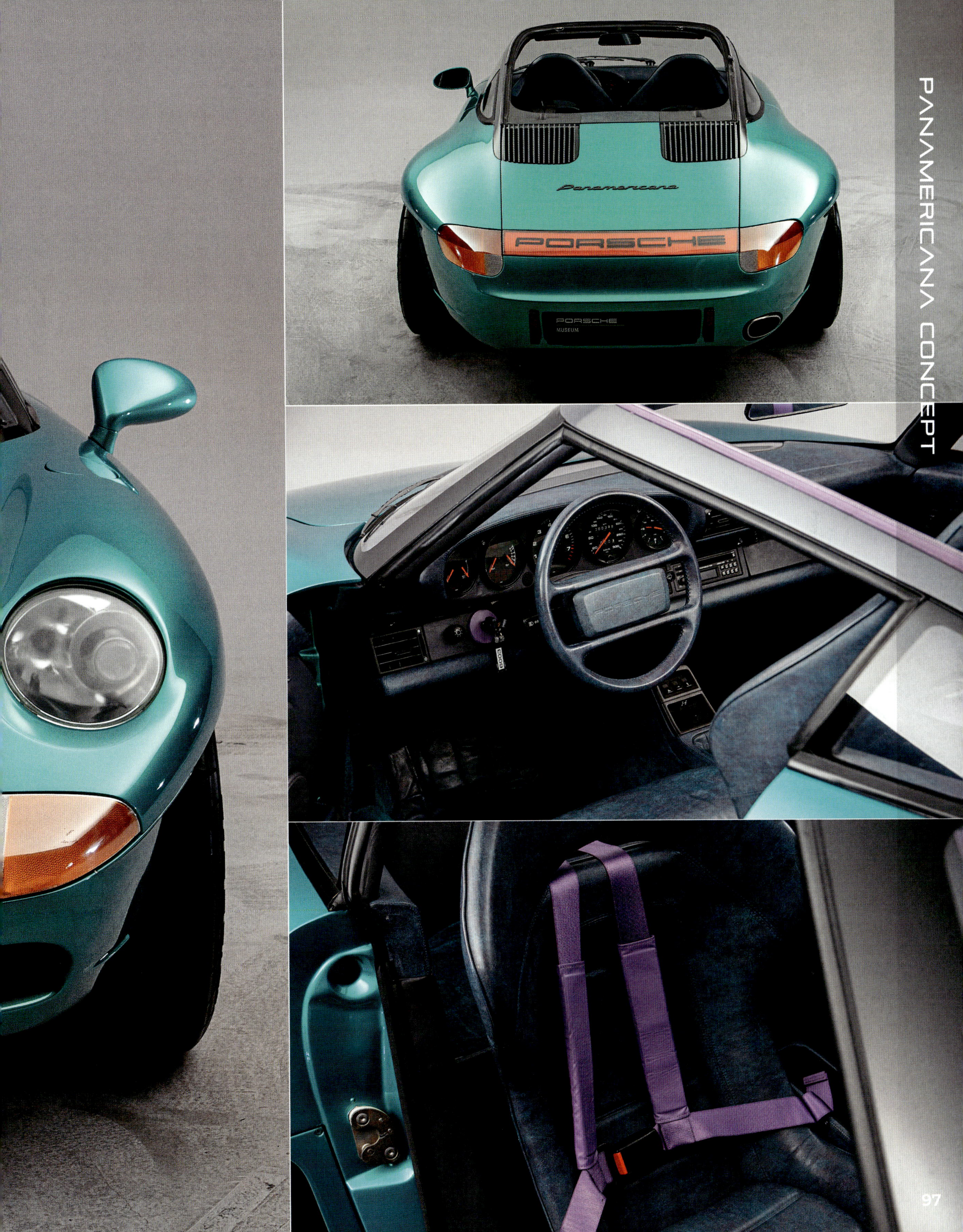

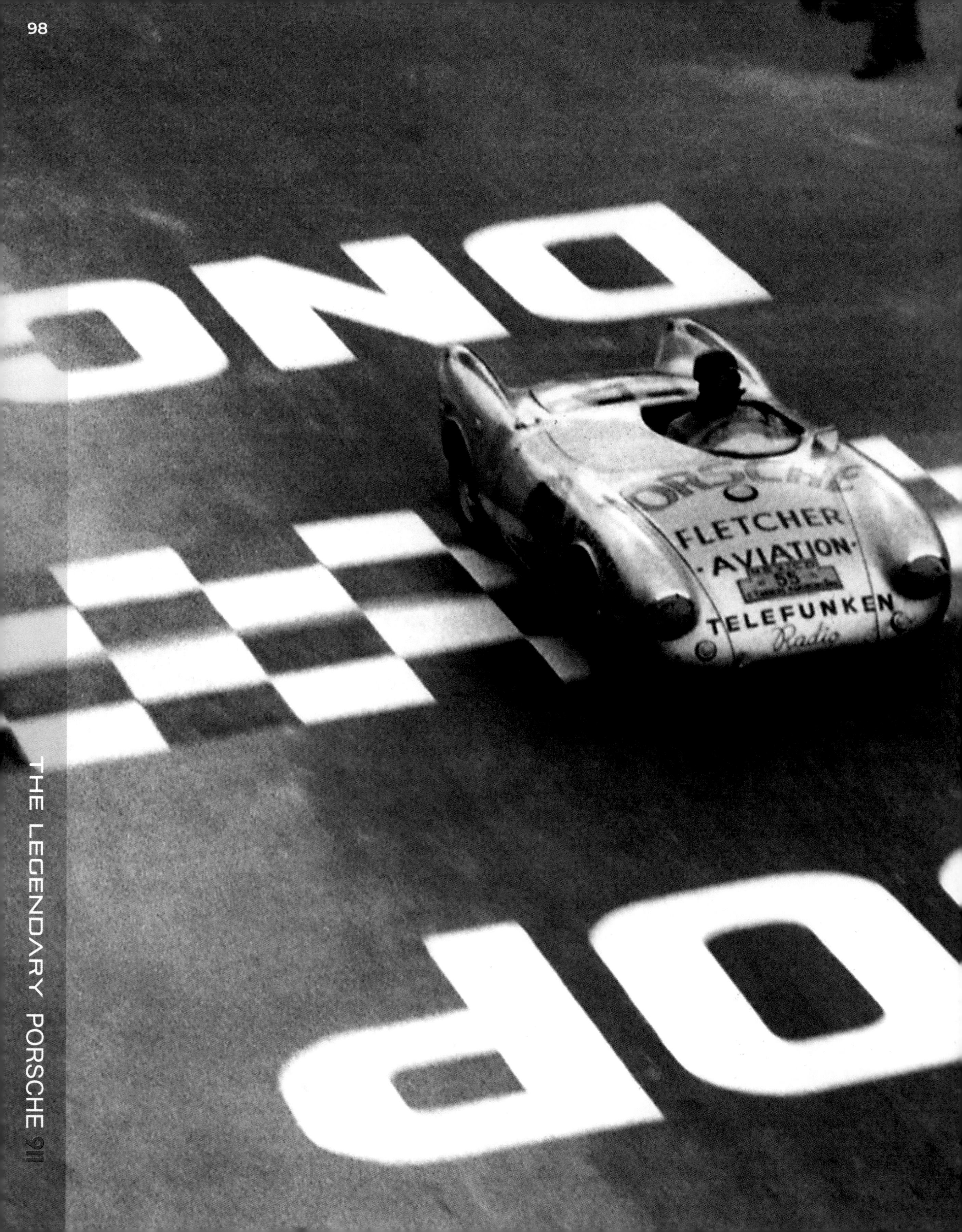

PORSCHE
FLETCHER
AVIATION
55
TELEFUNKEN
Radio

# THE CARRERA PANAMERICANA

The name of Porsche's Tourmaline green metallic concept here is the product of inspiration from a famous race in the 1950s, which delivered considerable success for the company. The Carrera Panamericana was a race through Mexico, administered by the Mexican government to celebrate completion of the Mexican leg of the Pan American highway. Running from Alaska right down to Ushuaia, the planet's southern-most city, this was a network of roads spanning more than 19,000 miles, and was built to connect the Americas and improve intercontinental travel and trade.

The Mexicans celebrated their slice of the achievement with this gruelling race from the top of the country down to the bottom, via 3,000 miles of roads. The race was fraught with danger, largely because it took place on public roads, and rules were few and far between. The first vehicle across the line was deemed to be the winner, and that was that!

First staged in 1950, the field was comprised of four-seat sedans, before sports cars were allowed to enter from 1951. This is where Porsche got involved, claiming a series of stage wins with its 550 Spyder, before dominating what would be the last race in 1954. Hans Herrmann, who would later taste success with Richard Attwood at Le Mans in 1970, won the small sports car category (Porsche claiming six of the top seven positions) and finished third overall – a huge achievement on the other side of the planet for Stuttgart's then fledgling sports car company.

The race was abandoned after 1954 on safety grounds, but the Carrera Panamericana was considered Porsche's greatest international success in the days prior to the Targo Florio, the feat immortalized in the radical SUV concept car in this section.

# BUTZI'S
# SPEEDSTER



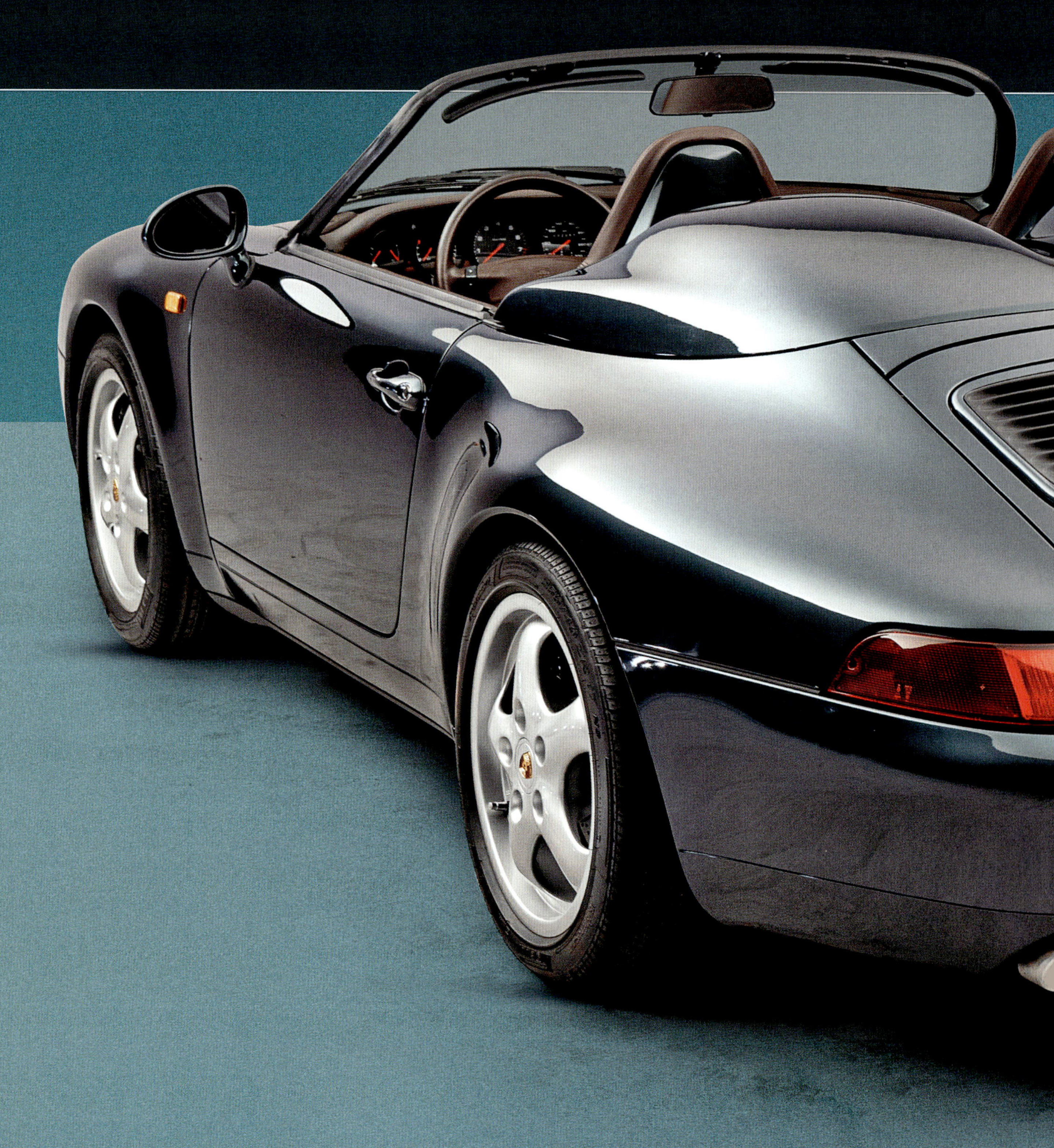

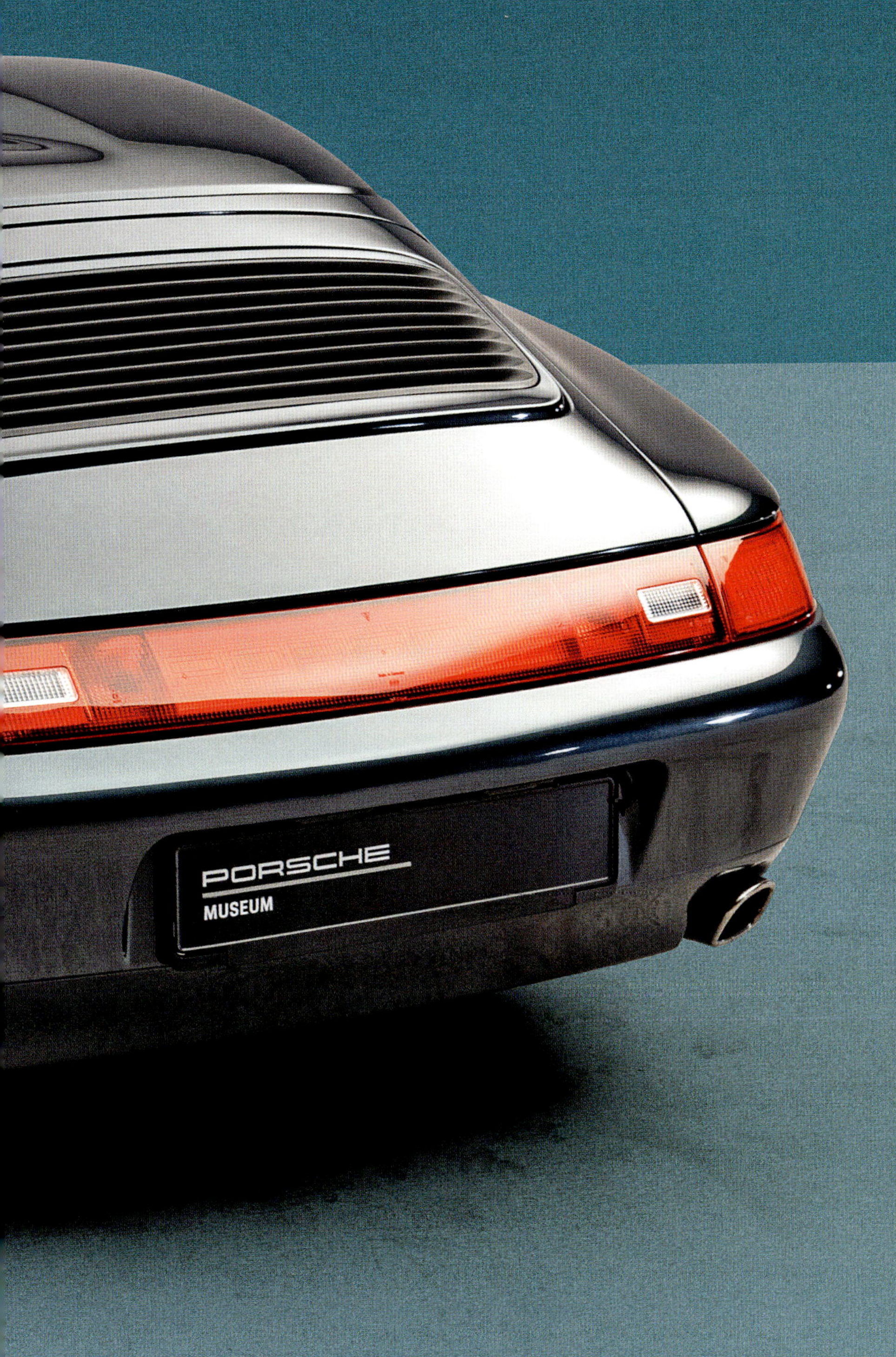

356, G-body, 964, 997, 991. Random names and numbers to some, these are of course the generations and internal model codes for one of Porsche's most revered product lines: Speedster.





## 993 SPEEDSTER
(1995)

### ENGINE
**Capacity:** 3,600cc
**Compression ratio:** 11:3.1
**Maximum power:** 285hp @ 6,100rpm
**Maximum torque:** 340Nm @ 5,250rpm
**Transmission:** Four-speed Tiptronic

### SUSPENSION
**Front:** Independent; MacPherson strut; anti-roll bar
**Rear:** Independent; multi-link; anti-roll bar

### WHEELS & TYRES
**Front:** 7x17-inch; 205/50/ZR17
**Rear:** 9x17-inch; 225/40/ZR17

### DIMENSIONS
**Length:** 4,245mm
**Width:** 1,735mm
**Weight:** Unknown

### PERFORMANCE
**0-60mph:** Not tested
**Top speed:** Not tested

This journey to what is arguably the ultimate expression of the topless sports car began in 1952 with the 356 1500 America Roadster. Widely seen as the forefather of the Porsche Speedster, it flopped, incidentally, after costing more to make than sell, driving coachbuilder Heuer-Glaser to bankruptcy in the process.

Lessons were learned, with production moving in-house at Porsche, the Speedster now a cut-down version of the Cabriolet and running off the same production line as other 356s. In 1954, the Porsche Speedster as we know it was born, chiefly to boost the appeal of Stuttgart's fledgling sports car company in the United States under the tutelage of importer Max Hoffman.

The Speedster enjoyed instant commercial success Stateside, and over 70 years later its name is synonymous among enthusiasts with embodying everything Porsche stands for: a raw, emotive drive, its genius lying chiefly with its simplicity. 356 Speedster production ended in 1958, replaced by the Convertible D, but that raked windscreen, low-slung profile and spartan interior would actually realise its place on the 911 some 30 years later.

Debuting on the 3.2 Carrera, the 911 Speedster then featured on the subsequent 964 generation. For the 993 though, a production Speedster was just not to be: with the 911's profitability dwindling, such an exotic variant which would ultimately sell in small numbers was not deemed worthwhile by Porsche, which by the mid-Nineties was ploughing efforts into design of the first water-cooled 911 in the 996. It was a move which would ultimately save the company from going bust.

This didn't mean that enthusiasts were robbed entirely of the spectacle of that Speedster profile attached to the body of the last air-cooled 911. In the best Porsche tradition, such occurrences are of course possible as one-offs, only via Porsche Exclusive Manufaktur, the department born out of a need to fulfil well-heeled customers' special wishes.

Your eyes are not, therefore, deceiving you: the 911 in our pictures is indeed a genuine 993 Speedster, built as a special wish, and for a special person. This was not an ordinary customer, but a member of the Porsche family itself. The 993 Speedster you see here was for Ferdinand Alexander 'Butzi' Porsche.

It might seem strange that the person who penned the Neunelfer's iconic, flowing shape – as a Coupe, no less – should seek out an open-topped version of the car in its final, air-cooled iteration. However, Porsche's predilection for the Speedster predates even that of its treasured 911, and so the historical reverence behind this stunning marriage of two iconic Porsche designs is palpable.

Based on a narrow-bodied 993 Cabriolet, Butzi's Speedster features the shorter, raked windscreen and reprofiled side windows from the 964 Speedster before it, along with a double-humped clamshell and low slung (and manual) hood. Riding above 17-inch wheels, the body was finished in Aventurine green, in keeping with the Porsche family tradition in taking delivery of green-hued cars.

This stunning vehicle was presented to Butzi on his 60th birthday on 11 December 1995. The car would be used by the 911's inventor for sunny drives through the Austrian mountains between his Porsche Design studio and the long-time family home in Zell am See. Clearly used and adored by Butzi, the Speedster wears 2,065 kilometres on its clock today, though the odometer hasn't rolled on much since 2012. As unfortunately, Mr Porsche sadly passed away aged 76 on 5 April of that year.

**As with all Speedsters, the manual hood was only ever intended for emergency use**

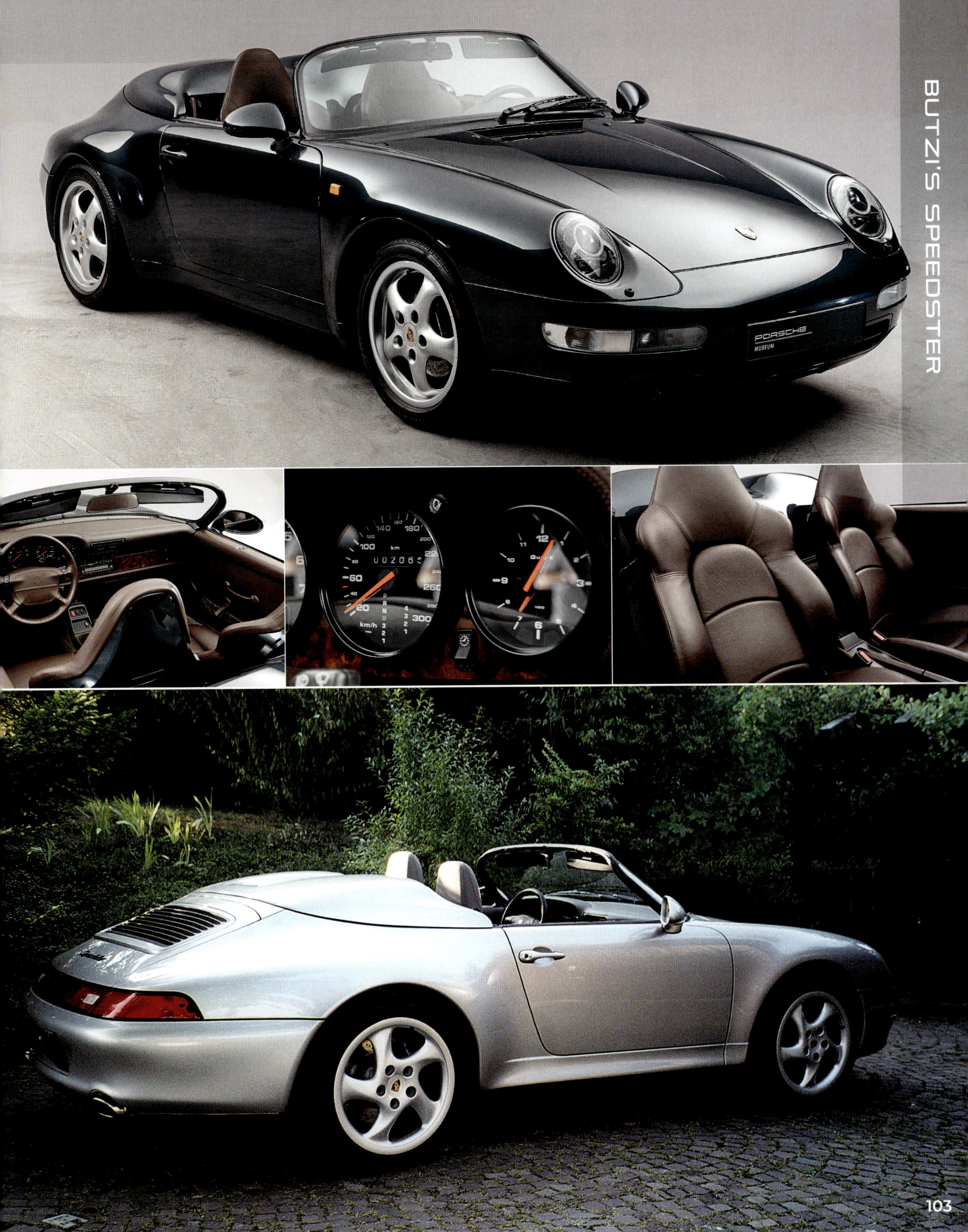

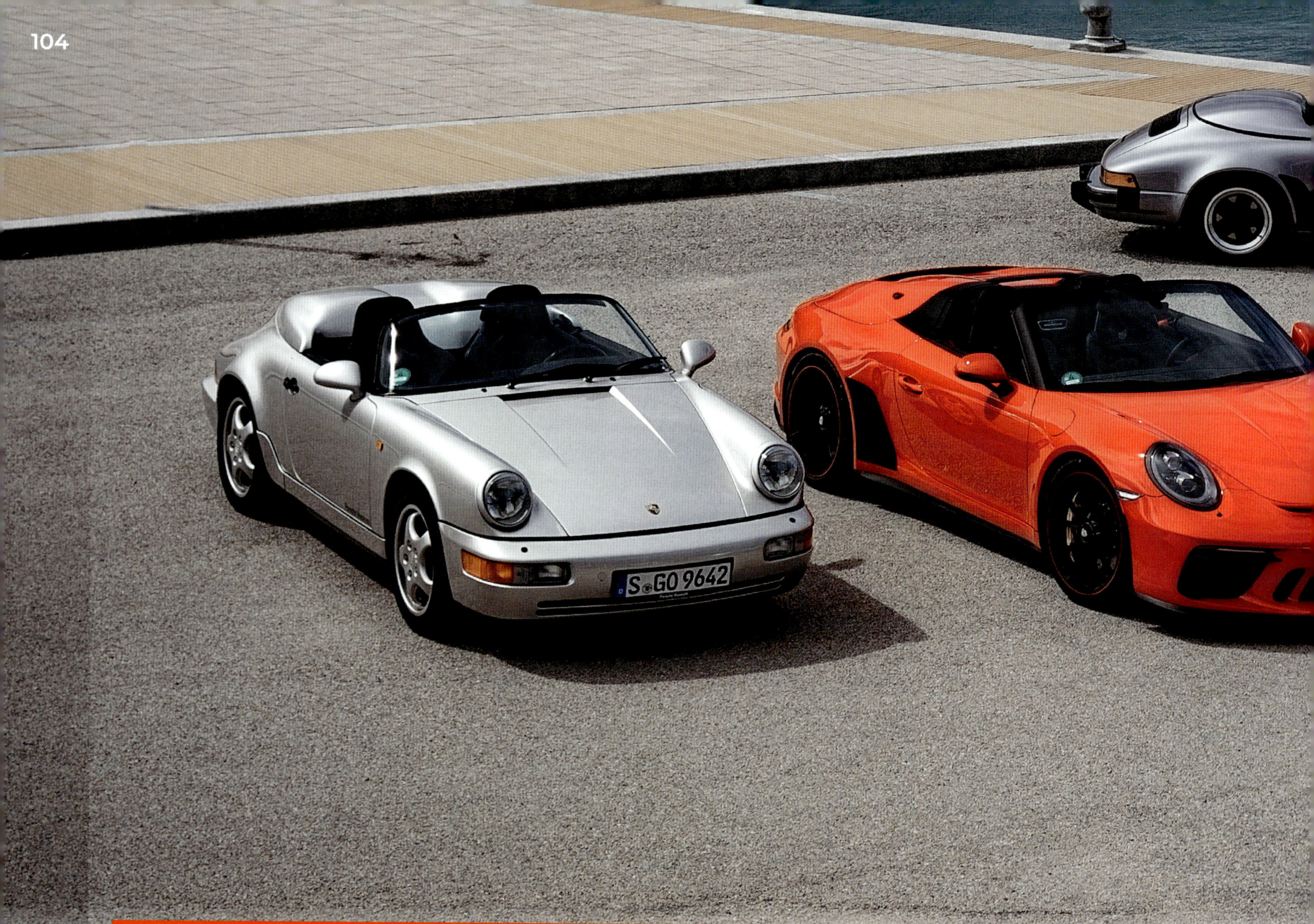

## PORSCHE'S SPEEDSTER TIMELINE

### 356

**Production years: 1954-58**
**Production numbers: 3,676**

Porsche's Speedster concept owes much to Max Hoffman, the storied importer of Porsche sports cars to the United States, which remains an important territory for the brand today. Hoffman told Ferry Porsche that for his brand to succeed in the US, it needed a smaller, simpler sports car that was priced more competitively than the 356 range of the time. The Porsche Speedster was duly born with just two bucket seats in an otherwise spartan interior. Its design concept would resonate with future designs of the Porsche Speedster as it joined the 911 family tree.

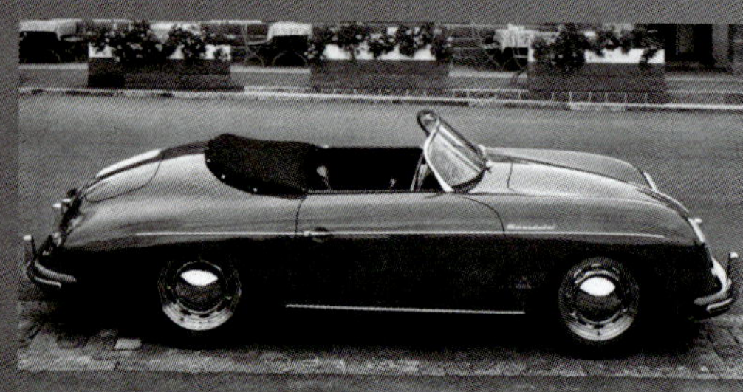

### 3.2 Carrera

**Production years: 1989**
**Production numbers: 2,274**

Project managed by designer Ben Dimson, the first 911 Speedster was originally conceived for the 964 generation but brought forward to boost sales at the end of the G-series era. Using engine and running gear from a base Carrera, the Speedster was treated to a bespoke windscreen and rear clamshell. Available in narrow and wide body, the former is extremely rare, though both iterations are collector-grade cars today.

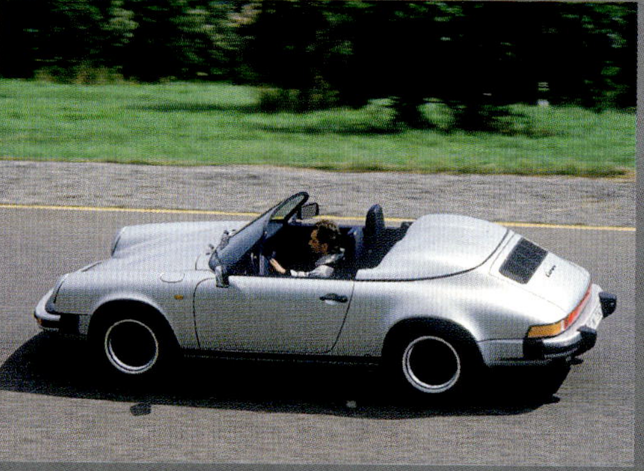

### 964

**Production years: 1992-94**
**Production numbers: 936**

The original 911 Speedster design was finally realised at the end of the 964 era, though it didn't sell in the volumes expected (Porsche had set aside VIN numbers for some 3,000 to be produced). Based on a RWD Carrera 2 Cabriolet, it served as a crossover between that and a 964 RS, thanks chiefly to its spartan 'Clubsport' trim, which was in keeping with the ethos of the original 356 Speedster. Most were narrow-bodied, though 20 wide-bodied 964 Speedsters were produced via Porsche Exclusive.

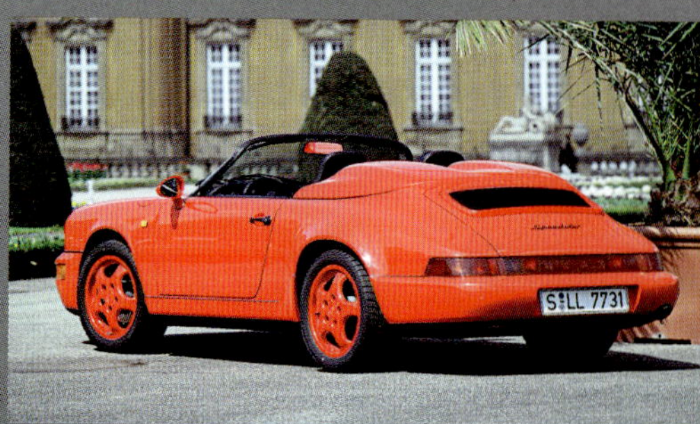

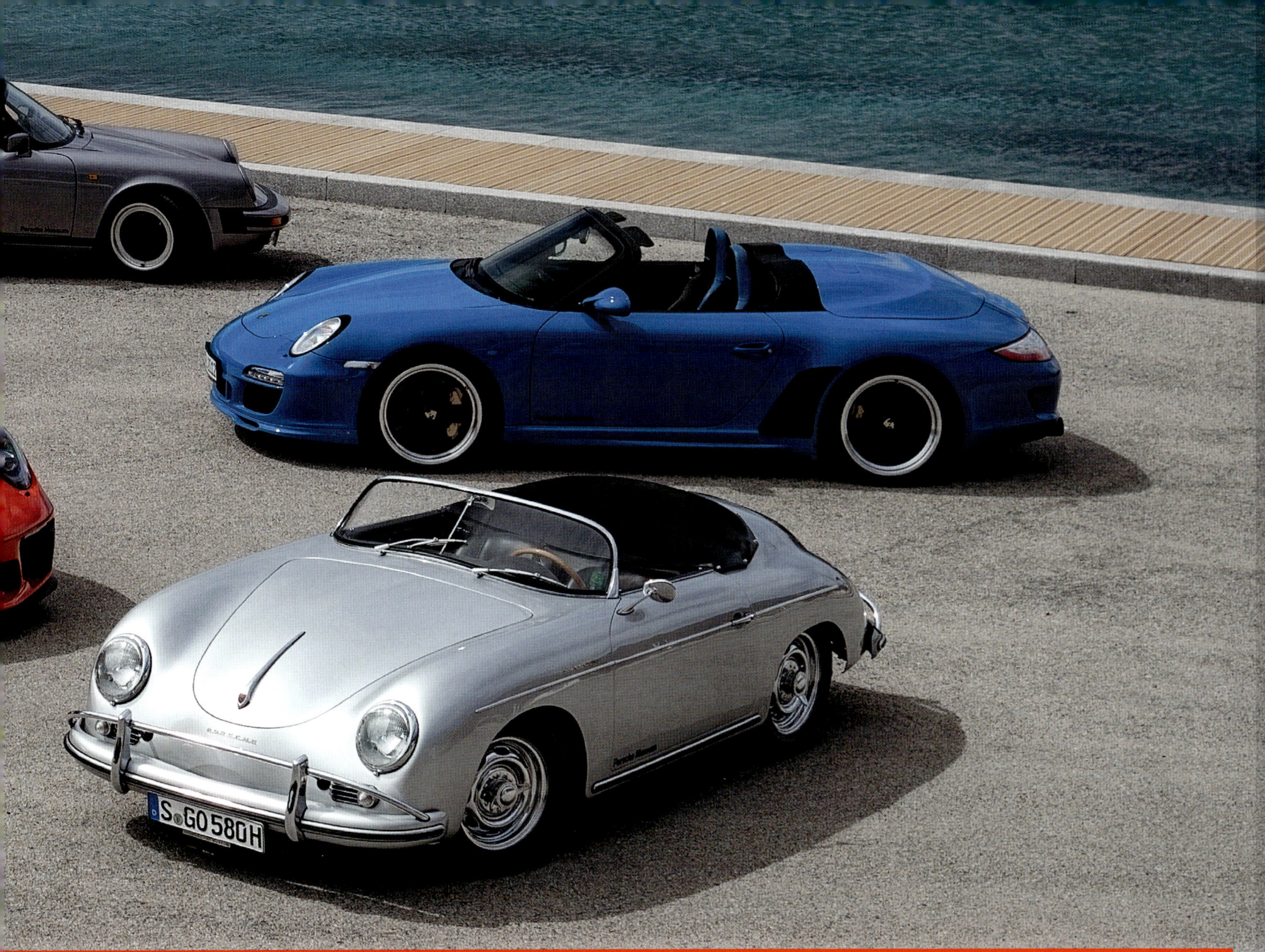

## 997
**Production years: 2010**
**Production numbers: 356**

The rarest iteration of Speedster, the 997 was hand built to a high specification by Porsche's Exclusive department, its wide body available in either Pure blue (a bespoke colour for the model) or Carrara white. It shared its 408bhp flat six with the Sport Classic and 997 GTS, though it was available as PDK-only. Its high specification and relatively hefty weight means it is most at odds with that original Speedster design, though its low production numbers means it's highly sought after by collectors.

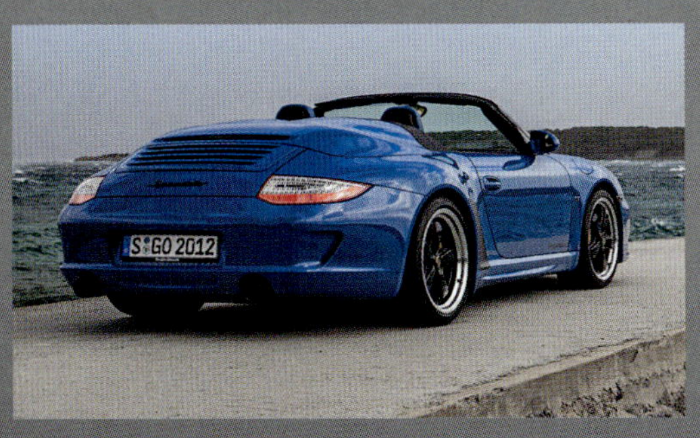

## 991
**Production years: 2018-19**
**Production numbers: 1,948**

Revealed as a special edition to celebrate 70 years of Porsche sports cars, the 991 Speedster was created by Andreas Preuninger's GT department. Using a Carrera 4 body, its powerful, high-revving and naturally aspirated flat six engine, along with its accomplished chassis, has lead many to call it a topless GT3 in all but name. They're not far wrong in our book. The latest Speedster is brilliantly engineered to feature that same sloping roofline and clamshell, which is electrically powered for the first time.

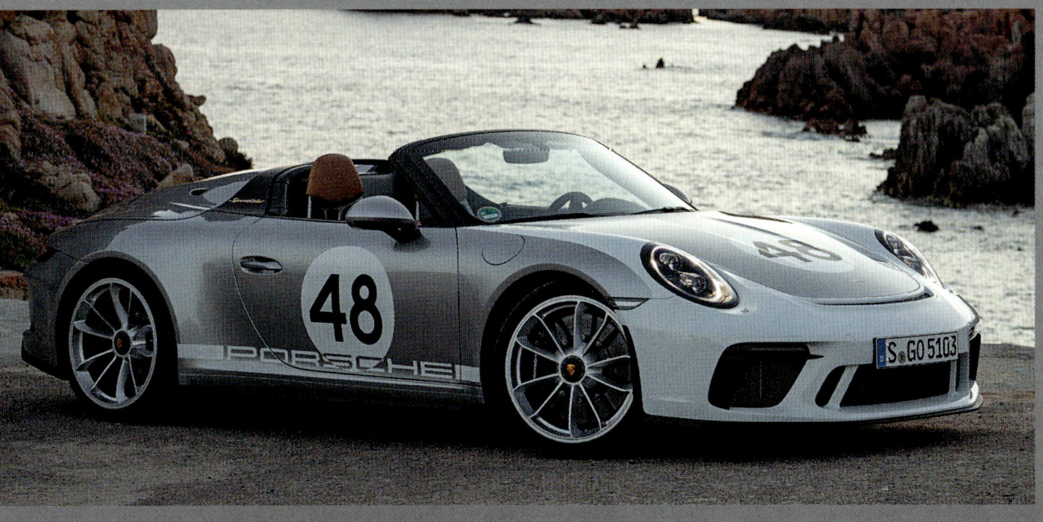

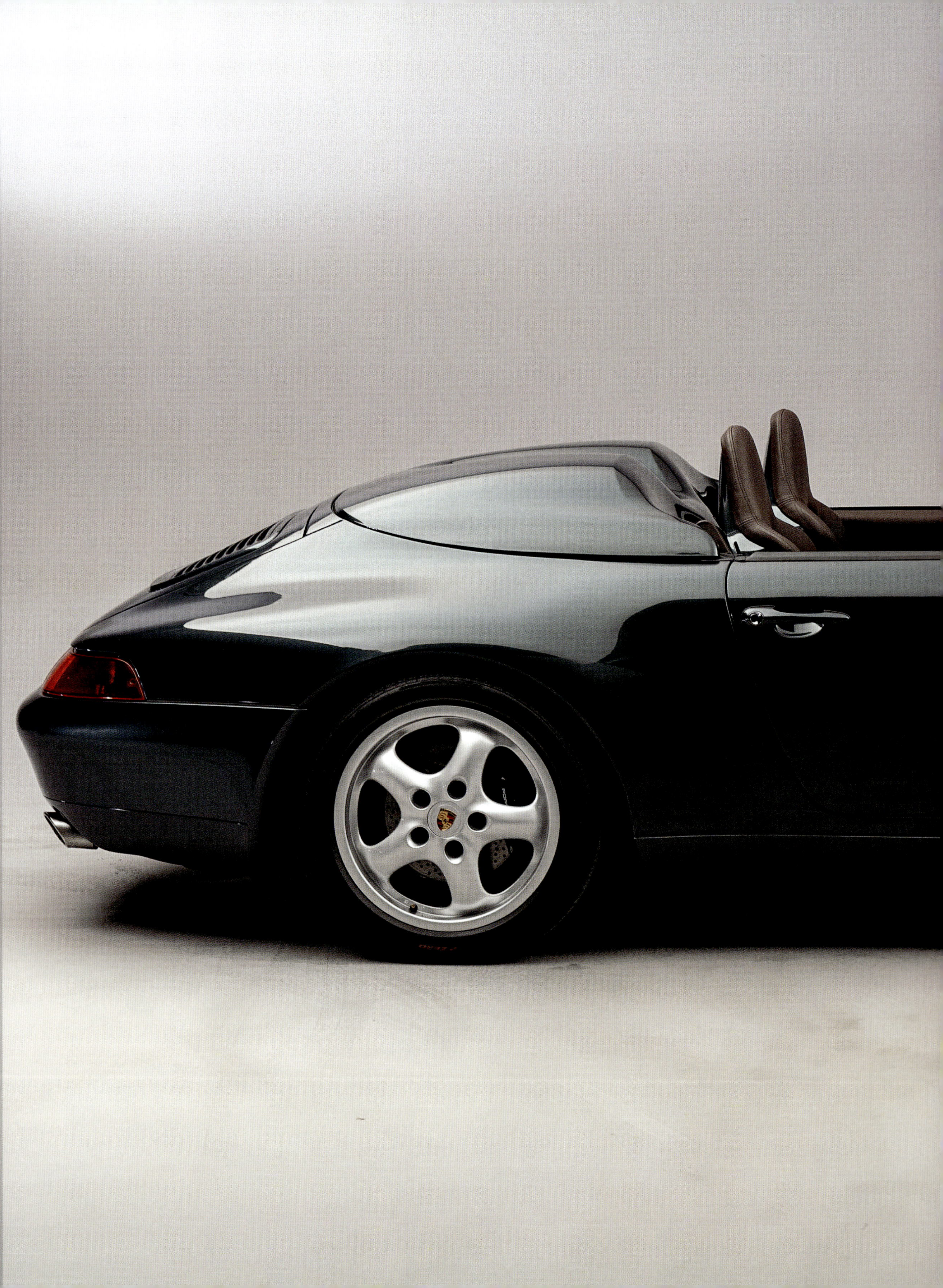

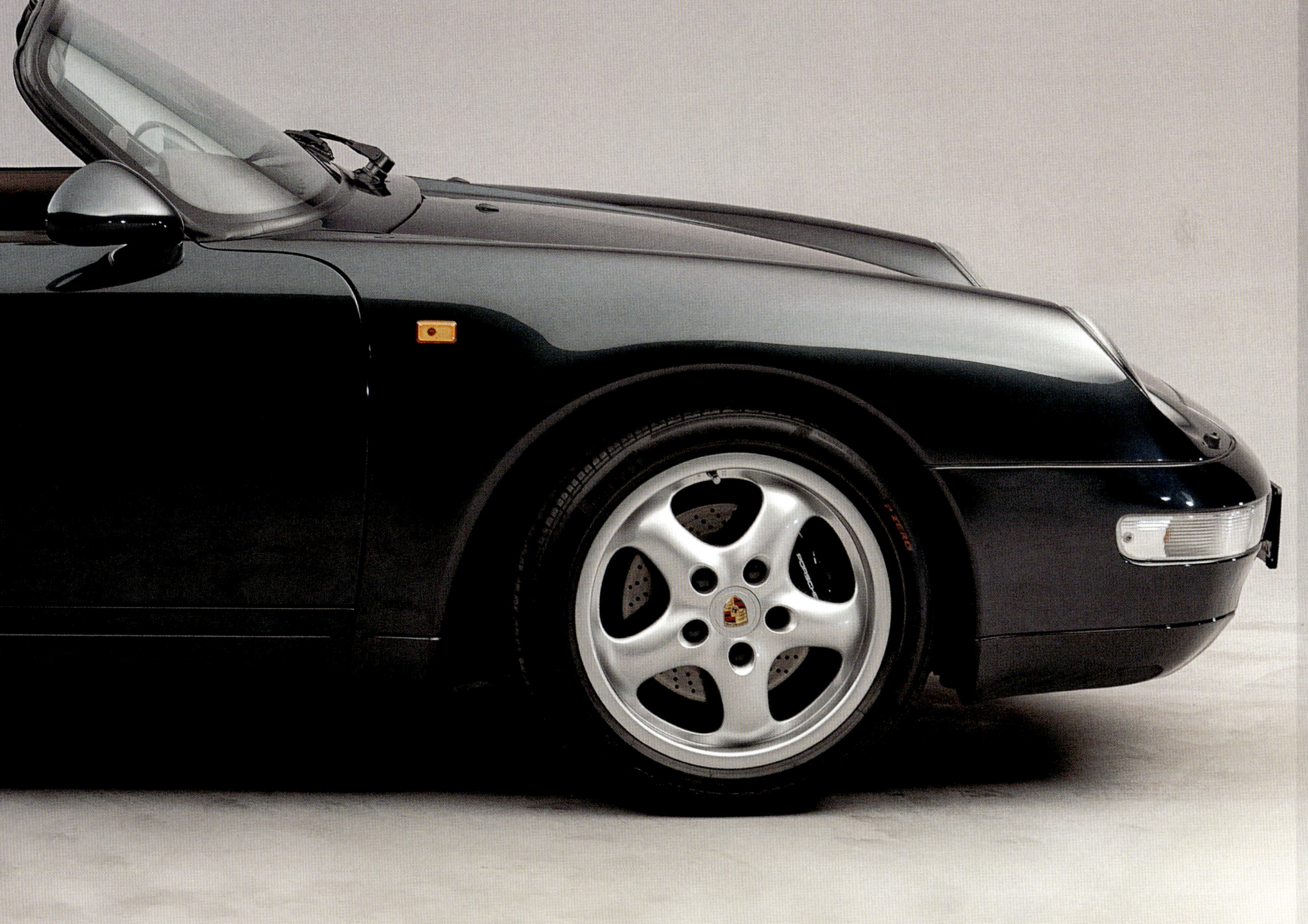

# ONE MILLIONTH

# 991

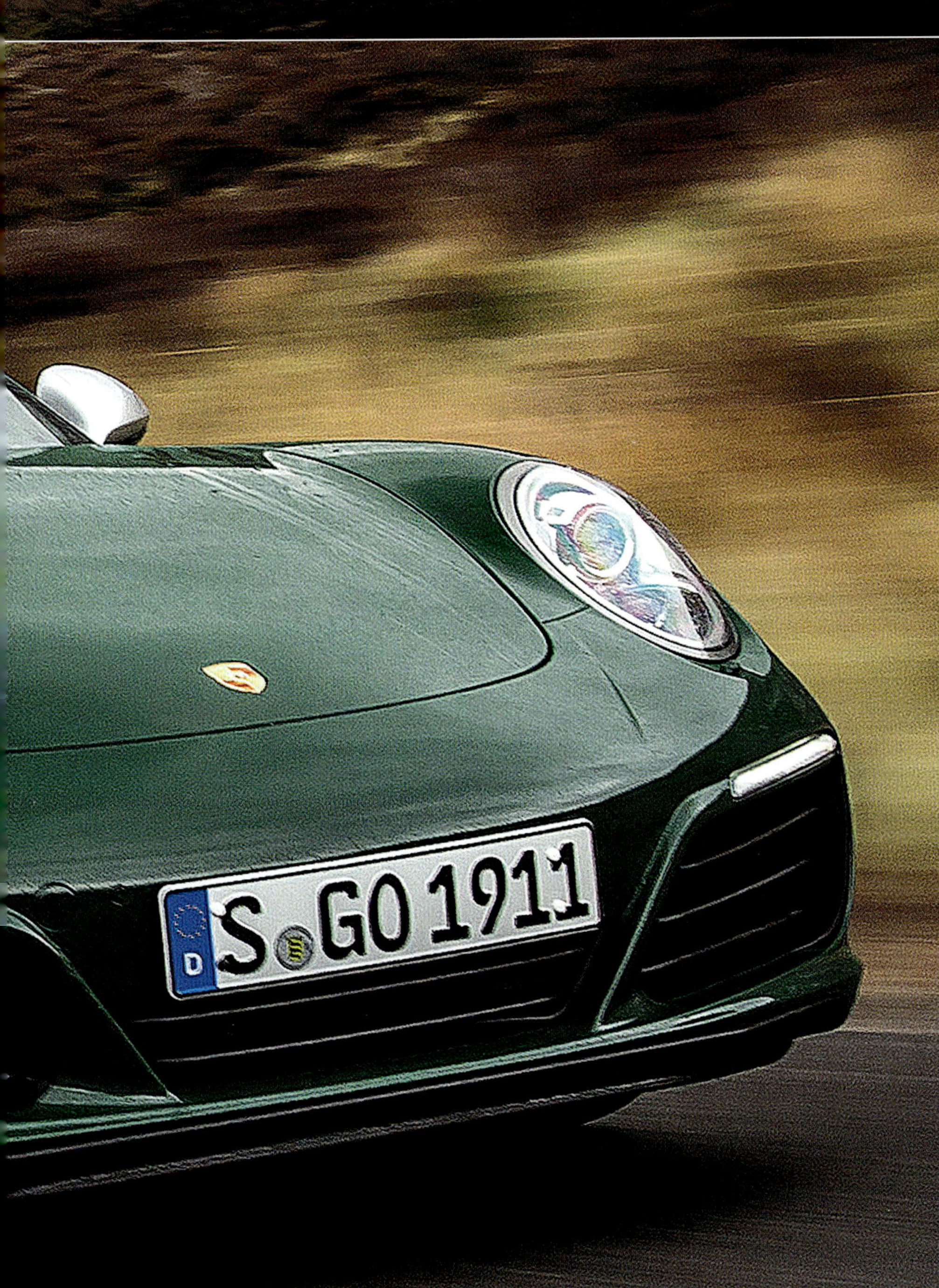

On 11 May 2017, the millionth Porsche 911 rolled off the Zuffenhausen production line in Germany. Think about that for a moment: one million 911s – and counting – that was an incredible feat for any car, let alone a premium sports car.





# MILLIONTH 911

(2017)

### ENGINE

**Capacity:** 2,981cc

**Compression ratio:** 10:0.1

**Maximum power:** 450bhp @ 6,500rpm

**Maximum torque:** 550Nm @ 2,150–5,000rpm

**Transmission:** Seven-speed manual; rear-wheel drive

**Modifications:** Exclusive Powerkit (+30bhp)

### SUSPENSION

**Front:** Independent; MacPherson strut; PASM; anti-roll bar

**Rear:** Independent; Multi-link; PASM; anti-roll bar

### WHEELS & TYRES

**Front:** 9x20-inch; 245/35/ZR20

**Rear:** 12x20-inch; 305/30/ZR20

### DIMENSIONS

**Length:** 4,528mm

**Width:** 1,852mm

**Weight:** 1,450kg

### PERFORMANCE

**0-60mph:** 4.1 secs

**Top speed:** 194mph

Since its introduction the 911 has become a sports car icon, defining the marketplace, dominating race circuits and being symbolic and relevant in every decade it's existed. That's as true today as it was when it was introduced back in 1963; the 911 might be something of a freak, a quirk of Porsche's engineering determination, and against the odds it's proved wildly successful. Even so, one million of them, that's absolutely extraordinary.

The specification of the one millionth 911 is basically that of a GTS, the S's unit featuring the same Powerkit that increases its power to 450hp – that increased output driving the rear wheels only. Sitting in the hound's-tooth-covered seats, with the warmth of the wooden steering wheel, it's a shame the gear knob's not similarly covered. A manual at least, which might be a retrospective nod in these big-selling PDK times, but it's the correct one, as a seven-speed stick shift features. There's little over 940 miles on the odometer when this privileged test driver got in it, and all I can think is I hope the previous occupant had the presence of mind to take a picture of it as it ticked over the 911 marker. It's all familiar, all 911, though the significance of its build number isn't lost on me. More irreplaceable than any other 911 I've been lucky enough to drive, I'm initially circumspect with it as I take it out on the open road. That caution quickly dissipates, the historical significance of the car forgotten as I just revel in driving it.

It feels very like the GTS, standard chassis aside here. It effectively is so, which is to say perhaps the most rounded, capable 911 you can buy. Or can't when specifically applied to this car. The steering is light, feelsome, the throttle immediate and the performance unerring, it being very much a modern 911. The 911 today epitomises the evolution of the car, any car, and the Millionth underlines that. The original was an agile, fast engaging and usable sports car at genesis, and today it remains so, only the march of modernity has brought with it refinements, more comfort, economy, greater performance and a huge advance in technology. For all of that, though, it remains utterly identifiable as a 911. No other car is so recognisable, so interesting, so unique, which is why it's endured so effectively, and seduced so many. One million, then, and counting...



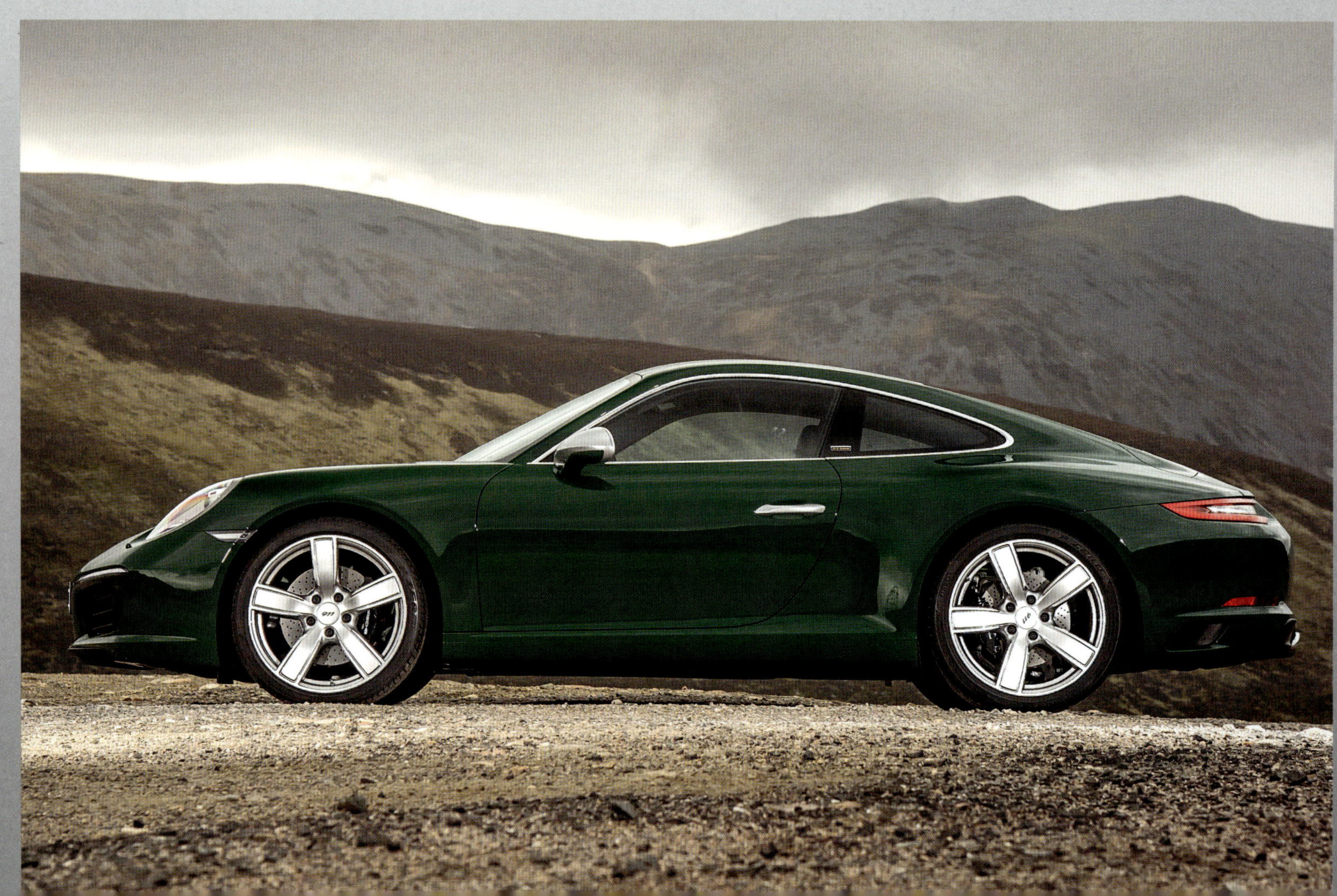

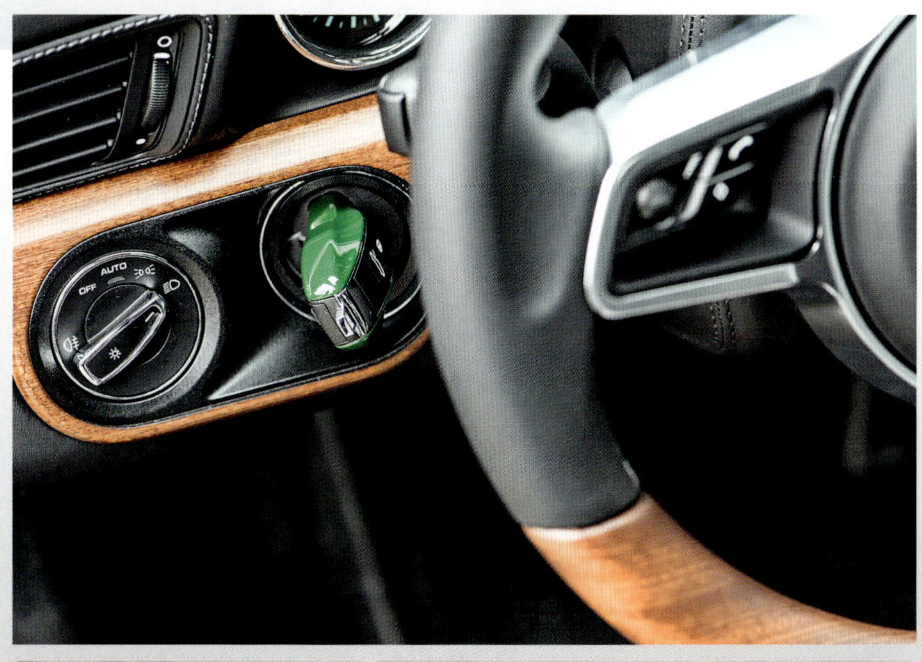

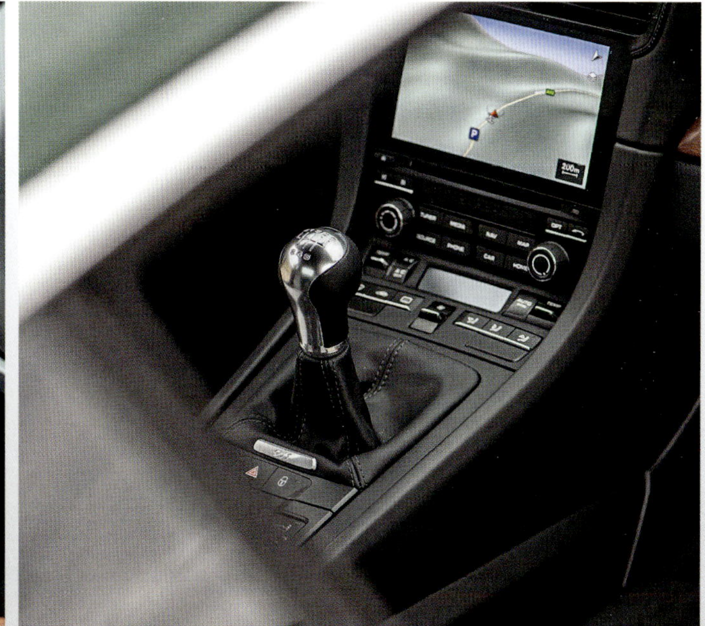

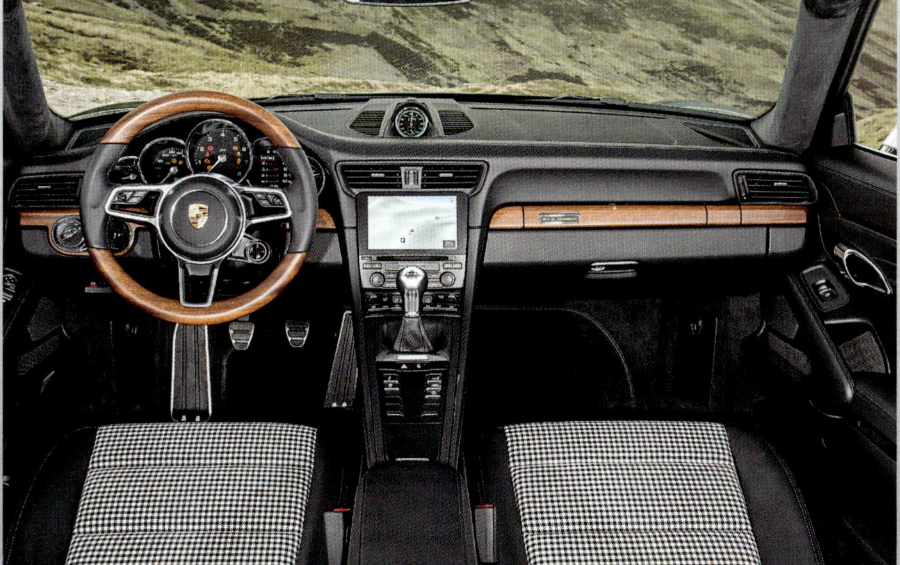

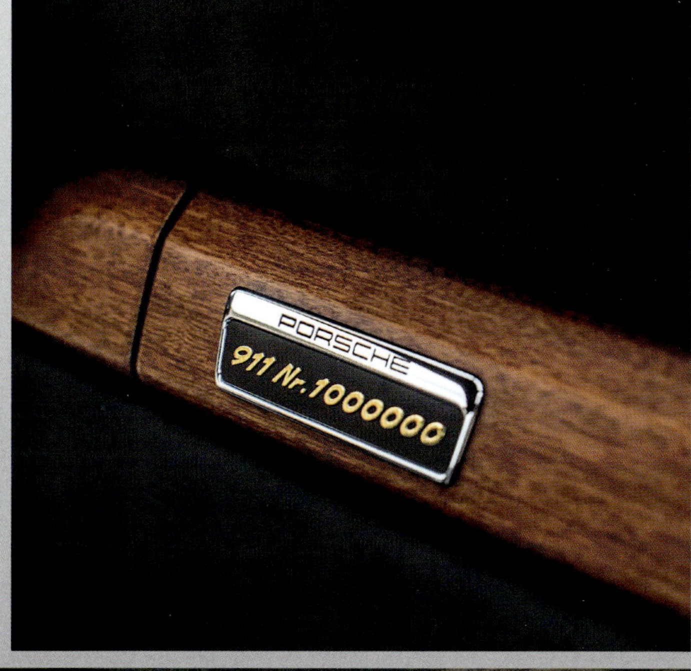

Inside, the Millionth 911 has been lavished with some Exclusive touches that evoke the trim of those early 911s

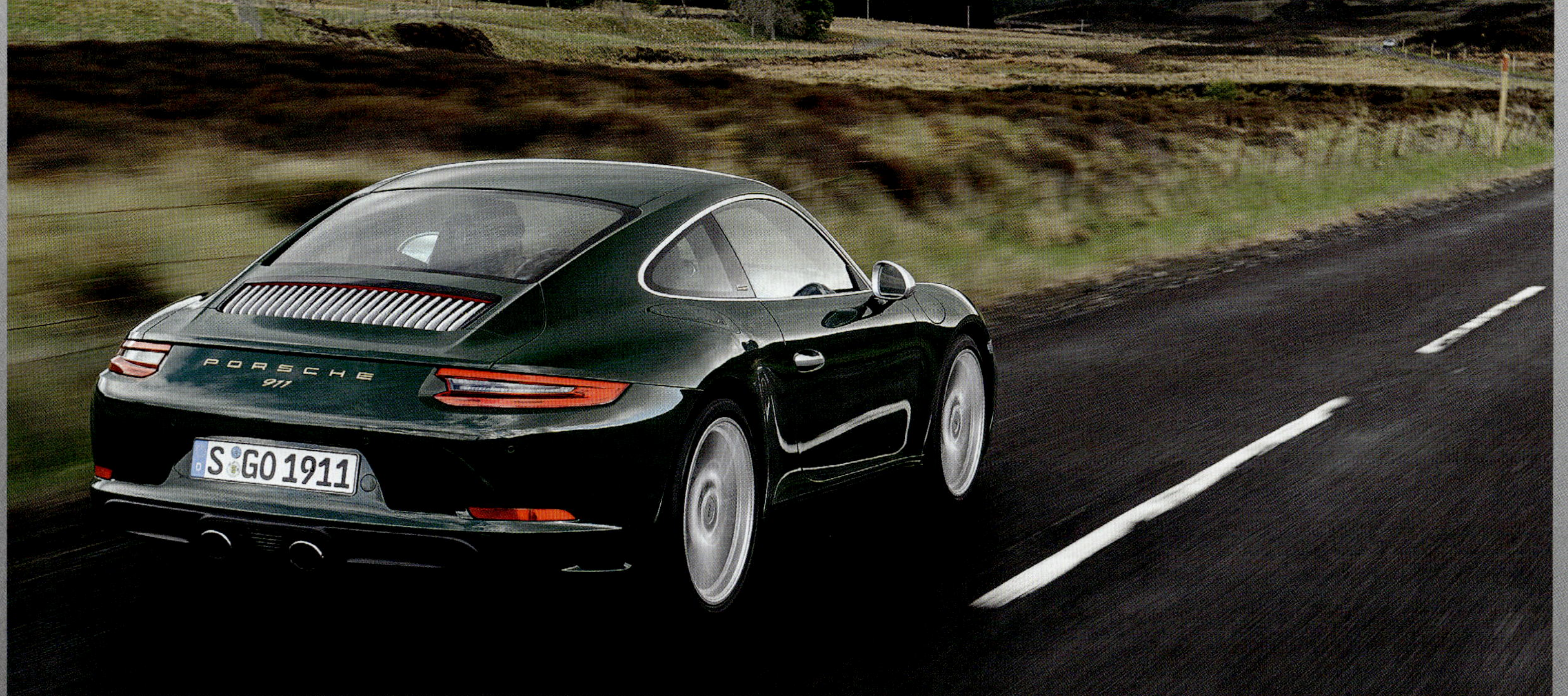

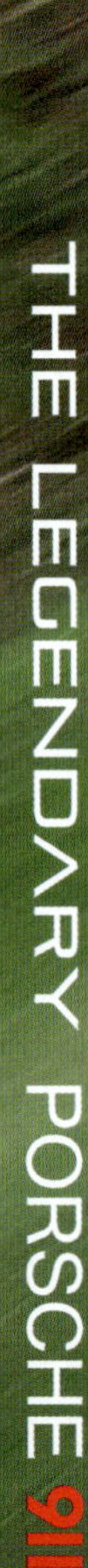

## BUILDING THE MILLION 911S

Every one of the million 911s has been built in Porsche's Stuttgart Zuffenhausen production line and, like the cars it produces, that line has under transformation since its inception. During the time those million 911s have been built, the world around it has changed and the line has undergone developments to reflect that. Modernisation of not just the product, then, but the manufacturing itself, from the introduction of hot zinc galvanization in the '70s, to new, more efficient production processes to cope with the increased demands in the 1980s. Spot-welding via robots was introduced in 1985, three-axis welding robots arriving three years later, with the 964 being the first fully robot-welded 911 to leave the production line.

Famously in the '90s, Porsche would turn to Toyota to help in adopting lean production techniques to improve efficiencies introduced under the then CEO Wendelin Wiedeking. The now single production line would produce all the current models, the 964 making way for the 993, then the 996 (as well as the Boxster). The line has continued to develop, new production processes being added to increase efficiencies, though there remains a highly skilled workforce who hand-assemble the 911 at various stages in its production cycle. That production line produces all the 911 series models, including the GT cars, though race cars are taken off the Zuffenhausen line for final finishing at the famous GT department at Weissach.

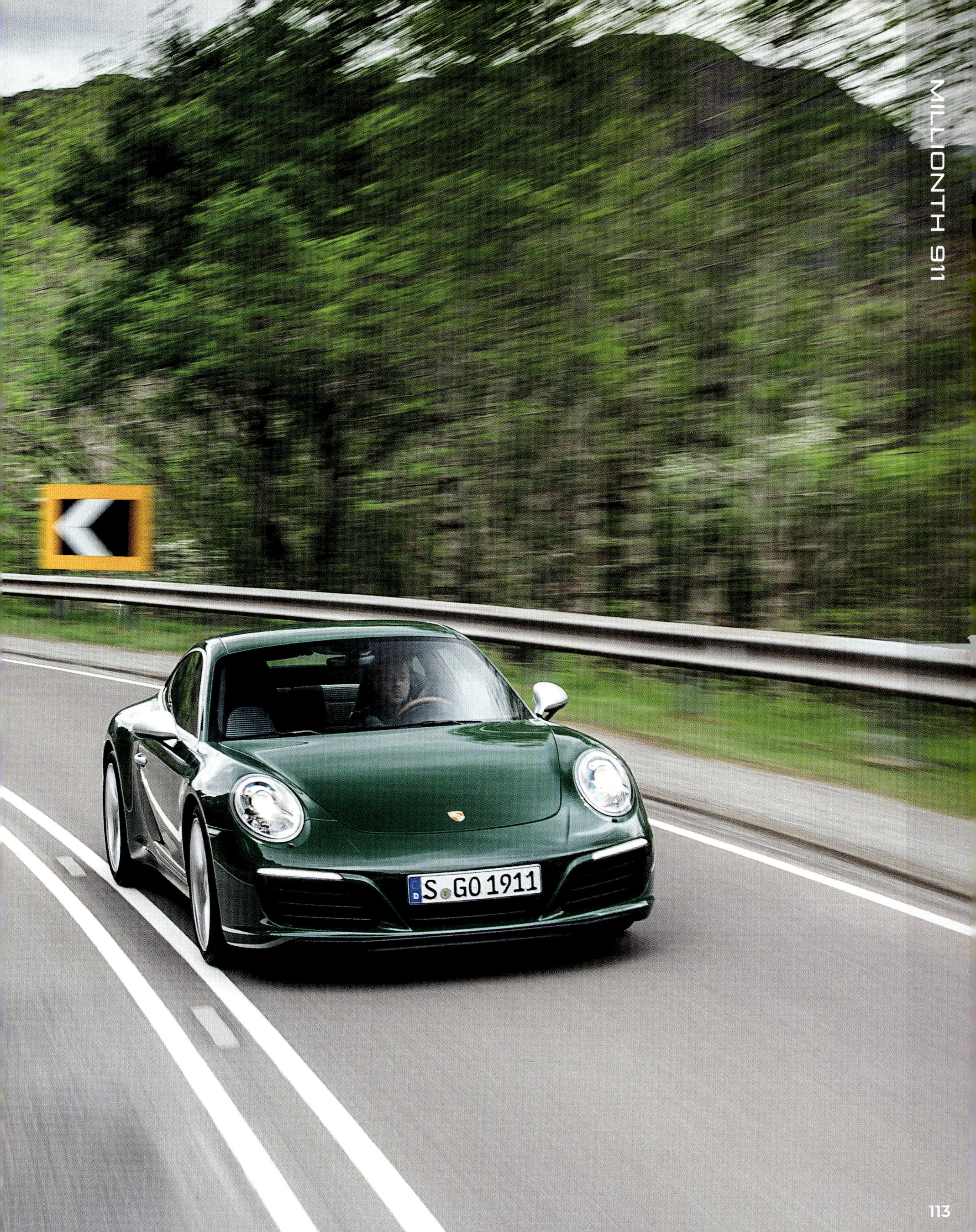
S · GO 1911

# CELEBRITY
# PORSCHE OWNERS

One of the myriads of Hollywood heavyweights to have fallen for Porsche, Keanu Reeves' love affair with the legendary sports car began when he was given a Matchbox replica as a child. The toy was a grey 911, and it made such an impression on the star of *The Matrix* and *John Wick* that years later he bought himself a Carrera 4S (993), a manual transmission and one of the last air-cooled 911s.

"I used any excuse to head up the Pacific Coast Highway [in California]," Reeves said, "onto the great canyon roads." Sadly his 911, which he affectionately dubbed 'The Sled' because it was "sleek and fast", was stolen but Porsche AG stepped in, modifying a new production 911 for the actor with a bespoke steering wheel and interior black trim.

Fellow movie icon Tom Cruise famously drove a 928 in his 1983 breakout film *Risky Business* but subsequently opted for a 911 in real life, owning a 1986 Targa with the full leather interior. Other actors to have taken the wheel of 911s include Jeremy Renner (C4 Cabriolet), Hilary Duff (Carrera S) and *The Office* star Steve Carell, who owns a 911 Turbo, while Michael Fassbender has actually raced the car in the Porsche 911 GT3 Cup.

Many sporting icons are 911 fans. In the 2010s, David Beckham spent £70,000 on a classic 1969 911 in slate grey. The England and Manchester United midfielder wanted the car because it was reminiscent of the 911 his idol Steve McQueen famously drove in *Le Mans*, which was given to the actor in 1971 after filming finished and after his premature death, sold at a charity auction in the States for £850,000.

Another athlete to have been seduced by the charms of the 911 is basketball star LeBron James. The four-time NBA champion and triple Olympic gold medallist has owned four Porsches, his favourite a 911 Turbo S Convertible boasting 640bhp. Football superstar Cristiano Ronaldo is the proud owner of a 911 Turbo S.

The music business also has a high proportion of 911 devotees. One Direction's Harry Styles, R&B star Rihanna, and rappers Eminem and Wiz Khalifa have all collected the keys for their 911s while, in 2024, the Indian hip-hop star MC Stan released a single from his new album entitled '911 Porsche'.

> ## "IT'S A VERY SIMPLE, STRAIGHTFORWARD LITTLE THING THAT GOES LIKE STINK. I LOVE IT."
>
> P.J O'ROURKE IN PRAISE OF HIS PORSCHE CARRERA GT

Beyond the realms of film, sport and music, the 911 has enamoured itself to a host of high-profile names. Microsoft mastermind Bill Gates bought a blue 911 Turbo as far back as 1979, four years after co-founding the company that made him his fortune. British supermodel Kate Moss celebrated her 40th birthday by gifting herself a 1970s edition of the car while the late American author and satirist P.J O'Rourke was a proud Carrera driver. "It's a very simple, straightforward little thing that goes like stink," he said. "I love it."

**Famous celebrity owners include (clockwise from top), Rihanna, Steve McQueen and LeBron James.**

The cachet of celebrity ownership over the years has only served to underline the 911's timeless popularity and pedigree.


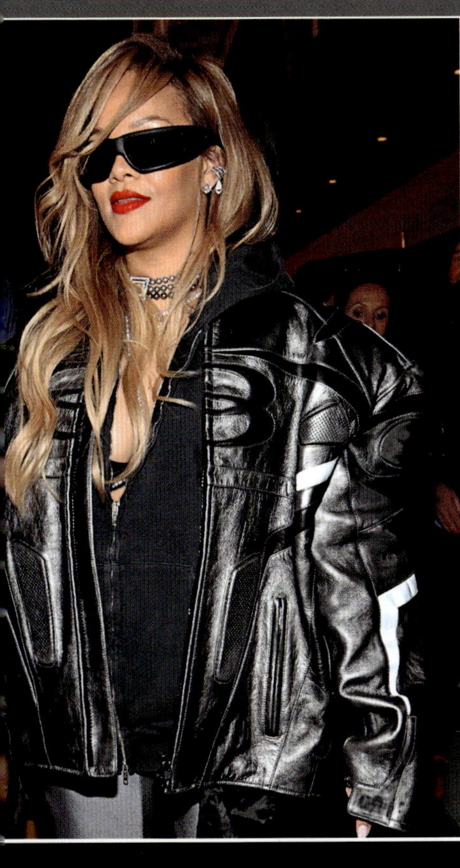

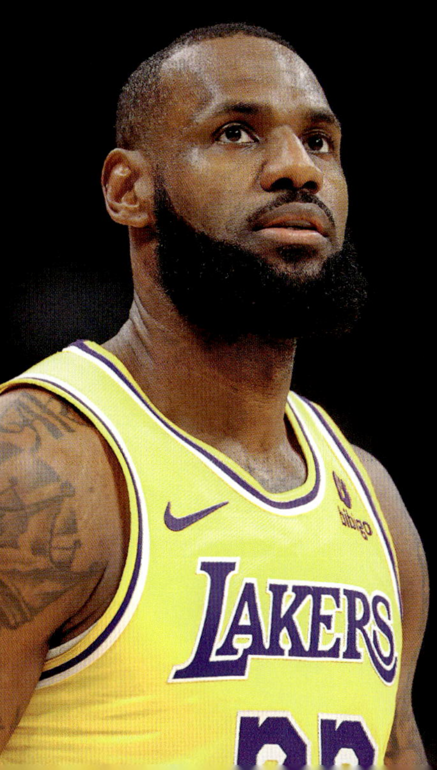

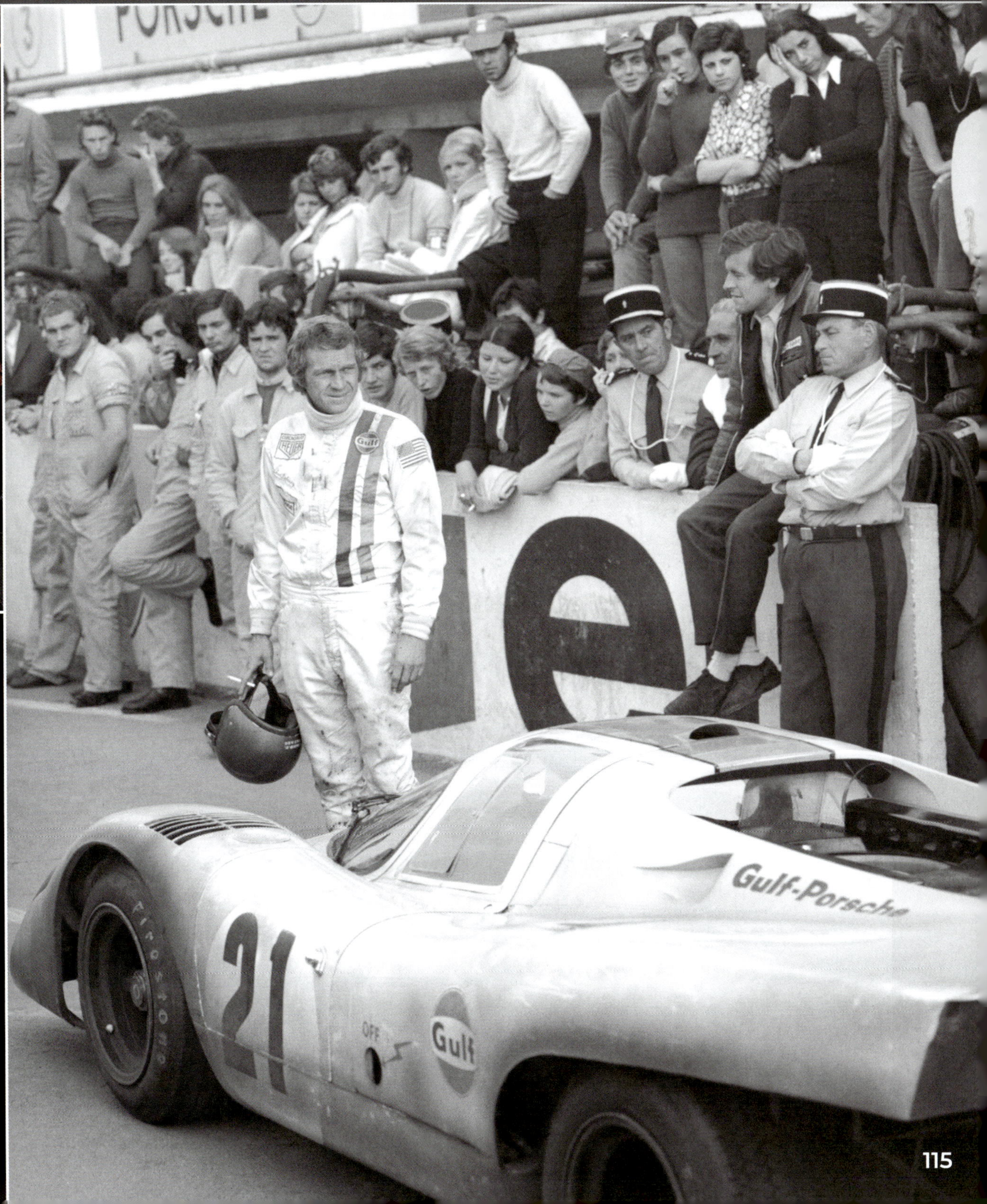

# PORSCHE
# AT THE MOVIES



t was Steve McQueen's celebrated slate-grey 911 S, which he famously drove in *Le Mans*, that undoubtedly accelerated the car's early popularity worldwide. The movie was released in 1971 and its images of 'The King of Cool' behind the wheel of his Porsche are some of the most iconic in cinematic history. As a token of their appreciation, the makers of Le Mans gifted McQueen the car after filming had wrapped.

But despite only being seven-years-old at the time, it was not the first time the 911 had shared screen time with a major Hollywood star. That distinction belongs to the bright yellow 911T, complete with a ski rack, that featured in 1969 film *Downhill Racer* starring Robert Redford. Snow-covered French Alpine mountains provided a stunning backdrop to the car while Redford found himself behind the wheel of another Porsche again in 2001 – this time a 912 in the thriller *Spy Game*.

Porsche's presence on the big screen ever since those two early appearances has been constant. When *Bad Boys: Ride or Die* was released in the summer of 2024, the fourth film in the Will Smith and Martin Lawrence franchise, a 911 Turbo S was to the fore. The first movie of 1995 saw a 911 Turbo (964) steal the show while *Bad Boys for Life* heavily featured a Carrera 4S (992) when it was released in 2020.

Two films in which a 911 plays a starring role are *No Man's Land* and *Against All Odds*. With Charlie Sheen in the lead role, the former hit cinemas in 1987 and tells the story of an undercover cop sent to dismantle a gang that is stealing 911s in Los Angeles. In *Against All Odds*, released three years earlier, one of the most memorable scenes sees Jeff Bridges' character race his 911 against James Woods' Ferrari 308 along Sunset Boulevard.

More recent appearances for the 911 in front of the cameras have come in films with cars at their core. Early in 2000's *Gone In 60 Seconds* a group of car thieves spectacularly smash a late 90s silver 996 through the glass frontage of a dealership. The Porsche was actually an air-cooled 1978 Porsche that had undergone cosmetic surgery in order to look like a more modern water-cooled 911, shedding weight to make the stunt safer.

A vivid light blue GT3 RS made a belated appearance for Porsche in the *Fast and Furious* franchise in 2011. The fifth film in the blockbuster series, the 911 was seemingly piloted by the late actor Paul Walker but in reality driven by Hollywood stuntman Rich Rutherford. The subterfuge didn't end there though; the RS was actually a 911 Carrera 2 in disguise.

The prize for the most 911s assembled together for a movie however goes to 1981 Cold War spy thriller parody *Condorman*. The scene in question sees a pack of five black 935s, driven by would-be KGB assassins, pursuing the film's hero through rural Yugoslavia.

Porsche in the movies (clockwise from top right), *Gone In 60 Seconds*, Spy capers with *Conderman* and Charlie Sheen in *No Man's Land*.

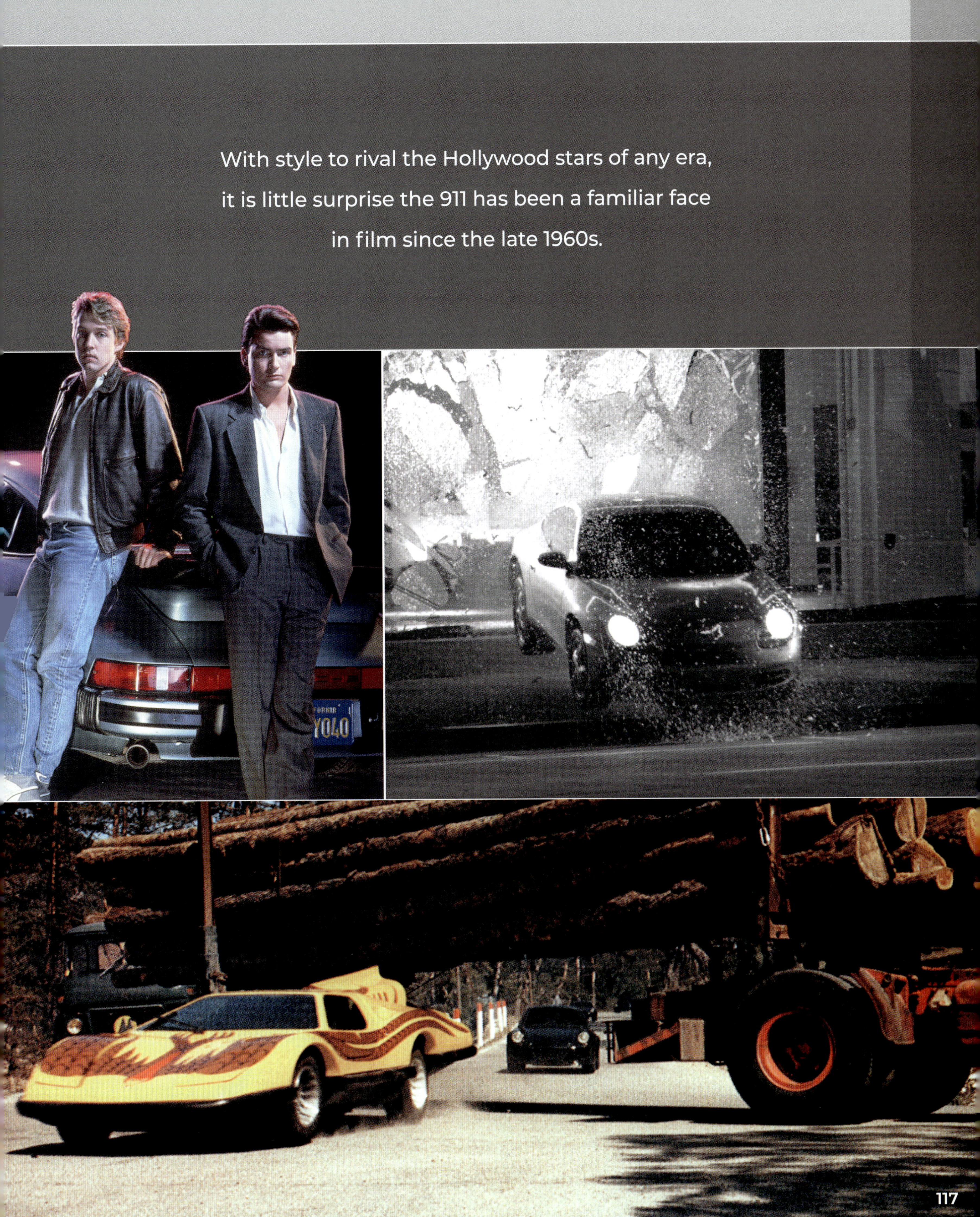


With style to rival the Hollywood stars of any era,

it is little surprise the 911 has been a familiar face

in film since the late 1960s.

# PORSCHE
# IN ADVERTISING

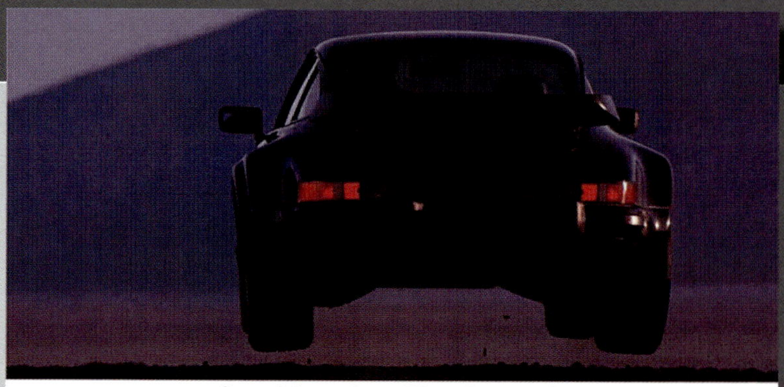



The early print adverts for the 911 were, in truth, prosaic rather than particularly funny. "Perhaps once in a generation, the opportunity arises to create an entirely new car," read one of the earliest, published in the US in the '60s. "Design and build –almost without compromise – the ultimate car for getting from here to there in the quickest, safest, most enjoyable manner possible."

By the 1970s one of the company's most popular and ubiquitous marketing slogans was 'Nothing even comes close' but by the '80s, however, the humour had began to permeate the messaging. "One ride and you'll understand why most rocket scientists are German," claimed a 1989 ad for the 911 Turbo. In the same year, Porsche insisted "In Germany it doesn't compete with cars. It competes with airplanes."

The car-buying public and beyond liked the deliberately wry self-promotion and in the '90s the advertising really got into its comedic stride. "Look at it this way," one advised, "it's either an expensive sports car or very reasonable race car." Another compared owning a Porsche to parenthood. "It's like children. You can't understand until you've had one." The most fondly remembered and famous line penned during the period was released in 1992 as part of an updated 911 Turbo campaign. "There are rational arguments for buying a new Porsche," it said, "but we won't bore you with them."

With a successful template in place, the advertising maintained its sense of humour after the 20th century had given way to the 21st. "Keeps the logical side of your brain pinned to the back of your skull," a 2001 ad for the 911 Carrera insisted. Two years later the new edition of the 996 Cabriolet was publicised with a timely if tongue-in-cheek warning for 911 drivers. "The hours a Porsche spends parked," it noted. "You don't get those back."

Some examples of Porsche ads have had a darker or more risqué tone. "It gets a little bit louder above 5,000 rpm," one explained, "so you can't hear the passenger scream." In 2003 Porsche were eager to extol the virtues of the 911 Turbo and decide to spread their gospel with an attention-grabbing slogan about the driving experience. "Calling it transportation," it said, "is like calling sex reproduction."

Different countries have adopted different but always comic approaches to getting the 911 message across. In Germany they appealed to the hunger of potential customers, claiming a new Porsche meant "you can stay longer for breakfast, you will be back for dinner sooner." Over in the States, the company hoped to boost sales in with an invitation to transport "the ultimate souvenir" across the Atlantic for American tourists. "Bring something back from Europe," it urged, "besides a bunch of slides."

As distinctive and unique as the iconic car itself, Porsche advertising campaigns over the past eight decades have relied heavily on humour to convey the 911's glorious idiosyncrasies.

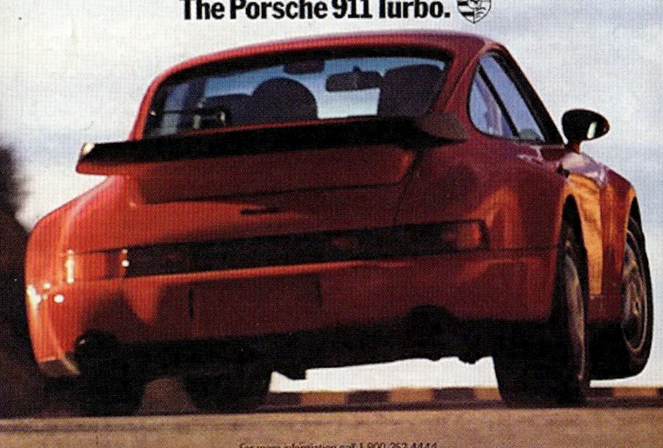


"LOOK AT IT THIS WAY, IT'S EITHER AN EXPENSIVE SPORTS CAR OR VERY REASONABLE RACE CAR."

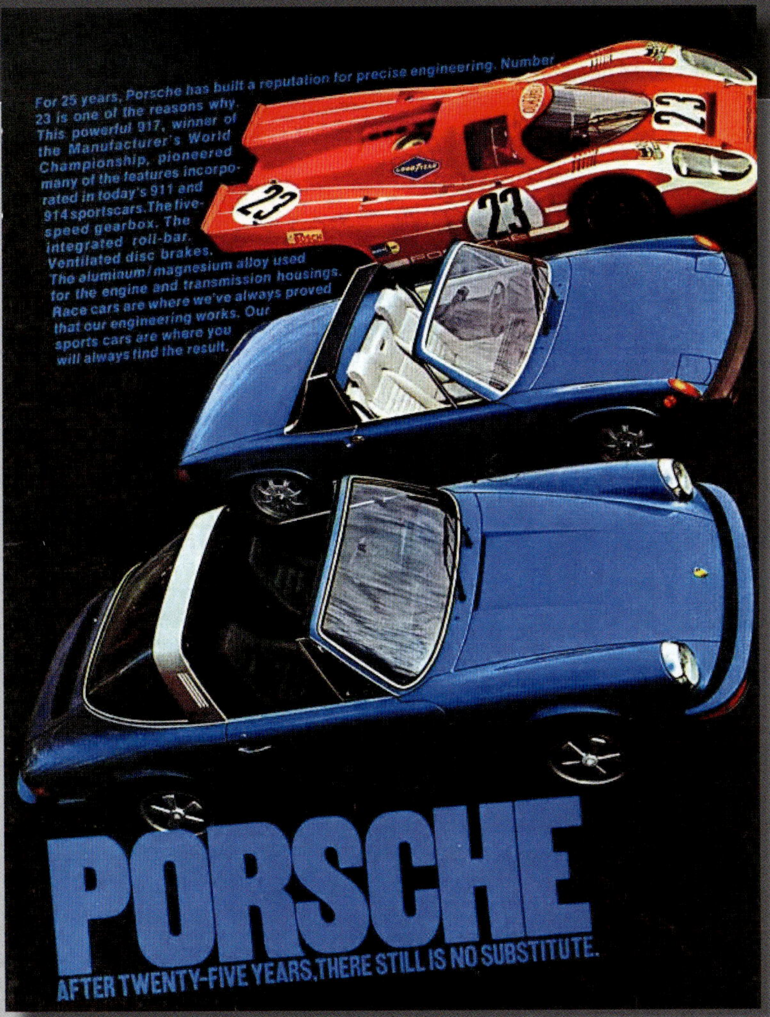


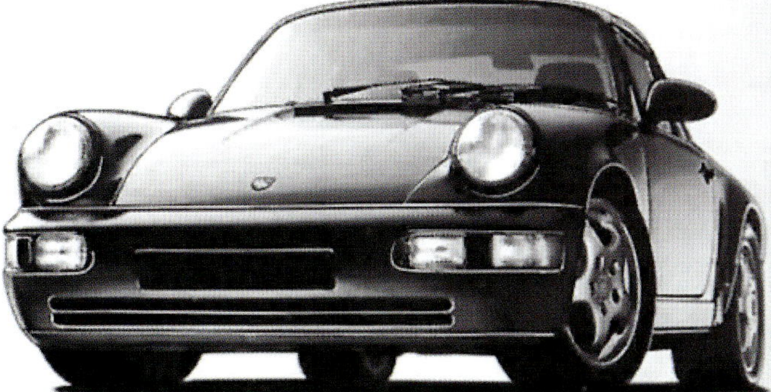


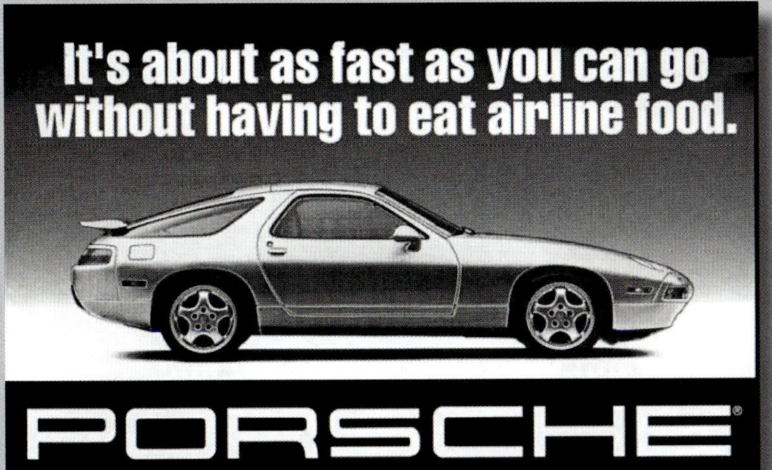

# PORSCHE
# RACE CARS



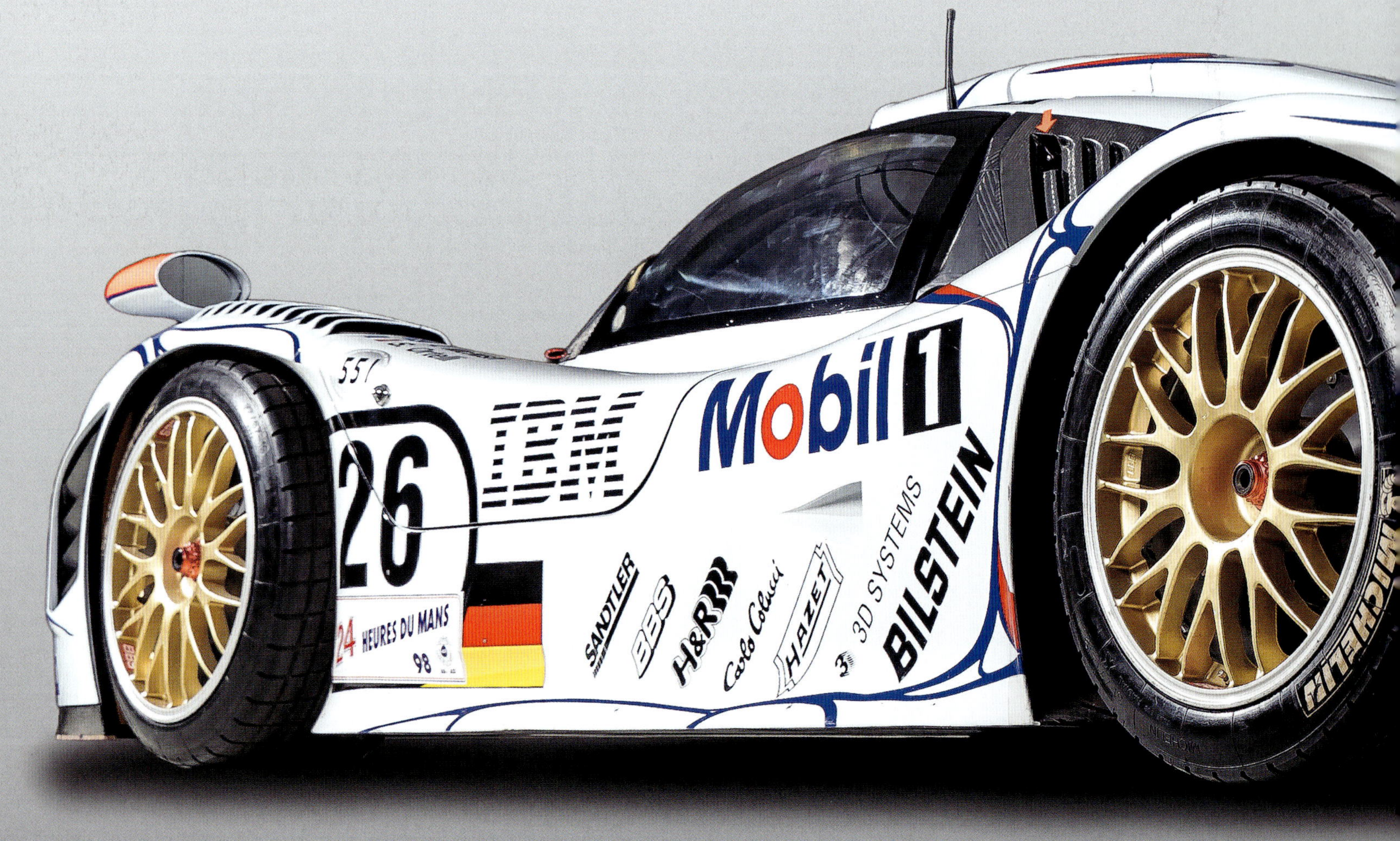

Become acquainted with some of the most renowned race cars in the history of Porsche: revel in the story of the Carrera RSR at the Targa Florio; learn why the Moby Dick is one of the most revered treasures at the Porsche Museum; take to the track at Goodwood in the one of the most fearsome track weapons of the 1990s – the 993 GT2 R; and discover how the mid-engined 911 GTI '98 conquered the iconic 24 Hours of Le Mans.

You will also find full coverage of the remarkable achievements of Porsche 911s at the world's oldest and most prestigious endurance races for sports cars, featuring the 24 Hours of Daytona, the 12 Hours of Sebring and the Targa Florio Classica, as well as the legendary Le Mans.

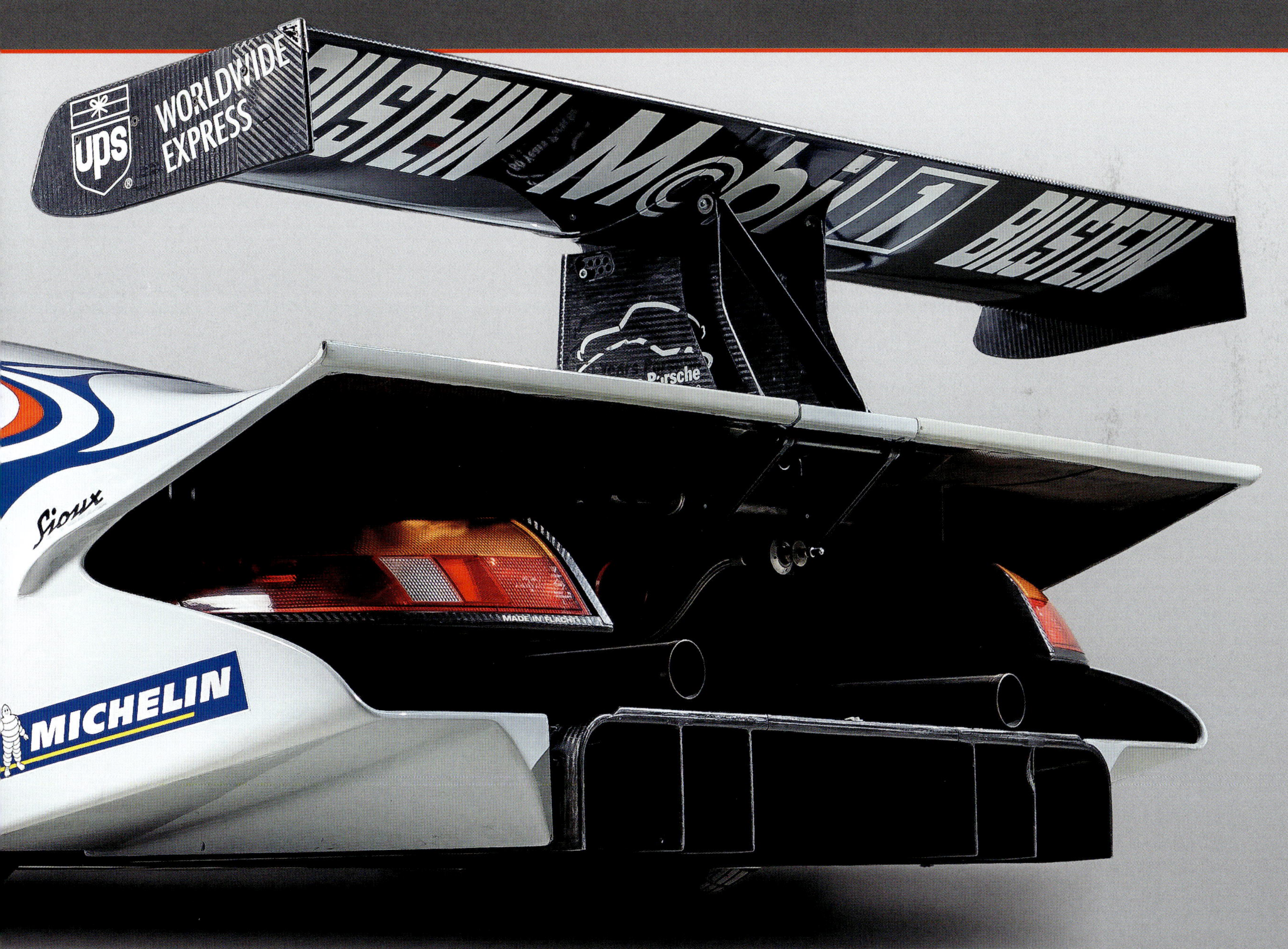

# CARRERA RSR

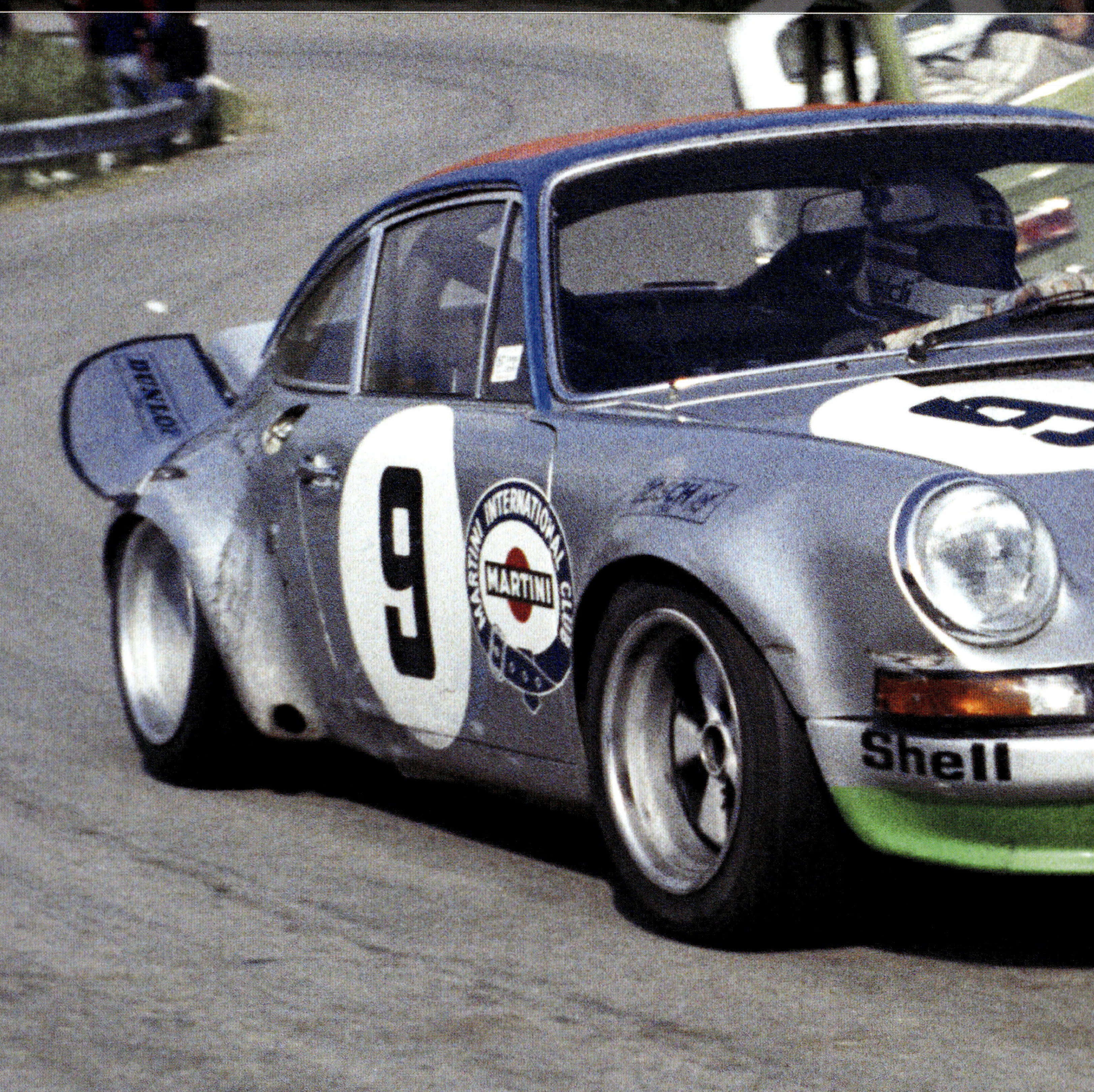

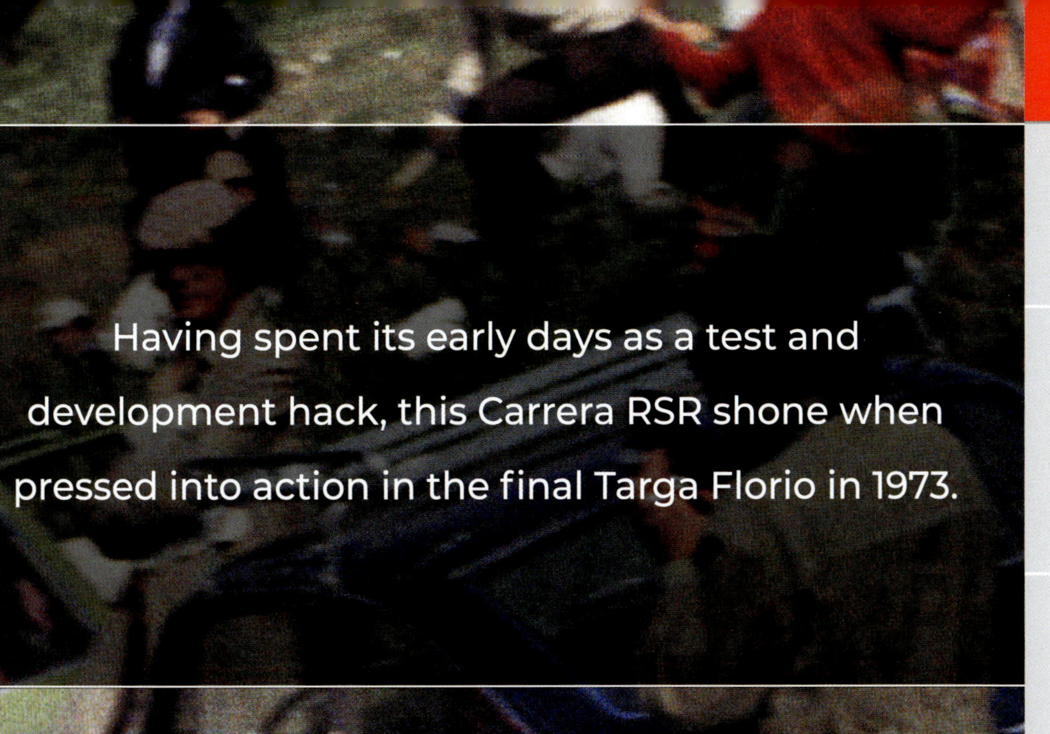

Having spent its early days as a test and development hack, this Carrera RSR shone when pressed into action in the final Targa Florio in 1973.

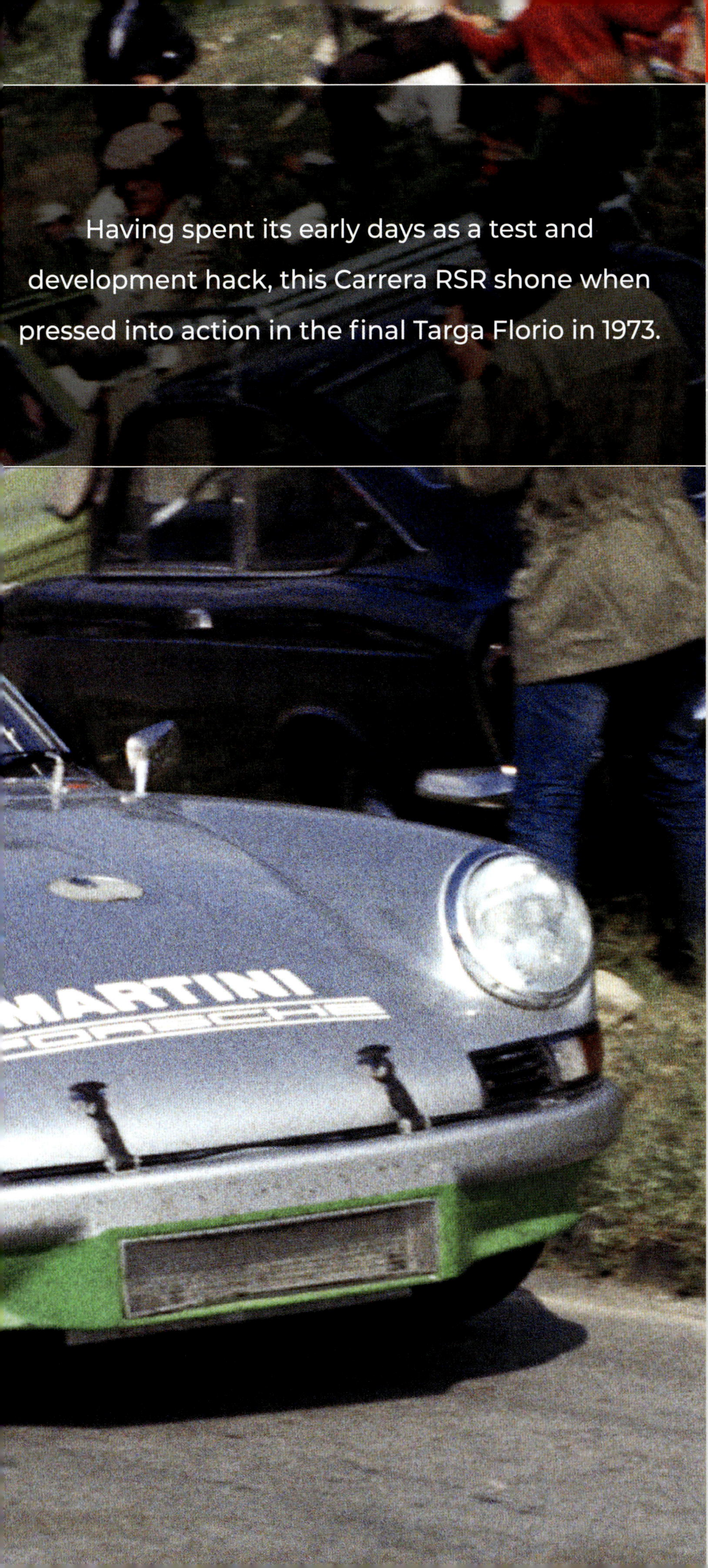

# CARRERA RSR
## ARGA FLORIO
(1973)

### ENGINE

**Capacity:** 2,806cc
**Bore x stroke:** 92.0 x 70.4mm
**Compression ratio:** 10:3.1
**Maximum power:** 300bhp @ 8,000rpm

### DIMENSIONS

**Wheelbase:** 2,271mm
**Track (front/rear):** 1,472/1,528mm
**Weight:** 1,360kg

### PERFORMANCE

**Top speed:** 260km/h

The year 1973 was significant for a couple of reasons. On 3 April that year, the first ever mobile phone call was made by a Motorola engineer in Manhattan, New York, and the world as we knew it was changed forever. The second reason – and perhaps more relevant to Porsche enthusiasts – was the introduction of the 911 Carrera RS, a high-performance road and race car that elevated Porsche's standing on the international motorsport stage.

Announced at the Paris Motor Show in October 1972, the 911 Carrera RS was powered by a 2.7-litre engine producing 210 horsepower, and featured a radical new aerodynamic device, the engine-lid ducktail. Porsche's intention was to create the next racing 911, but in order to do this it had to produce 500 road-going versions to meet the homologation requirements for entry in Group 4, the Special Grand Touring category, as documented in the Rennsport Icons chapter (see pages 26–31).

In short, so successful was the sales effort behind the Carrera RS, that 528 cars were produced between October '72 and February '73, but the official notification of the model's homologation was only received on 1 March 1973. This meant that the racing version, the Carrera RSR, would have to run in the prototype category at Daytona, scheduled for 3–4 February '73. It made little difference as the 2.8-litre Carrera RSR won the Daytona 24 Hours overall on its debut, easily outgunning the other GT class contenders for which it had been intended.

The development of the Carrera RSR involved taking a Carrera RS from the production line and transferring it to the Customer Service Department across the road in Zuffenhausen where it would have a fully race prepared 2.8-litre engine installed. This increase in bore over the production 2.7-litre unit was the largest displacement possible within the existing engine stud positions. Compression was increased by using higher-domed pistons, and Nikasil-coated liners were fitted, a technology used to great effect in the mighty 917 model. These modifications ensured the Carrera RSR was the first 911 to achieve that magical 300bhp figure.

The Carrera RSR was fitted with a much larger, centrally mounted oil cooler located in the front, below the bumper. Stopping power was significantly enhanced by the use of 917 finned calipers that gripped the cross-drilled discs and weren't as prone to fade, and a front/rear brake balance mechanism was also installed. A safety fuel cell was mounted in the front luggage compartment too.

The victory at Daytona no doubt bolstered the Porsche racing department's confidence sufficiently to send three cars to the Targa Florio of 1973 – as it transpired, it was to be the last ever iteration of this famous Sicilian race.

Despite chaotic practice sessions for the team, the #8 Carrera RSR was qualified in 5th place by Gijs van Lennep, but the #9 car was down in 15th place. The start of the race got underway as expected, with the Ferrari of Arturo Merzario speeding off into the distance, followed by Rolf Stommelen in his Alfa Romeo. The other Ferrari and Alfa Romeo were followed by the #8 Porsche 911 Carrera RSR, but after just two laps, Van Lennep found he had been promoted to 3rd place.

Our feature car, the #9 Carrera RSR, also began its climb up the ladder and in true Targa fashion, the rate of attrition amongst the faster cars was high. With just four of the eleven laps completed, the #8 Porsche 911 Carrera RSR of Herbert Müller and Van Lennep led the field, a position they would not relinquish. The #9 RSR made even greater headway as it climbed from its original starting position to finish in 3rd place, a little more than 18 minutes behind the #8 winning Porsche. The troubled #107 Carrera RSR of Günter Steckkönig and Giulio Pucci came home in a respectable 6th place overall. A star was born.

**R2 was originally restored as the Targa Florio-winning RSR, before being appropriately designated as the no.9 car**

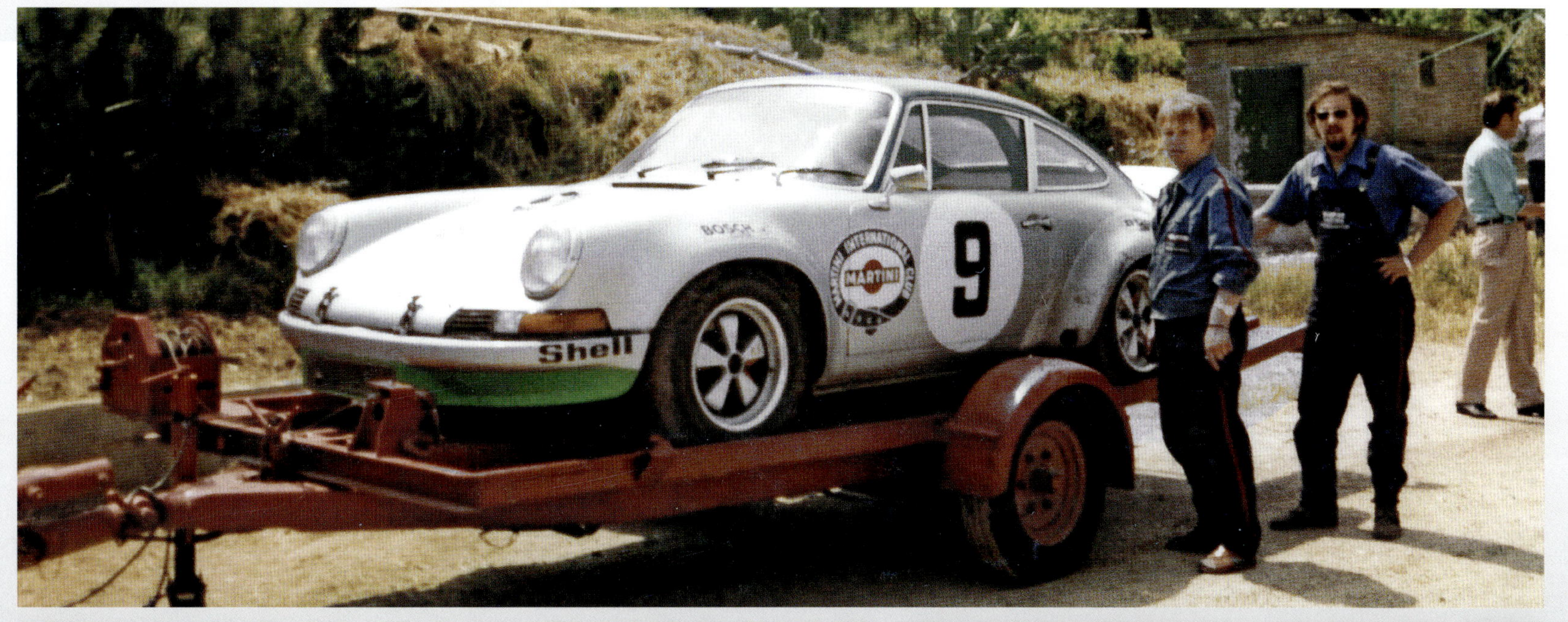

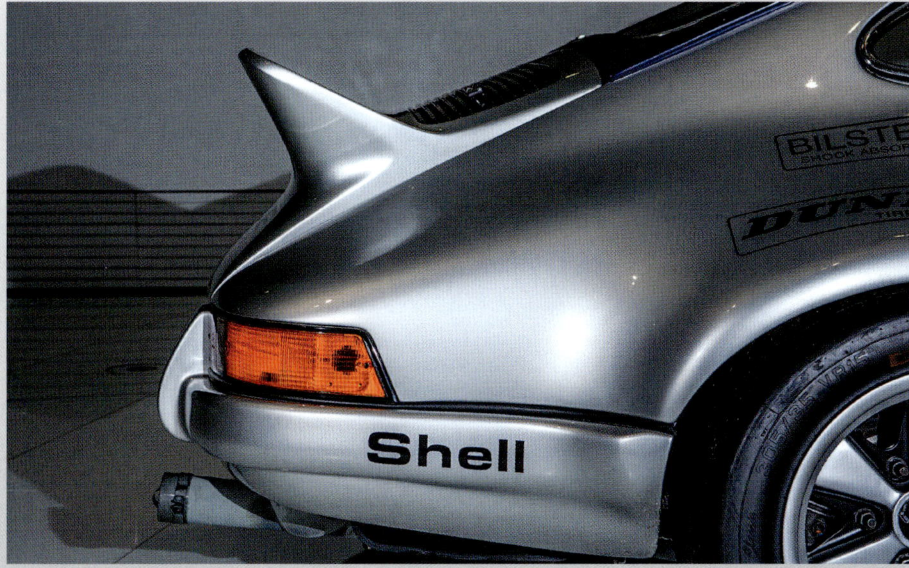

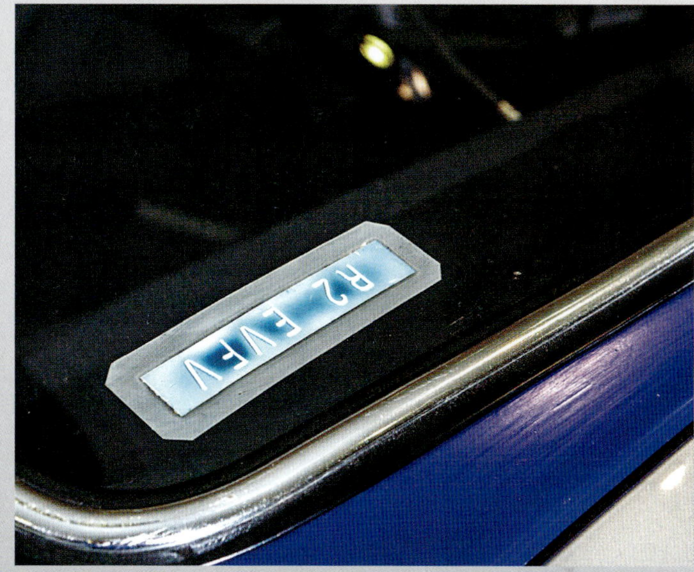

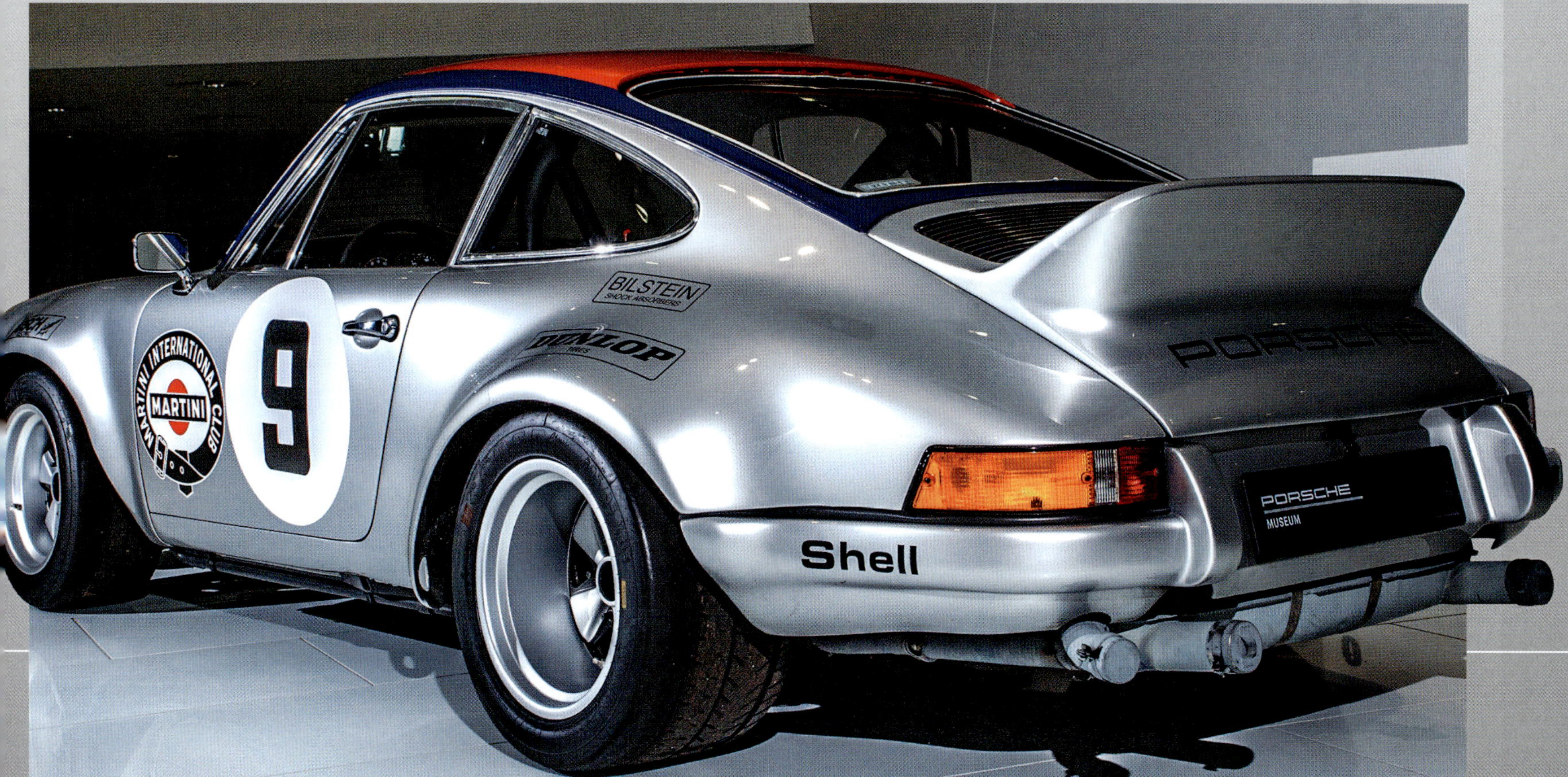

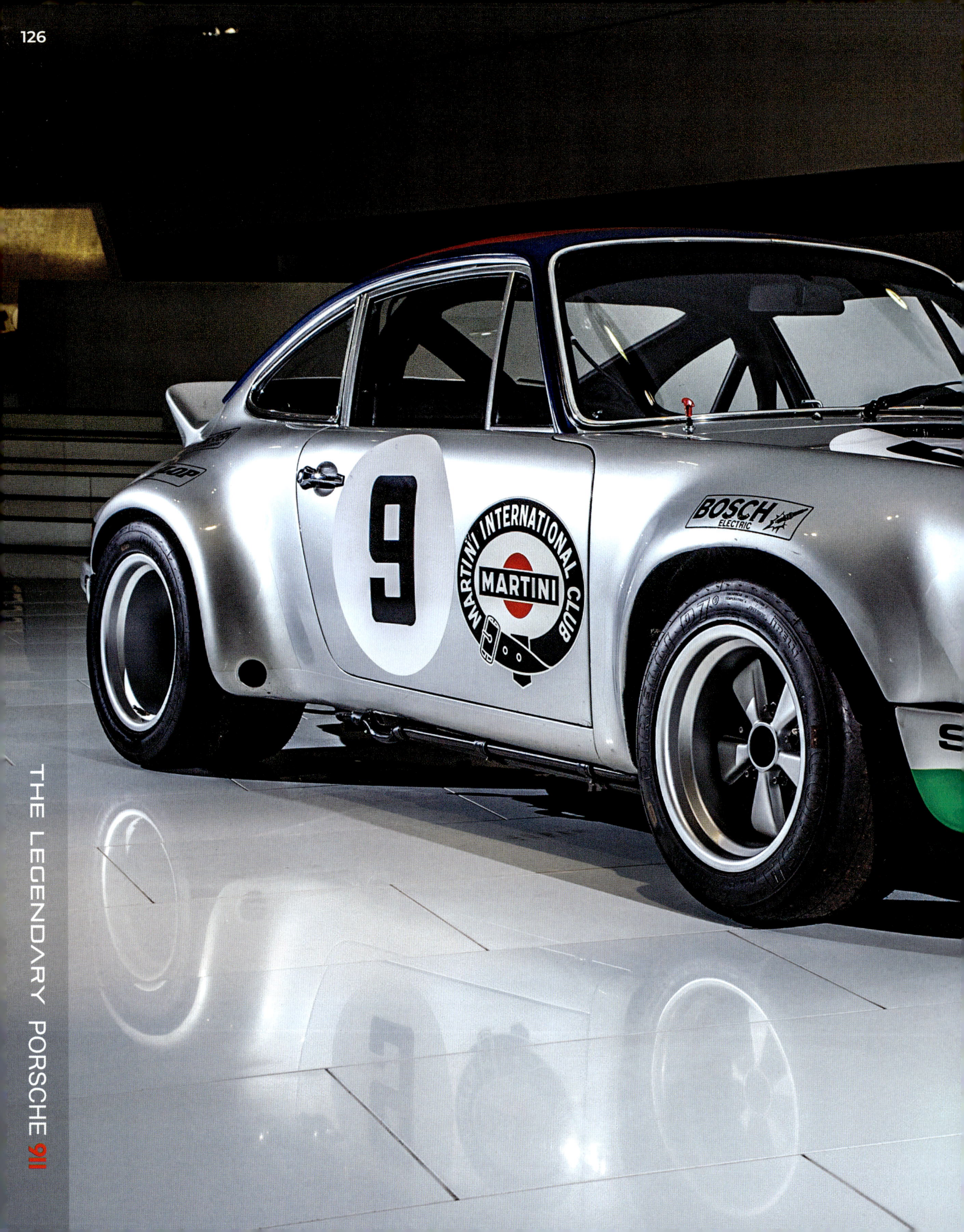
9
MARTINI INTERNATIONAL CLUB
MARTINI
BOSCH
ELECTRIC

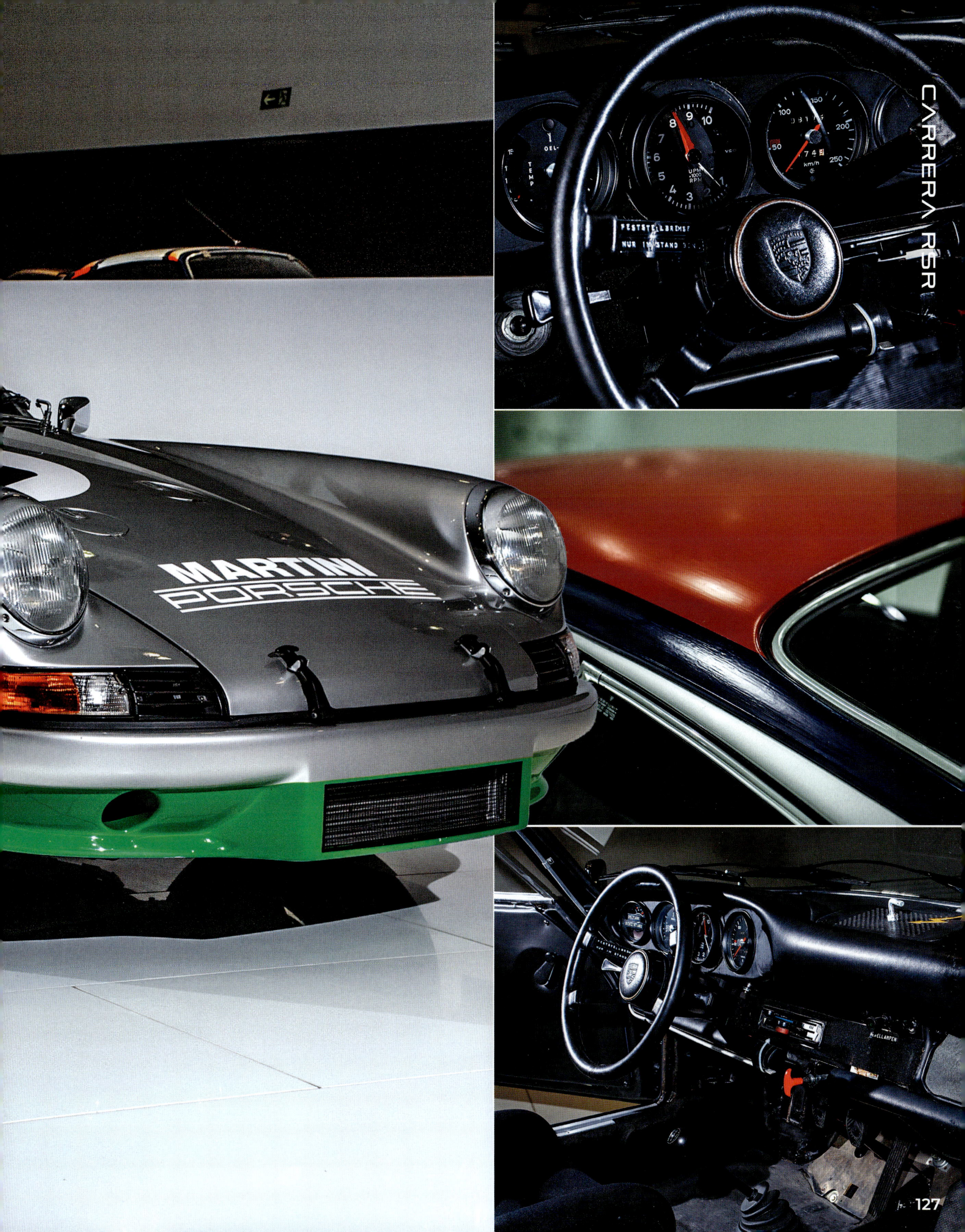

# MOBY DICK
# A BIG FISH

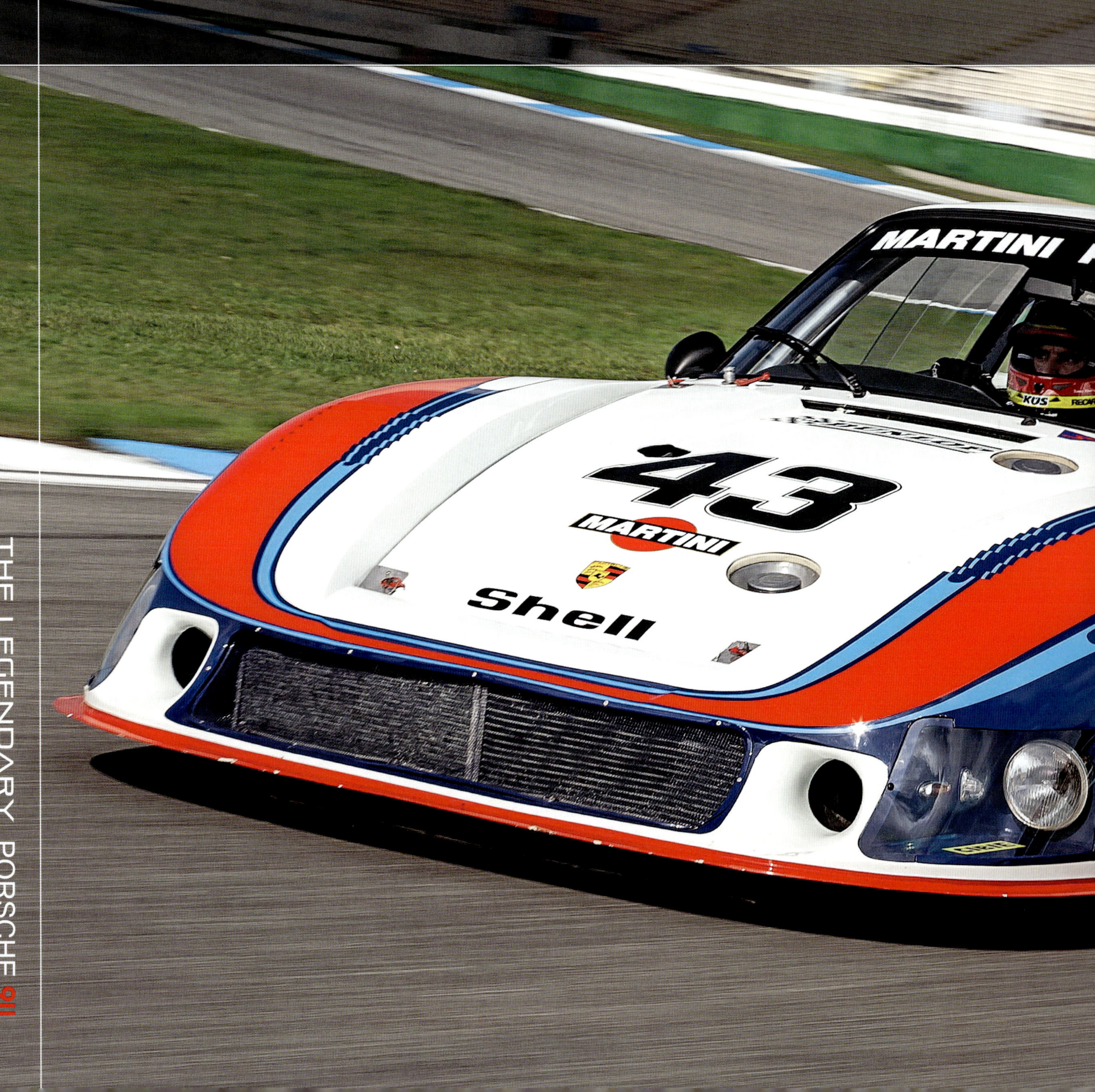

Group 5 rules offered manufacturers great freedom to modify their cars in the silhouette class, so doyen of racing engineers Norbert Singer pushed the rules to the limit and gave us the Porsche 935/78 'Moby Dick'.



# 935/78

(1978)

### ENGINE

**Capacity:** 3,211cc

**Compression ratio:** 7:0.1

**Maximum power:** 750bhp @ 8,200rpm (max: 845bhp @ 8,200rpm)

**Maximum torque:** 784Nm @ 6,600rpm

**Transmission:** Four-speed manual (Type 930/50)

### SUSPENSION

**Front:** Wishbones; MacPherson struts

**Rear:** Aluminium semi-trailing arms; Progressive rate coil springs; Bilstein gas-filled telescopic dampers

### WHEELS & TYRES

**Front:** 11x16-inch light alloy with centre-lock nut

**Rear:** 15x19-inch light alloy with centre-lock nut

### DIMENSIONS

**Length:** 4,890mm

**Width:** 1,990mm

**Weight:** 1,025kg

### PERFORMANCE

**0-60mph:** 4.5 secs

**Top speed:** 227mph

n the 1970s, Porsche had much going for it on the worldwide motorsport stage. Firstly, it learned how to dominate with turbocharging, and secondly, it had in Ernst Fuhrmann a CEO who believed in the commercial benefits of motorsport. Then there was one Norbert Singer, a motorsport engineer who originally wanted to work in aeronautics, but when a position at Porsche presented itself in March 1970 he elected to take that instead.

With an interest in aerospace, Singer's knowledge of aerodynamics and weight conservation came in handy when working with racing cars. Singer's first task at Porsche involved cooling on the mighty 917s, but in just a few short years he was already making his presence felt in Porsche's wider race department.

At the start of the 1976 season, Group 5 regulations referred to a 'silhouette' car, but any definition of what a 'silhouette' comprised was notable by its absence. This term, though, was deliberately loose in its meaning so that the manufacturers competing in Group 5 could develop race cars that looked like a production car, but were clearly powerful, all-out racing machines. Porsche's contender for Group 5 was the 935, but the model had to go through two evolutions before the third iteration, the mighty 935/78, or 'Moby Dick,' was born.

When the first version of the 935 appeared in 1976, it featured a flatter rear wing and headlights in their conventional position in the fenders, but the 1977 version already showed signs of where the ultimate 935 was heading. The headlights had been removed from the conventionally shaped fenders, which were now downward sloping and more streamlined.

The regulations required the manufacturer to keep the windows from the production car, so a new rear window was made, a kind of double window. The 935/78 was also fitted with a long tail, which maximised the air flowing off the modified rear bodywork, making the car almost as fast as the prototypes at the Le Mans 24 Hours. Engine development saw the introduction of a first for the company: water cooling in a 911. The regulations required a production engine block, with some machining permitted, but the heads could be modified. This worked perfectly for Porsche as this allowed it to retain traditional air cooling for the cylinders, but water-cooling for the heads allowed the introduction of four-valves per cylinder. This meant that the fan, which had to be retained by regulation, could now be smaller as it only had the cylinders to cool.

On 14 May 1978, Moby Dick rolled onto the Tarmac for the 6 Hours of Silverstone and delivered its first, and only, race victory. Jacky Ickx qualified the 935/78 in pole position, beating the second-placed car, another Porsche 935, by two seconds. The race itself started in wet conditions, and Jochen Mass made good his escape, and before long was so far ahead of the rest of the field that the following horde was unaffected by his spray. The Ickx/Mass car was never troubled, and romped home seven laps clear of the second-placed car.

While the car in period achieved significantly less than might have been expected, the 935 'Moby Dick' nevertheless represents a time when relative freedom and liberal interpretation of the motorsport rules allowed such outlandish cars to be built. Norbert Singer's interpretation of these loose rules was bordering on the outrageous, almost rebellious, but the silhouette era saw some of the most colourful and competitive racing in motorsport history. The Moby Dick is thus a special Porsche race car, and we are all the richer for such wild thinking, the likes of which we are unlikely to see ever again.

**Taking full advantage of a loophole in Group 5 rules, the Moby Dick is instantly recognisable for any Porsche fan for its outlandish silhouette rather than any on-track accomplishments, which were only loosely based on a 911 road car**

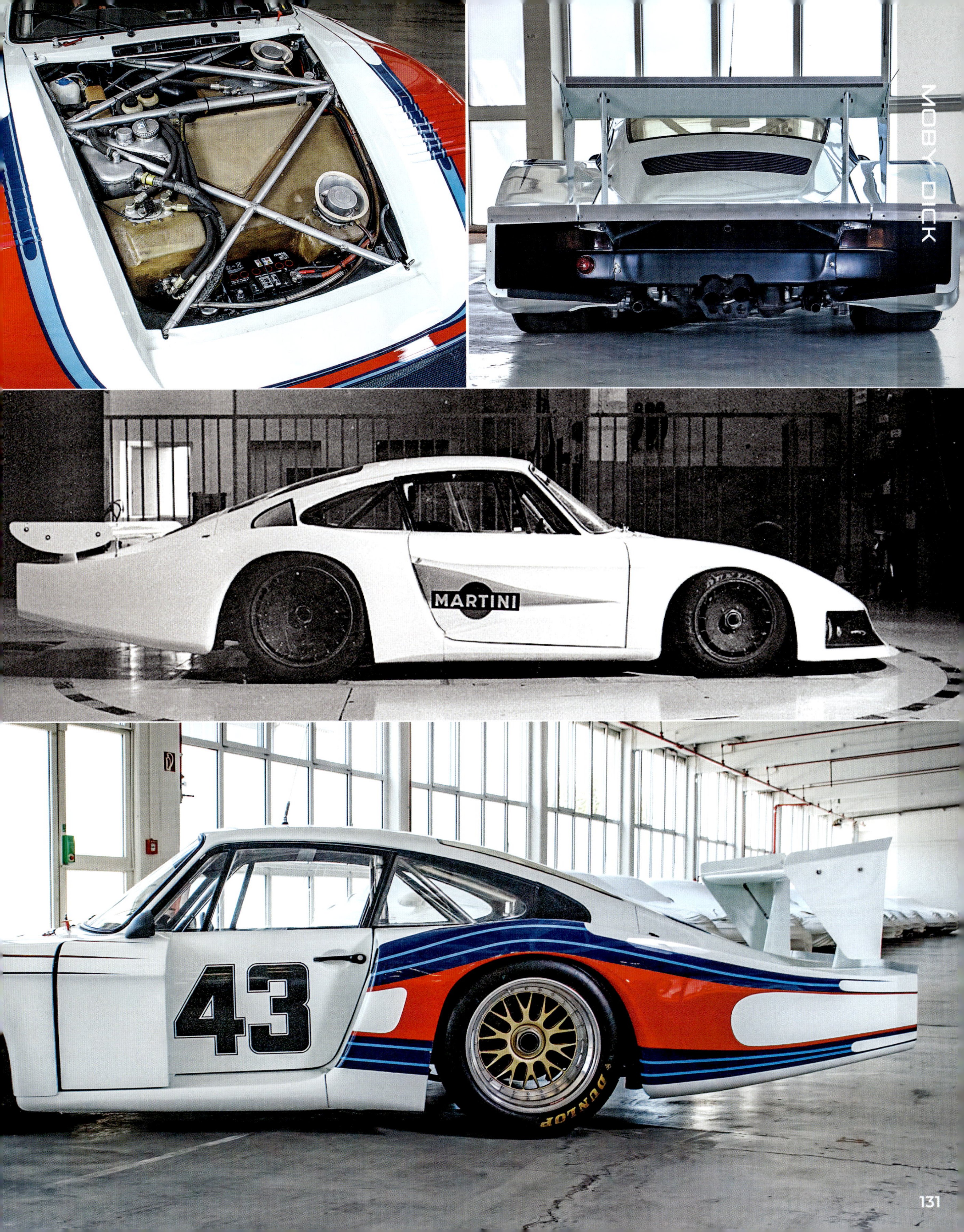

Seating position was moved to the right-hand-side on Moby Dick for better balance on predominantly clockwise circuits; gearbox oil cooler lay behind duct aft of driver's door

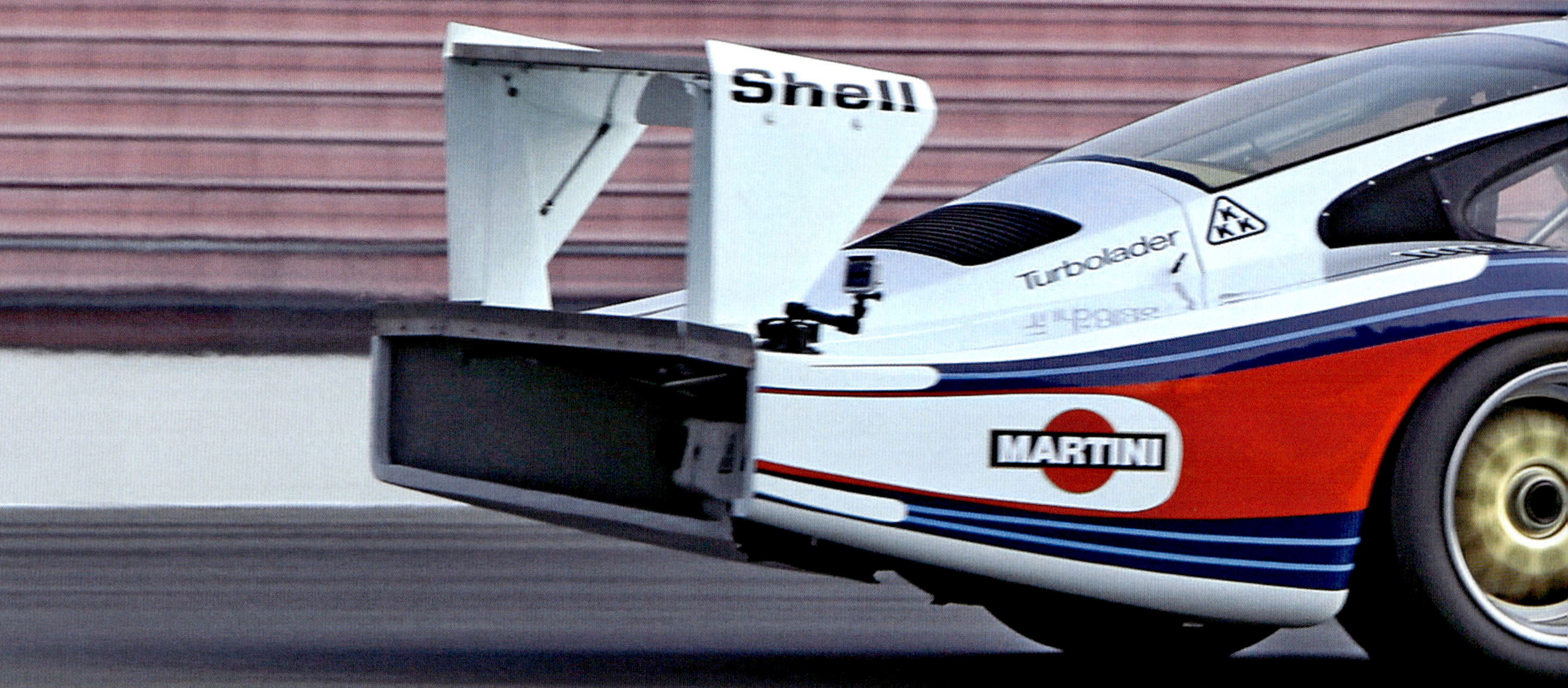




## THE MOBY DICK NAME

During the building process of Moby Dick, the car was on stands in the workshop at Weissach without wheels; this height made it easier to work on and for the mechanics to work under the car as required. Once the car was completed and ready for its first text run, the racer was painted completely in white.

Norbert Singer recalls with some humour the moment Moby Dick was rolled out: "You can imagine, after seeing the car for weeks at a certain level, you get used to it. Then you fit the wheels and bring it down to the floor, and the combination of being 8cm lower, the increased width, and with the car being much longer, it was quite a shock, and one of the mechanics said 'It looks like Moby Dick.' And that just stuck."

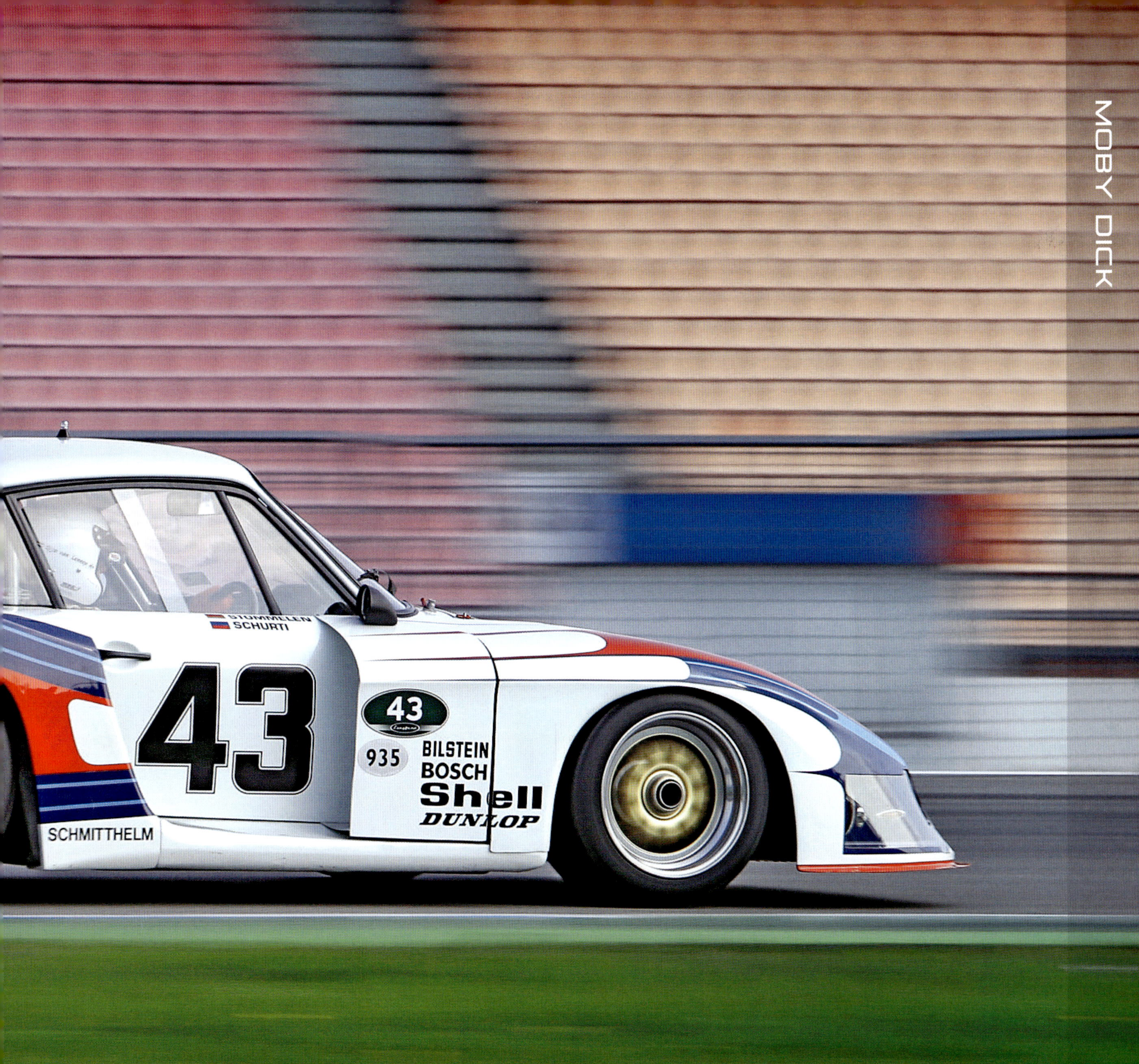
SCHURTI
43
43
935
BILSTEIN
BOSCH
Shell
DUNLOP
SCHMITTHELM

# SPEED FREAK

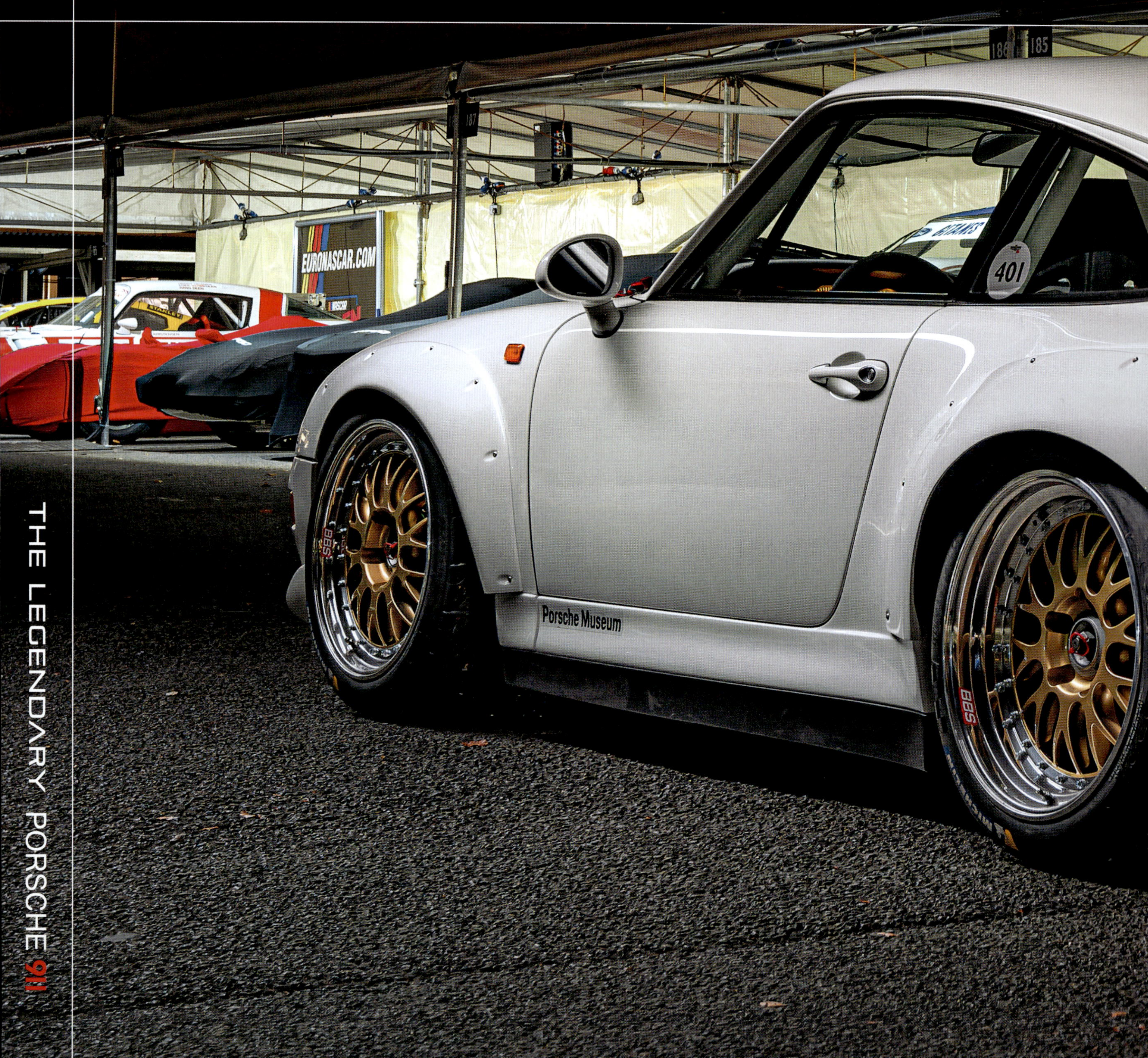

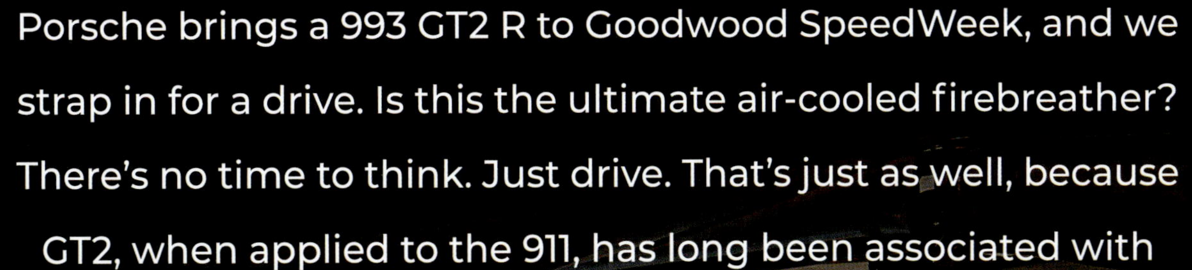

Porsche brings a 993 GT2 R to Goodwood SpeedWeek, and we strap in for a drive. Is this the ultimate air-cooled firebreather? There's no time to think. Just drive. That's just as well, because GT2, when applied to the 911, has long been associated with being a difficult, challenging car.

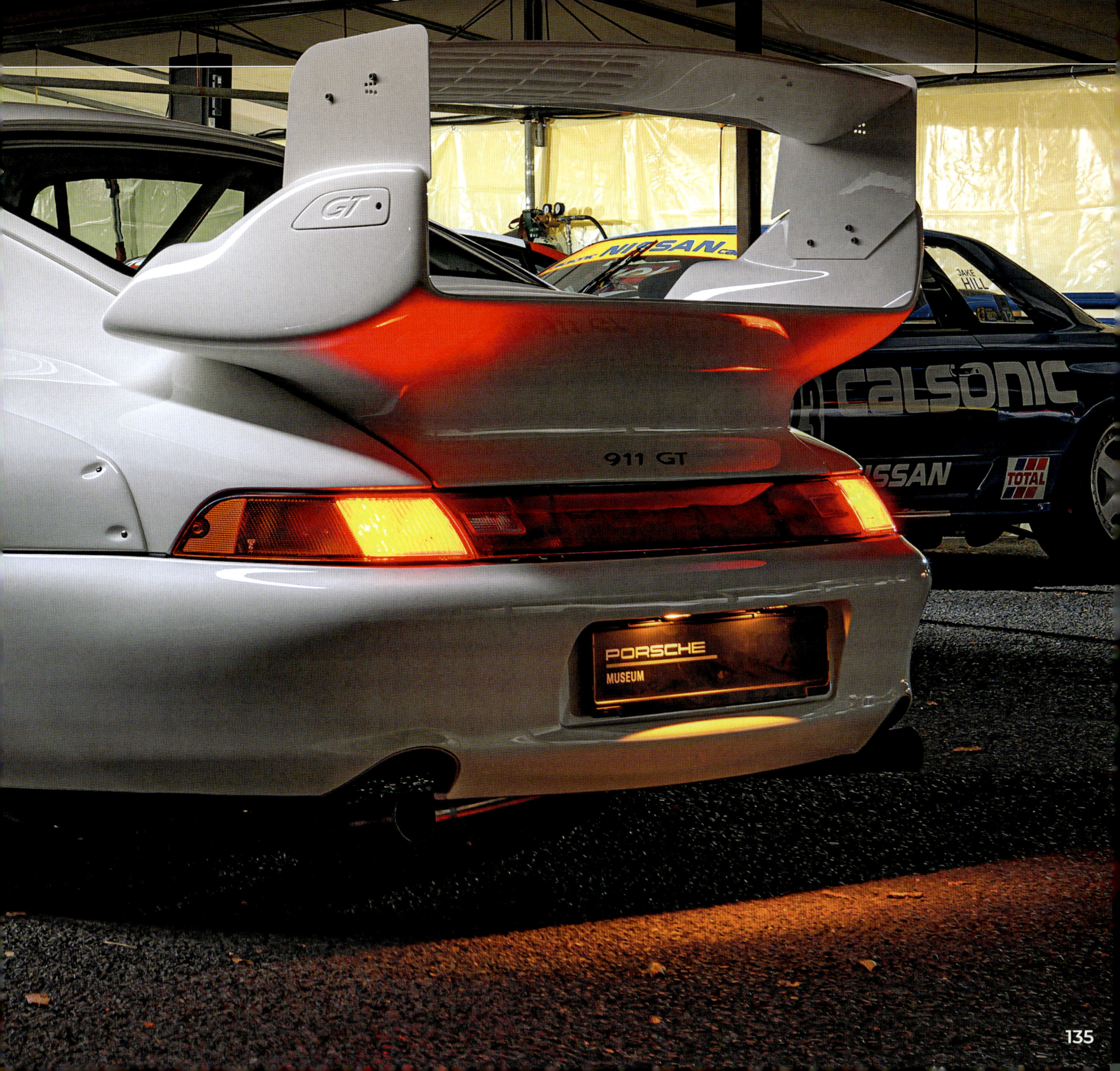

The GT2 is the definition of a race car, with its form entirely derived from function, those wild wheel arches covering 18-inch split rim wheels, the fronts being 10 inches wide and the rears 11 inches. You strap the six-point Sabelt harnesses on while clutched tightly by the embrace of the sole bucket seat in the stark interior. There's no trim inside, save for the dash top surrounding the instruments, simple door cards, and a bit of centre console containing a light for the fuel reserve plus a couple of switches.

A development of the flat six from the 993 Turbo, it's designated M64/60 R and comes with different KKK turbochargers, larger intercoolers, higher lift cam, and manually (rather than hydraulically) adjusted valves. It runs a higher boost pressure of 2.05-2.1 bar as well as a differing, freer-breathing exhaust system, while a TAG box, opposed to Bosch, is tasked with the engine management. That TAG unit is sat behind the seat, a finned black box with six LEDs on it, listing the words Power, Speed, Sensor, Ignition, Injection, Function and, somewhat ominously, Fatal Error respectively.

There's a green light alongside Power, which apparently is 450hp, as in line with the GT2 racing specifications. That is 20hp more than the GT2 road car, though as with any quoted figures from Porsche that's likely to be a little bit conservative. There's little to see from lifting the engine cover, with the intercooler taking up all the engine bay and more, fitting snugly under that lightweight wing. The gearbox is a racing version of the six-speed G50 transmission, with a separate oil pump feeding a cooler. Slightly shorter and more precise in its movement than a regular 993, but still familiar.

Given its fearsome reputation the GT2 R feels remarkably biddable on track. The steering, power assisted, is light and accurate, the turn-in having that familiar 911 quirk of needing a bit of patience, before settling in and working the tyres hard. A bit of trail braking helps get the nose to tuck in with a bit more authority, putting some weight on the nose and working down the gearbox. Doing so is a joy, the brake pedal firm and strong, it providing the perfect platform from which to roll off the side to rev-match those easy downshifts, the grip levels huge through the corner, with the traction being similarly mighty when exiting it.

As with any racing car it works better the quicker it's driven, and speed isn't something that's in short supply. The GT2 R's ability to gain it is relentless, it feeling light, and hugely accelerative when those two KKK turbos are fully lit. The GT2 R requiring all your attention, all of the time. Not in a fearsome manner – just involved and hugely enjoyable, the GT2 R is so communicative that it's surprisingly quick to get to grips with. That comes as something of a surprise, but then the GT2 R was built to be campaigned for hours at a time, not sprinted for mere moments. It feels resolute, strong and unendingly rapid. There's so much more on offer than a brief stint around Goodwood's fast circuit allows, though the eight laps (around 19 miles) in it underlines that it's about as pure a driving experience as you could have.

Devoid of stability or traction control systems, you're responsible for feeling the limits, while the manual transmission keeps you busy, with every shift up or down the 'box an absolute joy. No finger-flipped shifts here, the 993 GT2 R a physical, involving car, but all the better because of it. To have raced one must have been sensational, its arrival in the global GT2 series it was designed for seeing Porsche win plenty of silverware with it, and having experienced it, it's not difficult to see why.

**Lightweight motorsport wheels sit under signature GT2 arch extensions**

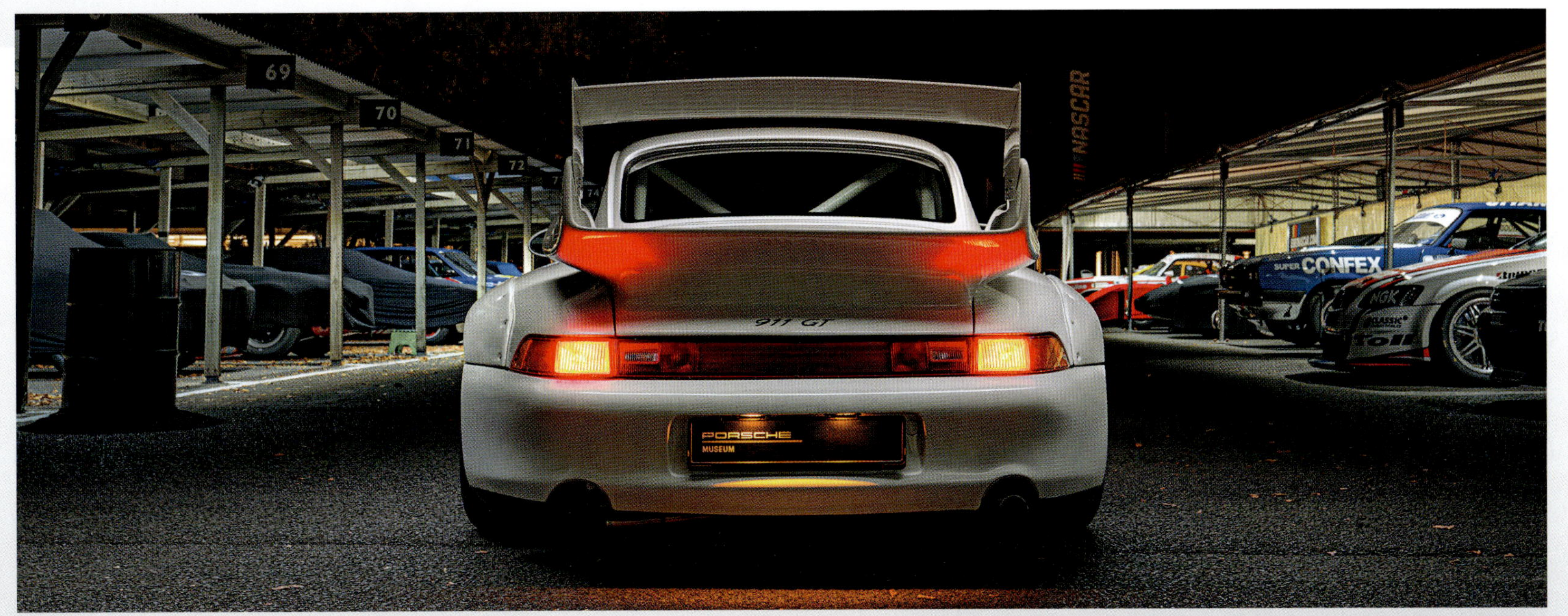

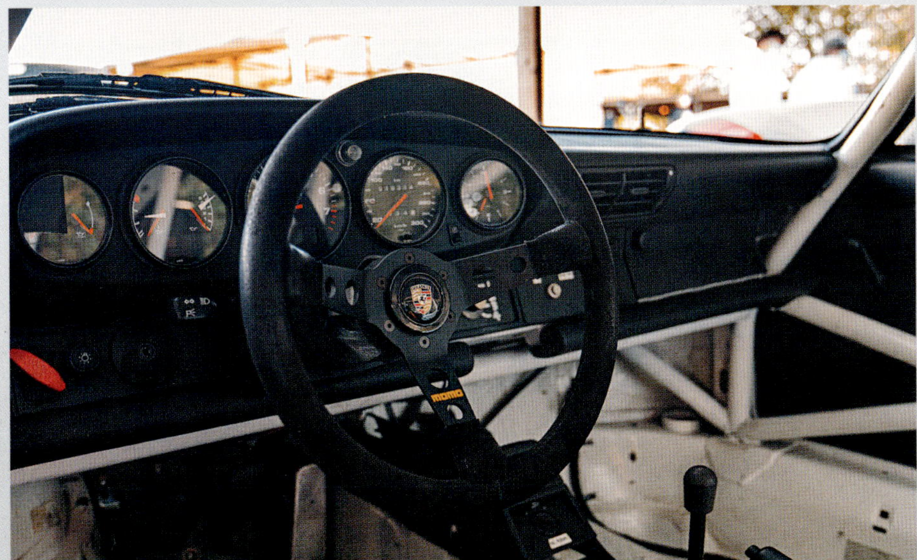

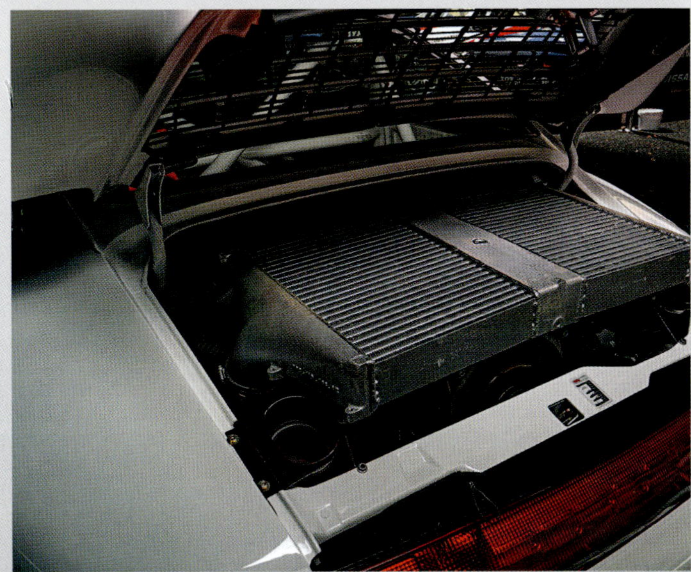

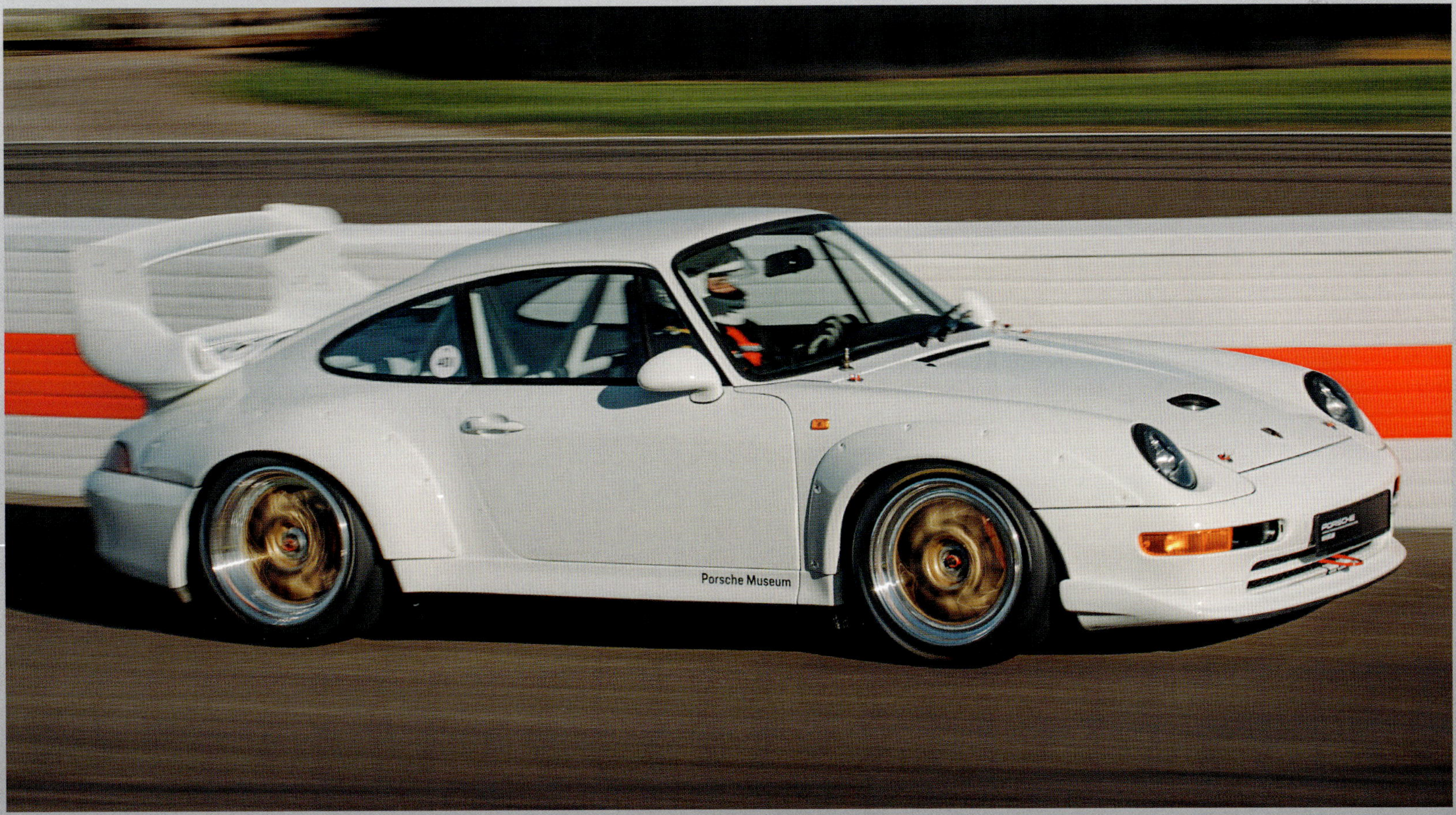

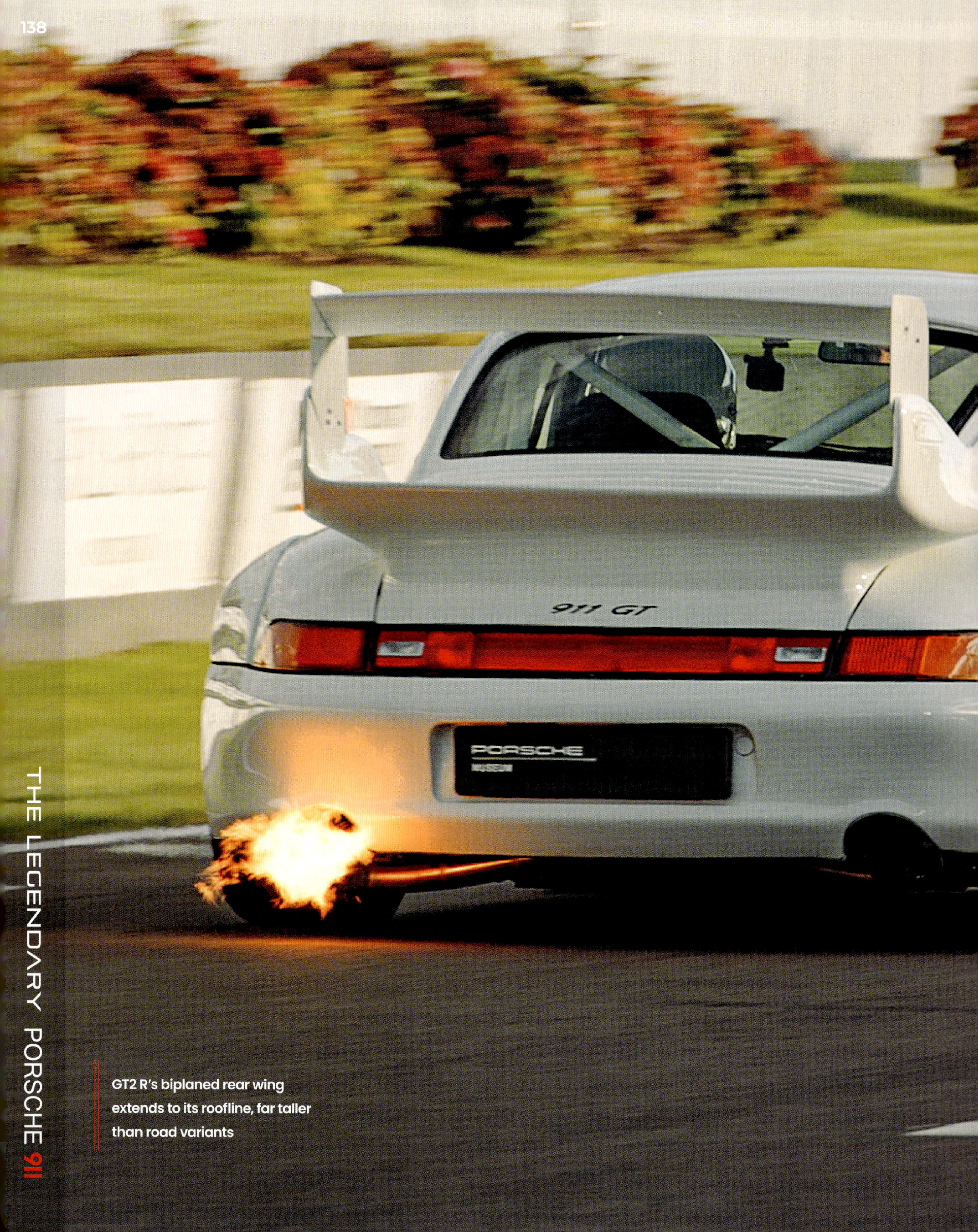





GT2 R's biplaned rear wing
extends to its roofline, far taller
than road variants

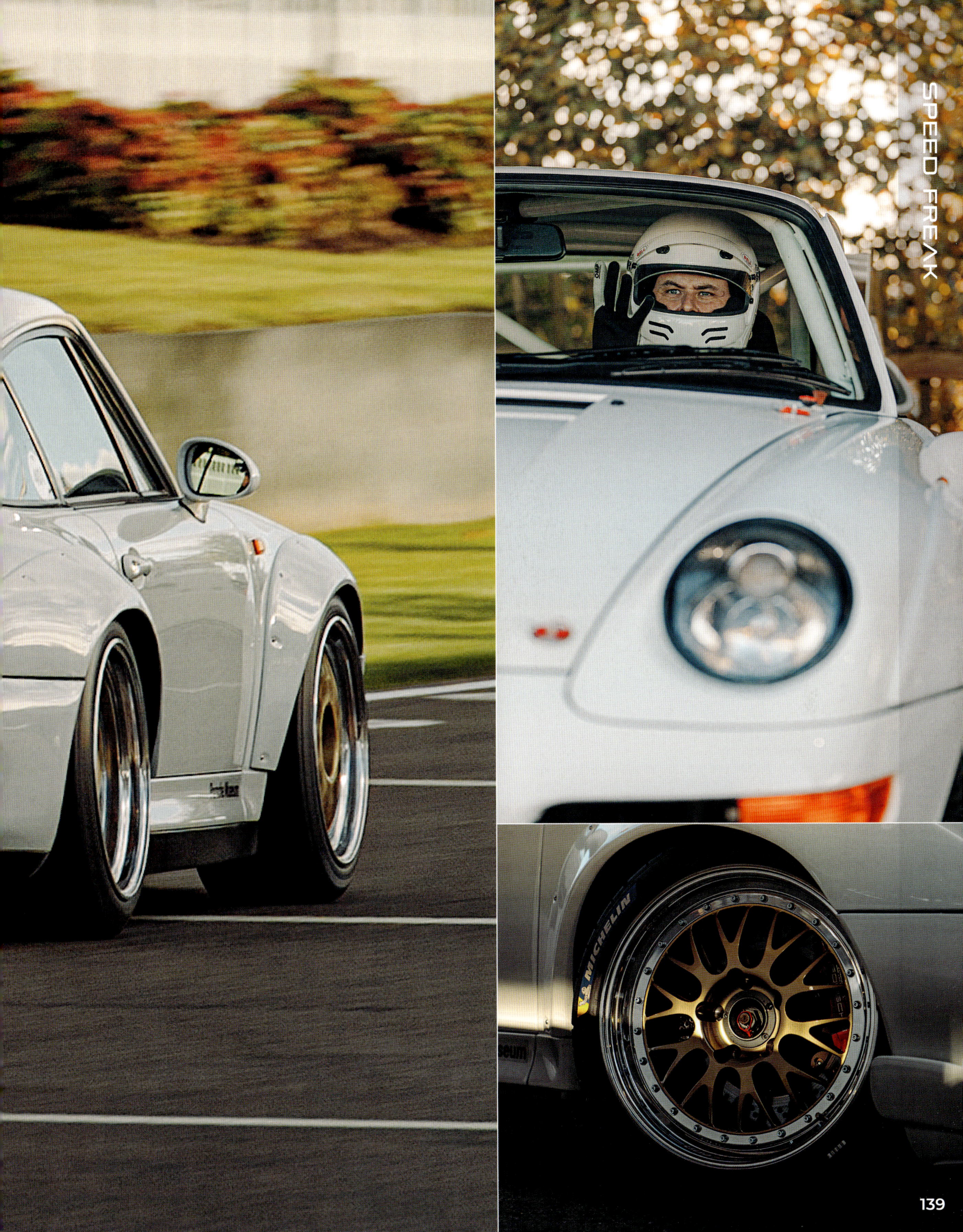
SPEED FREAK

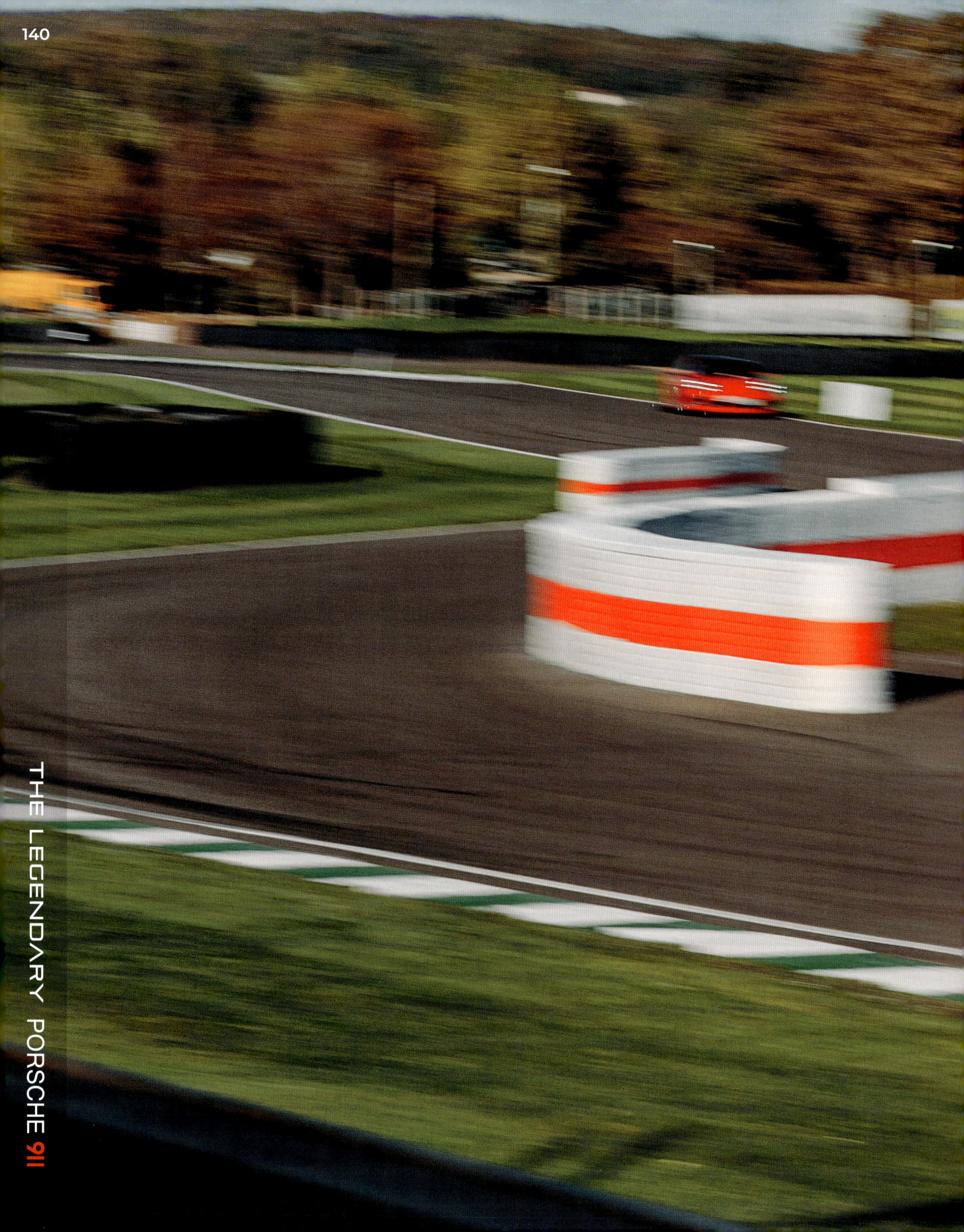

THE LEGENDARY PORSCHE 911

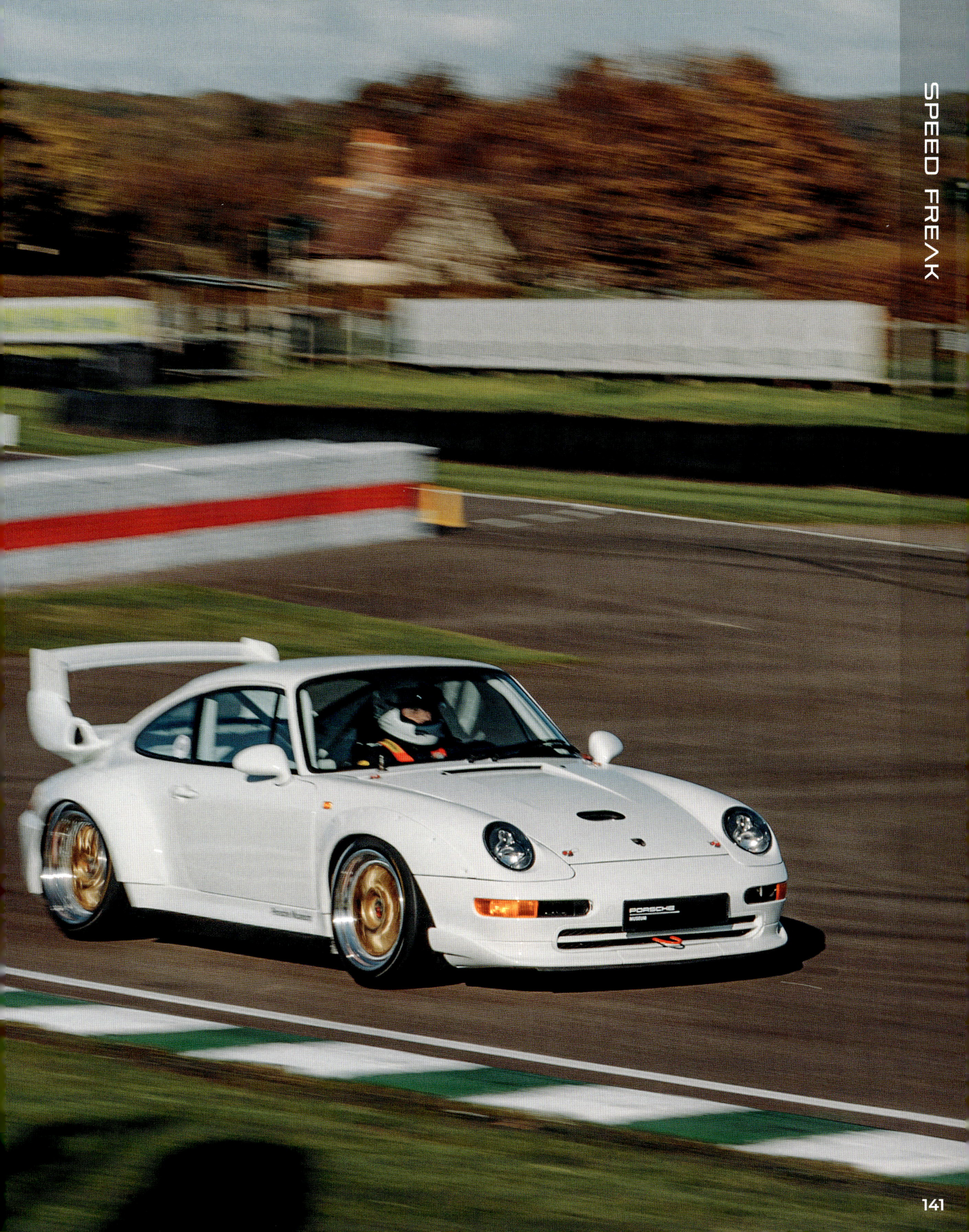
SPEED FREAK

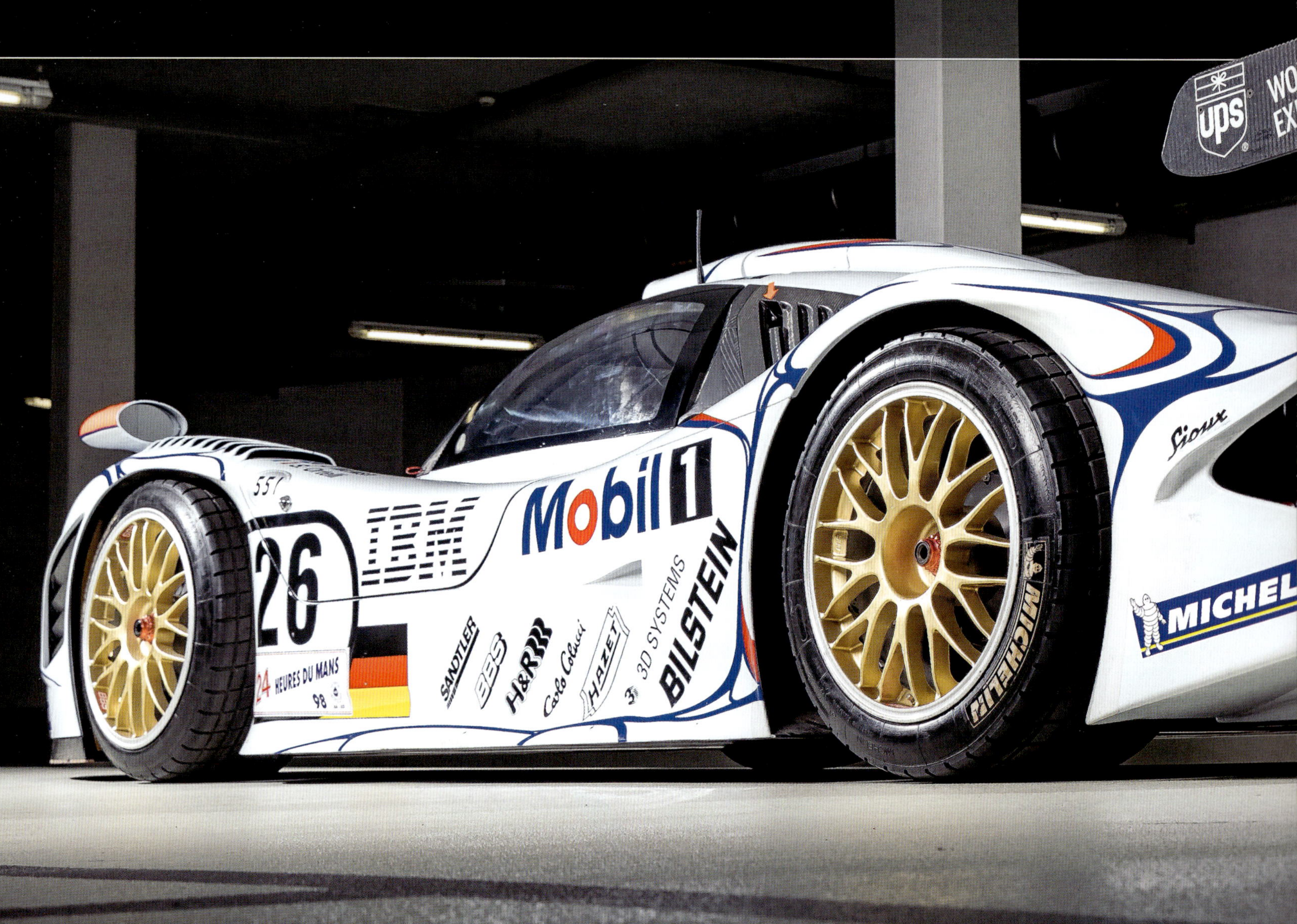
ULTIMATE
RACER

THE LEGENDARY PO

The 1990s proved a barren run for Porsche at Le Mans. That is until 1998, when the ultimate 911 incarnation returned Weissach to winning ways. Here is its story.





# GT1-98
(1998)

### ENGINE
**Capacity:** 3,198cc
**Compression ratio:** 9:0.1
**Maximum power:** 360bhp
**Maximum torque:** 630Nm @ 5,000rpm

### SUSPENSION
**Front:** Double wishbones; pushrods; telescopic dampers
**Rear:** Double wishbones; pushrods; telescopic dampers

### WHEELS & TYRES
**Front:** 11.5x19-inch; 27/67-19
**Rear:** 13x19-inch; 31/70-19

### DIMENSIONS
**Length:** 4,890mm
**Width:** 1,990mm
**Weight:** 940kg

### PERFORMANCE
**0-60mph:** Unknown
**Top speed:** Circa 217mph

**A**nyone with even a passing interest in Porsche's motorsport activities can't fail to be aware of its history at Le Mans, one that encompasses a record 20 outright victories. The most recent of those appearances on the winner's rostrum was in 2017 with the dominant 919 Hybrid, but two decades previously, the 1990s was a more barren affair at Le Mans for Porsche. The 15th win had been achieved in 1994 with the Dauer 962, a racer that was capable, but showing its age. It would take until 1998 to chalk up the 16th victory, and that would come courtesy of an entirely new, 911-derived design – the Porsche GT1.

The GT1 marked a number of firsts for Porsche, one of which was the use of a carbonfibre monocoque chassis, with the sections and panels constructed by English specialists, CTS. The new car was also 20 centimetres longer, five centimetres wider and three centimetres lower. The wheelbase had also grown slightly to 2.7 metres, the driver was relocated to the right-hand side, and as the road car-based, conventionally hinged doors of the older GT1s would no longer fit, the doors now hinged on the A-pillar, supercar-style. There was also a large, adjustable plastic rear wing, while the nose was noticeably lower, a development achieved by relocating the cooling radiators from the centre to the outer edges of the front end. In fact, the only recognizable elements from the Neunelfer were the 996-style headlights – Litronic units that had been enlarged and modified to incorporate the better lighting required for tackling the Mulsanne straight at night – and the tail lamps that had somehow been neatly incorporated above the massive rear diffuser.

Compared to what had gone before, the 1998 GT1 was a hugely impressive package, and Porsche had left no stone unturned when it came to meeting the challenges posed by the likes of Toyota and Nissan, not to mention arch-rival Mercedes-Benz with their mighty CLK-LM. There was an understandable sense of optimism within Weissach when it came to the new season, although it would initially prove to be a little misplaced. Except, that is, for the toughest and most famous race on the calendar. Resplendent in Mobil 1 livery, two cars were prepared for assault on the 1998 Le Mans: #25 was crewed by Jörg Müller, Uwe Alzen and Bob Wollek, while the #26 car was to be driven by the trio of Allan McNish, Laurent Aïello and Stéphane Ortelli. It's fair to say the omens weren't good, the GT1s having proved fast but a little fragile in previous outings, and at Le Mans it was Mercedes-Benz that took pole and 3rd positions on the grid, split by a Toyota GT-One. Porsche had to settle for 4th for #25 and 5th for #26.

Both cars spent time in the pits for minor repairs, and with 90 minutes of the race remaining it looked like Toyota would take the chequered flag. But it was struck by transmission failure, meaning the two Porsche spent the last hour in a one-two formation, and that's how it finished. The GT1 conquered Le Mans and delivered Porsche a fitting present on its 50th birthday. After 2,975 miles and 351 laps at an average speed of 123.9mph, the car of McNish, Aïello and Ortelli crossed the line in 1st place, bringing Porsche a historic 16th victory at the toughest race in the world. It was to be the swansong for the GT1, the remainder of the season garnering a 2nd-place finish by McNish and Yannick Dalmas at the Dijon 500km in July, and a clutch of 3rd places. But there is one final drama worth mentioning. In October 1998 the Petit Le Mans was held at the US circuit of Road Atlanta, and with Dalmas at the wheel the GT1 took off at high speed, completing a full somersault before landing back on its wheels and careering into the safety barriers. Although the car was badly damaged, the driver escaped without injury.



> **It may have adopted the 996.1's fried egg headlights and amber-lensed rear cluster, but in reality the mid-engined GT1 beared little resemblance to any road-based Porsche 911**

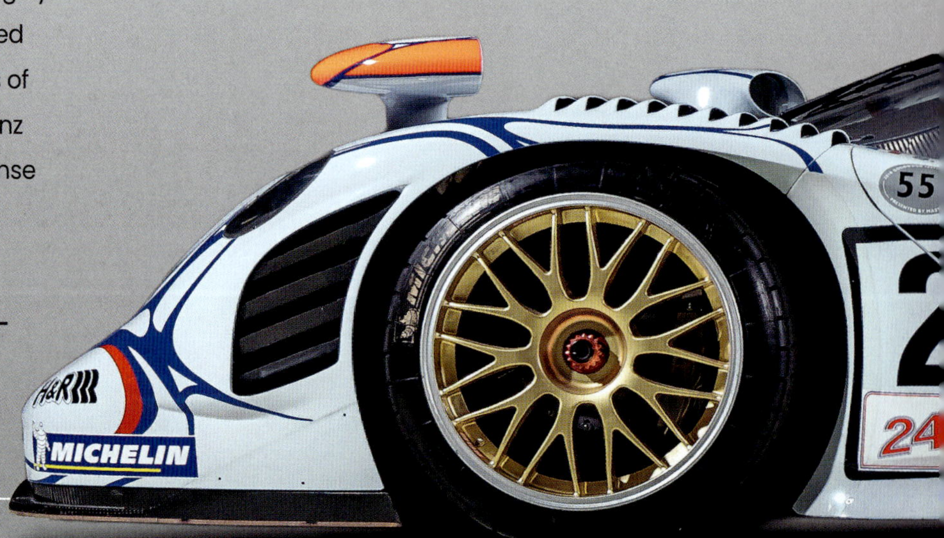

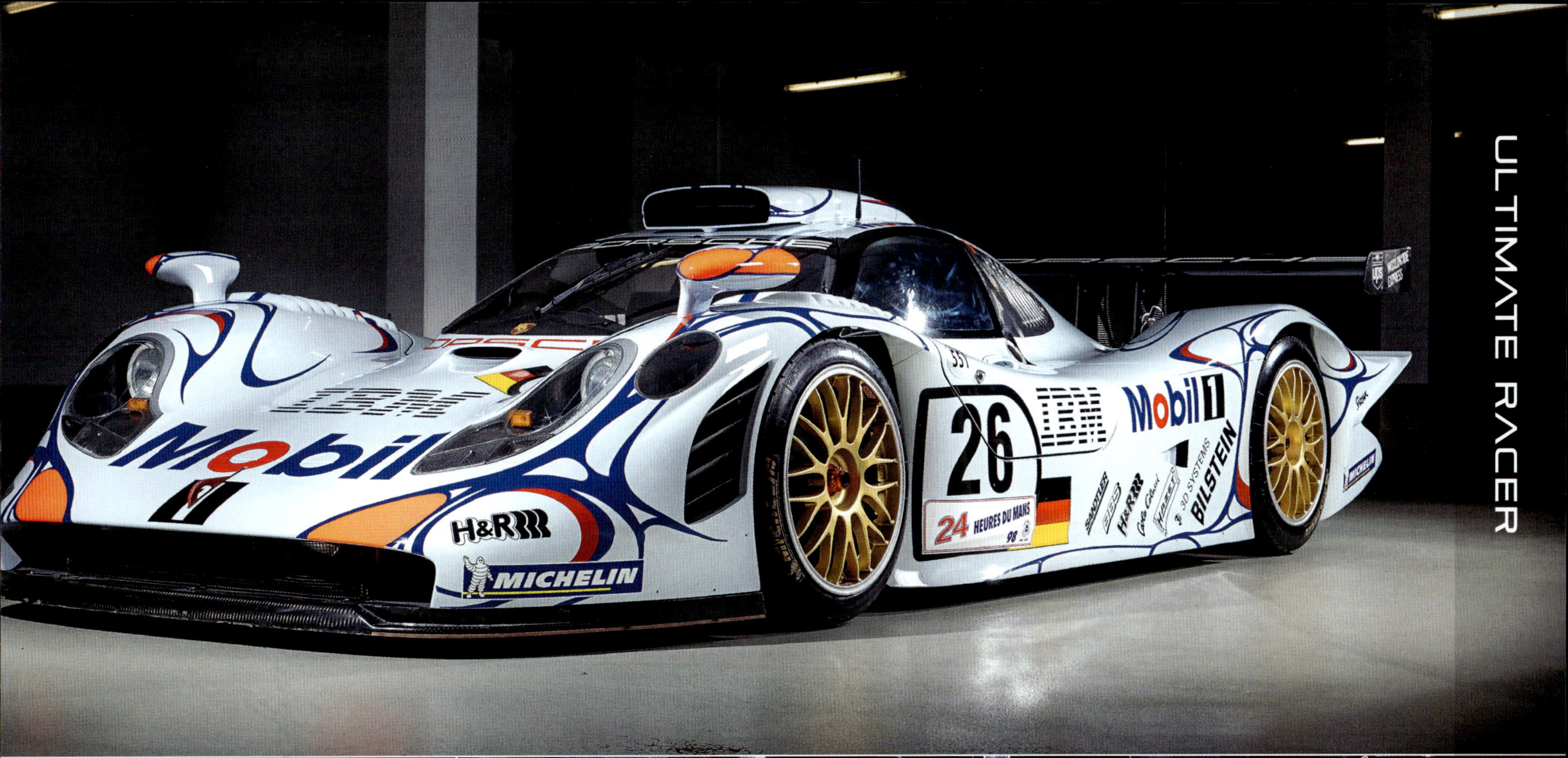

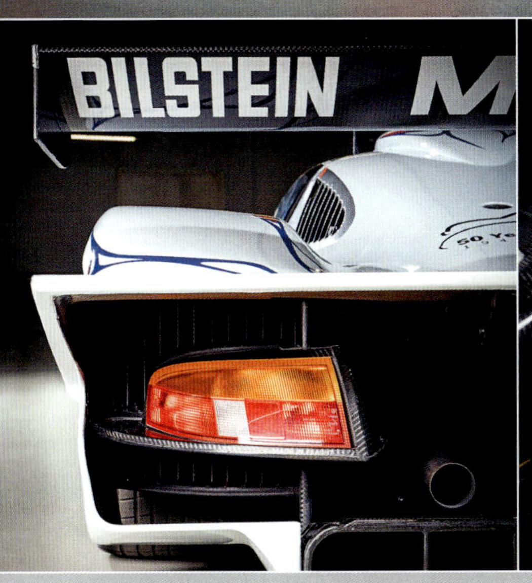

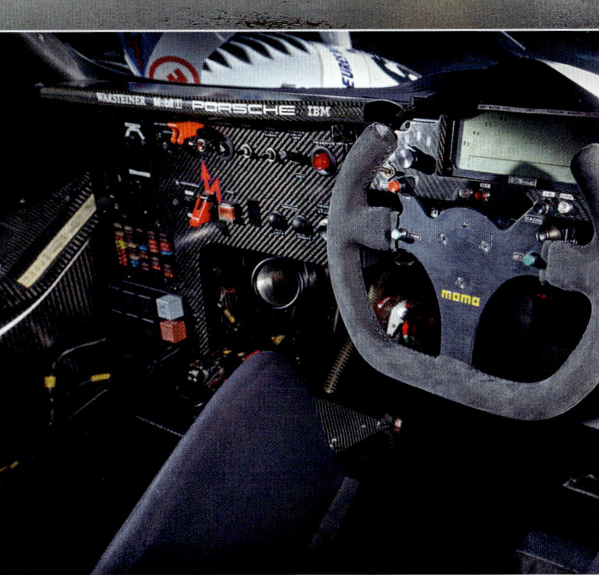

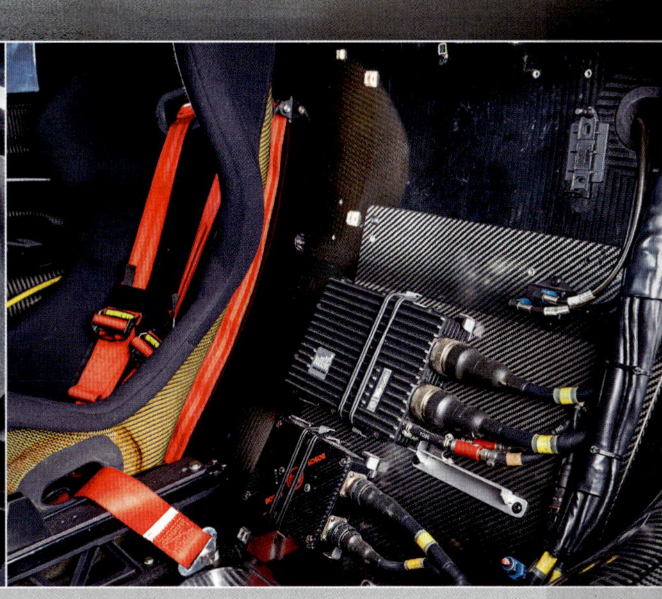

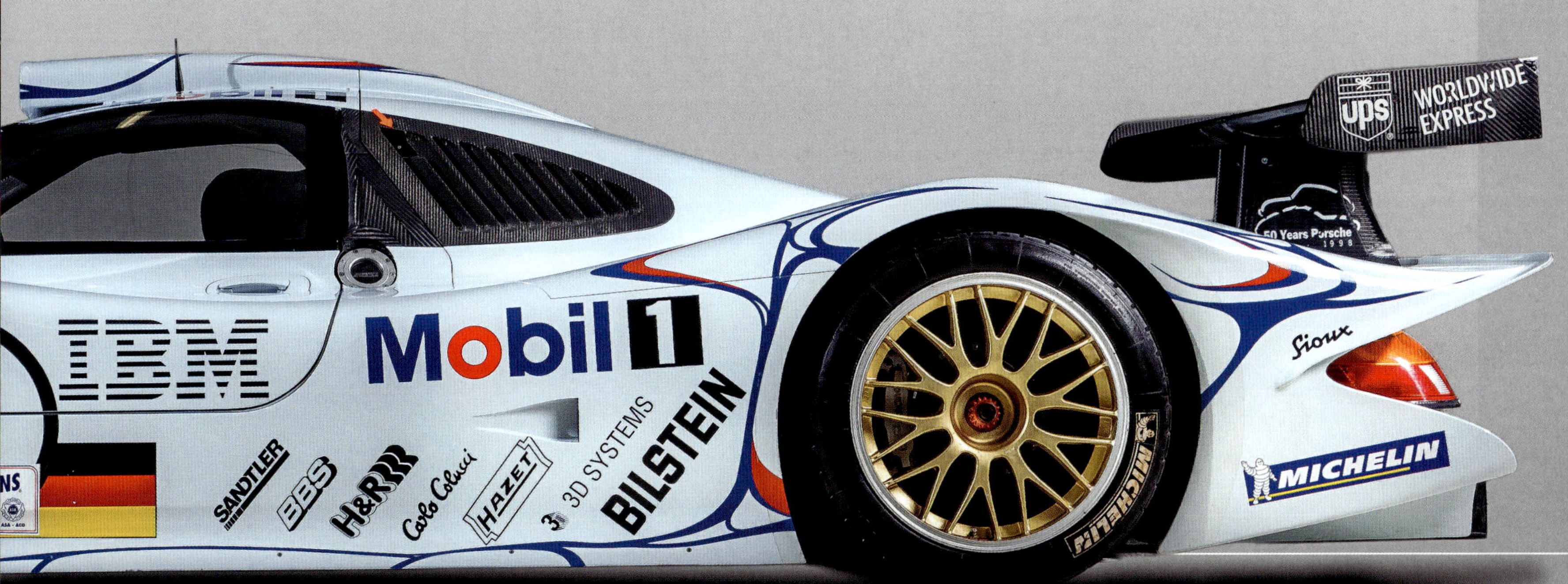

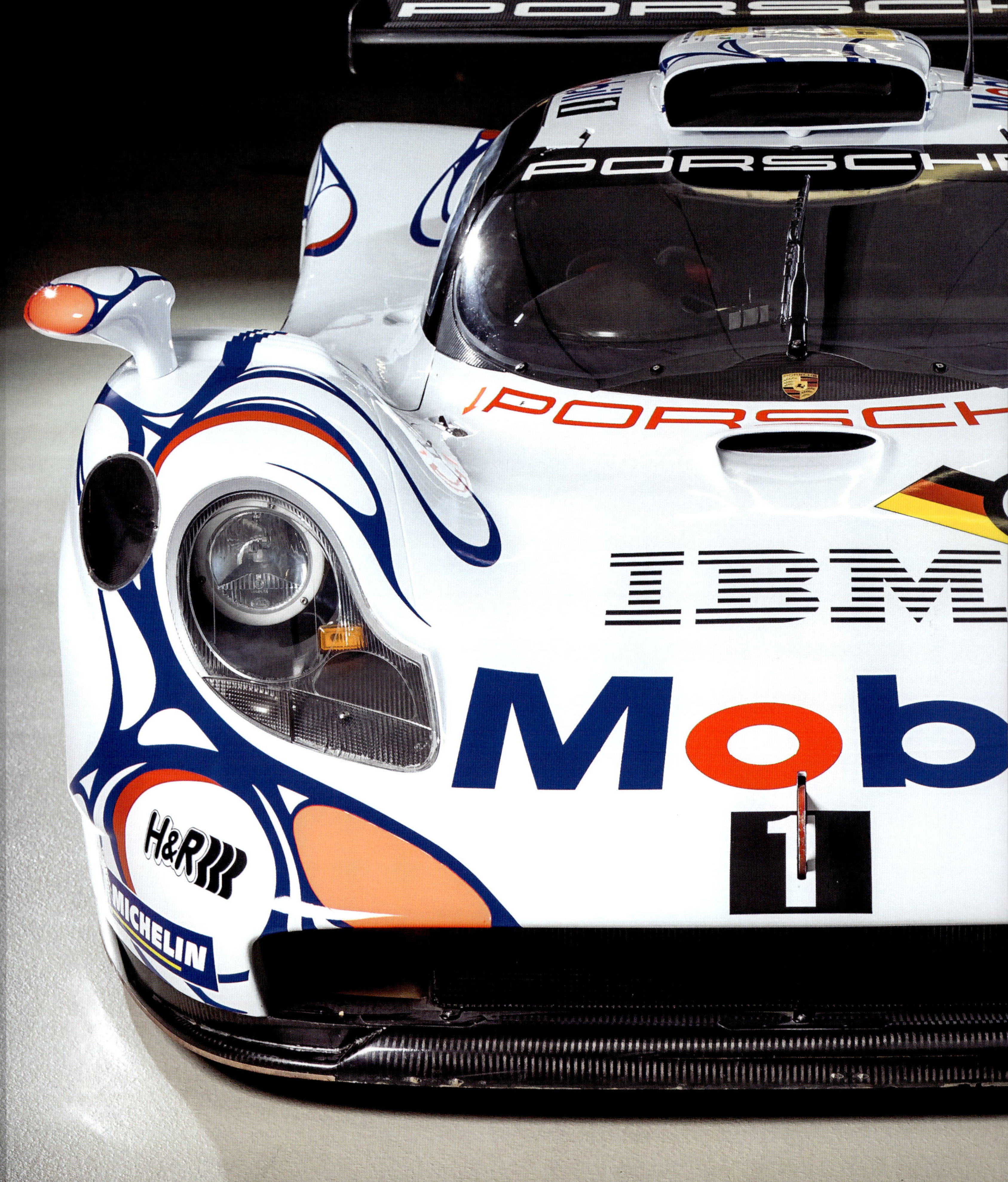

PORSCHE
PORSCHE
PORSCHE
IBM
Mobl
H&R
MICHELIN
1

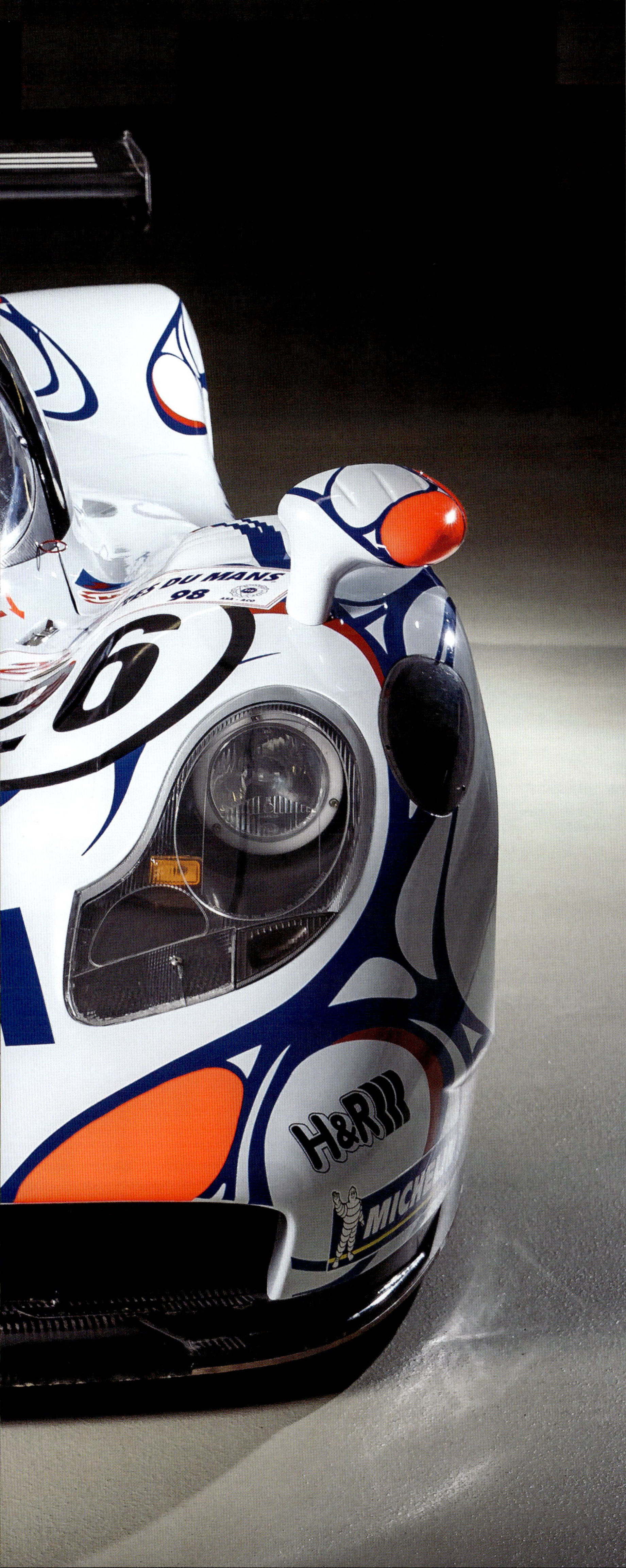

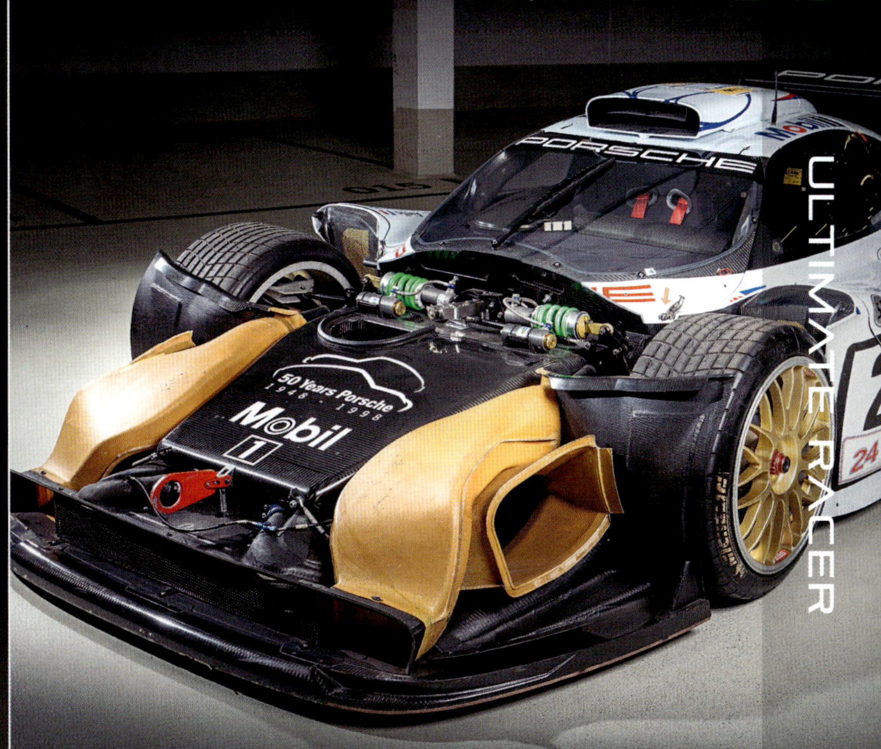

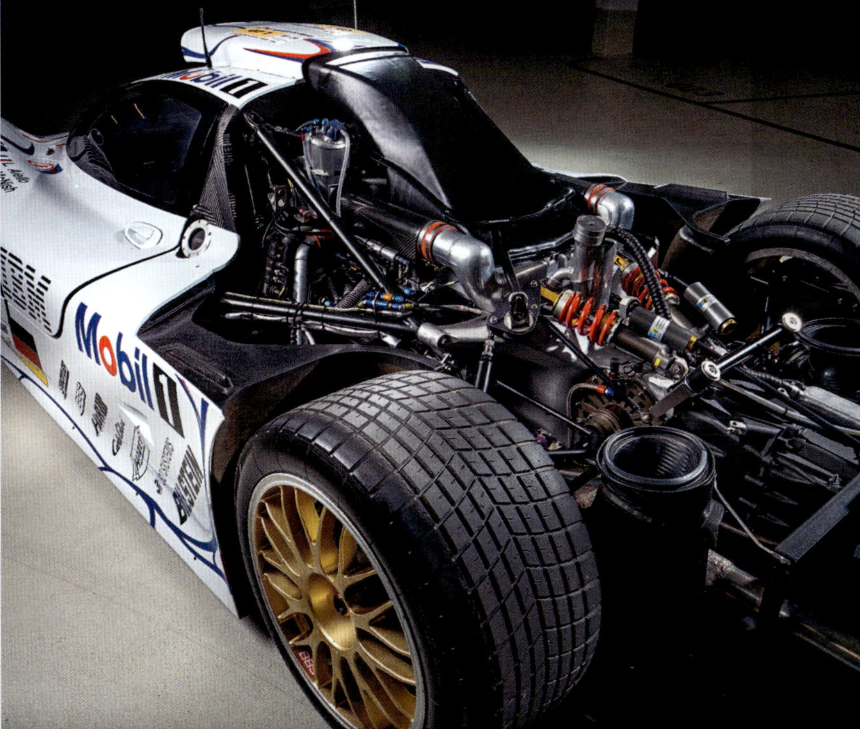

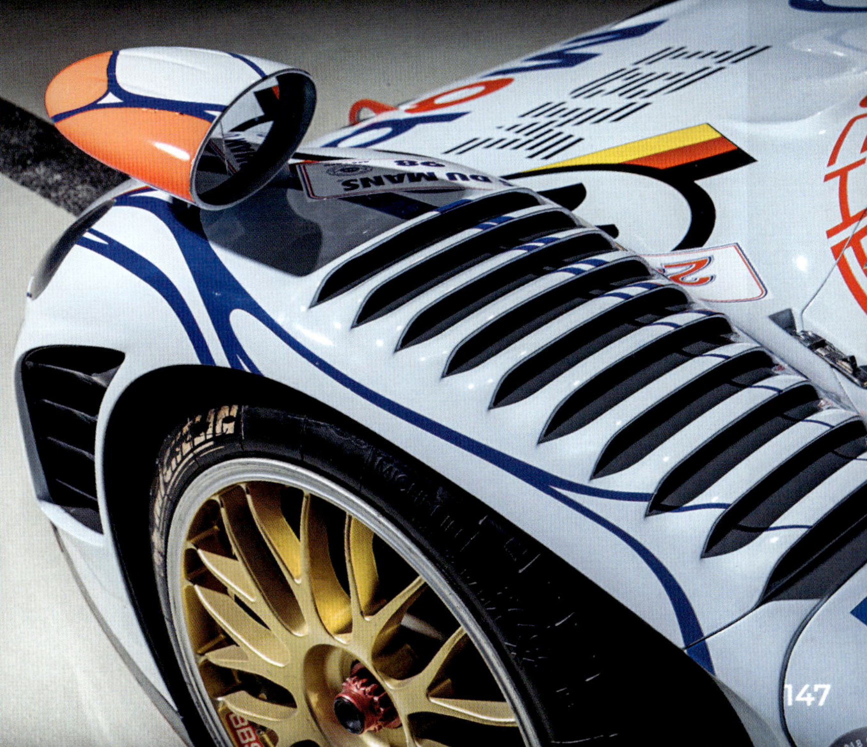

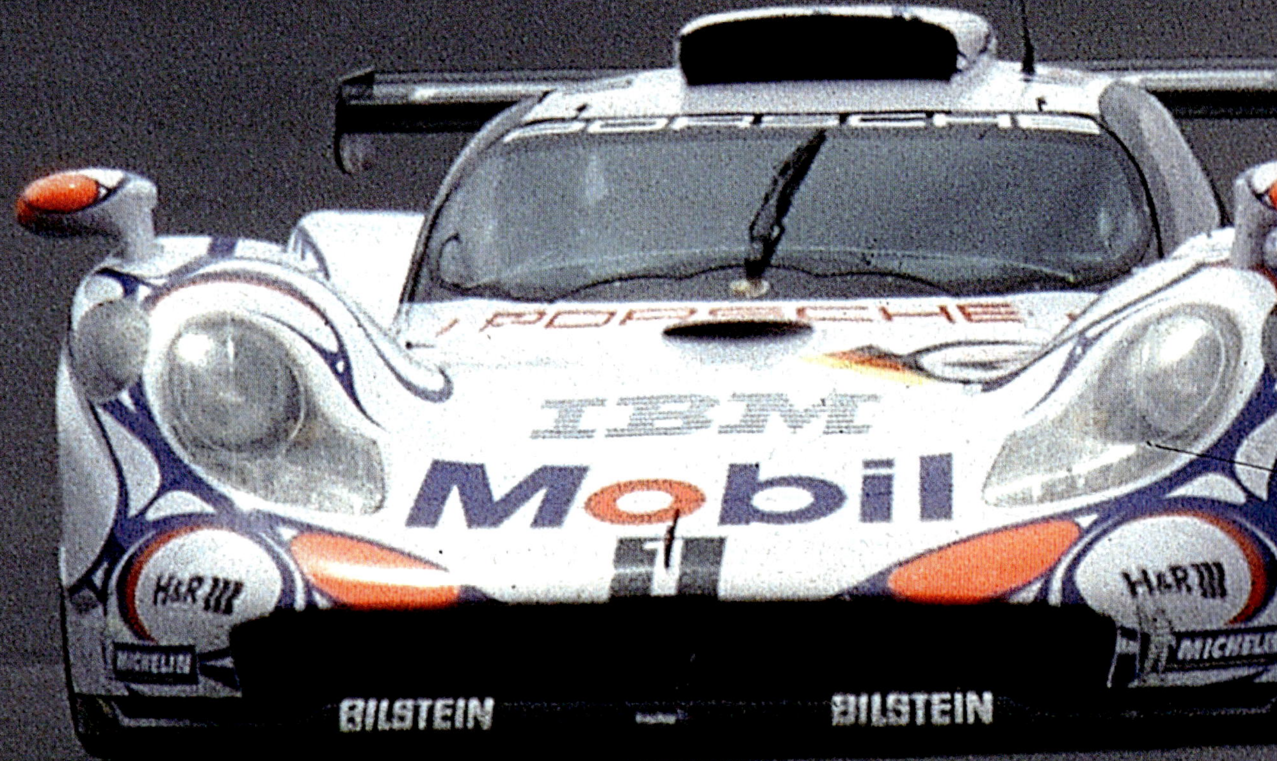

The no.26 car of Allan McNish, Laurent Aïello and Stéphane Ortelli spearheaded a Porsche one-two at Le Mans

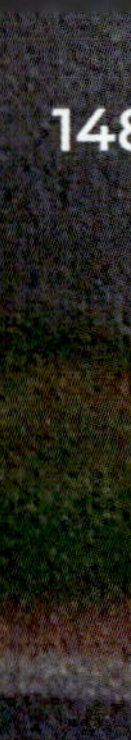



## THE GT1-98 WINNERS

Following his victory in 1998, Allan McNish went on to conquer Le Mans again with Audi a decade later. An unsuccessful stint in Formula One with the Toyota team began in 2001, but by 2013 he'd win at Le Mans again, as well as becoming the World Endurance champion.

He retired from full-time racing that year. Laurent Aïello switched to the British Touring Car Championship for 1999 – winning the title – and entered Le Mans with Audi the same year. After competing in the German DTM series he retired in 2005. Stéphane Ortelli enjoyed plenty more success with Porsche, winning the Supercup in 2002 as well as the GT World Championship N-GT Class in 2002 and 2003 in a 911 GTS RS. He was also successful in the Blancpain Endurance Series with Audi.

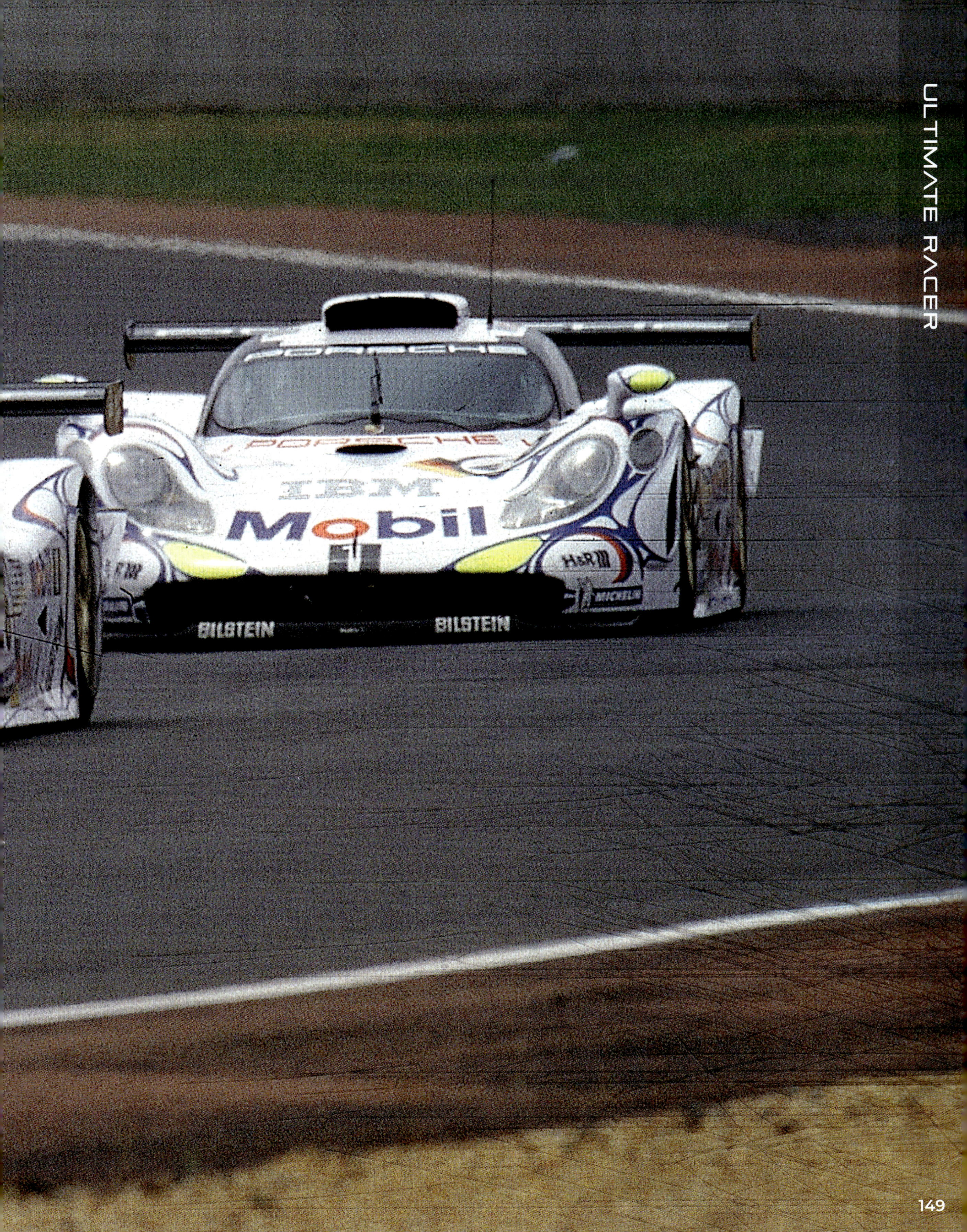

Mobil
IBM
H&R
MICHELIN
BILSTEIN
BILSTEIN

# PORSCHE
# AT THE RACES



The 911 was still in its infancy when Porsche first decided to test its racing mettle on the global stage. The decision to enter the company's new baby in the 1965 Monte Carlo Rally was a gamble, but the publicity the prestigious event offered was irresistible, and after a 2.0 Coupé in Ruby Red had been plucked from the production line in Stuttgart, the 911 was ready to make its competitive debut..

Driven by Herbert Linge and Peter Falk, the car set off from Bad Homburg near Frankfurt in January, battling snowstorms along the gruelling 2,500-mile journey through Germany, Holland, Belgium and finally France, and after four days on the road the Porsche pair registered a hugely encouraging fifth place in the overall classification.

It was only the first chapter in the 911's remarkable racing story. Three years after its Monte Carlo bow, a 911 T piloted by the British pairing of Vic Elford and David Stone held off the challenge of Renault Alpine to take the crown for Porsche for the first time, while the honours went to the 911 in 1969 and 1970 to complete a magnificent hat-trick in the Principality.

The inimitable sports car's stamina and speed was put to the test again in the 1980s. This time the revered and feared Paris–Dakar Rally was the proving ground and in 1984 the French duo of René Metge and Dominique Lemoyne famously took top spot on the podium behind the wheel of a 3.2 litre Carrera fitted with a new four-wheel drive system and a steel roll cage. Over 400

vehicles lined up for the start of the race on New Year's Day in the shadow of the Place de la Concorde in Paris, but almost three weeks later it was the 911 that was victorious in the Senegalese capital. Metge and Lemoyne repeated the trick two years later, with the legendary Jacky Ickx and Claude Brasseur completing a Porsche one-two in another 959.

The third leg of the unofficial Triple Crown of endurance racing along with the 24 Hours of Le Mans and Daytona, the 911 has enjoyed a long affair with the 12 Hours of Sebring. First held on a World War Two airfield in Florida in 1950, the 911 opened its Sebring account in 1973 when the American trio of Hurley Haywood, Peter Gregg and Dave Helmick dethroned the Ferrari 312 PB as champion car in a Carrera RSR.

The RSR returned to winning ways in 1976, clocking up 1,196 miles in the half-day of racing. The result was the start of an unprecedented period of 911 domination at Sebring with the car recording eight more consecutive overall triumphs. The sequence was brought to an end by a stablemate – a prototype 962 – in 1985 but of Porsche's record tally of 18 wins in Florida, 10 proudly belong to the 911.

**Need for speed (clockwise from top left): The 911 debuted at the world-famous Monte Carlo Rally in 1965; victory over 7,450 punishing miles in the 1984 Paris–Dakar Rally underlined the 911's pedigree; the RSR has claimed 10 crowns at the 12 Hours of Sebring in the USA.**

Porsches have registered more than 30,000 victories in motorsport since the 1950s, with the 911 taking the coveted chequered flag in some of the world's most celebrated races.

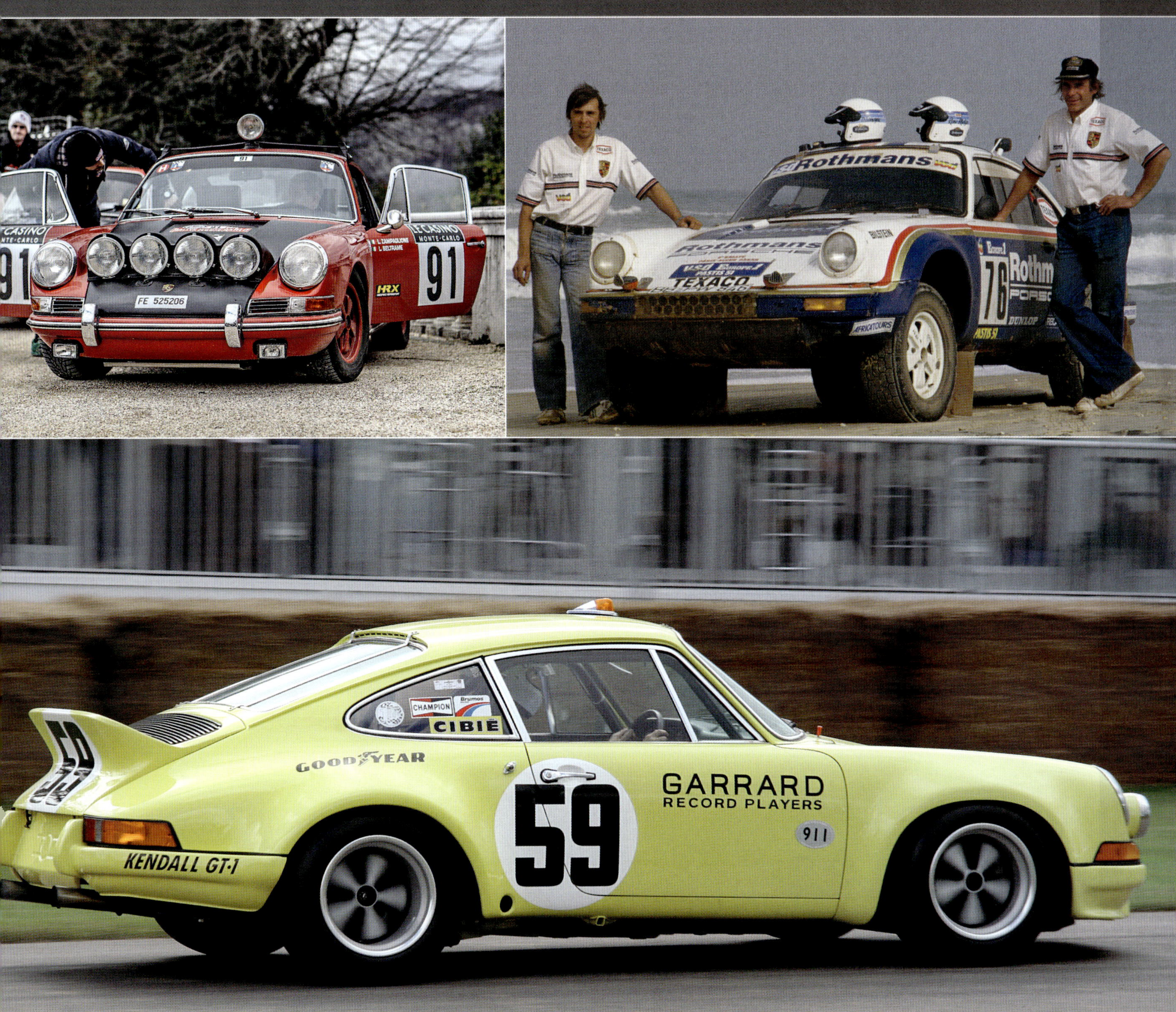

# MAGNIFICENT
# AT LE MANS

When the Automobile Club de l'Ouest staged the first edition of the 24 Hours of Le Mans back in 1923, Ferdinand Porsche was still eight years from founding the iconic company that would bear his family name. Porsche AG was born in the early 1930s, but it was not until 1951 that one of its cars finally took to the Circuit de la Sarthe in the shape of a 356 SL, which triumphed in its class.

Two years after it first went on sale, the 911 made its own Le Mans bow in 1966. The six-cylinder, 160bhp S model, driven by French duo Jacques Dewes and Jean Kerguen, finished 14th on debut but far greater things were to come from the 911.

The 1979 edition of the event garnered headlines worldwide before the race had even begun, the media frenzy created by the inclusion of Hollywood royalty Paul Newman in the Dick Harbour Racing line-up. They were driving Porsche 935s, but despite Newman's undisputed star quality, it was Kremer Racing team in their own 935s who ultimately stole the show.

In a race plagued by severe wet weather which significantly slowed the field, the Kremer trio of German Klaus Ludwig and American brothers Don and Bill Whittingham completed 306 gruelling laps of 8.5 miles over the 24 hours, seven more than Newman and his Kremer team-mates. Porsche registered a remarkable 1-2-3-4 finish in the overall final standings.

The 911 doubled up in 1998. This time Frenchman Laurent Aïello, Britain's Allan McNish and Monégasque Stéphane Ortelli were collectively behind the wheel of their upgraded GT1-98. On paper at least, Mercedes, BMW and Toyota had quicker cars on the starting line but fell victim to mechanical problems or collisions. That left Nissan and McLaren as the principal challengers, however, both struggled to match the 911's pace.

In the end, the Aïello–McNish–Ortelli combination was victorious by the narrowest of margins. They completed 351 laps in total, just one more than the second Porsche AG team in the same car.

Victory in 1998 proved a watershed for both Porsche and Le Mans. The result was the last time a road-legal car commanded top spot on the podium, while Porsche took a self-imposed sabbatical from the race after what was their 16th overall classification win. They were back in Le Mans action in 2014 and the following year returned with a team that included Formula One star Nico Hülkenberg. It was a triumphant return, the first of three successive victories, but their hat-trick of crowns came courtesy of a Porsche 919 Hybrid, underlining the modern era of petrol-electric engine domination of the event.

**French flair (clockwise from top left): Six 911s, including a Carrera RSR driven by Peter Gregg and Guy Chassueil, competed at Le Mans in 1973; the Automobile Club de l'Ouest first staged the iconic race in north west France in 1923; Porsche's famous win in 1998 was the last time a road-legal car triumphed in the marquee event.**

Motorsport's oldest endurance race, the annual
24-hour event in north west France has twice
witnessed 911s join the pantheon of Porsche greats
to lift the coveted winner's trophy.

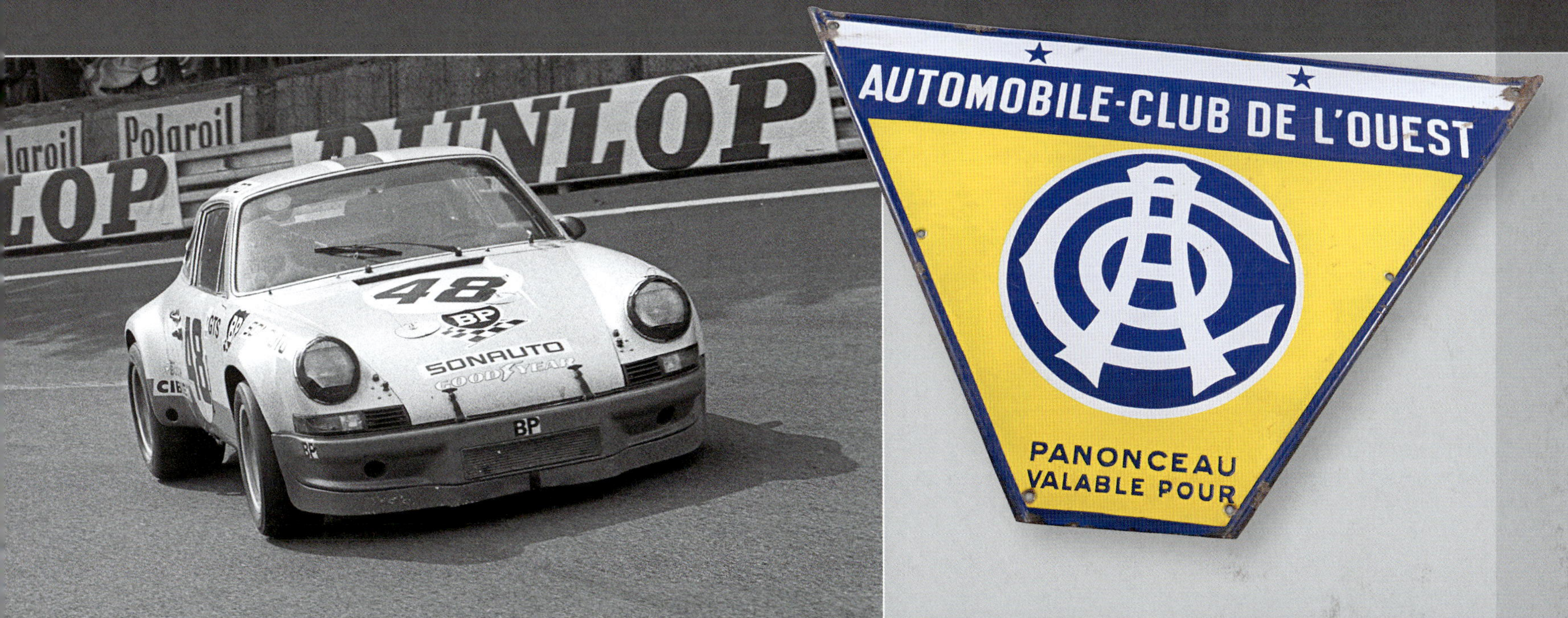

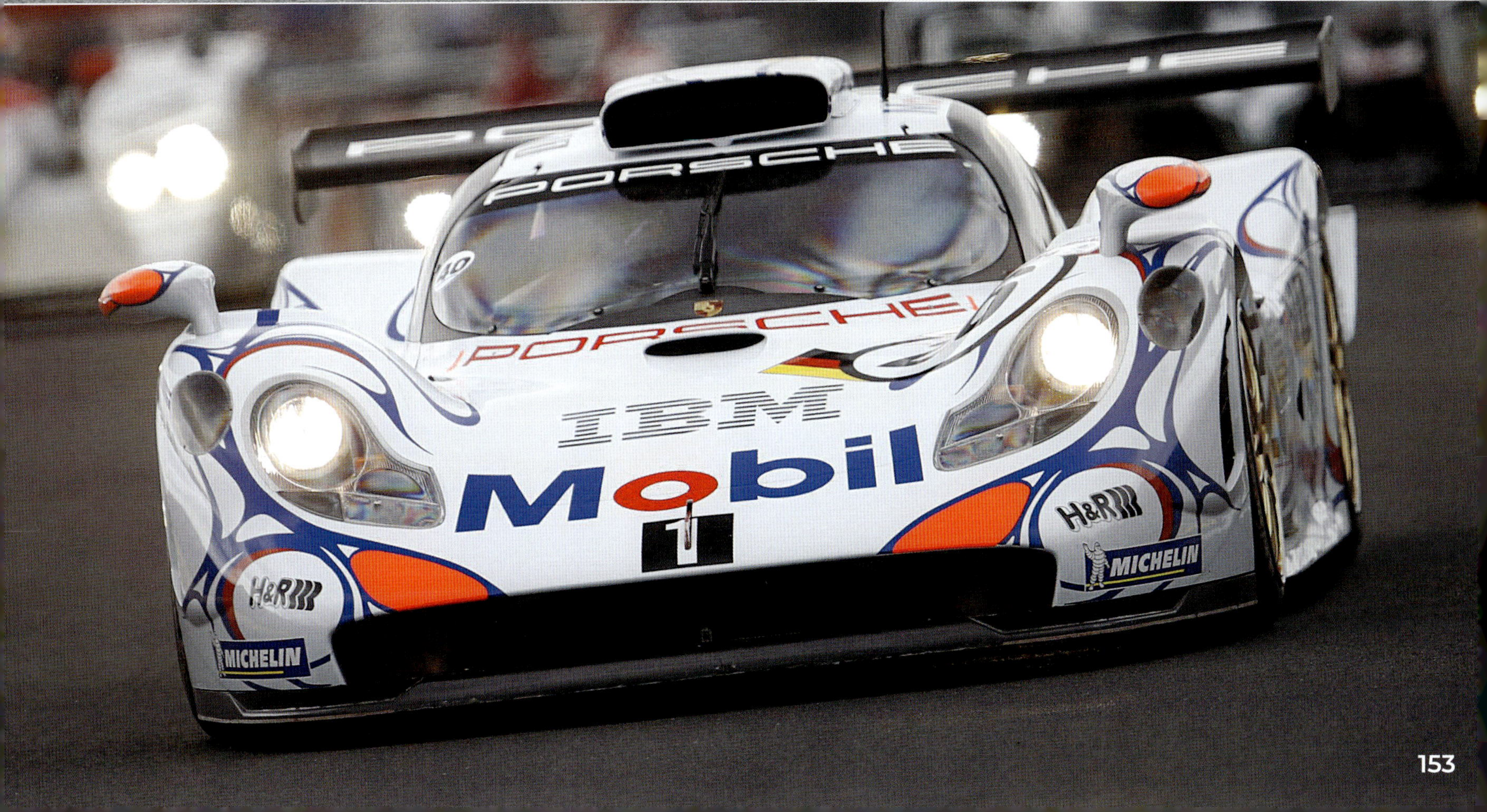

# KING OF DAYTONA



Striking in its contrasting black and white livery, Jack Ryan's 'No.18' 911 now sits in glorious retirement at the Revs Institute. The Florida museum in the city of Naples is home to over a hundred classic cars, but few on display are as iconic as the first ever 911 to tackle the precipitous banked walls and full-throttle straights of the Daytona International Speedway back in 1966.

A Volkswagen dealer from Atlanta, Ryan bought his first generation 911 with 30,000 miles already on the clock and despite its modest 130bhp, he decided to enter it for the fifth edition of the Daytona. Against the odds, his No.18 claimed victory in the GT Class and, in the process, gave the 911 its maiden triumph in a major international motorsport event. It was also the beginning of the 911's love affair with America's marquee endurance race.

Porsche's first overall win at Daytona came in 1968 when a right-hand drive 907 proved its stamina, clocking up more than 2,500 miles en route to the honours, but in 1973 the Brumos Racing team began an extended and unprecedented period of dominance for the 911, when their Carrera RSR outlasted the competition. The international oil crisis denied the team the chance to defend their crown in 1974, but the following year Brumos and the Carrera returned to Florida to register a second triumph.

From 1977 to 1983, the Carrera and then the 935 recorded a remarkable seven wins in succession. There was a third win for Brumos in 1978, this time with a 935, while the Ecurie Escargot, Interscope, L&M Joest, Garretson, JLP and Henn's Swap Shop teams also sent out victorious 911s, leaving the assorted Ferraris, Lancias and BMWs trailing in their rear-engined wake.

Porsche's success in Florida continued through the '80s, but it came in the shape of various high-powered prototypes rather than production models, an approach emulated by the other manufacturers. However, on the 20th anniversary of the Henn's team victory in 1983, the 911 roared back onto the top of the podium. Entered by The Racer's Group and driven by the German-American quartet of Kevin Buckler, Michael Schrom, Jörg Bergmeister and Timo Bernhard, the 996 GT3 RS powered through 695 laps of the 3.56 mile circuit – nine more than the second-placed Ferrari 360 Modena GT.

To date that 2003 triumph is the 911's most recent victory. A Porsche 963 prototype proved its staying power in 2025 to take Porsche's overall number of victories at Daytona to a record-extending 20 titles – 10 clear of nearest challenger, the US-based Riley Technologies – and of those 20 successes, half proudly belong to the irrepressible 911. No car has even come close to rivalling its spectacular pre-eminence of the 1970s and early '80s and the 911's magnificent roll call of nine triumphs in 11 all-conquering years.

**Stateside stamina (clockwise from top left): The Porsche 907 was the car to beat in Florida in 1968; the 996 GT3 RS relegated the Ferrari 360 Modena GT into second place in 1983; in 2003 overall victory and victory in the GT class went to the No. 66 Porsche 996 GT3 RS from The Racer's Group.**

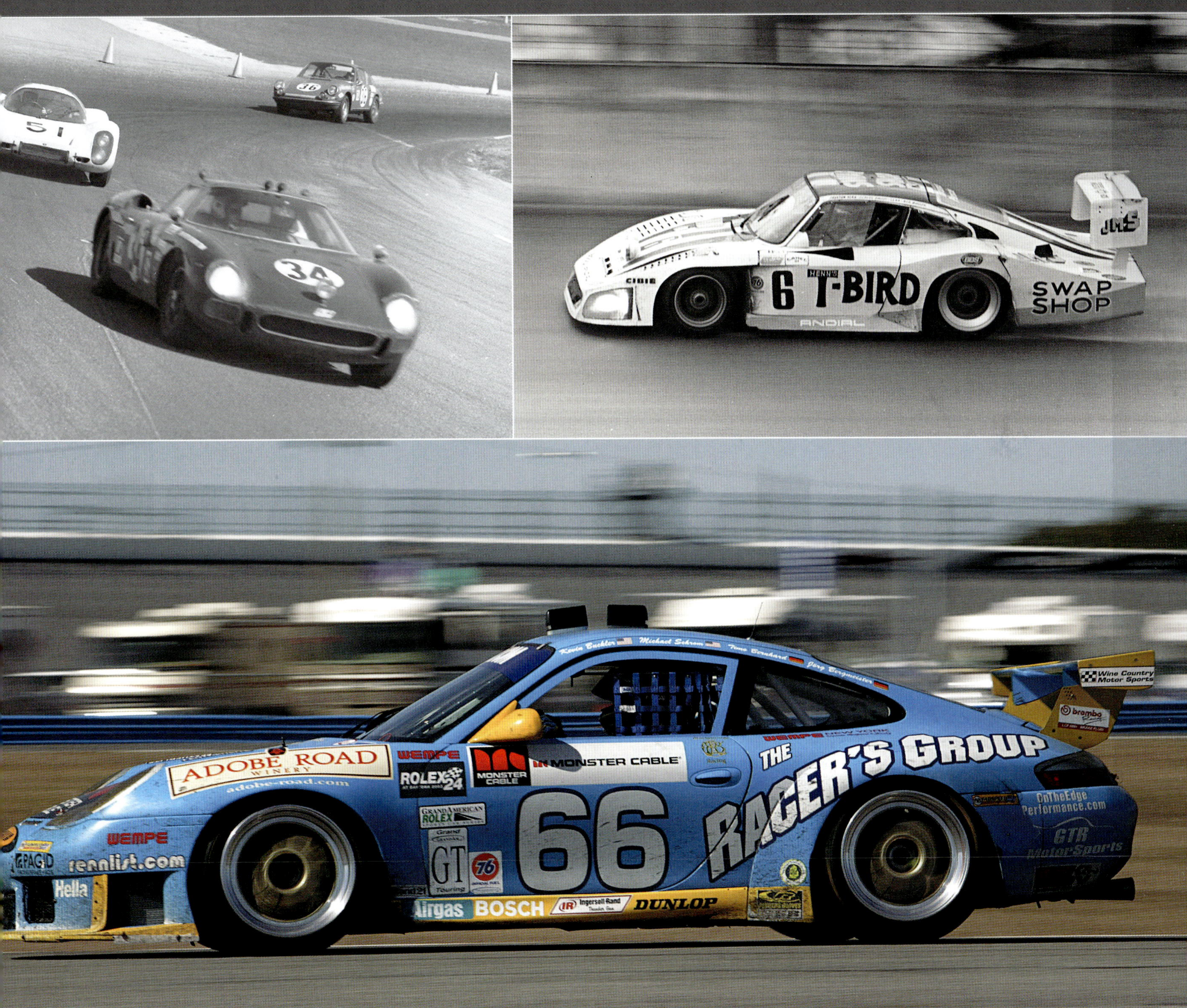

The most successful car in the history of the 24 Hours of Daytona, the 911 reigned supreme on the revered Florida circuit during the 1970s and '80s.

# THE FLORIO
# FAIRY TAIL



**B**y the time the trio of 911s lined up for the start of the 57th edition of the Targa Florio, staged high up in the frequently perilous Madonie Mountains on the island of Sicily, Porsche had already secured 10 titles in the prestigious event since the inaugural 1906 race. A 911, however, had never taken the chequered flag in Italy and faced with new FIA regulations, which precluded the racing prototypes that had distinguished themselves in the past, Porsche was forced to reluctantly press their production 911 RSR into service.

By the time the trio of 911s lined up for the start of the 57th edition of the Targa Florio, staged high up in the frequently perilous Madonie Mountains on the island of Sicily, Porsche had already secured 10 titles in the prestigious event since the inaugural 1906 race. A 911, however, had never taken the chequered flag in Italy and faced with new FIA regulations, which precluded the racing prototypes that had distinguished themselves in the past, Porsche was forced to reluctantly press their production 911 RSR into service.

Few gave the three 911s a prayer against a field which was bursting with bespoke one-offs from the likes of Alfa Romeo and Ferrari that significantly outclassed the Porsches in terms of aerodynamics, power and pedigree. With 300bhp and a specially fabricated plastic ducktail spoiler, the RSRs were quick, but with the cream of the competition enjoying at least 130bhp more, it should not have been a fight, fair or otherwise. Running some three minutes slower in practice than 1972 winner, Arturo Merzario in a Ferrari 312 PB, only underlined Porsche's underdog tag.

Staged over 11 laps of the Piccolo delle Madonie circuit, an undulating 45-mile course with at a conservative estimate 600 corners in total and over 1,000 metres in changes in elevation, the race began with the cars released at 20 seconds intervals. Co-piloted by Swiss Herbert Müller and Dutchman Gijs van Lennep, the best of the 911s began surprisingly brightly and luck was certainly on their side when Merzario's car suffered a puncture on the opening lap and later a broken driveshaft and was forced to retire.

Another of the fancied Ferraris and two of the Alfas also failed to finish and Müller and Van Lennep took full advantage of their rivals' various misfortunes, coming home more than six minutes ahead of the second-placed Lancia Stratos. The podium was completed by another of the RSRs driven by Leo Kinnunen and Claude Haldi, also under the Martini Racing banner, and the Targa Florio belonged to the 911s.

Victory was historic for two reasons. Although a number of Porsche's previous winners had some 911 DNA in them, 1973 was the first and only year a true 911 was triumphant. It was also a milestone result given it was the last time the race was part of the FIA-sanctioned World Sports car Championship, the sport's governing body withdrawing its seal of approval for the event due to ongoing safety concerns.

**Against the odds (far left): Gijs van Lennep and Herbert Müller became motorsport legends after their 1973 Targa triumph; (far right) the duo's Carrera RSR finished six minutes clear of the field.**

"Win a big race in a car that looks like a road car and it's good
PR," said Van Lennep in 2023, reflecting on one of the 911's most
famous if unlikely successes. "The locals liked to have an Italian
car winning, of course, but they were pleased for us. If you
win the last Targa Florio – and I have been five or six times to
Sicily in the last 50 years – you are a hero there. Even today if
you stop in a town square to have something to eat and drink
somebody will recognise you. In no time at all 200 people will
come from everywhere. You can win Le Mans – I did twice – but
if you win the Targa Florio, especially the last one, for me it is the
better achievement."

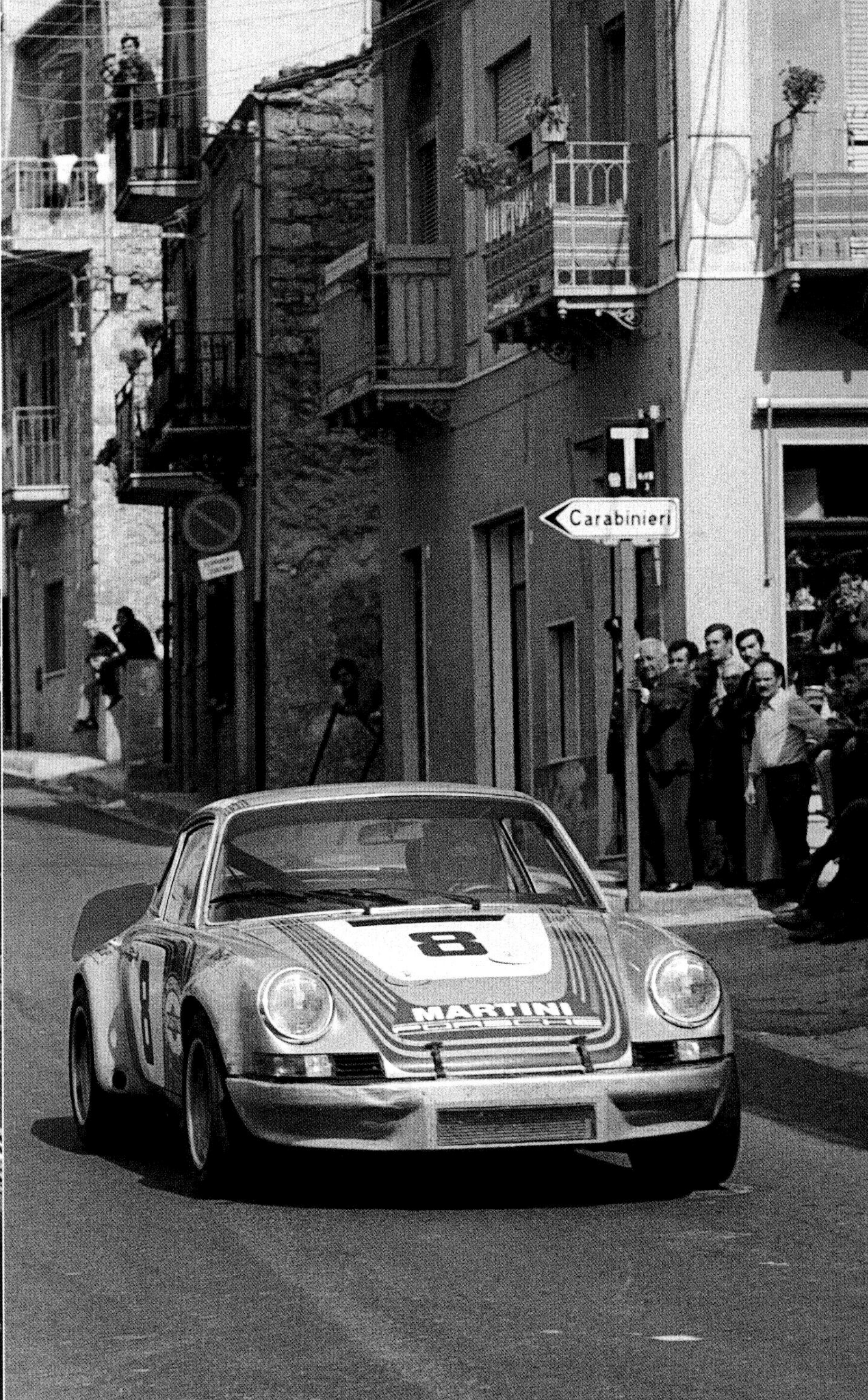

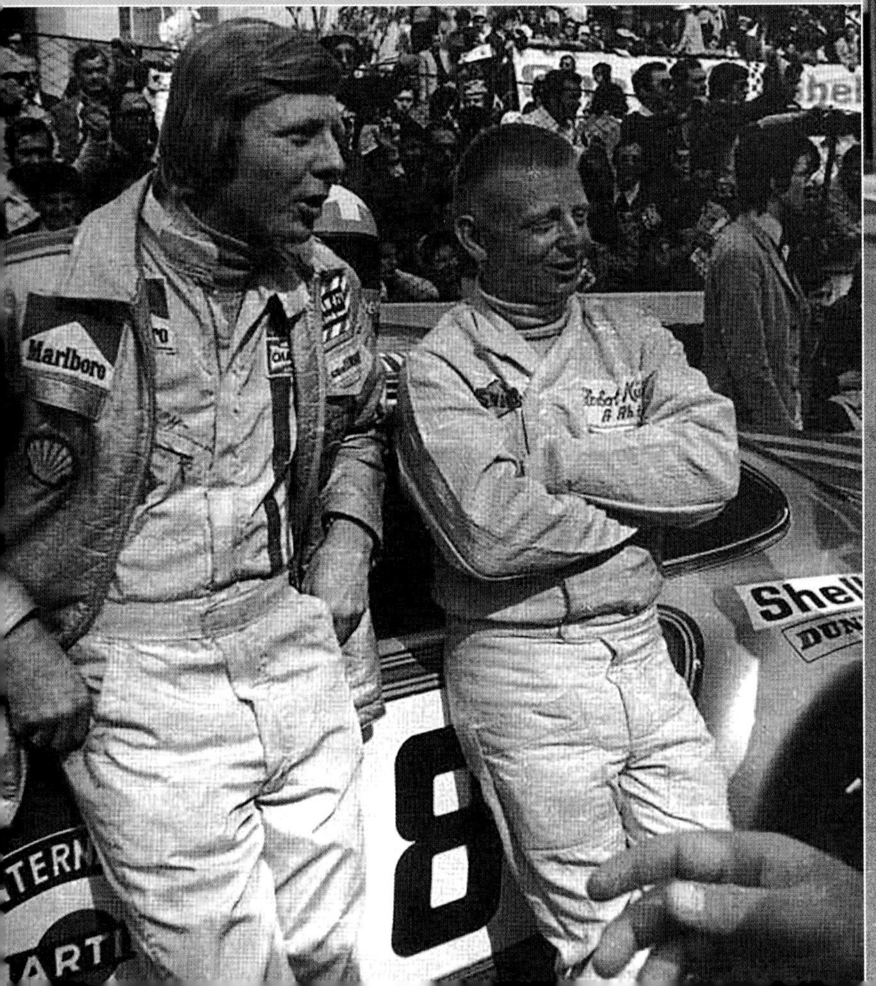

# MODIFIED
# RENNSPORTS



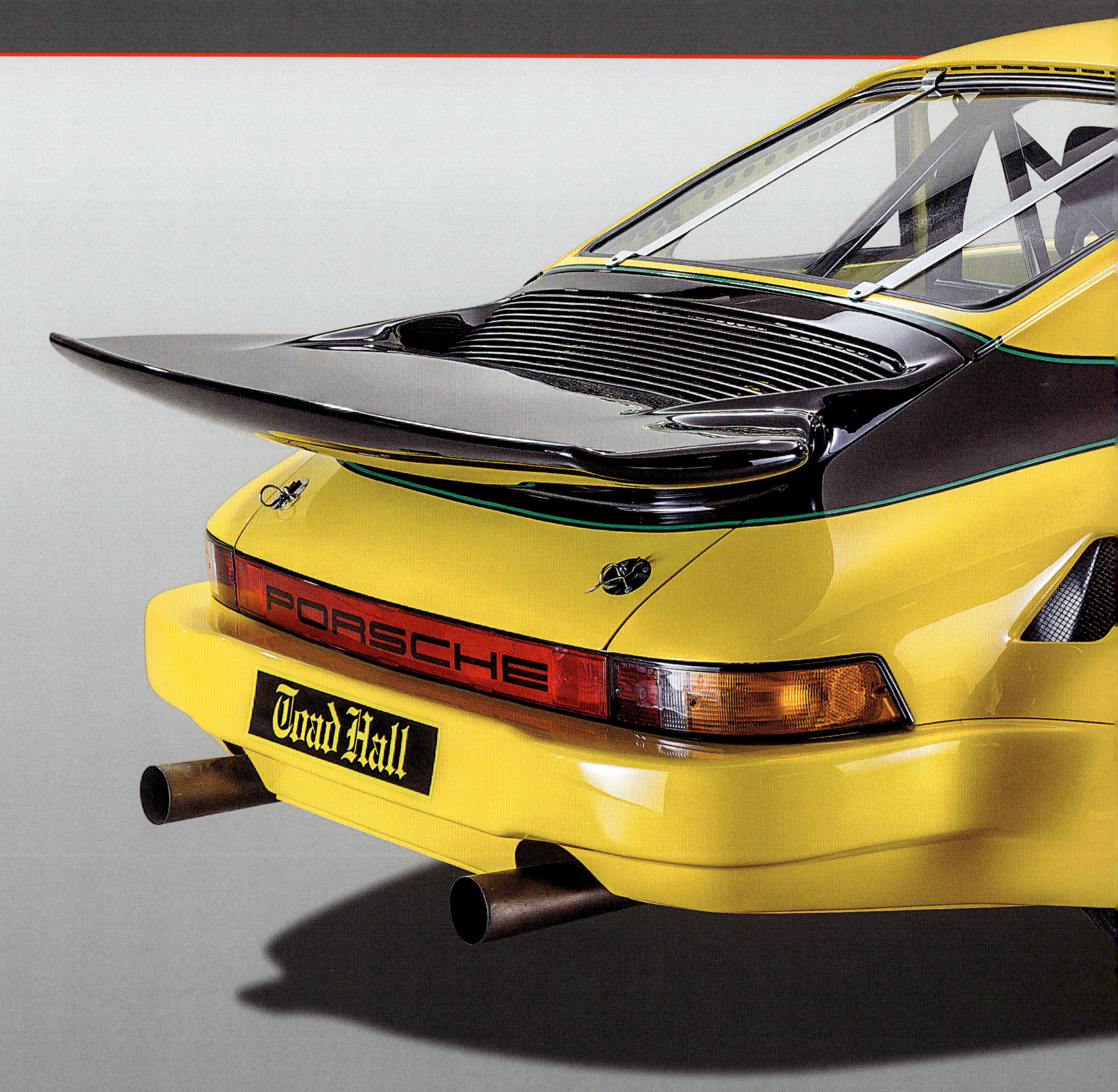

**Porsche's storied Rennsport programme is the stuff of automotive legend.**

A moniker conceived to take the company racing, it's since created a 60-year legacy of triumph on the world's most challenging stages. Victory on the race track has long bred success in the showroom too, and Porsche has no shortage of enthusiasts keen to indulge in the prowess of Weissach's race-bred engineering for their own 911, which comes courtesy of the company's acclaimed GT programme. The pinnacle for the road is the GT3 RS, best surmised as as damned near to a race car with licence plates as you can get. Above the GT3 RS there's the track-only 911 RSR, sitting at the top of the Porsche performance pyramid. Now read on and be amazed.

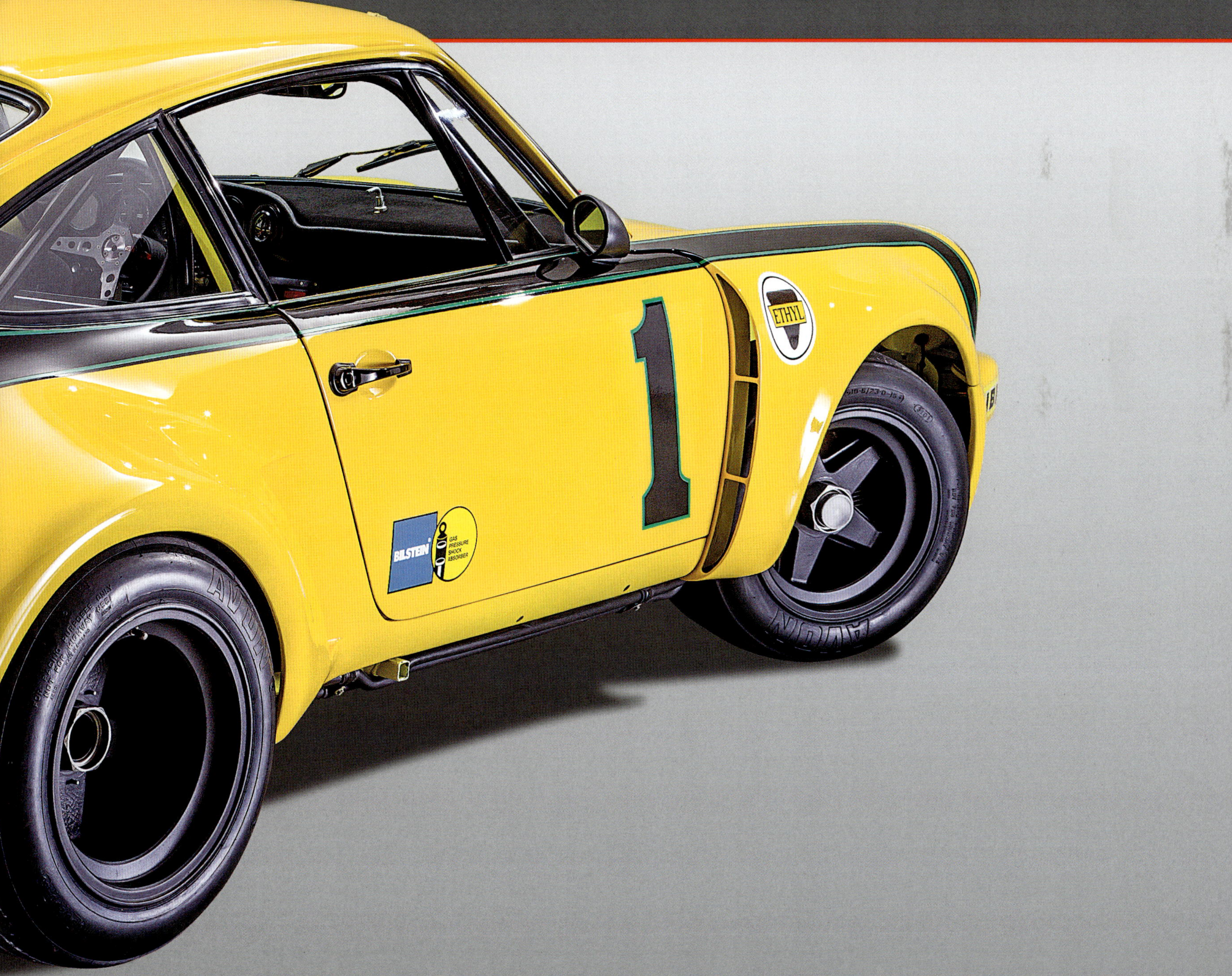

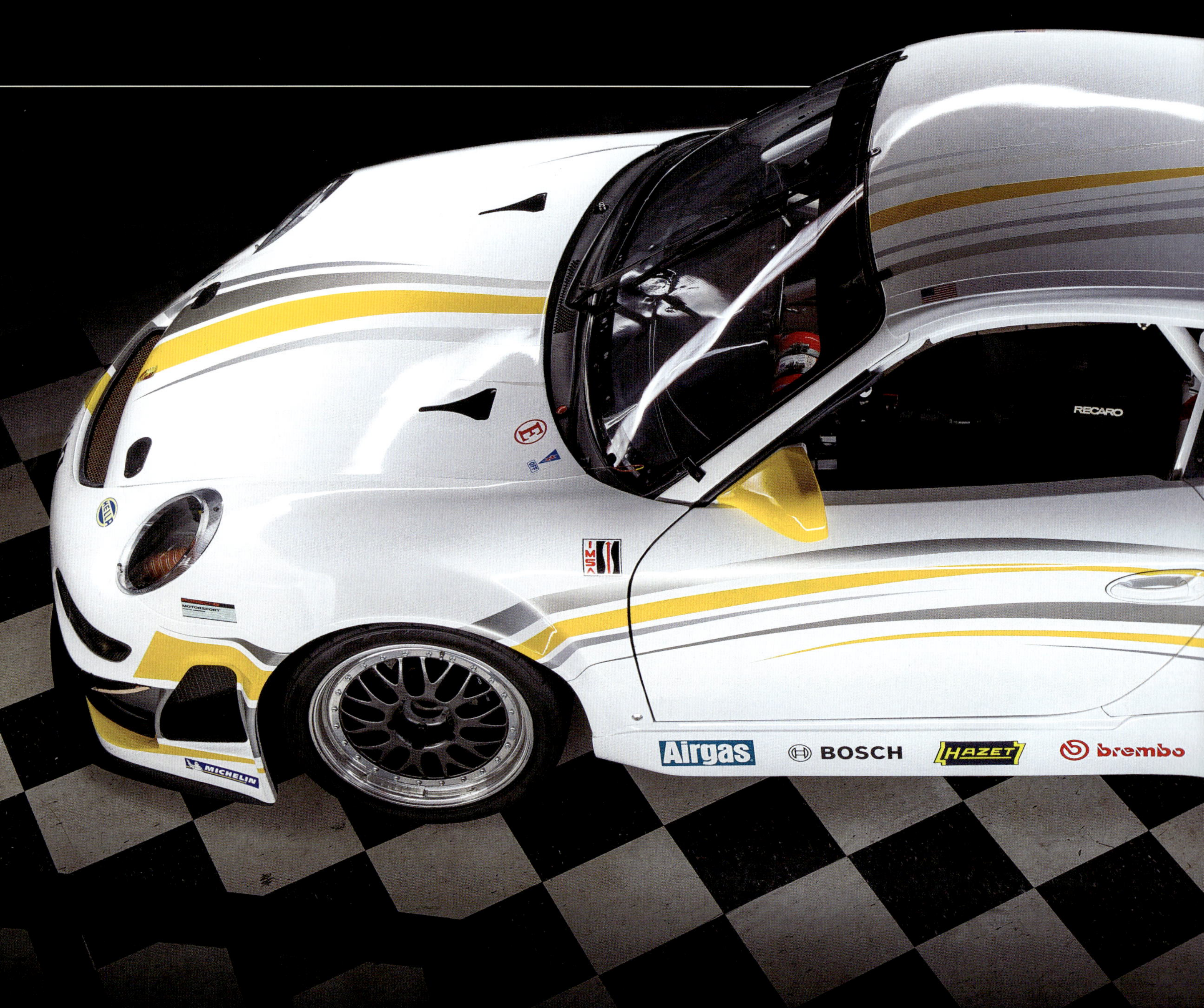

CARRERA
TO RSR
THE LEGENDARY PORSCHE 911

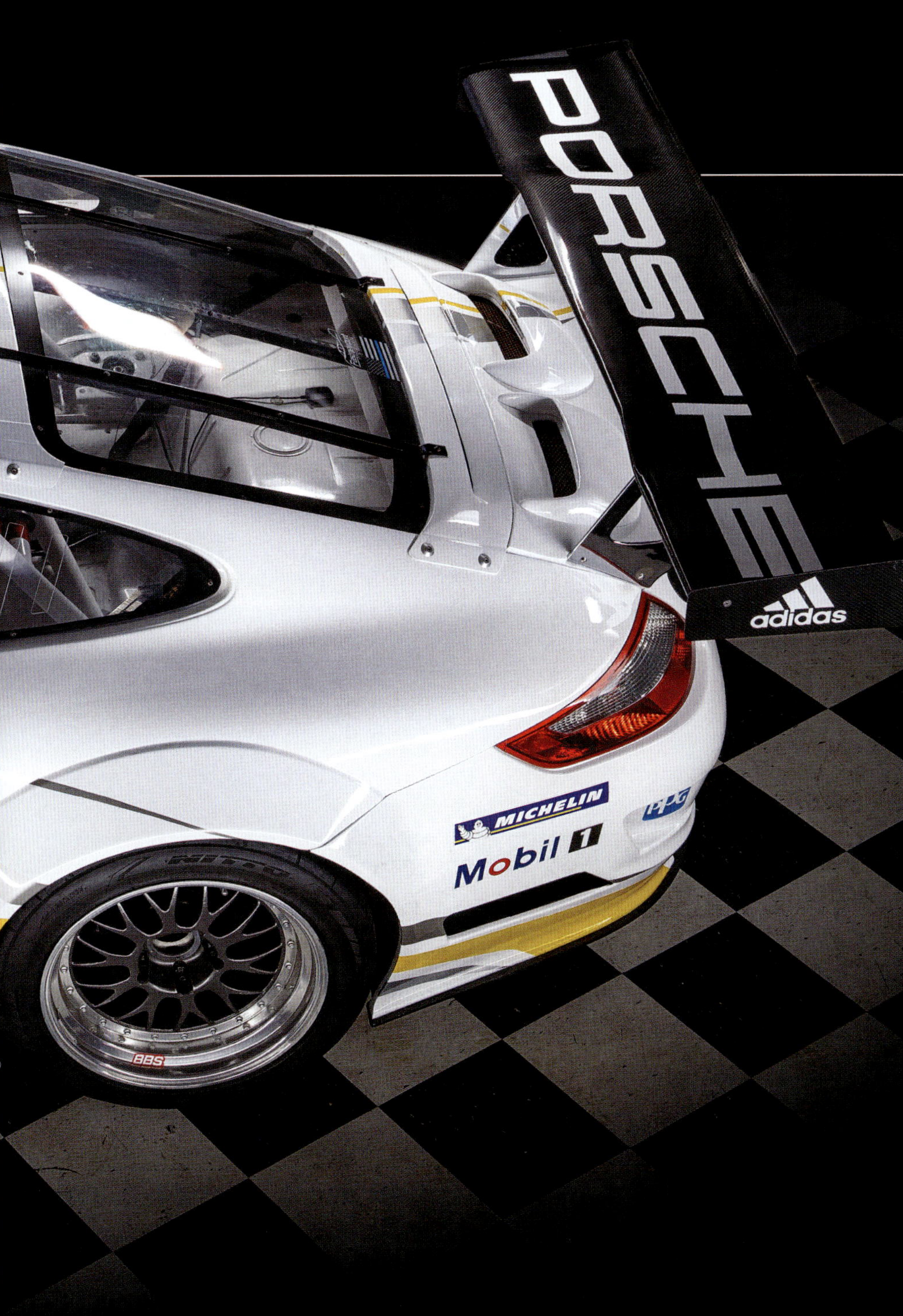


A GT3 RSR is the pinnacle of 997 performance, reserved exclusively for the race track – or is it?



# 996.1 CARRERA CABRIOLET TO 997 GT3 RSR

(2000)

### ENGINE

**Capacity:** 3,600cc

**Compression ratio:** 11:3.1

**Maximum power:** 320bhp @ 6,100rpm

**Maximum torque:** 340Nm @ 5,250rpm

**Transmission:** Six-speed manual

### SUSPENSION

**Front:** Independent, MacPherson strut; anti-roll bar

**Rear:** Independent, Multi-link; anti-roll bar

### WHEELS & TYRES

**Front:** 8x18-inch Cup 2; 225/40/ZR18

**Rear:** 10x18-inch Cup 2; 285/30/ZR18

### DIMENSIONS

**Length:** 4,245mm

**Width:** 1,795mm

**Weight:** 1,232kg

### PERFORMANCE

**0-60mph:** Not tested

**Top speed:** Not tested

**W**hat does it take to make a road-legal RSR? This Carrera project reveals all. Superior to other Porsche race cars such as Cup and GT3 R 911s, an RSR is a top-level racer, driven by the best on world-class stages in the leading GT class. As such they are far removed from the aspirations of the everyday enthusiast. That is, unless your name is Mark Cilani. His admiration for the ultimate 911 has led him to the purchase of his very own 997 GT3 RSR – albeit with some notable differences.

For a start, the car has a licence plate attached to the rear PU, a rather conspicuous giveaway that this is an RSR destined for the motorway rather than the Mulsanne. The second and less blatant detail of note lies in its chassis number. If you know your numbers, you'll see this chassis didn't leave Porsche as a 997 RSR at all… what you're looking at actually began life as a 996.1 Carrera Cabriolet.

The original owner went to great lengths to mimic every single visual RSR detail possible on this project. The base car was completely stripped before a full Cup-style cage was installed, including joins to the shock mounts and chassis with full-width knee and door bars. Mounts and brackets for the air jack tubes were then incorporated into the car, which was bead blasted and then powder coated in white in true Porsche Motorsport fashion. The rear wheel arches were retubbed to accommodate wider race tyres in line with factory RSR specifications.

The car's suspension is largely made up of genuine Porsche Motorsport North America parts, from track rods to top mounts. Fully rose jointed, there are no rubber mounts left on the car. Its lower control arms are from Fabcar with Porsche Motorsport NA spherical ends, with five-hole adjustable Motorsport anti-roll bars with Tarret drop links. Sachs Cup car shocks and Eibach main and helper springs take care of damping. The three-piece BBS wheels pay homage to the original, centre-locking RSR monoblocks – these too are centre-locking, but have been machined to accommodate the 996's five-nut stud pattern. Behind them reside the original 996 Brembo brakes with Porterfied R4 racing pads.

Back in Mark's car den, we ask to see the engine. Although we're soon looking at the wet-sumped flat six of a 996 M96 rather than an RSR-spec engine, plenty of work has gone on here. The 3.4-litre engine has been re-sleeved to 3.6-litre specification. The work includes new JE pistons and rings, Carillo con rods plus high-performance valve springs. The headers are stainless steel, with a Porsche Cup centre-exit muffler.

RSS supplied the underdrive pulley and engine mounts, the power-steering pump was deleted and the clutch and lightweight flywheel were balanced to help make shifts up and down the gearbox smoother. The gearbox itself is still the H-patterned, G96 six-speed manual as found in the 996, with a few upgrades including a raised shifter base for ease-of-use, Numeric Racing shift cables, RSS mounts and a Sachs racing pressure plate.

The race car conversion continues inside. Stripped down to its white paint, the interior comprises a Recaro halo seat with Schroth six-point belts, Simpson centre and window nets, and a Momo Mod. 07 wheel with, of course, quick release. As for electrics, a complete overhaul comprising the removal of the entirety of the old system took place, with all unwanted or unnecessary circuits removed to lighten the harness as much as possible. A Motec Club dashboard system has been housed in the carbon 997 dashboard, it programmed to talk to the car's stock ECU.

Back to that body. Made up of 19 pieces, all can be removed back down to the original chassis. Aside from the fibreglass roof, front and rear PUs, this reborn 997 features extensive carbon fibre: the lightweight doors are made from it, as are the rear wing, diffuser and Cup-style exterior mirrors. It's not all for show either: two NACA ducts in the hood supply an air feed to the driver, while carbon inlets at the front feed air to all three radiators.

Window glass has been removed all round, replaced with plexi, though there's no window whatsoever in the doors. A lightweight battery and two high-output Motorsport headlights complete the tantalising spec of this unique 911 racer. With little expense spared, the project to build this was scheduled to last two years.

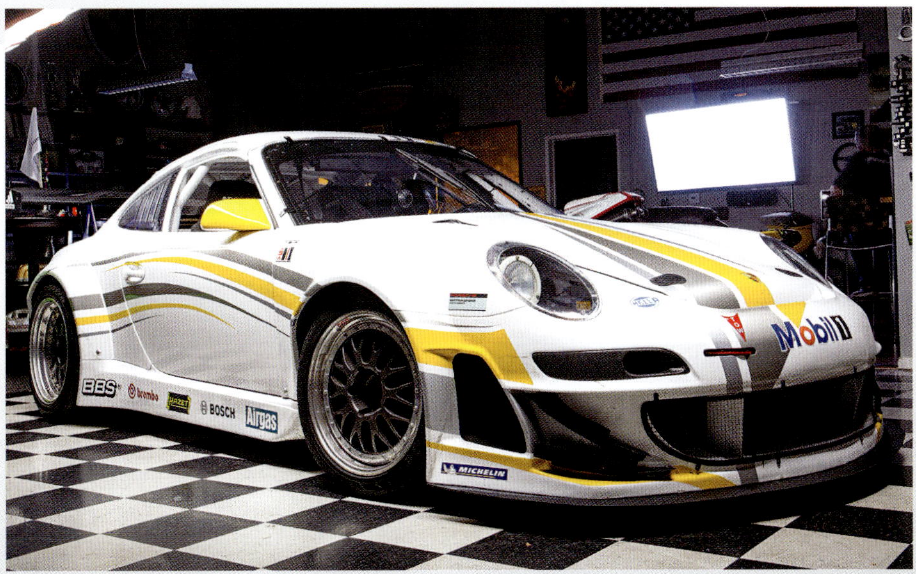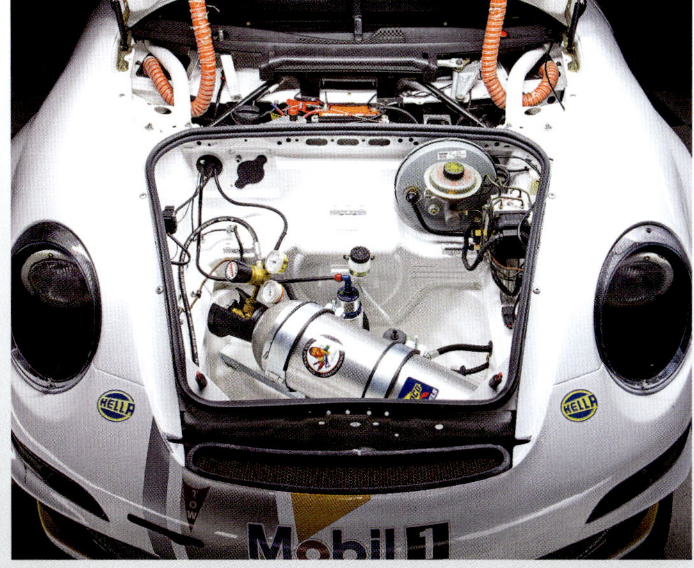

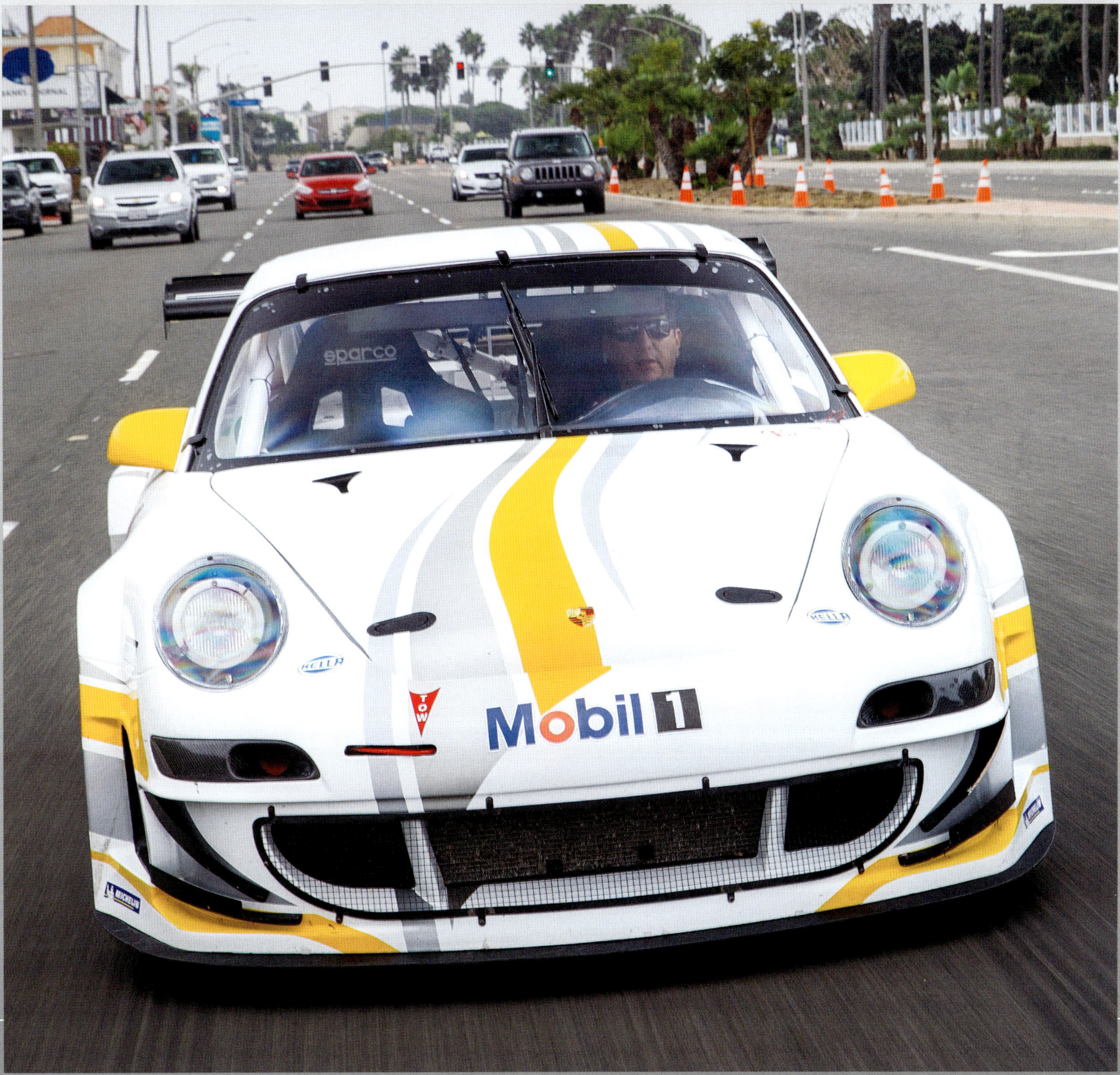

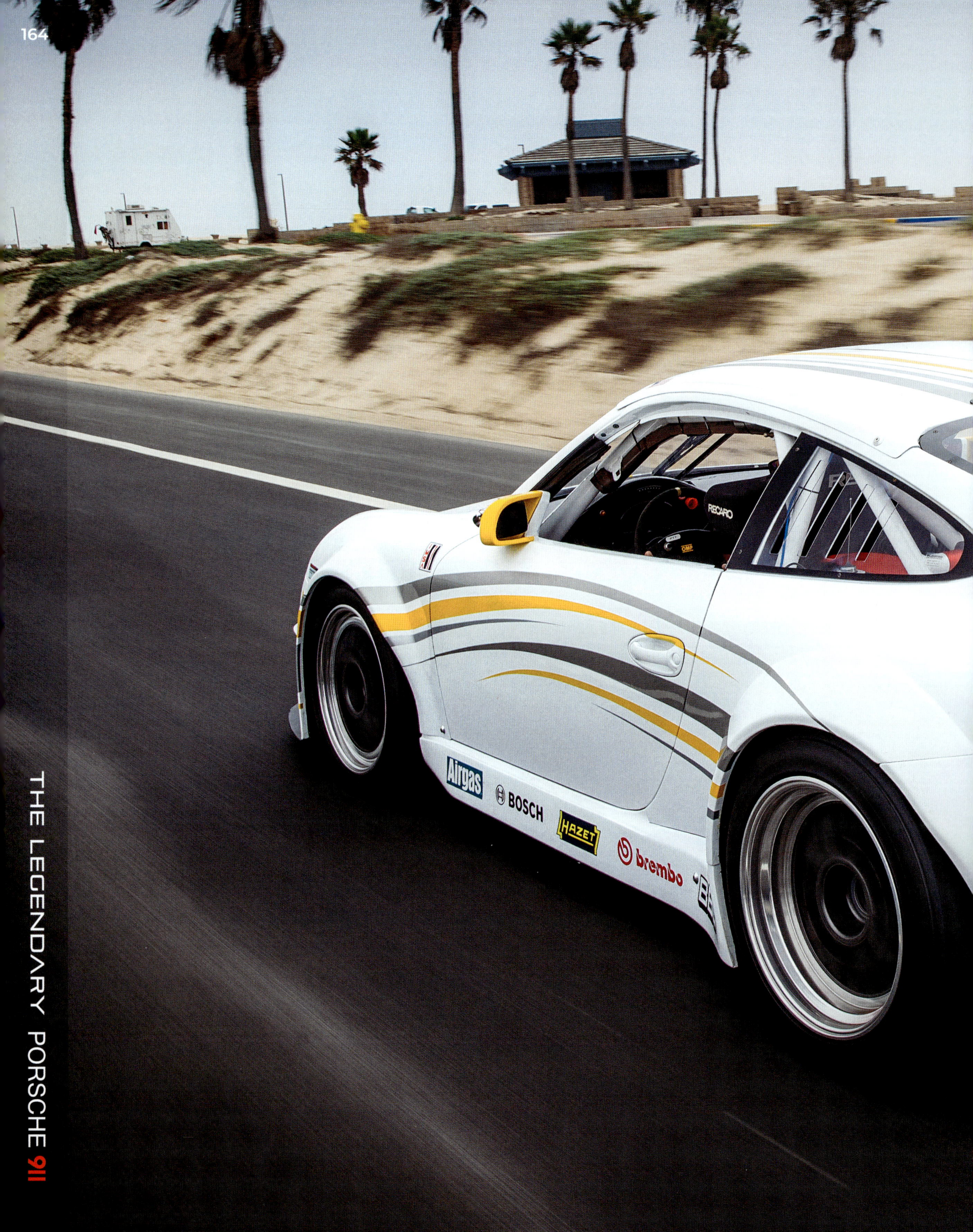

THE LEGENDARY PORSCHE 911

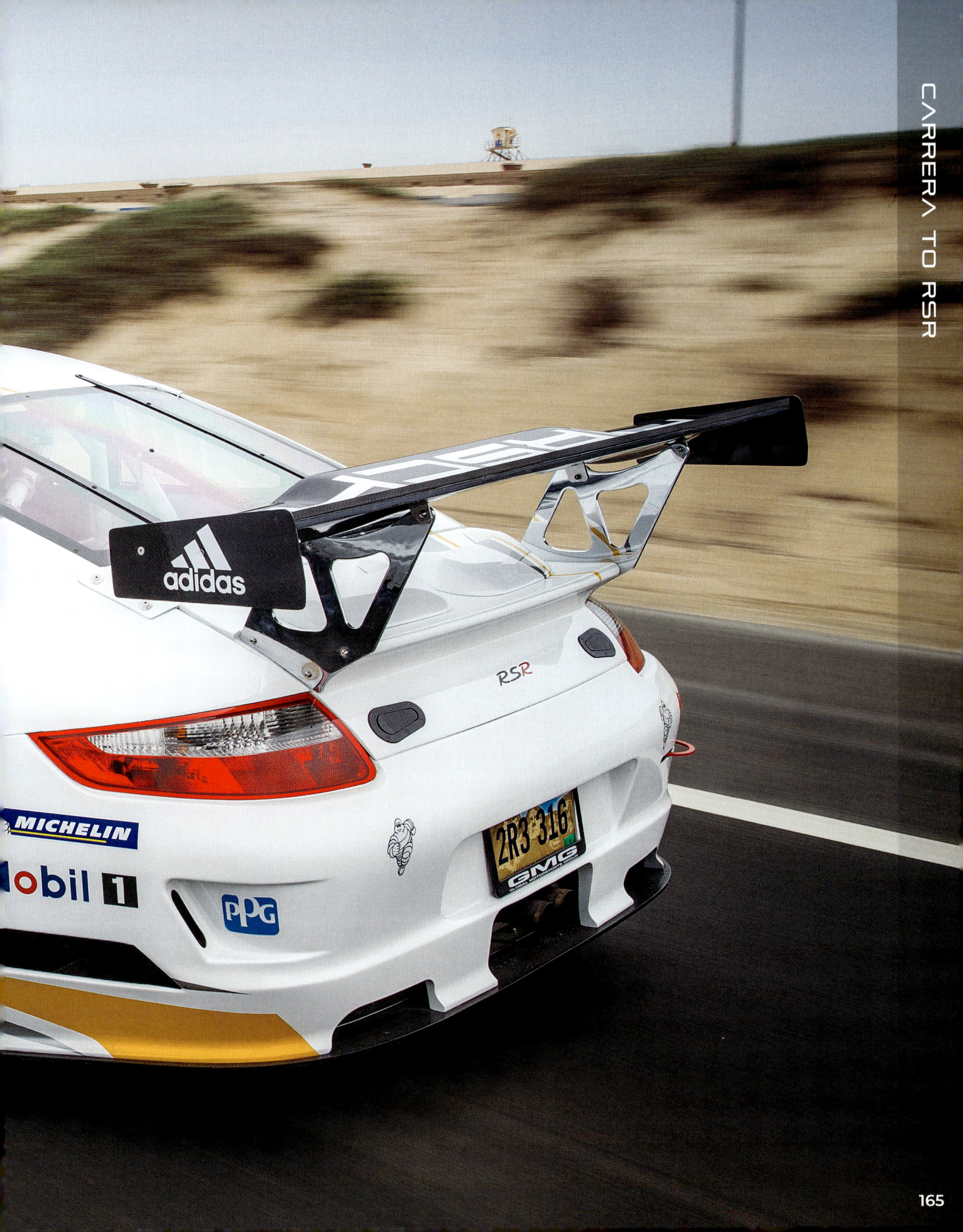
adidas
RSR
MICHELIN
obil 1
PPG
2R3·316
GMG

# THE GREATEST OF ALL TIME

## IROC

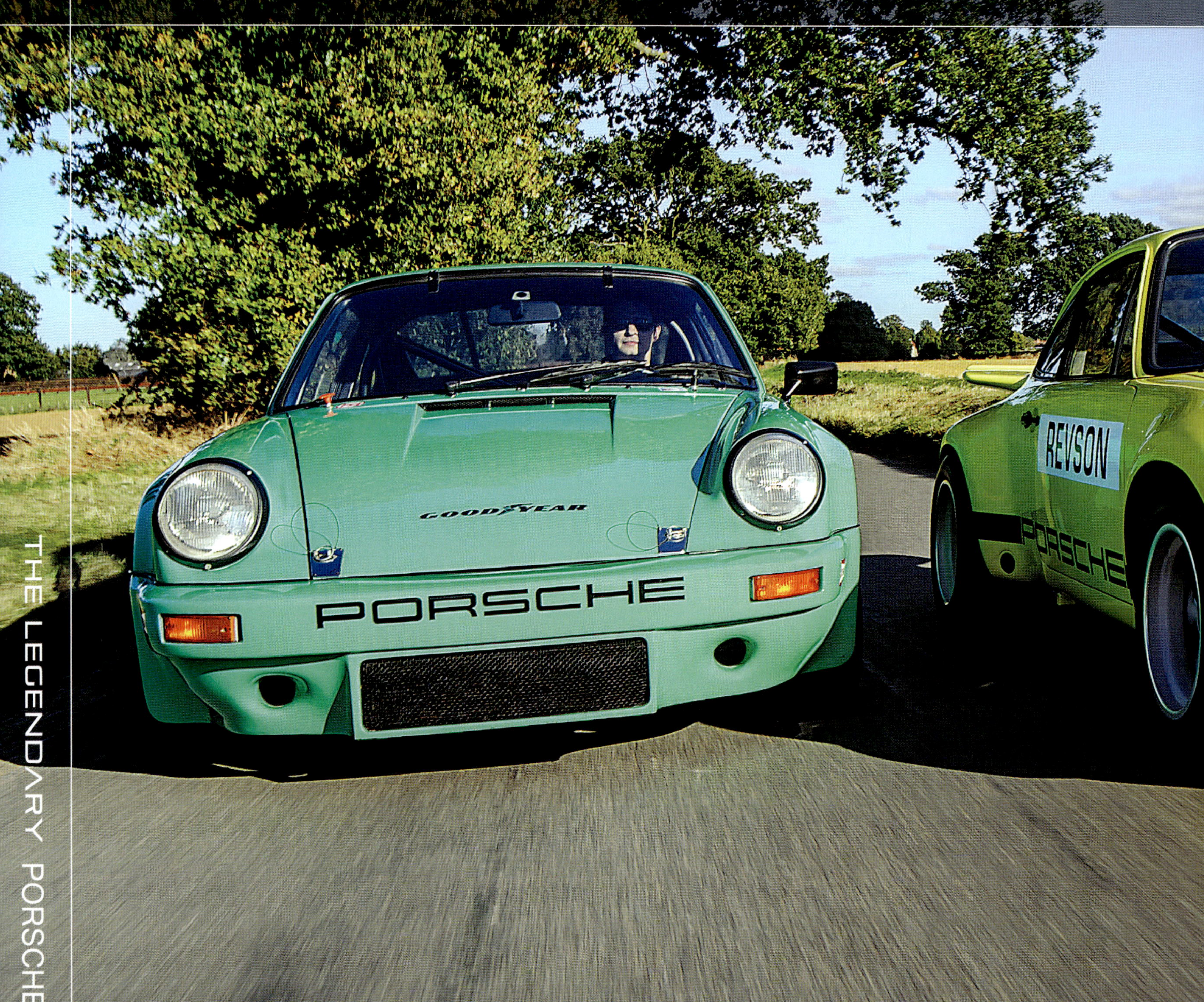

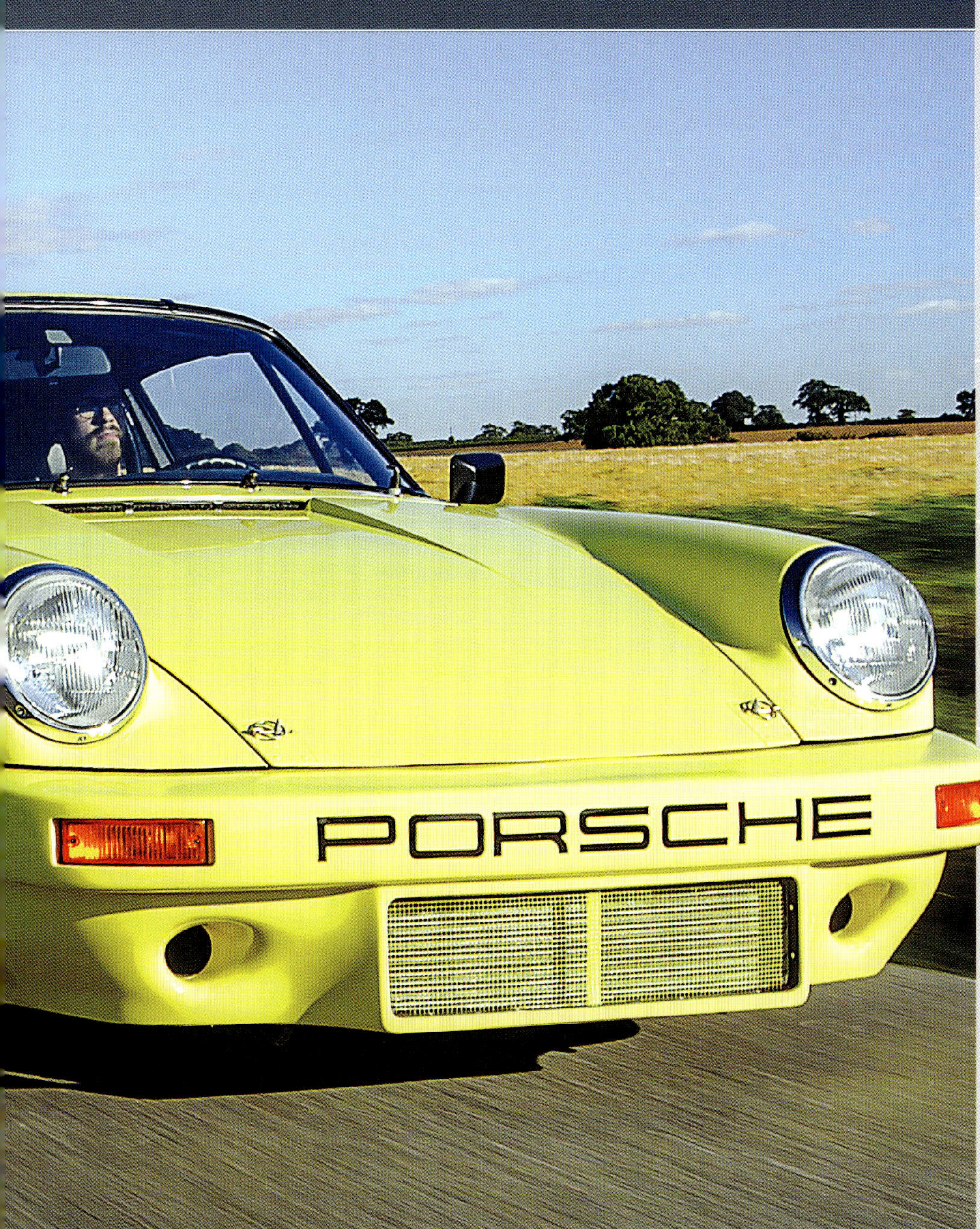

More than 50 years after Roger Penske founded IROC, two of the bespoke RSRs from that inaugural season are brought back together.



# CARRERA RSR IROC

(1973)

**ENGINE**
**Capacity:** 2,994cc
**Compression ratio:** 10:3.1
**Maximum power:** 316bhp @ 8,000rpm
**Maximum torque:** 310Nm @ 6,100rpm
**Transmission:** Five-speed manual

**SUSPENSION**
**Front:** Independent, MacPherson strut; Bilston damper; torsion bar; anti-roll bar
**Rear:** Independent, semi-trailing arm; Bilston damper; torsion bar; anti-roll bar

**WHEELS & TYRES**
**Front:** 9x15-inch Fuchs alloys; 215/55/R15 tyres
**Rear:** 11x15-inch Fuchs alloys; 295/40/R15 tyres

**BRAKES**
**Front:** 300mm cross-drilled discs; four-piston calipers
**Rear:** 300mm cross-drilled discs; four-piston calipers

**DIMENSIONS**
**Length:** 4,135mm
**Width:** 1,680mm
**Weight:** 967kg

**PERFORMANCE**
**0-60mph:** Unknown
**Top speed:** Unknown

**T**wo decades before the Porsche Supercup was even formed, Porsche was involved in another one-make series, one with a unique aim: to find out across the worlds of Formula 1, NASCAR, IndyCar and sports cars, who was the greatest driver of all. For North American motorsport enthusiasts, IROC will likely be more familiar in Chevrolet or Pontiac circles, while in Europe, the International Race of Champions enjoyed little publicity over its 30-year run. However, before the succession of Camaros and Firebirds, the first series was actually run using 15 identical Porsche 911s: the IROC RSRs.

Devised by legendary US team owner, Roger Penske, the IROC I championship would be contested over four races: three heats on the West Coast at Riverside and a grand finale at Daytona in the east four months later. A points structure would be applied at Riverside with only the six best racers making it to Florida. The whole thing would be televised on the popular Wide World of Sports programme after a deal was struck with broadcaster, ABC.

For the first season of IROC, Penske had arranged some of motorsport's biggest names, with the likes of F1 World Champions, Emerson Fittipaldi and Denny Hulme, going up against IndyCar stars Gordon Johncock and Bobby Unser. NASCAR was represented by legend-in-the-making Richard Petty (among others) while Can-Am champions George Follmer and Mark Donohue were invited.

Daytona was designed as a winner-takes-all event in 1974, the $6,000 prize for each win at Riverside dwarfed by the offer of $43,000 to the race winner at Daytona. Having decided to retire after the inaugural IROC series, Donohue was determined to win. However, despite starting from pole, Revson led the first lap before Donohue's 1972 Can-Am replacement, Follmer, took the lead. After pulling away from the pack, Donohue made his move before quarter-distance, forcing Follmer into a mistake that proved inconsequential when the latter's gearbox expired. In the latter stages, Pearson began to close in as Donohue started to struggle with fading brakes, however, the Penske star's victory was assured when Pearson lost third gear, allowing Revson into second and Unser onto the final step of the podium.

With the series concluded (and Donohue a total of $56,500 richer), the remaining IROC RSRs were also sold off to private racers, with many of the cars used over the next few years in various American endurance races. Penske, meanwhile, accepted an offer from Chevrolet to use Camaros in the next running of the International Race of Champions. Through the 1970s and early 1980s, the 15 lurid 911s were scattered ever further to the four winds, modified in various ways to keep up with the competition along the way. They were, after all, just old racing cars. However, at the turn of the century, the significance of the unique IROC RSRs began to be unearthed as the cars came into the hands of collectors, restoring them back towards their original specifications. And that brings us here to the Aladdin's Cave that is Maxted-Page, the internationally renowned classic Porsche specialist, where two genuine Porsche 911s from the first International Race of Champions lay in wait.

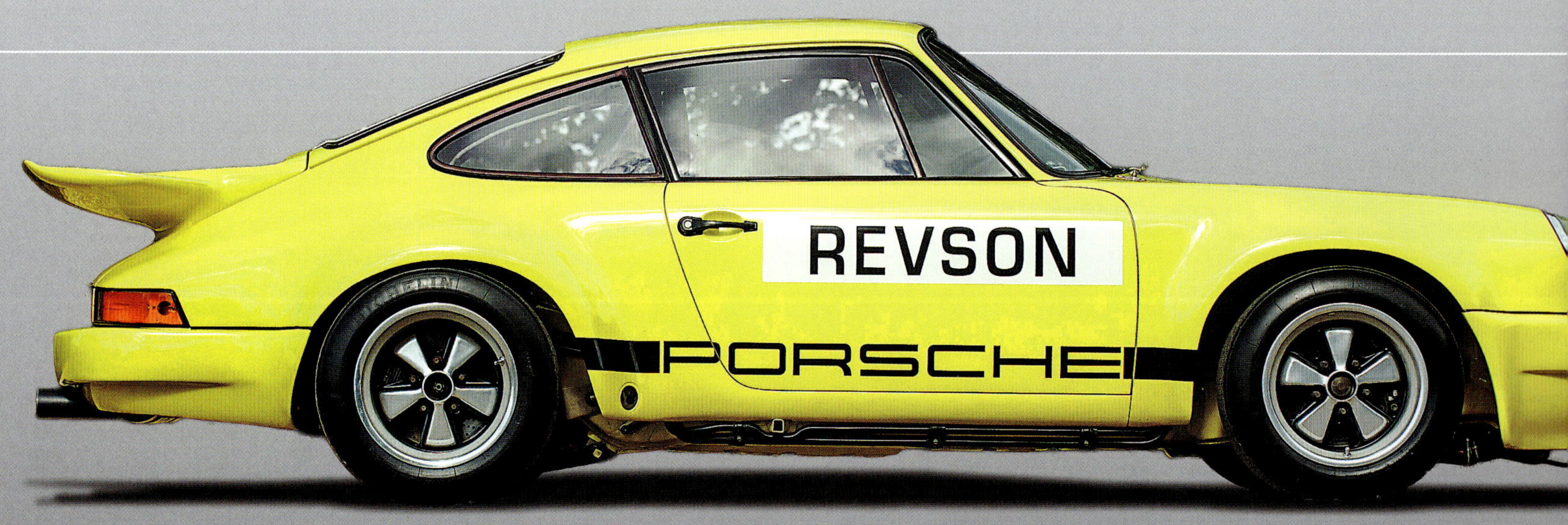

Finished in bright green, chassis no. 0042 was used in the three Riverside races by Petty, Foyt and Hulme, with the IndyCar star giving this particular IROC RSR a best finish of fifth in the second heat race. The car was one of the first seven cars sold off ahead of the Daytona finale, initially staying in California before passing between a trio of owners in France and Austria during the 1990s.

Nearly 45 years after battling each other on track, we've brought no. 0042 face-to-face with another genuine RSR from the inaugural IROC series, chassis no. 0016. If the bright yellow Porsche 911 looks familiar, it should do; earlier this year American comedian and car nut, Jerry Seinfeld, consigned the car to Gooding and Co's Amelia Island auction, where it sold for nearly twice its estimate to the Fica Frio Collection.

Venturing out onto the rural lanes, the huge yellow whaletail jutting out purposefully behind you is a moment to savour. Chasing the bright green ex-Hulme car along the snaking tarmac helps to confirm it too. When was the last time two IROC RSRs stretched their legs together? Daytona, 1974? It's hard to think too much however. Every thought in your mind is washed away in a cacophony of glorious flat-six music every time you bury the traditional organ pedal under your right foot toward the floor.

All too soon, we're back in the confines of Maxted-Page – back in the real world. It takes a while to process everything:

watching a genuine IROC RSR disappear into the distance ahead of you, all while piloting another 911 used in that first International Race of Champions. While I didn't come close to exploring the car's furthest limits, I am pretty happy with the company I've kept. After all, in the Porsche 911 world, there aren't many cars much more illustrious than the RSR from the International Race of Champions.

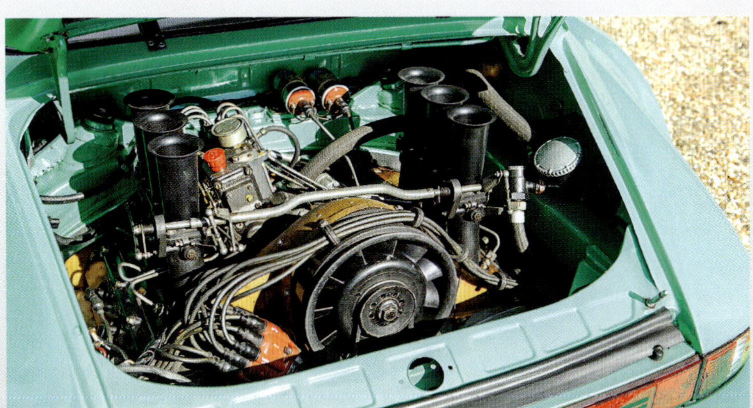

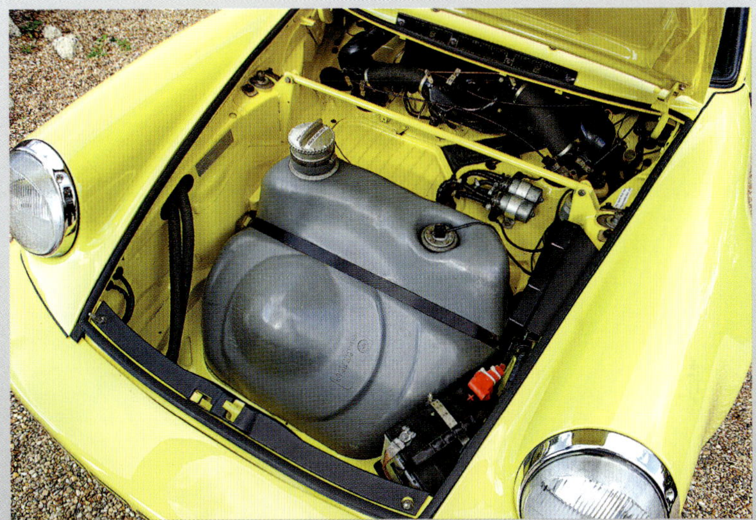

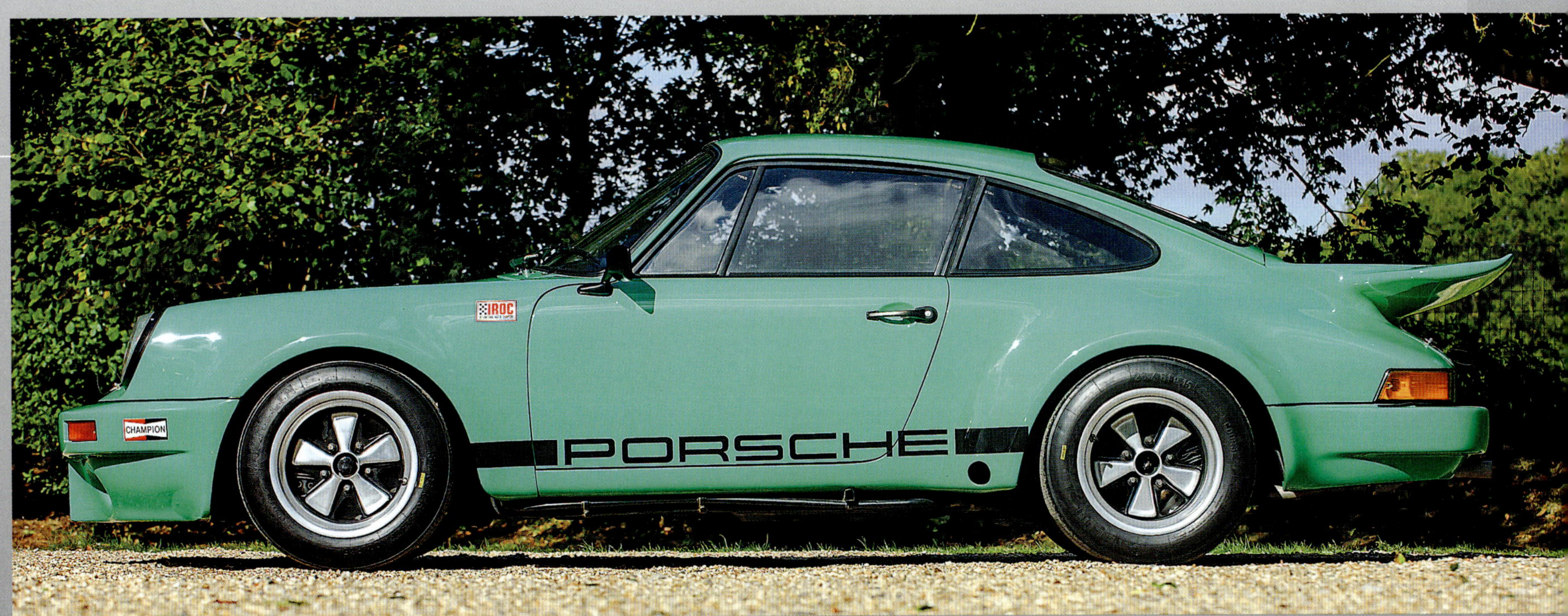

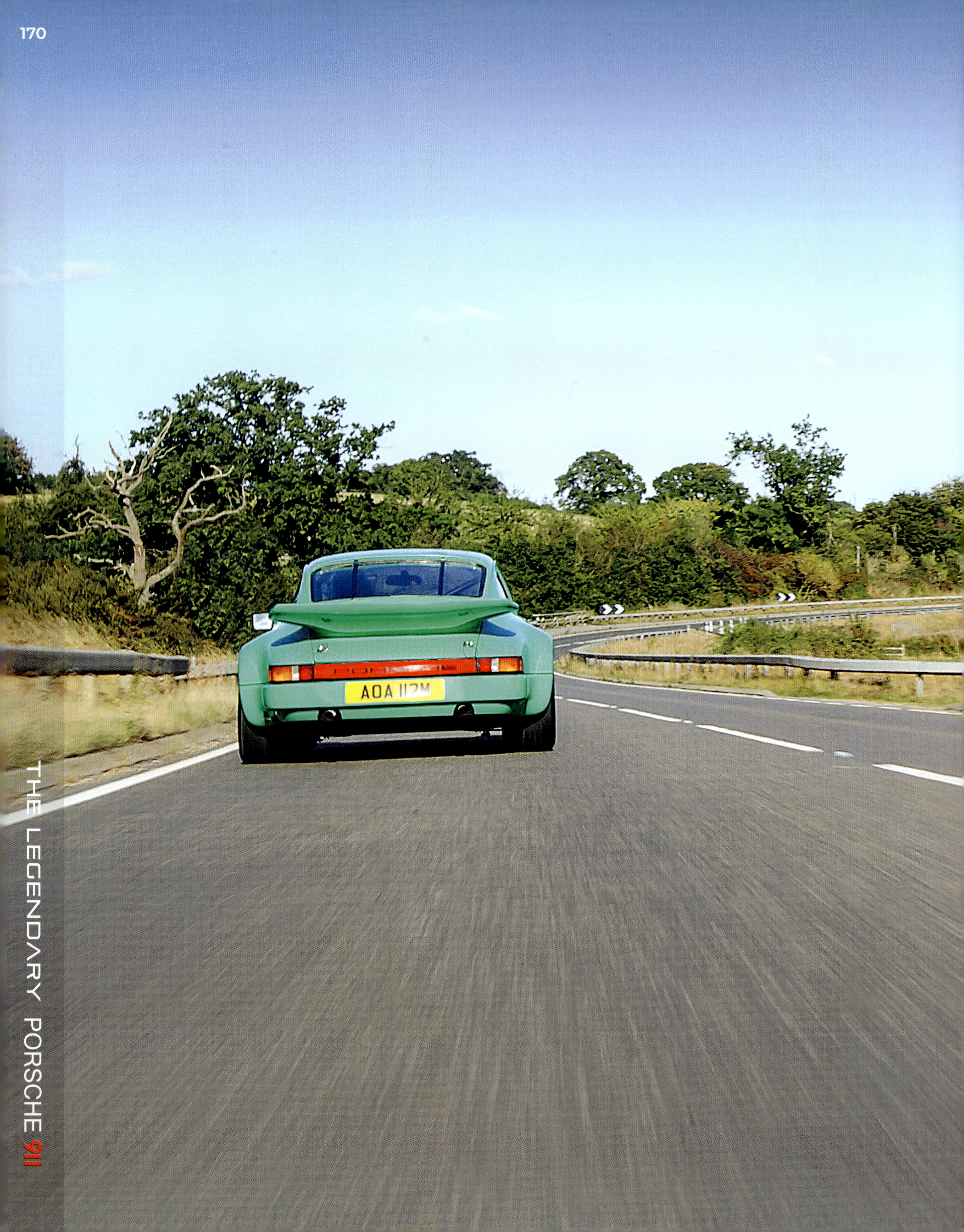

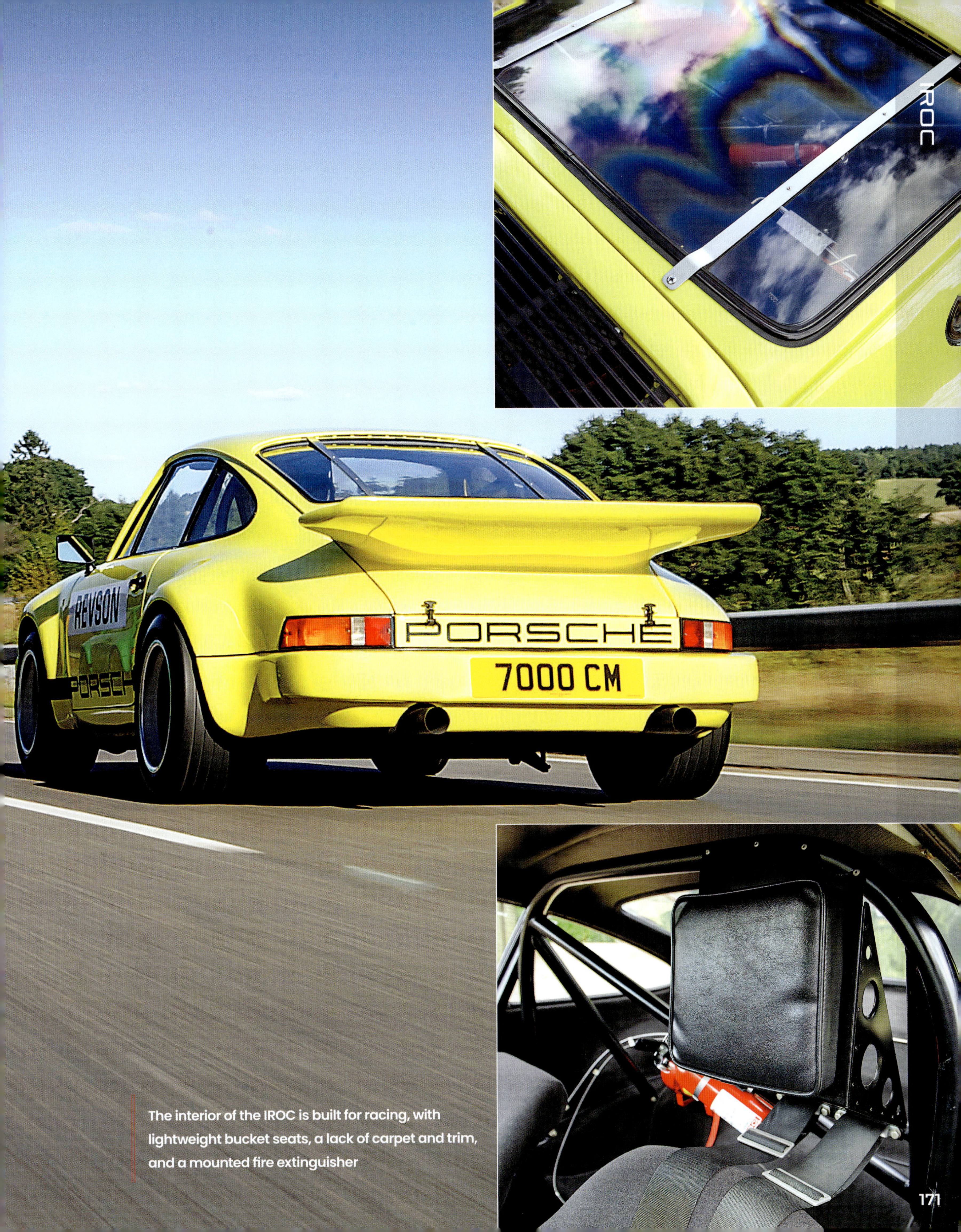




The interior of the IROC is built for racing, with lightweight bucket seats, a lack of carpet and trim, and a mounted fire extinguisher

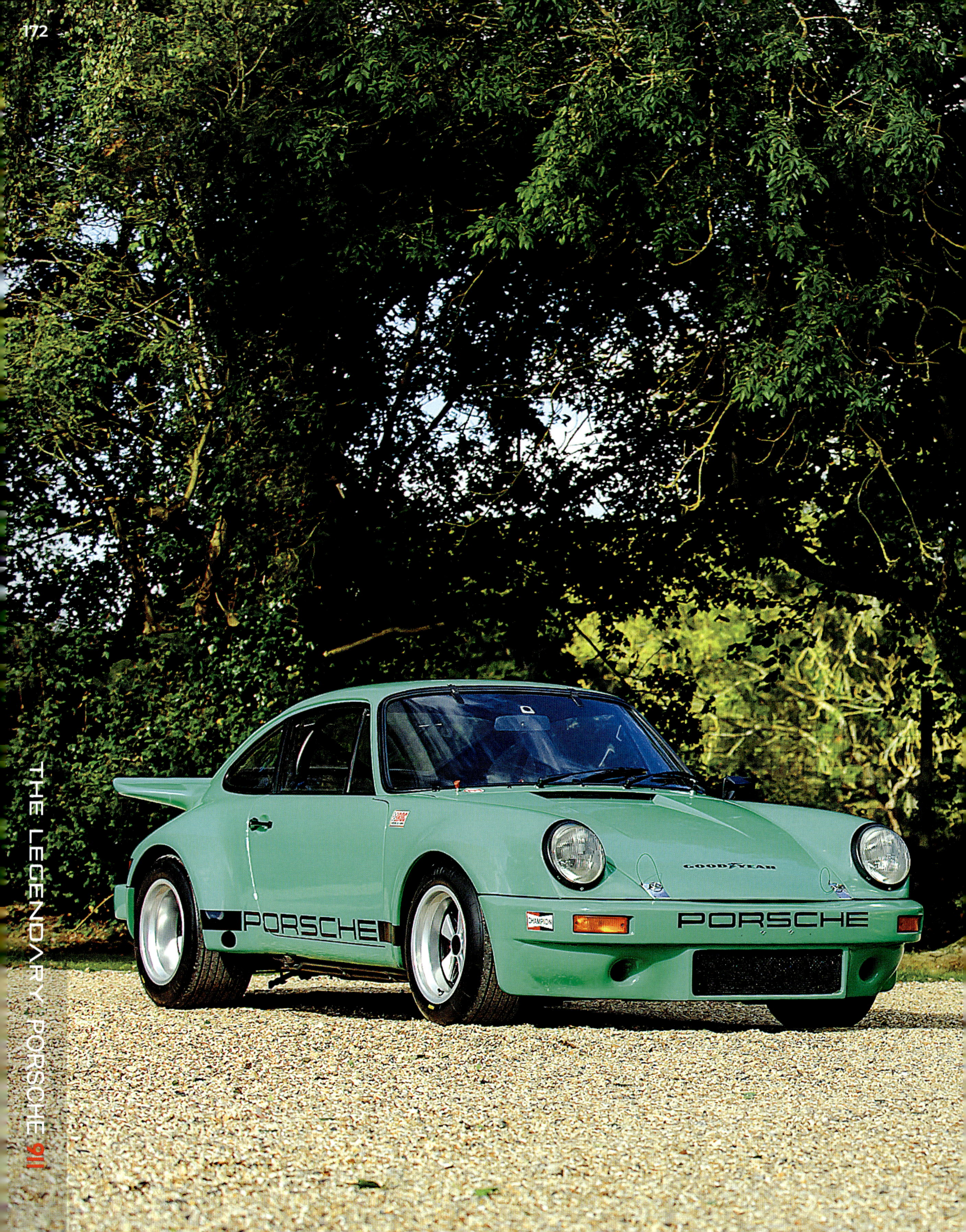

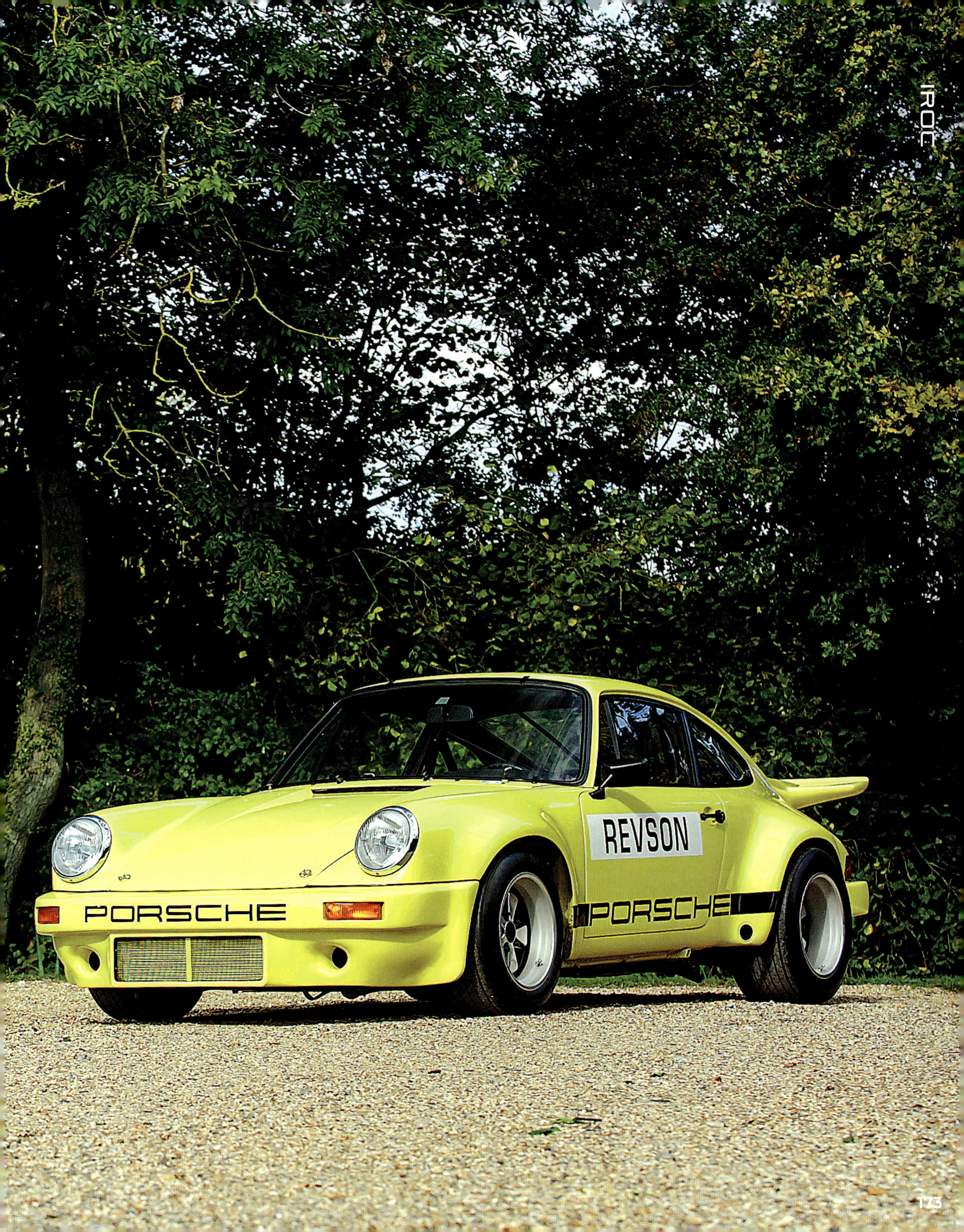
REVSON
PORSCHE
PORSCHE

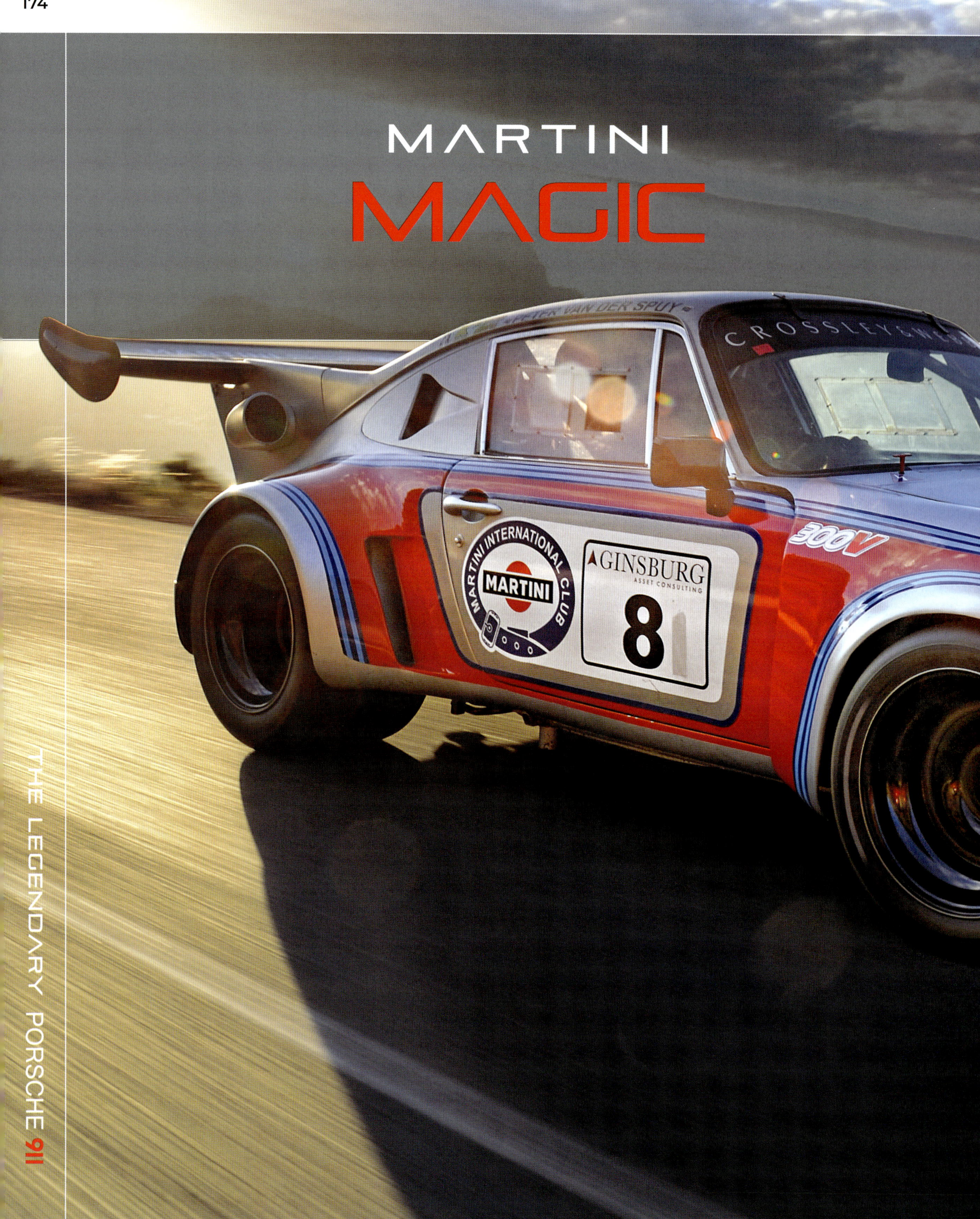
MARTINI
MAGIC

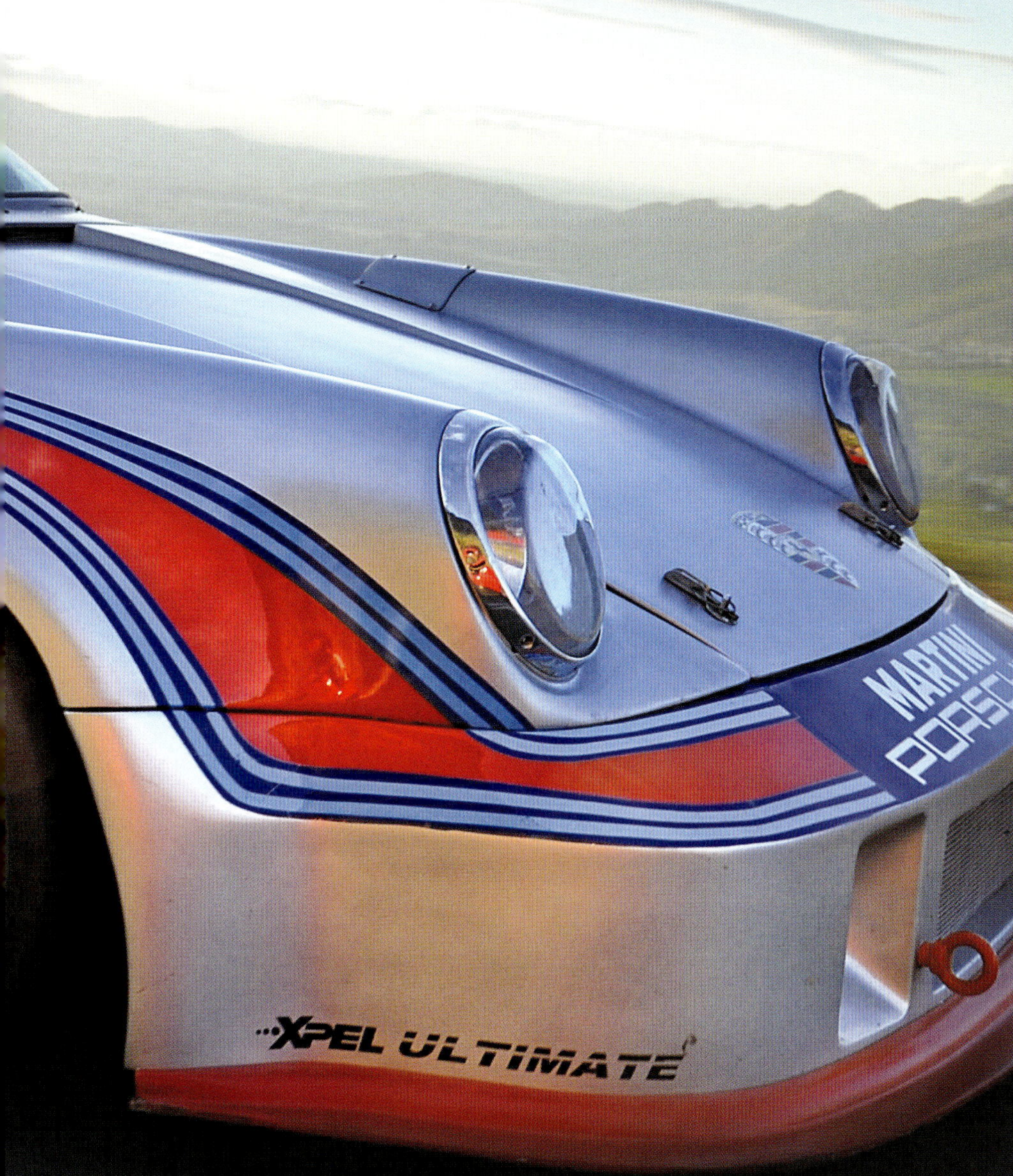

The original 2.1-litre Martini RSR offered the largest wing and the widest hips of any 911 when it was raced back in the early 1970s. Find out what it would have been like to drive the most fearsome turbo Rennsports Porsche ever to storm around the track.





# TURBO RSR REPLICA
(1972)

## ENGINE
**Capacity:** M64/01 bored to 3,800cc
**Compression ratio:** 8:5.1
**Maximum power:** 554bhp
**Maximum torque:** 680Nm
**Transmission:** G50 Five-speed manual
**Modifications:** Single turbocharger with two waste gates; GT2 Evolution camshafts; GT3 Cup oil cooling

## SUSPENSION
**Front:** MacPherson strut; coil springs; Sachs shocks; anti-roll bars
**Rear:** Swing arms; coil springs; Sachs shocks; anti-roll bars

## WHEELS & TYRES
**Front:** 23.7x11.5-16; Hoosiers
**Rear:** 27.0x14.0-16; Hoosiers

## DIMENSIONS
**Weight:** 1,250kg

## PERFORMANCE
**0-60mph:** 3.4 secs (est.)
**Top speed:** 168mph (est.)

t feels rather intimidating, but uniquely special and immensely exciting nonetheless. I'm ensconced in a Racetech racing seat with my legs almost parallel to the floor. I can hear every bit of road debris hitting the undercarriage of the car and I need to shout if I want to talk to my passenger, the owner of the car. In front of me is a plastic windscreen (a weight-saving measure), while the cabin is stripped out with only the necessary buttons and switches you associate with a race car. Above the windscreen, down the A-pillar and to my right, the silver poles of the full roll cage won't leave anyone in doubt that this is a full-on 911 race car.

With a quick glance in the interior mirror – as I won't need it again on this drive! – I observe one of the largest wings in Porsche's racing history. As I peer in the side view mirrors, the massive, widened rear arches and end tips of the rear wing come into view. This car fills the road with its size and presence unlike any air-cooled 911 I've ever driven. I need to feed in enough throttle to stop the car from stalling but also need to let the racing clutch out quickly, as any unnecessary slippage would damage the clutch. The steering wheel conveys oodles of feedback; it goes light for only a brief moment before it weights up again and gives your arms a proper workout. The G50 gearbox allows for quick and direct shifts, while the long metal gearlever and gearknob (with the very industrial-looking linkage system below) contributes to the solid shift action every time I change gear. This only further contributes to the solid nature of the car and ensures that you never miss a gear when shifting.

As I press the throttle harder, and following a minor delay as the turbo gets up to speed, the RSR pushes us forwards and towards the next corner with a rush of a modern-day supercar, only with much more noise, feedback and excitement. Goodness, you need to be awake! Ahead of me, the pronounced front wings are visible and through the steering wheel it is easy to experience how the front wheels sniff out any changes in the road camber and dive into bends like only a race car can. I realise that you need all your mental focus (and rather talented feet and hands) to get the most from this car. Maybe it is a good thing that there are almost no other vehicles on this road. This is a car best suited to the track!

However, this car's origin is the same as all other 911T production cars that left the factory in 1972. It rolled off the assembly line as a standard production car but 45 years on, it is raced on South Africa's competition circuits and receives much love and attention from its current owner. This 911 has been road registered every year since 1972. The owner says his car was already built (at great expense and with much effort) into a racing car by one of the previous owners. He bought the RSR a few years ago from a fellow 911 racer and enthusiast.

Following his purchase, he did the occasional race during the course of a year but soon realised that a full rebuild of the car was required. The result was that the car underwent a near two-year restoration. It was stripped, the wiring was redone, the chassis was straightened up and the entire car was repainted. Then, the engine was taken out, stripped and rebuilt, and the cooling system was upgraded, to name just a few of the alterations. The engine was originally a 3.6-litre engine from a 964 Carrera, which was of course turbocharged.

It might be a bit of a novelty that it is still road registered but long may it continue, as the owner has no intention of letting the licence lapse. It is, without a doubt, one of the most exhilarating 911s I've ever had the chance to drive on the road. Many Porsche aficionados despise the concept of a 911 replica, but replica is the wrong word to use in this instance. This Martini RSR is a well-developed race car that pays tribute to the original, a car that formed the very foundation of so many road and race Porsches since the 1970s…

**The Martini RSR had one of the largest and most agressive rear wings in Porsche's racing history**

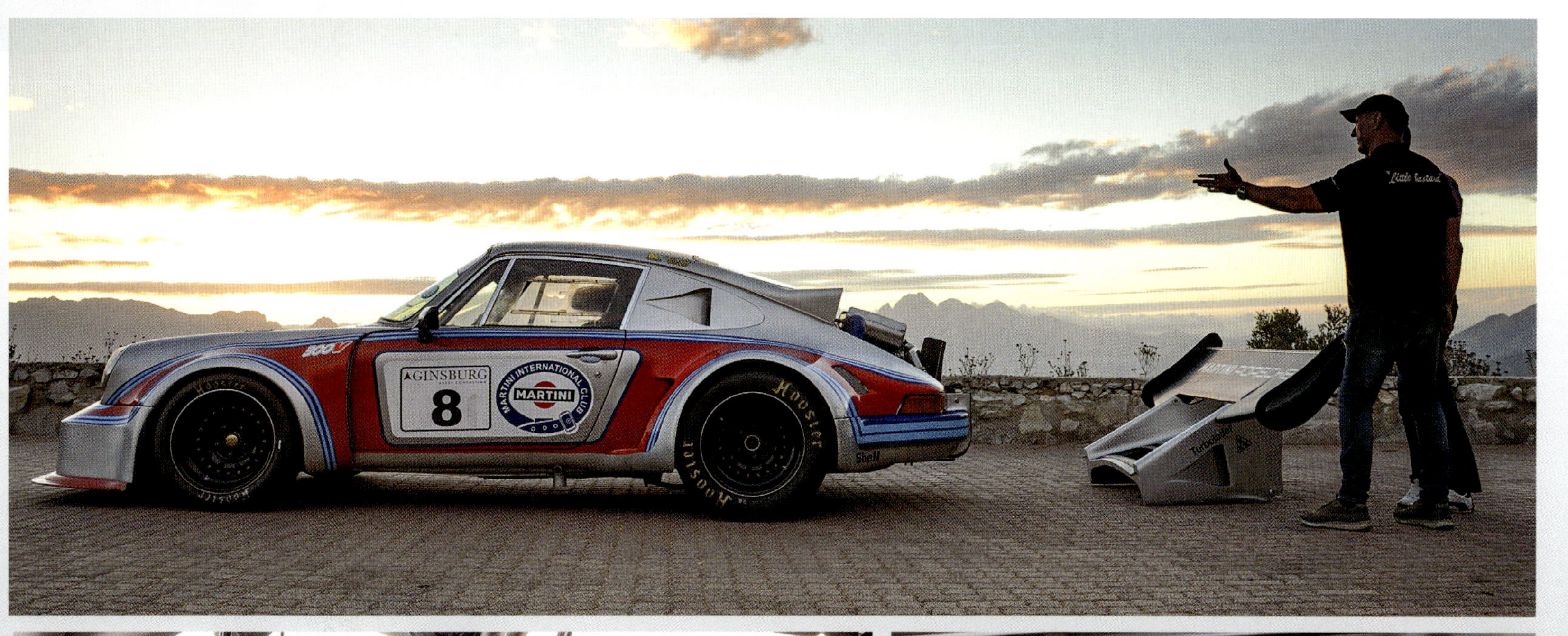

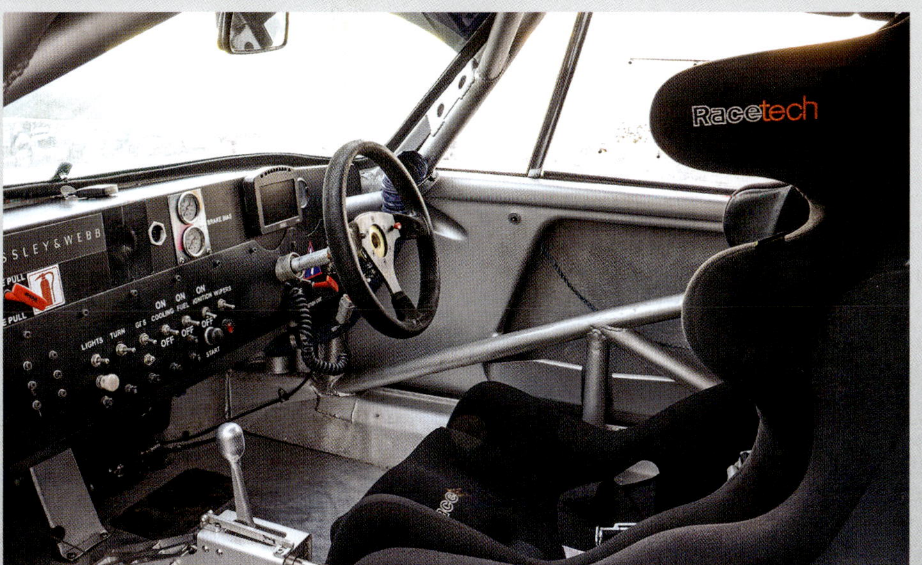

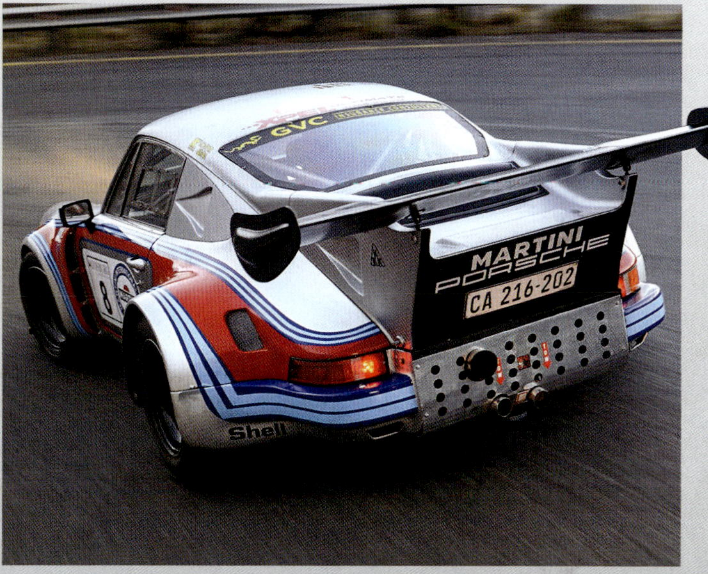

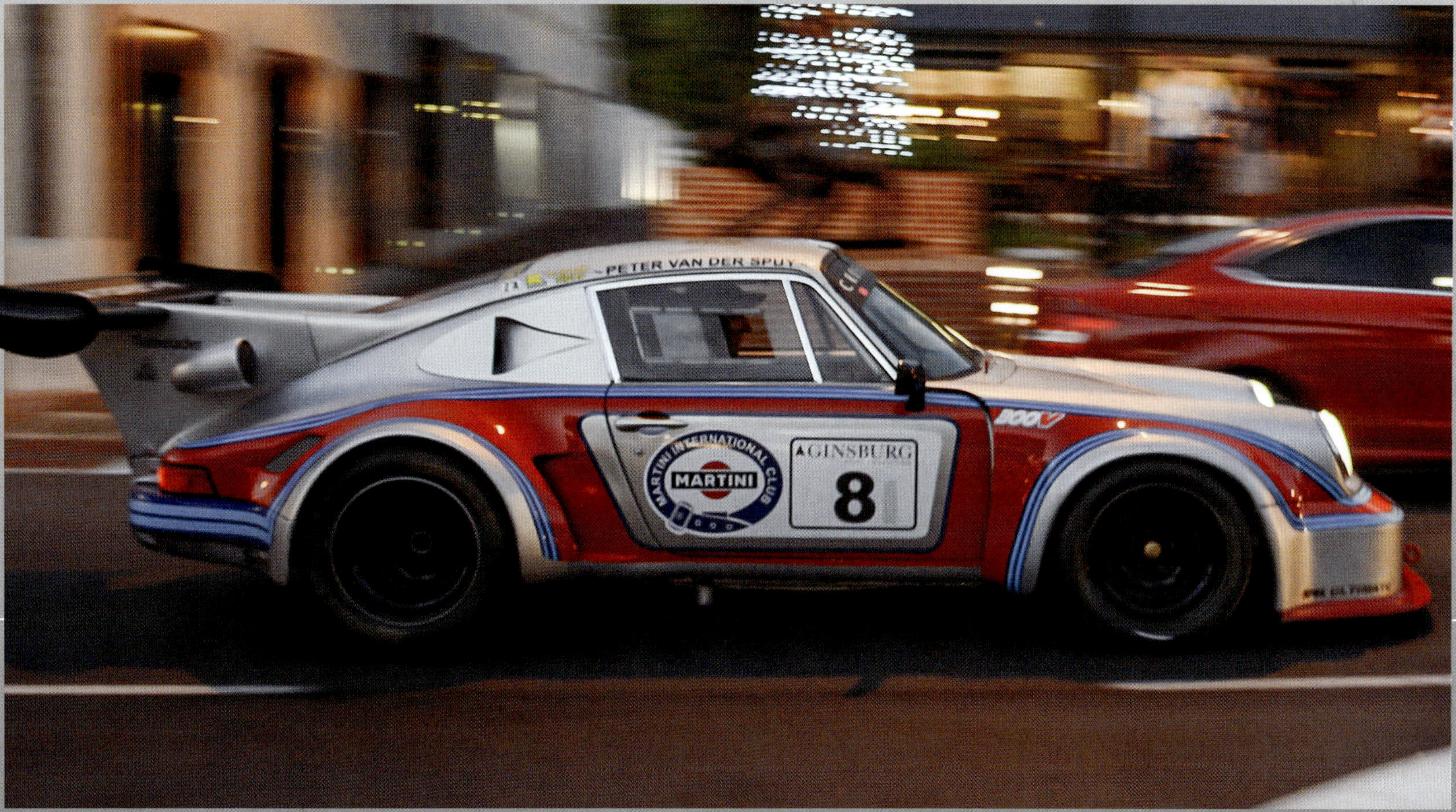

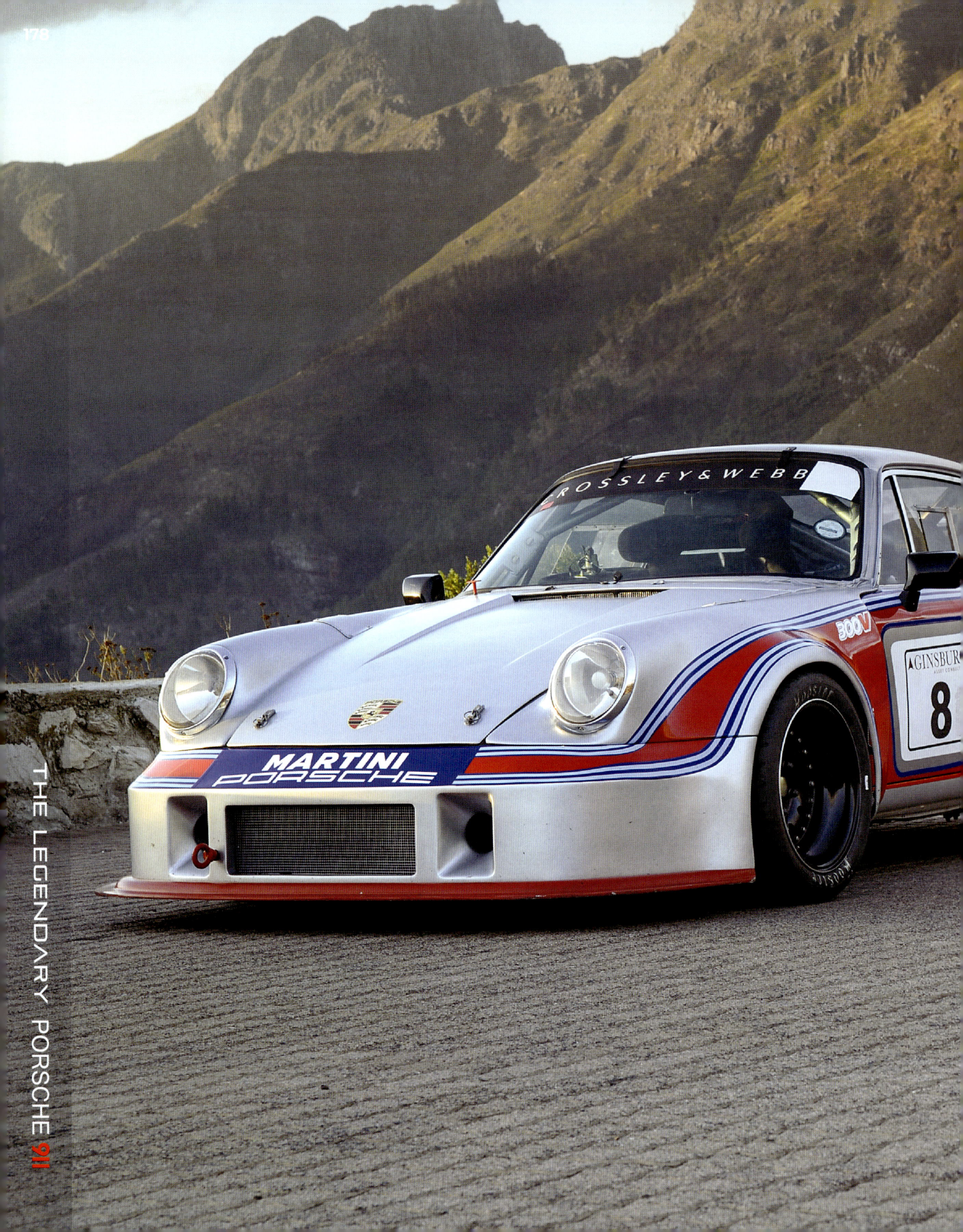
ROSSLEY & WEBB
300V
MARTINI
PORSCHE
GINSBUR
8

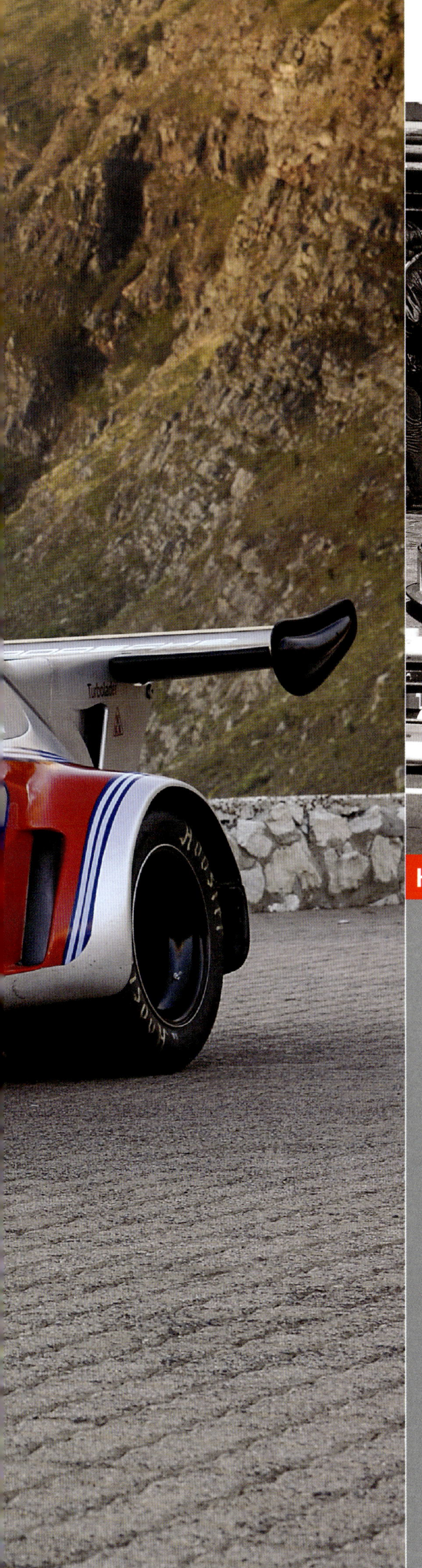

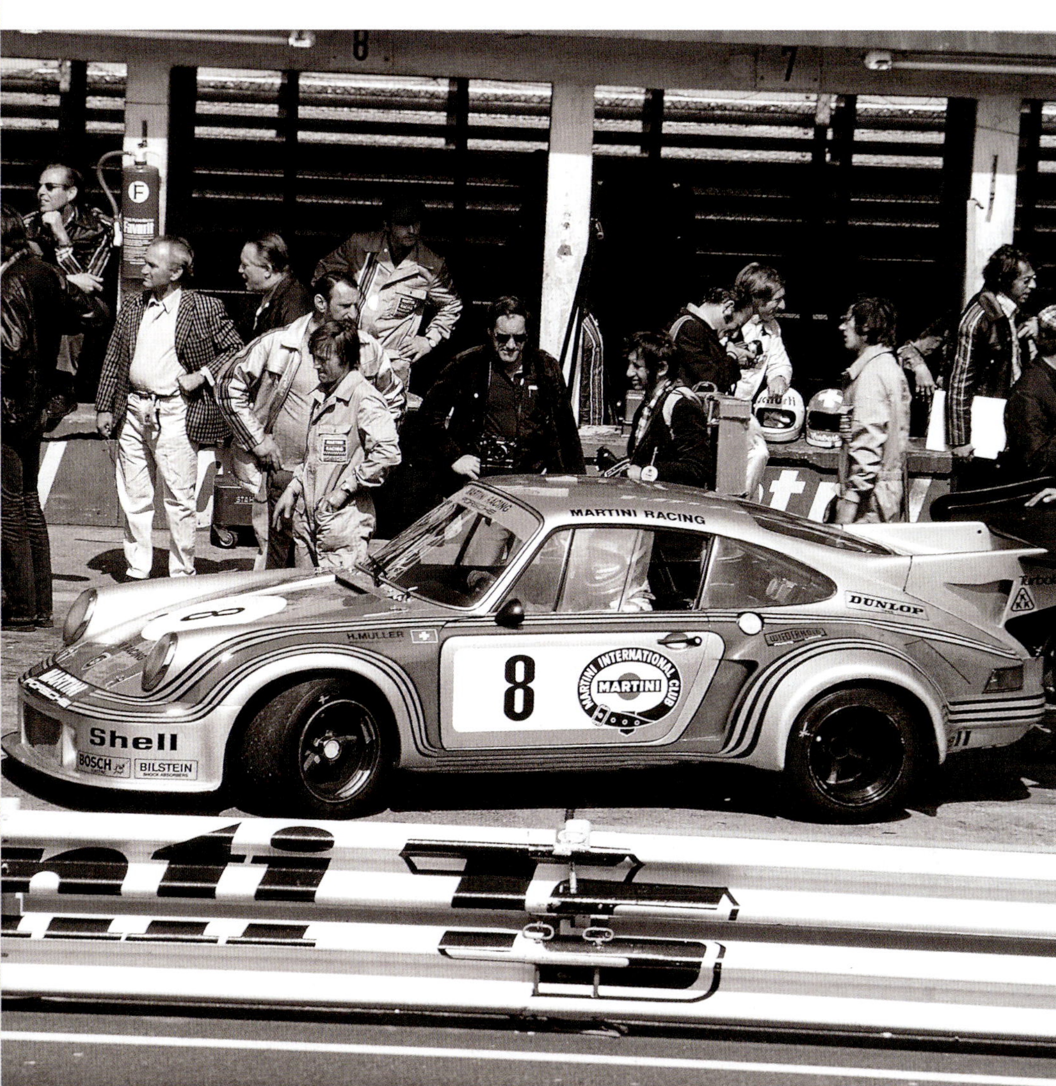

# HISTORY OF THE TURBO RSR

**The year 1973 heralded the introduction of wide-ranging changes for the World Championship for Makes. Porsche gained significant experience of turbocharging from the 917/10 and 917/30 race cars used the Can-Am and Interseries Championships, which the firm won in 1972 and 1973. Needless to say, the knowledge gleaned from the flat-12 engines could be easily transferred to the flat six. In accordance with the rules, this turbocharged engine's displacement was limited to 2.14-litres and suffice to say, the car was stripped of all unnecessary weight.**

As is still the case today with Porsche's race cars, the Turbo RSR, Porsche's first turbocharged 911, was up against much stronger competition with V12 engines. Even so, it achieved two very successful second places: at the Watkins Glen 6-hour endurance race and most notably at the 24-hour race of Le Mans in 1974. Behind the wheel were Gijs van Lennep and Herbert Müller with their no. 22 car. In both cases it was the Matra-Simca V12s that beat the little 2.1-litre Turbo.

The RSR Martini is undoubtedly one of the most impressive, jaw-dropping 911 race cars. After all, this race car gave birth to the lineage of 911 Turbo road cars that are widely celebrated as the most capable performance cars on the planet.

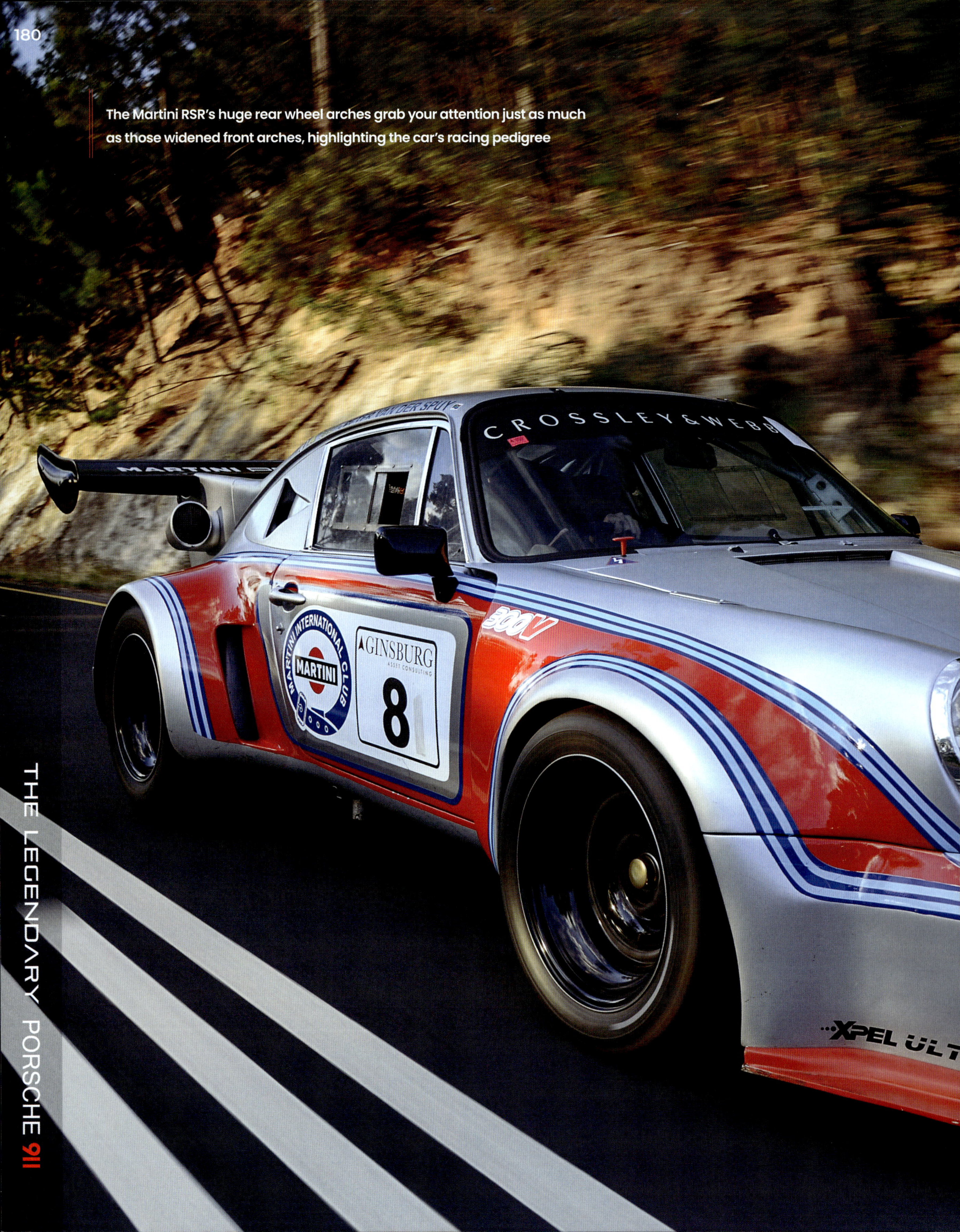

The Martini RSR's huge rear wheel arches grab your attention just as much as those widened front arches, highlighting the car's racing pedigree

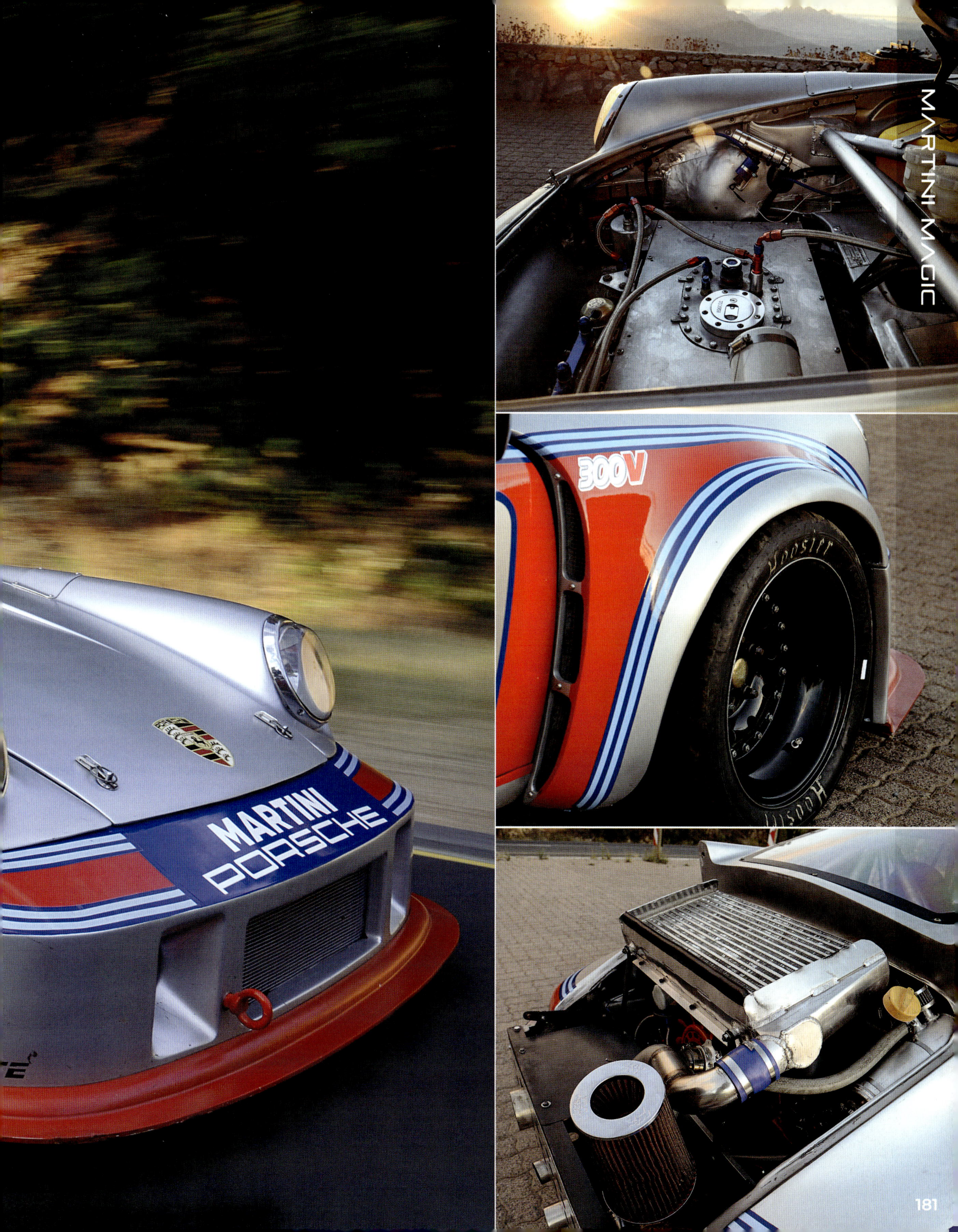
MARTINI PORSCHE
300V

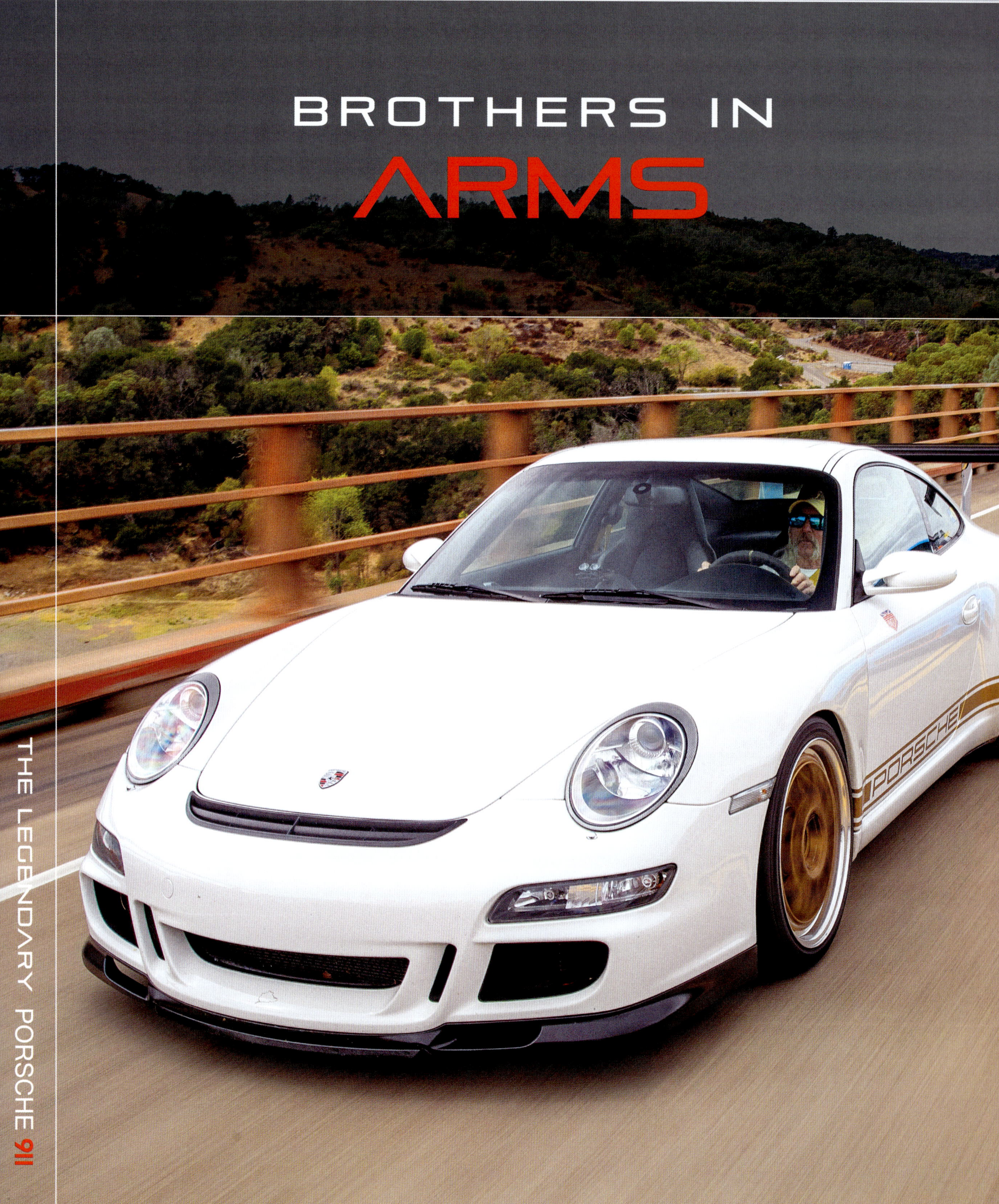


BROTHERS IN
ARMS

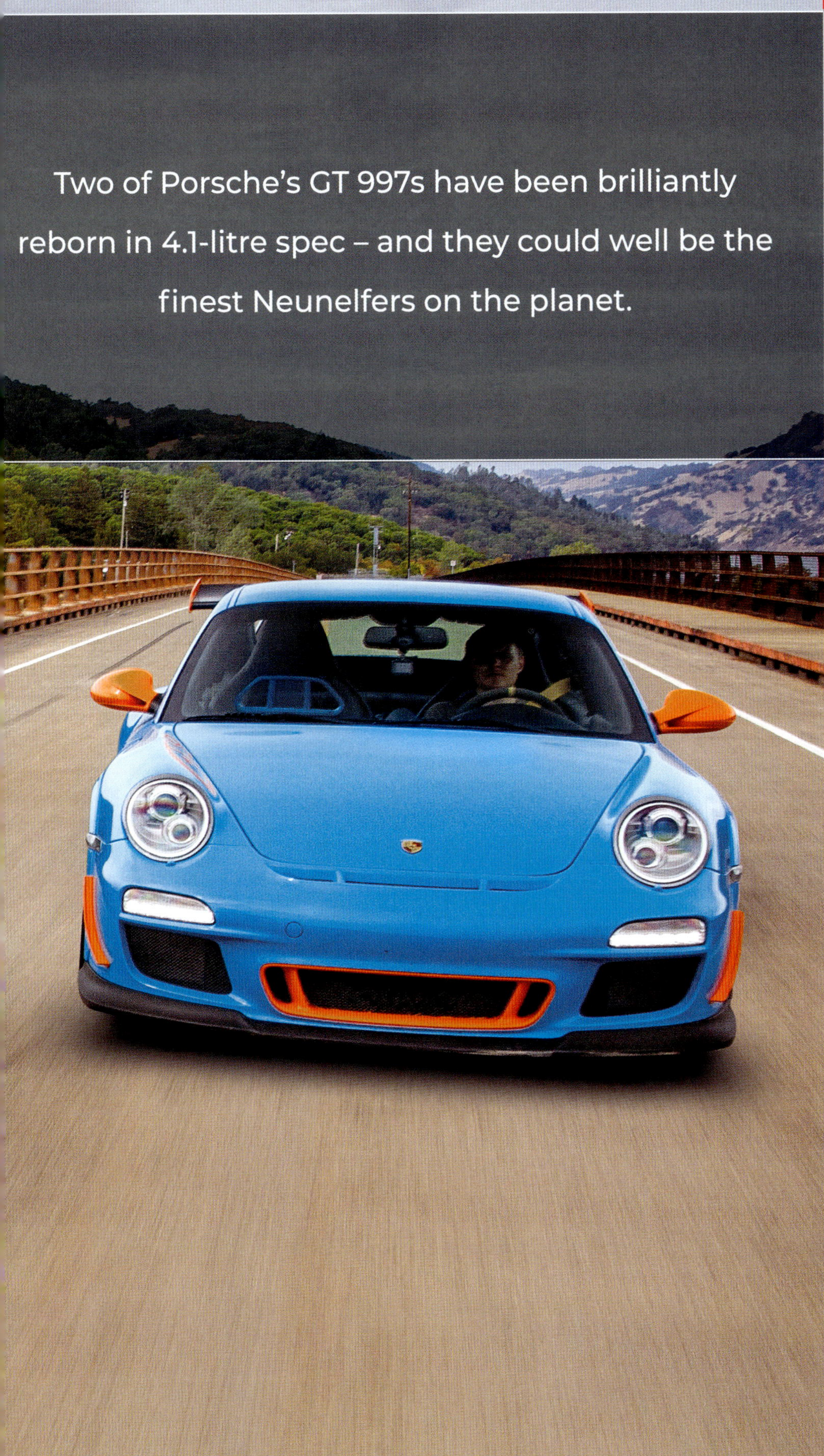

Two of Porsche's GT 997s have been brilliantly reborn in 4.1-litre spec – and they could well be the finest Neunelfers on the planet.



# 997.2 GT3 RS

(2011)

## ENGINE

**Capacity:** 4,150cc
**Compression ratio:** 13:1.1
**Maximum power:** 540bhp @ 7,950rpm
**Maximum torque:** 542Nm @ 5,300rpm
**Transmission:** Six-speed manual gearbox

## SUSPENSION

**Front:** Independent; RSS inner monoballs and adjustable thrust arm bushings; Bilstein Clubsport coilovers; anti-roll bar
**Rear:** Independent; RSS/SharkWerks rear adjustable links; RSS/SharkWerks bump steer/toe steer kit and lock-out plates; Bilstein Clubsport coilovers; anti-roll bar

## WHEELS & TYRES

**Front:** 9x19-inch Forgeline GA1R; 245/35/19 Michelin Cup 2
**Rear:** 12x19-inch Forgeline GA1R; 325/35/19 Michelin Cup 2

## DIMENSIONS

**Length:** 4,460mm
**Width:** 1,852mm
**Weight:** 1,344kg

## PERFORMANCE

**0-60mph:** 3.6 secs
**Top speed:** Not tested

I n the world of Porsche, superior engine size has never formed part of the agenda. While Lamborghini's first car in 1963 was the 3.5-litre, V12r 350GT, for example, Porsche's original 911 had a measely 2.0-litre flat six. Lamborghini still uses the V12 in its Aventador today, while Audi's R8 is powered by a 5.0-litre V10, and Ferrari's V8 and V12 powerplants are considered legendary among the wider car enthusiast population. Despite this the plucky 911 sports car has continued to battle successfully against its bigger-engined rivals on the circuit, sticking fiercely to its winning recipe of a robust flat six and an exquisite chassis.

It is this approach which Alex Ross, owner of Californian Porsche tuners SharkWerks, has always found favour with. British born, his extracurricular indulgence in Lotus is therefore forgiveable, but the overachieving 911 has always been the primary source of his motoring aspirations. This, fused with a hint of the "bigger is better" American way, is what has given us the SharkWerks 4.1.

Acquired in 2011 before being 'run in' with a 2,600-mile jaunt across the USA, Alex and the SharkWerks team found tuning potential in its 3.8-litre Mezger engine, this becoming the trailblazer for its pioneering 4.1-litre programme. It all started before Porsche had even released its own 997 GT3 RS 4.0. The result of SharkWerks' efforts is a staggering 540hp, up nearly 100hp from stock 3.8-litre spec, and 542Nm torque on 93 octane fuel. Even better, SharkWerks says its revamping work also helps lengthen the life of the Mezger six. Needless to say, it's a positively intoxicating experience behind the wheel. Make no mistake: this 'Bluefin', as Alex calls it, is still the undisputed best in our book.

However, the white 997.1 GT3 sitting next to it today represents what is arguably an even greater engineering feat. That's because it too is now resplendent in near-identical 4.1-litre specification, though in being a 3.6-litre GT3 to begin with has simply had more ground to make up to the majesty of its RS brother.

The GT3 obviously differs in its chassis dimensions, its body and track widths being narrower than the Gen2 GT3 RS, and a different intake system and intake manifold means it's down on power by around 25hp, but its aero is more extreme, making use of a Cup wing and adjustable struts at the back, while a Cup spoiler better helps the flow of air at the front of the car. It's owned by Ralph Jackson, who worked for Vasek Polak as a teenager in the 1950s and 1960s. Ralph has Porsche on the brain and 100 octane petrol pumping through his veins, and also counts the 800hp GT2 built by SharkWerks in his extensive Porsche ownership history.  That he's put 15,000 miles on the clock in the seven months since its conversion is some testament to what he thinks of its results. However, we're itching to have a go ourselves on the fabulous roads of the northern California coast.

We hop in 'Bluefin' first to reacquaint ourselves with its charm which, once it's fully up to temperature, doesn't take long at all. The exhaust note is first to arouse our senses: it's still got that full-bodied, 997.2 GT3 RS howl, yet it's been upped a note or two. Impressively there's no drone at low revs, but an application of the throttle pedal unleashes a fierce resonance that ascends into pure banshee as the RS 4.1 screams to 8,800rpm. Without question, though, the jewel in the 4.1's crown is that brilliantly reworked flat six. Its ability to rev so freely and so willingly – and for so long – is simply astonishing. If its twin wasn't patiently waiting for its own appraisal, we simply wouldn't want to swap out this seat for anything.

SharkWerks' GT3 4.1 is dominated from the outside by that frankly outrageous aerodynamic aid struts, the Cup wing with delicate Gurney flap on its trailing edge is monstrous even compared to the raised wing of the RS 4.1, the chunky end plates at either extremity almost usurping the width of the GT3's arches. From the outset this GT3 feels every bit as on par with its 4.1-litre forebear. The engine is, again, sublime. I can't get past the intensity of its rush right to the redline, which surely won't ever be beaten by anything out of the factory.

Since our first test drive of SharkWerks 4.1-litre 997.2 GT3 RS, nothing from the factory or otherwise has really gotten near it. However, this thrilling Rennsport is finally joined on its pedestal by its brother in arms, the 4.1-litre 997.1 GT3. We depart by telling Ralph we think his is the best 911 we've driven, ever, but he already knows it. A long-time Porsche owner, he says it's his best and therefore last 911. Talk about bowing out at the top.

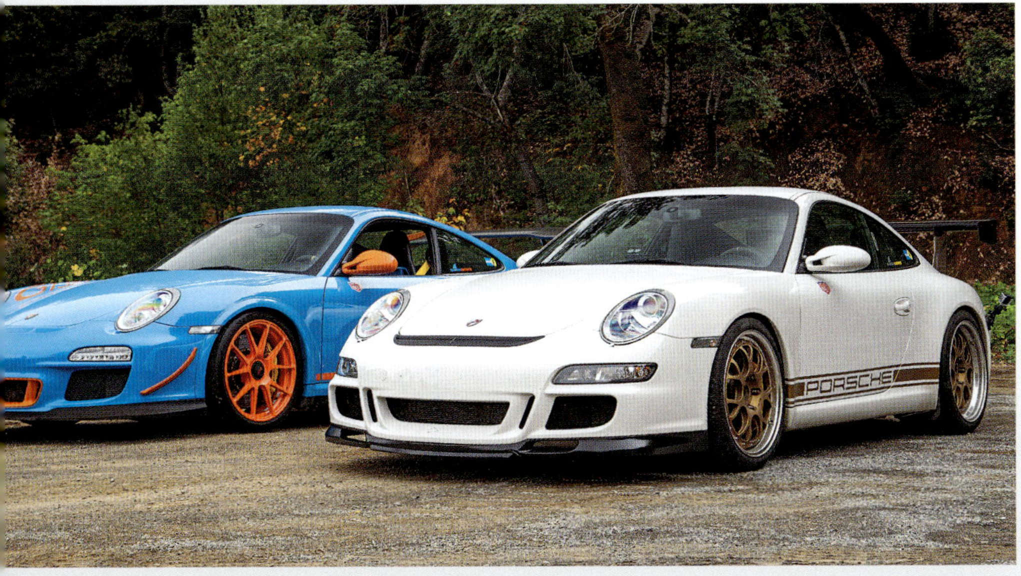

As well as unbeatable performance, SharkWerks' 4.1s have been built to last, with tens of thousands of real-world development miles under their belt

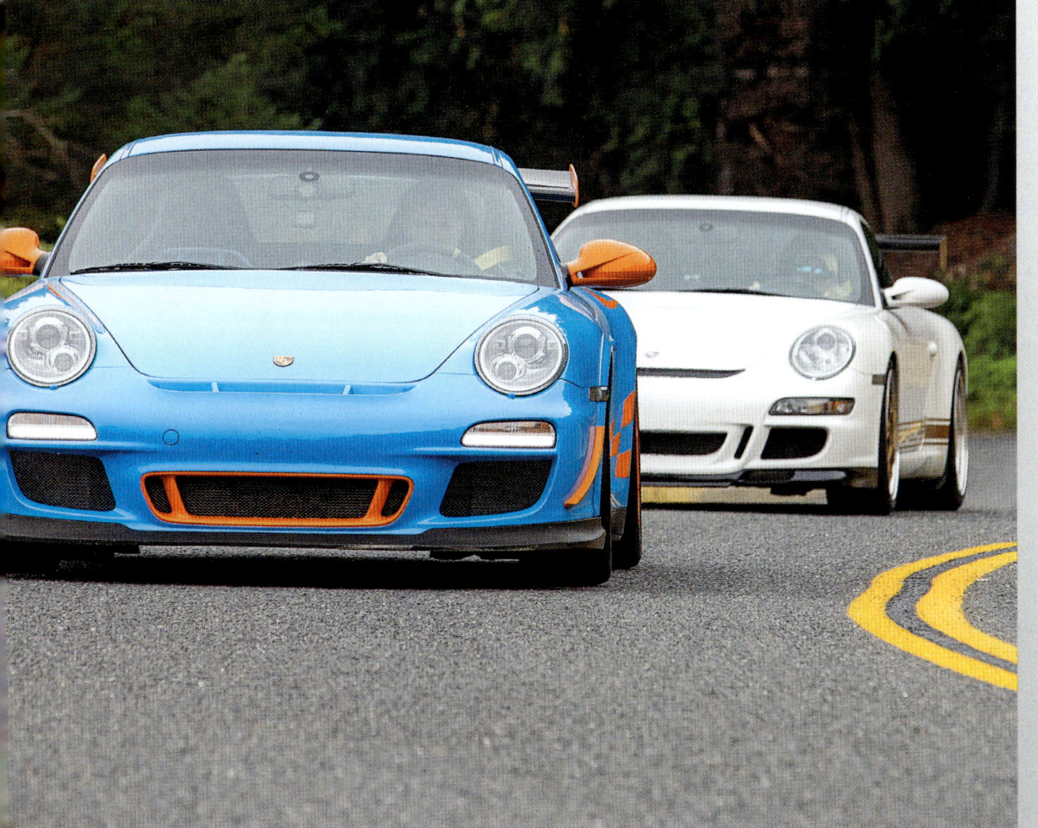

SPECIFICATION

# 997.1 GT3
(2007)

### ENGINE
**Capacity:** 4,150cc
**Compression ratio:** 13:1.1
**Maximum power:** 515bhp @ 7,950rpm
**Maximum torque:** 542Nm @ 5,300rpm
**Transmission:** Six-speed manual gearbox

### SUSPENSION
**Front:** Independent; RSS inner monoballs and adjustable thrust arm bushings; Bilstein Clubsport coilovers; anti-roll bar
**Rear:** Independent; RSS/SharkWerks rear adjustable links; RSS/SharkWerks bump steer/toe steer kit and lock-out plates; Bilstein Clubsport coilovers; anti-roll bar

### WHEELS & TYRES
**Front:** 9x19-inch Fifteen52 Apex RSR forged three-piece; Michelin Cup 2 305/30/19
**Rear:** 12x19-inch Fifteen52 Apex RSR forged three-piece; Michelin Cup 2 305/30/19

### DIMENSIONS
**Length:** 4,445mm
**Width:** 1,808mm
**Weight:** 1,365kg

### PERFORMANCE
**0-60mph:** 3.6 secs
**Top speed:** Not tested

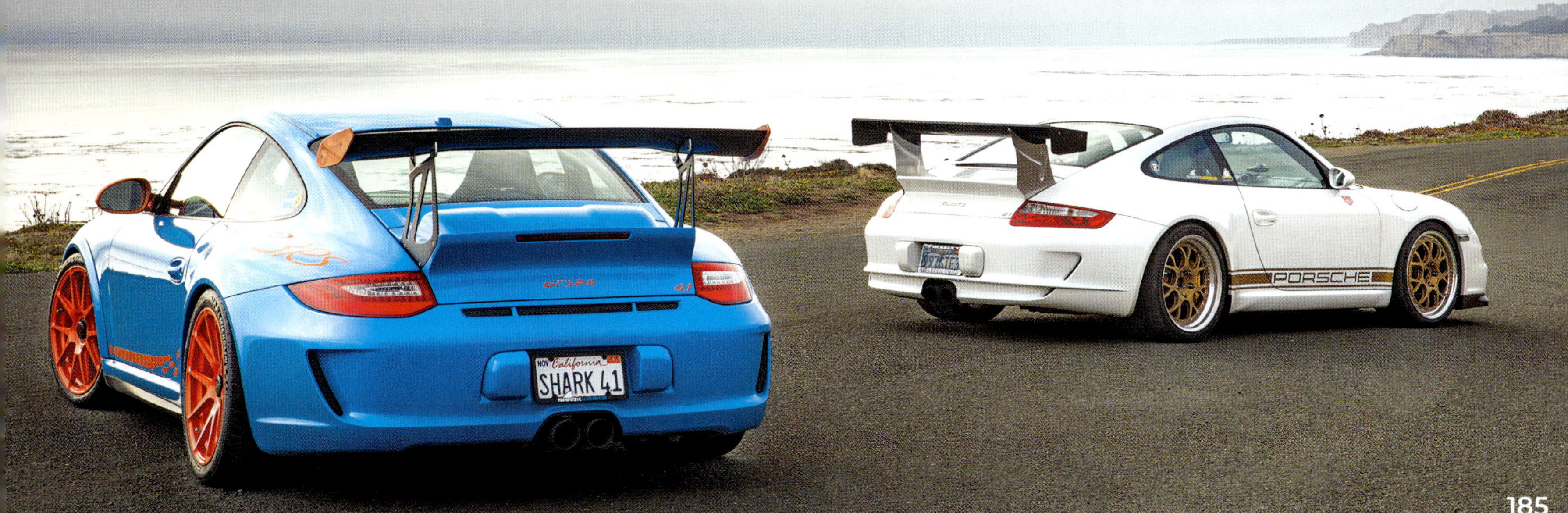

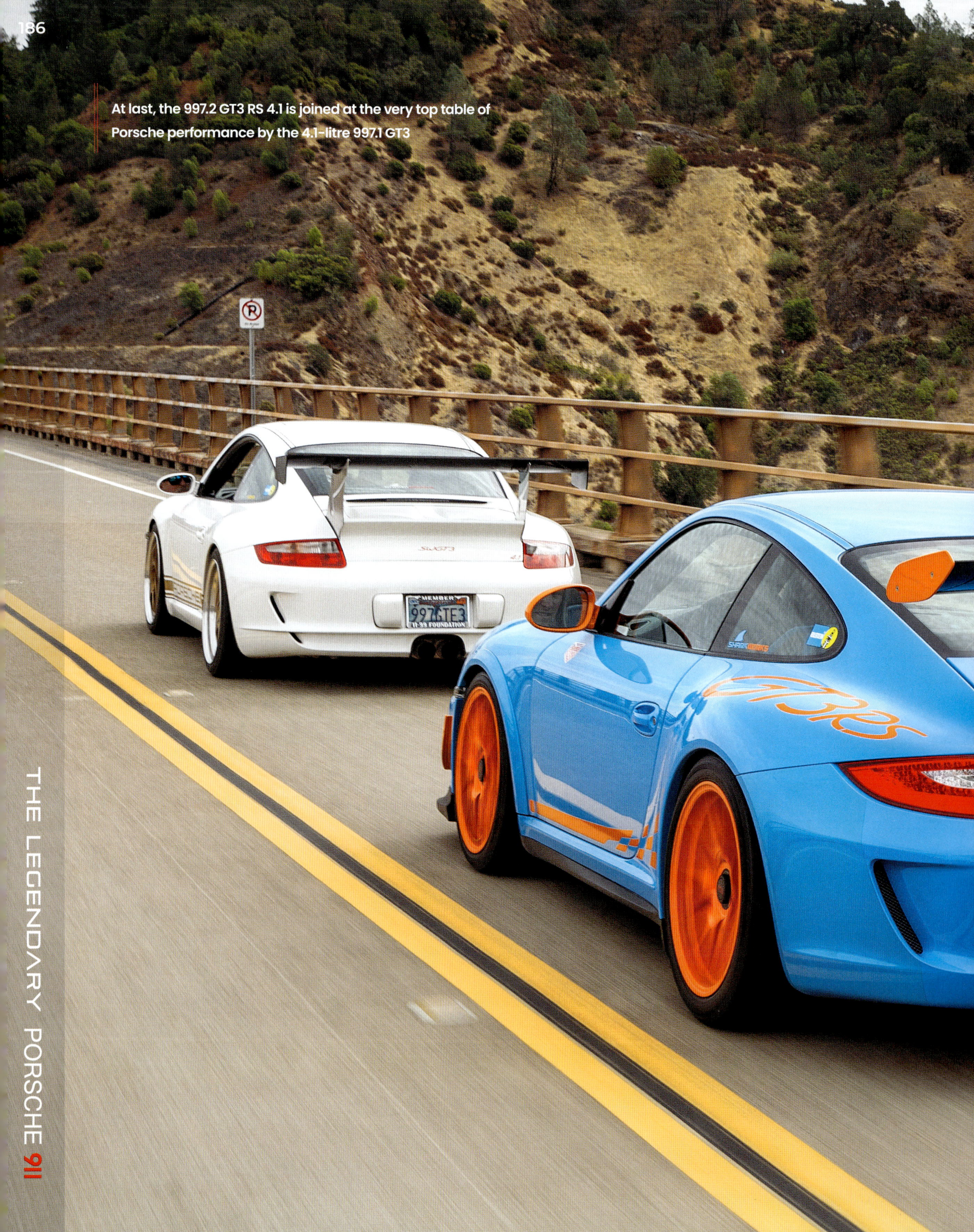


At last, the 997.2 GT3 RS 4.1 is joined at the very top table of Porsche performance by the 4.1-litre 997.1 GT3

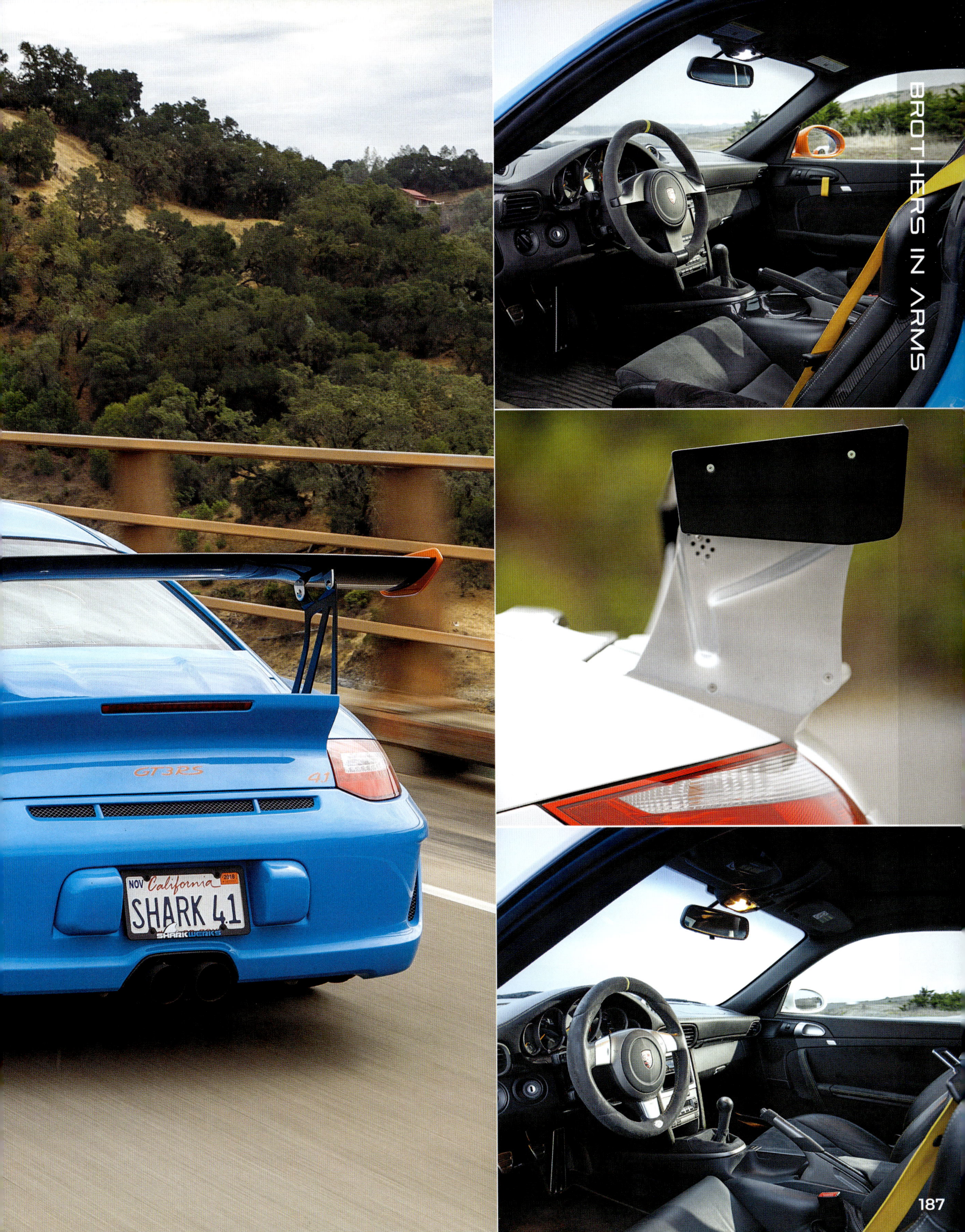

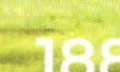



# THE RAREST
# RENNSPORT

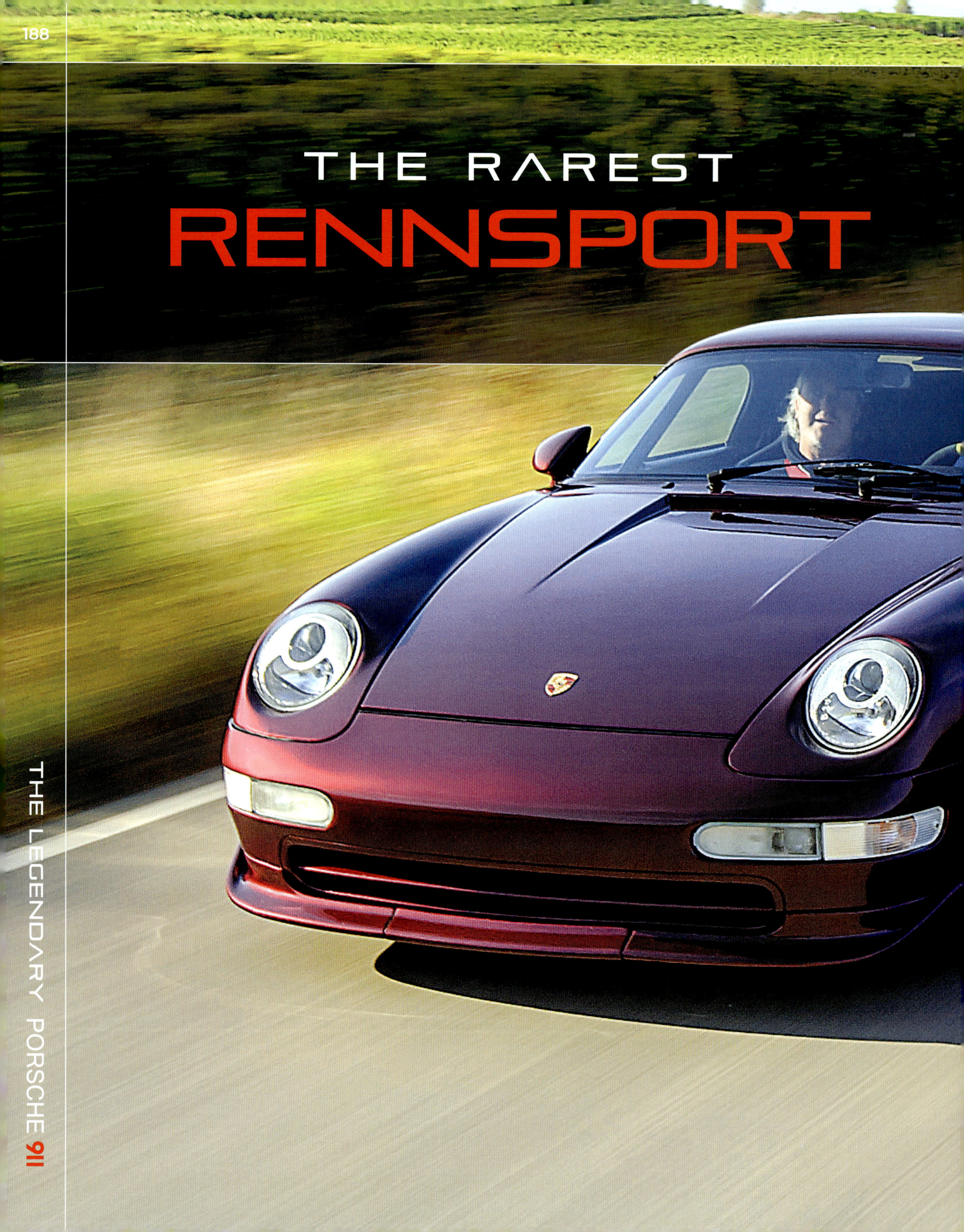

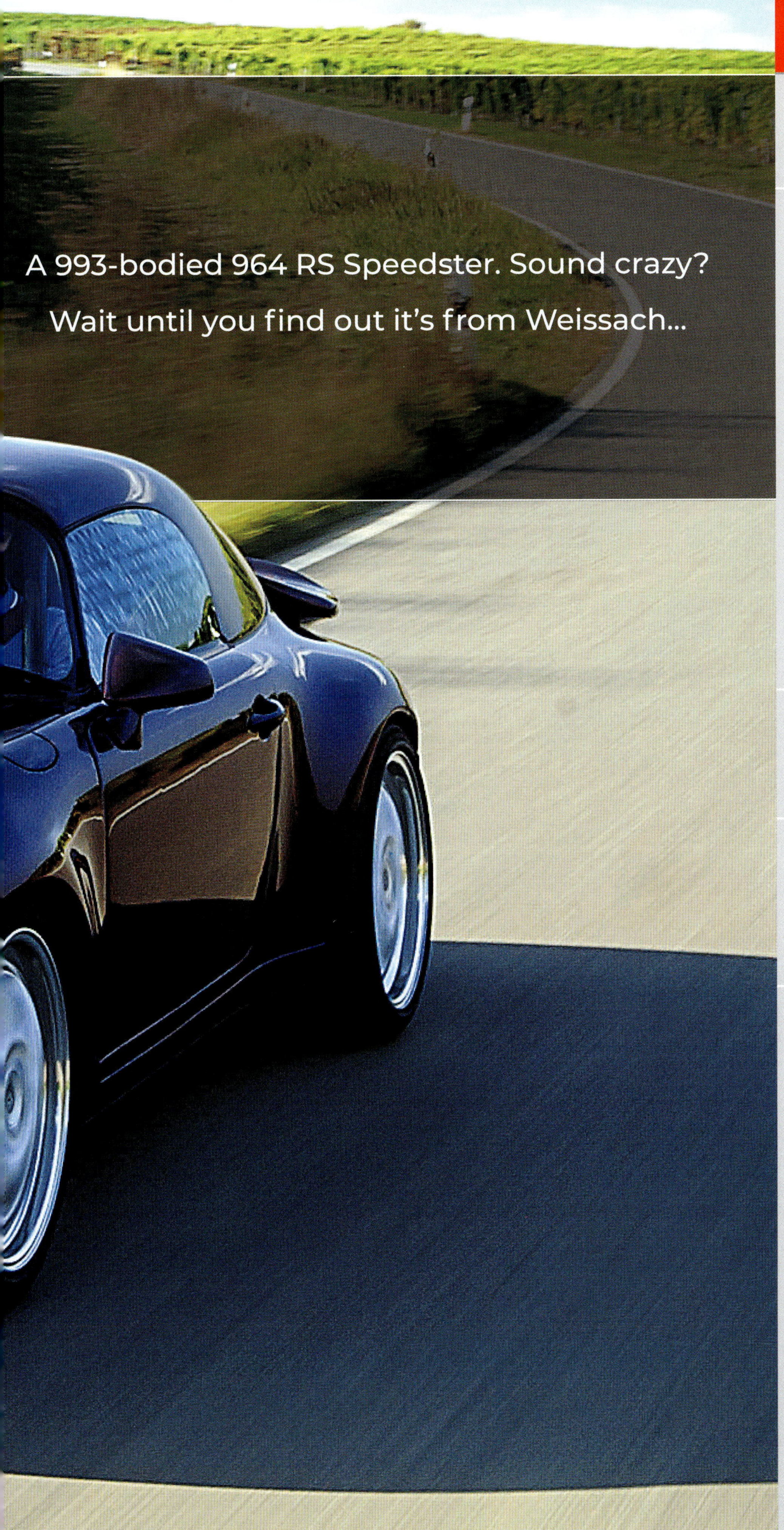




# 964 RS SPEEDSTER
(1994)

## ENGINE

**Capacity:** 3,746cc

**Compression ratio:** 11:6.1

**Maximum power:** 310hp

**Maximum torque:** 680Nm

**Modifications:** Factory 964 RS body converted to 993 Speedster including 993 RS body with 993 Turbo preproduction rear wing, GT2 front lip and GT2-spec Speedline wheels; M64/04 engine mated to G50/31 gearbox; custom stainless steel exhaust including manifolds, downpipe and heat exchangers; 964 Turbo 3.6 rear axle; Momo Sport steering wheel; carbon-Kevlar hardtop and side mirrors from Strosek

## WHEELS & TYRES

**Front:** 8x18-inch Speedline wheels; 225/40/ZR18 tyres

**Rear:** 10x18-inch Speedline wheels; 285/30/ZR18 tyres

## DIMENSIONS

**Length:** 4,245mm

**Width:** 1,735mm

**Weight:** 1,210kg

## PERFORMANCE

**0-60mph:** Unknown

**Top speed:** 189mph

Just when you think you've seen it all, a car like this crops up. What is particularly unusual is for such a car to hail from the Porsche factory itself. The base car is actually a 1991 model year 964 RS, originally equipped with the 3.6-litre Rennsport engine. The story goes that the car's current owner saw the 993 Speedster 'birthday present' for Herr Porsche being built at Weissach and asked for an example to be built for him, too. His friends at the company agreed, but he had to supply the car for the conversion. This, of course, means the Speedster shown here is the only such car to be based on an RS (the car made for Ferry Porsche, incidentally, uses a Carrera engine with a Tiptronic gearbox).

The mammoth conversion to Speedster-spec was carried out at the end of 1993: apparently Weissach engineers first started on repairing crash damage found on the Rennsport's body (this was not structural) before the factory conversion to Speedster. Huge works here involved removing the 964 RS roof, pillars and all glass before the updated 993 bodywork could be painted in its original 964-spec Amethyst hue and fitted to the car's body.

Completed by spring 1994, the Speedster came with a few choice additions at the request of its owner, reflecting his own motorsporting background. For example, to aid body stiffness, an N/GT-style Matter roll cage with door bars was fitted to the new-look Rennsport Speedster, along with a lightweight carbon-Kevlar fixed hardtop. Road registered, the car was given back to the owner to complete the first of its 62,000-kilometres as the world's most positively insane factory Porsche 911 Speedster.

The evolution doesn't stop there, however. In 1996, the body received some aerodynamic improvements including a wing from the pre-production 993 Turbo and a front splitter from the 993 GT2, along with 18-inch Speedline wheels (fitted at the time using spacers) and a revised exhaust system with duel pipes.

Then in 2001, the owner's own team oversaw the Speedster's final, eccentric upgrade, replacing the 3.6-litre M64/03 flat six with the M64/04 engine from the 964 RS 3.8-litre (in standard form this engine produces 359Nm of torque but 400Nm was achieved for the RS Speedster thanks to some subtle engine work). A six-speed G50/31 gearbox from the later 993 RS was then mated to this larger flat-six firecracker, before the 964 RS rear axle was swapped out for the wider axle of the 964 Turbo, which meant the Speedlines could be mounted without spacers. A final, altogether subtler touch to the Speedster was the fitting of a Momo Sport steering wheel.

So what's the thinking behind this enigmatic Porsche 911 in the first place? Our owner is forthright with his answer: "As a former racing driver I wanted something different for my collection, but something that was still heavily performance oriented, rather than just a show car. The project, as you can see, has evolved over a number of years, but I've always loved driving this thing. It's so different to any other Porsche 911 you'll ever drive."

And with that I'm thrown the keys to what is, quite comfortably, the wildest Porsche Speedster on the planet. Turning the key, the engine quickly catches, before settling to a smooth idle despite a raucous thrumming of the flat six reverberating through the bare cabin. The clutch, pleasantly, is lighter than expected, and after slotting the shifter into first, the biting point is found easily. In no time at all, Speedster and driver are away.

I soon let fly, aware I'm on public (albeit very quiet) roads, but it's clear this Speedster can climb to a ludicrously heady speed at an absurd rate. What's truly astonishing though, is the Speedster's ability to dispatch of corners at such frightening pace for an air-cooled 911. Grip is inspirational and, propelled vehemently by that guttural 3.8-litre engine, I'm shooting through long, fast turns at the pace of a 993 Turbo. If the tyres weren't as old I'd be taking them even faster.

Stepping out from the car and handing the keys back to their owner, I try to make sense of what I've just experienced. Its concept may be as bizarre as its story, but what is undeniable is this is a truly exquisite creation made to the very highest calibre. This 964 Speedster is one of the most exciting 911s I've ever driven; its many parts marry beautifully together and the real shame lies in the fact this is the only one of its kind.

Weeks on from my test drive, it's still hard to believe a car like this even exists. That it has credible proof as a Weissach work of art is even more startling. As for the fact it's been driven – hard – for more than 62,000 kilometres on our public roads for the last decade? I think, at last, we really have now seen it all.

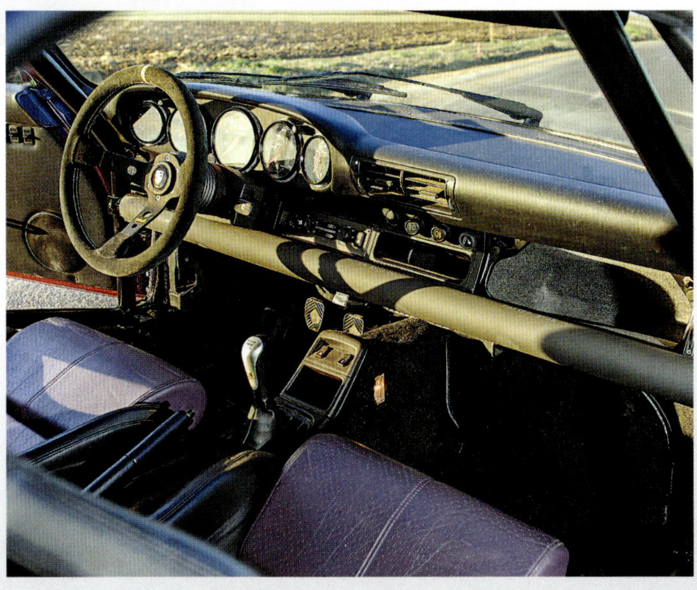

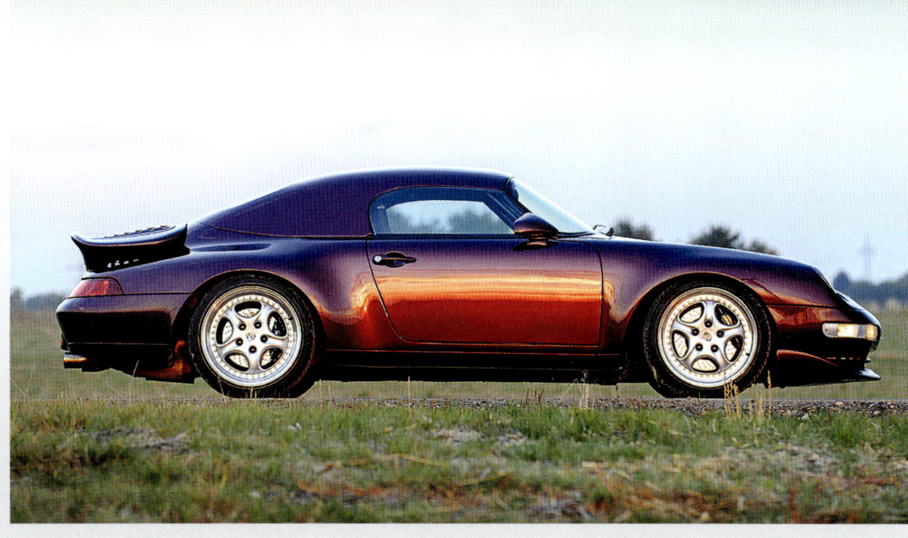

The cabin unmistakably heralds from 964-generation of RS, identifiable thanks to dashboard, colour-coded leather Recaros, and pared back door cards. Original tachometer masks the redline of the Speedster's larger 3.8-litre Rennsport flat six

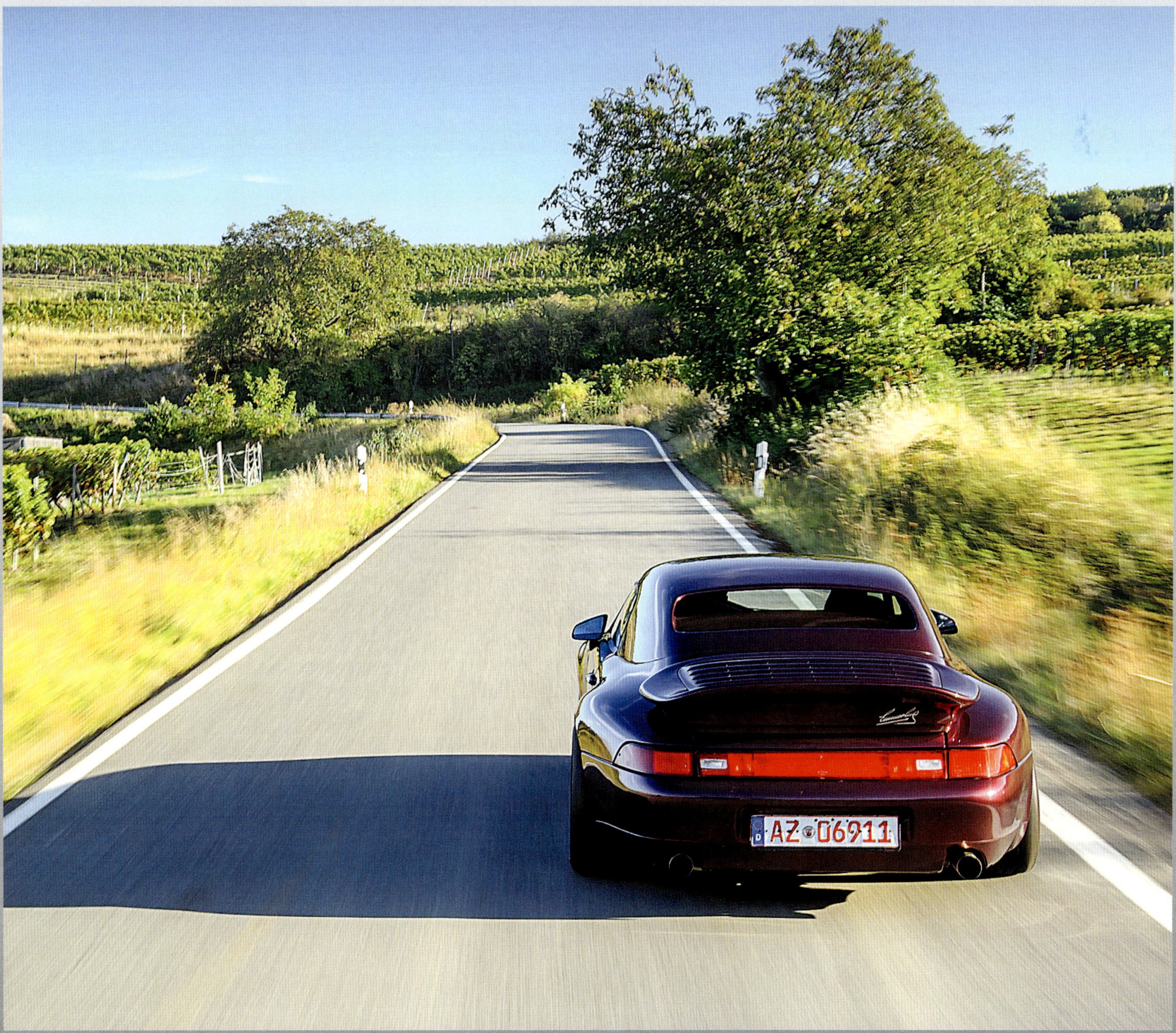

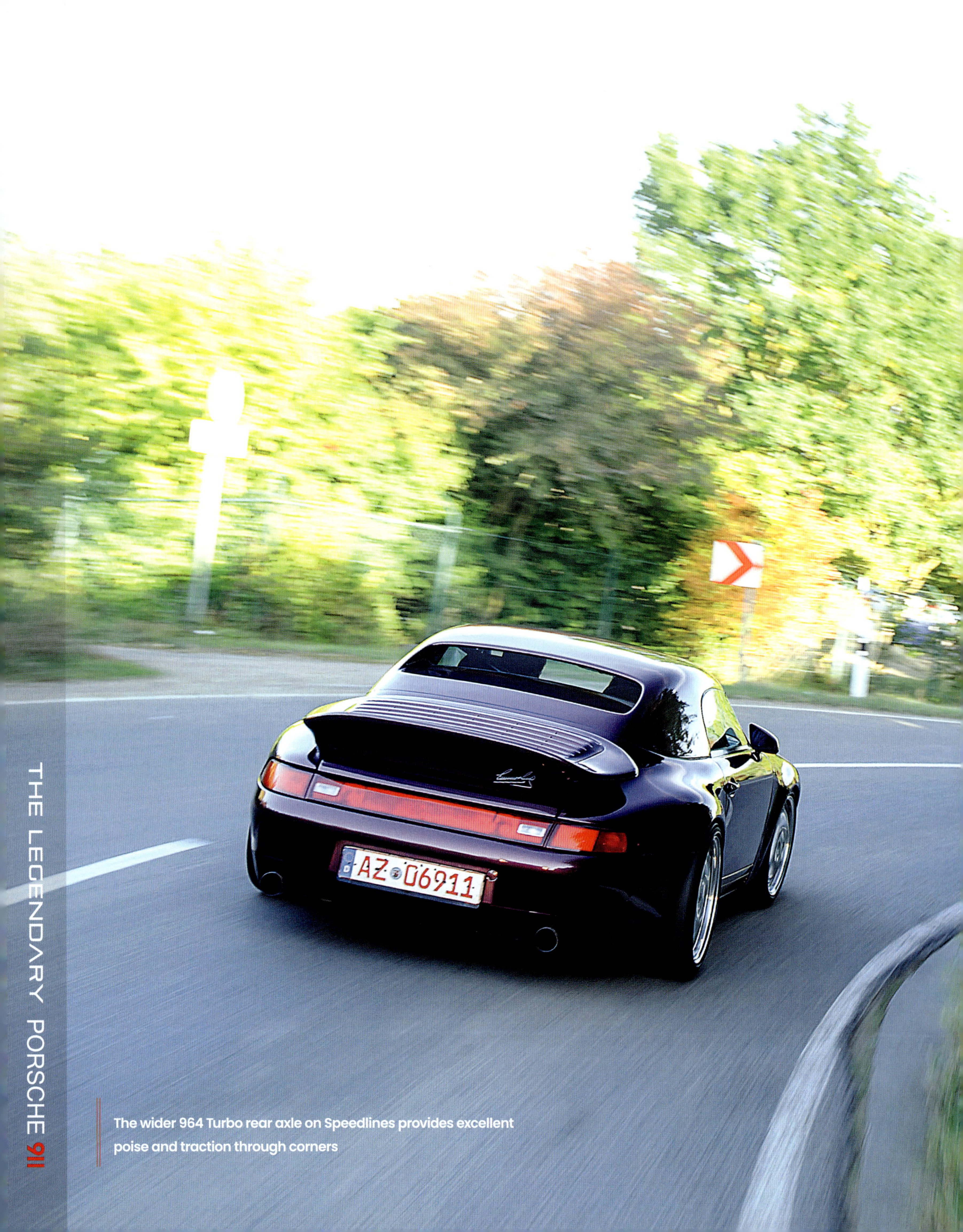

The wider 964 Turbo rear axle on Speedlines provides excellent poise and traction through corners

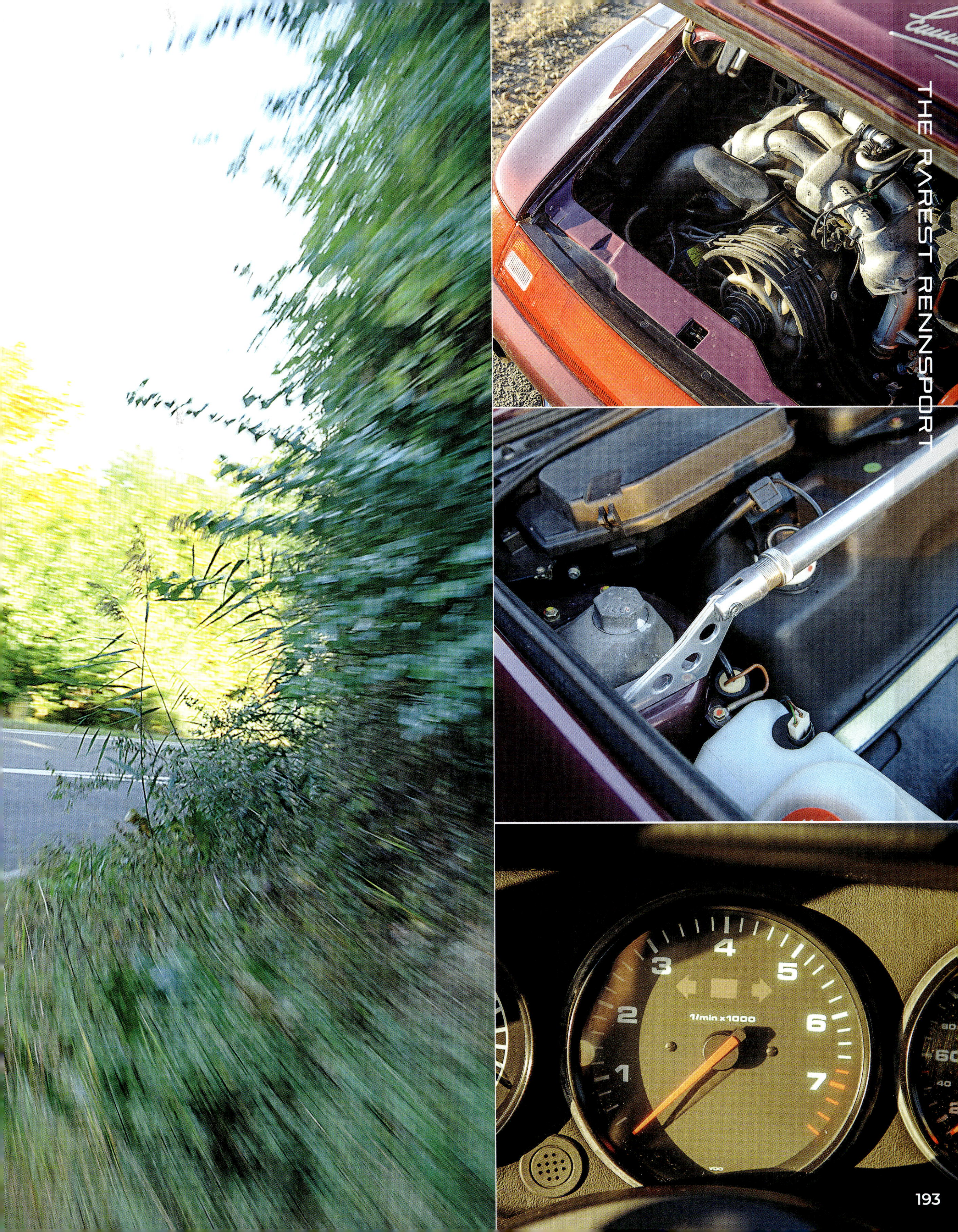

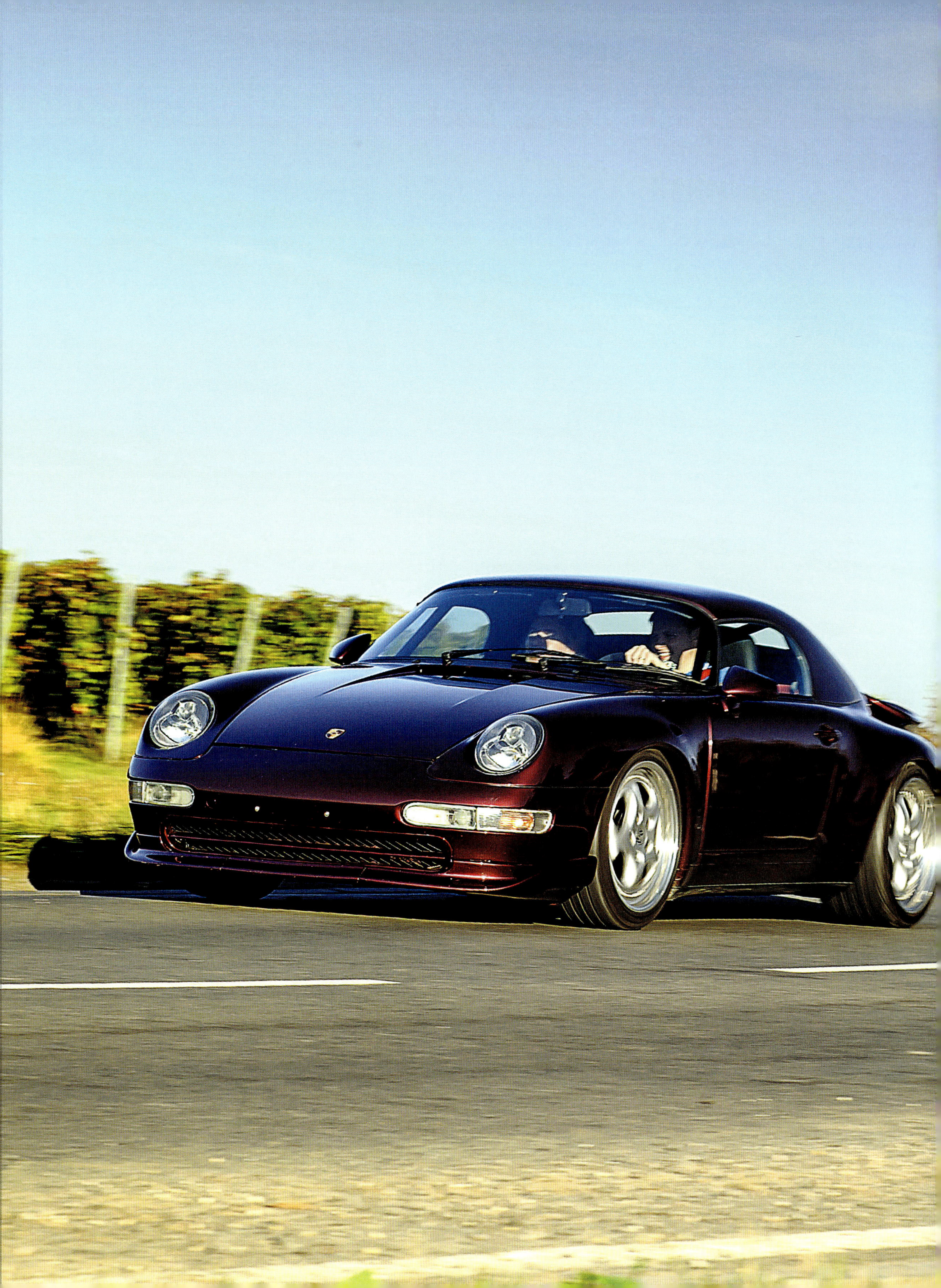

# TOAD HALL'S
# WILD RIDE

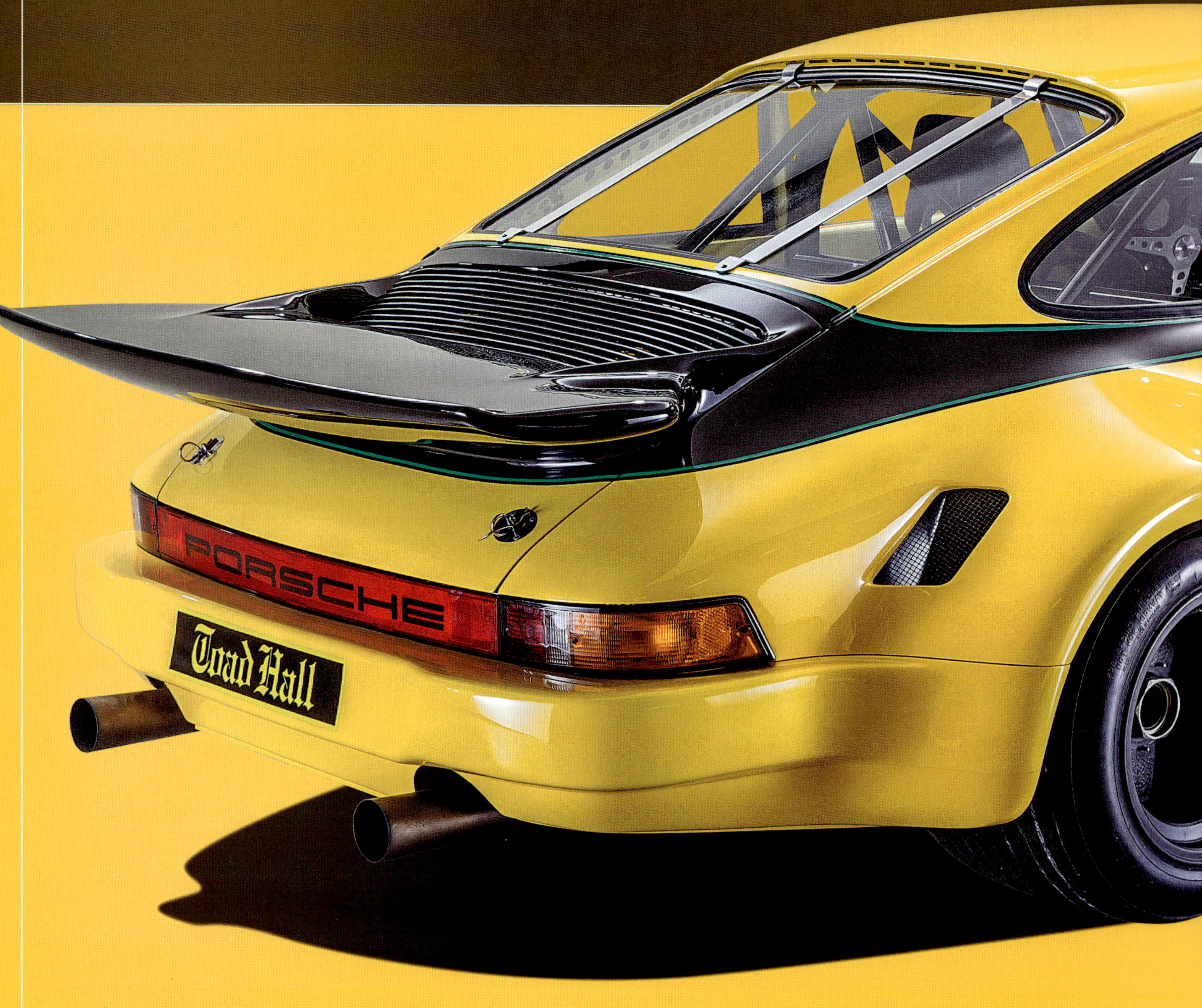

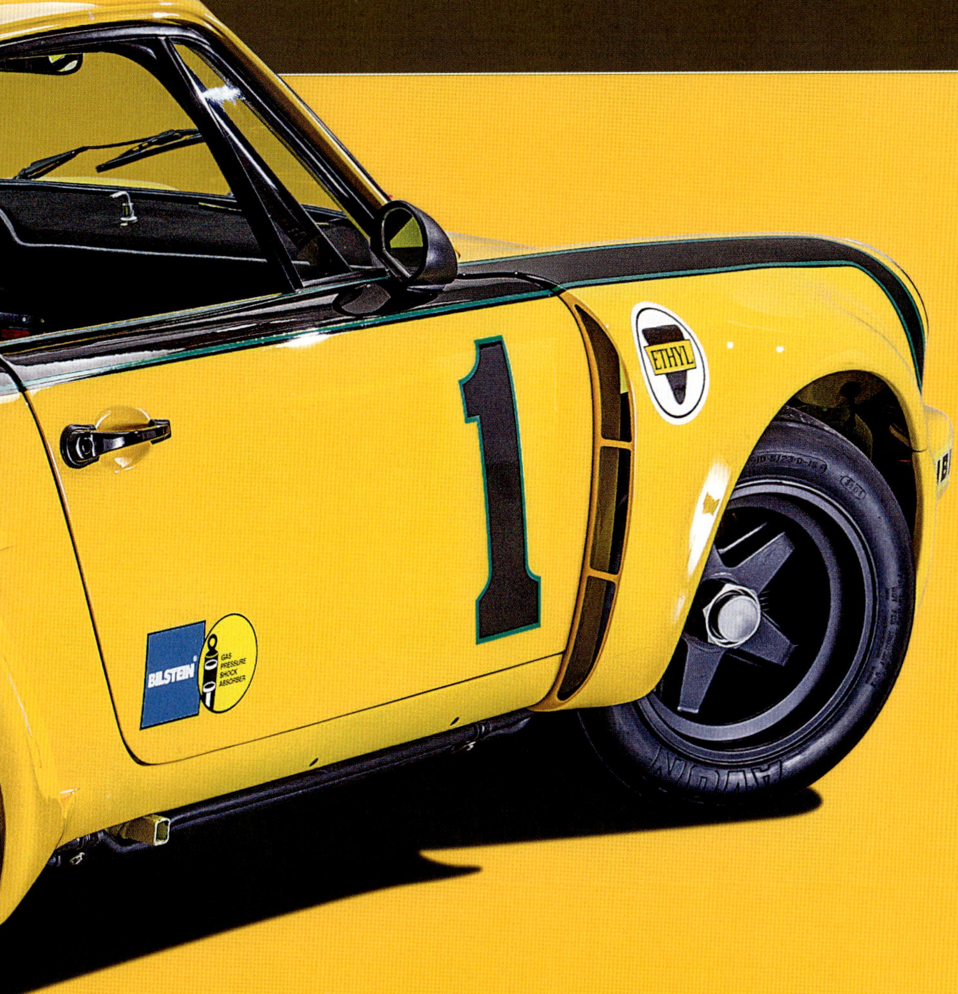

Relive the story of this famously liveried American race car, one of the most successful 3.0 RSRs to take to the track in the United States and beyond.



# CARRERA RSR

(1974)

**ENGINE**

**Capacity:** 2,996cc
**Compression ratio:** 10:5.1
**Maximum power:** 330bhp
**Maximum torque:** 314Nm
**Transmission:** Five-speed manual (type 915)

**SUSPENSION**

**Front:** MacPherson struts, lower wishbones, coil springs over
**Rear:** Trailing arms, coil springs over telescopic dampers

**WHEELS & TYRES**

**Front:** 10x15-inch magnesium alloys; 10.5/23.0-15 slick tyres
**Rear:** 13x15-inch magnesium alloys; 13.0/25.0-15 slick tyres

**DIMENSIONS**

**Length:** 4,350mm
**Width:** 1,896mm
**Weight:** 900kg

**PERFORMANCE**

**0-60mph:** Not tested
**Top speed:** 179mph (est)

The 917 was the first car to give Porsche an overall win at the 24 Hours of Le Mans. However, that success would prove to be short-lived, as the FIA promptly banned it at the end of the 1971 season for being such a dominant force. Thus, Porsche needed to go back to the drawing board. This time around, they conceived a production-based, naturally aspirated race car that would go on to become one of the most sought-after race cars ever – the Carrera RSR.

The RSR started out as a 2.8-litre, 280-horsepower racer that was run by both privateers and Porsche's works team. However, by 1974, the team were already elbows-deep in their attempt to create a turbocharged production-based car – a project that would go on to spawn both the 934 and 935, venerable champions in their own right. Thus, when Porsche created the 330-horsepower RSR 3.0, it was only ever raced by private teams. Approximately five dozen RSR 3.0s were created and sent to private teams around the world. One of those, 911 460 9049, is the one you see featured here.

Porsche's 3.0 RSR represented a serious departure from the smaller 2.8-litre models. Aside from increasing displacement, the 3.0-litre replaced the magnesium crankcase with an aluminium variant, in order to better handle the physical forces that came with this bump in output. The 3.0-litre complemented its increase in power by way of wider wheel arches, a full-width front spoiler and the ubiquitous 'whale tail' rear wing. In lieu of torsion bars, the 3.0's suspension was updated to utilise coil springs as well.

This specific car, the third 1974 RSR 3.0 ever built, was sold directly from the factory to Michael Keyser of the Toad Hall Racing Team, for use in the 1974 IMSA Camel GT championship season. The year 1974 was the only occasion that the Camel GT series would leave the United States, undertaking races in both Mexico and Canada.

That same year, Toad Hall and 9049 took its act overseas, competing in the 1974 24 Hours of Le Mans. Primary drivers Keyser and Milt Minter were joined by Swiss driver Paul Blancpain, and the trio would race to an 11th-place finish in the GT class, coming 20th overall. Their 246 laps wasn't enough to compete with the best-performing RSR, run by Porsche Club Romand, which completed 312 laps for a third in class, seventh overall

finish. This would however be the first and last time chassis 9049 participated at Le Mans, but certainly not the last time the car would venture overseas for top-level endurance racing.

Keyser and Toad Hall took 9049 back to the 1975 IMSA Camel GT series, starting with the 24 Hours of Daytona in December 1974. Milt Minter was replaced with two Mexican endurance racers, Guillermo 'Billy' Sprowls and Andres Contreras. The three would go on to achieve a second-place at Daytona; again, their efforts were stymied by yet another 3.0 RSR, this time driven by Peter Gregg and Hurley Haywood of the Brumos team.

In 1976, Toad Hall sold the car to John Wood, an American driver. Wood's goal was to use 9049 to run in the SCCA Trans-Am series, but the car was not within the specifications laid out by the SCCA. Thus, 9049 underwent some bodywork revisions to adhere to these regulations. The two most serious changes to the car were the addition of a 1976 911 Turbo rear wing, and a reduction in the width of the rear fender flares.

In 1978, just after the 24 Hours of Daytona but prior to the 12 Hours of Sebring, 9049 was once again sold off. This time, it would land in the hands of the Miami Auto Racing team, helmed by drivers Jack Refenning and Dr. Ray Mummery. Oddly, 9049 traded hands without an engine being involved; thus, Miami Auto Racing had a blank slate on their hands. The narrow Trans-Am bodywork would prove to be a good fit in the IMSA Camel GT GTU class, but the team needed an engine that would work with the regulations. Therefore a 2.5-litre engine was sourced, and the car was sent to the 12 Hours of Sebring.

In 2002, the car was sold to the Blackhawk Collection in California, where it sat for two years prior to its arrival at Canepa. After purchasing the car from Blackhawk, Canepa once again tore the car down, preparing the vehicle for historic racing. After an extensive teardown, rebuild, and subsequent track test, 9049 was ready, its Toad Hall livery as bright as the day it left the factory.

Shortly after its restoration at Canepa, it was sold off to a private owner. We can only hope that the new owner sees 9049's incredible pedigree and continues to take it out to historic racing events, be it in the United States or elsewhere. One of the most successful U.S. RSRs should not be left to languish, after all.

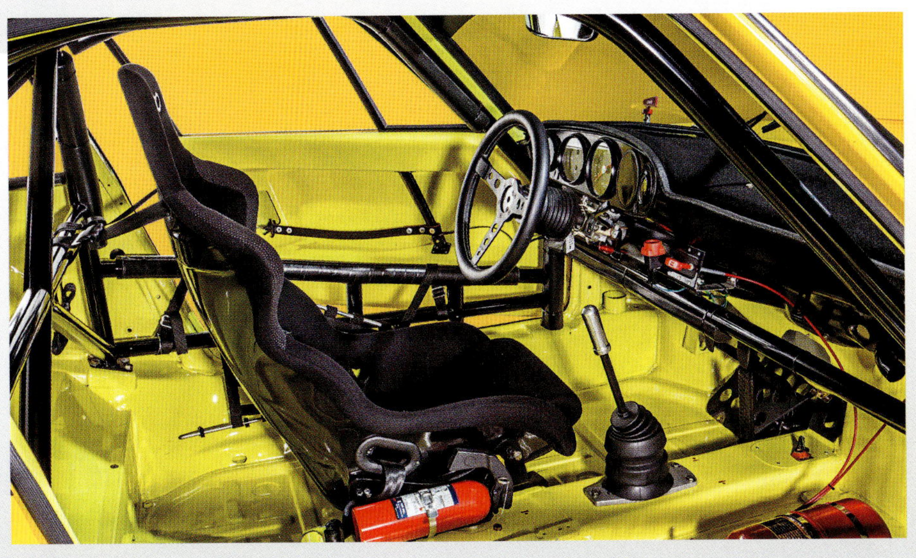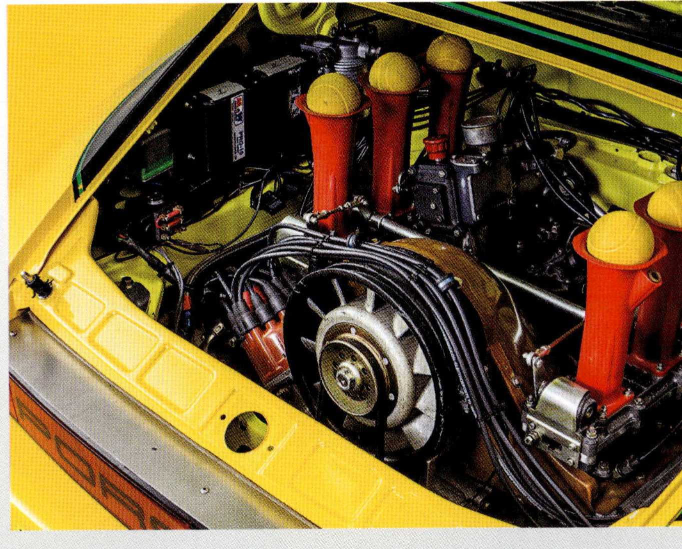

After racing with a 2.5-litre engine for some years, a correct 3.0-litre flat six was returned to power the Toad Hall RSR. The car remains primed for racing, with a front-mounted fuel tank and pared back interior

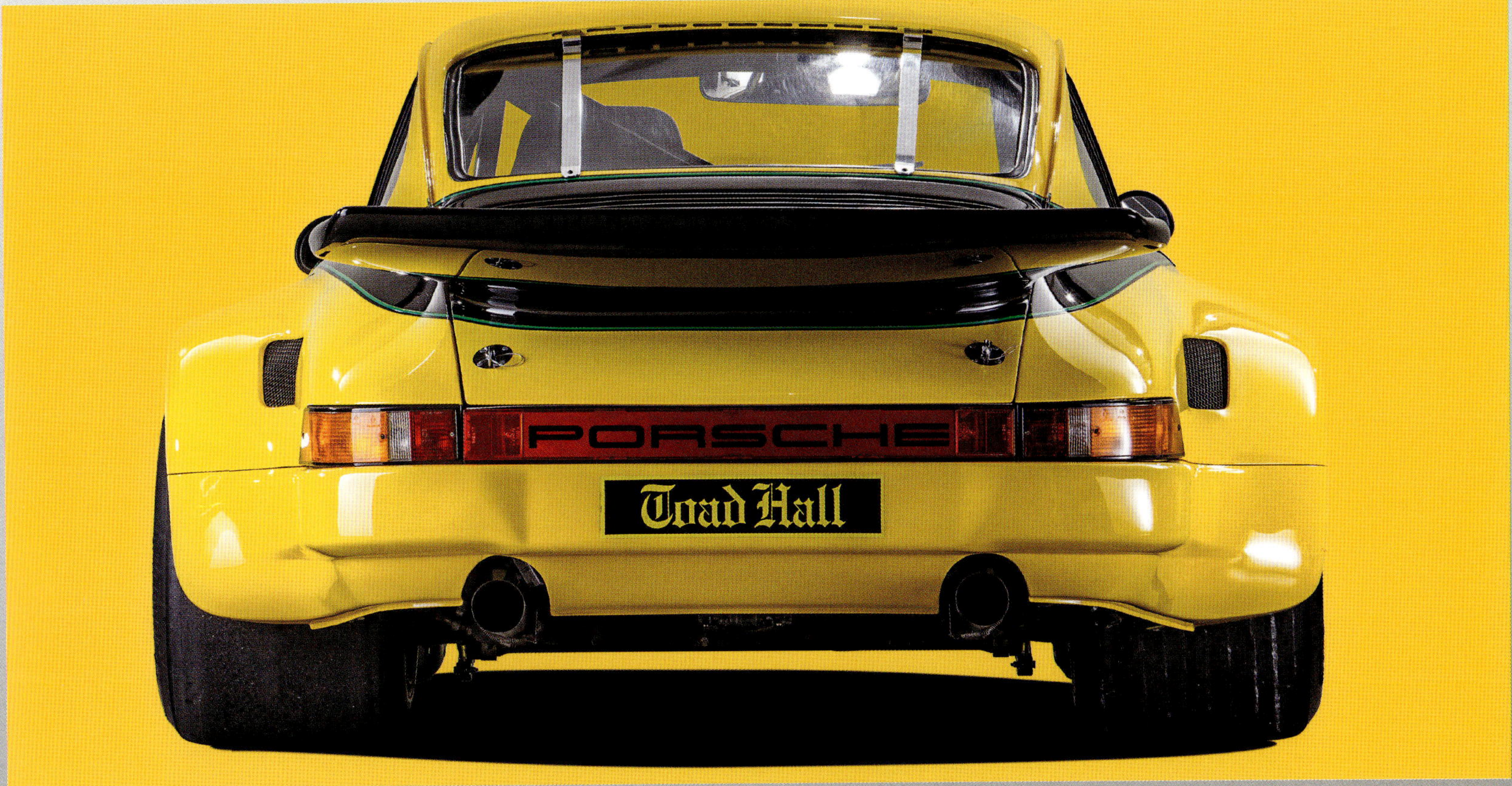


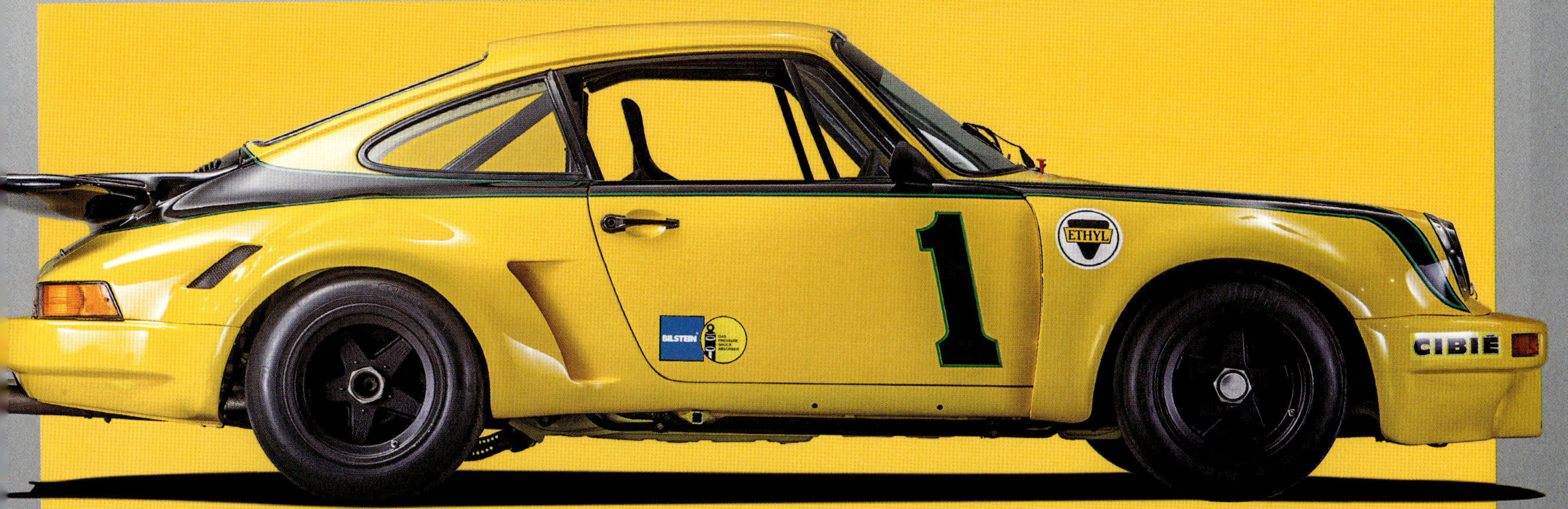

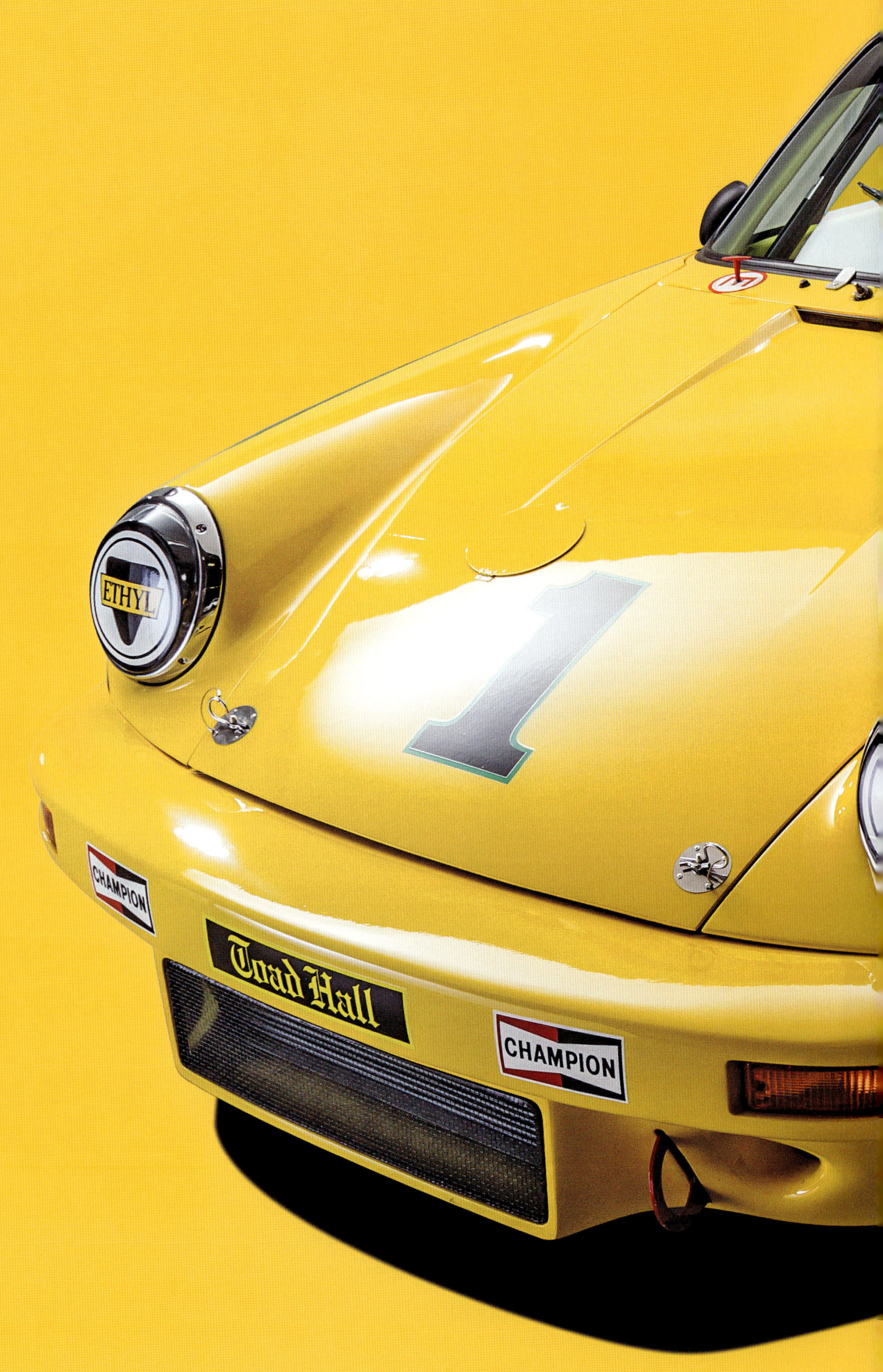
ETHYL
1
CHAMPION
Toad Hall
CHAMPION

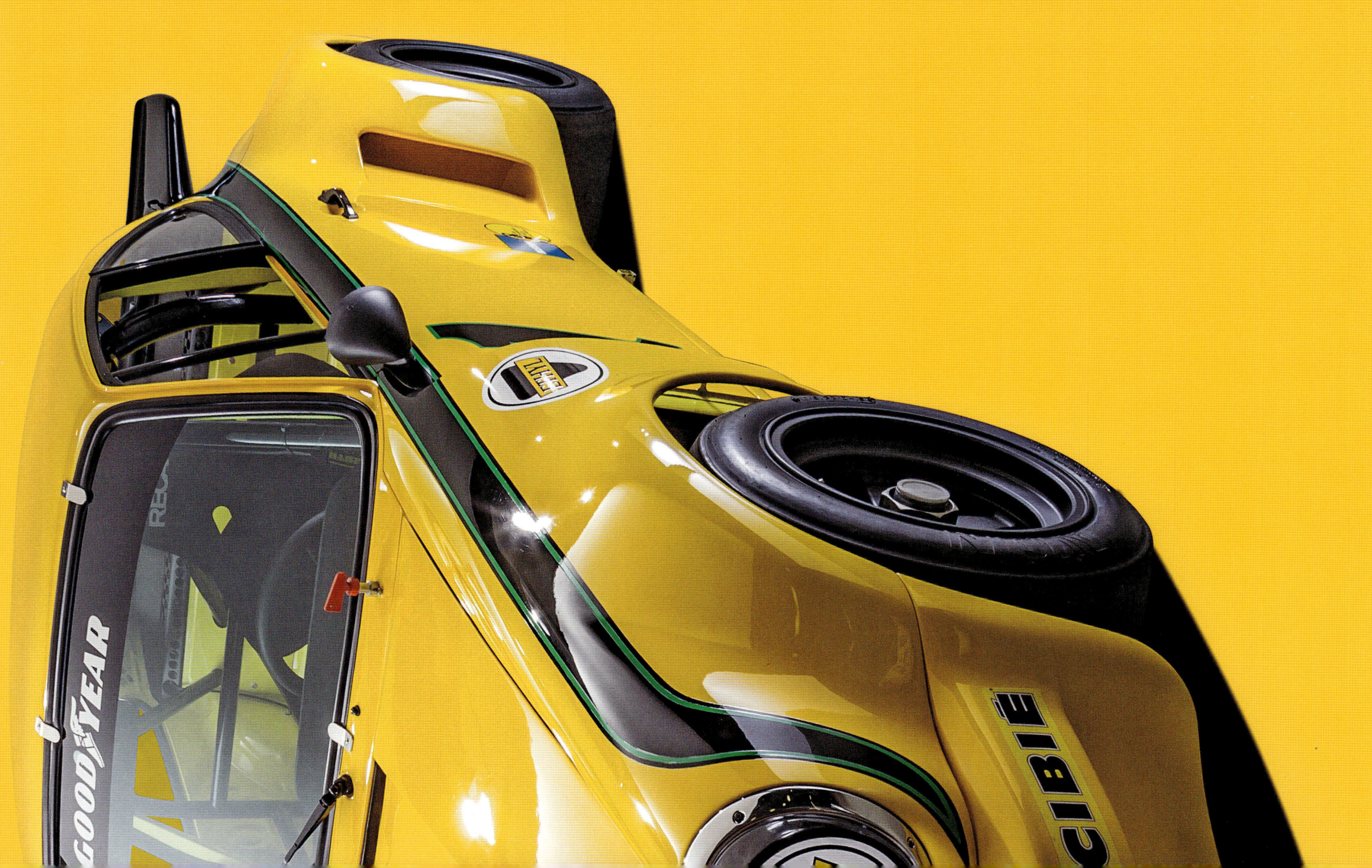

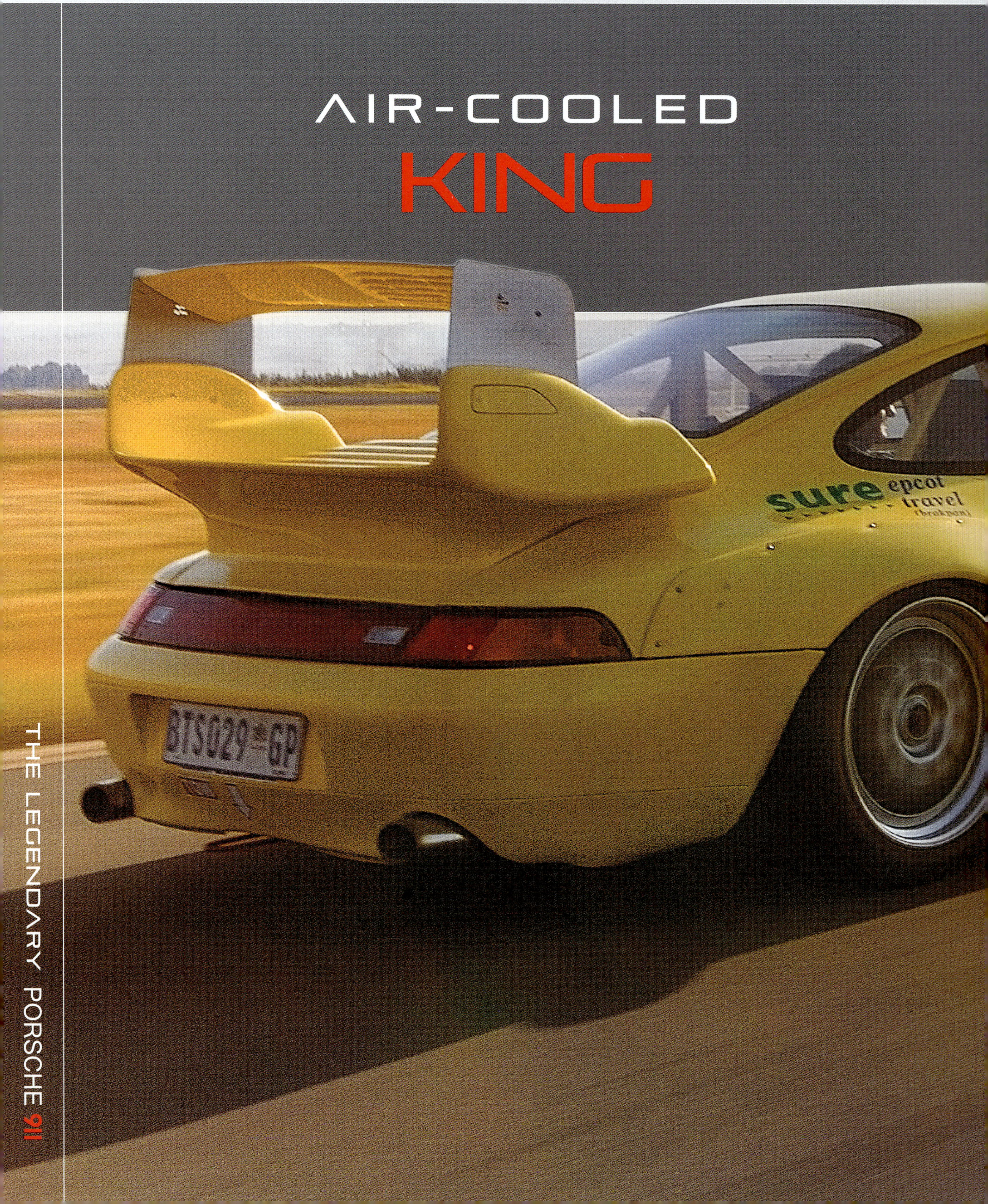

# AIR-COOLED
## KING

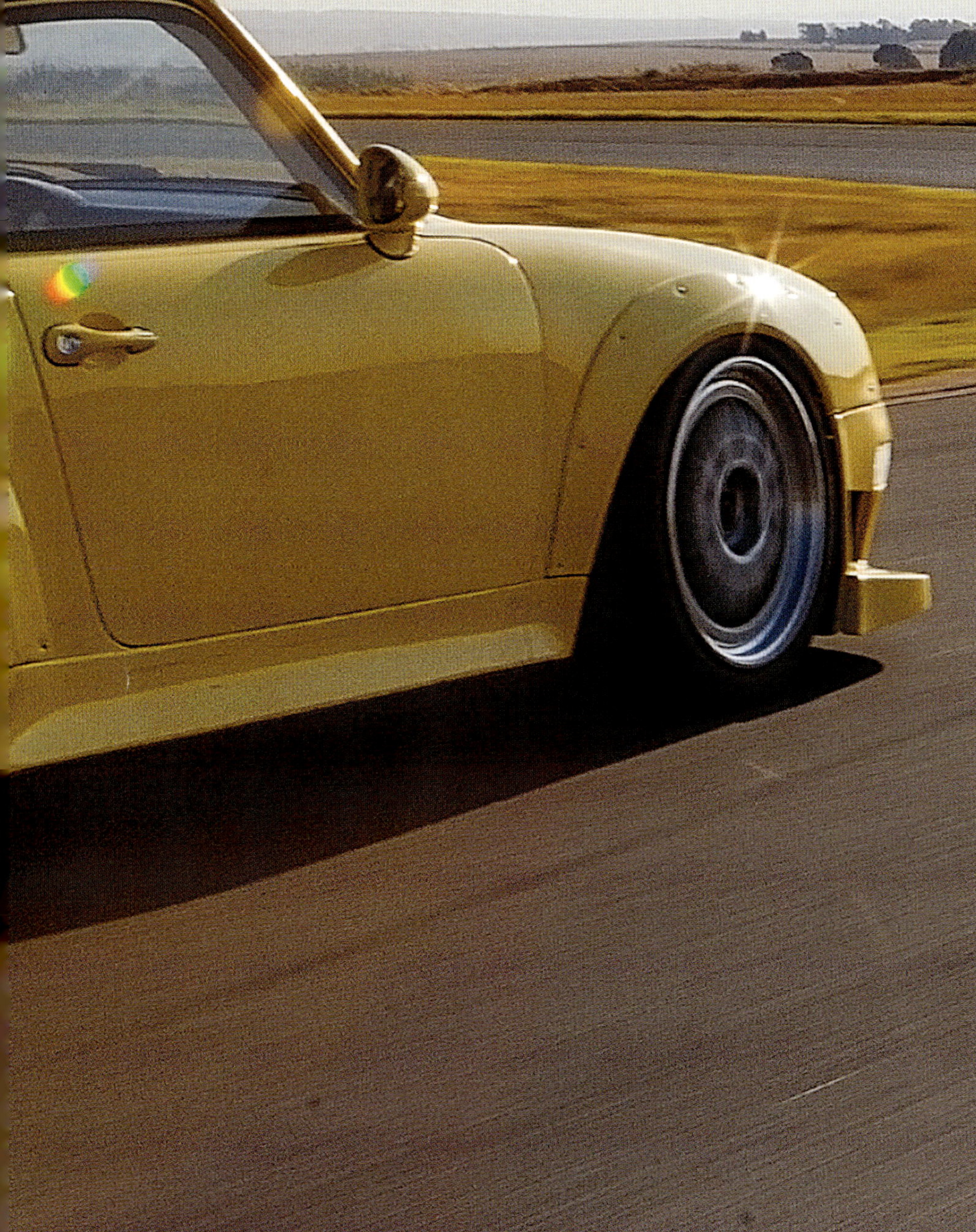

For many, the 993's engine is the pinnacle of air-cooled engineering. Here we put its most extreme iteration through its paces.



# 993 CUP RSR 3.8 RSR

(1998)

## ENGINE

**Capacity:** 3,746cc

**Compression ratio:** 11:4.1

**Maximum power:** 325bhp @ 6,900rpm

**Maximum torque:** 353Nm @ 5,500rpm

**Transmission:** Six-speed manual, straight cut gears

**Modifications:** Factory lightweight package; restrictors removed

## SUSPENSION

**Front:** MacPherson struts; coil springs; adjustable gas dampers; anti-roll bar

**Rear:** Multi-link; coil springs, gas dampers, anti-roll bar

## WHEELS & TYRES

**Front:** Split-rim wheels; Dunlop SP Sport 250/640 R18 slicks

**Rear:** Split-rim wheels; Dunlop SP Sport 280/640 R18 slicks

## DIMENSIONS

**Length:** 4,245mm

**Width:** 1,735mm

**Weight:** 1,120kg

## PERFORMANCE

**0-60mph:** 4.0 seconds

**Top speed:** 162mph

Even if you are not of the opinion, like several 911 fans, that the 993 should be put on a pedestal, you have to admit that it was, and still is, an exceptional era in the 911s heritage. Not only is its smooth exterior design a visual delight, but being the last of the air-cooled generation gives it a unique place in the 911's history.

Dig a little deeper, and the 993 RS is one of a handful of 993s that most of us lust after. Until its design, the RS featured the same base engine as used in race cars such as the 964 RSR, the largest capacity engine fitted to a production 911. This engine was also the foundation of other race cars.

However, in terms of naturally aspirated 993 engines, its zenith was reached in the design of the 993 RSR. Here the 3.8-litre engine developed depending on the literature you have read, between 315bhp and 340bhp. There are also a few companies that would actually enlarge this engine's capacity to either 3.9 or 4.0 litres in size.

Today that power figure might not seen like much, but take into account that the RSR tips the scales at only 1,120 kilograms, and it is suddenly a very attractive result. This specific car was ordered with the lightweight package; the car has a different front splitter, and the doors and all the windows (except the windscreen) are lighter compared to a standard 993 RSR. The lighter windows also included the sliding mechanism for the driver's window.

One of the most attractive facts about this car is the fact that it is actually road-registered (the owner admits that more than half the 5,500 miles the car has done were actually done on the road!). The rest has been done on the track, although admittedly not all of it while racing. Even though it would have been quite an experience to drive this race car on the road, the track is the perfect environment on which to experience the epitome of Porsche's naturally-aspirated, air-cooled development. This, of course, is the final evolution of the flat six before it adopted water-cooling.

If you are used to road cars, the details of this car include the peculiar tyre sizes, the fact that the wheels are pushed up into those wide wheel arches, the split-rim wheels and most notably, the bi-plane rear wing. The RSR really does look hunkered down and ready to tackle the next endurance race. A simple turn of the key kicks the 3.8-litre engine into life. The sound from the engine and exhaust is not as loud as I thought it would be – this is owing to the exhaust system which has been replaced with another, quieter, system, and offers a balance for both road and track use (the owner admits the original system would have had the authorities knocking on his door).

However, as soon as the engine catches, the cabin is filled with the harshest of clunking metal sounds that you could ever imagine. If you haven't experienced straight cut gears before, you will seriously think that the gearbox is about to rumble itself to pieces. Press the clutch in, though, and all those noises disappear. I select first gear, let the clutch out and we are off. The gearbox has the same slick and easy shift action as that of other 993s, although here it has a springy action to it, assisting you as you move the lever out of each slot.

The first lap I take very easy. Suddenly my brain seems to forget all about the noise, focusing entirely on the directness of the steering system and the lightness of the car instead. As I become more comfortable with the RSR, I start to rev the engine that bit harder. It does feel like a massive punishment to the drivetrain, though. The engine actually only picks up speed as it swings past 5,000rpm, but by then the sound is already borderline ear-splitting. Then the needle simply swings faster and I quickly slot the next gear home a few 100revs before 7,000rpm. It is an intensive, raw and grinding sound. There is no doubt that the engine is built to be driven at high revolutions all the time.

I do a final lap and try my utmost to enjoy it, but at the same time take in every conceivable aspect of the drive. For a moment I can imagine what racers must experience, the intensity, both physically and mentally, of piloting such a car lap after lap, must be wholly draining but also extremely exhilarating. Mention RSR and most enthusiasts will think of the 2.8 and 3.0-litre RSRs of the 1970s, and maybe even the recent endurance versions. But back in 1997 and 1998, Porsche built just 30 of these cars and after driving this example, my top five 911 wish list has been well and truly shuffled.

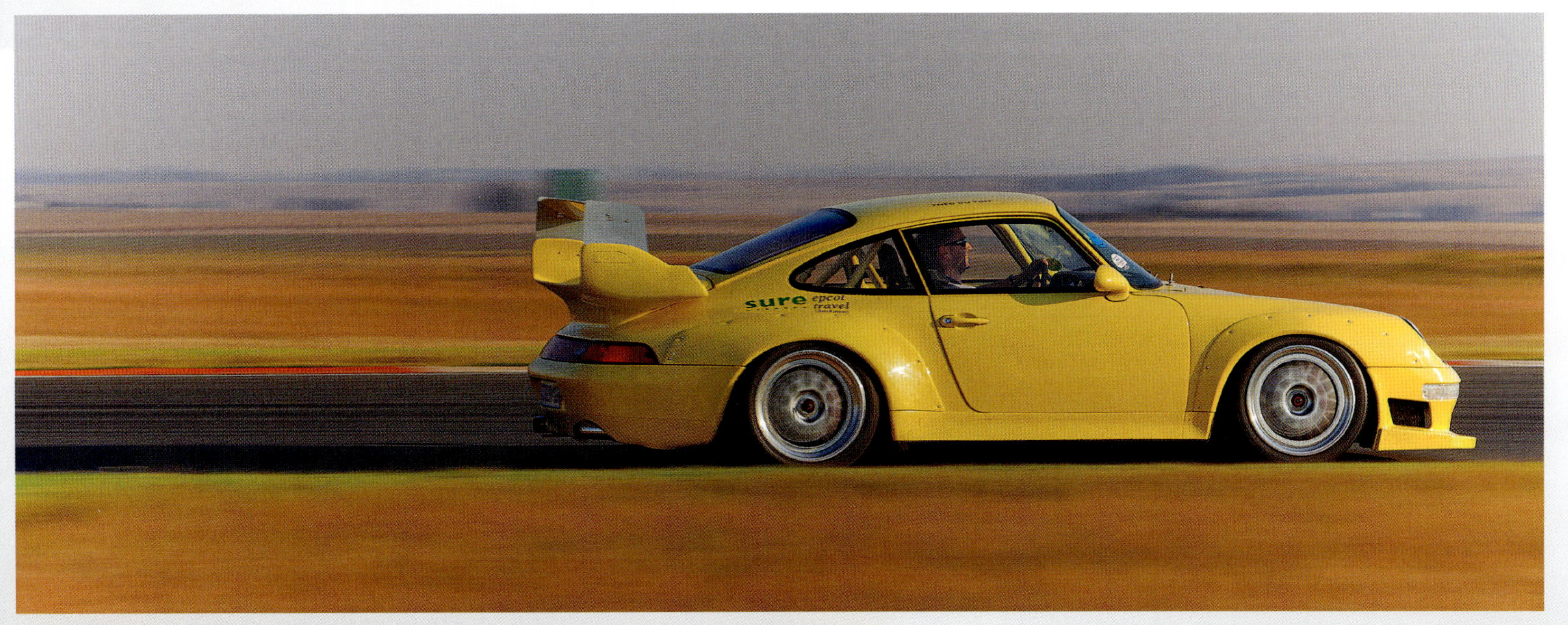

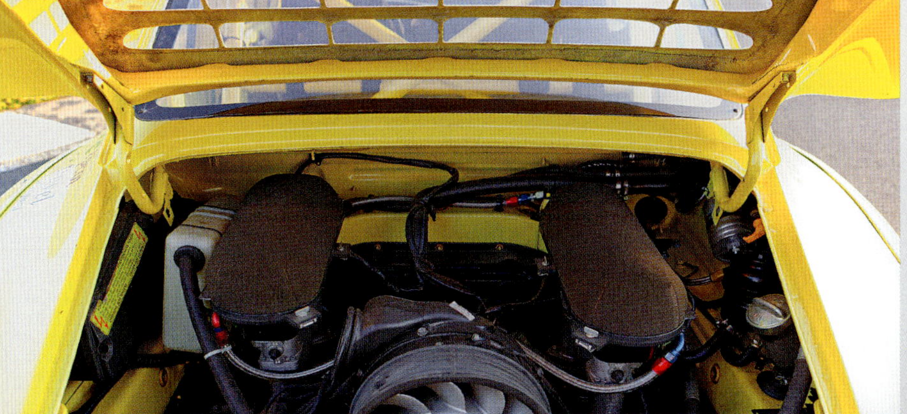

Kerb weight of just 1,120 kilograms is sprightly, making good use of the 325 available horsepower

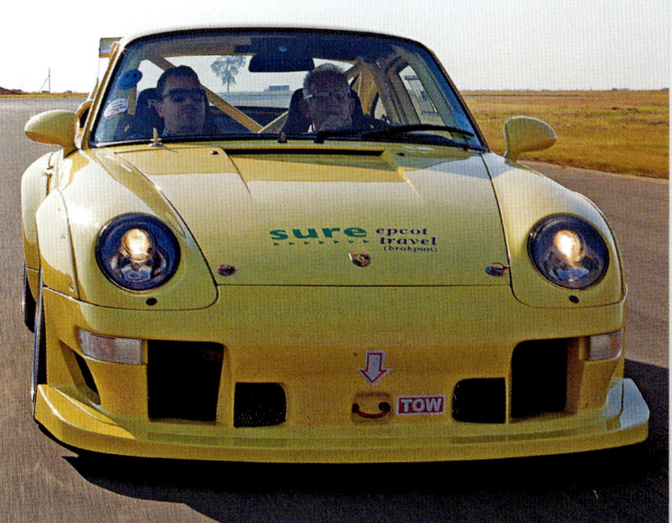

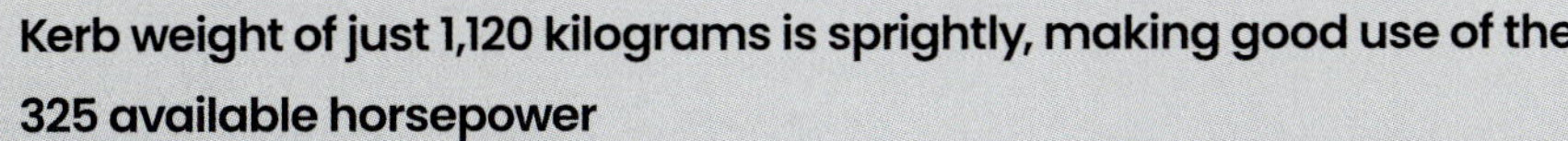

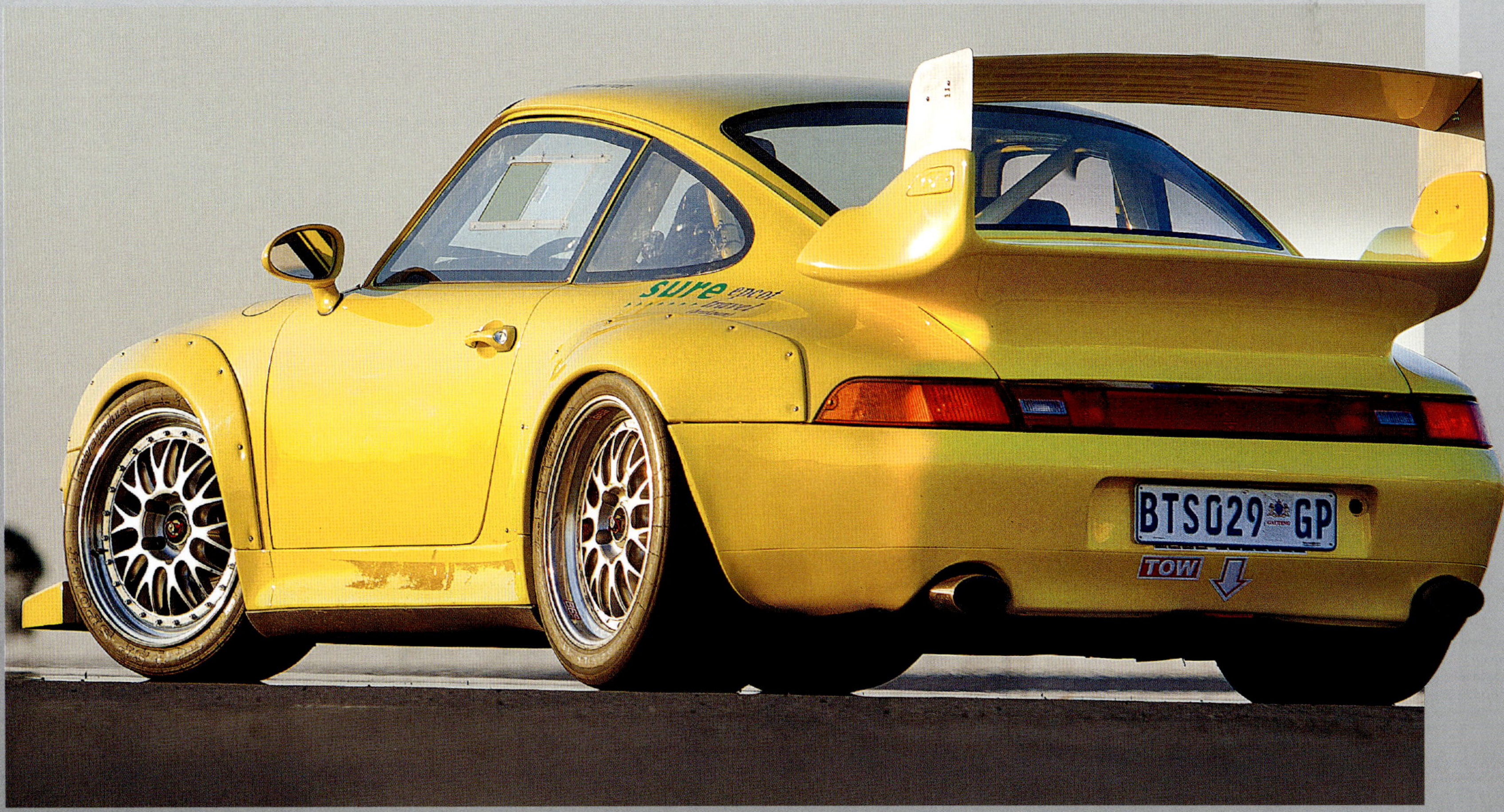

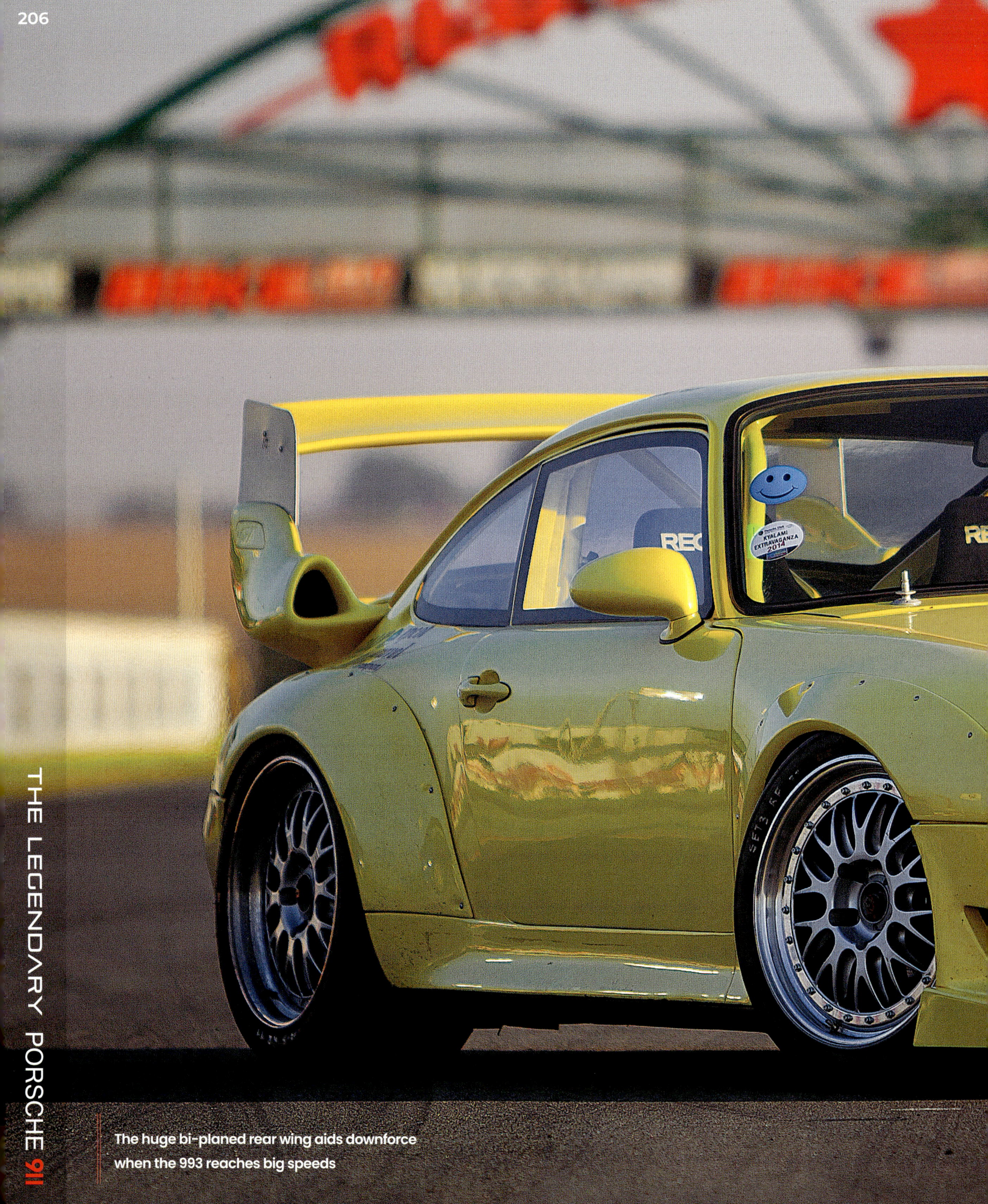



The huge bi-planed rear wing aids downforce
when the 993 reaches big speeds

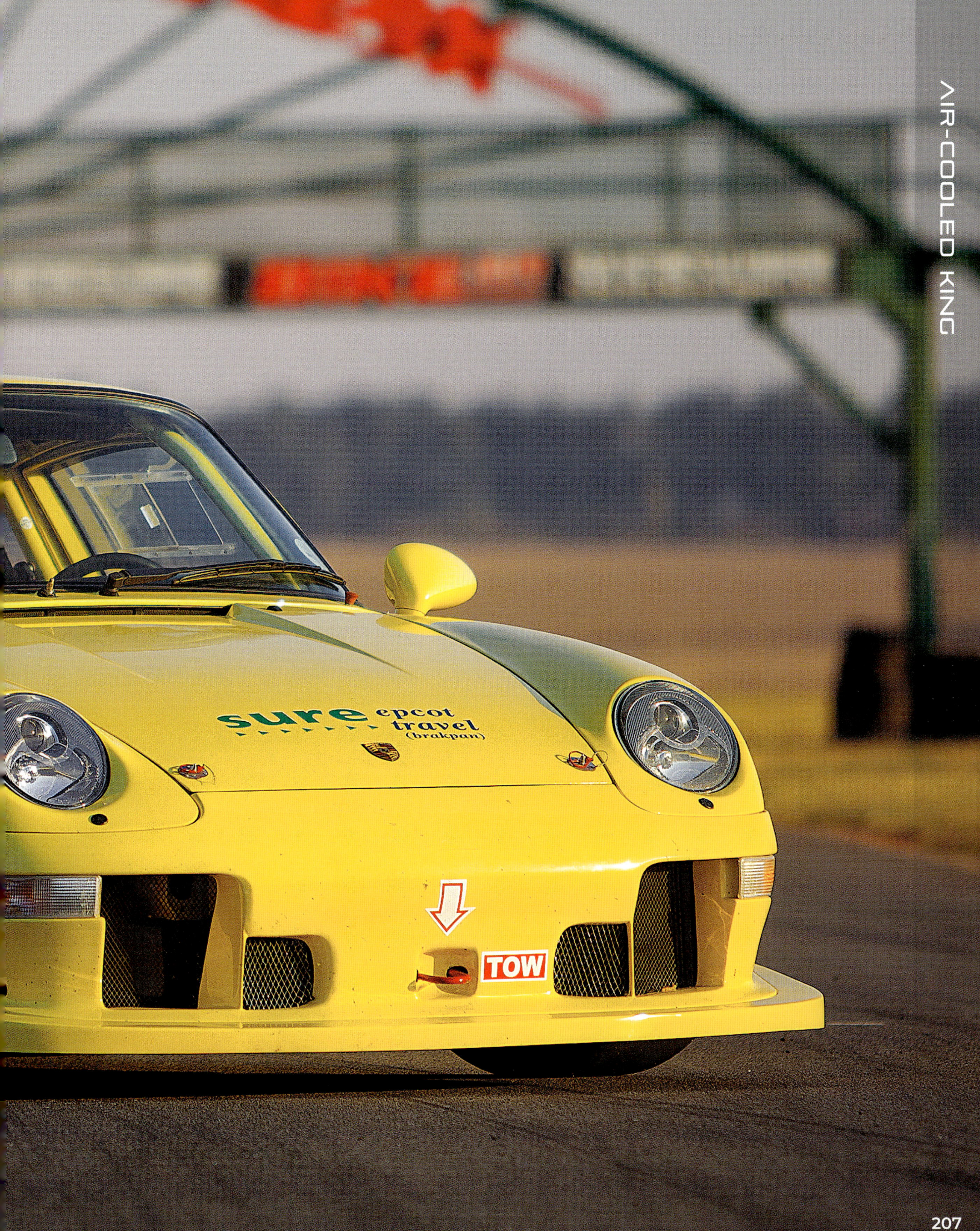
sure epcot
travel
(brakpan)
TOW

# ULTRA RARE
# PORSCHE 911S

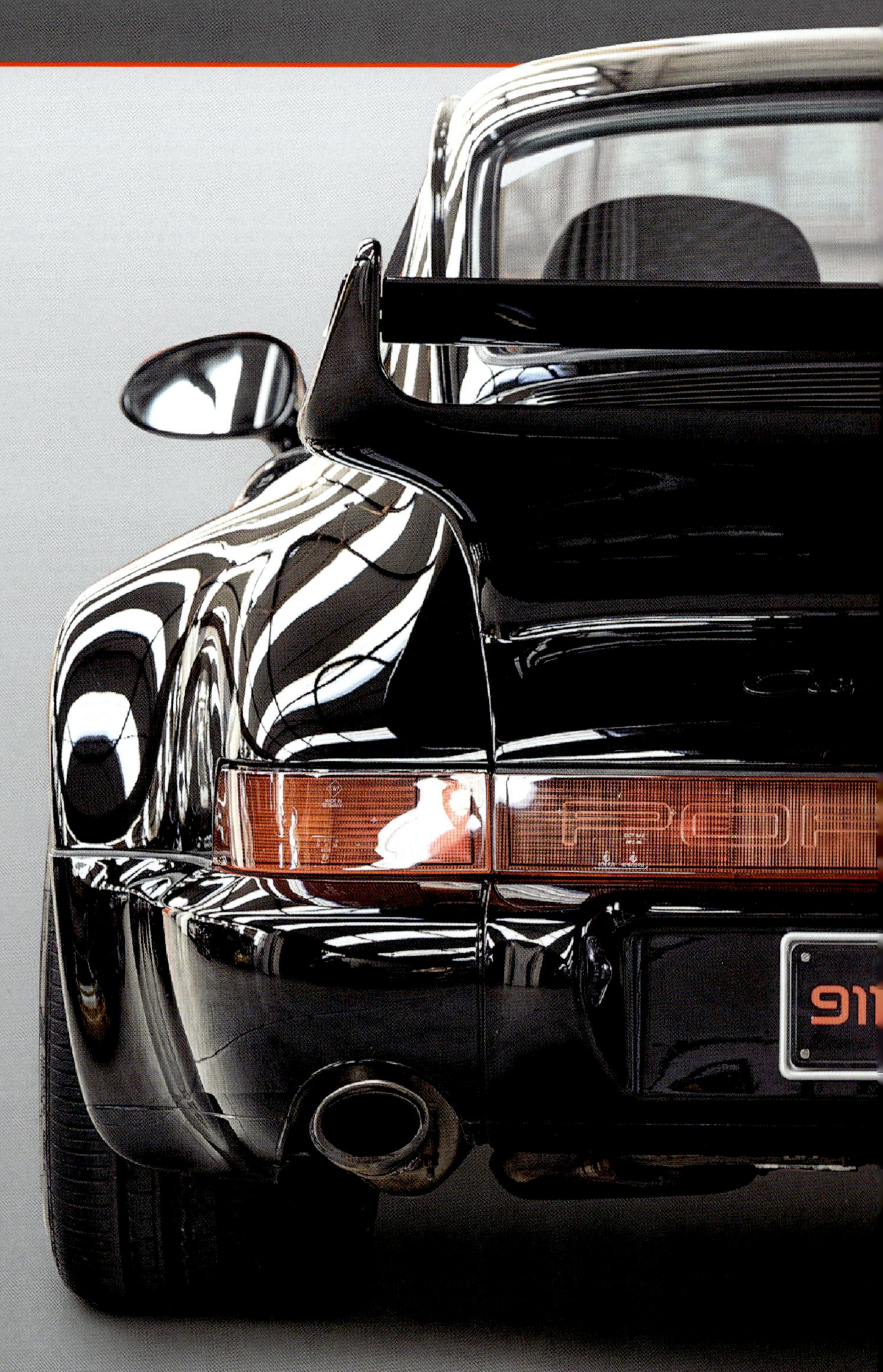

When it comes to making low-production specials, there are few better automotive manufacturers than Porsche – particularly when it comes to its legendary 911. Though there are now more than 1 million 911s gracing our planet, over its 64-year lifespan (and counting), Porsche has sought to create numerous variations of its darling sports car that are extra special.

Whether it's a track-ready RS or a bespoke, limited-edition model, these cars are particularly coveted by the enthusiast who seeks that extra dose of exclusivity from their 911. As the 911's stock has soared since its 50th birthday celebrations in 2013, these rarest of models have sky rocketed in price as collectors realise their value as key milestones in Porsche motoring history. But what models are the rarest, and, most importantly, how do they drive? This chapter will count down some of the rarest 911s Porsche has ever created, presented to not only put you behind the wheel of one of these low-numbers specials but, if your pocket allows, help you to acquire your own slice of Porsche motoring legend for real.

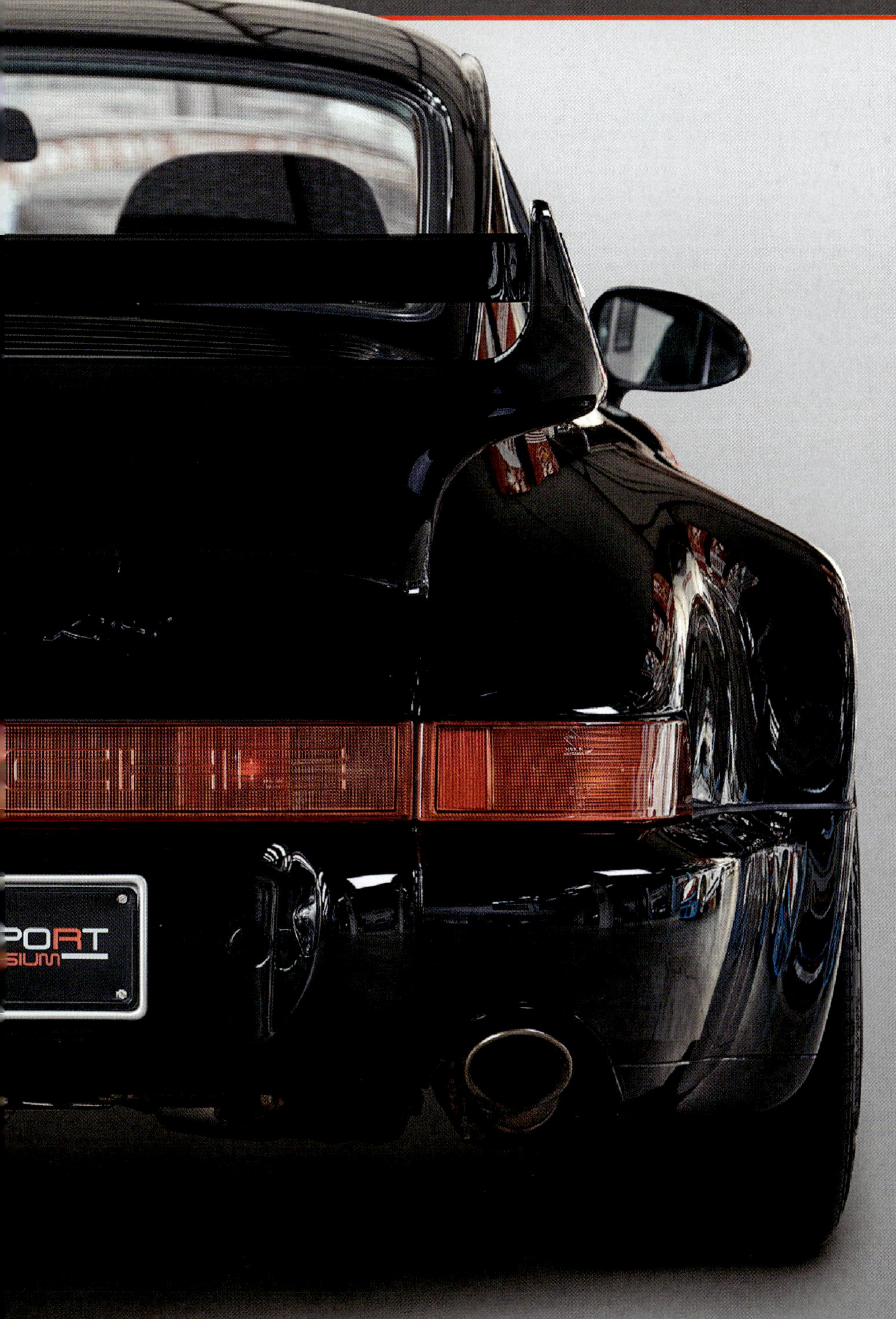

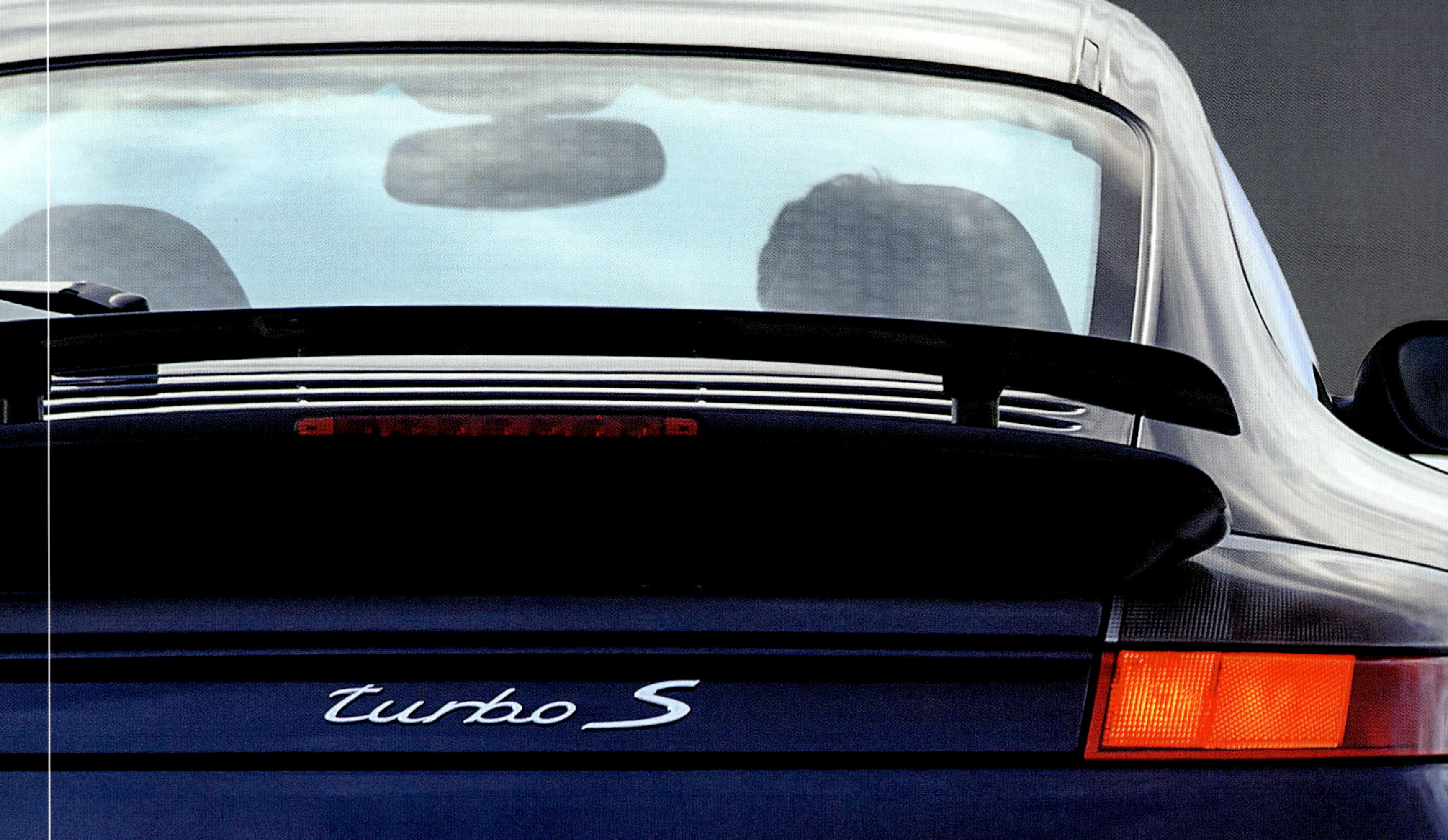
turbo S
RA05 OPO

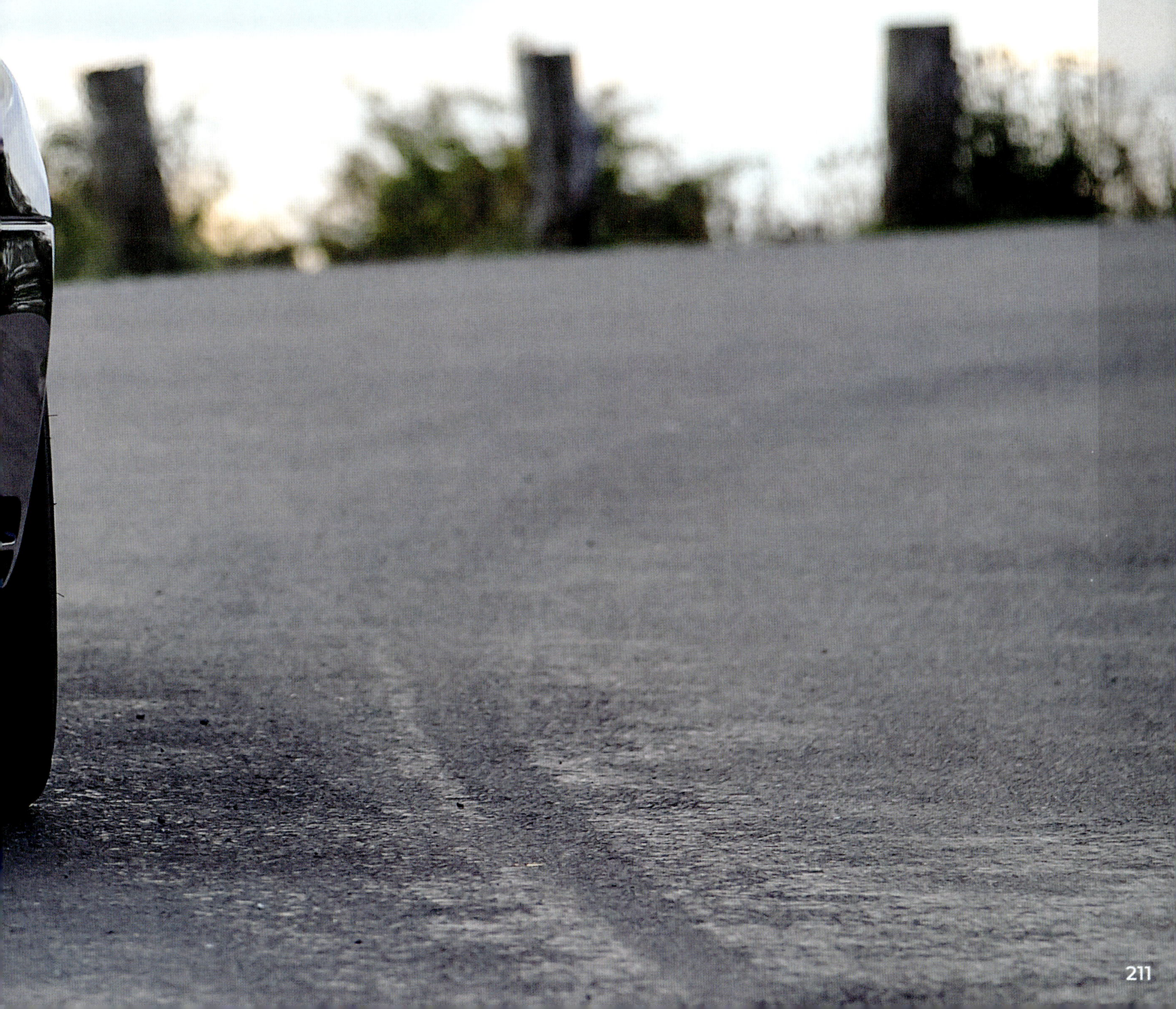

ONLY 1,563 MADE
996 TURBO S

While flames of the 996 v 997 Turbo debate continue to be fanned by respective owners, there is an oft-ignored yet particularly special car available for similar money: the 996 Turbo S.

Boasting a production run of just over 1,500 units, the 996 Turbo S came at the very end of the 996 production cycle in 2005, just before the start of 997 Turbo production, and was given the full-house treatment of options.

The 996 Turbo S is powered by a 3.6-litre twin turbocharged engine with double overhead camshafts operating four valves per cylinder and dry sump lubrication, just like its 996 Turbo counterpart. The engine is fitted with VarioCam Plus, a further development of the familiar VarioCam system, which changes both the intake camshaft timing (by as much as 25°) as well as the intake valve lift. Fitted with bigger turbos as part of the X50 Powerkit – standard on the Turbo S – power was boosted to 450bhp and the car's top speed broke through that magic 300km/h barrier, boasting a maximum of 190mph (307km/h) and placing it firmly in supercar territory.

The Turbo S was given Porsche's ceramic brakes with tell-tale yellow calipers, beefing up the car's stopping performance. Porsche stated at the time of launch that the ventilated and drilled ceramic discs would last for an astonishing 186,000 miles. These ceramic brake discs were made of carbon fibre fused with silicon carbide, and being 50 per cent lighter than the steel discs, significantly reduced unsprung mass and thereby improved the car's handling. The 996 Turbo S was also fitted with the latest Bosch ABS 5.7 anti-lock braking system.

The Turbo S was available in either Coupe or Cabriolet form – in fact, the open version was produced in far greater numbers (963 units) than the closed car (600 units). Selling for around £100,000 when new, the 996 Turbo S took an awful hit in the market in the years that followed, dropping down to as little as £30,000 by 2012, and is now wedged between the many 996 and 997 Turbos on the market.

The top speed is just 9mph short of the magic double ton, an incredible feat for such a well-appointed sports car made two decades ago and, despite its incredible performance and somewhat firm suspension, the 996 Turbo S can still be effortlessly docile around town, just like the 996 and 997 Turbos that share its price range.

Sleek in style, with its huge performance largely masked behind discreet 911 coachwork, the 996 Turbo S is a model that clearly has the power and performance of several supercars many times its value. Though this can be said of the 996 and 997 Turbos, what they lack is the exclusivity of the 996 Turbo S and its ultra-lavish specification straight out of the box.

The 996 Turbo S is a superb and exceptionally fast Porsche grand tourer for a true arbiter of taste – the biggest problem a buyer will likely have is finding one.



## TURBO S TIMELINE

### 930 S

**Power hike over 930: 30bhp**
Thanks to the success of the 935 race car, Porsche enjoyed a captive audience who wanted the same 'flat nose' look. It featured a lower streamlined nose with pop-up lights and aggressive rear fender air inlets. 948 units were produced.

### 964 TURBO S

**Power hike over 964 Turbo: 61bhp**
Turbo S Lightweight featured side air inlets ahead of the rear wheels, a flatter rear spoiler and a weight saving 180kg, all contributing to a 0–62mph of 4.6 seconds, nearly a half second quicker than the standard turbo.

### 993 TURBO S

**Power hike over Turbo: 42bhp**
The 993 Turbo S was the last to be completed by Porsche Exclusive. Now with a 4WD setup, power was lifted to 450bhp by fitting two larger turbos, a modified control unit and an additional oil cooler. Only 345 cars were made.

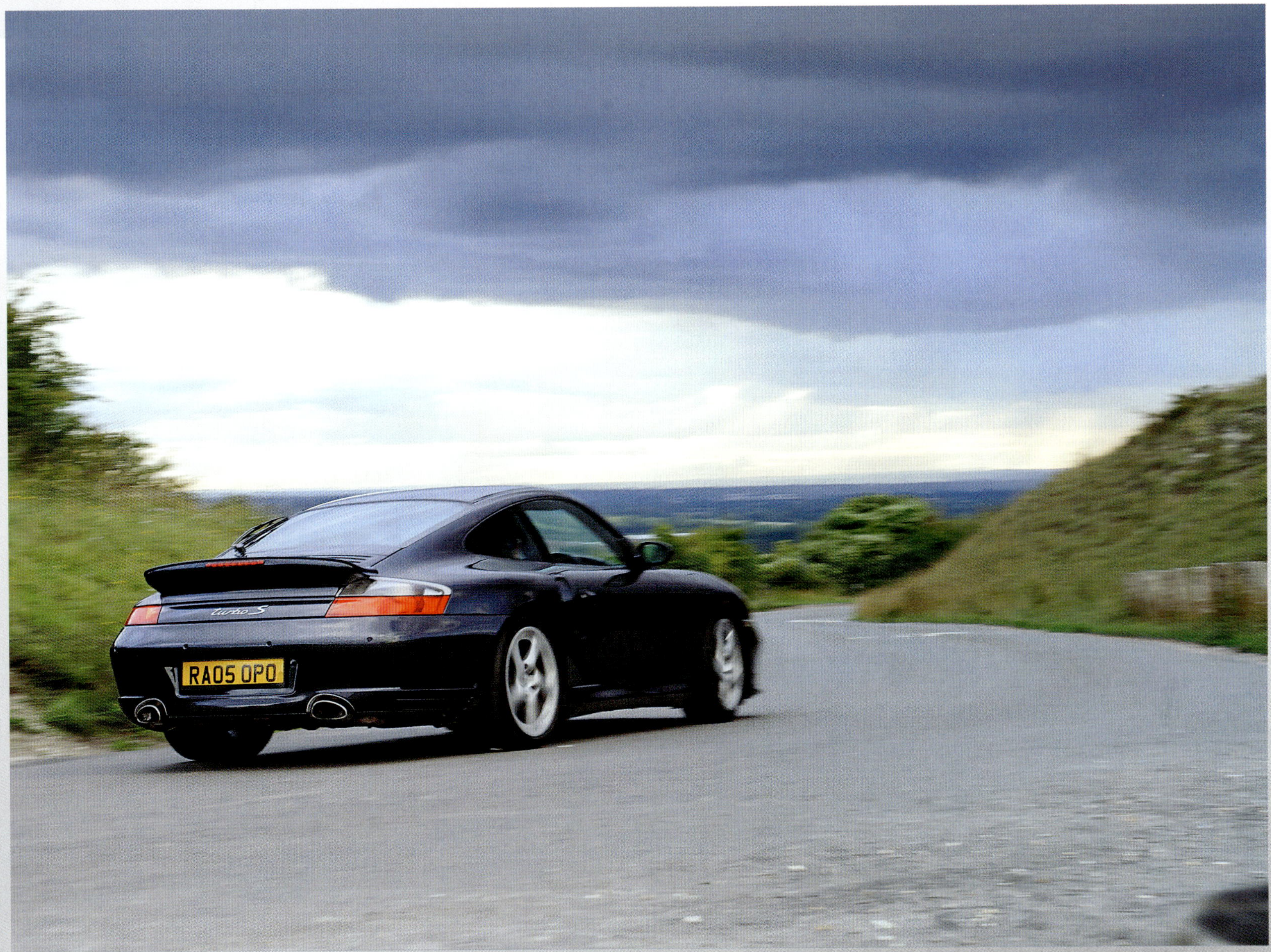

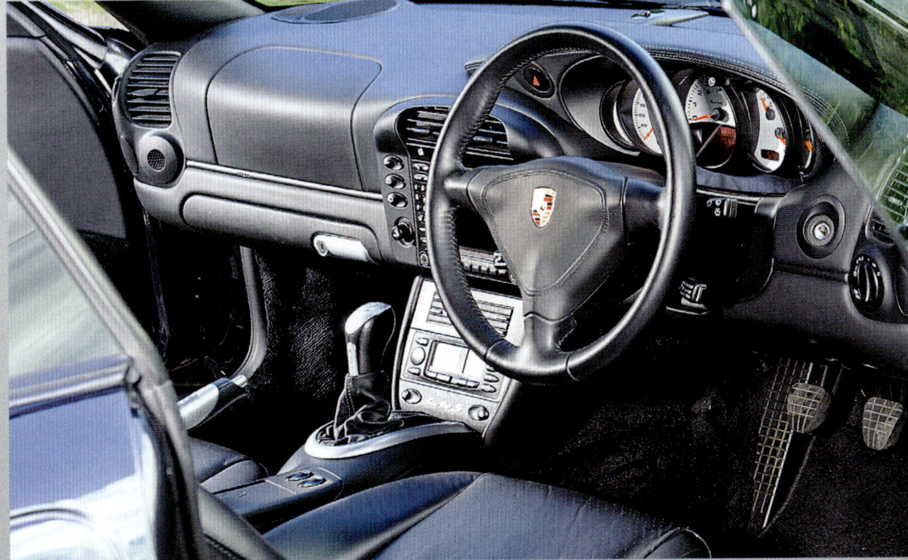

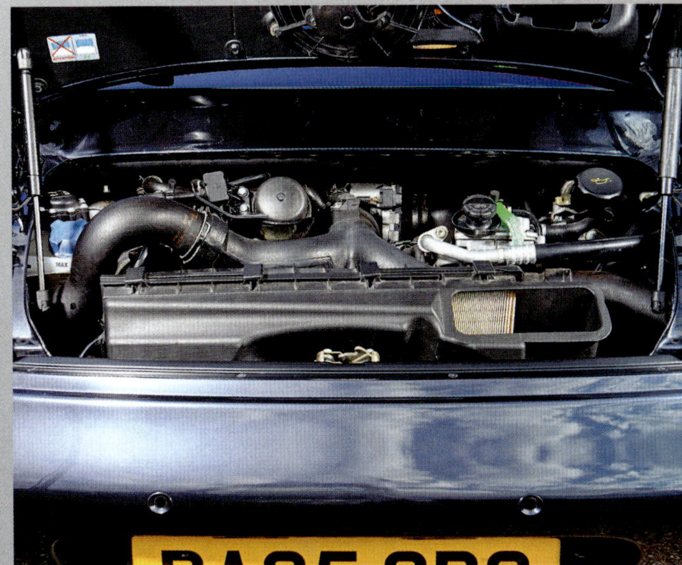

### 996 TURBO S

**Power hike over Turbo: 30bhp**
To cope with the extra performance, the Turbo S was fitted with PCCB. Metallic paint, Xenon headlights, BOSE audio system, Porsche Communication Management system, full leather trim and 18-inch alloys were all fitted as standard.

### 997 TURBO S

**Power hike over Turbo: 30bhp**
Fitted with Porsche's latest seven-speed gearbox, the Turbo S returned the same fuel consumption as the regular Turbo model, but acceleration from 0-62mph was now a blistering 3.3 seconds with a top speed of 195mph.

### 991 TURBO S

**Power hike over Turbo: 40bhp**
Once again, 3.8-litre twin-turbo engine was modified to produce an astonishing 560bhp. To speed crept up to 197mph, while the 62mph dash was achieved in just 3.1 seconds.

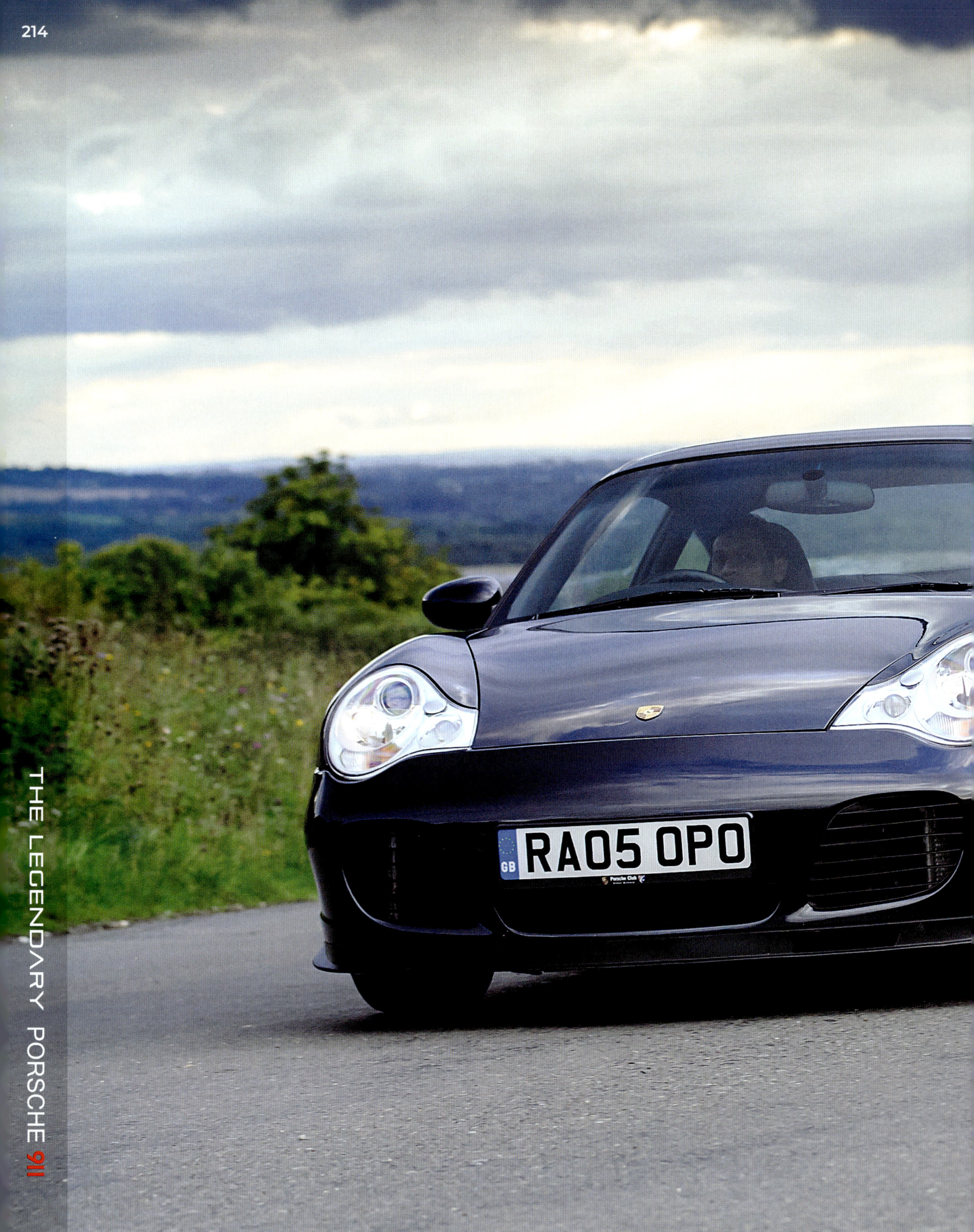
RA05 OPO
GB

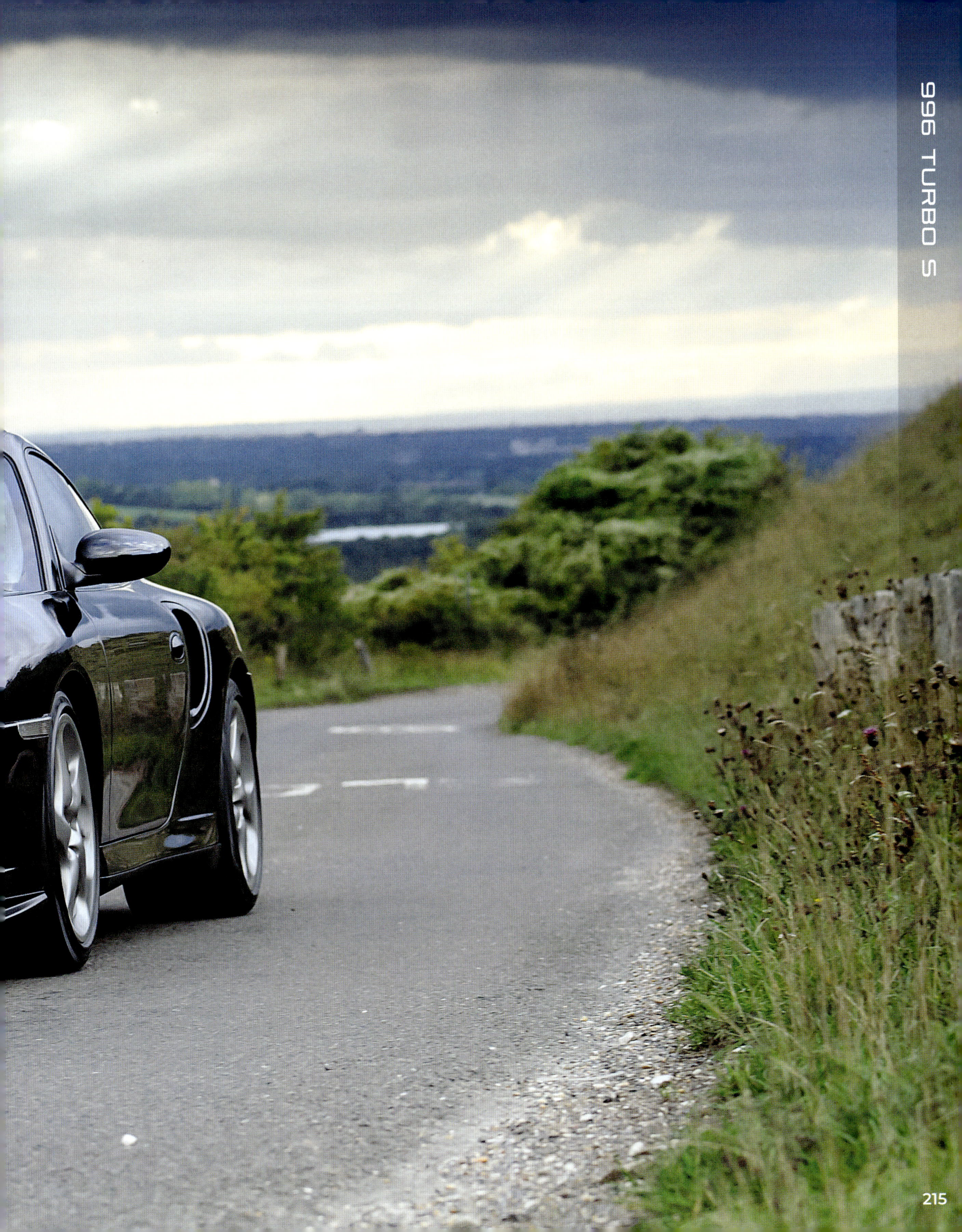

# ONLY 1,437 MADE
# 964 TURBO 3.6



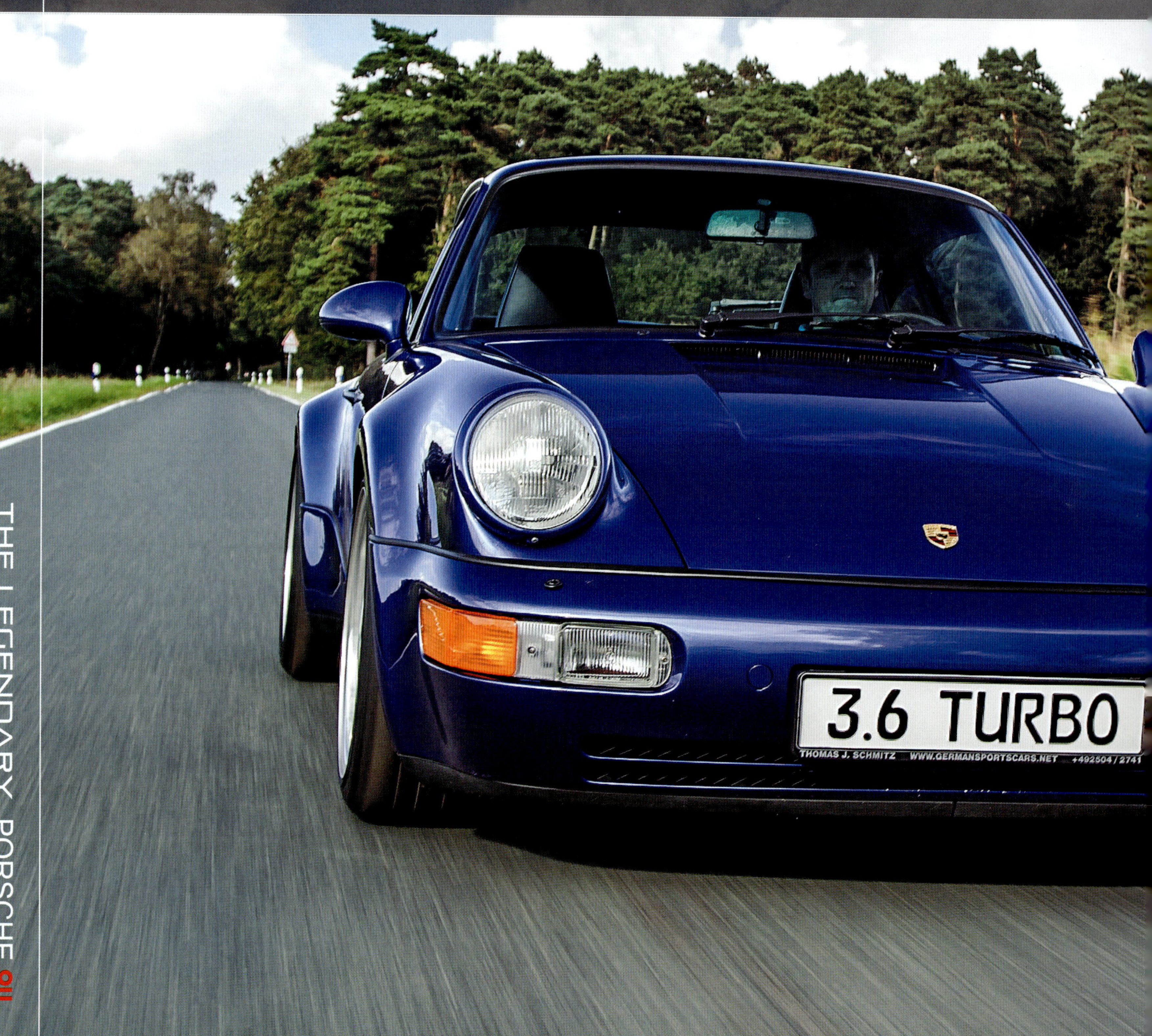

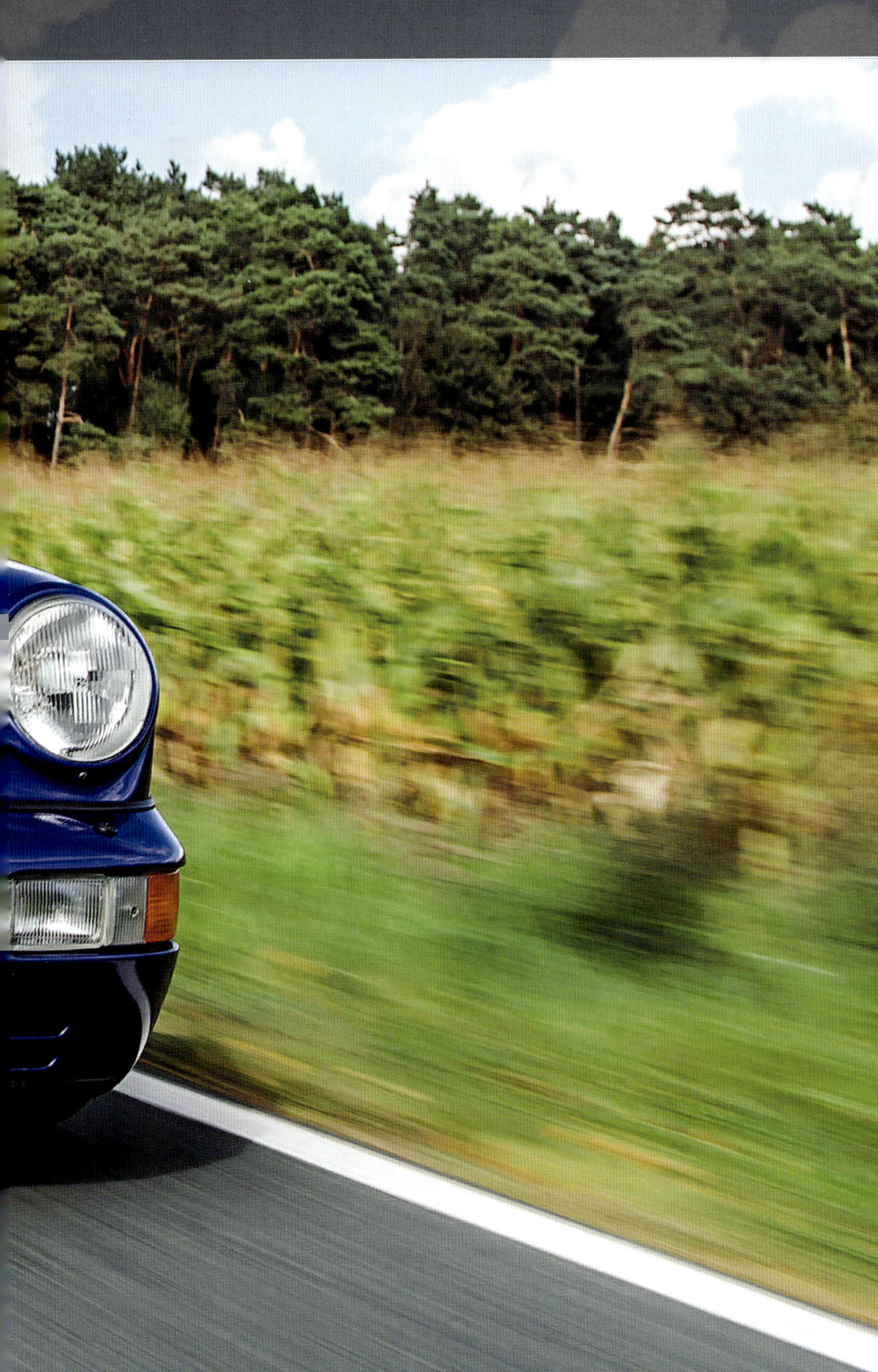

After 15 years of tweaking the 3.3-litre engine in the forced-induction 911, the 3.6-litre 964 proved to be a welcome addition to the evolution of the Turbo story...



# 964 TURBO 3.6

(1993)

### ENGINE

**Capacity:** 3,600cc

**Compression ratio:** 7:5.1

**Maximum power:** 360bhp @ 5,500rpm

**Maximum torque:** 520Nm @ 4,200rpm

**Transmission:** Five-speed manual

### SUSPENSION

**Front:** Independent suspension by transverse links; single coil spring, anti-roll bar; twin-tube gas-pressure shocks

**Rear:** Independent suspension by semi-trailing arms;  single coil spring, anti-roll bar; twin-tube gas-pressure shocks

### WHEELS & TYRES

**Front:** 8x18-inch Speedlines; 225/40ZR18

**Rear:** 10x18-inch Speedlines; 265/35ZR18

### DIMENSIONS

**Length:** 4,250mm

**Width:** 1,775mm

**Weight:** 1,470kg

### PERFORMANCE

**0-60mph:** 4.8 seconds

**Top speed:** 174mph

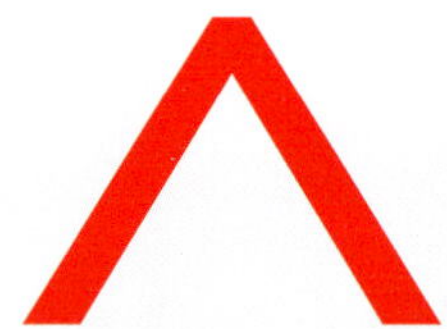

**A**fter 15 years of tweaking the 3.3-litre engine in the forced-induction 911, the 3.6-litre 964 proved to be a welcome addition to the evolution of the Turbo story...

At the Paris Motor Show in autumn of 1992, Porsche introduced its third and final iteration of the 964 Turbo, now featuring a 3.6-litre engine. In reality, this model was only going to be made for just one year, as the 964 was to be replaced by the all-new 993 series at the following year's Frankfurt Motor Show. This almost guaranteed that the 3.6 would become a sought-after model in time, with only 1,437 units being produced during that year.

An additional three millimetres on the bore and two millimetres on the stroke resulted in an increase in capacity of 300cc. Combined with the Turbo-optimised cylinders, pistons and crank train, and an increase in the compression ratio from 7.0 to 7.5:1, the Turbo 3.6's power was boosted to 360bhp. Torque was increased significantly to 520Nm at 4,200rpm, up from 450Nm at 4,500rpm in the earlier, 3.3-litre 964 Turbo, but importantly this range was available from as low as 2,400rpm right up to 5,500rpm.

Gone were the days of waiting for the needle to crawl round the tacho before the sudden kick of inertia. The turbocharger with primary and bypass catalytic converter and intercooler system was taken over, unchanged, from the 3.3-litre. In a move to reduce internal and external noise levels, the engine and gearbox were mounted on hydro-mounts, which combined the acoustic isolation function of a conventional rubber mount with balanced damping performance. These mounts ensured effective vibration isolation of the drive unit from the chassis.

Previously the reserve of the limited edition Turbo S, the three-piece Speedline aluminium 18-inch wheels made a fitting addition to the 3.6, clad with much wider 225/40 front and 265/35 rear rubber. Visible through the wheels were the same red four-pot brake calipers and ventilated/drilled discs back and front as used on the Turbo S. Moreover, the chassis of the 3.6 Turbo is 20mm lower than the earlier 3.3 model, and with the spring rates 12 per cent firmer, this reduced pitching, lift under acceleration and roll in cornering.

The body of the Turbo 3.6 was noticeably wider than the standard 964 by 25mm in order to accommodate the bigger tyres and increased track. The wider fenders and large rear spoiler gave the car a meaningful and powerful presence, while a smooth underbody ensured an efficient aero, and accordingly the coefficient of drag, 0.35, was down slightly on its predecessor.

The overwhelming impression given by this car is that of being thoroughly civilised, predictable and smooth in its behaviour. It is a world away from the earlier Turbo models. On-board comfort included air-conditioning, a computer with turbo boost indicator, electric seat adjustment, leather upholstery, headlamp washer, an alarm, airbag for driver and passenger, and either a radio/cassette player or radio/CD player. Lavish in specification, the Porsche press kit called it "what a sports car should be".

In a way the 964 Turbo 3.6 represented the end of an era, being the last of the mono-turbo 911s with rear-wheel drive. The 964 3.6 Turbo represents a marked improvement over the 3.3-litre variant in terms of performance – and its sophistication in delivering that performance. Twinned with that presence on the road, the last forced-induction 964 makes for a formidable Turbo experience.



**Porsche executed numerous tweaks to the engine aside from its obvious increase in capacity, also carrying over the braking system from the 3.3-litre 964 Turbo S**

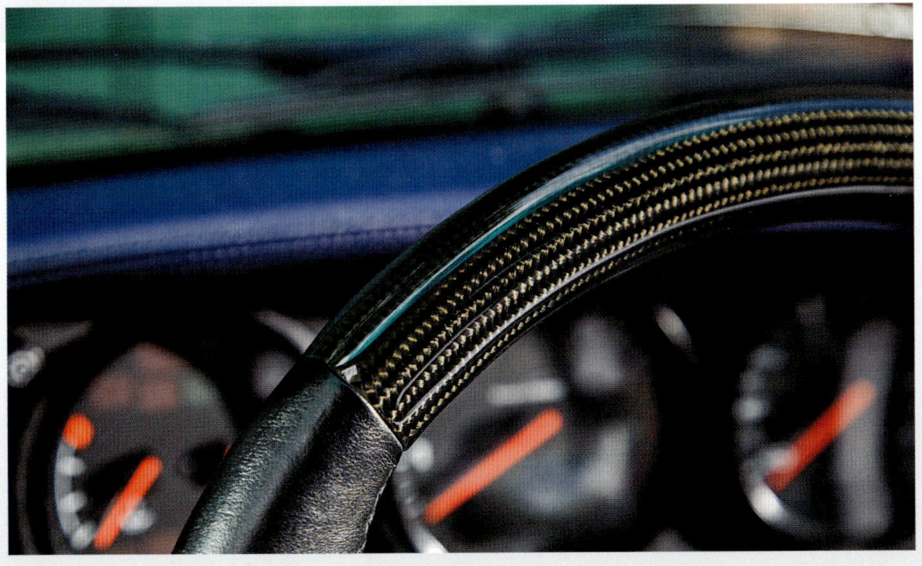

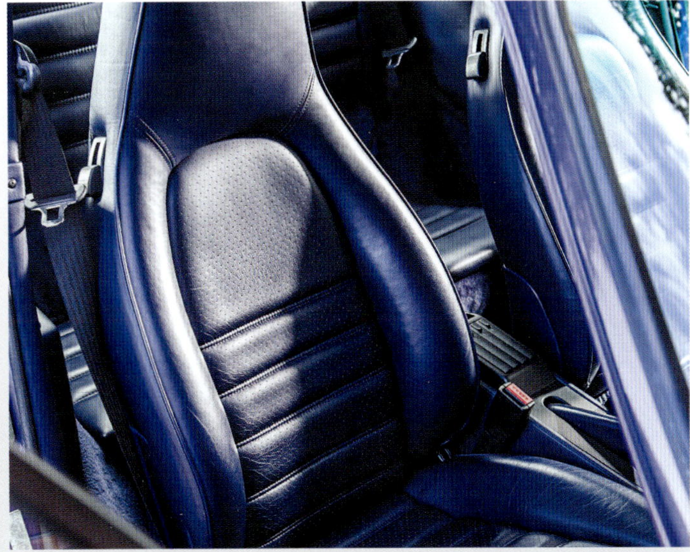

The opulence from the 3.3-litre 964 Turbo was carried over to the 3.6-litre variant, though the carbon-rimmed steering wheel here has in fact been sourced from a 993 Turbo S

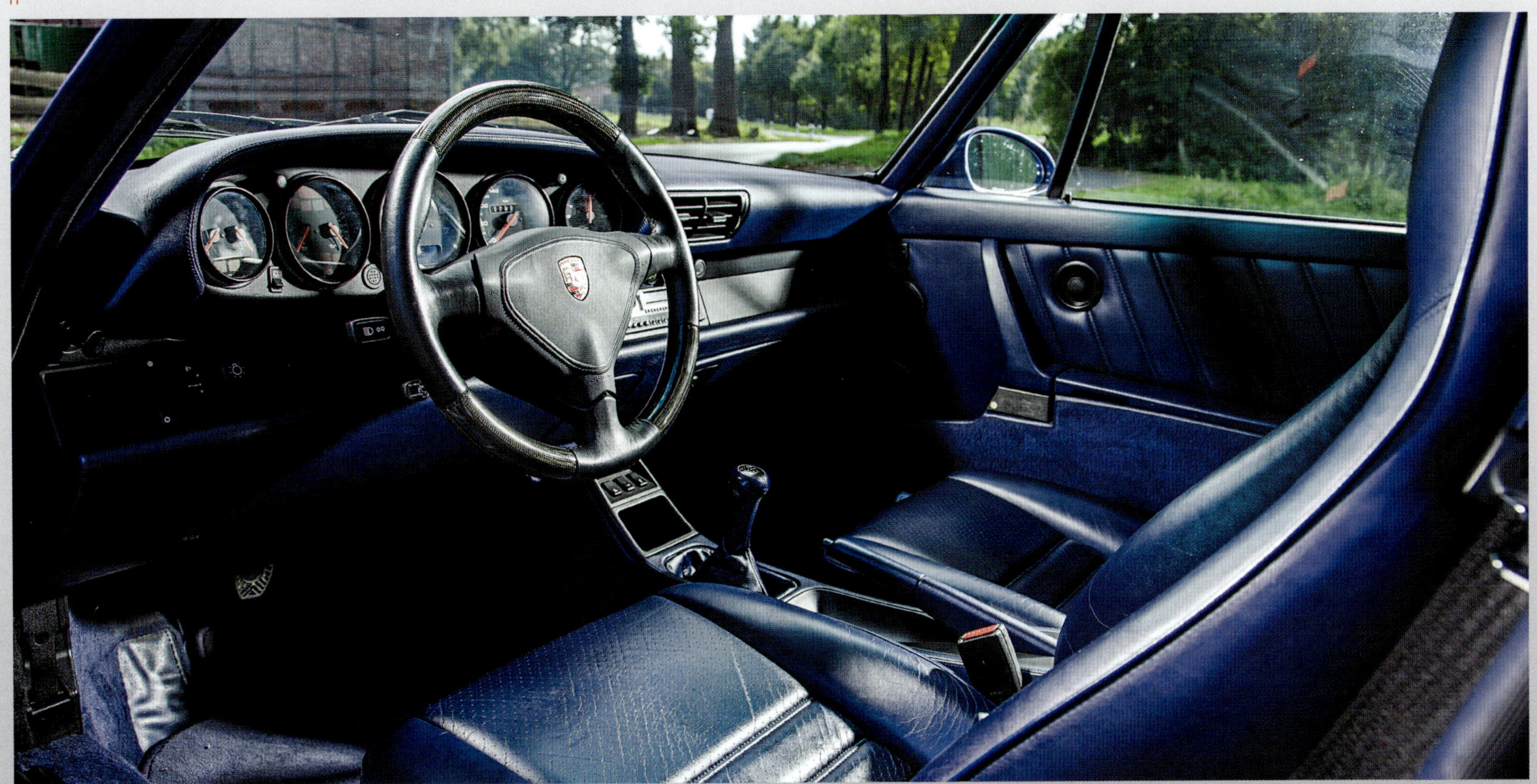

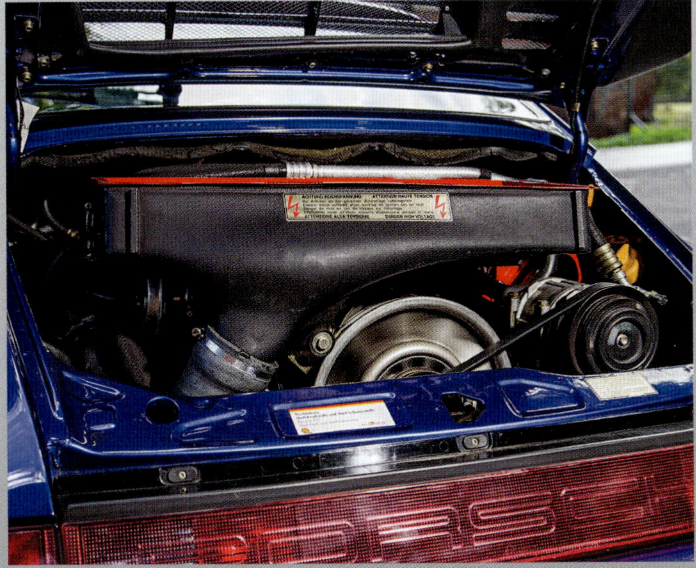

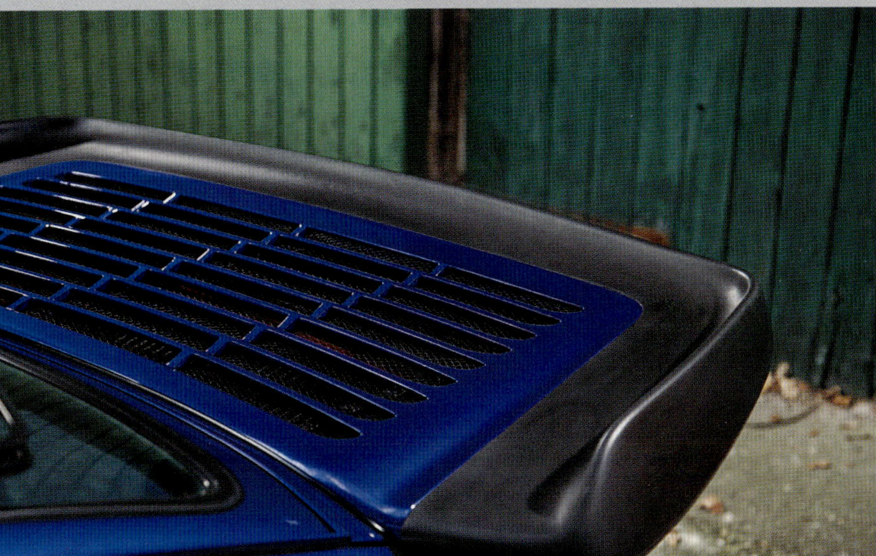

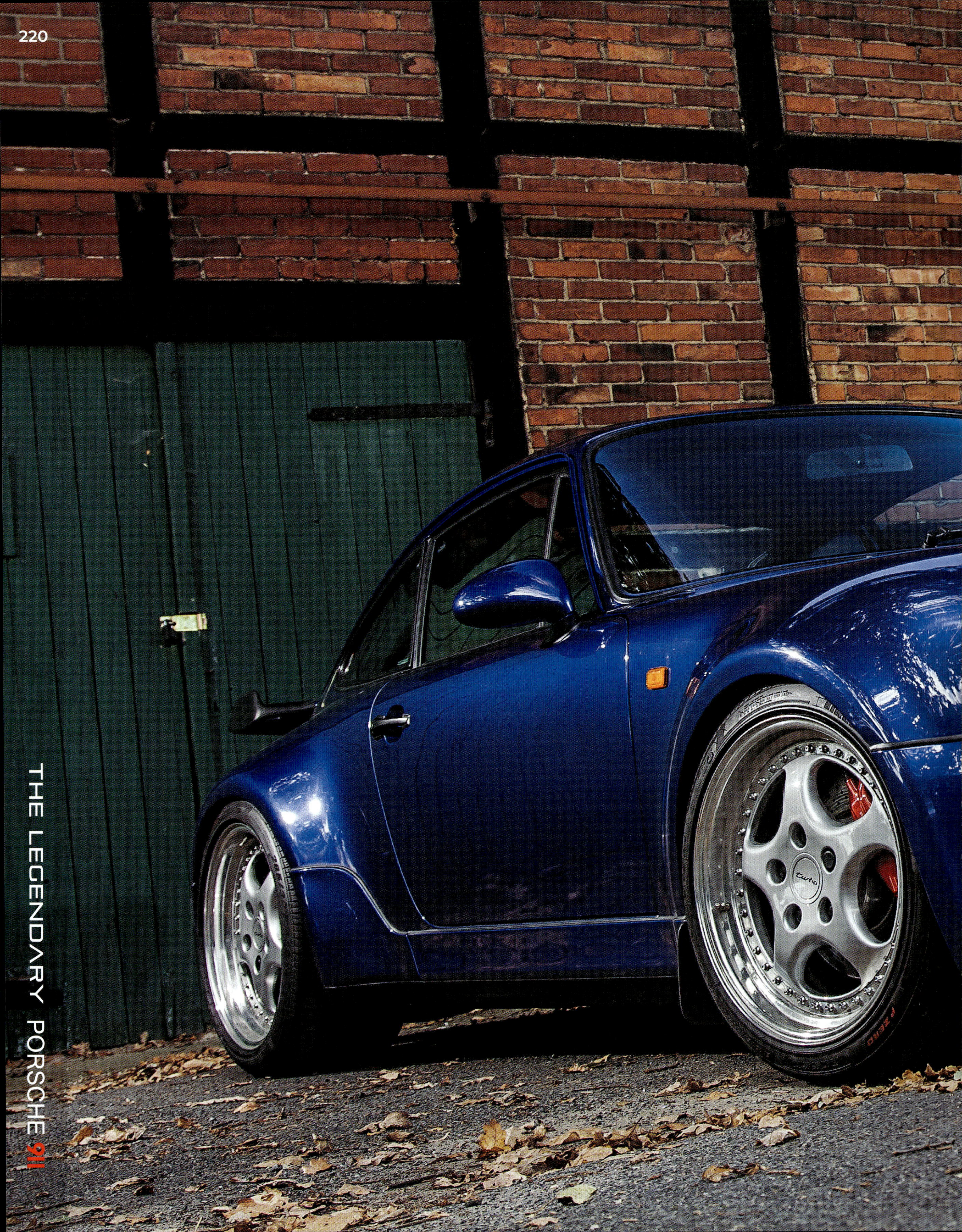

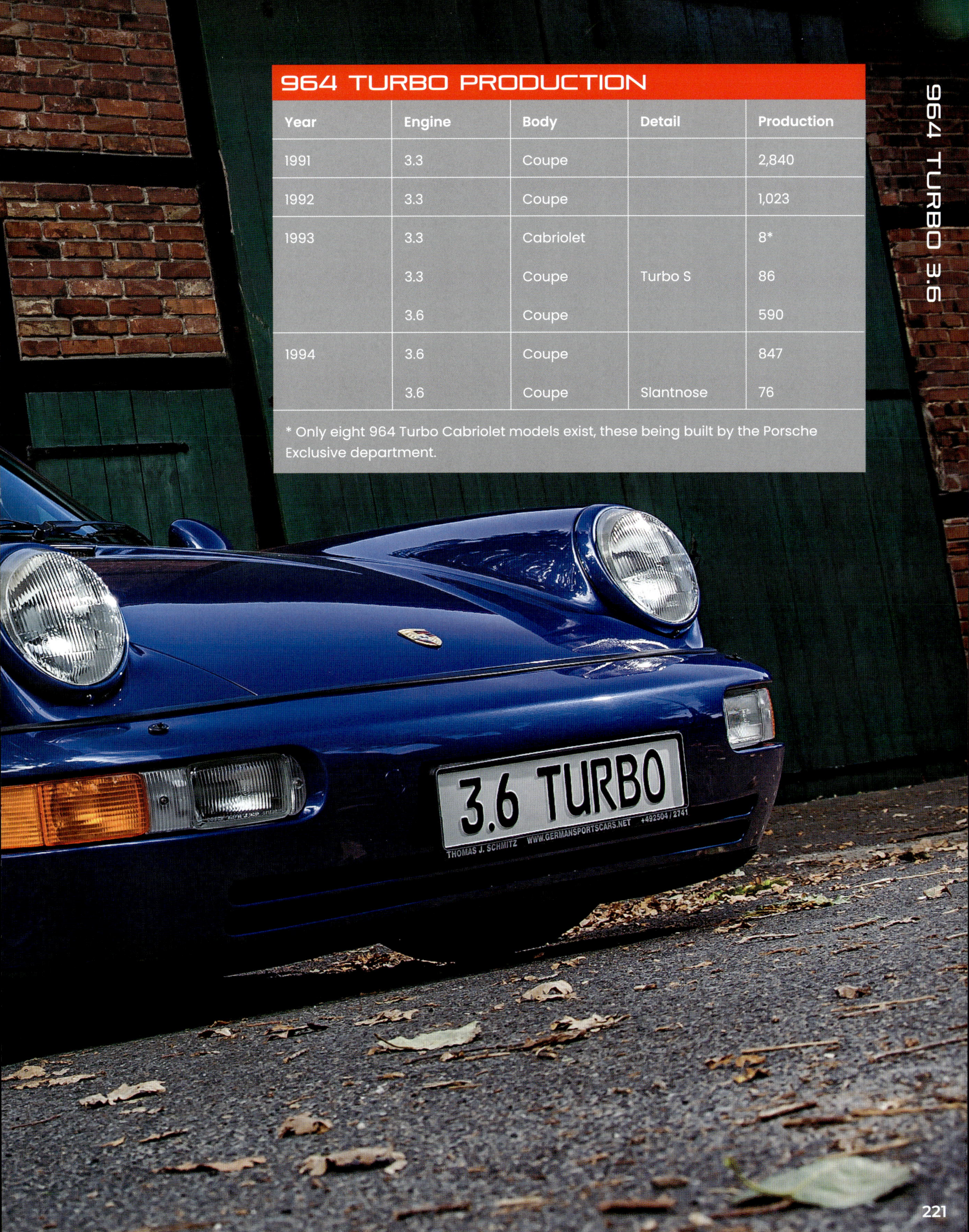




## 964 TURBO PRODUCTION

| Year | Engine | Body | Detail | Production |
| --- | --- | --- | --- | --- |
| 1991 | 3.3 | Coupe | | 2,840 |
| 1992 | 3.3 | Coupe | | 1,023 |
| 1993 | 3.3 | Cabriolet | | 8* |
| | 3.3 | Coupe | Turbo S | 86 |
| | 3.6 | Coupe | | 590 |
| 1994 | 3.6 | Coupe | | 847 |
| | 3.6 | Coupe | Slantnose | 76 |

* Only eight 964 Turbo Cabriolet models exist, these being built by the Porsche Exclusive department.

# ONLY 1,287 MADE
# 996 GT2

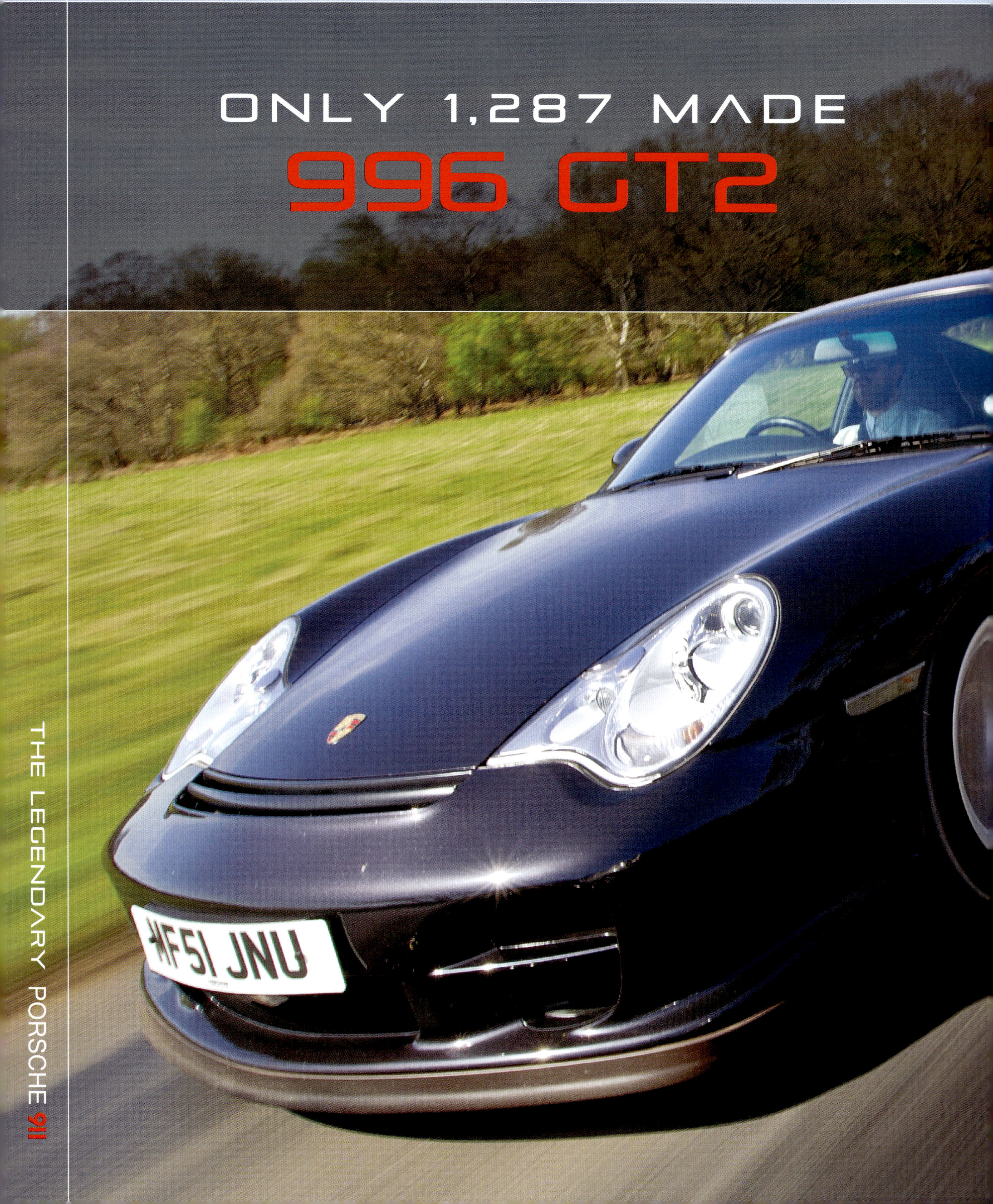

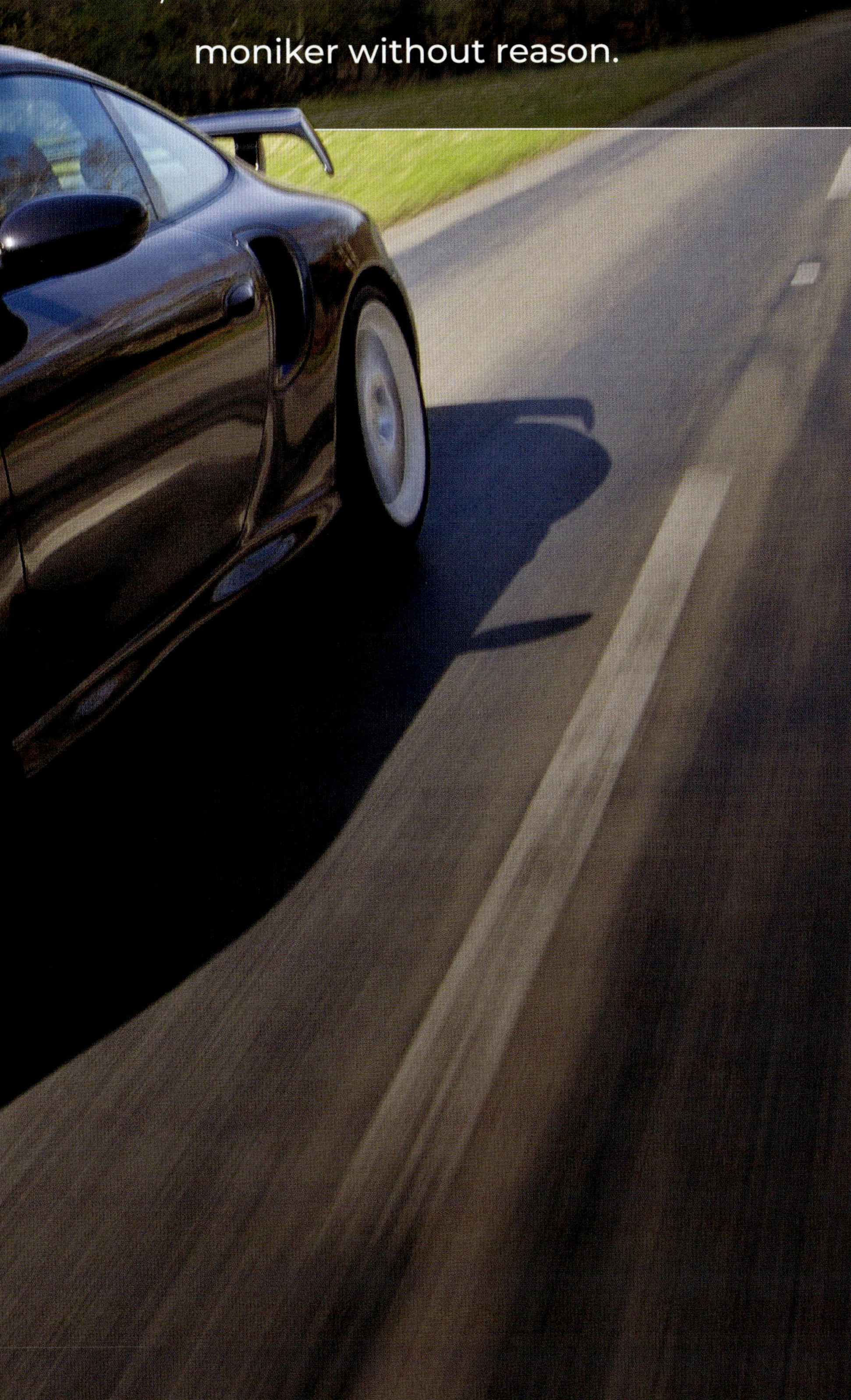

With no racing pedigree, the 996 era marked a fresh start for the GT2. Despite this, the newcomer retained its entire hardcore DNA. Despite many people's protestations, including Porsche's, the GT2 didn't earn its 'Widowmaker' moniker without reason.



# 996 GT2

(2001-2002)

### ENGINE

**Capacity:** 3,600cc
**Compression ratio:** 9:4.1
**Maximum power:** 462bhp @ 5,700rpm
**Maximum torque:** 620Nm @ 3,500-4,500rpm
**Transmission:** Six-speed manual, rear wheel drive

### SUSPENSION

**Front:** Independent suspension by transverse links; single coil spring, anti-roll bar; twin-tube gas-pressure shocks
**Rear:** Independent; multi-link with telescopic dampers; coil springs; anti-roll bar

### WHEELS & TYRES

**Front:** 8x18-inch alloys; 235/40/R18 tyres
**Rear:** 12x18-inch alloys; 315/30/R18 tyres

### DIMENSIONS

**Length:** 4,450mm
**Width:** 1,830mm
**Weight:** 1,440kg

### PERFORMANCE

**0-60mph:** 4.1 seconds
**Top speed:** 196mph

Like the renowned 2.7 RS, the Porsche 993 GT2 was a homologation special: a racer for the road built so Weissach could go racing on the track. It was envisaged that the original GT2 would take the fight to the then-dominant McLaren F1 (an outright winner at Le Mans in 1995). That plan proved to be a step too far for Porsche's rear-engined sports car, necessitating the frankly bonkers mid-engined GT1 racer that would eventually take Weissach's 16th Le Mans victory in 1998, the same year the 911 road car range would make the move to water-cooling.

By the turn of the 21st century, the 911s at the top of the motorsport tree were no longer turbocharged. The GT3 era had dawned; the GT2 was dead. The naturally aspirated Mezger engine was now the Porsche powerplant with sporting pretensions. There was no need for Porsche to launch a 996 GT2, but in 2001 Weissach did just that. "Thank goodness" is all one can say to that.

The 996 generation of 911 was certainly not the prettiest. However, the 996 GT2 is easily the best-looking neunelfer that rolled out of Stuttgart between 1998 and 2004. Where the 993 was all tacked-on arches and huge wing, the 996 GT2 is a much subtler affair – especially in Basalt black – yet it doesn't lose any of its menacing appeal. From the twin radiator exit louvres and imposing rear-arch intercooler feeds to the fixed rear wing and gaping vents in the deep 'air dam' front bumper, the GT2's styling shows it means business. Along with the use of the Turbo's wide body shell – something neither the 996 GT3 nor GT3 RS benefitted from – the GT2 is certainly not found wanting when it comes to imposing itself visually.

The GT2's reputation often precedes it, but from behind the wheel, it is more controllable than the stats on a piece of paper suggest. Another rear-wheel-drive, forced-induction 911, the 930 suffered from a similar rap thanks to its long gear ratios and epic turbo lag, but with a bit of common sense, both of these turbocharged titans can make incredibly swift, incredibly hair-raising progress through the countryside. It may have been one of the first 21st-century 911s, but the 996 GT2 is a truly old-school driving experience wrapped up in a modern, reliable package. By the turn of the 997, though, the 911 GT2 moniker had evolved further still...

**In Comfort guise the 996 GT2's cockpit remains very well appointed, with carbon trim adding a motorsport feel. Removal of the rear seats means the aural theatre provided by the flat six penetrates inside the cabin more**

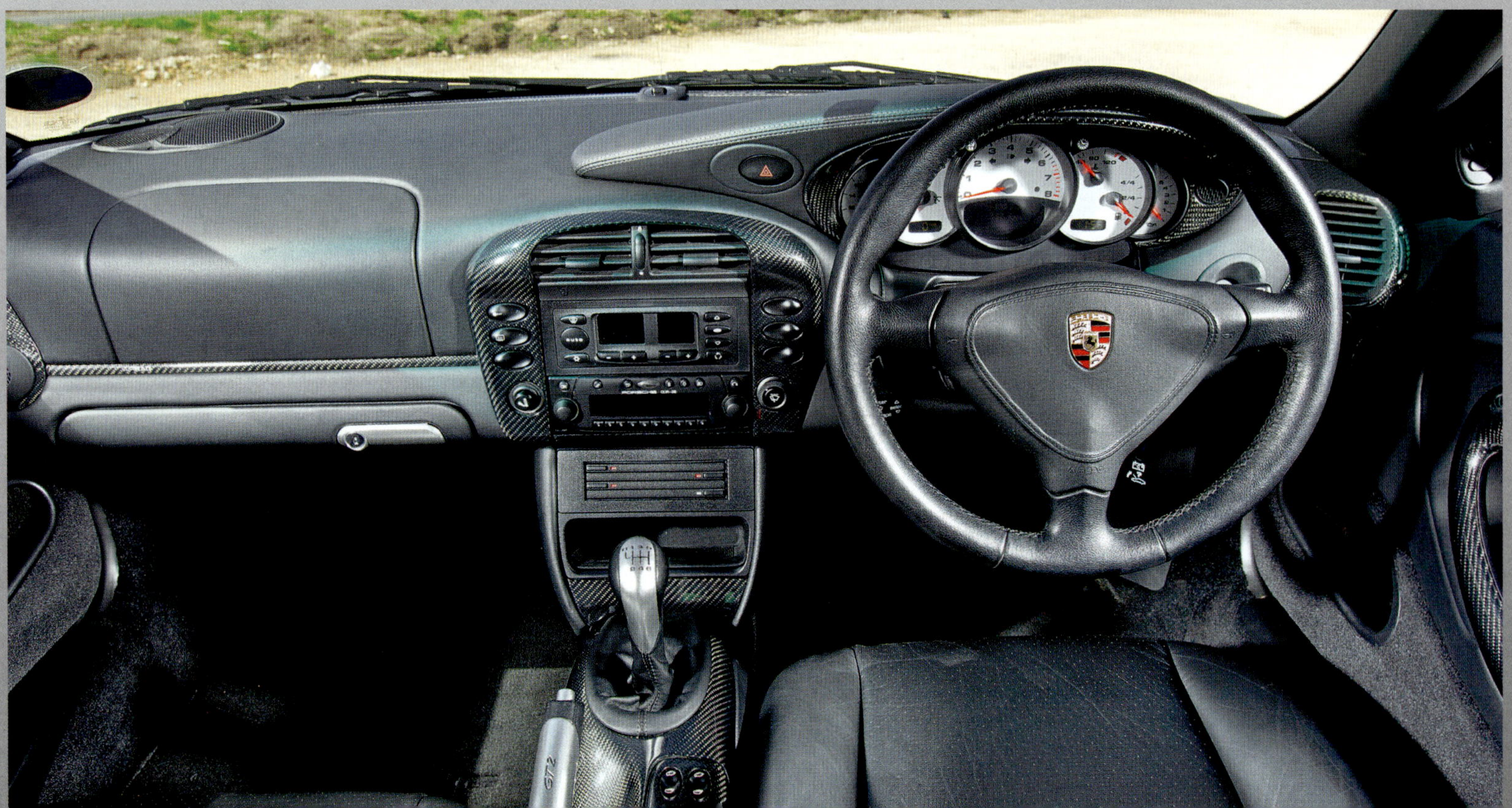

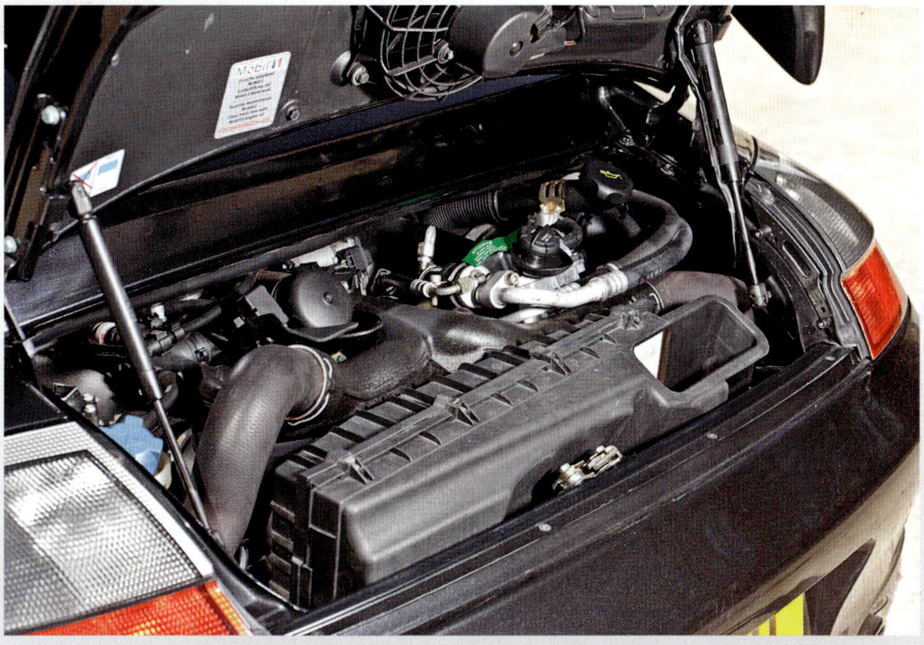

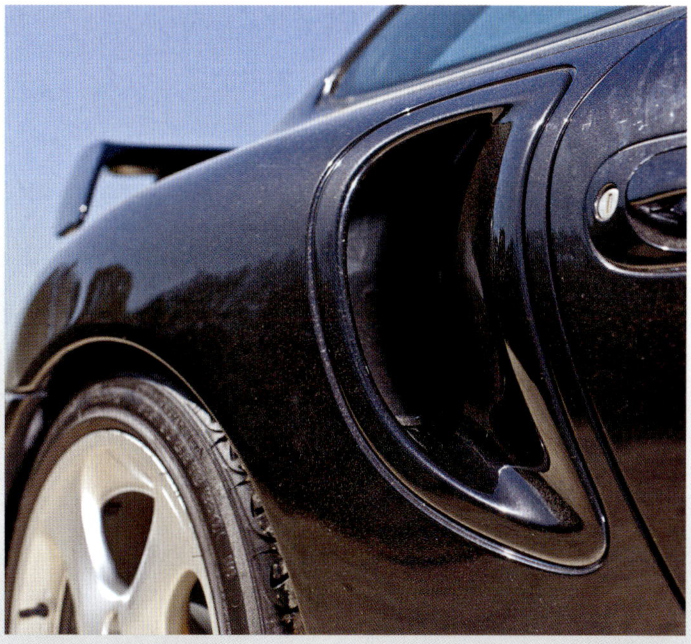

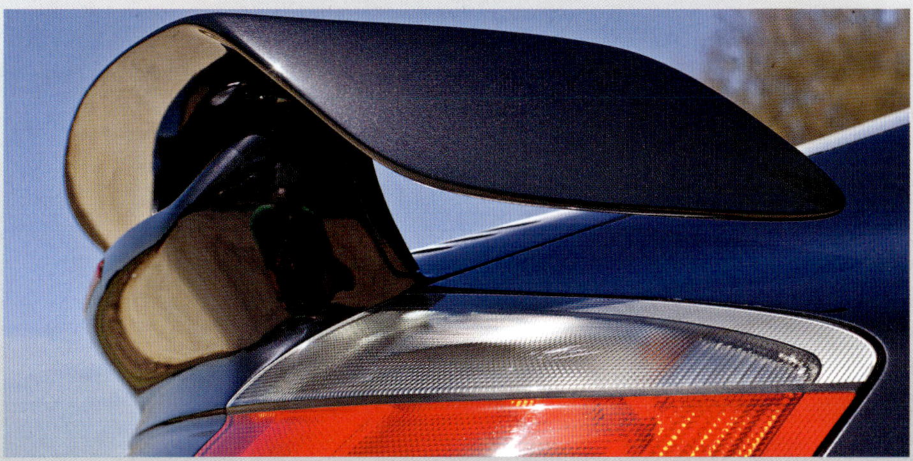

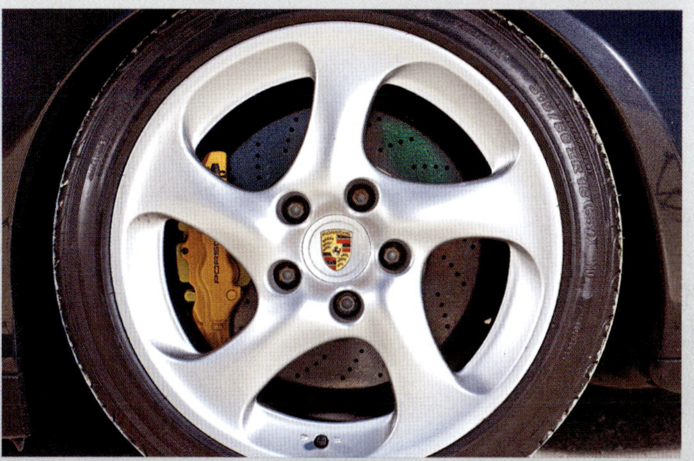

The 996 GT2 utilised the Turbo's wider body shell with side air vents for intercoolers plus hollow-spoked wheels, yet PCCB, a large fixed rear wing and a heavily revised engine were all pure GT2 specification

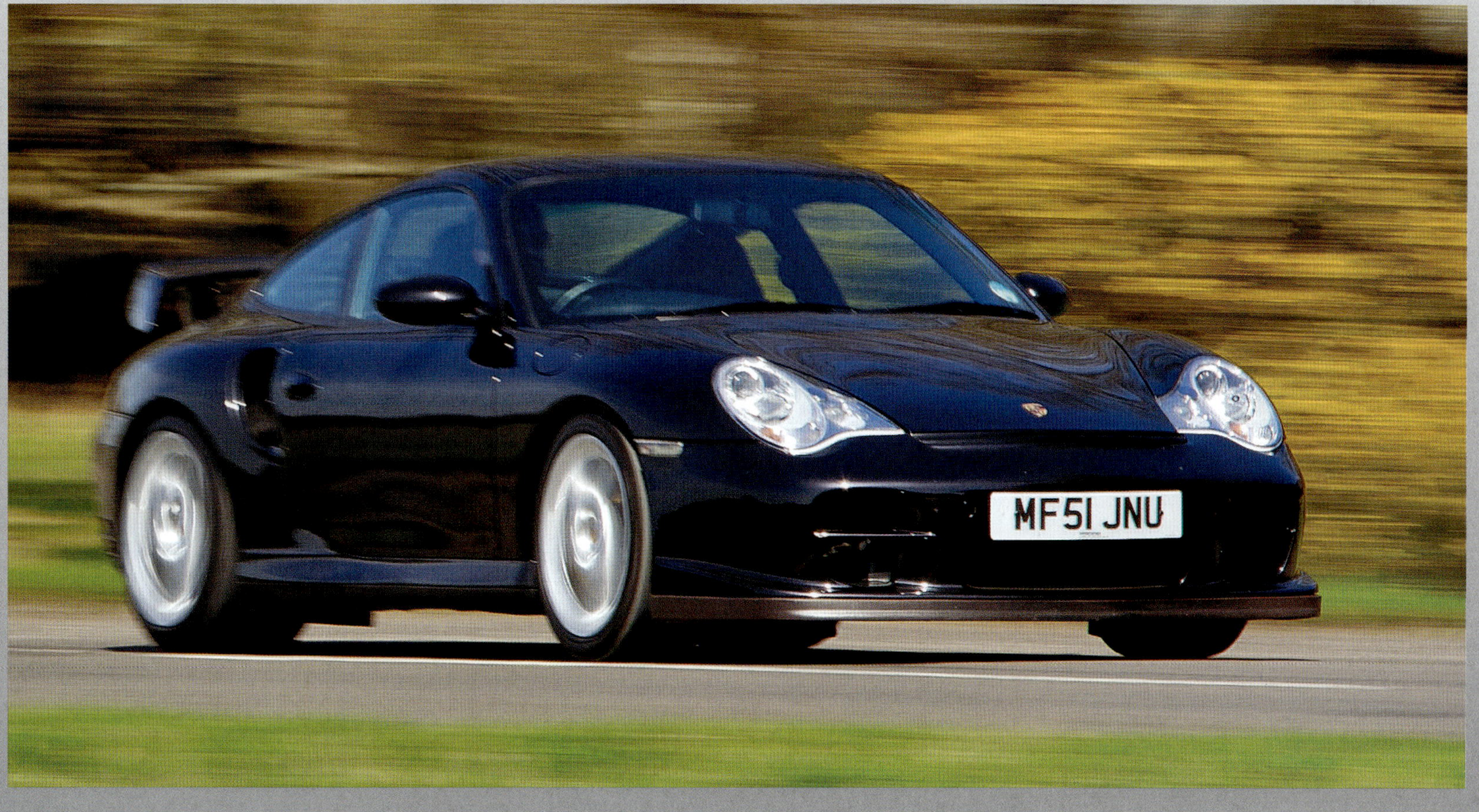

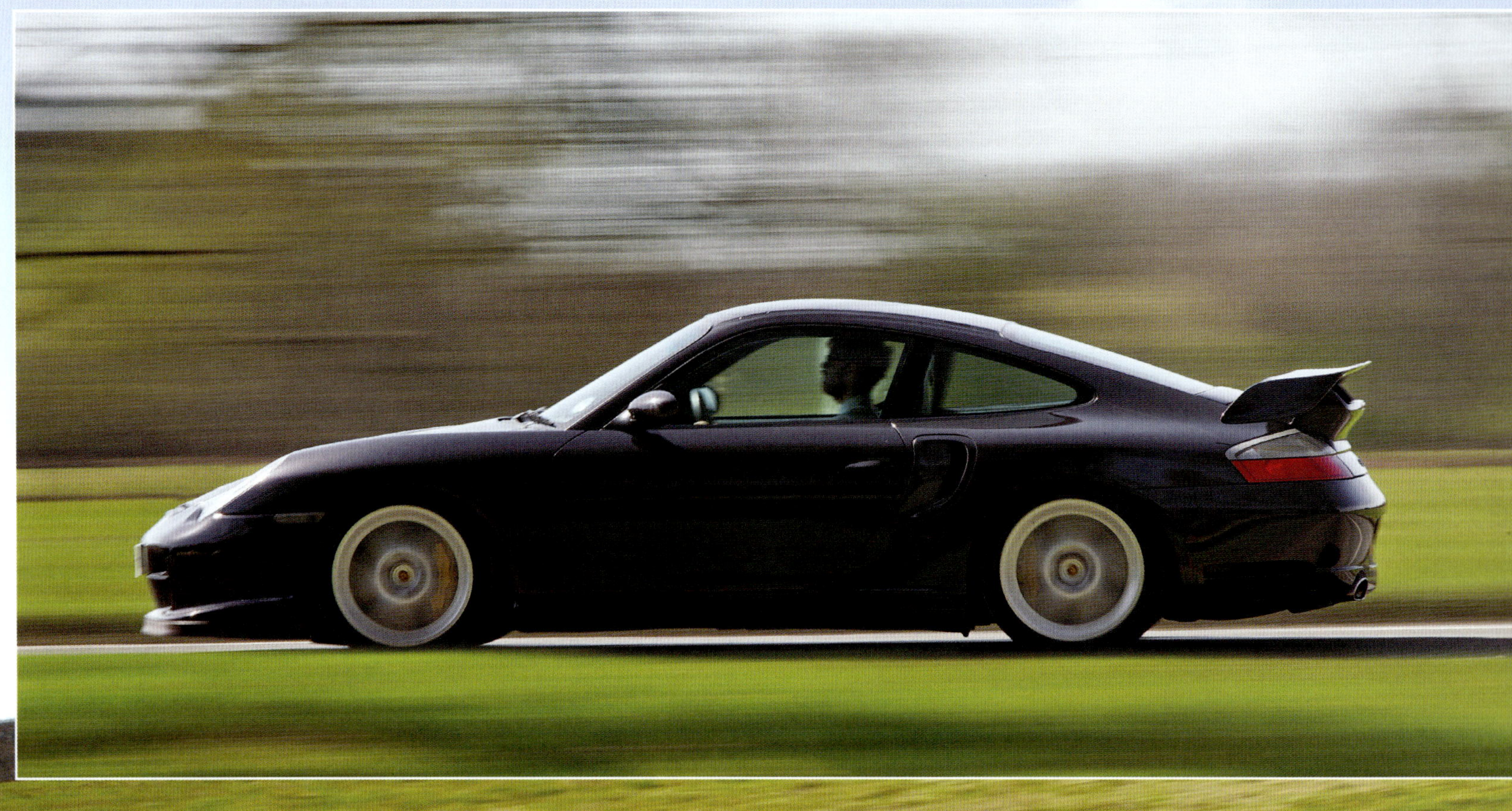



## THE WATER-COOLED GT2 IN COMPETITION

While the Porsche 993 GT2 enjoyed a successful international motorsport career – including class victories at the 24 Hours of Le Mans in 1996 and 1997 – the 996 version was never intended for official competition use. However, while Weissach never chose to slap a number on the water-cooled GT2's door, a prominent Californian 911 enthusiast did just that in the Pikes Peak International Hill Climb.

Convinced of the GT2's turbocharged potential, Zwart returned to Pikes Peak in 2010, this time in a 997 GT2 RS (pictured), clocking a new 2WD Time Attack course record of 11 minutes and 31.1 seconds on the now smooth-surfaced hill climb.

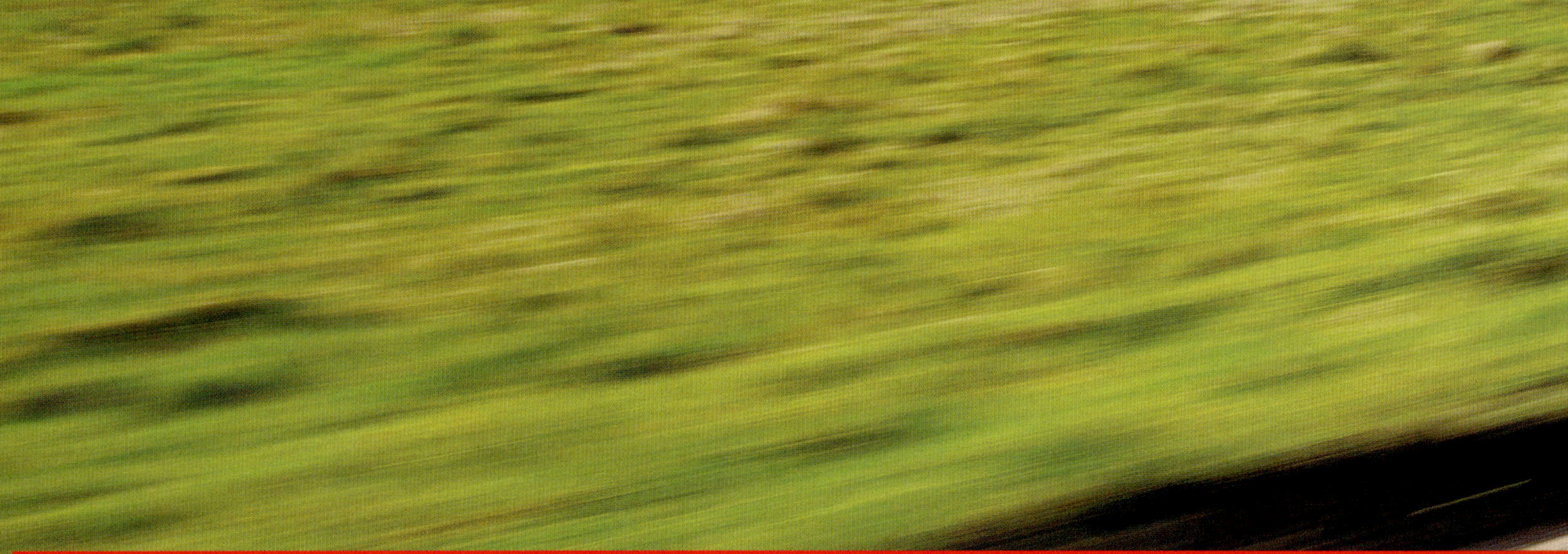

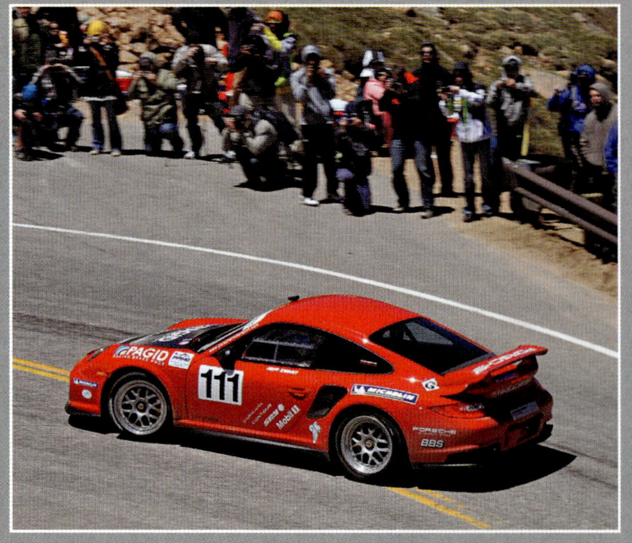

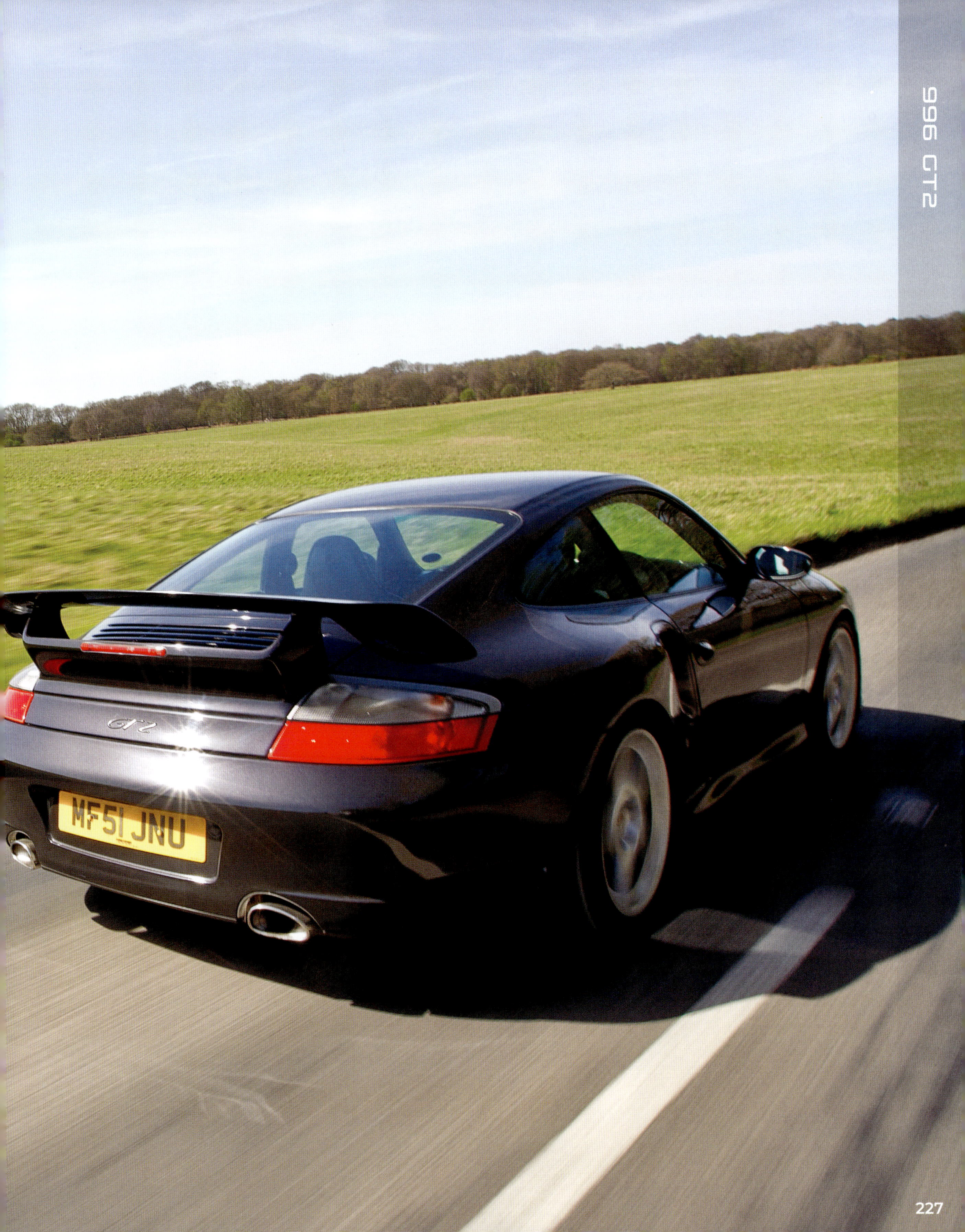

# ONLY 22 MADE
# 911R

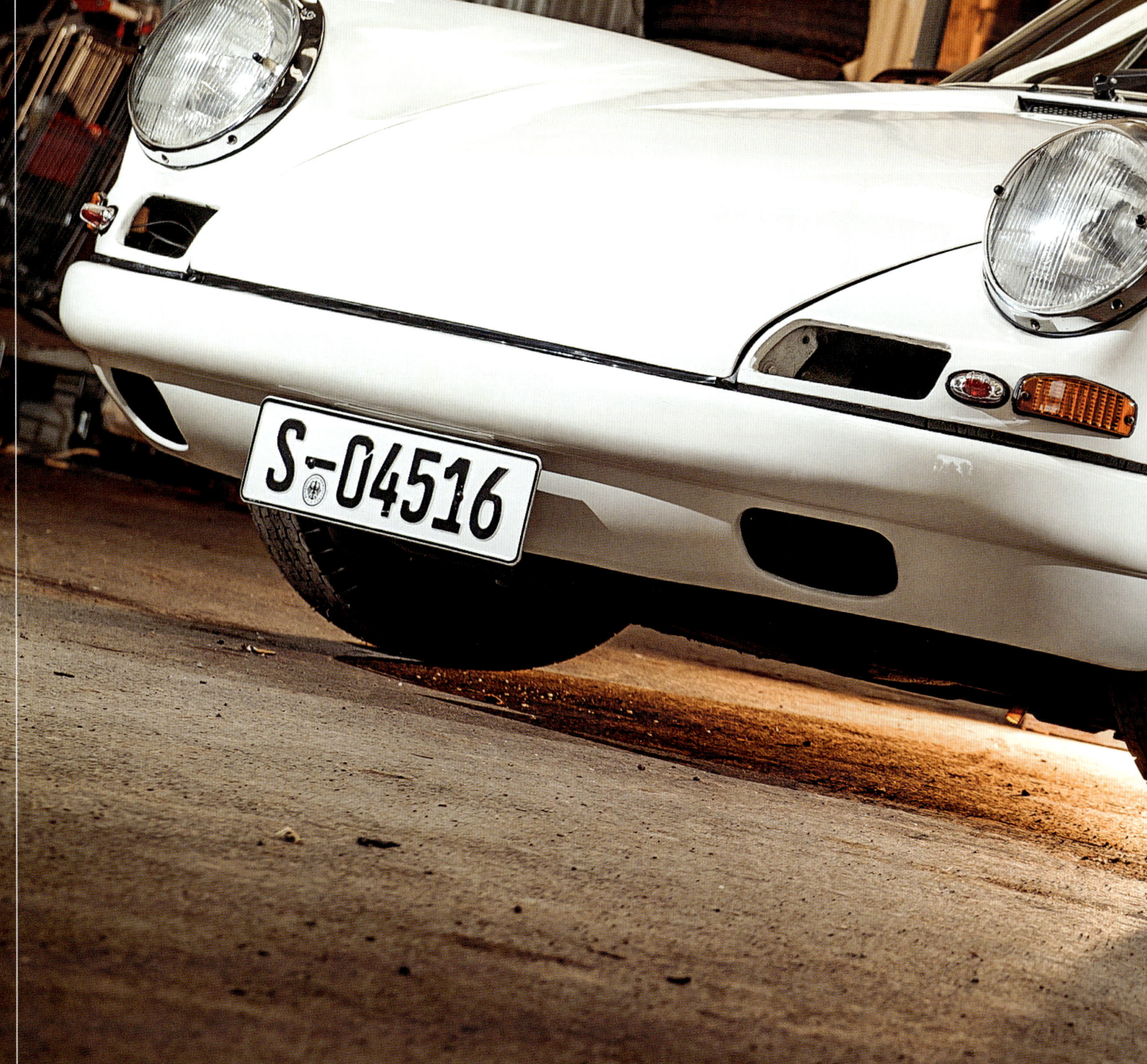

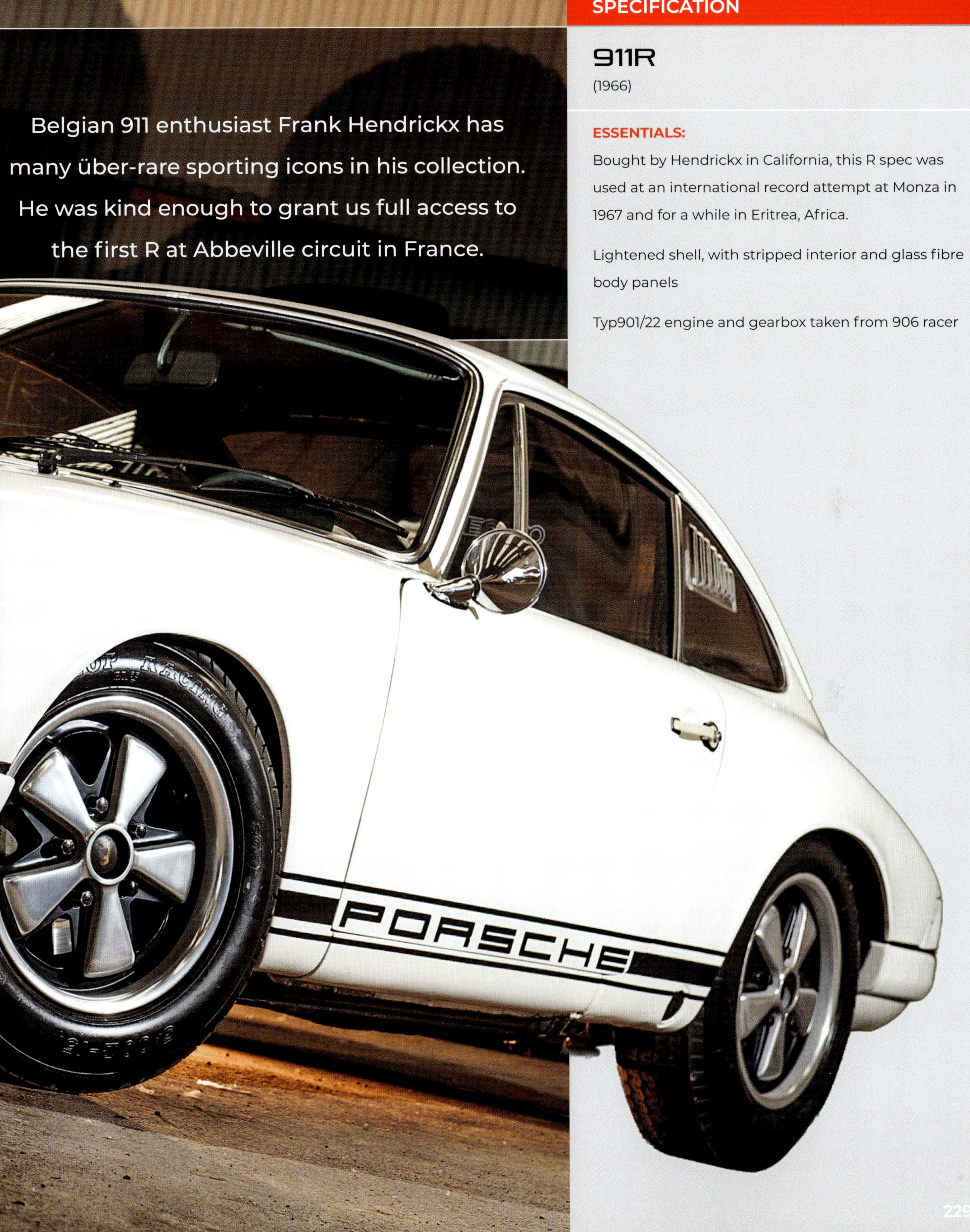

Belgian 911 enthusiast Frank Hendrickx has many über-rare sporting icons in his collection. He was kind enough to grant us full access to the first R at Abbeville circuit in France.

SPECIFICATION

911R
(1966)

ESSENTIALS:
Bought by Hendrickx in California, this R spec was used at an international record attempt at Monza in 1967 and for a while in Eritrea, Africa.

Lightened shell, with stripped interior and glass fibre body panels

Typ901/22 engine and gearbox taken from 906 racer

PORSCHE

You have to be a determined – not to mention well heeled – 911 enthusiast to have the 911R in your Porsche collection. However, Frank Hendrickx is no ordinary collector, having spent over a decade tracking down some of these cars. What matters to him is the absolute authenticity of his 911s that requires a commitment bordering on obsession, Frank begins by explaining to us how he caught the 911 virus.

That came in 1991, when Frank paid a deposit on the then-recently launched RS 964. He became a total recidivist, and today his collection includes, aside from the car we're about to introduce, other 911 exotica such as the Ruf CTR, SC RS, and the C4 Leichtbau. But indubitably, the R is the most special...

The earliest 'special' 911 in the collection is the 911 R, a car that was a casebook study in removing weight. The 160bhp S was already proving successful in competition, but technical director Ferdinand Piëch realised that a ground-up racer was required to win at the highest level, so he had the 911 significantly lightened.

The 'R', for Rennen (racing), was assembled by coach-builder Karl Bauer, who fitted doors, bonnets and engine covers, as well as bumpers in glass fibre. The windscreen used 4mm-thick glass (instead of 6mm) and perspex replaced the other windows. Aluminium hinges and simplified catches were employed throughout, and steel bulkheads everywhere were drilled to eliminate vital ounces. The interior was stripped and the dash cut back to three instruments. The standard suspension was lowered, and the 210bhp engine and gearbox of the 906 racer fitted.

Weighing not much over 800kg, the R proved to be fast and reliable, and achieved a series of international speed records, but it never got beyond the prototype stage, as the Porsche board refused to sanction production of the necessary 500 units to qualify the R for production car racing – which was Piëch's aim. So only 22 of this, the lightest 911 ever made, were built. With no racing category available to them, it took Porsche a couple of years to find customers for the Rs.

What a contrast 40 years on, when these Porsches sell for well into six figures. Hendrickx tracked his car down in California, where documents showed that this was the second R built, and that it was used as the back-up car at the international speed record attempts at Monza in May 1967 before becoming a works racer, being sold when the 911 model went to 2.2 litres. The buyer was an Italian, Dr Daolio, who took the R to Asmara in Eritrea, where he worked, and the 911 R competed extensively in local rallies and street races before going to a Japanese collector when the doctor returned to Italy in 1980. The R saw almost no use for the next 30 years – when Frank acquired it, the clocks showed only 32,000km.

On Abbeville's smooth tarmac, the R is a delight to drive. The steering is light and very direct, the gear change with its dog leg first requires no effort, and on winter tyres this racing 911 drifts beautifully through tight corners. The engine is amazingly responsive: Frank has weighed the car at 820kg – exactly its ex-factory weight – and the engine delivers 216bhp according to the dynamometer, a power to weight ratio unmatched by naturally aspirated production 911s until the first GT3.

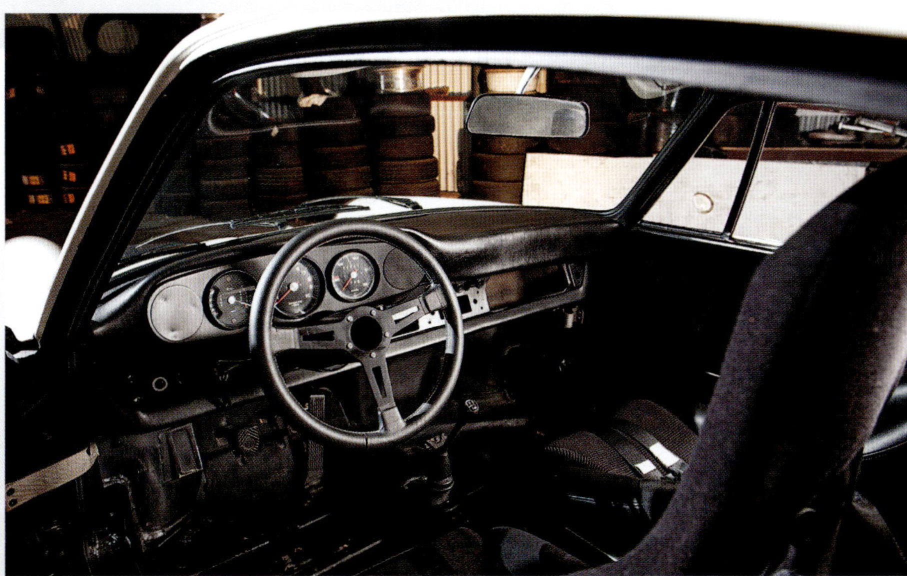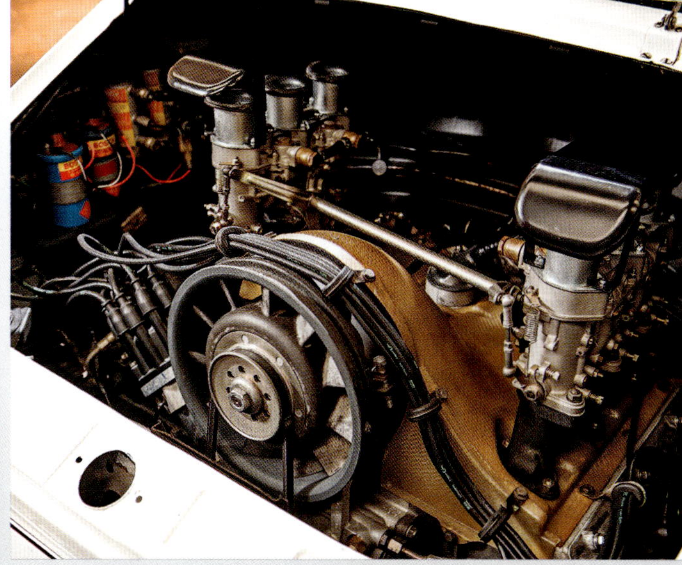

Weight-saving measures on the 911R included drilling holes in the bulkhead and cutting back the dashboard. The Typ 901/22 2.0-litre engine from the 906 was used in the 911R, producing 210bhp

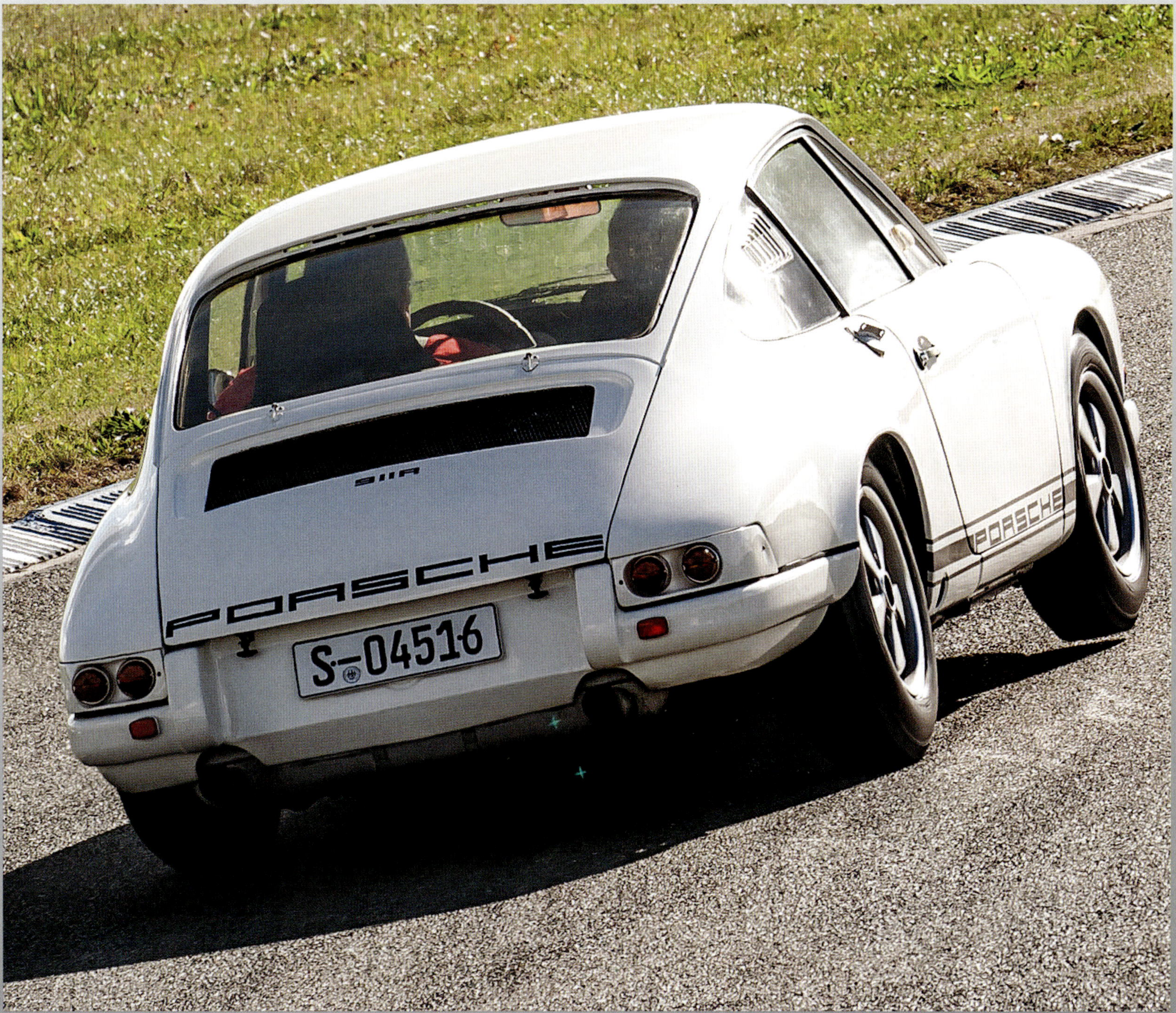

# 964 SPEEDSTER

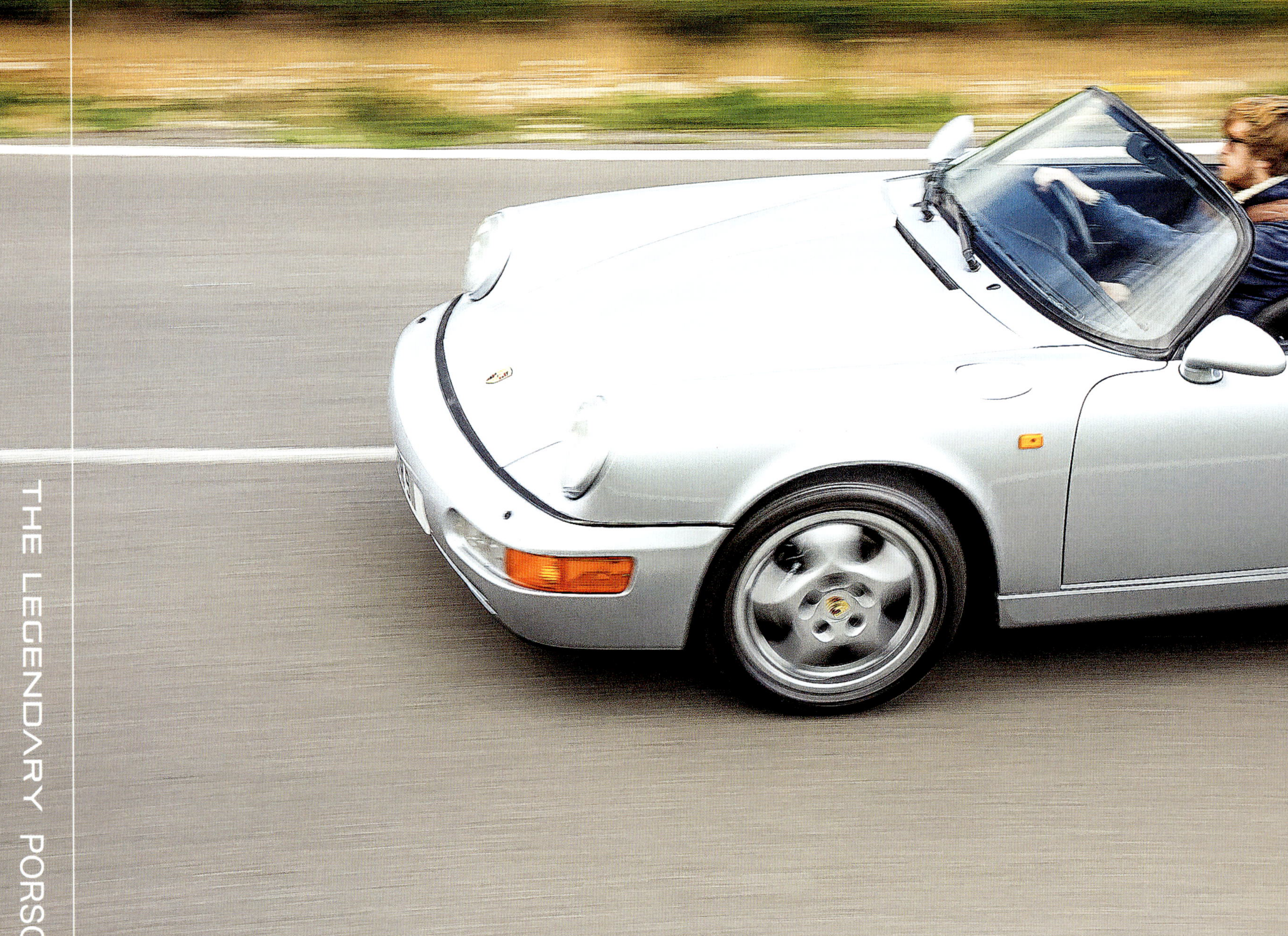

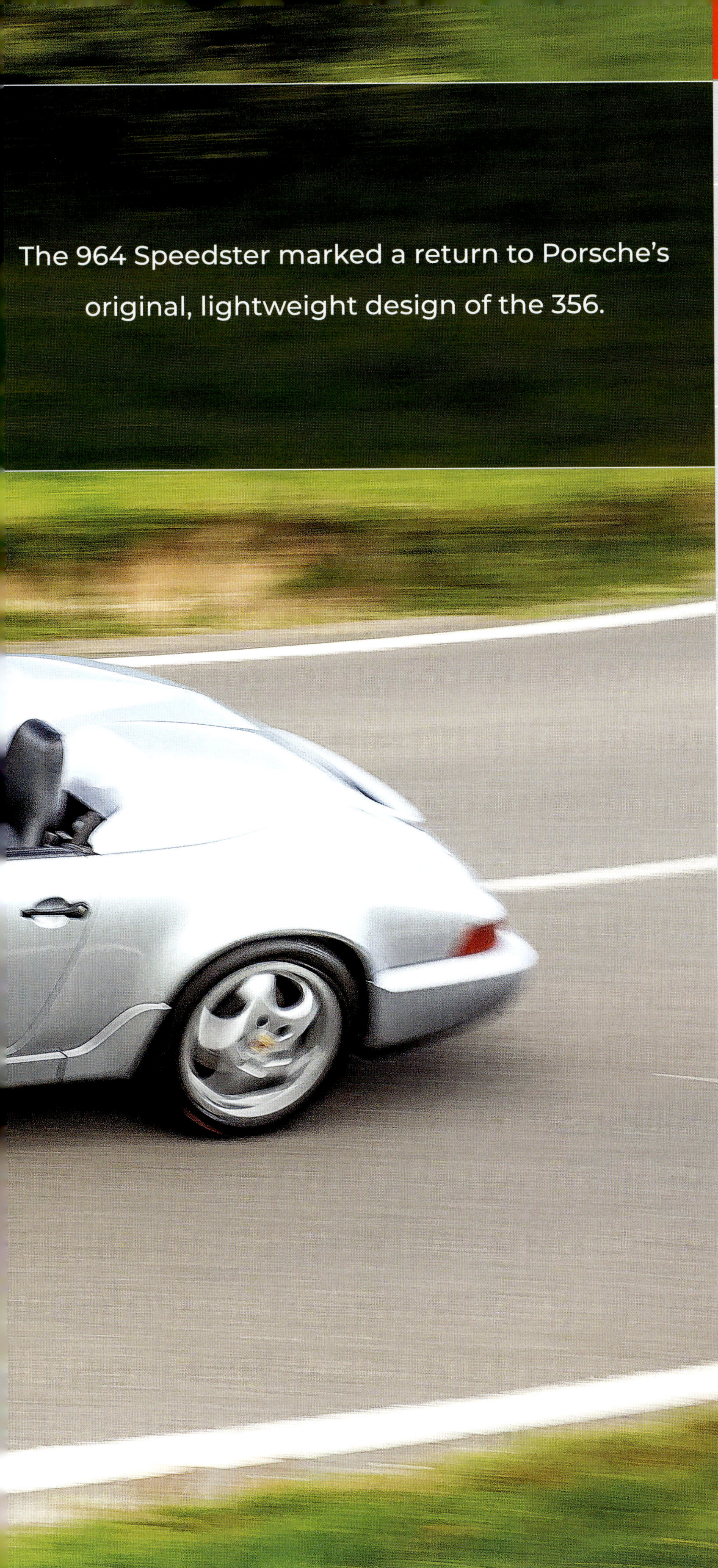





# 964 SPEEDSTER

( 1993-94)

### ENGINE

**Capacity:** 3,600cc

**Compression ratio:** 11:3.1

**Maximum power:** 250bhp @ 6,100rpm

**Maximum torque:** 310Nm @ 4,800rpm

**Transmission:** Six-speed manual

### SUSPENSION

**Front:** Lower wishbones and MacPherson struts with combined coil springs and dampers; anti-roll bar

**Rear:** Semi-trailing arms with combined coil springs and dampers; anti-roll bar

### WHEELS & TYRES

**Front:** 7x17-inch Fuchs alloys; 205/50/ZR17 tyres

**Rear:** 9x17-inch Fuchs alloys; 255/40/ZR17 tyres

### BRAKES

**Front:** 320mm vented discs

**Rear:** 299mm vented discs

### DIMENSIONS

**Length:** 4,250mm

**Width:** 1,652mm

**Weight:** 1,340kg

### PERFORMANCE

**0-60mph:** 5.5 seconds

**Top speed:** 161mph

Speedster: undoubtedly the nine coolest letters in the Porsche lexicon. One mention of this legendary Zuffenhausen moniker brings to mind images of the glamour of the Hollywood scene in the Fifties. First appearing in pre-A 356 form in 1954, the Speedster became intrinsically linked with American car culture and Porsche's formative years. However, the iconic status garnered by the original car meant that the Porsche Speedster sub-brand soon transcended its early US-based roots.

While it may have been intended for the American market, the decision to reimagine the Speedster aesthetic on certain generations of 911 has seen Stuttgart create some of the most sought after cars in the company's history. During the Porsche 911's formative years, however, the Speedster's legend appeared to have been largely forgotten by the Zuffenhausen elite as engineers set about creating the Targa and, later on, Cabriolet body styles, providing ample open-top choice for Porsche buyers. The Speedster's absence was not helped either by Stuttgart's financial struggles during the late Seventies and early Eighties; a special edition car would surely have been the straw that broke the camel's back.

However, Porsche brought out its first 911 Speedster in 1989, to critical acclaim. Backed by what turned out to be strong sales of the first Speedster in 911 guise, Porsche were buoyed into producing another variant just four years later under the 964 programme. Based on the rear-driven Carrera 2, the 964 Speedster featured, like its predecessor, no rear bench and a manually-operated hood that folded neatly under a double-bubble glass fibre panel behind the seats. The hood, much like the raked windscreen, was borrowed from the earlier 3.2 Speedster and simply fitted to the 964's newer coachwork. Limited specification once again was the order of the day –

manually operated exterior mirrors were housed in the later 'teardrop' covers, with RS-style door cards and a choice of Recaro buckets or Sports seats.

The majority of 964 Speedsters sold were narrow bodies sitting atop 17 inch Cup alloys – usually colour coded to match the hue of the bodywork – with just nine wide body cars known to be in existence. A right-hand drive 964 Speedster, such as the Polar silver example shown here, is also a rarity, as only 14 were built to this specification. However, a 964 Speedster of any iteration is considered a rare find today as just over 900 examples were eventually built (the actual number is 936), with Porsche blaming tough economic conditions at the time for its relative sales flop.

Arguably, the 964 could be considered to be the least prettiest of Porsche's Speedster quartet. Usurped by its wider-bodied company, the 964 purveys a very different look to the broad, squat visuals associated with a traditional Speedster. Its ride height looks almost unnaturally high, though this is a flaw that befalls every example of this second-generation 911 Speedster.

At the wheel of the 964 the sensations are very different, though. While not matching the sporting finesse of a fixed-roof equivalent, the 964 boasts a beautiful blend of organic Speedster experience mated to improved handling that the comparatively antiquated G-series just can't match. ABS-assisted brakes for the first time provide ample stopping power when called upon, while the 964's powertrain is equally impressive. It's M64 engine produces a zesty 250bhp that's entirely usable on public roads, delivered to the rear wheels via a G50 gearbox that boasts an effortlessly crisp throw. All in all, it's a great shame so few 964 Speedsters saw the light of day. Those 936 examples that did get built were far short of the 3,000 that Zuffenhausen were rumoured to have predicted.

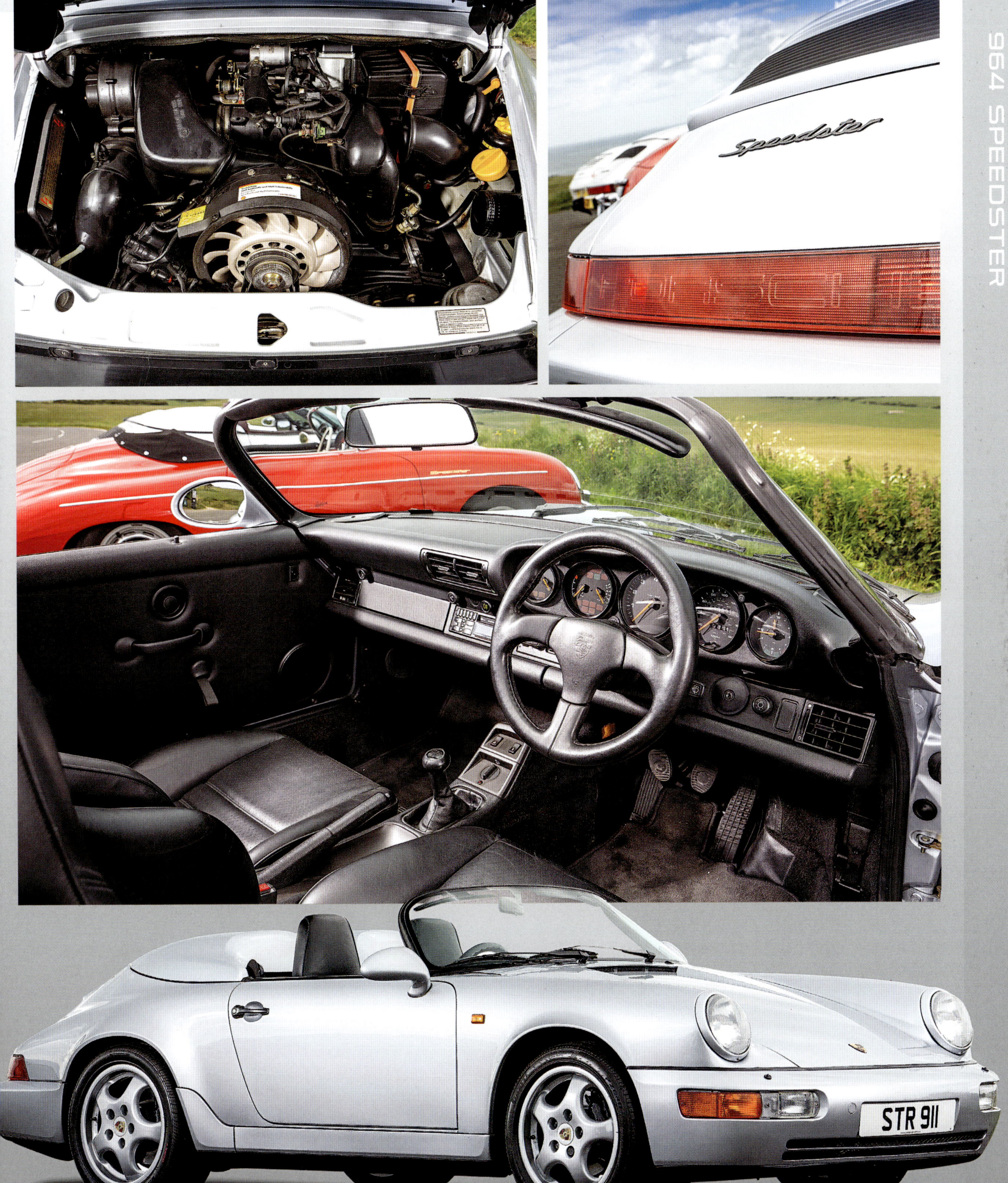

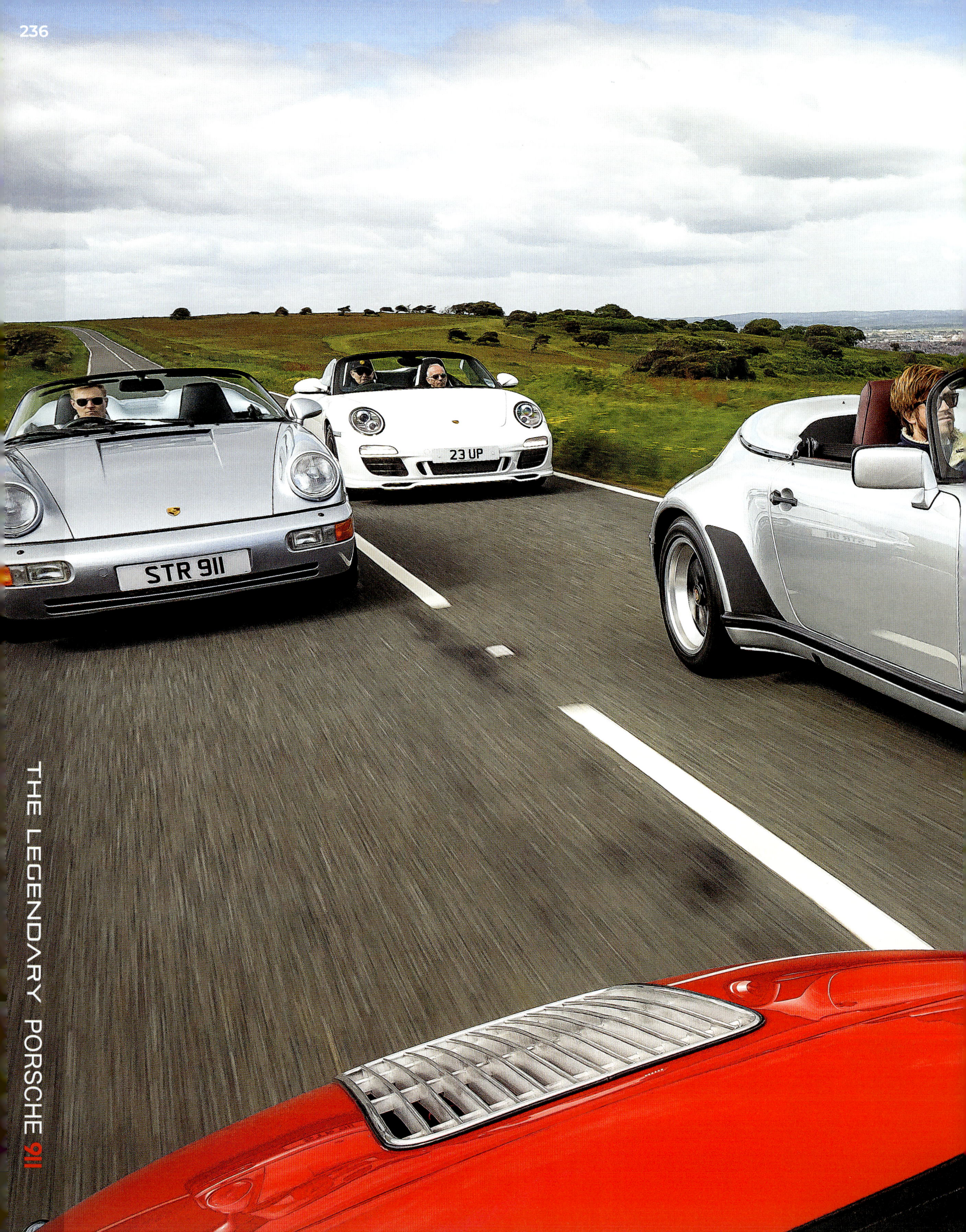

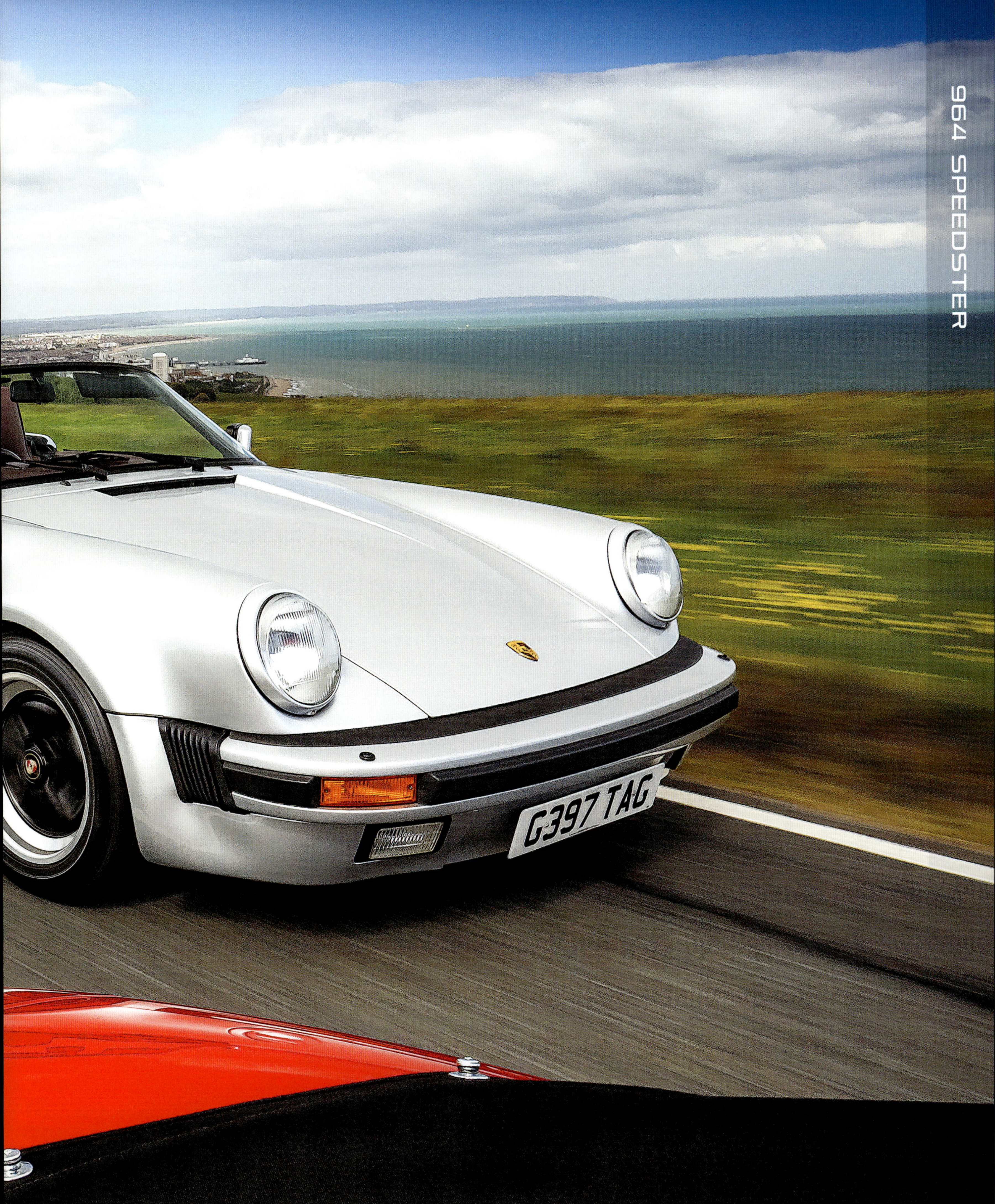
964 SPEEDSTER

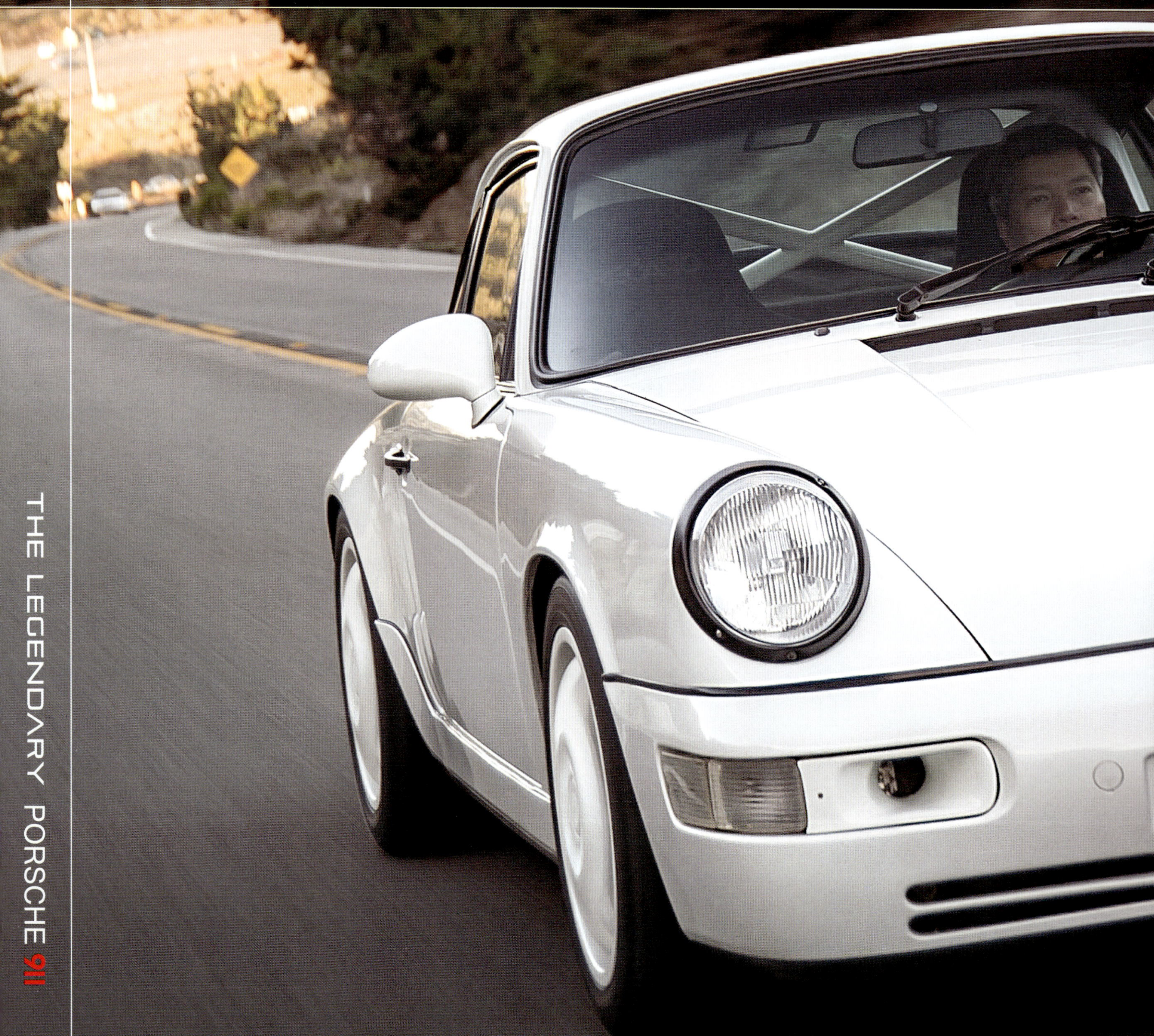

ONLY 701 MADE
964 RS
AMERICA

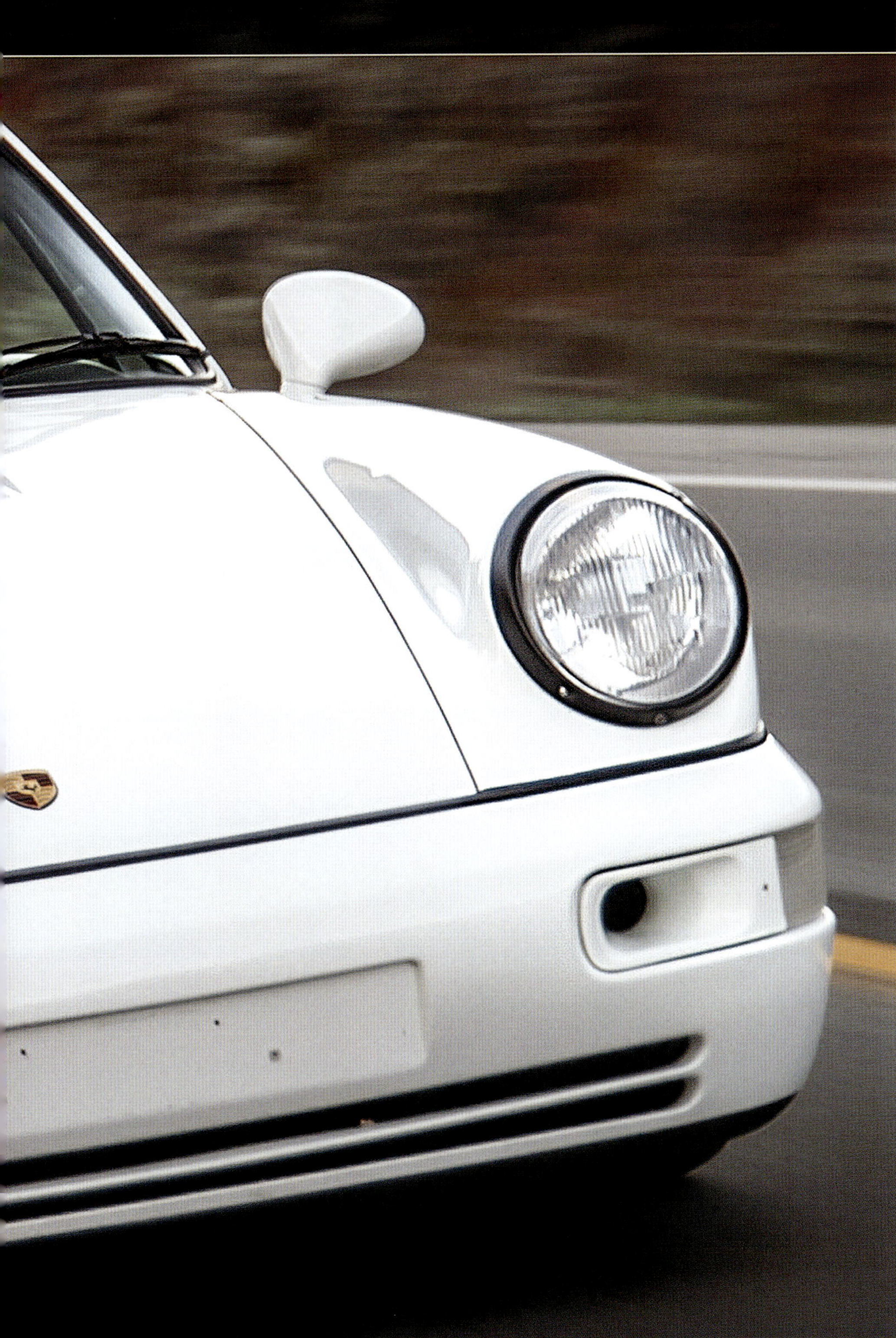

The 964 RS America was built during anxious times for Porsche, when sales were in the doldrums and funds were low. But save the excuses; these cars are exciting. All you need is a sunset to chase



## 964 RS AMERICA

(1993)

### ENGINE

**Capacity:** 3.6 litres
**Compression ratio:** 11.3:1
**Maximum power:** 250bhp
**Maximum torque:** 228lb ft @ 4,800rpm
**Transmission:** G50/21 Euro close-ratio six-speed box with LSD, LSD repacked by Guard Transmission

### SUSPENSION

**Front:** Bilstein adjustable PSS10 coilovers, Kokeln Alloy strut brace
**Rear:** Bilstein adjustable PSS10 coilovers

### WHEELS & TYRES

**Front:** 8x17-inch Porsche Cup 1 wheels, Nitto NT01 225/45 ZR17 tyres
**Rear:** 9x17-inch Porsche Cup 1 wheels, Nitto NT01 255/40 ZR17 tyres

### BRAKES

**Front:** 'Big Red' 964 RS calipers, OEM Textar pads
**Rear:** 'Big Red' 964 RS calipers, OEM Textar Pads

### DIMENSIONS

**Length:** 4,275mm
**Width:** 1,651mm
**Weight:** 1,340kg

### PERFORMANCE

**0-60mph:** 5.4 secs
**Top speed:** 163mph

**T**oday, many enthusiasts regard the 964 line as the final flourish of the original 911 design. The styling certainly supports this argument, with the classic swooping rain gutters topping the same window profile found on the very first 901 models. This is the Porsche line, and aficionados just love it.

Launched at the Detroit Show in January 1992, the RS America was closer to the US-spec 964 Carrera 2 than the 964 RS. While the RS engine was blueprinted, which Porsche said added 10hp, the American engine was standard at a basic 247hp. The car carried less equipment than standard, with sports suspension and wider wheels and tyres.

As per Porsche marketing strategy, the 964 RS America was promoted with a hand on the 1973 2.7 911 Carrera RS. The press release read: "Porsche commemorates the 20th anniversary of the Porsche 911 RS with the creation of the Porsche RS America. Released in late spring of 1992 as a 1993 model, the RS America is available only in North America. The 1993 RS America captures the spirit of the original RS with its emphasis on performance." Factory RS Americas had a fixed rear wing, similar in

appearance to the Carrera 3.2. Inside were electric windows and a rear seat delete. A sunroof and air conditioning were optional, while the only other choices were a limited-slip differential and a radio upgrade. Paint could also be upgraded, with a metallic option at modest cost and colour-to-sample for a little bit more.

Unlike in Europe, where less equipment in a factory Porsche usually means a higher price, the 964 RS America sold for $53,900 (approximately £36,000) – $10,000 less than a Carrera 2. Hardcore 911 fans were about the only people still buying Porsches in America, and the company was keen to keep them on board. If there was disappointment at the lack of real RS-ness in the America-only version, it didn't register too loudly on the sales charts. Porsche made 701 RS Americas: 617 for the 1993 model year, and 84 more in 1994. Accounting for almost 17 per cent of 3,713 units sold in the US and Canada for 1993, the 964 RS America more than justified its existence.

Kudos to the plucky 964 RS America: perhaps it lacked a blueprinted engine and it may not have the DNA of a bona fide 911 Rennsport, but it delivered driving pleasure that was the match any 964 RS ever made.



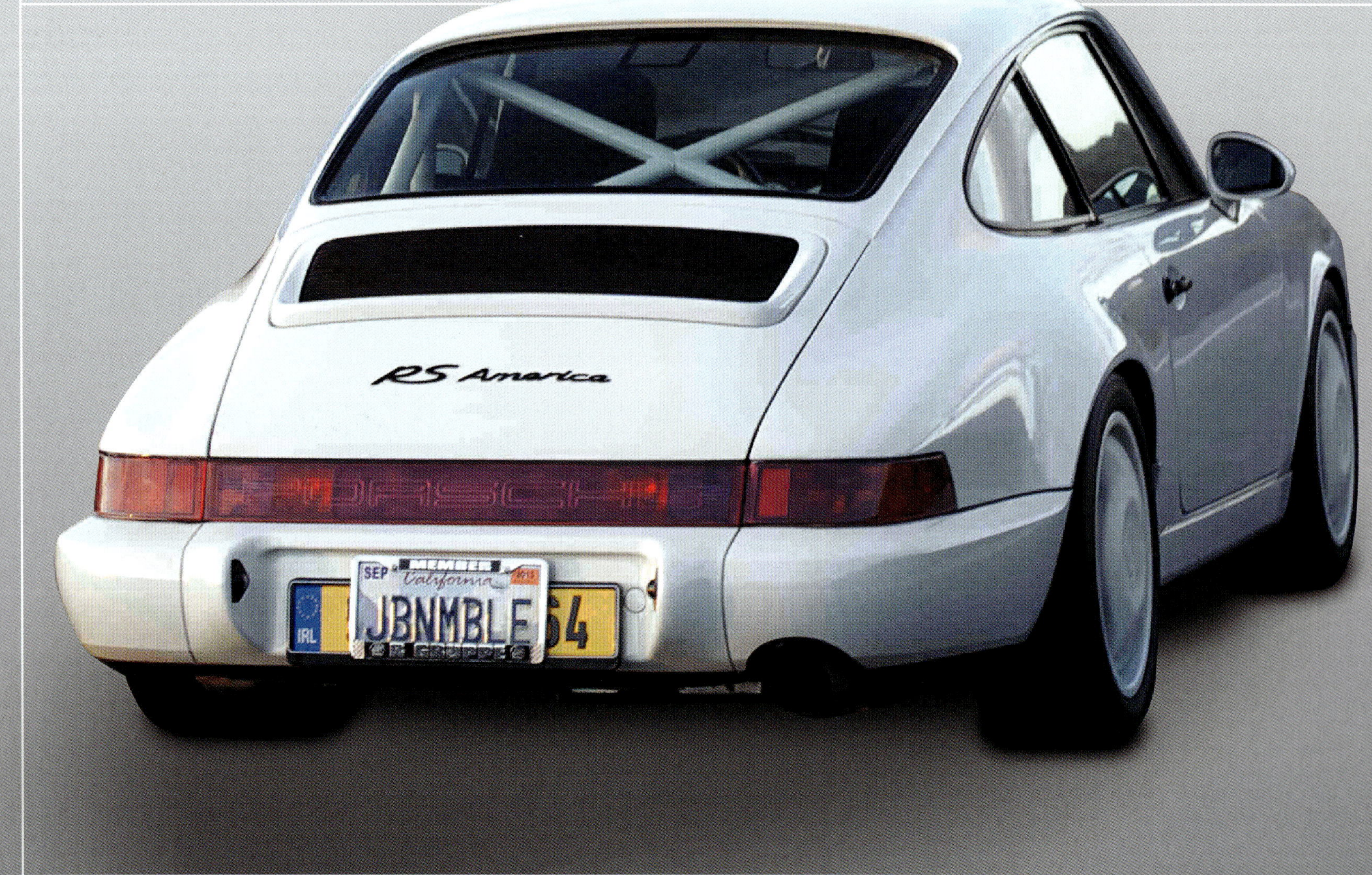

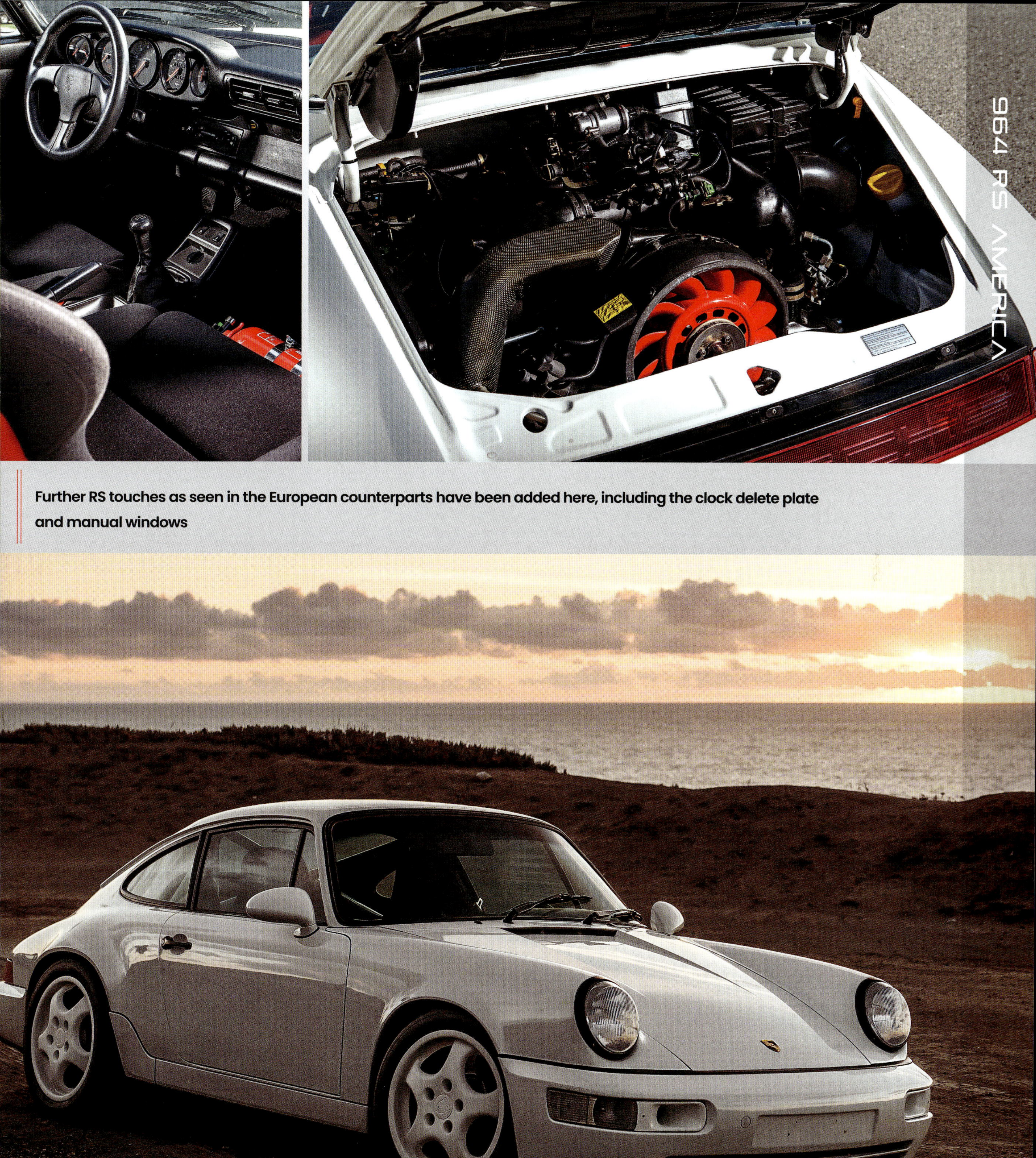

Further RS touches as seen in the European counterparts have been added here, including the clock delete plate and manual windows

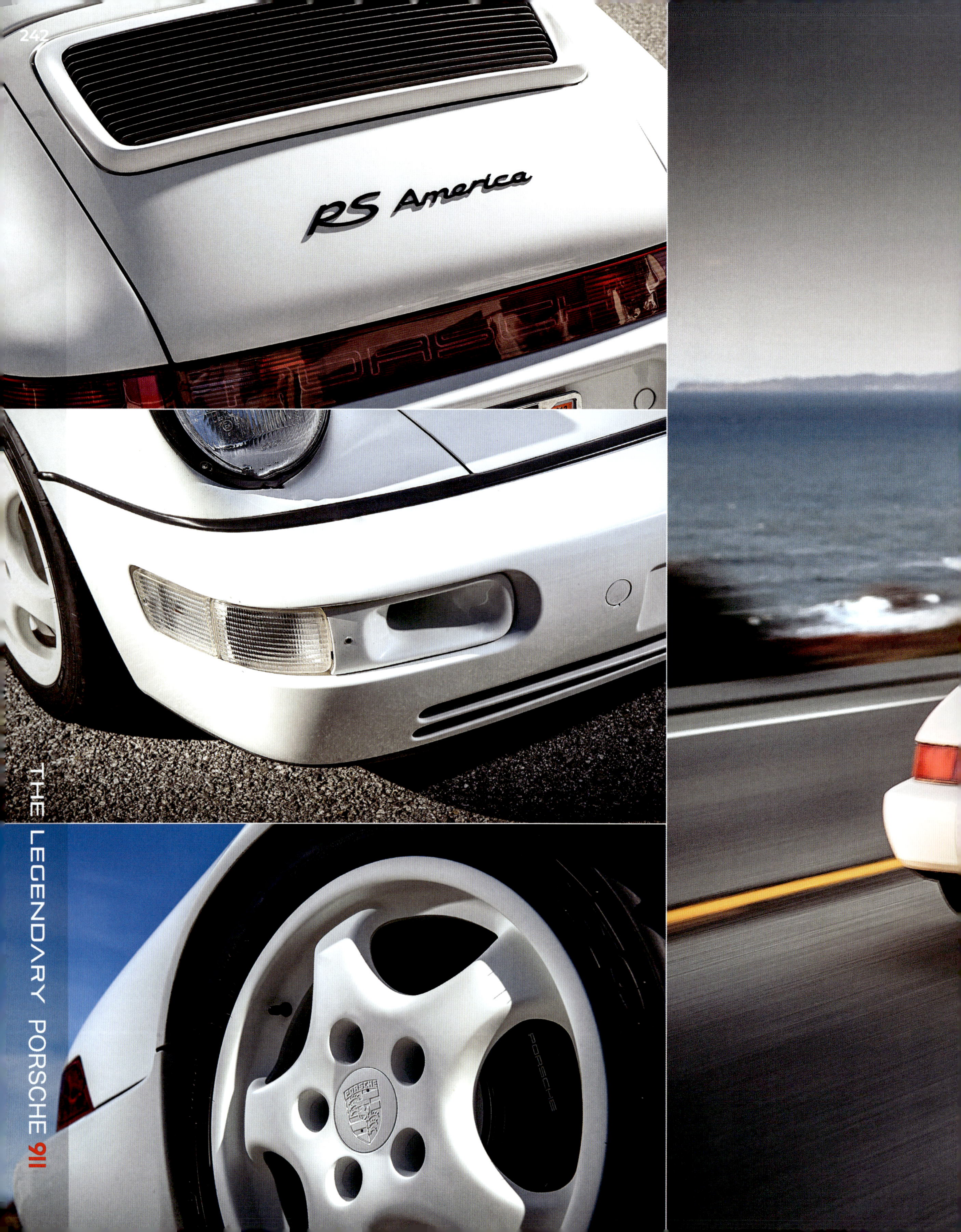
RS America

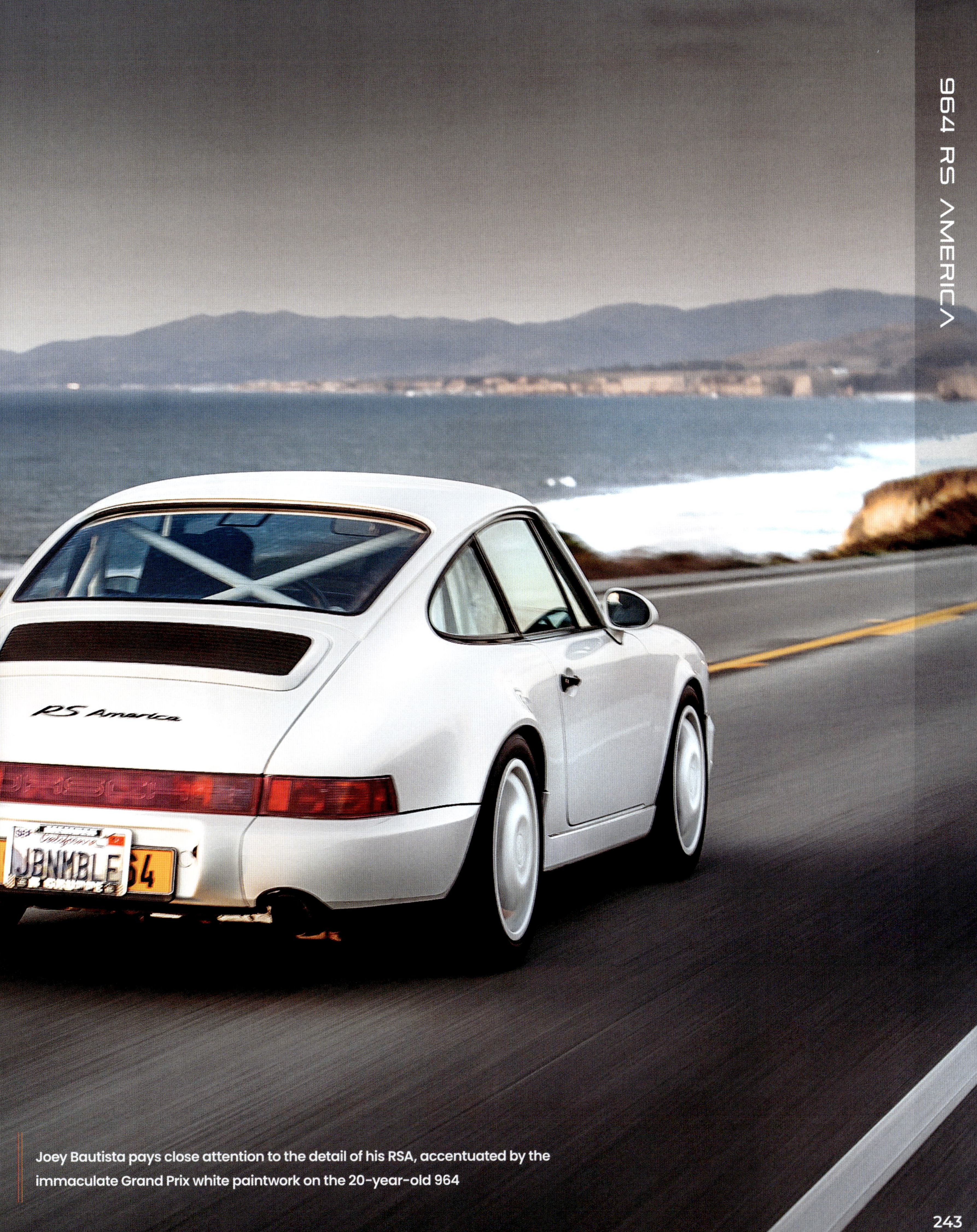



Joey Bautista pays close attention to the detail of his RSA, accentuated by the immaculate Grand Prix white paintwork on the 20-year-old 964

# ONLY 682 MADE
# 996 GT3 RS

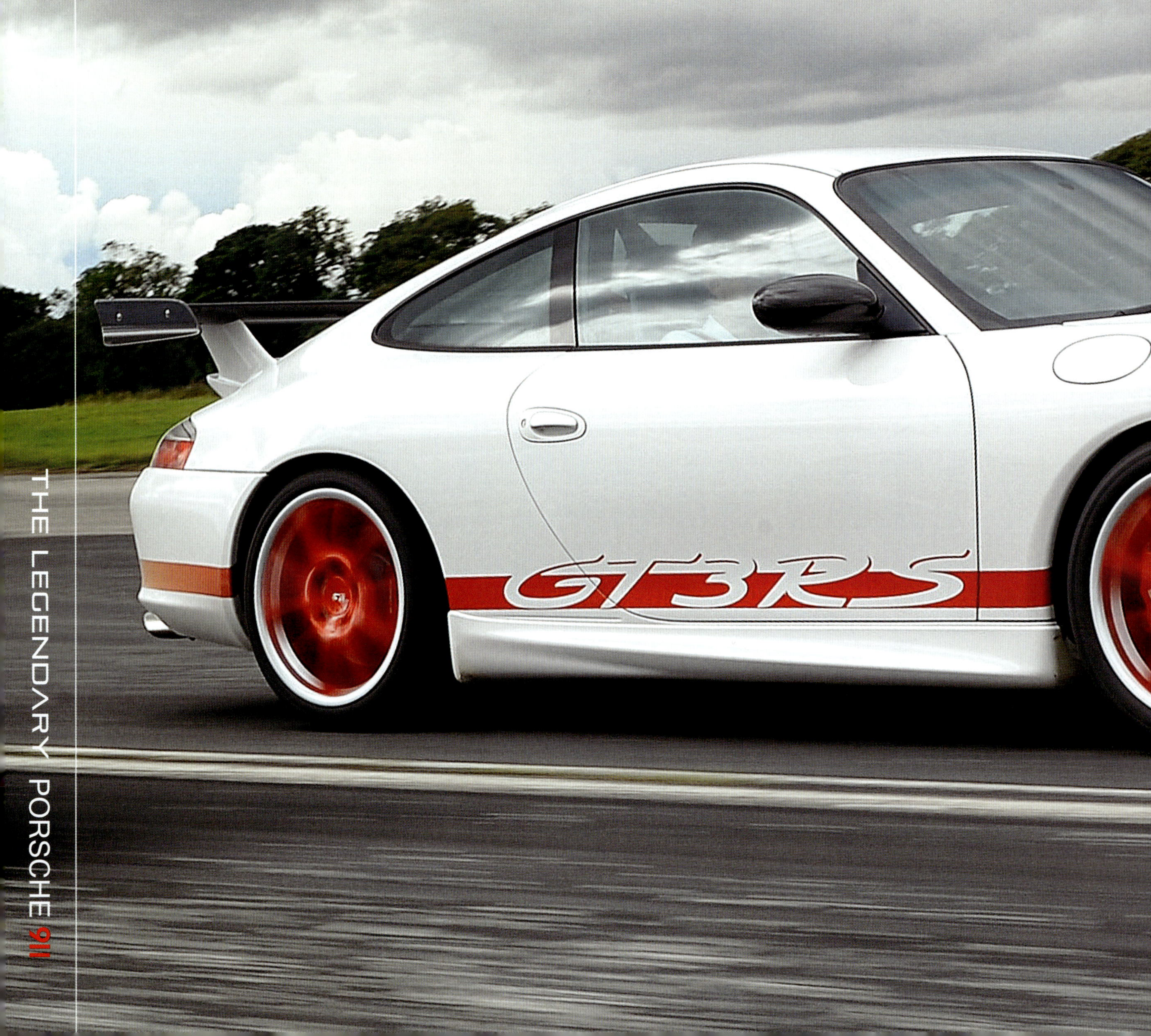

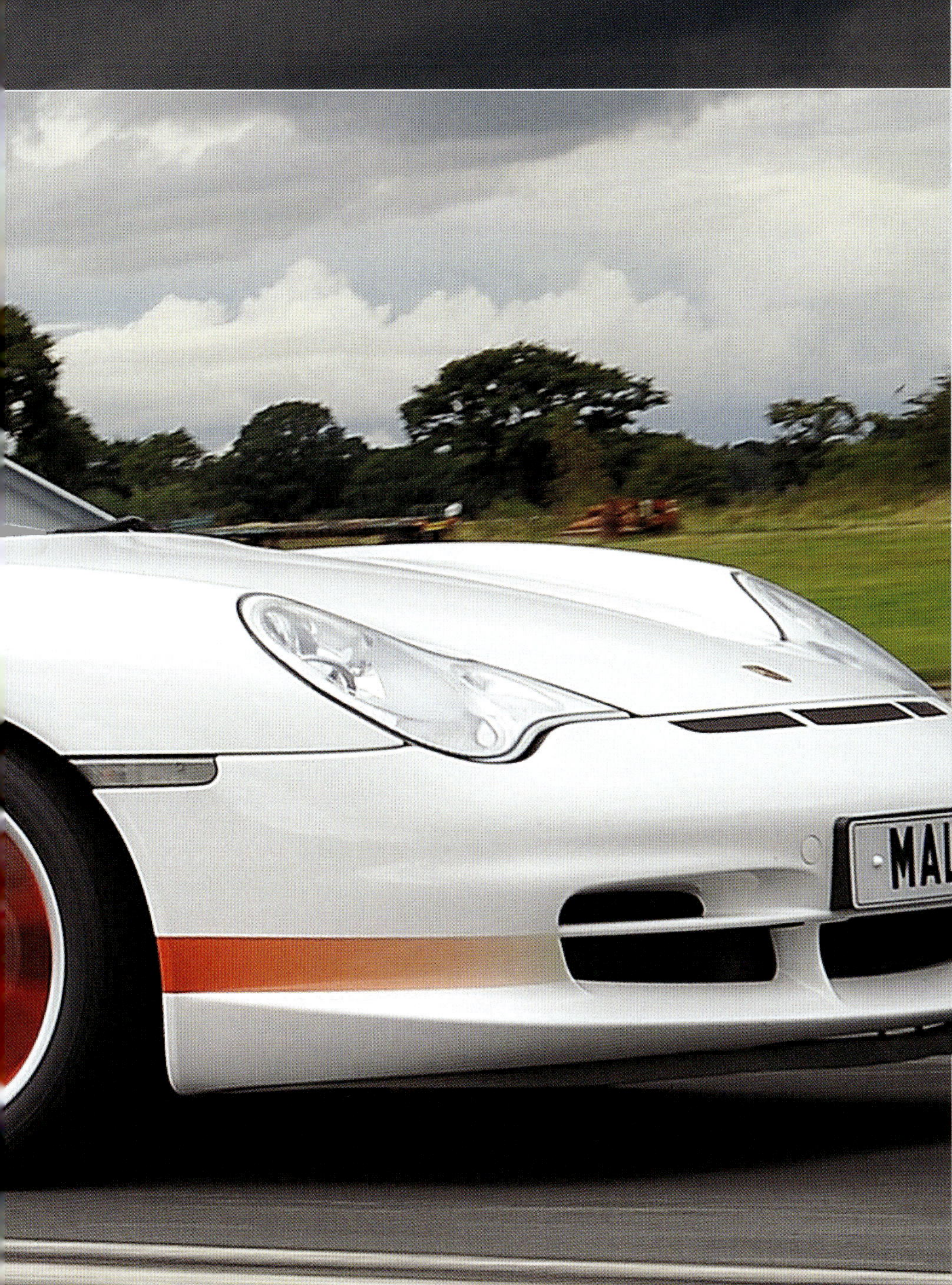

Porsche has a peerless history of producing pared-back 911s for purity of performance. Here, we delve into the pedigree of the first water-cooled lightweight that sticks to the Stuttgart axiom 'less is so much more'.





# 996 GT3 RS
(2004)

### ENGINE
**Capacity:** 3,600cc
**Compression ratio:** 11:7.1
**Maximum power:** 381bhp @ 7,400rpm
**Maximum torque:** 385Nm @ 5,000rpm
**Transmission:** Six-speed manual

### SUSPENSION
**Front:** MacPherson struts with with anti-roll bar
**Rear:** LSA multi-link; anti-roll bar

### WHEELS & TYRES
**Front:** 8.5x18-inch GT3 wheels; 234/40/ZR18 tyres
**Rear:** 11x18-inch GT3 wheels; 295/30/ZR18 tyres

### DIMENSIONS
**Length:** 4,435mm
**Width:** 1,770mm
**Weight:** 1,360kg

### PERFORMANCE
**0-60mph:** 4.4 seconds
**Top speed:** 190mph

**P**erhaps more than any other car manufacturer, Porsche has an evangelical ethos of seeking to improve performance by creating lighter editions of its sports cars in the quest for purity in performance. Particularly evident throughout the 911's entire lineage, the Porsche achievement of enhanced performance and durability with reduced weight stands above and beyond its peers.

The 2.7 RS, introduced after ten years of 911 production and achieved motorsport fame before becoming the holy grail of car investment legend. Later, its Carrera Rennsport successors did the same, with the water-cooled GT3 RS creating a resurgence in Porsche Cup popularity and some giant-killing performances in GT racing. Here, we take a look at the first such water-cooled Rennsport, the 996 GT3 RS.

Of course, it was the 996 GT3 RS that brought lightweight 911s into the modern era of water cooling. The 996 GT3 RS's announcement in 2004 was spectacular, despite shaving only 20 kilograms off the weight of the lightest 996 Gen2 GT3. As we now know, further iterations of GT3 RS followed, each shaving vital kilograms from the performance-enhanced GT3 variants on which they were based. This marks out a formidable lineage of lightweight 911s to date then, with each iteration enjoying soaring market values to boot. Some view this as changing forever the image of the 911 as the 'everyman super car', while to others it's an acknowledgement in wider circles that the Porsche 911 has been under-valued for many years, and is now finding its true place as a collectable car.

In some ways the GT3 RS feels very modern. The ethos of weight saving and attention to detail allows that tactile 'lightweight' 911 interface to shine through in a remarkably common way. The GT3 RS is a motorsport hero designed to achieve homologation and GT racing victories. You wouldn't really want it as your daily driver, as it's too stiff and uncompromising for that, but as a track day car or weekend indulgence it is nothing short of fantastic. I find it sad that this car's value means it will now rarely be driven.

Indeed, the common theme here, as with other ultra rare Porsches, is value. The GT3 RS was always going to be a blue-chip value car, and never really dropped much below its original invoice price, yet at today's prices, the car is valued at around £350,000. As time goes on, that figure is absolutely certain to head onwards and upwards, with only 682 ever being produced by Weissach. If you're a GT3 RS owner then, you're faced with the usual question: to drive it, or not to drive it and watch its value rocket? With such a blistering performance weapon at your disposal, there is surely only one option: get out and drive it exactly like it was built for!



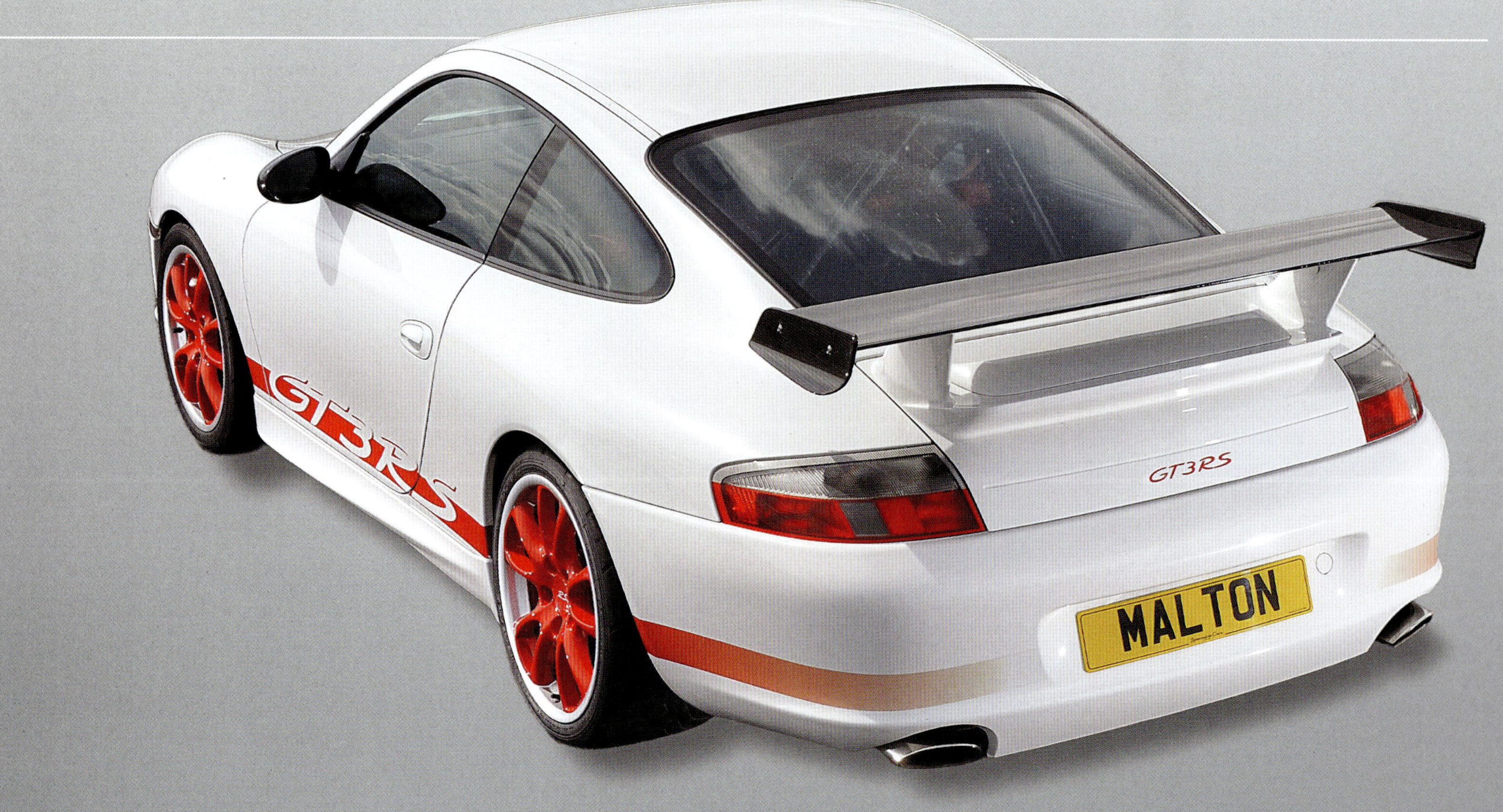

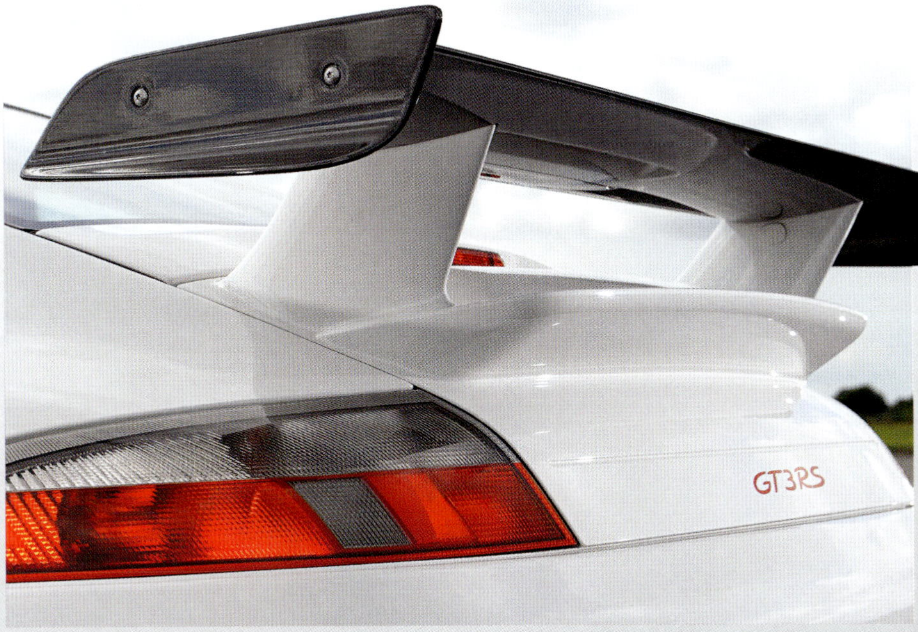

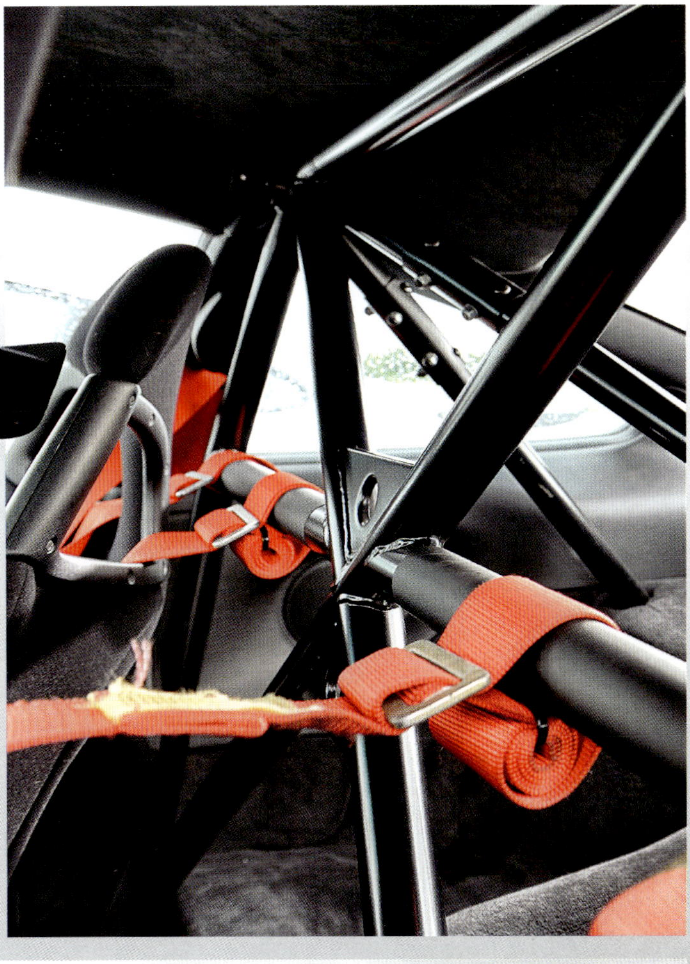

Porsche describe the first GT3 RS as an uncompromising vehicle with the purity of a genuine racer

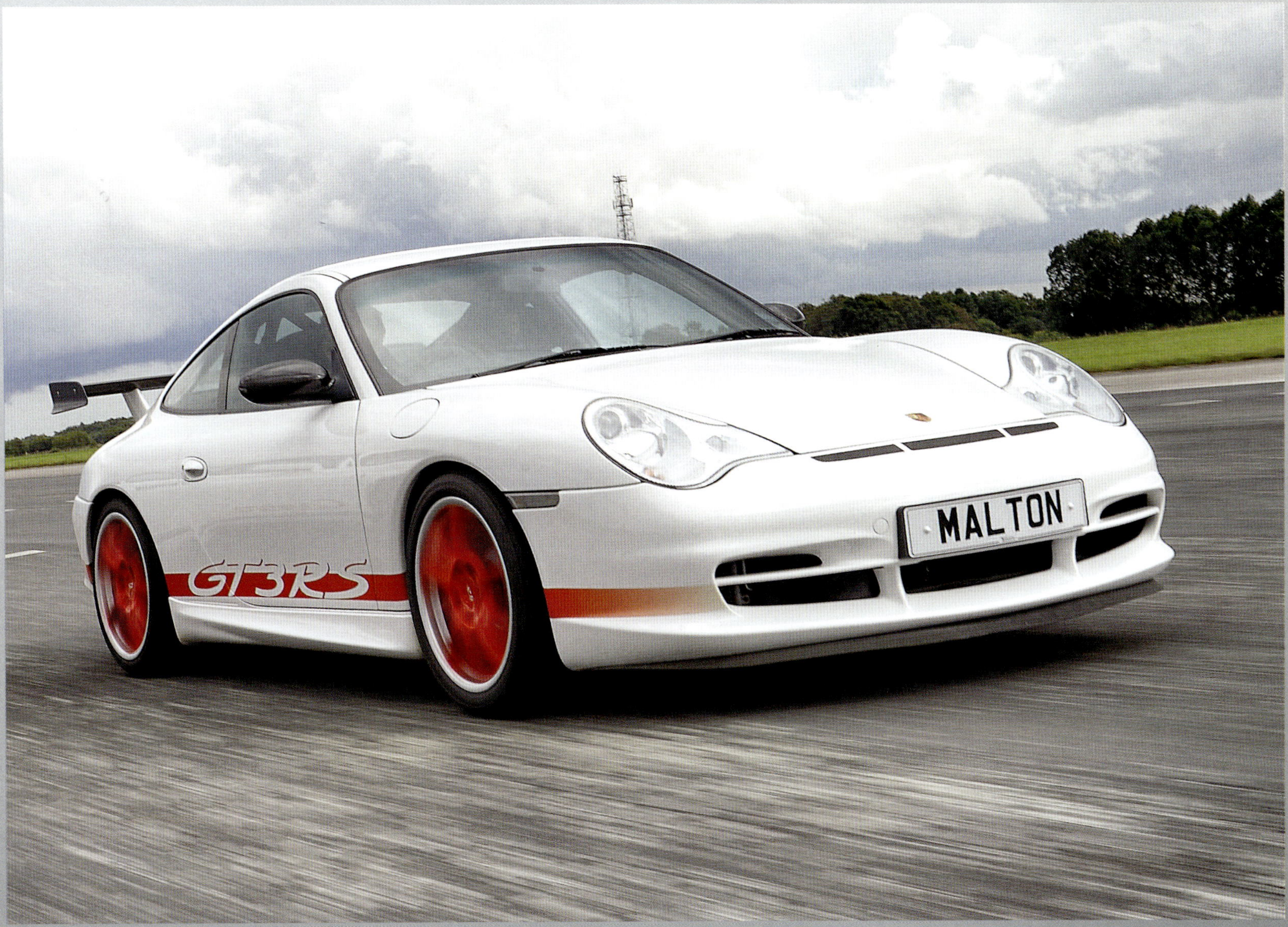

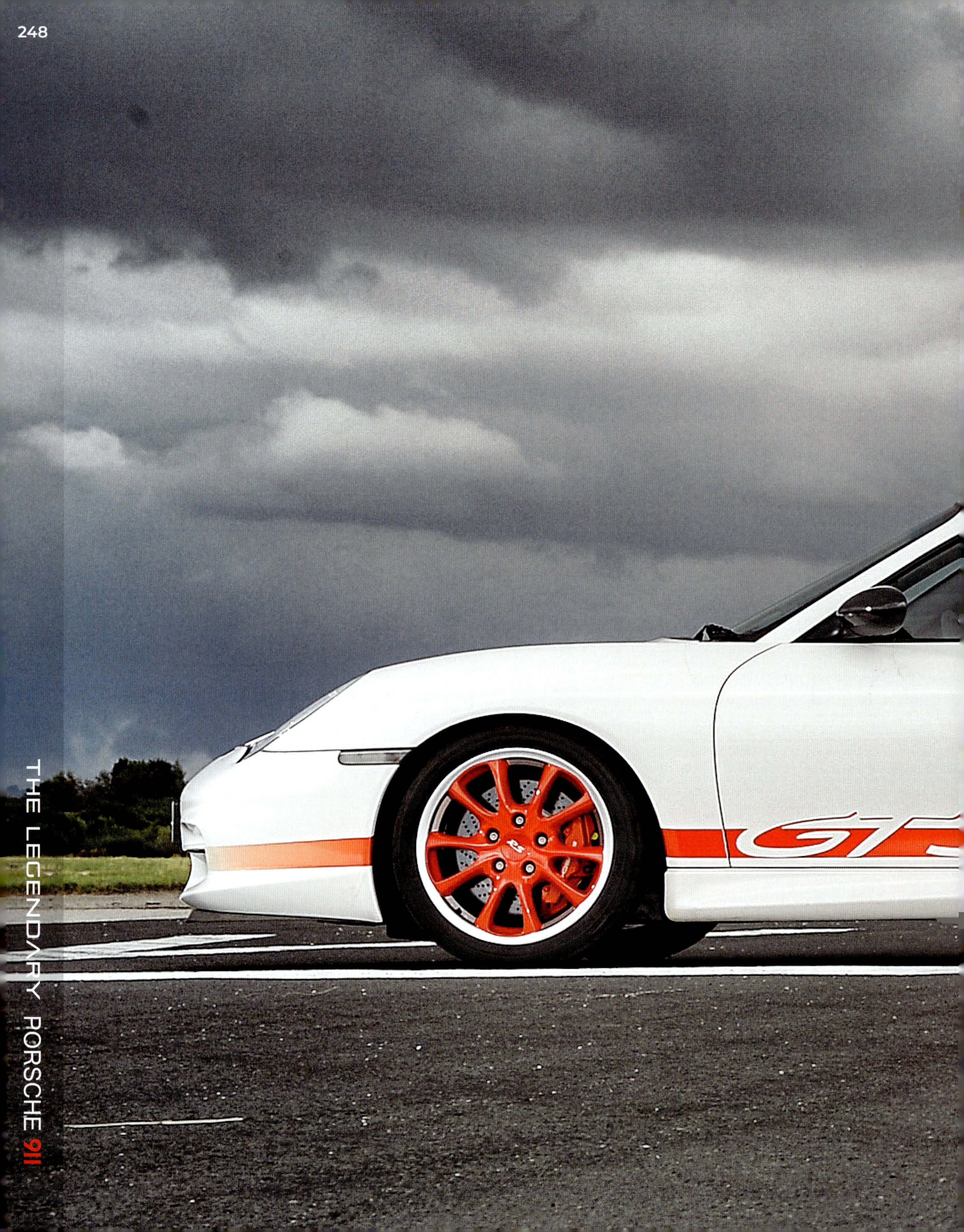

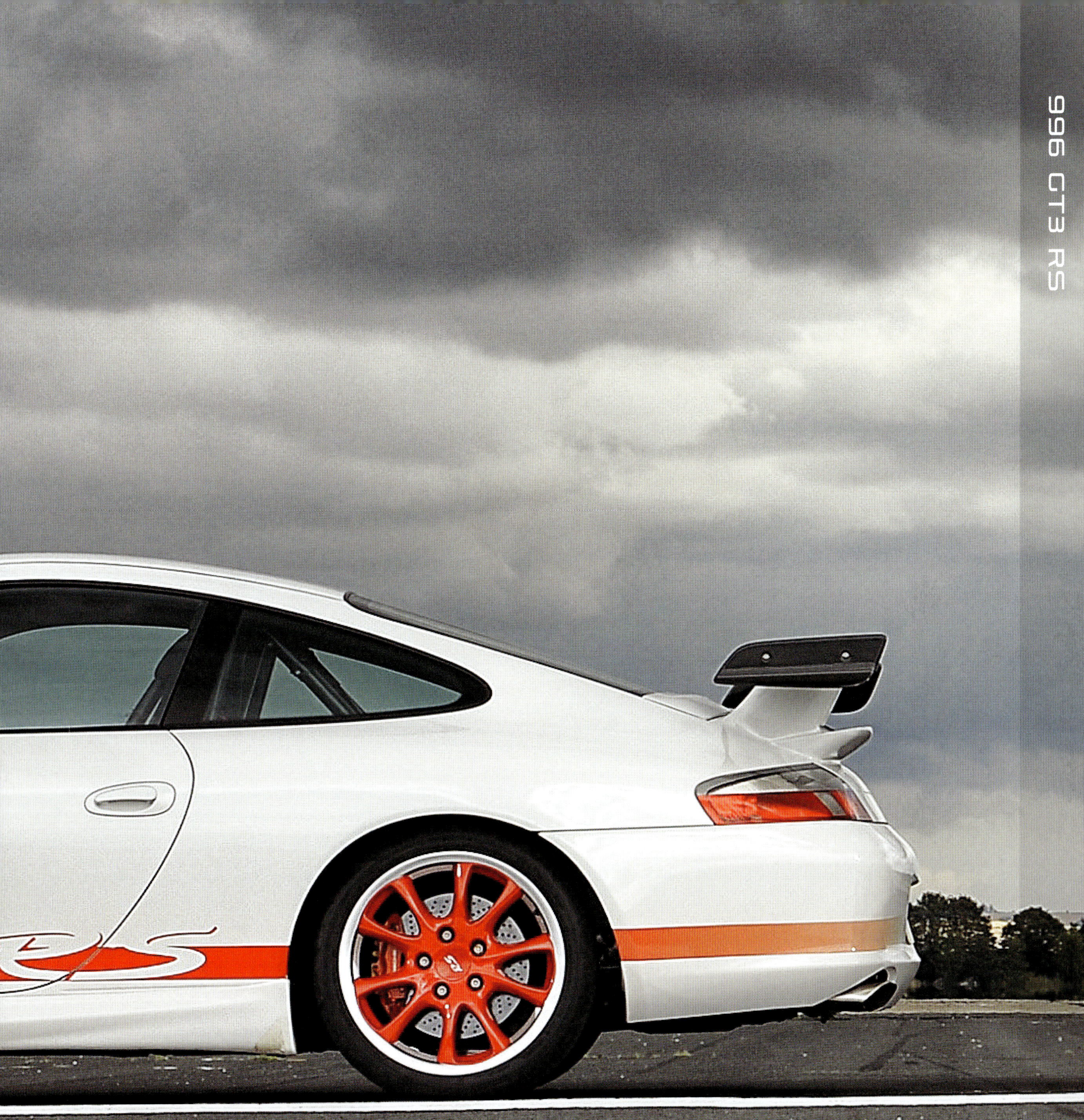

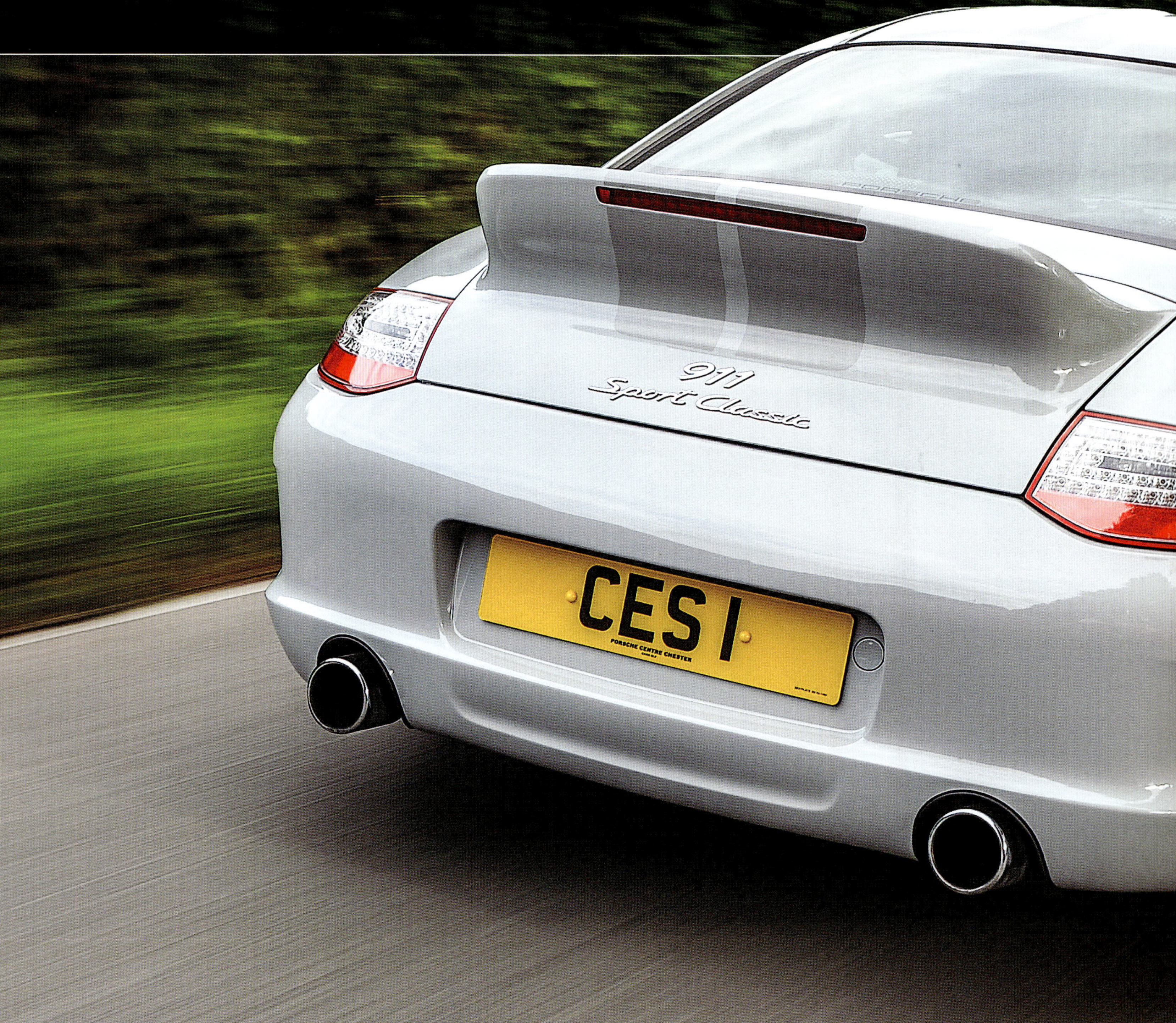
ONLY 250 MADE
997 SPORT CLASSIC
911
Sport Classic
CES 1

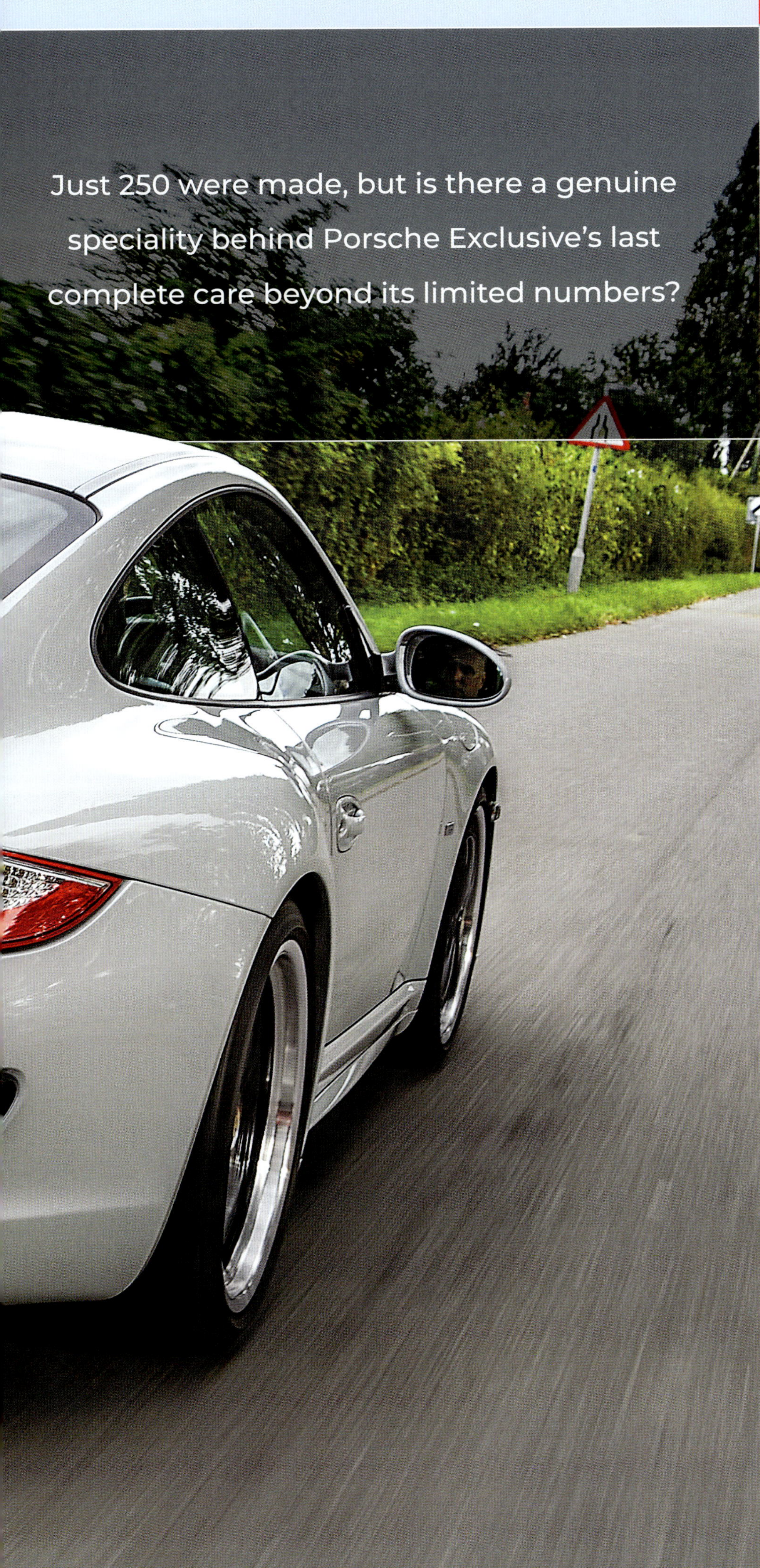





# 997 SPORT CLASSIC

(2010)

## ENGINE

**Capacity:** 3,800cc

**Compression ratio:** 12:5.1

**Maximum power:** 408bhp @ 7,300rpm

**Maximum torque:** 420Nm @ 4,200-5,600rpm

**Transmission:** Six-speed manual

**Engine modifications:** Porsche Exclusive Powerkit

## SUSPENSION

**Front:** Independent; MacPherson strut; anti-roll bar

**Rear:** Independent; Multi-link; PASM

## WHEELS & TYRES

**Front:** 8.5x19-inch Fuchs; 234/35/ZR19 tyres

**Rear:** 11x19-inch Fuchs; 305/30/ZR19 tyres

## DIMENSIONS

**Length:** 4,435mm

**Width:** 1,852mm

**Weight:** 1,425kg

## PERFORMANCE

**0-60mph:** 4.6 seconds

**Top speed:** 187mph

**I** will be the first to admit that my initial response to the Sport Classic was less than stellar. Introduced in 2010 at a time when the backdate 911 craze was in full frenzy, I rather casually viewed the Sport Classic press release as a spot of opportune mid-life badge engineering by Porsche. At a price point of £140,000, it was a healthy premium over even a well-specced 997, for what appeared to be simple cosmetic trinkets. I suspect many others thought the same. We were all wrong.

Walking towards the Sport Classic, I begin to realize that, when you see one in the metal, any cynical dismissals of black-centred wheels and that ducktail were a mistake. All 250 Sport Classics are finished in this understated shade of 'Sport Classic grey'. There's something uniquely retro about the colour, which the design team allegedly saw on a Porsche 356 and fell in love with. Opening the driver's door, there's deep brown 'Espresso' leather, with retro houndstooth-style panelling. As I climb inside, I can't help but glance rearwards over the wide wheel arches and beyond to that ducktail rear wing. It shouldn't really work on a modern 911, yet it looks so right.

Over the years of Porsche Exclusive design, customers were free to choose some rather bizarre 'enhancements' which, when viewed retrospectively, can be less than easy on the eye. From solid gold gearlevers to wooden dashboards and purple leather trimmed Motorolas, today they are right up there with shoulder pads and braces. Despite Porsche Exclusive's remit to create whatever the owner wished, clearly the customer does not always know best. But in this final model, wholly created by Porsche Exclusive as a genuine special, the Sport Classic took

those decisions away from the buyer and the department used their decades of skill, tasteful judgement and sense of what is appropriate to create a 911 that will stand the test of time. It's as if they looked at the misguided tastes of the 1980s and created a final masterpiece that said: "We are the experts at 911 DNA." There were no options with the Sport Classic; you either understood it or you didn't.

The Sport Classic was the final model to be created by the Exclusive department. In these days of automated production lines, emissions scandals and homologation tests, it seems Porsche and their clientele no longer have the freedom they once had. Symptomatic of this is the fact that the Sport Classic was never sold in North America due to a small production run and changes that the US deemed significant enough to homologate a new model, making it unviable.

There is no single element of the Sport Classic that is the defining winner. It's the overall effect of the carefully thought-out changes by Porsche Exclusive that come together to make the car so special. But the Sport Classic is not just visually different. Putting the car through its paces, that taught handling, short shift gearlever, carbon ceramic brakes, Sports steering wheel and the suspension setup all give an analogue connection to the car; this is a modern era 911 with all the classic feelings that cynics say have been removed from modern 991s.

And so the Sport Classic is a fitting tribute to Porsche Exclusive. Far more than just a cool grey paint scheme and motorsport styling touches, it's a great drive. This is quite probably my favourite 911.

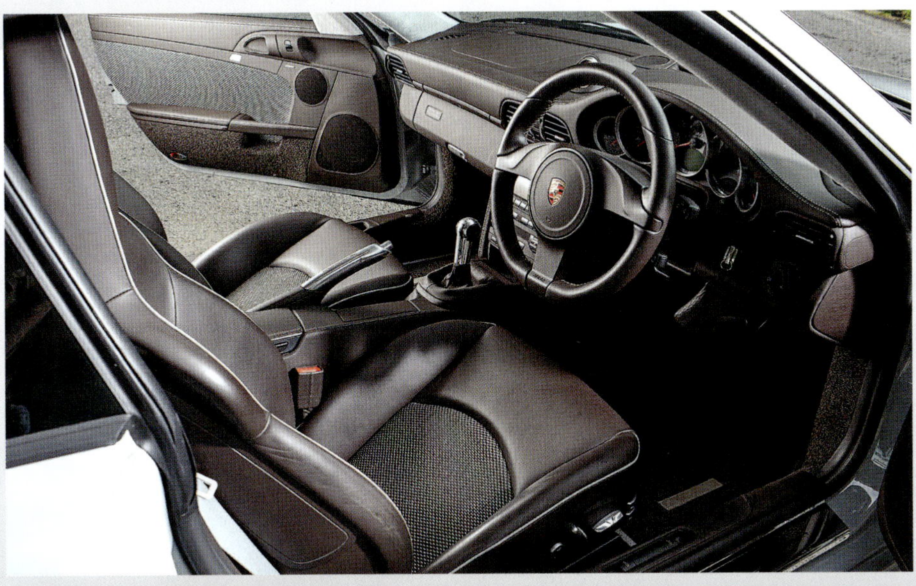

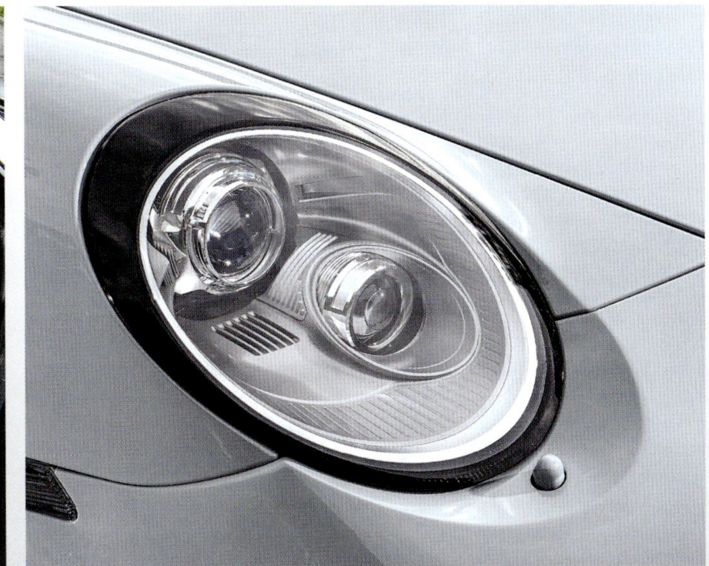

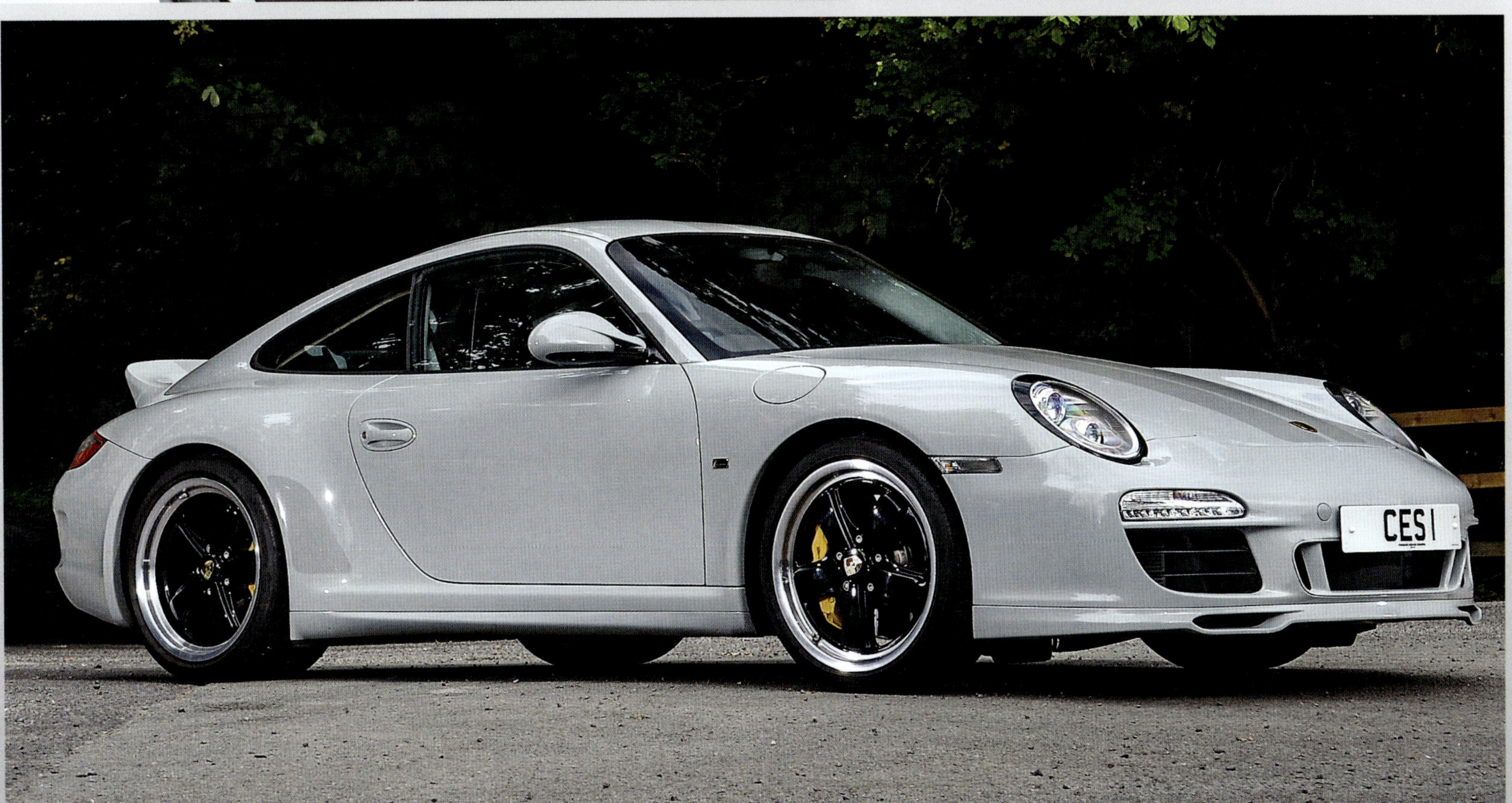

Just 250 997 Sport Classics were produced by Porsche Exclusive, all of which were in this special 'Sport Classic grey' paint

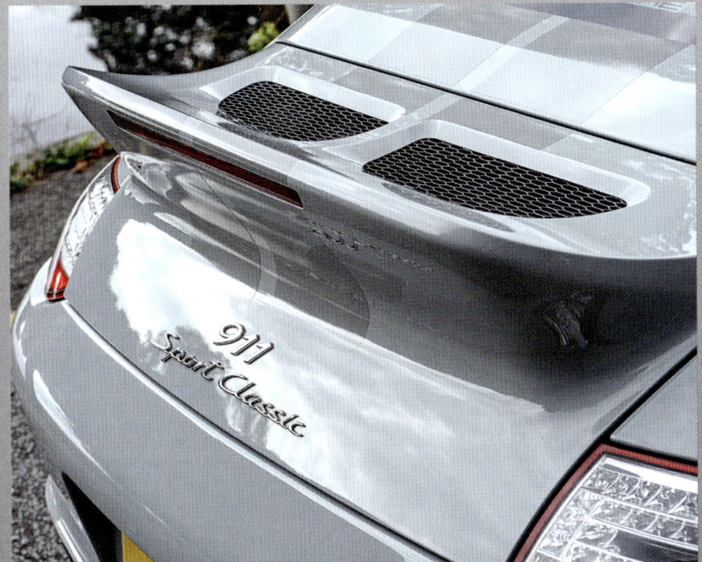


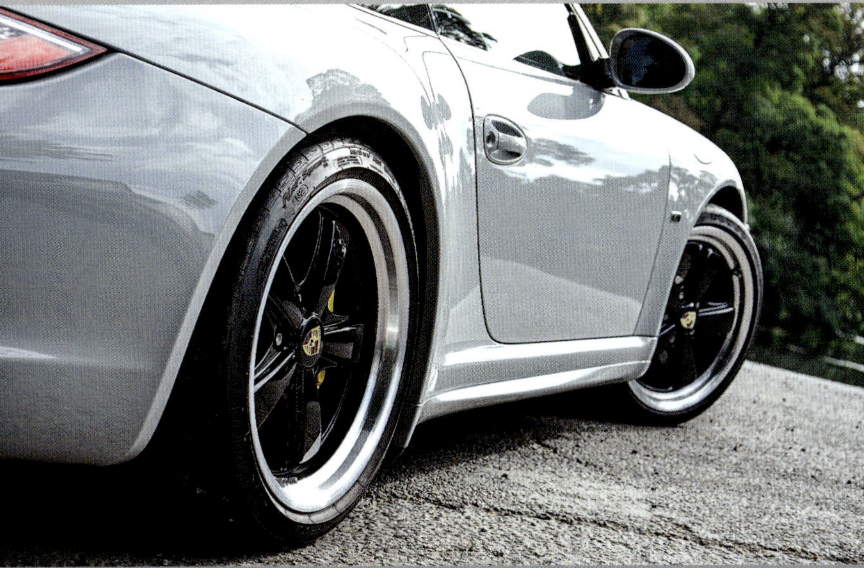

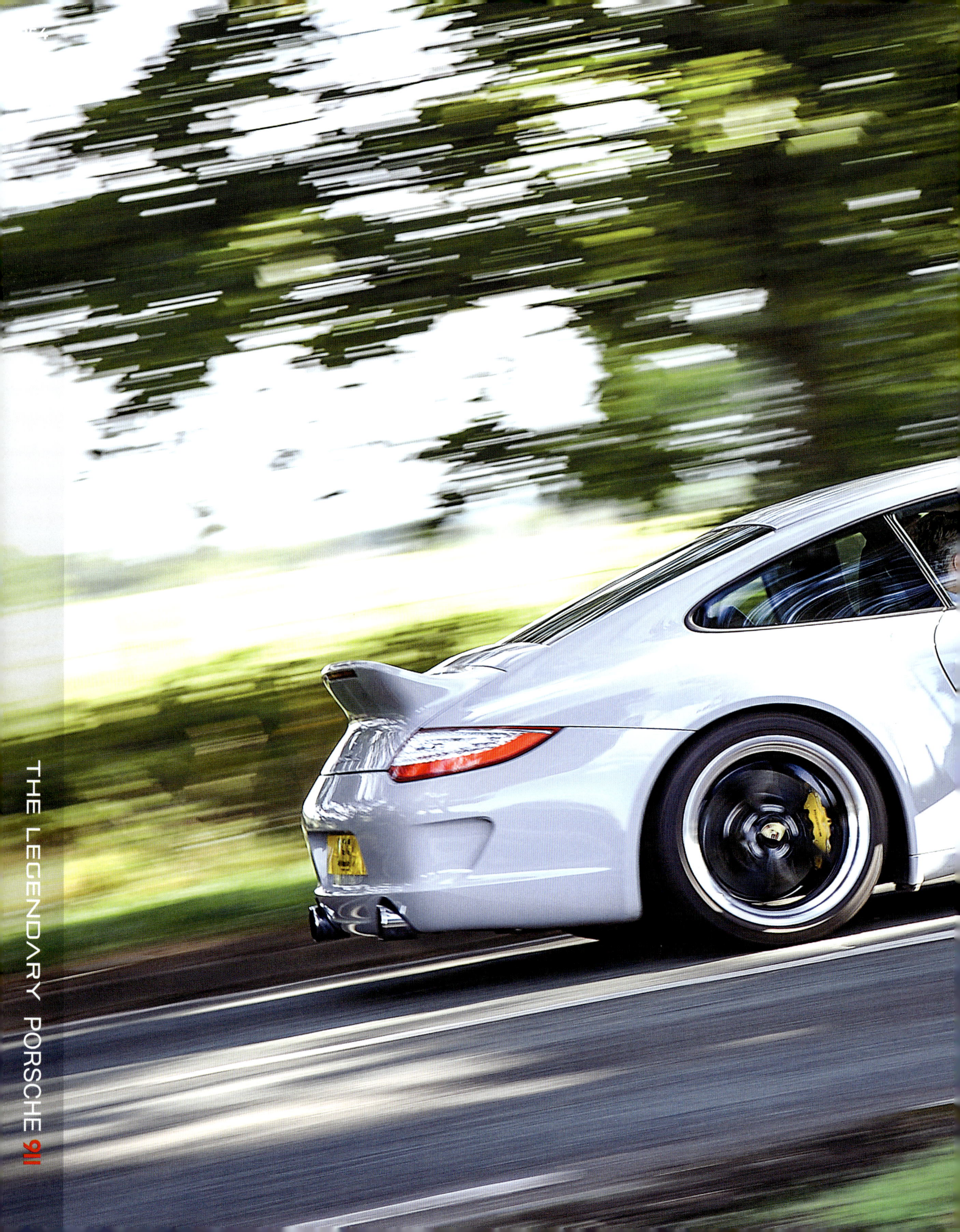
THE LEGENDARY PORSCHE 911

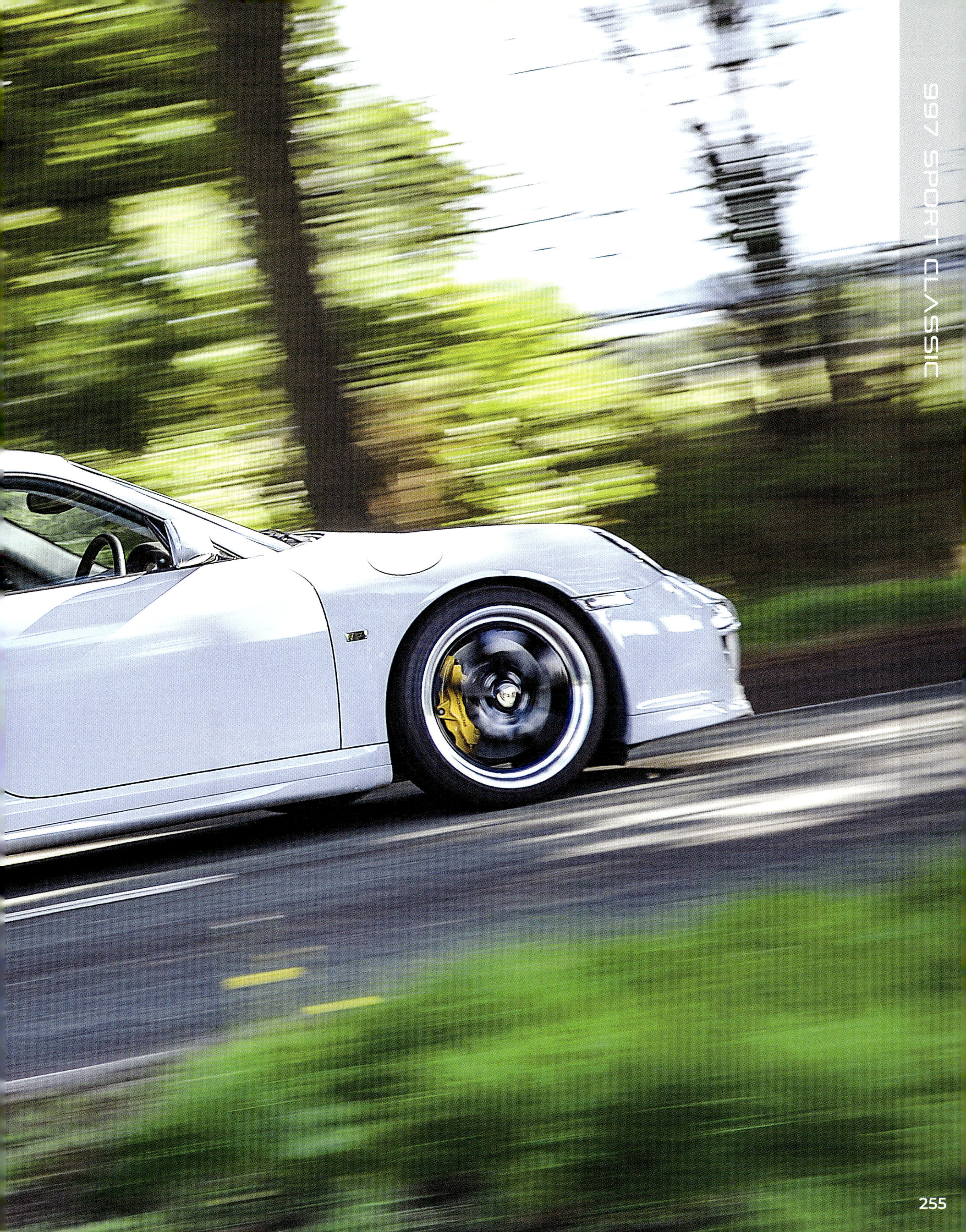
997 SPORT CLASSIC

# THE PORSCHE
## MUSEUM



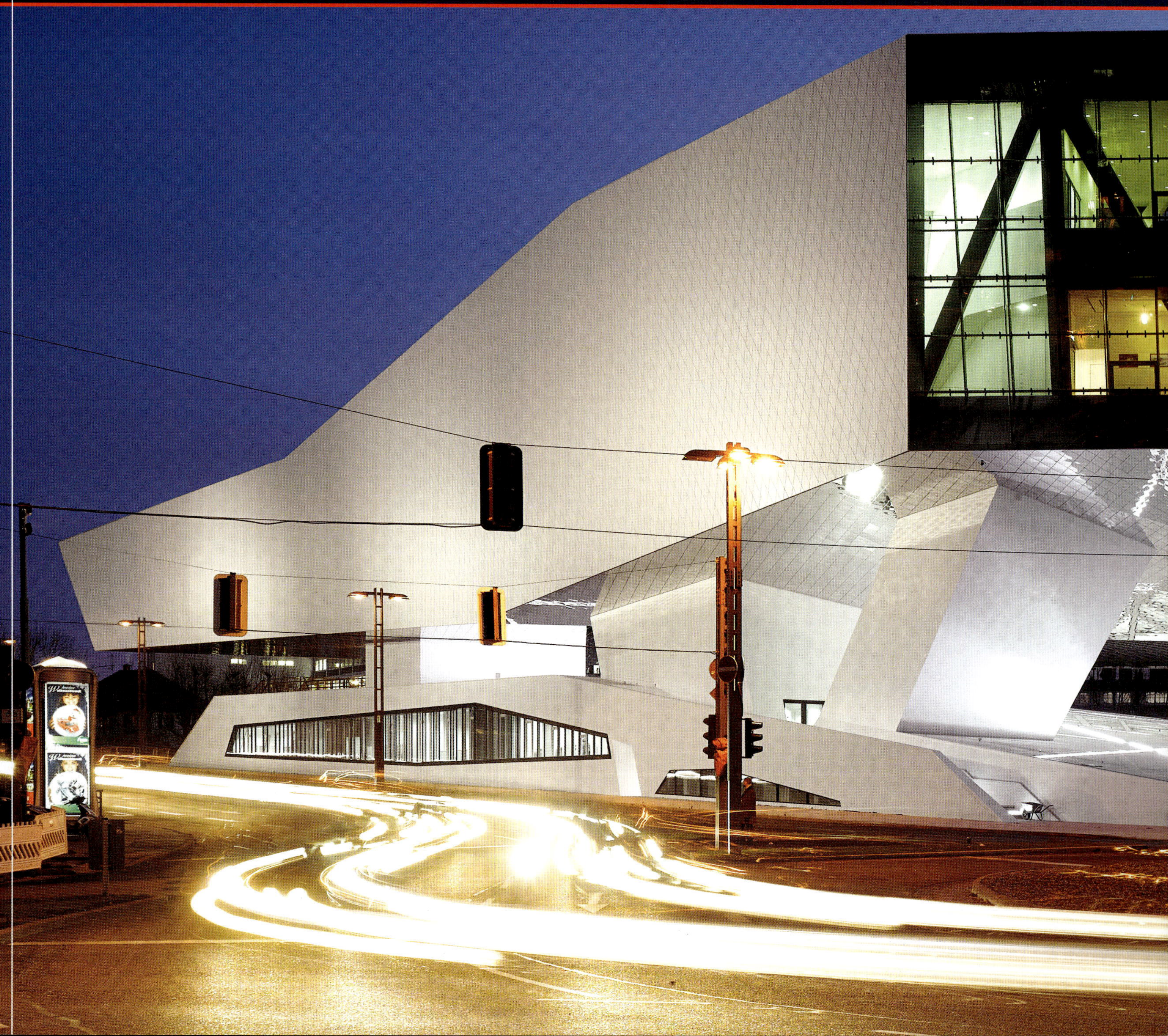

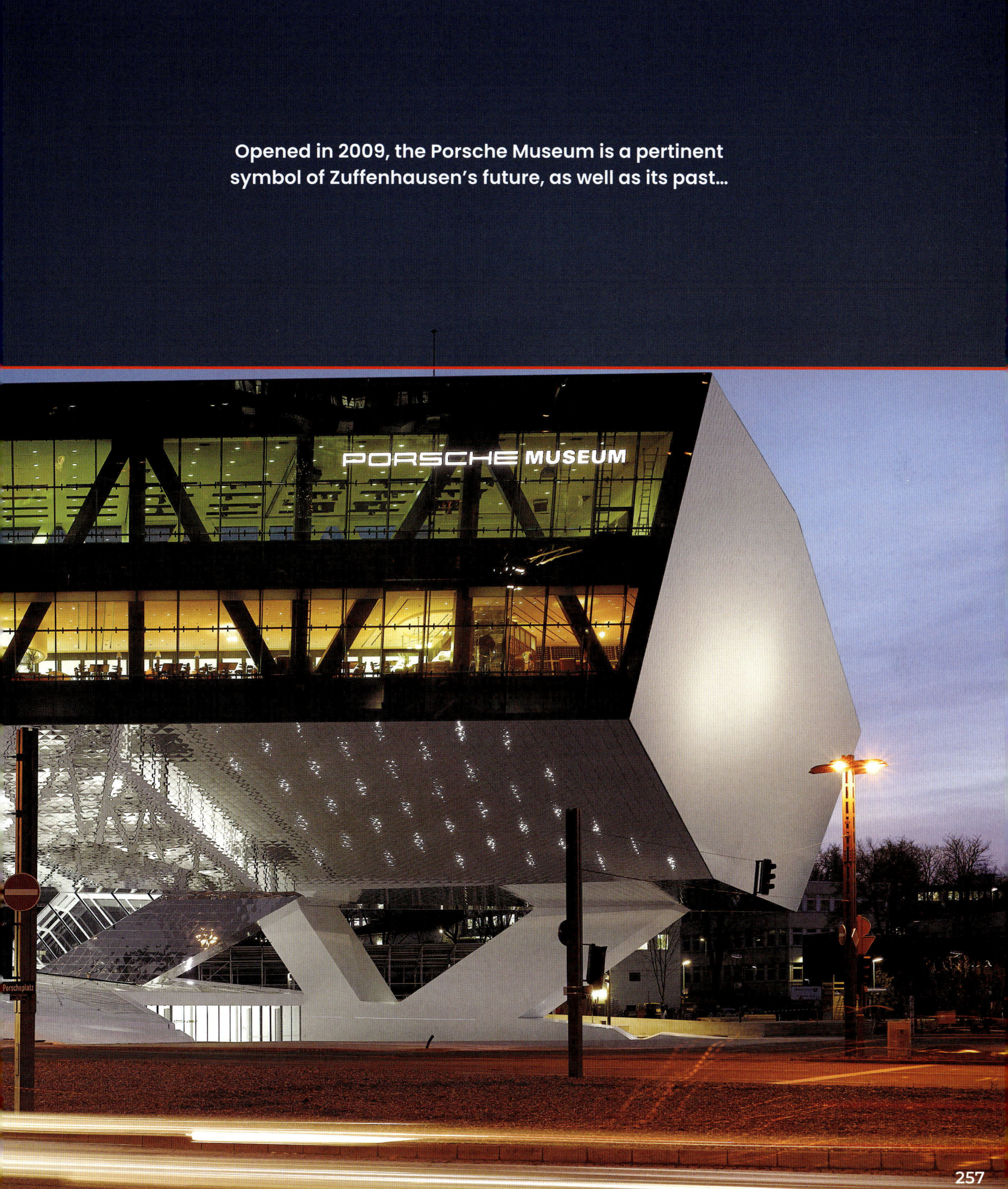

Opened in 2009, the Porsche Museum is a pertinent symbol of Zuffenhausen's future, as well as its past...
PORSCHE MUSEUM
Porscheplatz

You'll see the unmistakable, unorthodox silhouette of the Porsche Museum protruding into the Stuttgart skyline long before you recognise the rest of Porscheplatz. This isn't down to the height of the building; nearby factory structures spread over the home of Dr. Ing. h. c. F. Porsche AG reaching further skywards, but these carry function strictly over form and so they are otherwise nondescript, even ugly, in appearance. In stark contrast, it's the beauty of the Museum that immediately draws your eyes towards it.

At first it looks like the main structure of the Museum is suspended in the air (in fact, it is supported by only three V-shaped columns), and its form appears to change drastically as you walk around its perimeter. No matter what angle, there's a crisp yet complex illusion emanating from it. Even from the outside then, there's no denying this entire complex is a fine example of architectural art.

The building itself was designed by Viennese architect office Delugan Meissl, whose design was chosen by the Porsche board from over 170 different entrants for the project. Construction work started in early October 2005 to implement those design renders, and on January 31st 2009, the building was officially opened to the public. Inside, you'll find a 5,600-square metre exhibition space with a variety of motoring relics and icons spread eloquently over two spiralling floors, outlining the entire history of Porsche from Ferdinand's birth in 1875 to the present day.

Owned by Porsche AG, the Museum inhibits a special, innovative way of presenting the history of the manufacturer to the public, so much so that you could visit the displays two or three times in a year and enjoy an entirely difference experience, each time learning new things. It is this which helps the Museum attract so many visitors – more than 500,000 fans and enthusiasts now make the pilgrimage each year.

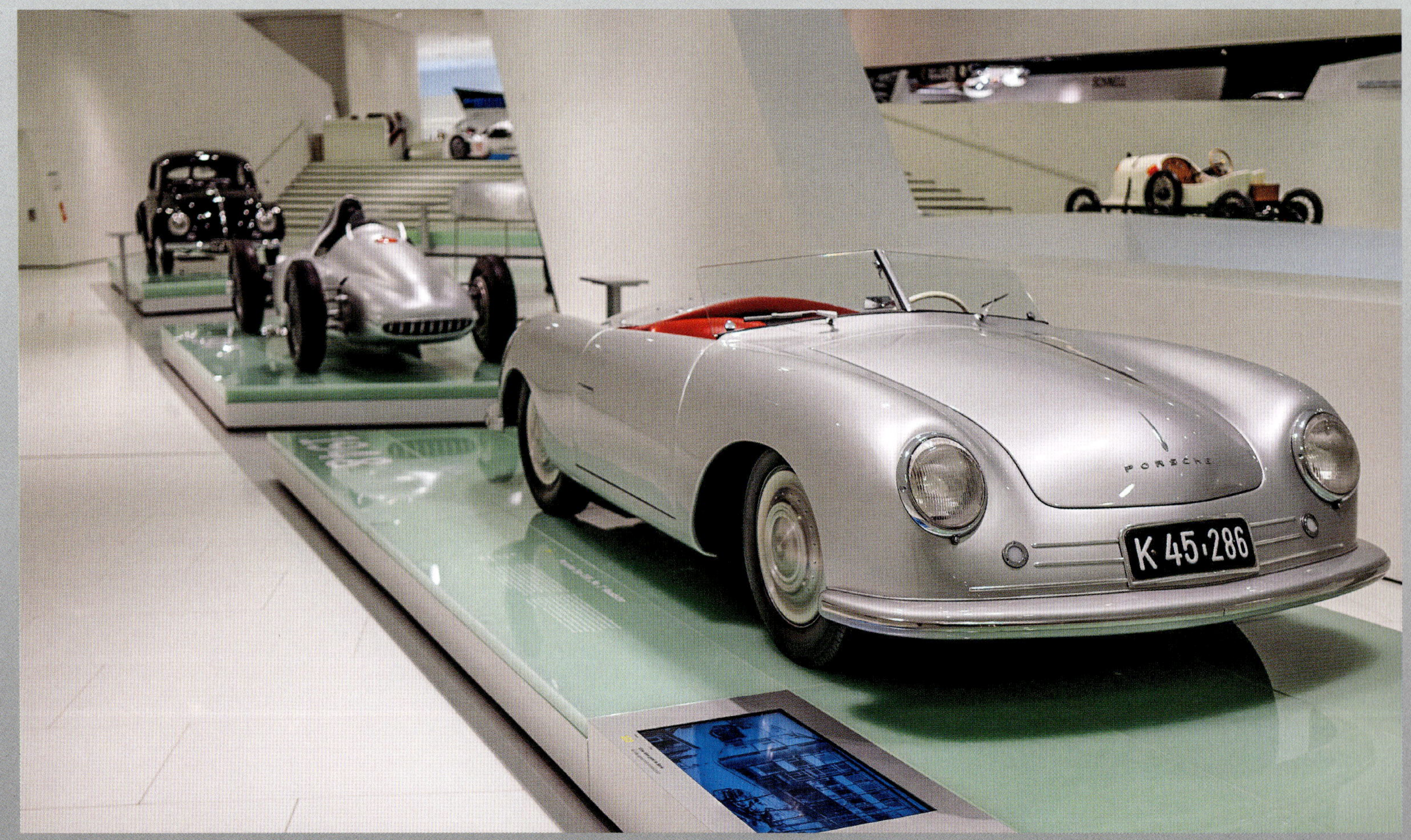

**911 or not, the Museum presents the entire history of Porsche through a variety of engaging displays**

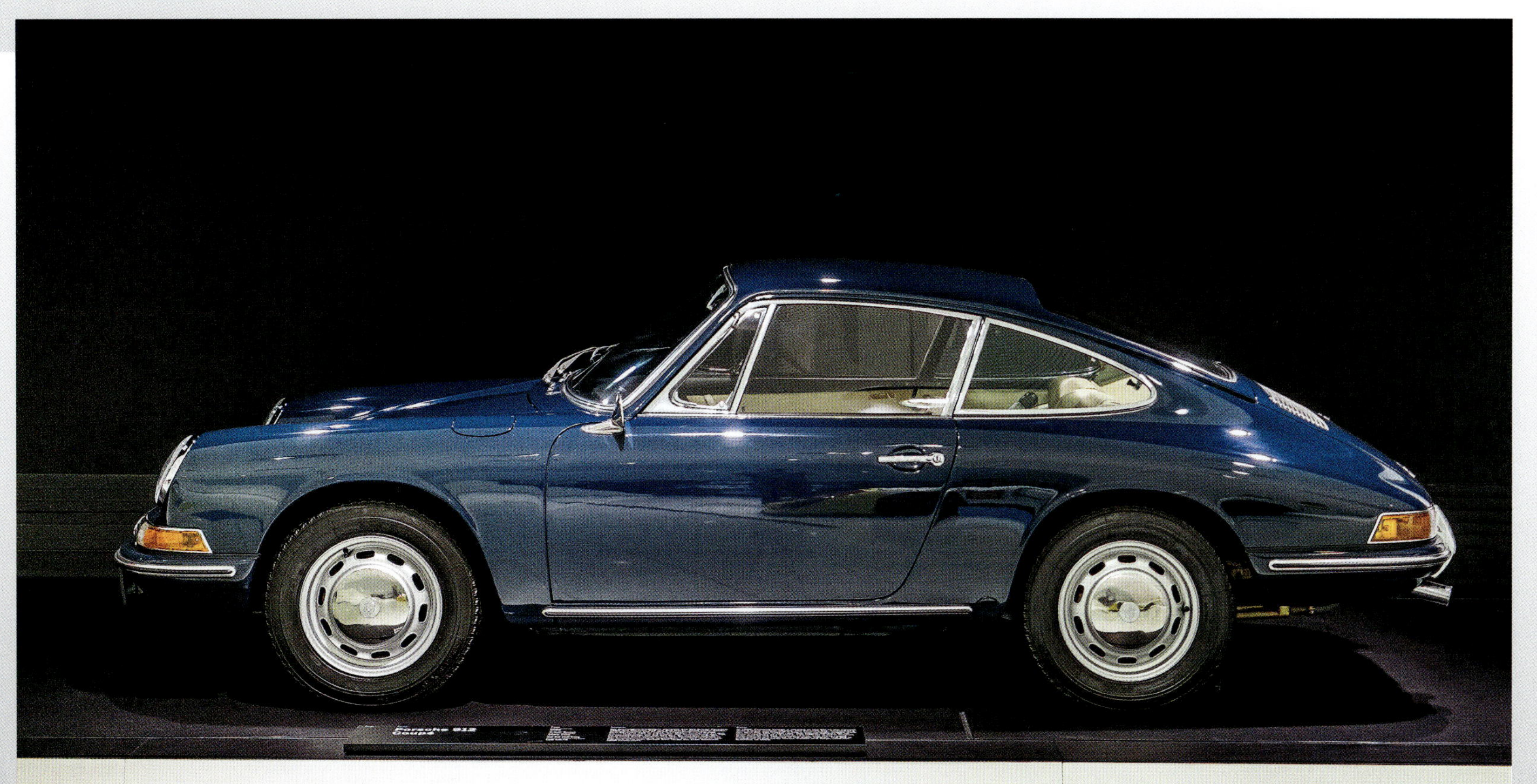

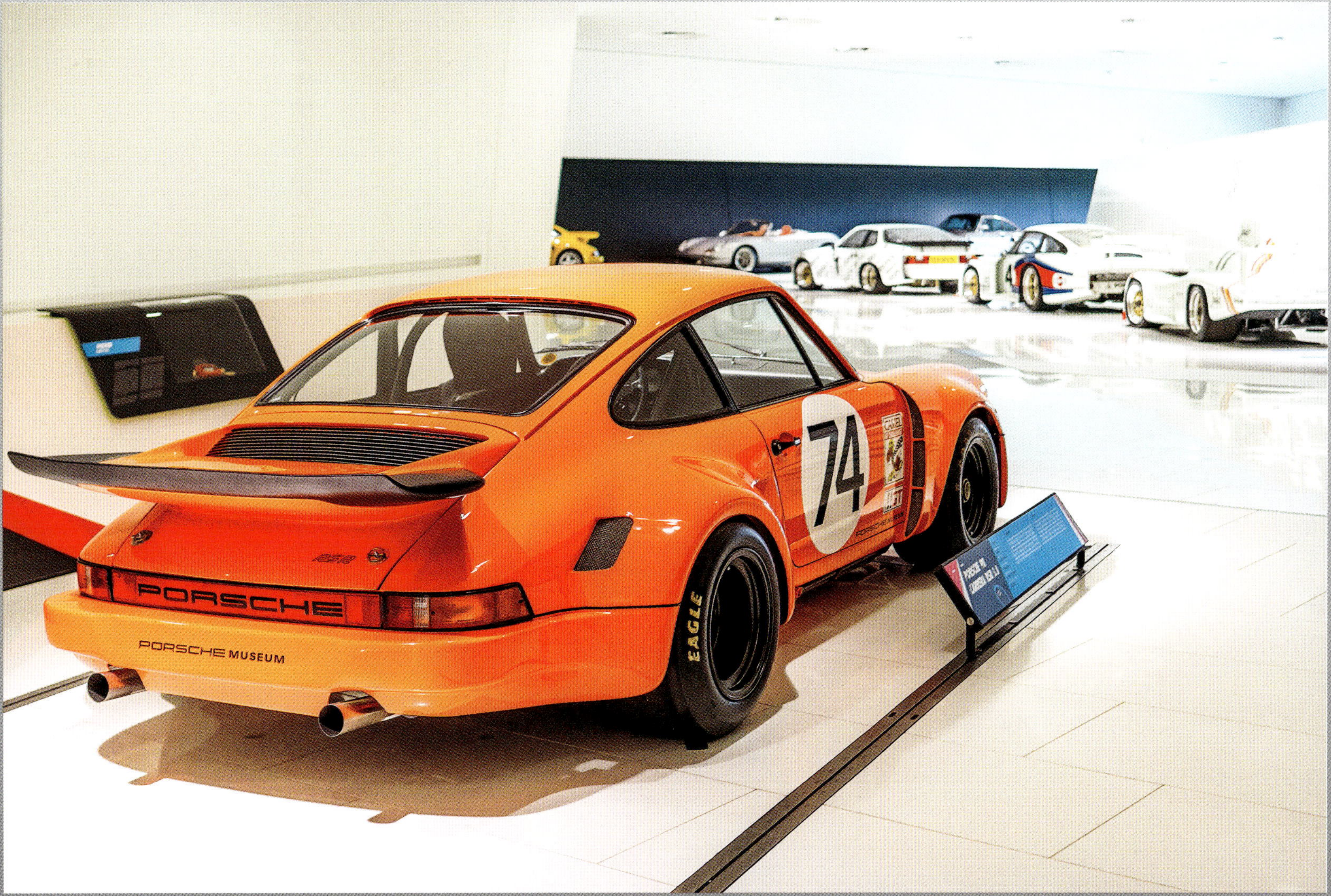

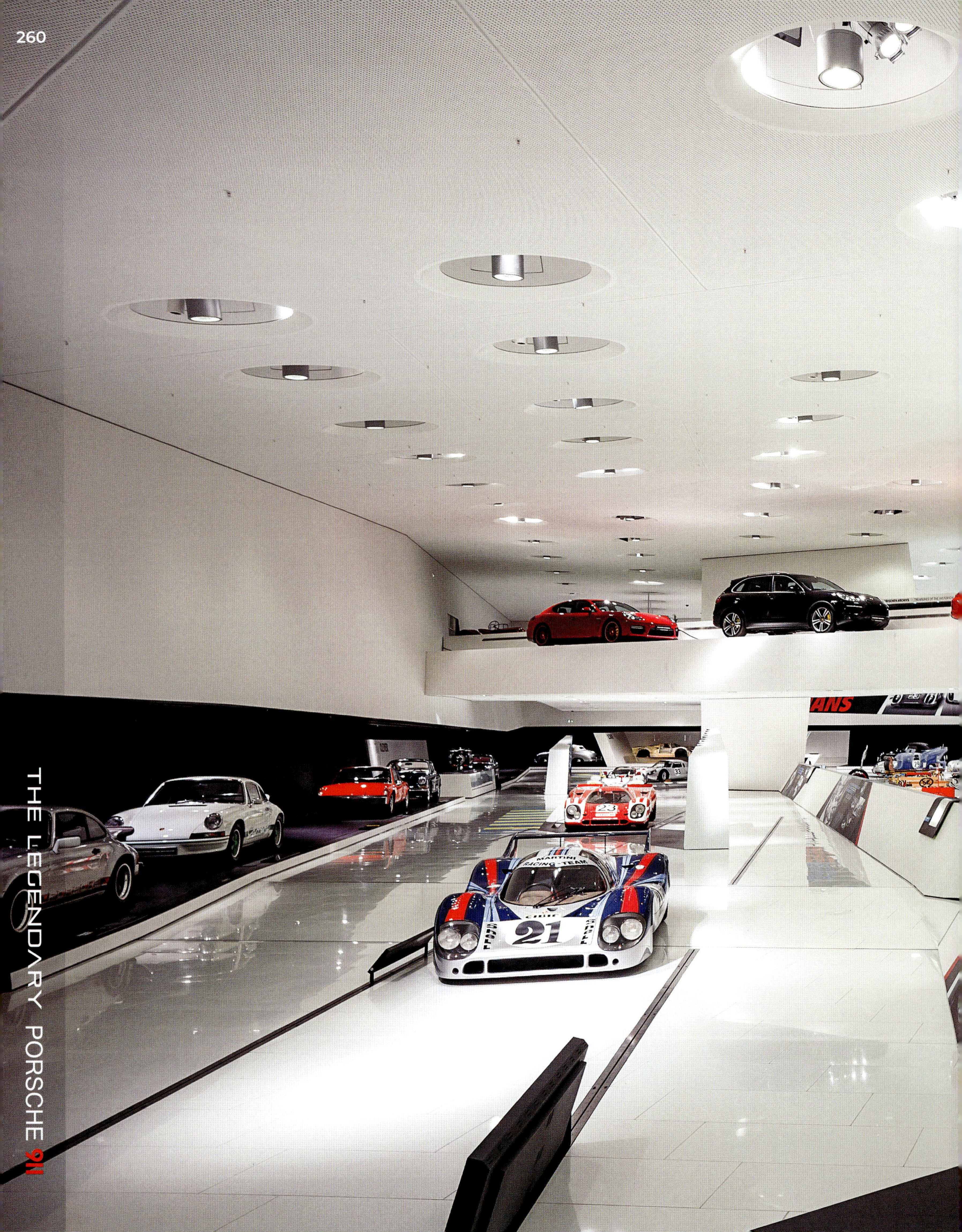
260
THE LEGENDARY PORSCHE 911

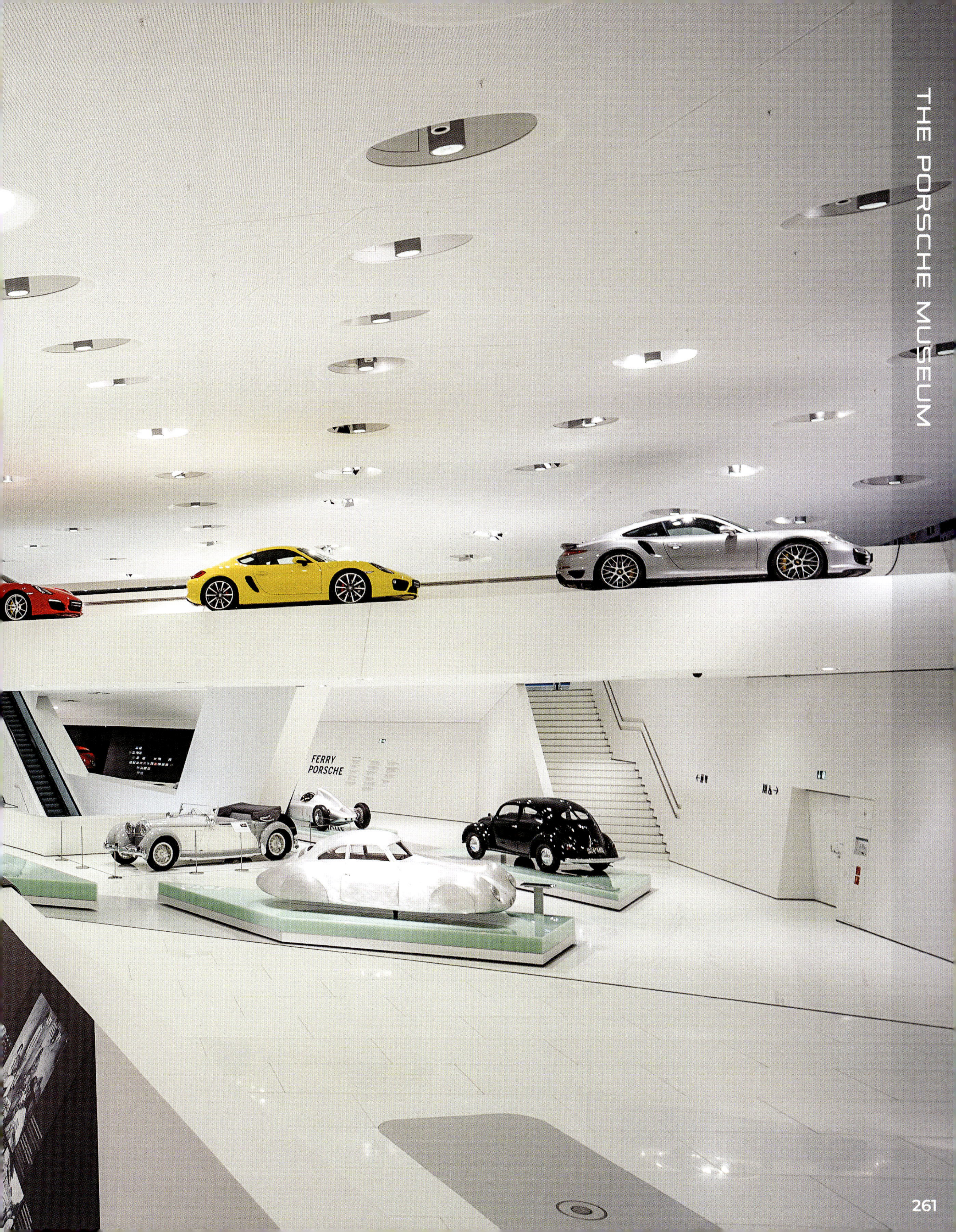

FERRY
PORSCHE

Displays are always centered around the visions that shaped the company. Here, you will find out more about Zuffenhausen's remit of lightweight construction, clever use of technology, fast and powerful performance, an intensity in sporting excellence, and a consistency in high standards as the blueprint for any car produced by Porsche.

What's more, the Museum operates by organising its exhibitions according to themes. Typically, two to three themes prevail in a 12-month cycle, each lasting several months. The Museum's management constantly liaise with Alexander Klein, from Porsche Archive, to decide on display themes relevant to the company, which can be time sensitive. For example, the display theme during our most recent visit was 'Le Mans', using Porsche's rich racing history at La Sarthe to mark Weissach's dominance in the top class of the race over the years.

Once a display theme is in place for the Museum to present historically, plans are then made with Klein over suitable sports cars to pull from storage to ensure a glorious ensemble of Porsches are permanently on display at Porscheplatz 1. "Of course, this is a difficult task," Klein tells me, "because some of the cars in storage could be going through a restoration or have one scheduled, and so we must carefully match which high brow cars should go on display with the cars that can."

After a comprehensive hitlist of suitable cars is put in place to help illuminate each theme, detailed floor plans are then Klein continues: "The cars you see in the Museum are not placed there just because we feel like it; they are there as a result of careful planning. As well as looking at what can be displayed from our history, we look at how the car can be displayed – for example, look at the 956, which is mounted upside down to highlight its superior downforce capabilities. Of course, such a presentation takes a lot of time for us to organise."

In a bid to appeal to the younger generation of Porsche fan (school and college visits here are not uncommon), classic Zuffenhausen relics are often presented in a fresh, modern way, with current technology deployed to aid the evocative learning experience. The sensory overload is welcoming: as well as being able to run your eyes fastidiously over each and every sports car on display, there are clever touch pods that allow

you to hear the different engine notes of a 356's flat four, an early 911's flat six, or even the howl of a 956 charging down the Mulsanne Straight. Then there's the sensations of smell: despite an otherwise corporate environment, get close to the cars and you can smell the faint whiff of oil from the rear of classics above the quaint aura of polish and leather. Up to 80 sports cars are on display at any one time in the Museum, and to ensure each theme retains its appeal over prolonged periods of time, a select few cars are swapped out every few weeks.

As well as providing an open display for the paying public to learn about the Porsche brand, the Museum also engages with enthusiasts by staging events at the venue. At least one conference event is held here a week, for what the Museum terms as 'big customers'. The premises also stages one-off occasions for the public to get closer to the Porsche experience, for example during Le Mans when you could rock up and watch the entire 24-hour race from inside the Museum itself.

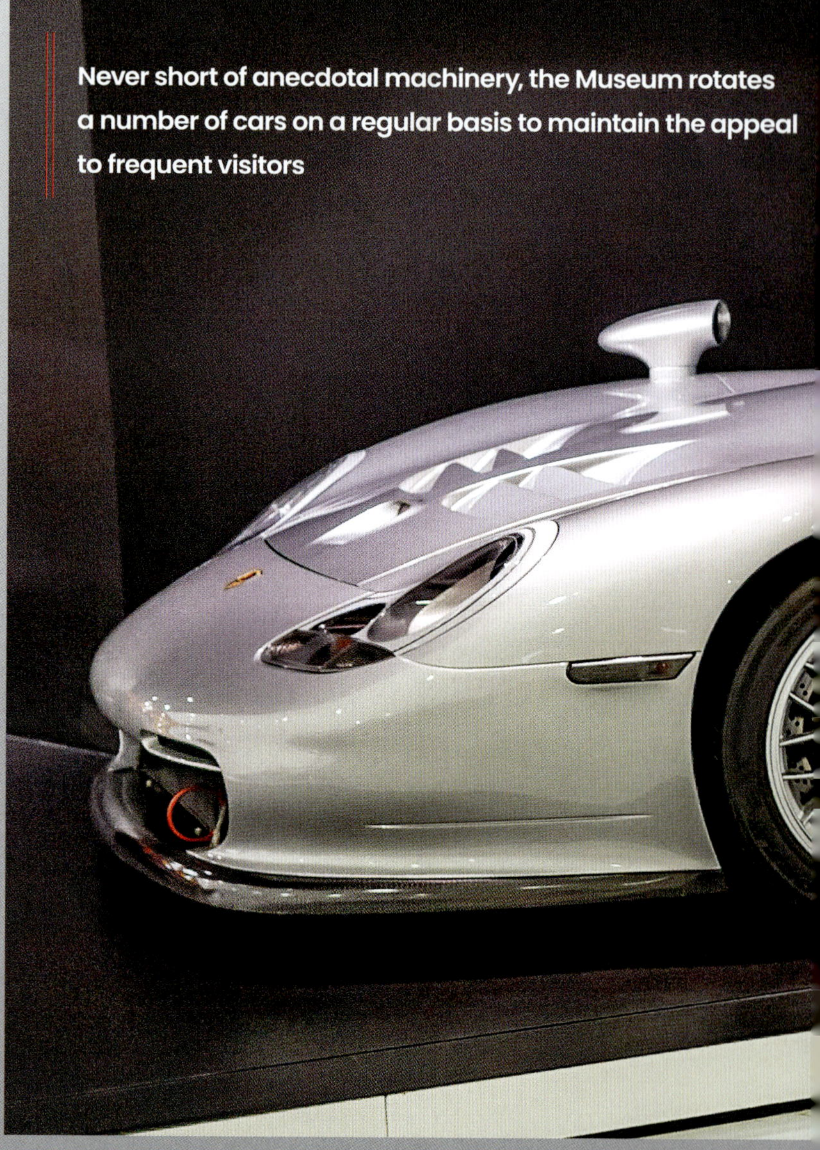

Never short of anecdotal machinery, the Museum rotates a number of cars on a regular basis to maintain the appeal to frequent visitors

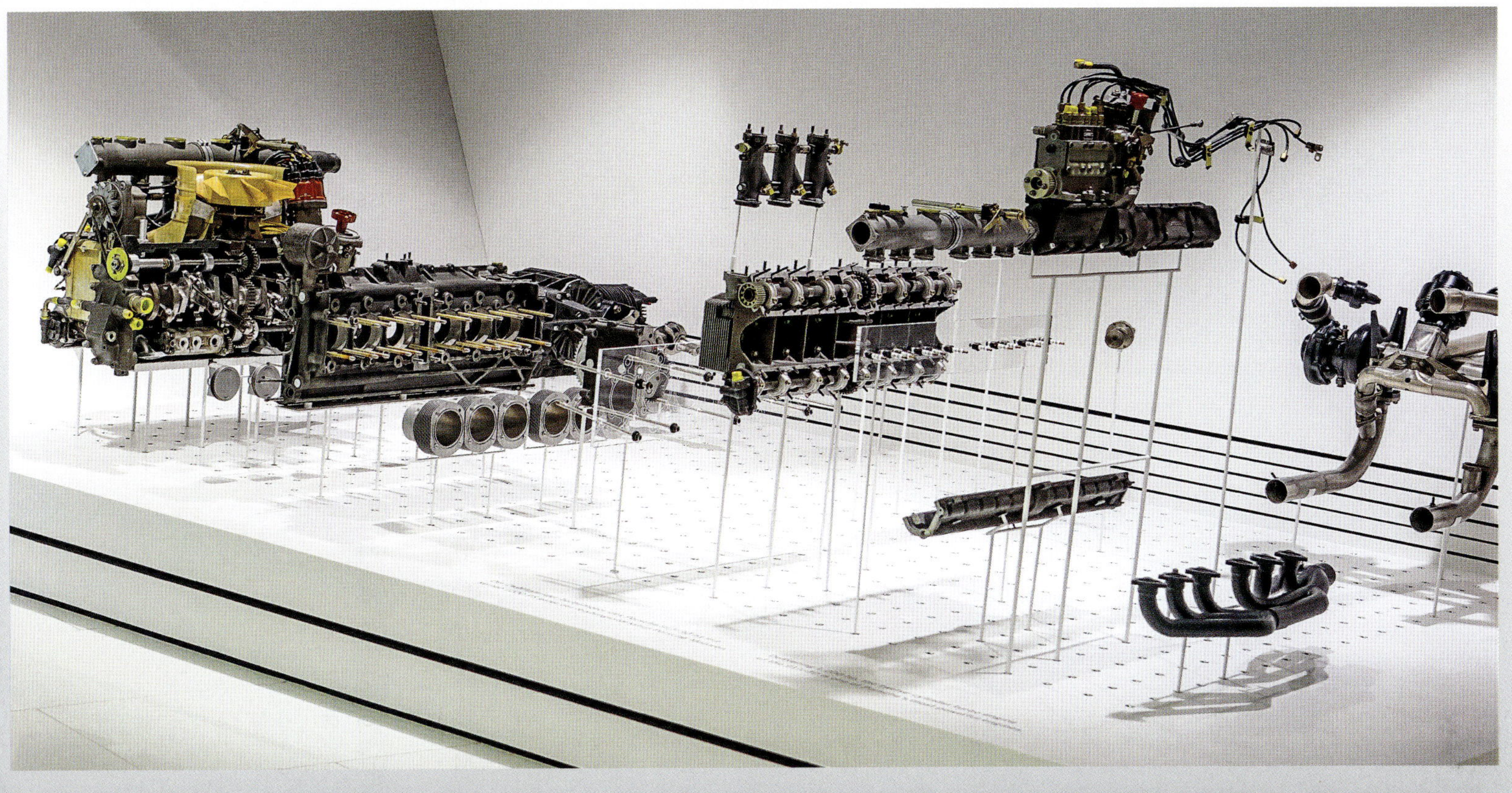

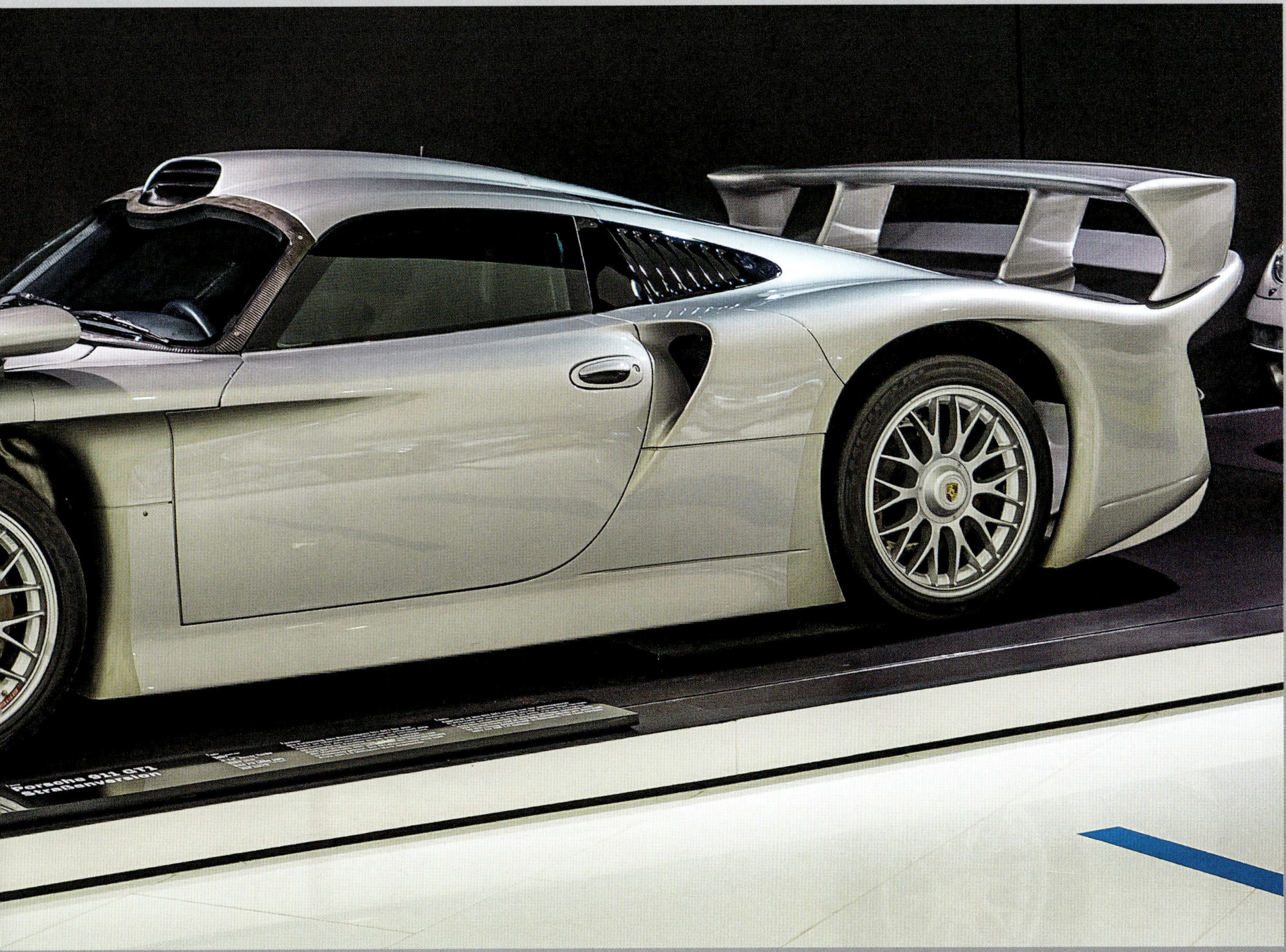

There's much more to the Museum than merely presenting highly polished Porsche motoring artefacts and showing how a 911 et al is created and engineered, though. There's a Museum workshop on the complex, as well as the Boxenstopp and Christophorus restaurants.

Today, the Museum is much more than just a swanky holding lot for motoring relics to be displayed for adoring members of the public. Step outside afterwards, and you will realise that the Museum acts as the epicentre of Porscheplatz. Sports cars being built in the adjacent factory and then displayed in the Stuttgart Porsche dealership over the road all get their identity from the cars inside the Museum, and Porsche AG know it: it's the whole reason for the complex existing in the first place.

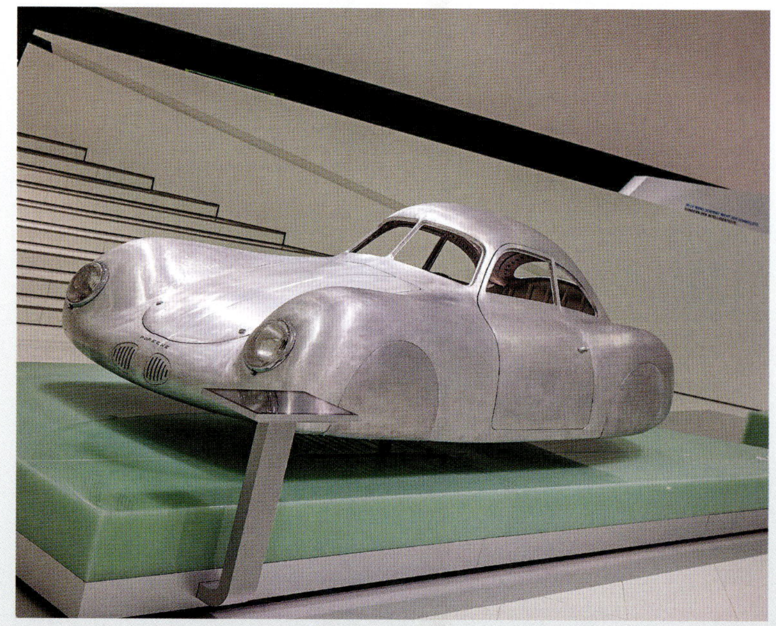

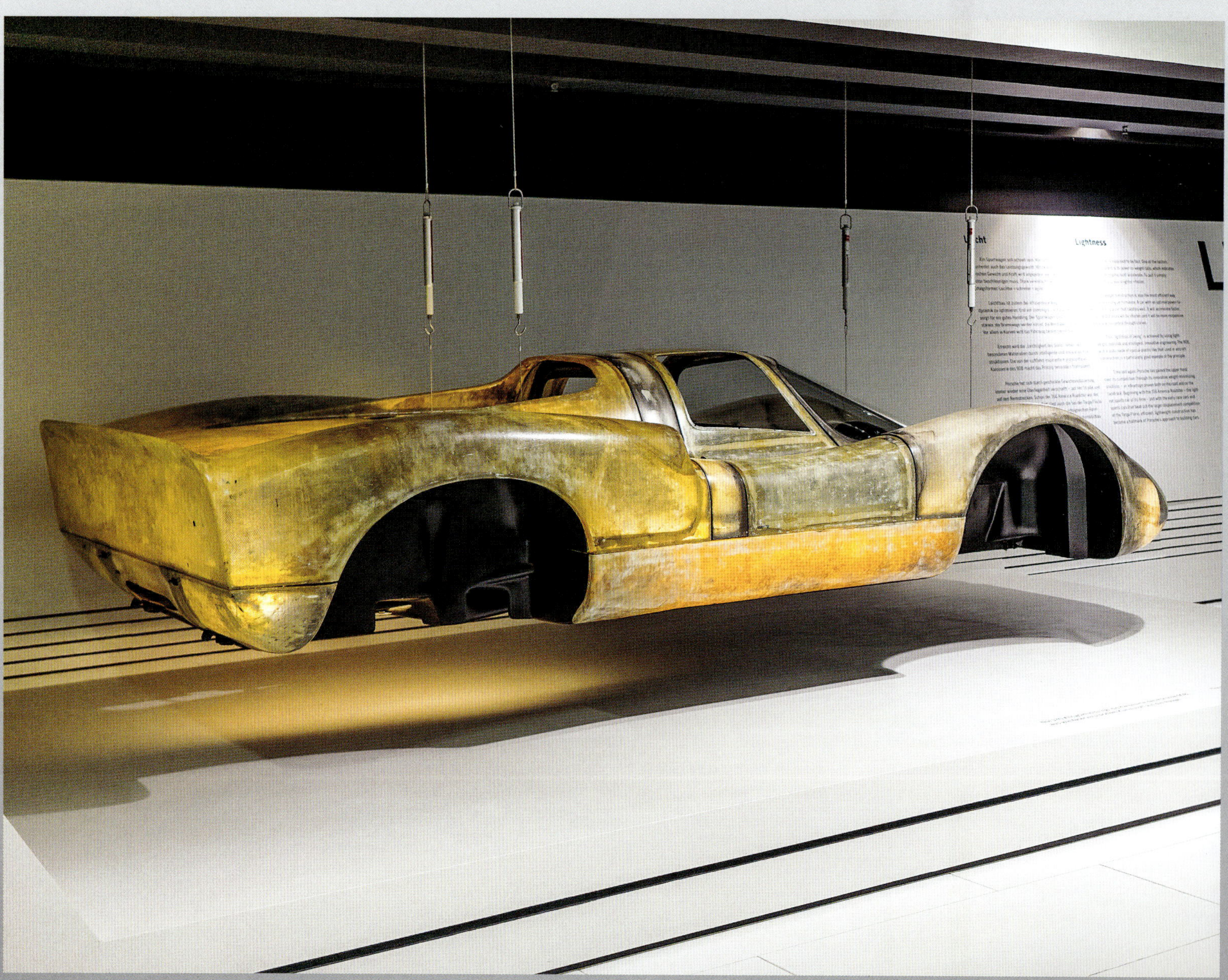

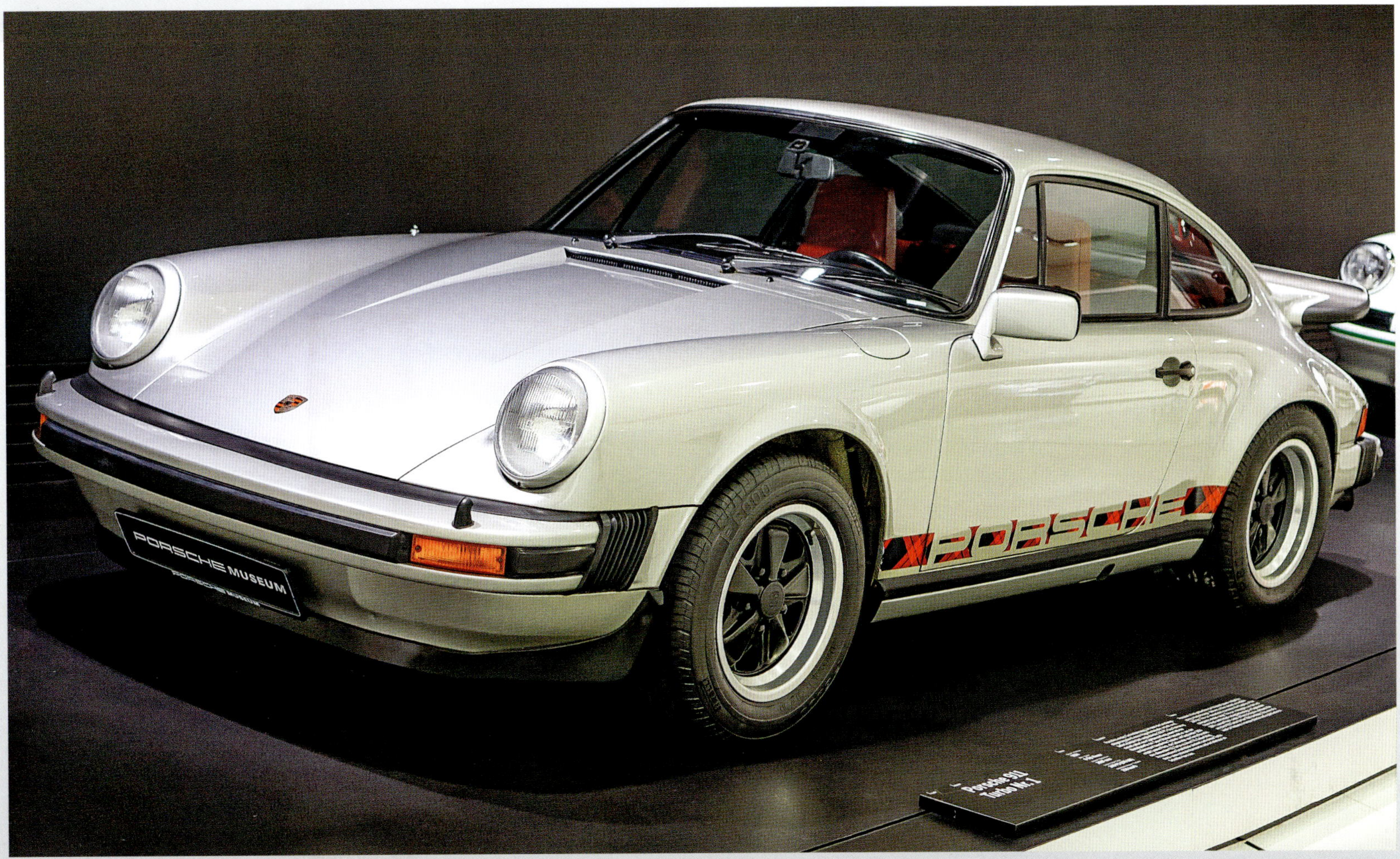
PORSCHE
PORSCHE MUSEUM

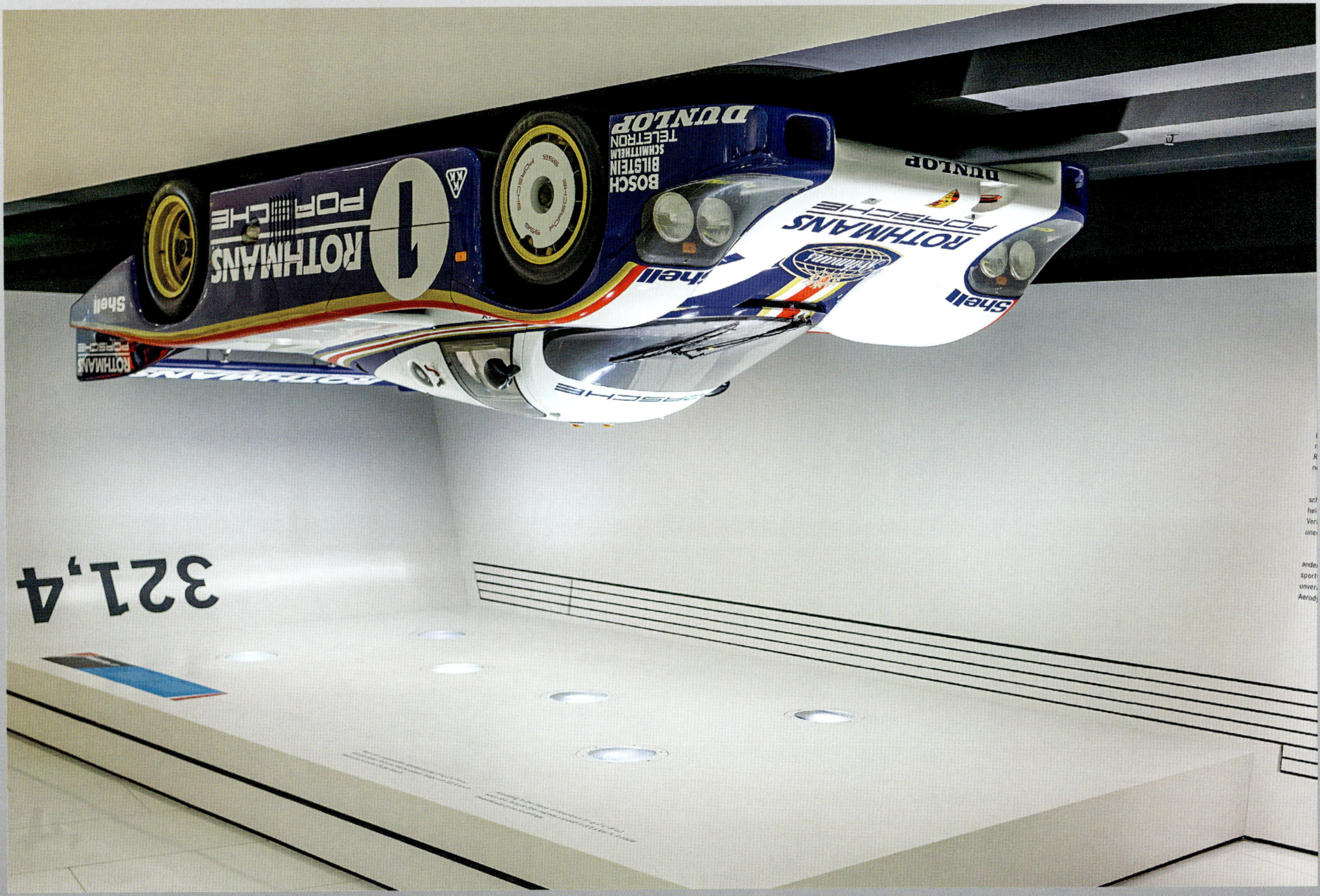
ROTHMANS
PORSCHE
DUNLOP
BOSCH
BILSTEIN
TELETRON
Shell
321,4

The area is just as special for enthusiasts too: throughout the day, 911s will constantly pull up onto the concourse in front of the Museum so owners can get a quick snap of their Porsche back on 'home turf'. They come from afar too – one Australian Porsche owner told me how he'd travelled to Europe on business and couldn't resist a quick stop at the place that built his beloved 997.2 C4S. "It doesn't disappoint here, does it?" he says as we ogle at our reflections in the mirrored roof high above our heads. It certainly doesn't. If you haven't yet been, you're simply missing out.

"THE ENTIRE PORSCHEPLATZ COMPLEX IS A FINE EXAMPLE OF ARCHITECTURAL ART"

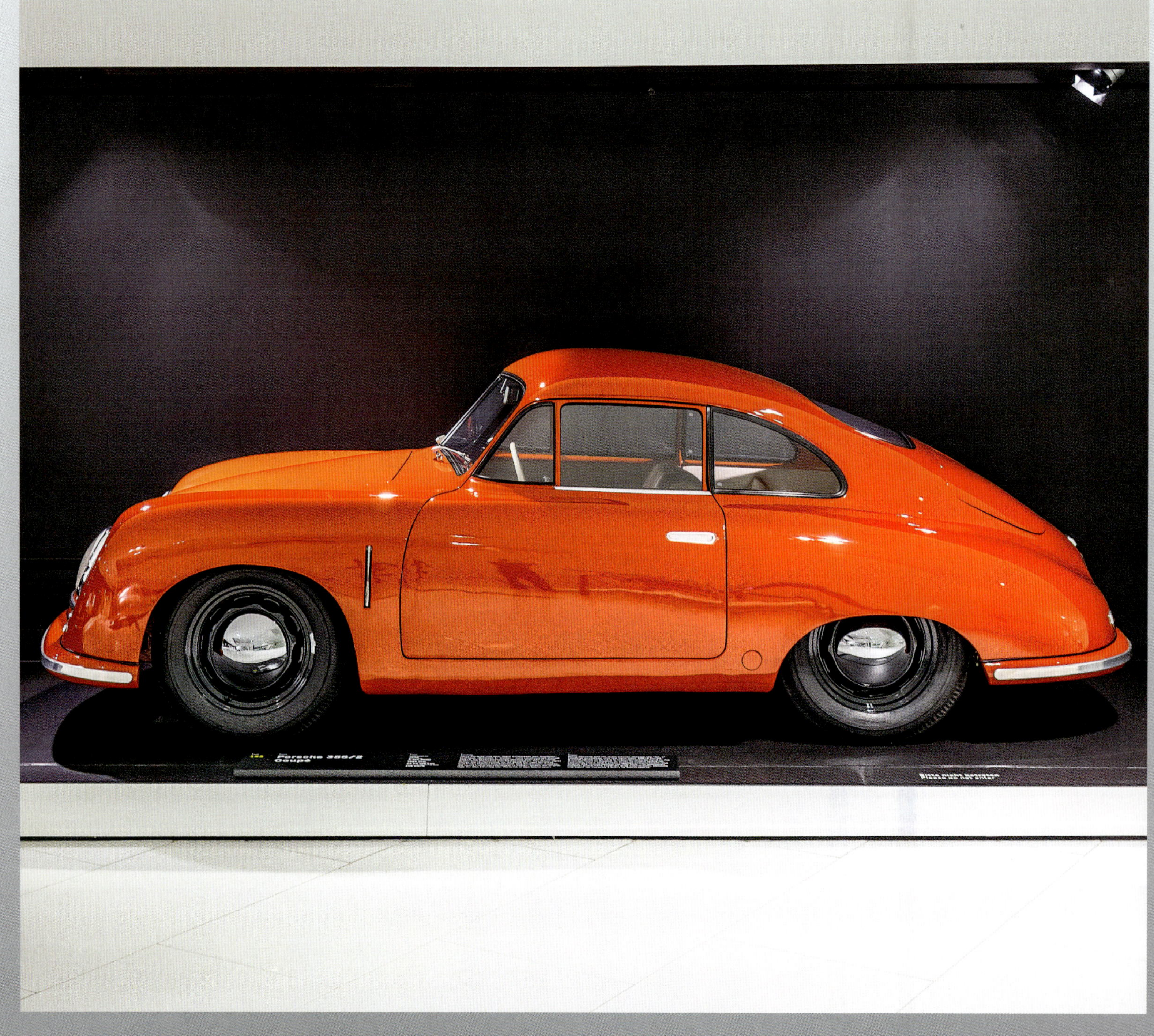

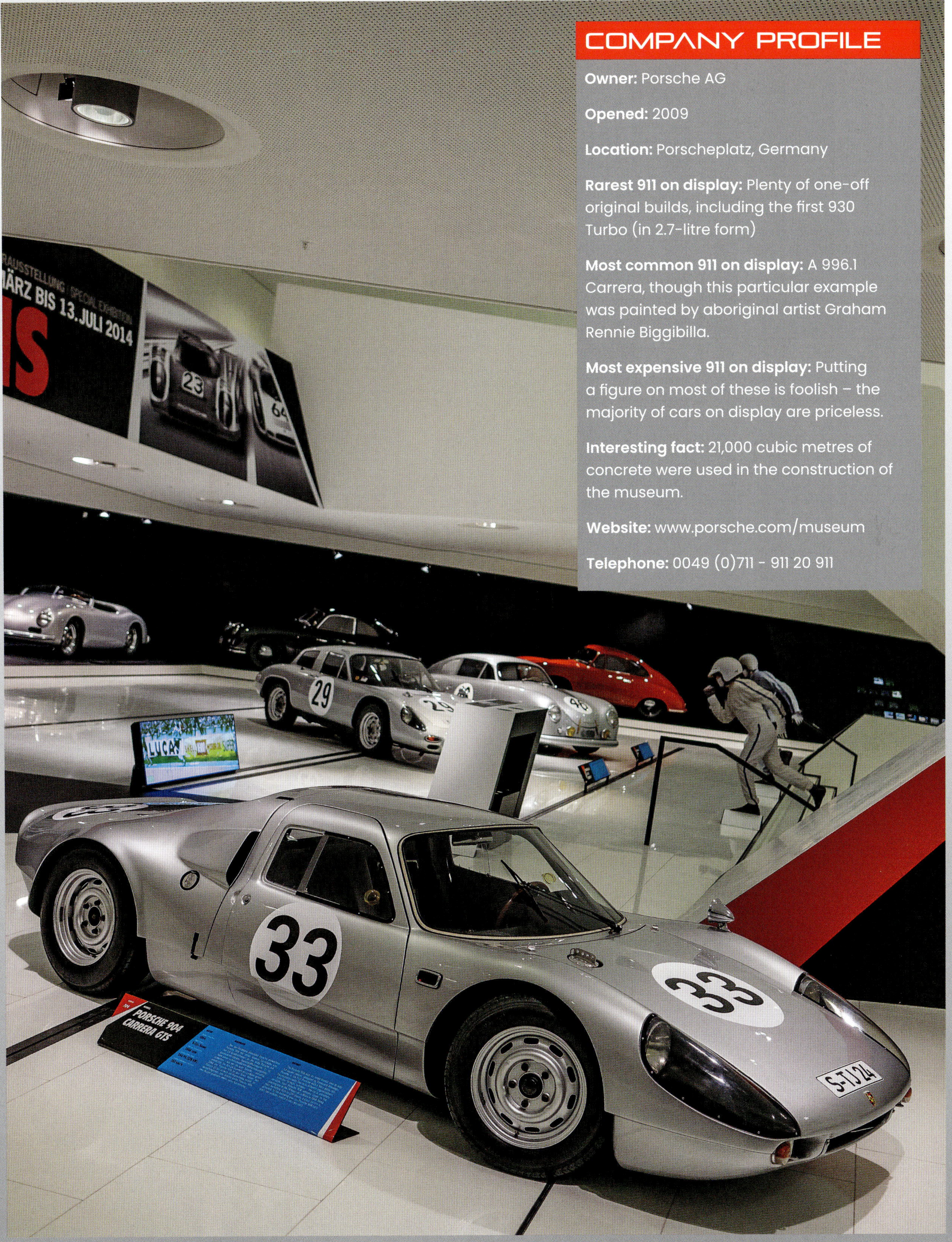


COMPANY PROFILE

**Owner:** Porsche AG

**Opened:** 2009

**Location:** Porscheplatz, Germany

**Rarest 911 on display:** Plenty of one-off original builds, including the first 930 Turbo (in 2.7-litre form)

**Most common 911 on display:** A 996.1 Carrera, though this particular example was painted by aboriginal artist Graham Rennie Biggibilla.

**Most expensive 911 on display:** Putting a figure on most of these is foolish – the majority of cars on display are priceless.

**Interesting fact:** 21,000 cubic metres of concrete were used in the construction of the museum.

**Website:** www.porsche.com/museum

**Telephone:** 0049 (0)711 - 911 20 911

# PORSCHE
# STATISTICS & FACTS

## PORSCHE MODELS (1963– PRESENT)

Original 911 (1964–1973)

G series (1974–1989)

964 (1988–1994)

993 (1993–1998)

996 (1997–2005)

997 (2004–2012)

991 (2011–2019)

992 (2018– present)

## PORSCHE 911 AWARDS

World Performance Car of the Year: 2021, 2014, 2021

Evo Car of the Year: 1998, 1999, 2000, 2003, 2004, 2007, 2010, 2011, 2013, 2016, 2023, 2024

Motor Trend Best Driver's Car: 2012, 2020

Car and Driver Editor's Choice: 2011, 2019

Motor Week Driver's Choice Award: 1994, 1998, 2018

Motor Week Best Dream Machine: 2002, 2017

Automobile Magazine's 'All-Stars Award': 2001, 2003, 2009

Edmunds.com 'Most Wanted Coupe': 2006

Road & Track's 'Best Dream Car': 2004

Auto Week's 'America's Best' Award: 2003

Popular Mechanics' 'Design & Engineering" Award: 2001

Automobile Magazine's 'Best Luxury Sports Cars': 2000.

## CURRENT 911 MODELS

911 Carrera

911 Carrera S

911 Carrera GTS

911 Carrera 4 GTS

911 Carrera T

911 Carrera Cabriolet

911 Carrera S Cabriolet

911 Carrera GTS Cabriolet

911 Carrera 4 GTS Cabriolet

911 Carrera 4 T Cabriolet

911 Targa 4 GTS

911 Turbo 50 Years

911 GT3

911 GT3 with Touring Package

911 GT3 RS

911 S/T

## TARGA FLORIO

Winner

**1973**

Drivers: Herbert Müller (SWI), Gijs van Lennep (NED)

Team: Martini Racing

Car: Carrera RSR

Distance: 492.13 miles

Laps: 11

## 24 HOURS OF LE MANS

Winners

**1979**

Drivers: Klaus Ludwig (GER), Bill Whittington (USA), Don Whittington (USA)

Class: GP5 SP

Team: Porsche Kremer Racing

Car: Porsche 935 K3

Distance: 2593.56 miles

Laps: 307

**1998**
Drivers: Laurent Aïello (FRA), Allan McNish (GB), Stéphane Ortelli (MON)
Class: LMGT1
Team: Porsche AG
Car: Porsche 911 GT1-98
Distance: 2,972.504 miles
Laps: 365

## 24 HOURS OF DAYTONA

Winners

**1973**
Drivers: Peter Gregg (USA), Hurley Haywood (USA)
Team: Brumos Porsche
Car: Carrera RSR
Distance: 2,552.7 miles
Laps: 670

**1975**
Drivers: Peter Gregg (USA), Hurley Haywood (USA)
Team: Brumos Porsche
Car: Carrera RSR
Distance: 2,606.04 miles
Laps: 679

**1977**
Drivers: Hurley Haywood (USA), John Graves (USA), Dave Helmick (USA)
Team: Brumos Porsche
Car: Carrera RSR
Distance: 2,615.04 miles
Laps: 681

**1978**
Drivers: Peter Gregg (USA), Rolf Stommelen (GER), Toine Hezemans (NED)
Team: Brumos Porsche
Car: Porsche 935
Distance: 2,611.2 miles
Laps: 680

**1979**
Drivers: Hurley Haywood (USA), Ted Field (USA), Danny Ongais (USA)
Team: Brumos Porsche
Car: Porsche 935
Distance: 2,626.56 miles
Laps: 684

**1980**
Drivers: Rolf Stommelen (GER), Volkert Merl (GER), Reinhold Joest (GER)
Team: L&M Joest Racing
Car: Porsche 935
Distance: 2,745.6 miles
Laps: 715

**1981**
Drivers: Bobby Rahal (USA), Brian Redman (GB), Bob Garretson (USA)
Team: Garretson Racing
Car: Porsche 935
Distance: 2,718.72 miles
Laps: 708

**1982**

Drivers: John Paul Sr. (USA), John Paul Jr. (USA), Rolf Stommelen (GER)

Team: JLP Racing

Car: Porsche 935

Distance: 2,760.96 miles

Laps: 719

**1983**

Drivers: A.J. Foyt (USA), Preston Henn (USA), Bob Wollek (FRA), Claude Ballot-Léna (FRA)

Team: Henn's Swap Shop Racing

Car: Porsche 935

Distance: 2,373.12 miles

Laps: 618

**2003**

Drivers: Kevin Buckler (USA), Michael Schrom (USA), Timo Bernhard (GER), Jörg Bergmeister (GER)

Team: The Racer's Group

Car: 911 GT3-RS

Distance: 2,474.2 miles

Laps: 695

**2025**

Drivers: Felipe Nasr (BRA),
Nick Tandy (GBR),
Laurens Vanthoor (BEL)

Team: Porsche Penske Motorsport

Car: Porsche 963

Distance: 3,560 miles

Laps: 781



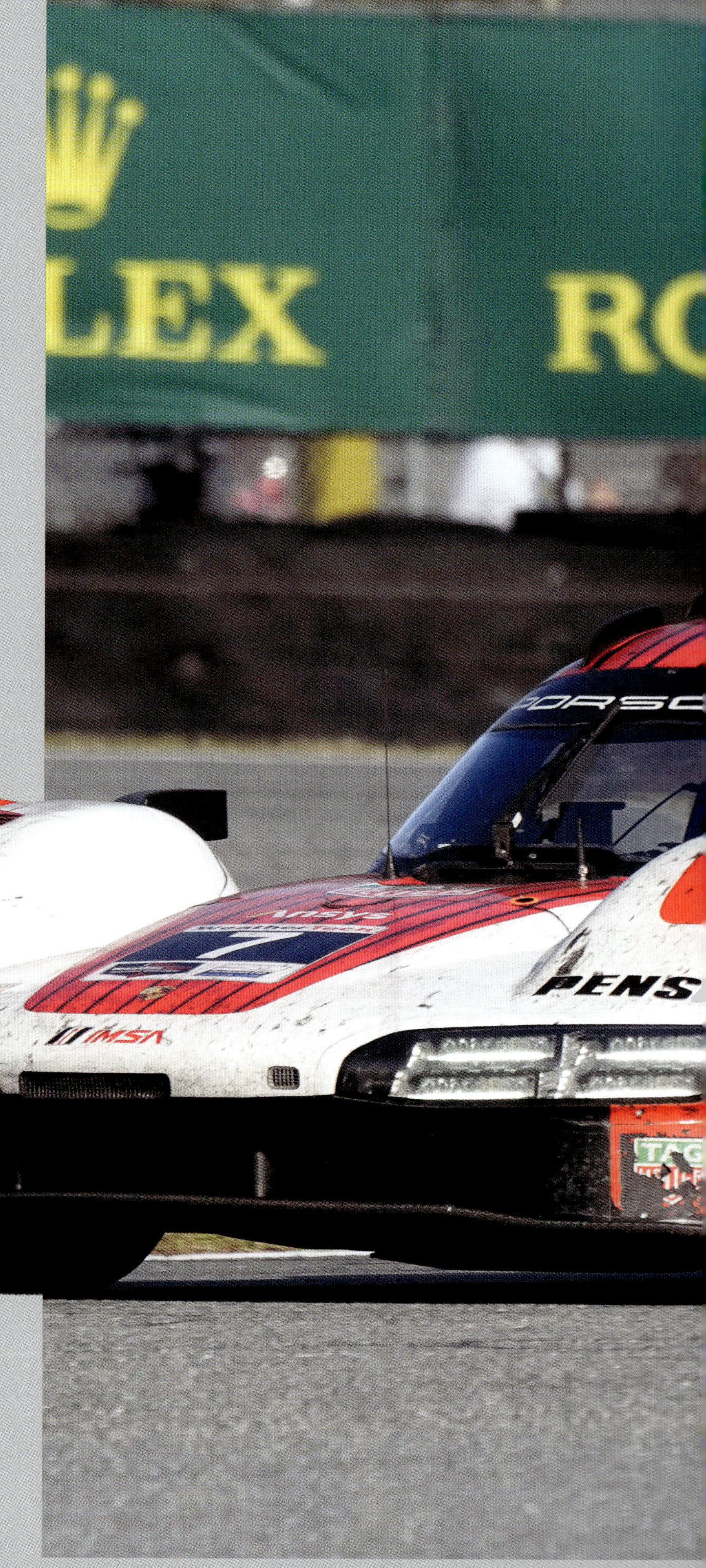

Laurens Vanthoor, of Belgium, comes out of a turn in the Porsche 963 during IMSA Rolex 24 hour auto race at Daytona International Speedway in 2025

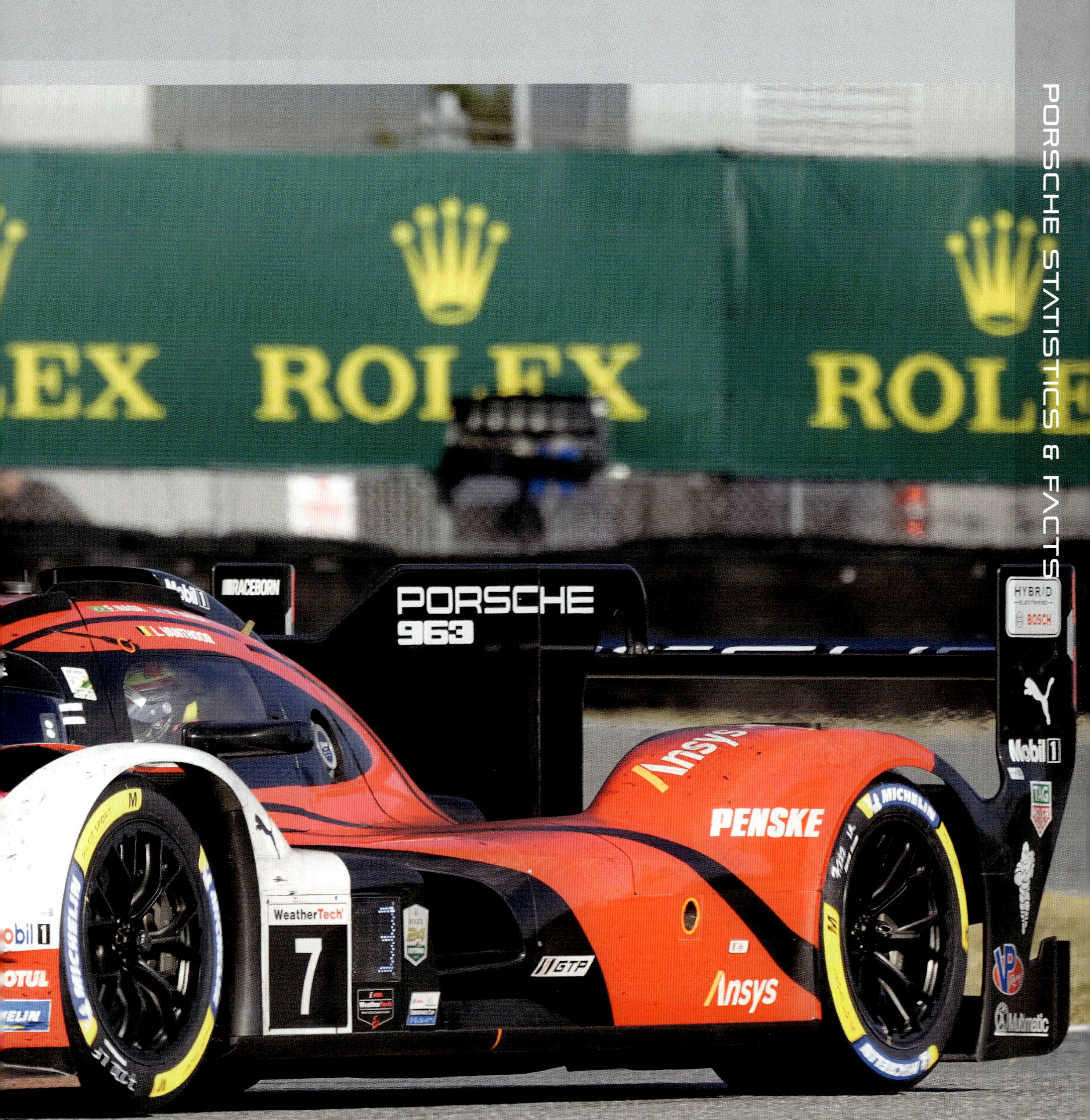

PORSCHE
963
WeatherTech
7
PENSKE
Ansys
GTP

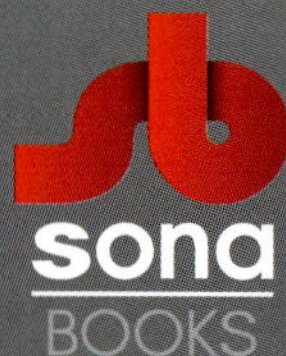


### Car photography:

Duwyne Aspeling (174-181), Damian Blades (92-97, 100-107), Ali Cusick (26-37, 60-67, 216-221),
Malcolm Griffiths (222-227), Roland Halbe (256), Steve Hall (166-173, 188-195, 210-215), Barry Hayden (21),
James Lipman (238-243), Tim Moolman (202-207), Richard Pardon (68-75), Laurens Parsons (228-231),
Daniel Pullen (15, 54-59, 142-147, 160-165, 182-187, 232-237), Mark Riccion (134-141),
Glen Smale (86-91, p122-133), Dean Smith (21, 108-113), Phil Steinhardt (38-53, 258-267),
Andrew Tipping (196-201), Chris Wallbank (244-255)

### All other images Alamy, Getty, Porsche Archives and Wiki Commons:

| | | |
|---|---|---|
| ©Sutton Motorsports | Entertainment Pictures | National Motor Museum |
| A7A Collection | Formula 1 | Phil Talbot |
| Associated Press | Goddard Automotive | Photo 12 |
| Auto Images | Grzegorz Czapski | r-photography.info |
| B.O'Kane | Heritage Images | Reinhold Möller |
| Bernard Cahier | IMAGO | Right Light Media GmbH |
| Brian Snelson | ISC Images and Archives | Rossen Gargolov |
| Brian Snelson | John Raoux | Sotheby's |
| Charles01 | Justin Tafoya | Tristan Fewings |
| dan74 | Manuel Hollenbach | Wirestock, Inc. |
| David Becker | Michael Ochs Archives | Xinhua |
| DPPI Media | Mr.choppers | Zuma Press |

Every effort has been made to acknowledge correctly and contact the source and/or copyright holder of each picture and Sona Books apologises for any unintentional errors or omissions, which will be corrected in future editions of the book.

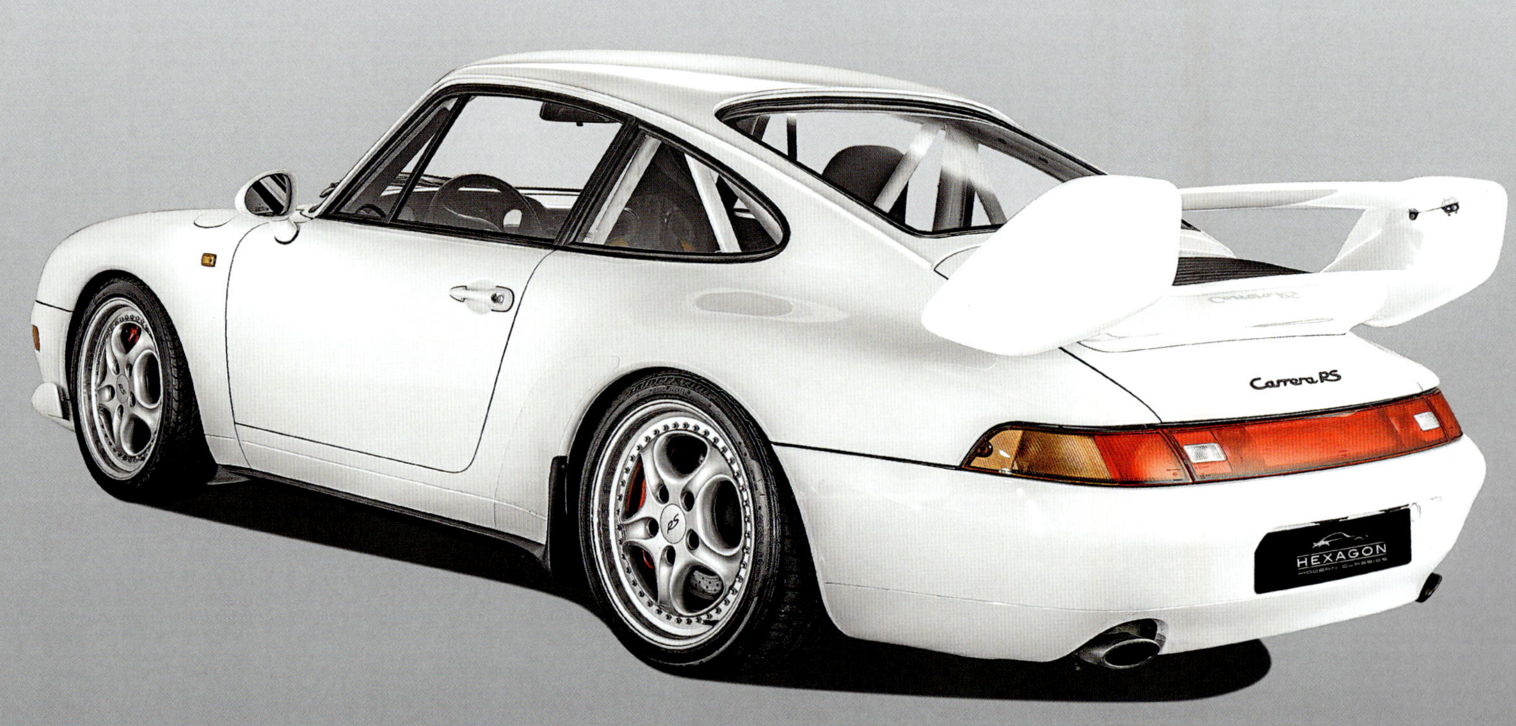